THIRD EDITION

MANAGEMENT ACCOUNTING

A STRATEGIC APPROACH

WAYNE J. MORSE
Rochester Institute of Technology

JAMES R. DAVIS
Clemson University/Gordon College

AL L. HARTGRAVES
Emory University

THOMSON

SOUTH-WESTERN

Australia · Canada · Mexico · Singapore · Spain · United Kingdom · United States

Management Accounting: A Strategic Approach, 3e
Wayne J. Morse, James R. Davis, and Al L. Hartgraves

Editor-in-Chief:
Jack W. Calhoun

Vice President/Team Director:
Melissa S. Acuña

Acquisitions Editor:
Steven W. Hazelwood

Developmental Editor:
Rebecca von Gillern

Marketing Manager:
Mignon Tucker

Production Editor:
Salvatore N. Versetto

Manufacturing Coordinator:
Doug Wilke

Production House:
Litten Editing and Production, Inc.

Compositor:
GGS Information Services, Inc.

Printer:
Quebecor World Versailles
Versailles, KY

Design Project Manager:
Christy Carr

Internal Designer:
Ramsdell Design, Cincinnati, OH

Cover Designer:
Ramsdell Design, Cincinnati, OH

Cover Photo:
© 2002 John Shotwell/The Image Bank

Media Developmental Editor:
Sally Nieman

Media Production Editor:
Lora I. Craver

Library of Congress Cataloging-in-Publication Data
Morse, Wayne J.
    Management accounting : a strategic approach / Wayne J. Morse, James R. Davis, Al L. Hartgraves.—3rd ed.
        p. cm.
    Includes index.
    ISBN 0-324-11997-6 (alk. paper)
    1. Managerial accounting. I. Davis, James Richard, 1947-II. Hartgraves, Al L. III. Title.

HF5635 .M865 2002
658.15′11—dc21   2002019660

PREFACE

Strategic position analysis, value chain, value added, virtual integration, process mapping, upstream, downstream, internal failure, external failure, structural cost drivers, cost hierarchy . . . What in the world? Can this be management accounting? Yes! These are just some of the cutting edge topics you will discover as you read this edition of *Management Accounting*. While there are plenty of traditional topics, it's the big-picture, decision oriented, integrated presentation of new and traditional topics required for success in the competitive environment of the twenty-first century that make this, page for page, the most complete text in the market. So get ready for the most exciting entry into management accounting ever developed. Much awaits you as you read the 13 chapters that follow.

Management accounting is concerned with the use of financial and related information, by managers and other persons inside specific organizations, to make strategic, organizational, and operational decisions. It provides a framework for identifying and analyzing decision alternatives and for evaluating success in accomplishing organizational goals. Although accountants play an important role in the management accounting process, management accounting is more of a managerial tool than an accounting process. Furthermore, in an era of global competition, continuous improvement, process reengineering, and employee empowerment, management accounting is used by decision makers at all levels, rather than just by personnel traditionally classified as "managers." **The purpose of this book is to introduce students to management accounting as it is practiced today.**

Because this is an introductory text, we have elected to provide a survey of many topics, carefully relating them to each other. Whereas this book is written for a general business audience, we have strived to place management accounting in a broad context, relating management accounting to other subject areas. We have left the in-depth coverage of many topics to more specialized books on cost accounting, finance, production, statistics, marketing, policy, and so forth. We hope this book, like the trunk of a tree, will serve as a strong base for the future growth of knowledge and as a means of unifying the branches of management.

We emphasized the use of management accounting information for decision making within the context of an organization's strategy. The organization and content of *Management Accounting, 3e*, reflects our belief that students who understand the big picture have a better basis for learning, are better decision makers, and are better able to apply what they learn to new situations. If you have or know how to develop a map of the forest, you are less apt to get lost among the many individual trees. The following points illustrate the big picture and decision orientation of *Management Accounting, 3e*.

- **Strategic Position Analysis.** *Management Accounting, 3e*, is based on concepts in the management literature originally developed by Michael Porter, such as strategic position analysis. Strategic position analysis concerns a fundamental choice regarding how a business plans to compete in the market place, e.g. low price/cost, product differentiation/innovation, or market niche. This choice affects management's need for and use of accounting information. See Chapter 1 pages 9–12 for an example of this feature and approach.
- **Structural, Organizational, and Activity Cost Drivers.** Most management accounting texts consider only activity cost drivers. *Management Accounting, 3e*, is based on a more comprehensive set of cost driver concepts first developed in the management literature and introduced into the accounting literature by John

Shank. These concepts recognize decisions regarding size, location, and target customers as structural cost drivers, decisions regarding the organization of processes and design of products or services as organizational cost drivers, and the performance of tasks as activity cost drivers. This broader framework facilitates learning that costs must be managed when making structural and organizational decisions rather then when performing activities. See Chapter 1 pages 17–20 and Chapter 5 pages 178–179 for an example of this approach.

- **Activity-Cost Concepts Emphasize Decisions.** Activity cost concepts are first introduced within the context of cost analysis/planning, profitability analysis/planning, and decision making rather than as an alternative approach to product costing. This decision orientation within the framework of core management accounting topics provides a broader framework for understanding the usefulness of activity-cost concepts for activity-based management. It also assists students in thinking outside the product costing box. We believe that introducing ABC as an alternative approach to product costing is flawed in that it places students in a product costing box that instructors must then help them get out of. See Chapter 2 pages 54–58, Chapter 3 pages 98–101, and Chapter 4 pages 123–128 for examples of this approach.

- **Deemphasize Product Costs vs. Period Costs.** *Management Accounting, 3e*, is based on a belief that the accounting distinction between product and nonproduct costs (introduced early in virtually all management accounting texts) should not be the central theme of a management accounting text, is misleading, diverts attention from the analysis of the complete value chain, and forces an unnecessary distinction between manufacturing and nonmanufacturing organizations.

- **Unit Level-Hierarchical Framework for Analysis.** *Management Accounting, 3e*, uses a unit level-hierarchical framework to show how activity-based approaches to cost estimation, profitability analysis, and budgeting relate to, yet differ from, approaches based on the variable–fixed cost dichotomy. This text indicates when each is appropriate and the dangers of the unit level approach in situations involving variations in the complexity or volume of products or services. See Chapter 2 pages 40–54 & 60–64, Chapter 3 pages 84–88 & 98–101, and Chapter 11 pages 465–467 for examples of this approach.

- **Value Chain, Internal Processes, Activities within Processes.** *Management Accounting, 3e*, places activities within the broader context of internal processes and the external value chain for a product or service. This big picture orientation, first introduced into the accounting literature by John Shank, provides a broad context for learning and applying activity concepts. It also helps students retain a frame of reference while immersed in the details of activity management. To foster big-picture learning, the first example of ABC is extended across all internal processes, rather than being limited to product costing. See Chapter 5 pages 173–178 for an example of the value chain orientation and pages 184–193 for an example of ABC across all internal processes.

- **Activity-Based Costing and Organizational-Based Costing.** *Management Accounting, 3e*, relates product costing applications of ABC to traditional costing concepts, which are identified as organizational-based costing. Our belief is that context and reference points foster learning and retention, as well as provide a basis for the extension of concepts to new situations. See Chapter 6 pages 230–231 for an example of obtaining information for financial reporting from full activity-based costs, Chapter 7 pages 293–297 for a discussion of organizational-based costing and the product costing continuum, and Chapter 8 pages 340–342 for inventory valuation comparisons from the Theory of Constraints to full ABC.

As the above comments suggest, we take a cost driver approach within the context of an organization's entire value chain. We believe the result is a book that is more relevant, interesting, and usable for students whose primary concerns are something other than financial reporting. Traditional financial reporting issues related to inventory costing are deferred until after students have studied cost drivers, the value chain, activity-based management, and activity-based costing. Students use the knowledge gained in the early chapters to critically examine inventory cost system alternatives, rather than using basic "product costing" concepts (originally developed for financial reporting) as a foundation for learning. By taking this approach, the instructor also avoids the need to explain the shortcomings of traditional approaches to product costing to students who have just completed their first few weeks of studying management accounting.

ORGANIZATION

The book contains 13 chapters:

1. Management Accounting: A Tool for Decision Making
2. Activity Cost Analysis and Planning
3. Profitability Analysis and Planning
4. Contribution Analysis for Decision Making
5. Value Chain Analysis and Activity-Based Management
6. Product Costing and the Manufacturing Environment
7. Designing Product Cost Systems
8. Inventory Valuation Approaches and Just-in-Time Inventory Management
9. Strategic Management of Price, Cost, and Quality
10. Strategic Management of Capital Expenditures
11. Operational Budgeting
12. Performance Assessment
13. Profitability Analysis of Strategic Business Segments

Two additional chapters are available in a supplement, *An Introduction to Financial Statement* and *Cash Flow Analysis*, prepared by the authors:

1. Financial Statement Analysis
2. Statement of Cash Flows

Developing a book that can be used in a single semester, while integrating many new concepts, required careful attention to organization. Chapters build on each other, and issues raised in early chapters are revisited in later chapters. Although some chapters (such as Chapters 8 and 10) or portions of some chapters (such as portions of Chapters 12 or 13) and appendix materials may be omitted, we recommend assigning chapters in numerical order. Chapter 1 is important and worthy of study, rather than being a light overview that may be lectured on but not assigned. In most management accounting texts, Chapter 2 is primarily concerned with terminology. To limit the number of chapters, we avoided the use of a terminology chapter and, instead, introduced terms where needed.

All chapters contain learning objectives linked to major chapter headings. Key terms are in bold type when they are first introduced, listed at the end of each chapter, and defined in a comprehensive glossary at the end of the text. Suggested readings that may be used by students interested in learning more about chapter materials, as an initial reading list for papers, or as additional assignment material, are available on our Web site http://morse.swcollege.com.

Global business activities, employee empowerment, the value chain, process management, activity-based costing, and competition on the basis of cost, quality, and service are so woven into the text that it is difficult to single out examples of these topics. Ethics also receives extensive coverage. Ethics is introduced within the context of measurement and management in Chapter 1 and discussed further in Chapters 4, 9, and 11. "What's Happening" features in Chapters 1, 10, 11, and 12 also highlight the importance of ethics in management accounting. Assignment material dealing with ethics are included in Chapters 1, 2, 3, 4, 5, 9, and 11.

CHANGES IN THIS EDITION

Although we retained the structure of the second edition, there are numerous revisions to update and strengthen text materials. Over forty percent of the What's Happening and Research Shows features are new or significantly revised. Assignment materials are revised to include current dates and improve clarity. Furthermore, more than twenty percent of the Exercises, Problems, and Discussion Questions and Cases are either new or revised to such an extent that they have new solutions. While there are numerous changes improving the presentation or updating text material, the following changes will be noticeable to users of previous editions:

CHAPTER 3
- Added appendix coverage of sales mix analysis.

CHAPTER 5
- Rewrote the primary example of a value chain.
- Relocated and rewrote the discussion of activity-based management to follow the discussion of activity-based costing.
- Added discussion of the ABC Cross.
- Added new topic of Mission-Based Processes and Activities.

CHAPTER 6
- Modified Exhibits 6–6, 6–7, and 6–8.
- Added discussion of ERP systems.
- Added Appendix with discussion of Journal Entries for Recording Product Costs.

CHAPTER 7
- Rewrote section on Production and Service Department costs.
- Substantially rewrote the Organization Based Costing allocation topic.
- Added section on "Uses and Evolution of Activity-Based Costing."
- Added new Appendix on "Linear Algebra Method of Service Department Cost Allocation."

CHAPTER 8
- Reduced coverage of reconciling absorption versus variable costing income.

CHAPTER 9
- Increased coverage of target costing.
- Increased coverage of benchmarking.

CHAPTER 10
- Increased coverage of capital budgeting procedures.

CHAPTER 11
- Reduced appendix coverage of manufacturing budgets.

CHAPTER 12
- Deleted material on budgeting and planning feedback, already in Chapter 11.
- Reduced number of exhibits.
- Revised material related to direct labor and assembly, increasing coverage of direct labor.
- Revised Appendix B, adding coverage of capacity variance.

CHAPTER 13
- Substantially revised and rewrote Chapter 13. Rewrote the entire discussion of centralization, decentralization, and segment reporting.
- Rewrote much of the transfer pricing material and added a discussion of international transfer pricing.
- Rewrote the section on "Investment Center Income."
- Rewrote and expanded discussion of EVA.
- Expanded discussion of balanced scorecard to include more coverage of nonfinancial measures and added new section on the Balanced Scorecard and Strategy Implementation.

SPECIAL FEATURES
- **Welcome to Management Accounting,** immediately before Chapter 1, orients students to the text and its various features.
- **Opening scenarios,** discussing how managers of real organizations apply text materials, are at the beginning of each chapter.
- **"What's Happening"** features illustrate how real companies utilize management accounting concepts.
- **"Research Shows"** report on applied management accounting research.

ASSIGNMENT MATERIALS
A variety of assignment materials accompany *Management Accounting, 3e*. Each chapter contains one or two review problems. Solutions to review problems are at the end of each chapter's assignment materials (rather than immediately following the review problem) to encourage students to solve the problems before reviewing the solutions. Chapters contain a range of assignment materials in the form of review questions, exercises, problems, discussion questions, and cases. Although many assignment materials deal with new concepts, there are ample materials dealing with important traditional topics.

- **Review questions,** sequenced in the order of materials presented in the chapter, focus on the recall of basic chapter materials.
- **Exercises** are relatively short and straightforward applications of individual chapter topics. They focus on recall and application.
- **Problems** contain more rigorous and comprehensive applications of chapter materials, often requiring the ability to organize and present information. Many problems also contain straightforward requirements calling for decisions, interpretation, or "what if " analysis.
- **Discussion questions** typically require students to conceptualize chapter materials and, sometimes, relate them to materials in previous chapters. They focus on comprehension, synthesis, and evaluation. Discussion questions can be used as written assignments or, with relatively limited amounts of advanced student preparation, as a basis of classroom or group discussion.
- **Cases** involve rigorous analysis, synthesis, and evaluation. They often integrate materials contained in several chapters and require students to extend their thought processes to new situations. While the coverage of cases, especially at the undergraduate level, will likely require the guidance of the instructor, the selective use of case materials helps prepare students for the difficult transition from the classroom to the business world. The cases are also excellent for group assignments.

ANCILLARY MATERIALS

This textbook is part of a comprehensive and carefully prepared educational package that offers various forms of assistance to both instructors and students. A variety of ancillary materials is available.

- A **solutions manual,** prepared by the authors, contains detailed solutions to all assignment materials.
- **Transparency acetates** for the solutions to assignments requiring extensive computations are available to adopters.
- **Power Point Slides,** prepared by *Douglas Cloud of Pepperdine University,* enhances the classroom presentation of text materials.
- A **test bank,** prepared by *Russell Madray of Clemson University,* is available in printed and electronic (ExamView) versions. A collection of problems, questions, and exercises, the test bank is designed to save time in preparing and grading periodic and final exams.
- A **study guide,** prepared by Professor Stephen V. Senge of the Simmons Graduate School of Management, reemphasizes and reinforces basic concepts and techniques.
- **An Introduction to Financial Statement and Cash Flow Analysis,** a soft-cover supplement covering financial statement analysis and cash flows in management accounting, has been prepared by the authors in recognition of the fact that some schools find it necessary to cover these topics in management accounting courses. The materials in this supplement, Financial Statement Analysis, Chapter 1, and Statement of Cash Flows, Chapter 2, may be used before or after the other text materials. Solutions to the supplement assignments are available on our Web site at http://morse.swcollege.com.

We were motivated in our approach to organizing this book by speakers at numerous meetings, conversations with businesspeople, returning graduate students with professional experience, participants in executive development programs, colleagues in accounting and other disciplines, and researchers working on the cutting edge of management accounting. The writings of many of these people are included in the suggested readings. We were especially influenced by Peter Drucker's numerous writings on management, Robert Kaplan's and Robin Cooper's work in the areas of activity-based costing and activity-based management, John Shank's and Vijay Govindarajan's writings on the value chain and strategic cost management, and Michael Porter's writings on strategic position analysis and the value chain.

Six books that influenced our conceptual framework for thinking about management accounting are: Megatrends by John Naisbitt, published by Warner Books; The Third Wave by Alvin Toffler, published by William Morrow & Co.; Relevance Lost: The Rise and Fall of Management Accounting by H. Thomas Johnson and Robert S. Kaplan, published by the HBS Press; Strategic Cost Management by John K. Shank and Vijay Govindarajan, published by The Free Press; Reengineering the Corporation by Michael Hammer and James Champy, published by Harper Business; and Cost and Effect by Robin Cooper and Robert Kaplan, published by HBS Press. These books helped us put management accounting within the context of the broad sweep of events affecting business and society at the start of the twenty-first century.

We are indebted to the following professors who served as reviewers for the third edition and offered helpful comments on the manuscript:

- James L. Bierstaker (University of Massachusetts Boston)
- John Giles (North Carolina State University)
- Eleanor G. Henry (State University of New York at Oswego)
- Gail Pastoria (Robert Morris College)
- Maryanne Rouse (University of South Florida)
- Edward L. Summers (The University of Texas at Austin)

We appreciate the assistance of Sheila Viel (University of Wisconsin—Milwaukee) who provided a complete review of the solutions to assignment materials and extend a very special thank you to Steve Senge (the Simmons Graduate School of Management) who developed the opening scenarios for most chapters. Steve has encouraged and supported us on this and previous projects. His efforts have helped make the text materials come alive.

We appreciate the tolerance and the feedback of our students as we tested many of the new ideas and assignment materials contained in this book. Finally, we appreciate the encouragement, support, and detailed suggestions for improvement provided by Melissa Acuña, Jennifer Codner, Sam Versetto, and Rebecca von Gillern of South-Western/Thomson. Working with them has been a pleasure.

Appreciation is extended to the Institute of Certified Management Accountants for permission to use adaptations of problem materials from past Certified Management Accounting Examinations—these materials are identified as "CMA Adapted." We are also indebted to the American Institute of Certified Public Accountants for permission to use materials from the Uniform CPA exam—these materials are identified as "CPA Adapted."

Despite the efforts of the many people who assisted in this project, there is always room for further improvement. To assist us in continuously improving this product so that it better fits your needs and the needs of your students, comments and suggestions are most welcome. Users wishing to contact us with comments, suggestions, or questions, may send us correspondence via our Web site in the **Instructor's Resource** under **Comments & Feedback.**

Wayne J. Morse	James R. Davis	Al L. Hartgraves
Rochester, NY	*Clemson, SC*	*Atlanta, GA*

Wayne J. Morse, a hiking and canoeing enthusiast, is Professor of Accounting and Associate Dean of the College of Business at Rochester Institute of Technology. An author or co-author of more than fifty published papers, monographs, and textbooks, he was a founding member of the Management Accounting section of the American Accounting Association. His most significant writings are in the areas of learning curves, human resource accounting, and quality costs. He was a member of the IMA Committee on Research and an AICPA Board of Examiners subcommittee, and he has served on the editorial boards of *Advances-in-Accounting, Trends in Accounting Education, Issues in Accounting Education,* and *Management Accounting Research*. A Certified Public Accountant, he received his Ph.D. from Michigan State University. Prior to joining RIT, he was on the faculty of the University of Illinois, Duke University, the University of Tennessee, Clarkson University, and the University of Alabama in Huntsville.

James R. Davis, who enjoys gardening in his spare time, is Professor of Accounting at Gordon College and Professor of Accountancy Emeritus at the School of Accountancy and Legal Studies at Clemson University in Clemson, South Carolina. A co-author of three textbooks, he has authored or co-authored numerous journal articles and professional meeting proceedings. His primary areas of interest are managerial accounting, information systems, and professional ethics. He has served on several editorial boards and professional committees and has been very active with the ICMA Examination Project. He is a Certified Management Accountant and has held numerous offices in local IMA Chapters. He received his Ph.D. from Georgia State University. His international experience has included several teaching and consulting positions in New Zealand and Portugal, the most recent being a visiting lecturer at Universidade de Algarve in Faro, Portugal.

Al L. Hartgraves, who relaxes on the links, is Professor of Accounting at the Goizueta Business School at Emory University in Atlanta, Georgia. He is also a frequent Guest Professor at Johannes Kepler University in Linz, Austria and at the Helsinki School of Economics and Business Administration in Finland. His published scholarly and professional articles have appeared in *The Accounting Review, Journal of Accountancy, Management Accounting*, and many other journals. He has been selected by students at Goizueta Business School on four occasions as the Outstanding Educator of the Year, and he has received the Donald Keough Award for Outstanding Service to the school. He was listed as an Outstanding Faculty Member in the *Business Week Guide to the Best Business Schools*. He is a Certified Public Accountant and a Certified Management Accountant, having received the Certificate of Distinguished Performance on the CMA exam. He received his Ph.D. from Georgia State University.

BRIEF CONTENTS

CONTENTS

Contents

Chapter 10: Strategic Management of Capital Expenditures   408

WELCOME TO MANAGEMENT ACCOUNTING

"Accounting," according to management philosopher Peter Drucker, "has become the most intellectually challenging area in the field of management, and the most turbulent one." Drucker believes this rebirth of accounting is taking place because accounting is the primary discipline attempting to answer questions "few executives yet know how to ask: What information do I need to do my job? When do I need it? and From whom should I be getting it?" Drucker believes accounting is being shaken to its roots by reform movements aimed at moving it away from being merely financial (dealing with assets, liabilities, and cash flows) and toward being operational.[1]

The purpose of this book is to help you learn how to ask and answer the questions posed by Drucker, as well as other questions requiring the analysis of financial information. Our ultimate goal as authors is to help you succeed in your chosen career—be it accounting, actuarial science, agriculture, business administration, financial management, engineering, hospital administration, marketing, retail management, or any other field. We hope to accomplish this by introducing you to **management accounting,** a discipline concerned with the financial and related information used by managers and other persons inside specific organizations to make strategic, organizational, and operational decisions.

Each chapter begins with five to seven learning objectives you should achieve after completing the chapter. These objectives represent both a preview of the chapter's contents and specific learning outcomes. The opening of each section within a chapter contains a reference to the learning objective (LO) of that section. Next comes an opening scenario that illustrates the importance of chapter material in the management of actual companies. In addition to covering technical material, chapters contain numerous examples of how real companies, from Amazon.com to Xerox, utilize management accounting concepts. Particularly interesting examples are set out in a feature called "What's Happening?" Where appropriate, we report on applied research in the area of management accounting. Results that are especially interesting are summarized in a feature called "Research Shows."

The materials at the end of each chapter include suggested readings (a useful starting point for a research paper), one or more review problems (the answers are included), review questions, exercises, problems, discussion questions, and cases. We recommend that you solve the review problems to ensure your understanding of basic technical material, answer the review questions on your own, and prepare solutions to other materials selected by your instructor.

- Review questions focus on the recall of basic concepts. They are sequenced in the order materials are presented in the chapter. Hence, you should be able to answer each question and then page through the chapter to find the solution.
- Exercises are relatively short and straightforward applications of individual chapter topics.
- Problems contain more rigorous and comprehensive applications of chapter materials, often requiring the ability to organize and present information. Many problems have requirements calling for discussion, interpretation, or "what if" analysis.
- Discussion questions focus on comprehension, synthesis, and evaluation. While the focal point is on materials in the current chapter, the questions may require relating these materials to that found in other chapters. As the title suggests, answers to discussion questions will, and should, vary.
- Cases involve rigorous analysis, synthesis, and evaluation. They often integrate materials from several chapters (and sometimes from other courses). They may

---

[1]Peter Drucker, "Be Data Literate—Know What to Know," *The Wall Street Journal*, December 1, 1992, p. A16.

require the extension of thought processes to new situations. Like the "real world," many cases deal with ambiguous situations where you will simply have to develop the best solution you can with the available information. Again, cases do not have simple or absolute answers.

We hope you come to appreciate that accounting is much more than record keeping. Far from being an isolated back-room activity, accounting is an integrating force that ties the diverse elements of an organization together to develop and achieve common goals. Because goal accomplishment is affected by numerous specific decisions, we repeatedly illustrate how decisions are influenced, for better or worse, by the quality of financial information. We are convinced that you cannot be a successful product manager, store manager, design engineer, production supervisor, marketing representative, or participant on any project team without understanding and applying management accounting concepts.

We believe that knowledge is interrelated and go out of our way to point out these interrelationships. It is this approach that distinguishes this text and helps make management accounting a leveraging tool to help organizations succeed and to help you achieve your professional goals.

MANAGEMENT ACCOUNTING: A TOOL FOR DECISION MAKING

After completing this chapter, you should be able to:

LEARNING OBJECTIVE 1 — Contrast financial and management accounting and explain why financial accounting is not sufficient for internal decision makers.

LEARNING OBJECTIVE 2 — Explain how an organization's mission, goals, and strategies affect management accounting.

LEARNING OBJECTIVE 3 — Discuss the fundamental changes affecting the nature of competition.

LEARNING OBJECTIVE 4 — Differentiate among structural, organizational, and activity cost drivers.

LEARNING OBJECTIVE 5 — Explain how technology has influenced cost drivers and cost behavior.

LEARNING OBJECTIVE 6 — Discuss the impact employee empowerment can have on the activities used to serve customers and how management accounting can be an important part of employee empowerment.

LEARNING OBJECTIVE 7 — Explain the nature of the ethical dilemmas managers and accountants often confront.

COMPETITION, STRATEGY, AND MANAGEMENT ACCOUNTING

In the late 1990s, a corporate chief executive officer observed, "If you don't have competition, you're in the wrong business." This observation captures an essential element of the modern manager's environment. No matter how well a manager's organization serves customers, manages costs, or innovates, another firm is trying to do all of those things better. Firms employ various strategies to compete in product or service markets, and the strategies employed by the technology firms Hewlett-Packard and Dell during the early 2000s illustrate two sharply contrasting competitive approaches.

In September 2001, the chief executives of Hewlett-Packard (HP) and Compaq announced that their firms planned to merge in a $25 billion deal. At the time the proposed merger was announced, the combined firms held market share leadership positions in personal computers, servers, and printers. The merged firms

3

would become the largest computer hardware firm in the world, and HP management intended to rely on the efficiencies of size to provide an array of contemporary hardware, software, and service solutions for clients. HP managers stressed the importance of research and development expenditures to support a stream of product and service innovations. Citing the benefits of being first to market with an innovative product, CEO Carly Fiorina discussed HP's success in the high-margin handheld computer appliance market. In her view, a business model without innovation is not sustainable. In late 2001, however, several powerful HP shareholders opposed the merger. These shareholders commented that Compaq's position and profitability in PCs was in jeopardy since Dell had made the PC market "a cost game." They also felt that the merger would dilute HP's successful printer business. As a result, the HP-Compaq merger was in doubt as 2001 closed.

With a personal computer market share of 13–14 percent in late 2001, Dell relentlessly pursues market share with a high-volume, low-margin strategy. In 2000, managers at Dell began cutting prices in the personal computer market— a competitive strategy based on the firm's cost and efficiency advantage. Since rivals had to match Dell's price cuts, these reduced prices took their toll on other firms' profitability. Between the beginning of the price war in 2000 and late 2001, Dell earned $361 million of income while competitors collectively lost $1.1 billion in this market. Within this overall business model, Dell constantly refines it's operating polices to enhance efficiency. By taking orders directly from customers—50 percent of whom order online; limiting operating expenses to 10% of revenues while HP's range between 15–17 percent; holding only four days' inventory compared with Compaq's 24 days; and spending only 1.5% of revenues on research and development, Dell has solidified its position as the personal computer market's cost leader. Competitors comment that Dell is playing a dangerous game in a market where profit margins don't rebound since customers are accustomed to constantly lower cost technology. Dell's managers respond with their intention to extend this business model to the markets for networking, storage, and computer services.

The competition between Hewlett-Packard and Dell continuously tests both management teams' abilities to succeed with their respective business models: innovation and differentiation versus low cost and efficiency. Managers at these and other firms often employ an array of management accounting tools to assist them in making these strategic decisions.

Source: Based on: "Sheltering from the Storm," *The Economist,* September 8, 2001, p. 34; Peter Burrows and Andrew Park, "Where's the Upside?" *Business Week,* September 17, 2001, pp. 40–43; Eric Nee, "The Hard Truth Behind a Shotgun Wedding," *Fortune,* October 1, 2001, pp. 109–114; Andrew Park and Peter Burrows, "Dell the Conqueror," *Business Week,* September 24, 2001, pp. 92–102, and "A Stunning Reversal for HP's Marriage Plans," *Business Week,* November 19, 2001, p. 42; and Janice Revell, "A Marriage Only Dell Could Love," *Fortune,* October 1, 2001, p. 184.

The purpose of this chapter is to provide an overview of the factors that make management accounting increasingly important to successful businesses. We begin by distinguishing between financial and management accounting and by investigating how competitive strategy affects the way organizations, such as Hewlett-Packard and Dell, use management accounting information. Next, we explore how the emergence of global competition and changes in technology have increased the need to understand management accounting concepts. We also provide an overview of factors that influence costs in an organization and how these factors have changed between the beginnings of the twentieth and the twenty-first centuries. Finally, we consider how management accounting assists employees in making better decisions, and we examine the interrelationships among measurement, management, and ethics.

LEARNING OBJECTIVE 1

FINANCIAL ACCOUNTING IS INSUFFICIENT FOR MANAGEMENT

Many of you have had at least one course in **financial accounting,** an information-processing system that generates general-purpose reports of financial operations (income statement and statement of cash flows) and financial position (balance sheet) for an organization. Although financial accounting is used by decision makers inside and outside the firm, financial accounting courses typically emphasize external users, such as security investors and lenders. Adding to this external orientation are external financial reporting requirements determined by law and generally accepted accounting principles.

Financial accounting is also concerned with keeping records of the organization's assets, obligations, and the collection and payment of debts. An organization cannot survive without converting sales into cash, paying for purchases, meeting payroll, and keeping track of its assets.

The **income statement** is a summary of economic events during a period of time, showing the revenues generated by operating activities, the expenses matched to those revenues, and any gains and losses attributed to the period. The **statement of cash flows** is a summary of resource inflows and outflows stated in terms of cash. The **balance sheet** is a picture of the economic health of an organization at a specific time, showing the organization's assets and the claims on those assets. These financial statements, typically prepared quarterly and annually, report on the past affairs of the organization.

Managers often use income statements and balance sheets as a starting point in evaluating and planning the firm's overall affairs. Because financial accounting data are widely available, managers learn a great deal by performing a comparative analysis of their firm and competing firms. Corporate goals are often stated using financial accounting numbers, such as net income, or ratios, such as return on investment and earnings per share of common stock.

Despite financial accounting's importance, internal decision makers often find it of little value in managing day-to-day operating activities. They often complain that financial accounting information is too aggregated, prepared too late, based on irrelevant past costs, and not action oriented. For example, the costs of all items produced and sold or all services rendered are summarized in a single line in most financial statements, making it impossible to determine the costs of individual products or services. Financial accounting procedures, acceptable for costing inventories as a whole, often produce misleading information when applied to individual products. Even when they are accurately determined, the costs of individual products or services are rarely detailed enough to provide the information needed for decisions concerning the factors that influence costs. Financial accounting reports, seldom prepared more than once a month, are not timely enough for use in the management of day-to-day activities that cause excess costs. Finally, financial accounting reports are based on historical costs rather than on current or future costs. Because managers make decisions about the future, they are more interested in future costs than in historical costs such as last year's depreciation. While financial accounting information is useful in making some management decisions, its primary emphasis is not on internal decision making.

MANAGEMENT ACCOUNTING ASSISTS INTERNAL DECISION MAKERS

Management accounting provides both a framework to evaluate information in light of an organization's goals and information to managers and other persons inside the

As Competition Intensifies, More People Use Management Accounting Information

After studying several highly competitive, world-class companies, noted accounting researcher Robin Cooper observed that "with the emergence of the lean enterprise and increased global competition, companies must learn to be more proactive in the way they manage costs. For many, survival is dependent upon their abilities to develop sophisticated cost management systems that create intense pressure to reduce costs. . . ."

He further observed that "as cost management becomes more critical to a company's survival, two trends emerge. First, new forms of cost management are required, and second, more individuals in the firm become actively involved in the cost management process." Cooper goes on to suggest that with the large number of nonaccountants involved in the cost management process, there will be an increased need for management accounting information (and people who know how to use it) and a decreased need for traditional management accountants.

Source: Robin Cooper, "Look Out, Management Accountants," *Management Accounting,* May 1996, pp. 20–26.

organization. Because the information needs of internal decision makers can be known in advance, management accounting reports can be designed to meet their specific needs. Top management may need only summary information prepared once a month for each business unit. An engineer responsible for hourly production scheduling may need continuously updated and detailed information concerning the cost of alternative ways of producing a product.

Because of the intensity of competition and the shorter life cycles of new products and services, many influential business executives now believe management accounting is too important to be left solely to accountants. **Management accounting** is a process of obtaining and analyzing relevant information to help achieve organizational goals. Every manager must understand the financial implications of decisions. While accountants are available to assist in obtaining and evaluating relevant information, individual managers are responsible for requesting information, analyzing it, and making the final decisions. The increased use of accounting information is further examined in Research Shows 1–1.

Management accounting information exists to serve the needs of management. Hence, it is subject to a cost-benefit analysis and should be developed only if the perceived benefits exceed the costs of development and use. Also, while financial measures are often used in management accounting, they are not used to the exclusion of other measures. Money is simply a convenient way of expressing events in a form suitable to summary analysis. When this is not possible or appropriate, nonfinancial measures are used. Time, for example, is often an important element of quality or service. Hence, many performance measures focus on time, for example:

- Federal Express keeps detailed information on the time required to make deliveries.
- Fire departments and police departments measure the response time to emergency calls.
- Delta Air Lines monitors the number of on-time departures and arrivals.

No external standards (such as requirements of the Securities and Exchange Commission) are imposed on information provided to internal users. Consequently, management accounting information may be quite subjective. In developing a budget, management is more interested in a subjective prediction of next year's sales than in an objective report on last year's sales. The significant differences between financial and management accounting are summarized in Exhibit 1–1.

EXHIBIT 1-1

DIFFERENCES BETWEEN FINANCIAL AND MANAGEMENT ACCOUNTING

Financial Accounting	Management Accounting
Reporting system	Decision-making tool
Information for internal and external users	Information for internal users only
General-purpose financial statements	Special-purpose information
Statements highly aggregated	Information may be aggregated or detailed, depending on need
Relatively long reporting period	Reporting period may be long or short, depending on need
Report on past decisions	Oriented toward future decisions
Often required by law or generally accepted accounting principles	Not required by law or generally accepted accounting principles
Must conform to external standards	No external standards
Emphasizes objective data	Allows subjective data, if relevant

STRATEGIC COST MANAGEMENT PROVIDES THE BIG PICTURE

During recent years, the rapid introduction of improved products has shortened the market lives of products. Some products, such as personal computers, may be obsolete within two or three years after introduction. At the same time, the increased use of complex automated equipment makes it difficult to change production procedures after production begins. Combining short product life cycles with automated production results in an environment where most costs are determined by decisions made before production begins (decisions concerning product design and production procedures).

To ensure providing products and services that the customers want at the lowest possible price, businesses are working more closely with customers and suppliers. In examining challenges and opportunities, Hewlett-Packard routinely brings customers and suppliers together to discuss "business ecosystems" for products or services. "Most of the business managers are so busy minding their current businesses that it's hard to step out and see threats or opportunities," says Srinivas Sukumar, director of strategic planning for HP Labs. "By looking at the entire ecosystem, it provides a broad perspective to them. It gets people out of their boxes."[1]

In response to these trends, a new approach to management accounting, referred to as *strategic cost management,* has emerged. According to John Shank, a major proponent of this new approach, strategic cost management has emerged from a blending of three themes:

1. **Cost driver analysis**—the study of factors that cause or influence costs.
2. **Strategic position analysis**—an organization's basic way of competing to sell products or services.
3. **Value chain analysis**—the study of value-producing activities, stretching from basic raw materials to the final consumer of a product or service.[2]

We define **strategic cost management** as making decisions concerning specific cost drivers within the context of an organization's business strategy, internal value chain, and position in a larger value chain stretching from the development and use of resources to final consumers. Cost driver analysis and business strategy, including strategic position analysis, are introduced in this chapter. Value chain analysis, a notion similar to that of the business ecosystem, is introduced in Chapter 5.

[1]John A. Bryne, "Strategic Planning," *Business Week,* August 26, 1996, p. 50.
[2]John K. Shank, "Strategic Cost Management: New Wine, or Just New Bottles?" *Journal of Management Accounting Research,* Fall 1989, p. 50.

<table><tbody><tr><td>Learning Objective 2</td><td>

ORGANIZATIONS: THEIR MISSIONS, GOALS, AND STRATEGIES
</td></tr></tbody></table>

An organization's **mission** is the basic purpose toward which its activities are directed. Organizations vary widely in their missions. According to the late Roberto Goizueta, former chairman and CEO of the Coca-Cola Company, the mission of the Coca-Cola Company is "to create value over time for the owners of our business." He went on to note:

> Our society is based on democratic capitalism. In such a society, people create specific institutions to help meet specific needs. Governments are created to help meet social needs. Churches are created to help meet spiritual needs. Businesses such as ours are created to meet economic needs. The common thread between these institutions is that they can flourish only when they stay focused on the specific need they were created to fulfill.
>
> "When institutions try to broaden their scope beyond their natural realms, when for example they try to become all things to all people, they fail. Take, for example, the failure of the former Soviet Union.[3]

Mr. Goizueta believed that Coca-Cola best contributes to society and helps government and other organizations fulfill their missions by staying focused on its shareholders. He believed this keeps a company financially healthy, and a healthy company fills its responsibilities. Conversely, a bankrupt company is incapable of paying taxes, employing people, serving customers, supporting charitable institutions, or making other contributions to society.

We frequently distinguish between organizations on the basis of profit motive. **For-profit organizations** have profit as a primary mission, whereas **not-for-profit organizations** do not have profit as a primary mission. Clearly, the Coca-Cola Company is a for-profit organization, whereas the city of Chicago and the Red Cross are not-for-profit organizations.[4] Regardless of whether a profit motive exists, organizations must use resources wisely. Every dollar United Way spends for administrative salaries is a dollar that cannot be used to support charitable activities. Not-for-profit organizations, including governments, can go bankrupt if they are unable to meet their financial obligations. All organizations, for profit and not for profit, should use management accounting concepts to ensure that resources are used wisely.

A **goal** is a definable, measurable objective. Based on the organization's mission, management sets a number of goals. The mission of a paper mill located in a small town is to provide quality paper products in order to earn a profit for its owners. The paper mill's goals might include earning an annual profit equal to 10 percent of average total assets, maintaining annual dividends of $2 per share of common stock, developing a customer reputation for above-average quality and service, providing steady employment for area residents, and meeting or exceeding environmental standards.

A clear statement of mission and well-defined goals provides an organization with an identity and unifying purpose, thereby ensuring that all employees are heading in the same direction. Having developed a mission and a set of goals, employees are more apt to make decisions that move the organization toward its defined purpose.

A **strategy** is a course of action that will assist in achieving one or more goals. Much of this text will focus on the financial aspects of selecting strategies to achieve goals. For example, if an organization's goal is to improve product quality, possible strategies for achieving this goal include investing in new equipment, implementing additional quality inspections, prescreening suppliers, reducing batch size, redesigning products, training employees, and rearranging the shop floor. Management accounting

---

[3]Roberto Goizueta, "Why Shareholder Value?" *CEO Series Issue No. 13*, February 1997, Center for the Study of American Business, Washington University in St. Louis, p. 2.

[4]The term *nonprofit* is frequently used to refer to what we have identified as not-for-profit organizations.

information will assist in determining which of the many alternative strategies for achieving the goal of quality improvement are cost effective. The distinction between mission, goals, and strategies is illustrated in Exhibit 1–2.

STRATEGIC POSITION ANALYSIS

In competitive environments, managers should make a fundamental decision concerning their organization's goal for positioning itself in comparison to competitors. This goal is referred to as the organization's **strategic position.** Much of the organization's strategy depends on this strategic positioning goal. Michael Porter,[5] a highly regarded authority on business strategy, has identified three possible strategic positions that lead to business success:

1. Cost leadership
2. Product or service differentiation
3. Market niche

According to Porter, cost leadership

> requires aggressive construction of efficient-scale facilities, vigorous pursuit of cost reductions from experience, tight cost and overhead control, avoidance of marginal customer accounts, and cost minimization in areas like R&D [research and development], service, sales force, advertising, and so on. A great deal of managerial attention to cost control is necessary to achieve these aims. Low cost relative to competitors becomes the theme running through the entire strategy, though quality, service, and other areas cannot be ignored.[6]

Achieving cost leadership allows an organization to achieve higher profits selling at the same price as competitors or by allowing the firm to aggressively compete on the basis of price while remaining profitable. One of the first companies to successfully use a cost leadership strategy was Carnegie Steel Company, founded by Andrew Carnegie in the late nineteenth century.

> Carnegie's operating strategy was to push his own direct costs below his competitors so that he could charge prices that would always ensure enough demand to keep his plants running at full capacity. This strategy prompted him to require frequent information showing his direct costs in relation to those of his competitors. Possessing that information and secure in the knowledge that his costs were the lowest in the industry, Carnegie then mercilessly cut prices during economic recessions. While competing firms went under, he still made profits. In periods of prosperity, when customers' demands exceeded the industry's capacity to produce, Carnegie joined others in raising prices.[7]

Southwest Airlines and Dell are current examples of successful businesses competing with a strategy of cost leadership. Although Amazon.com uses the Internet to differentiate itself from traditional booksellers, its primary strategic position is price leadership.

Product or service differentiation involves creating something that is perceived as unique and worth a premium price. Possible approaches to differentiation include a market image (the Energizer bunny and Chiquita bananas), technological leadership (Hewlett-Packard printers), and customer service (Lands' End).

Even when differentiation is a strategic theme, costs must be managed. For this strategy to succeed, the resulting price premium must exceed the seller's cost of differentiation yet not exceed the differential value to the buyer. Although Borders Books'

[5]Michael E. Porter, *Competitive Strategy* (New York: The Free Press, 1980), p. 35.
[6]Porter, p. 35.
[7]H. Thomas Johnson and Robert S. Kaplan, *Relevance Lost: The Rise and Fall of Management Accounting* (Boston: Harvard Business School Press, 1987), pp. 33–34.

EXHIBIT 1-2

MISSION, GOALS, AND STRATEGIES

Mission—The basic purpose toward which activities are directed, typically ongoing and not precisely measureable. Achieving a monetary profit by providing outdoor mountain adventures may be the mission of a mountain guide.

Goal—A definable, measurable target or objective based on the organization's mission. One of a mountain guide's goals might be for his or her clients to reach the peak of a notable mountain.

Strategy—A course of action that will assist in achieving one or more goals. The mountain guide needs to select a safe and cost-effective strategy to reach the peak.

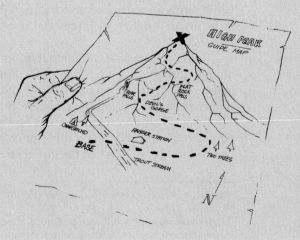

strategic position is product differentiation achieved by providing customers with product availability, a knowledgeable staff, and a pleasant shopping environment, management must ensure that Borders' prices do not rise too far above those of Amazon.com.

Conversely, while an organization may compete primarily on the basis of price, management must take care to ensure their product or service remains attuned to changing customer needs and preferences. In the late 1920s, General Motors employed a differentiation strategy, focusing on the rapid introduction of technological change in new automobile designs to overcome the market dominance of the Model T produced by Ford Motor Company. While successfully following a cost leadership strategy for years, Ford made the mistake of excluding other considerations such as vehicle performance and customer desires for different colors.[8] What's Happening 1–1 reports on the success of a Massachusetts textile mill that has become a world-class competitor through a product differentiation strategy with attention to competition on the basis of quality and service.

The third possible strategic position, focusing on a specific market niche such as a buyer group, segment of the product line, or geographic market

> *rests on the premise that the firm is thus able to serve its narrow strategic target more effectively or efficiently than competitors who are competing more broadly. As a result, the firm achieves either differentiation from better meeting the needs of the particular target, or lower costs in serving the target, or both. Even though the focus strategy does not achieve low costs or differentiation for the market as a*

1–1 WHAT'S HAPPENING?

PRODUCT DIFFERENTIATION AND MANAGEMENT/EMPLOYEE LOYALTY HELP MAKE MALDEN MILLS A MASSACHUSETTS TEXTILE SUCCESS

Most textile makers fled Massachusetts long ago due to scarce land, strict government regulation, high taxes, and high labor costs. While Malden Mills was tempted to move, management elected instead to follow a strategy of producing high-tech specialty fabrics rather than one of producing low-margin "commodity" products such as plain polyester sheets. Management believed that this strategy would allow them to pay higher labor costs while utilizing the skills of loyal employees.

Malden's first breakthrough came from working with outdoor garment-maker Patagonia to improve Polarfleece®, a double-faced fleece material originally developed by Patagonia. While the success of the new Polarfleece® attracted imitations, Malden Mills stayed ahead of the competition by continuing to develop new products, including Polartec®, an active-wear fabric used in high-priced clothing.

To improve quality and control costs, profits have been reinvested in the business. The business has gone from labor intensive to capital intensive and semiautomatic. Automation allows Malden to produce weekly 1.4 million yards of fabric in 140 styles and 5,000 colors. Even with automation, financial success, reflected in an increase in sales from $119 million to $403 million during the past decade, has resulted in an increase in the labor force to 3,200 employees.

Further illustrating company and employee loyalty is the response to a December 1995 fire that destroyed a significant portion of Malden Mills factory complex and left 1,400 workers fearing for their jobs. The company president indicated Malden Mills would continue paychecks and health benefits and rebuild the plant. When asked why, he responded, "It was the right thing to do." To which an employee commented, "And that is the kind of man I want to work for."

Source: Susan Diesenhouse, "A Textile Mill Thrives by Breaking All the Rules," *The New York Times,* July 24, 1994, p. F5, and a CBS news report of December 25, 1995.

---

[8]William J. Abernathy and Kenneth Wayne, "Limits of the Learning Curve," *Harvard Business Review,* September–October 1974, pp. 109–119.

whole, it does achieve one or both of these positions vis-à-vis its narrow market target.[9]

Following a focused strategy, regional breweries that cater to local taste preferences, such as Iron City Beer® in Pittsburgh, have prospered, while Miller®, Coors®, and Budweiser® dominate the U.S. market. Learjet follows a focused strategy in designing and building corporate aircraft, leaving the market for larger passenger aircraft to firms such as Boeing and the market for smaller private planes to firms such as Piper Aircraft.

According to Porter, firms that do not set one of these competitive strategies as a goal or that try to be all things to all people are doomed to be "stuck in the middle." Unable to effectively compete on the basis of price or differentiation in the market as a whole or in a particular market niche, firms stuck in the middle are doomed to low profitability.

The 1997 bankruptcy of Montgomery Ward is an example of the consequences of being stuck in the middle. In the early 1980s, Montgomery Ward and Sears Roebuck were America's largest mall-based retailers. In response to low-cost competitors such as Wal-Mart and "category killers" such as Circuit City, Sears decided to emphasize established brands, service, and pleasant surroundings. Wards elected to reduce prices and costs by stocking a lower grade of merchandise. Unfortunately, Wards ended up "stuck in the middle," unable to compete with the low prices of Wal-Mart or the higher grade of merchandise and service offered by retailers such as Sears and J.C. Penney.[10]

Research Shows 1–2 considers cost leadership and product or service differentiation among the working principles for twenty-first century corporations.

1-2   RESEARCH SHOWS

WORKING PRINCIPLES FOR TWENTY-FIRST CENTURY CORPORATIONS

A *Business Week* editorial reinforced the importance of competing on the basis of a business strategy of price or differentiation. However, recognizing the transitory nature of differentiation in a competitive environment, the editorial used the term "innovation" in place of "differentiation." According to *Business Week,* the first three working principles of the twenty-first century corporation are as follows:

1. *Everything gets cheaper faster.* "The Net destroys corporate pricing power. It allows customers, suppliers, and partners to compare prices from 100 or 1,000 sources, not just two or three, and erases market inefficiencies. It rapidly commoditizes all that is new, reducing prices fast. . . ."
2. *Cutting costs is the answer.* "In an economic universe of downward pressure on margins, one path to profitability will be to reduce expenses. . . ."
3. *Innovation builds profits.* "There is one way for corporations to circumvent principle No. 1 and raise prices. In an information economy, companies can gain an edge through new ideas and products. . . ." However, this advantage is temporary, so corporations following this strategy must innovate rapidly and continuously.

The editorial also points out that human capital is the only asset. In a twenty-first century corporation, creativity is the sole source of growth and wealth. Consequently, the "value of education raises exponentially in an economy based on ideas and analytic thinking."

Source: Based on "The Twenty-First Century Corporation," *Business Week,* August 28, 2000, p. 278.

---

[9]Porter, pp. 38–39.
[10]Kevin Mundt, "Why Sears Survived—and Ward and Woolworth's Didn't," *The Wall Street Journal,* July 28, 1997, p. A18.

THE ROLE OF MANAGEMENT ACCOUNTING IN GOAL ATTAINMENT

A major purpose of management accounting is to support the achievement of goals. Hence, determining an organization's strategic position goal has implications for the operation of an organization's management accounting system.

Careful budgeting and cost control with frequent and detailed performance reports are critical with a goal of cost leadership. When the product is difficult to distinguish from that of competitors, price is the primary basis of competition. Under these circumstances, everyone in the organization should, like Andrew Carnegie, continuously apply management accounting concepts to achieve and maintain cost leadership. In this case, the management accounting system should constantly compare actual costs with budgeted costs and signal the existence of significant differences. Presented is a simplified version of a performance report for costs during a budget period:

Budgeted (planned) Costs	Actual Costs	Deviation from Budget	Percent Deviation
$560,000	$595,000	$35,000 unfavorable	6.25

Frequent and detailed comparisons of actual and budgeted costs are less important when a differentiation strategy is followed. This is especially true when products have short life cycles or production is highly automated. In these situations, most costs are determined before production begins and there is little opportunity to undertake cost reduction activities thereafter.

With short product lives or automated manufacturing, exceptional care must go into the initial design of a product or service and the determination of how it will be produced or delivered. Here, detailed cost information assists in design and scheduling decisions. Presented is a simplified version of the predicted costs of producing a specialty product.

Engineering/Scheduling (12 hours @ $70) . . .	$ 840
Materials (detail omitted)	3,500
Equipment setup (2.5 hours @ $100)	250
Machine operation (9.5 hours @ $90)	855
Materials movement	150
Packing and shipping	675
Total	$6,270

When a differentiation strategy is followed, it often pays to work closely with customers to find ways to enhance the perceived value of a product or service. This leads to an analysis of costs from the customer's viewpoint. The customer may not want a costly feature. Alternatively, the customer may be willing to pay more for an additional feature that will reduce subsequent operating costs.

In designing its 777 aircraft, Boeing invited potential customers to set up offices in Boeing plants and to work with Boeing employees designing the aircraft. Many design changes were made to reduce customer costs. United Airlines, for example, convinced Boeing to move the location of the 777's fuel tanks to reduce servicing costs.

PLANNING, ORGANIZING, AND CONTROLLING

The process of selecting goals and strategies to achieve these goals is often referred to as **planning**. The implementation of plans requires the development of subgoals and the assignment of responsibility to achieve subgoals to specific individuals or groups within an organization. This process of making the organization into a well-ordered whole is called **organizing**. In organizing, the authority to take action to implement plans is delegated to other managers and employees.

Developing an **organization chart** illustrating the formal relationships that exist between the elements of an organization is an important part of organizing. An organization chart for Crown Department Stores is illustrated in Exhibit 1–3. The blocks represent organizational units, and the lines represent relationships between the units. Authority flows down through the organization. Top management delegates authority to use resources for limited purposes to subordinate managers who, in turn, delegate to their subordinates more limited authority for accomplishing more structured tasks. Responsibility flows up through the organization. People at the bottom are responsible for specific tasks, but the president is responsible for the operation of the entire organization.

A distinction is often made between line and staff departments. *Line departments* engage in activities that create and distribute goods and services to customers. *Staff departments* exist to facilitate the activities of line departments. In Exhibit 1–3, we see that Crown Department Stores has two levels of staff organizations—corporate and store. The corporate staff departments are Purchasing, Advertising, Treasurer, and Controller. Staff departments at the store level are Personnel, Accounting, and Maintenance. All other units are line departments. A change in plans can necessitate a change in the organization. For example, Crown's plan to discontinue the sale of hardware and add an art department during the coming year will necessitate an organizational change.

EXHIBIT 1–3

CROWN DEPARTMENT STORES' ORGANIZATION CHART

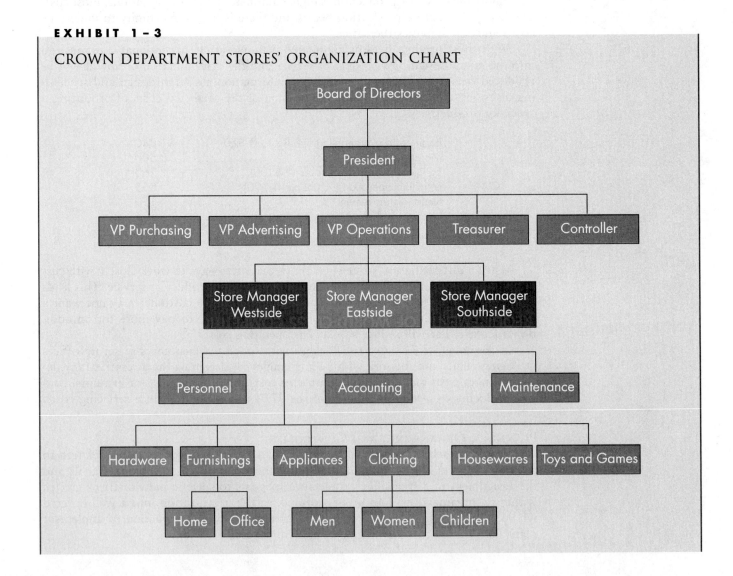

Controlling is the process of ensuring that results agree with plans. A brief example of a performance report for costs was presented previously. In the process of controlling operations, actual performance is compared with plans.

With a cost leadership strategy and long-lived products, if actual results deviate significantly from plans, an attempt is made to bring operations into line with plans, or the plans are adjusted. The original plan is adjusted if it is deemed no longer appropriate because of changed circumstances.

With a differentiation strategy and short-lived products, design and scheduling personnel will consider previous errors in predicting costs as they plan new products and services. Hence, the process of controlling feeds forward into the process of planning to form a continuous cycle coordinated through the management accounting system.

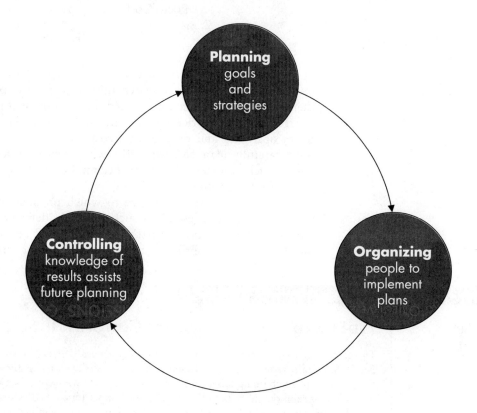

<table>
<tr></tr>
</table>

LEARNING OBJECTIVES 3

REQUIREMENTS OF WORLD-CLASS COMPETITION

For the past fifty years, the move away from isolated national economic systems toward an interdependent global economic system has become increasingly pronounced. International treaties, such as the 1993 North American Free Trade Agreement and the 1994 General Agreement on Tariffs and Trade, merely recognize an already existing and inevitable condition made possible by advances in

- Telecommunications to move data,
- Computers to process data into information, and
- Transportation to move products and people.

The labels of origins on goods (Japan, Germany, Canada, Taiwan, United States, and so forth) only scratch the surface of existing global relationships. Behind labels designating a product's final assembly point are components from all over the world.

The move toward a global economy has heightened competition and reduced selling prices to such an extent that there is little or no room for error in managing costs

or pricing products. Moreover, customers are not just looking for the best price. Well-informed buyers routinely search the world for the product or service that best fits their needs on the three interrelated dimensions of price/cost, quality, and service.

To customers, price includes not only the initial purchase price but also subsequent operating and maintenance costs. To compete on the basis of price, the seller must carefully manage costs. Otherwise, reduced prices might squeeze product margins to such an extent that a sale becomes unprofitable. Hence, price competition implies cost competition.

Quality refers to the degree to which products or services meet the customer's needs. Service includes things such as timely delivery, helpfulness of sales personnel, and subsequent support. What's Happening 1–2 takes a look at how Federal Express and United Parcel Service compete on the basis of quality, service, and price.

1-2   WHAT'S HAPPENING?

FedEx and UPS Stage Battle Customer Is Sure to Win

To increase customer service in the $18 billion express delivery business, Federal Express introduced FedEx Shipr, a personal computer-based system that lets even its smallest customers use a modem to order pickups, print shipping labels, and track deliveries. "We have to stay ahead of the competition" was the theme of remarks describing this service by Dennis Jones, FedEx's chief information officer.

Almost immediately, United Parcel Service announced a similar service. Responding to a reporter's question, Joe Pyne, vice-president of marketing at UPS, commented, "There's no question we track FedEx, just like they track us."

Both companies invest heavily in equipment and infrastructure to continue to meet increasingly tight delivery deadlines. In the late 1990s, UPS invested $120 million in sorting hubs for air shipments while FedEx invested $1.8 billion in new aircraft. To better utilize this equipment, FedEx entered into an arrangement with the U.S. Postal Service to ship some USPS packages while the USPS placed FedEx boxes in selected Post Office buildings.

A recent article in *Business Week* reported that UPS has gained at least a temporary advantage by utilizing information technology to integrate its traditional strengths in ground transportation with its overnight air transportation system. According to the article, "UPS, like FedEx, still uses planes to make most (overnight) deliveries. But in the past two years, its logisticians have also figured out how to make quick mid-distance deliveries—as far as 500 miles in one night—by truck, which is much less expensive than by air. As a result, UPS's overall cost structure per package is $6.64, compared with FedEx's $11.89."

While both companies battle to improve or at least maintain profitability, customers benefit from continuously improving quality and service at lower and lower costs. FedEx and UPS have cut prices in recent years for large-volume customers, reducing their profit margins on each sales dollar by one-third.

Source: Based on David Greising, "Watch Out for Flying Packages," *Business Week* (November 14, 1994), p. 40; and Charles Haddad, "Ground Wars: UPS's Rapid Ascent Leaves FedEx Scrambling," *Business Week*, May 21, 2001.

Managers of successful companies know they compete in a global market with instant communications. Because the competition is hungry and always striving to gain a competitive advantage, world-class companies must continuously struggle to improve performance in these three interrelated dimensions: price/cost, quality, and service. Throughout this text, we will examine how firms can successfully compete on these three dimensions. As a starting point in our journey, we introduce cost driver concepts and consider how cost drivers and cost functions have changed during the twentieth century.

LEARNING OBJECTIVE 4

COST DRIVERS INFLUENCE COSTS

An **activity** is a unit of work. To serve a customer at a restaurant, a waiter or waitress might perform the following units of work:

- Seat customer and offer menu
- Take customer order
- Send order to kitchen
- Bring food to customer
- Replenish beverages
- Determine and bring bill to customer
- Collect money and give change
- Clear table

Each of these is an activity, and the performance of each activity consumes resources that cost money. To manage activities and their costs, it is necessary to understand how costs respond to **cost drivers**, the factors that cause or influence costs.

The most basic cost driver is customer demand. Without customer demand for products or services, the organization cannot exist. To serve customers, managers and employees make a variety of decisions and take numerous actions. These decisions and actions, undertaken to satisfy customer demand, drive costs. While these cost drivers may be classified in a variety of ways, we believe that dividing them into the three categories of structural, organizational, and activity cost drivers (as summarized in Exhibit 1–4) provides a useful foundation for the study of management accounting.

STRUCTURAL COST DRIVERS

Structural cost drivers are fundamental choices about the size and scope of operations and technologies employed in delivering products or services to customers.[11] The types of activities and the costs of activities performed to satisfy customer needs are influenced by an organization's size, its location, the scope of its operations, and the technologies used. Decisions affecting structural cost drivers are made infrequently, and once made, the organization is committed to a course of action that will be difficult to change. For a chain of discount stores, possible structural cost drivers include:

- *Determining the size of the stores.* This will affect the variety of merchandise that can be carried and operating costs.
- *Determining the type of construction.* While a lean warehouse type of construction may be less expensive, it may not be an appropriate setting for selling high-fashion clothing.

---

[11]John Shank (1989); and John Shank and Vijay Govindarajan, building on the work of Riley, identify five structural and six executional cost drivers. We identify their executional drivers as operational drivers and add the third category of activity cost drivers. See Daniel Riley, "Competitive Cost-Based Investment Strategies for Industrial Companies," *Manufacturing Issues* (New York: Booz, Allen, Hamilton, 1987).

EXHIBIT 1–4

STRUCTURAL, ORGANIZATIONAL, AND ACTIVITY COST DRIVERS

Structural cost drivers are fundamental choices about the size and scope of operations and technologies employed in delivering products or services to customers. General Motors' decision to locate the new Saturn automobile plant near Nashville, Tennessee, is an example of a structural cost driver.

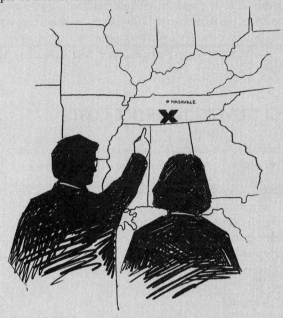

Organizational cost drivers are choices concerning the organization of activities and the involvement of persons inside and outside the organization in decision making. Authorizing employees to make decisions is an example of an organizational cost driver.

Activity cost drivers are specific units of work (activities) performed to serve customer needs that consume costly resources. Assembling a product is an example of an activity cost driver

- *Determining the location of the stores.* Locating in a shopping mall may cost more and subject the store to mall regulations but provide for more customer traffic and shared advertising.
- *Determining the type of technology to employ in the stores.* A computerized system for maintaining all inventory and sales data requires a large initial investment and fixed annual operating costs while providing more current information. However, the computerized inventory and sales systems may be less expensive at high sales volumes than a less costly system relying more on clerks taking physical inventory.

ORGANIZATIONAL COST DRIVERS

Organizational cost drivers are choices concerning the organization of activities and the involvement of persons inside and outside the organization in decision making. Like structural cost drivers, organizational cost drivers influence costs by affecting the types of activities and the costs of activities performed to satisfy customer needs. Decisions that affect organizational cost drivers are made within the context of previous decisions affecting structural cost drivers. In a manufacturing organization, previous decisions about plant, equipment, and location are taken as a given when decisions impacting organizational cost drivers are made. Examples of organizational cost drivers at a manufacturing organization include:

- *Deciding to work closely with a limited number of suppliers.* This relationship enables obtaining the proper materials in the proper quantities at the optimal time. Developing linkages with suppliers may also result in suppliers' initiatives that improve the profitability of both organizations.
- *Providing employees with cost information and authorizing them to make decisions.* This helps improve decision speed and reduce costs while making employees more customer oriented. Production employees may, for example, offer product design suggestions that reduce manufacturing costs or reduce defects.
- *Deciding to reorganize the existing equipment in the plant so that sequential operations are closer.* This more efficient layout reduces the cost of moving inventory between workstations.
- *Designing components of a product so they can fit together only in the correct manner.* This may reduce defects as well as assembly time and cost.
- *Deciding to manufacture a low-volume product on low-speed, general-purpose equipment rather than high-speed, special-purpose equipment.* Assuming the special-purpose equipment is more difficult and costly to set up for a new job, this decision may increase operating time and cost while reducing setup time and cost.

ACTIVITY COST DRIVERS

Activity cost drivers are specific units of work (activities) performed to serve customer needs that consume costly resources. Several examples of activities in a restaurant were mentioned previously. The customer may be outside the organization, such as a client of an advertising firm, or inside the organization, such as an accounting office that receives maintenance services. Because the performance of activities consumes resources and resources cost money, the performance of activities drives costs (see the following diagram).

The basic decisions concerning which available activities will be used to respond to customer requests have already been made. At this level, execution of previous plans

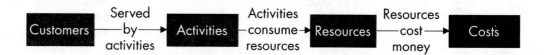

and following prescribed activities are important. All of the examples of structural and organizational cost drivers contained decision-oriented words. In the following list of activity cost drivers for a manufacturing organization, note the absence of the decision-oriented words.

- Placing a purchase order for raw materials
- Inspecting incoming raw materials
- Moving items being manufactured between workstations
- Setting up a machine to work on a product
- Spending machine time working on a product
- Spending labor time working on a product
- Hiring and training a new employee
- Packing an order for shipment
- Processing a sales order
- Shipping a product

In managing costs, management makes choices concerning structural and organizational cost drivers. These decisions affect the types of activities required to satisfy customer needs. Because different types of activities have different costs, management's decisions ultimately affect activity costs and profitability. Hence, good decision making at the level of structural and organizational cost drivers requires an understanding of the linkages among the three types of cost drivers and knowledge of the costs of different activities. We will examine these linkages throughout our study of management accounting.

LEARNING OBJECTIVE 5

CHANGING COST DRIVERS AND COST FUNCTIONS

As technology has advanced and competition has intensified, the management of most organizations has made decisions affecting their organizations' cost drivers. Perhaps the most fundamental shift in manufacturing organizations has been the movement from labor-intensive to automated assembly techniques. These changes have influenced the activities performed to meet customer needs and the responsiveness of costs to changes in the activity sales.

At the beginning of the twentieth century, products had long life cycles, production procedures were relatively straightforward, production was labor based, and only a limited number of related products were produced in a single plant. It was said of the Model T Ford that "you could have any color you wanted, as long as it was black." The largest cost elements of most manufactured goods were the cost of raw materials and the wages paid to production employees. Both of these costs were highly related to the number of units manufactured. In Exhibit 1–5, line A illustrates the traditional relationship between total costs and annual unit sales found at the start of the twentieth century.

The twentieth century has seen an accelerating shift from traditional labor-paced activities with a large portion of costs that vary with sales toward production procedures requiring significant investments in automated equipment. In the past, production employees used equipment to assist them in performing their jobs. Now employees spend considerable time scheduling, setting up, maintaining, and moving materials to and from equipment. They spend relatively little time on actual production. The equipment does the work, and the employees keep it running efficiently. Increased complexity of production procedures and an increase in the variety of products produced in a single facility have also caused a shift toward more support personnel and fewer production employees. The result has been a decrease in costs that change with the volume of production, illustrated by the flatter slope of line B.

The investment in automated equipment and the costs of maintaining such equipment have resulted in a significant increase in the basic costs that do not vary with

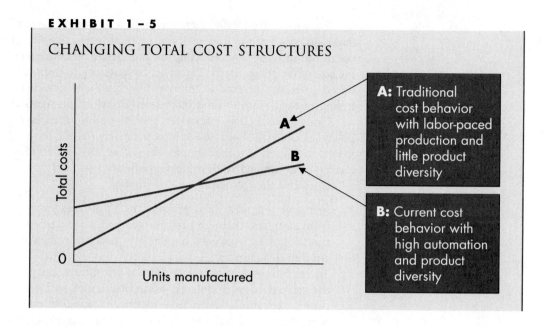

EXHIBIT 1-5

CHANGING TOTAL COST STRUCTURES

A: Traditional cost behavior with labor-paced production and little product diversity

B: Current cost behavior with high automation and product diversity

annual production. These costs are represented by the higher vertical axis intercept of line B.

Line B illustrates the relationship often found as we enter the twenty-first century. If units manufactured is used as the only independent variable, the new cost structure results in relatively higher costs at low volumes and relatively lower costs at high volumes. Both changes make it increasingly important to wisely manage manufacturing capacity and the costs that do not vary with units manufactured.

Given the variety and number of factors that drive costs, it is apparent that cost functions are multidimensional. What's more, the specific set of cost drivers differs from organization to organization. To manage costs, it is necessary to manage an organization's activities. Decisions about activities must be made in advance of the performance of an activity, requiring a detailed knowledge of alternative activities and their related costs. The need to understand and manage the multitude of structural, organizational, and activity cost drivers underlies Peter Drucker's observation that "accounting has become the most intellectually challenging area in the field of management."[12] We will examine the multidimensional nature of activity costs in the next chapter.

LEARNING OBJECTIVE 6

MANAGEMENT ACCOUNTING AS AN EMPOWERMENT TOOL

For many years, organizations experienced a growth in staff size as tasks performed by line personnel were taken over by staff specialists. Unfortunately, many advantages of staff specialization were offset by:

- Increased overall costs,
- A reduced feeling of achievement on the part of line personnel charged with implementing the decisions of others,
- Delays in decision making as coordination problems increased, and
- A tendency for employees in specific functional areas, such as marketing, engineering, and accounting, to view problems from the narrow perspective of their discipline.

[12]Peter Drucker, "Be Data Literate—Know What to Know," *The Wall Street Journal*, December 1, 1992, p. A16.

Since the early 1990s, there has been a movement toward empowering employees to make decisions at the lowest organizational level possible. This movement has flattened organization charts by reducing the number of management layers. It has also reduced the size of corporate staffs. Perceived benefits of the empowerment movement include reduced costs, an increase in the speed with which decisions are made, and an increased feeling of ownership of (and interest in) decisions on the part of line employees.

Gone are the costs associated with the eliminated layers of management and staff positions. Activities previously performed by people in these positions have been eliminated, assigned to other employees (often closer to the bottom of the organization chart), or combined with other activities.

Consider the following two examples:

1. In many organizations, production employees now order raw materials directly from suppliers through prearranged purchase agreements. This contrasts with the traditional approach of having all purchase orders processed by a separate purchasing department.
2. To encourage employees to take more interest in product quality and to reduce the related costs of defects, some businesses authorize workers to stop manufacturing operations when they identify a possible quality problem. This contrasts with the traditional approach of maintaining production and inspecting finished products for defects.

In both examples, delegating authority to lower levels results in a change in the activities performed and the costs incurred to fill customer needs. In the first example, the size of the purchasing department is reduced, the role of the purchasing department is changed, and the number of activities involved in placing a purchase order is reduced. Purchasing department employees now focus more on nonroutine tasks such as developing long-term relationships with a limited number of suppliers dedicated to helping both businesses prosper. Production employees perform the routine and streamlined activity of placing purchase orders.

In the second example, the activities involving the inspection of finished goods may be eliminated. More significantly, the activities of continuing to work on defective products and the reworking of defective products are reduced or eliminated. Again, production employees are now responsible for inspections. Ideally, this is done at lower cost as employees monitor production or move inventory.

These changes have required organizations to open their books to employees and to provide them with information previously regarded as confidential. They have also forced the remaining staff to focus more on the needs of line personnel, who are the staff's customers. What's Happening 1–3 illustrates how one company improved performance after opening its books to employees.

One specific result in the area of management accounting is the emergence of **activity costing**, which involves the determination of costs for specific activities (such as packaging an order) performed to fill customer needs. The cost to fill the customer's needs is then determined as the sum of the cost of all related activities.

When coupled with an analysis of alternative ways of filling customer needs or manufacturing a new product, activity cost information empowers line personnel to better manage activities under their control. Other examples of management accounting concepts developed to empower employee decision making include value chain analysis and quality cost measurements. These and related concepts will receive extensive treatment in subsequent chapters.

<table>
<tr><td>LEARNING OBJECTIVE 7</td><td>

MEASUREMENT, MANAGEMENT, AND ETHICS

</td></tr>
</table>

Performance measurement, also referred to as **outcomes assessment,** is the determination of the extent to which actual outcomes correspond to planned outcomes. It is a

1-3   WHAT'S HAPPENING?

EMPOWERMENT BRINGS SPRINGFIELD REMANUFACTURING FROM THE BRINK TO PROFITS

Although Springfield Remanufacturing Corporation is now profitable, in the late 1970s the company was bleeding red ink, and workers were so distrustful of management that they wore raincoats and galoshes to company meetings in preparation for another "snow job."

But when Jack Stack became president, he opened the books, providing employees with information on all aspects of operations, ranging from revenue and purchasing costs to management and labor expenses. According to Stack, this open-book policy is one of the actions responsible for bringing Springfield from the brink of bankruptcy to record earnings. "The more [employees] learned, the more they could do. . . .We matched up higher levels of thinking with higher levels of performance."

Candice Smalley, a nozzle rebuilder, says she didn't realize how much a factory floor worker could affect profits until she started seeing financials and hearing about usage and overhead. ". . . [I]t made us start trying to improve our quality." Denise Bredfeldt, the training director, says that before Springfield adopted an open-book policy, "people would just punch the clock and leave." Now, when things get bad, people start brainstorming about how to improve. Employees say they have a heightened sense of community and are willing to do whatever it takes to maintain competitiveness.

Source: "Company Wins Workers' Loyalty by Opening Its Books," *The Wall Street Journal,* December 20, 1993, pp. B1–B2.

management adage that "what you count is what you get." Because managers control what is being measured, successful organizations are very careful about what they measure. Selecting inappropriate performance measures may lead employees to take actions that do not support the attainment of organizational goals and plans.

If performance is measured by return on assets (net income/total assets), managers may be reluctant to replace inefficient, fully depreciated equipment with new equipment because the resulting increase in the denominator will reduce return on investment. If the performance of a case worker is measured on the basis of the number of cases being worked on, the case worker will be motivated to keep cases open in an effort to improve the performance measure, rather than being motivated to complete case assignments as soon as possible. If the performance of professional employees is measured on the basis of billable hours, the employees may be motivated to maximize billable hours, perhaps in an unethical manner. What's Happening 1–4 looks at an example of ethically questionable billing practices.

Performance measurement draws attention to whatever is being measured and causes people to improve performance on the dimension being measured. It also draws attention away from other variables that, in fact, may be more critical for success. If on-time delivery is critical to success but delivery costs, rather than delivery times, are reported in performance reports, employees will be more interested in minimizing delivery costs than maximizing on-time delivery.

OUTCOME ASSESSMENT

Outcome assessment is a critical element of success. Managers use outcome assessment information to improve processes, modify plans, or both. Management needs to determine the extent to which performance moves the organization toward its mission and goals. Outcome assessment requires the selection of performance measures

- That support, rather than hinder, the achievement of an organization's mission and goals.
- That are appropriate for the strategies being used to accomplish goals.
- That are cost effective, with perceived benefits exceeding the costs of measurement.

PERFORMANCE PRESSURES LEAD BAR ASSOCIATION TO TACKLE ETHICALLY QUESTIONABLE BILLING

On a six-hour trip, flying to consult a major client, a lawyer spends five hours preparing a brief for another client. What is the total time billed for services rendered?

Lawyers, among the few professionals who typically bill by the hour, are experts at finding creative ways to increase billable hours and revenues. According to Amy Stevens, "Their reasons are a potent mix of elementary economics and raw survival instinct. A firm's earnings are a function of the firm's billable hours, and time sheets are usually a factor in determining individual associates' promotions and bonuses as well as partners' profit shares." Hence, the flying lawyer might be tempted to double bill for eleven hours (6 hours and 5 hours), even though the total time involved in the trip was only six hours.

Concerned that questionable billing practices are contributing to a "discouraging" opinion of the profession, the American Bar Association (ABA) considered the possible need to rewrite its code of ethics to specifically prohibit double billing. The ABA Ethics Committee ultimately decided that "rather than looking to profit from the fortuity of coincidental scheduling . . . the lawyer who has agreed to bill solely on the basis of time spent is obliged to pass the benefits of these economies on to the client." In other words, double billing is unethical.

Source: Based on Amy Stevens, "ABA Tackles Firm's Tendencies for Creative Clockwork in Billing," *The Wall Street Journal,* December 17, 1993, p. B10; and an August 2001 search of http://www.abanet.org.

The systematic measurement and reporting of outcomes must also be timely and in a form that is easy to use. Managers should work with management accountants to identify appropriate measures and have them included in a systematic measurement and reporting system. See Exhibit 1–6 for an overview of this process.

It is possible to develop such long lists of potential performance measures that it becomes difficult to know where to begin. If an attempt is made to report on everything, the costs of assessment will certainly exceed the benefits. Additionally, a large number of items included in performance reports will make it difficult to address any of them. One possible solution is to agree on three or four measures most in need of immediate attention and focus on them in performance reports. When performance of these items has improved, they are replaced by other performance measures now deemed more in need of improvement. While it may not be possible to concurrently improve performance on all dimensions, this approach supports the notion of continuous improvement.

ETHICAL DILEMMAS

Ethics deals with the moral quality, fitness, or propriety of a course of action that may injure or benefit people. Ethics goes beyond legality, which refers to what is permitted under the law, to consider the moral quality of an action. Because situations involving ethics are not guided by well-defined rules, they are often subjective.

Although some actions are clearly ethical (working a full day in exchange for a full day's pay) and others are clearly unethical (pumping contaminated waste into an underground aquifer used as a source of drinking water), managers are often faced with situations that do not fall clearly into either category.

- Accelerating shipments at the end of the quarter to improve current earnings.
- Keeping inventory that is unlikely to be used on the books to avoid recording a loss.
- Purchasing supplies from a relative rather than seeking bids.
- Basing a budget on an overly optimistic sales forecast.
- Assigning some costs of Contract A to Contract B to avoid an unfavorable performance report on Contract A.

EXHIBIT 1 – 6

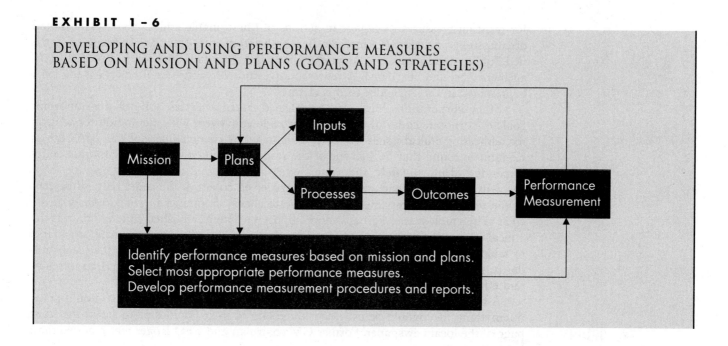

DEVELOPING AND USING PERFORMANCE MEASURES BASED ON MISSION AND PLANS (GOALS AND STRATEGIES)

Identify performance measures based on mission and plans.
Select most appropriate performance measures.
Develop performance measurement procedures and reports.

Many ethical dilemmas involve actions that are perceived to have desirable short-run consequences and highly probable undesirable long-run consequences. The ethical action is to face an undesirable situation now to avoid a worse situation later, yet the decision maker may prefer to believe that things will work out in the long run, be overly concerned with the consequences of not doing well in the short run, or simply not care about the future because the problem will then belong to someone else. In a situation that is clearly unethical, the future consequences are known to be avoidable and undesirable. In situations involving questionable ethics, there is some hope that things will work out.

- Next year's sales will more than make up for the accelerated shipments.
- The obsolete inventory can be used in a new nostalgia line of products.
- The relative may charge more but provides excellent service.
- You need to have more confidence in your sales staff.
- We can make up for the cost shift by working extra hard to be efficient with the remaining work on Contract B.

When forced to think about the situation, most employees want to act in an ethical manner. The problem faced by personnel involved in measurement and reporting is that while they may question the propriety of a proposed action, the arguments may be plausible, they want to be team players, and their careers can be affected by "whistleblowing." Of course, careers are also affected when individuals are identified as being involved in unethical behavior. The careers of people who fail to point out unethical behavior may also be affected, especially if they have a responsibility for measurement and reporting.

Major ethical dilemmas often evolve from a series of small compromises, none of which appears serious enough to warrant taking a stand on ethical grounds. Unfortunately, these small compromises establish a pattern of behavior that is increasingly difficult to reverse. The key to avoiding these situations is recognizing the early warning signs of situations that involve questionable ethical behavior and taking whatever action is appropriate.

CODE OF ETHICS

Codes of ethics have been developed by professional organizations to increase members' awareness of the importance of ethical behavior and to provide a reference point for resisting pressures to engage in actions of questionable ethics. These professional organizations include the American Bar Association, the American Institute of Certified Public Accountants, the American Medical Association, and the Institute of Management Accountants (IMA). A representative code of professional ethics for the IMA is presented in the appendix to this chapter.

Many corporations have also established codes of ethics. One of the important goals of corporate codes of ethics is to provide employees with a common foundation for addressing ethical issues. A survey conducted by two members of the IMA's Ethics Committee found that 56 percent of the responding companies have corporate codes of conduct. Unfortunately, the same survey also reported that although senior management and middle management usually received copies of the code, only 57 percent of the responding companies with corporate codes of conduct provided copies of the code to all employees.[13] Perhaps more important than a published code of ethics is the ethical tone set by top management. If employees perceive top management as capable of taking unethical actions or as less than 100 percent committed to high ethical standards, they will be less inclined to make the difficult decisions often required to maintain ethics.

A basic rule used by General Motors Corporation is that employees should never do anything they would be ashamed to explain to their families or to see in the front page of the local newspaper. Former GM chairman and CEO Roger Smith added that:

> *"ethical conduct in business goes beyond this, however. For example, one of the basic needs of top management is to receive reliable data and honest opinions from people throughout the organization. Too often, subordinates are reluctant to tell all the details of a project or assignment that has failed or is in trouble. This very human trait occurs in all walks of life, whether personal, business, or governmental, and contributes to the making of bad decisions. In short, ethics is an essential element of success in business."[14]*

Summary

Management accounting concerns the use of financial and related information by persons inside specific organizations and is primarily concerned with the future. It helps organizations determine goals and select strategies for achieving goals.

A fundamental goal of every organization concerns its strategic position in comparison to its competition. Careful budgeting with frequent and detailed performance reports is critical to achieving a strategic position of cost leadership. If the goal is product differentiation, management needs to view products or services from the customer's perspective and work to enhance the value of the organization's products or services to the customer. Activity cost information should be used to design products or services that meet customer needs at an acceptable price and cost to the seller.

World-class companies must constantly improve their performance on the dimensions of price/cost, quality, and service (including time). Success requires managing the multitude of factors that drive costs. These cost drivers are placed into three categories:

1. *Structural cost drivers*—choices about the size and scope of operations.
2. *Organizational cost drivers*—choices concerning the organization of activities and the involvement of persons inside and outside the organization in decision making.
3. *Activity cost drivers*—specific units of work performed to serve customer needs.

---

[13]Robert B. Sweeney and Howard L. Siers, "Survey: Ethics and Corporate America," *Management Accounting*, June 1990, pp. 34–40.

[14]Roger B. Smith, "Ethics in Business: An Essential Element of Success," *Management Accounting*, June 1990, p. 50.

The shift from traditional labor-paced activities toward automated production procedures and from the mass production of a limited number of long-lived products toward the limited production of a large number of short-lived products has made activity cost functions multidimensional. We will examine the multidimensional nature of activity costs in the next chapter.

Appendix

STANDARDS OF ETHICAL CONDUCT FOR PRACTITIONERS OF MANAGEMENT ACCOUNTING AND FINANCIAL MANAGEMENT

Competence

Practitioners of management accounting and financial management have a responsibility to:

- Maintain an appropriate level of professional competence by ongoing development of their knowledge and skills.
- Perform their professional duties in accordance with relevant laws, regulations, and technical standards.
- Prepare complete and clear reports and recommendations after appropriate analysis of relevant and reliable information.

Confidentiality

Practitioners of management accounting and financial management have a responsibility to:

- Refrain from disclosing confidential information acquired in the course of their work except when authorized, unless legally obliged to do so.
- Inform subordinates as appropriate regarding the confidentiality of information acquired in the course of their work and monitor their activities to assure the maintenance of that confidentiality.
- Refrain from using or appearing to use confidential information acquired in the course of their work for unethical or illegal advantage either personally or through third parties.

Integrity

Practitioners of management accounting and financial management have a responsibility to:

- Avoid actual or apparent conflicts of interest and advise all appropriate parties of any potential conflict.
- Refrain from engaging in any activity that would prejudice their ability to carry out their duties ethically.
- Refuse any gift or hospitality that would influence or appear to influence their actions.
- Refrain from actively or passively subverting the attainment of the organization's legitimate and ethical objectives.
- Recognize and communicate professional limitations or other constraints that would preclude responsible judgment of successful performance of an activity.
- Communicate unfavorable as well as favorable information and professional judgments or opinions.
- Refrain from engaging in or supporting any activity that would discredit the profession.

Objectivity

Practitioners of management accounting and financial management have a responsibility to:

- Communicate information fairly and objectively.
- Disclose fully all relevant information that could reasonably be expected to influence an intended user's understanding of the reports, comments, and recommendations presented.

RESOLUTION OF ETHICAL CONFLICT

In applying the standards of ethical conflict, practitioners of management accounting and financial management may encounter problems in identifying unethical behavior or in resolving an ethical conflict. When faced with significant ethical issues, practitioners of management accounting and financial management should follow the established policies of the organization bearing on the resolution of such conflict. If these policies do not resolve the ethical conflict, management accountants should consider the following courses of action.

- Discuss such problems with the immediate supervisor except when it appears that the supervisor is involved, in which case the problem should be presented initially to the next higher managerial levels. If satisfactory resolution cannot be achieved when the problem is initially presented, submit the issue to the next higher management level. If the immediate supervisor is the chief executive officer, or equivalent, the acceptable reviewing authority may be a group such as the audit committee, executive committee, board of directors, board of trustees, or owners. Contact with levels above the immediate supervisor should be initiated only with the supervisor's knowledge, assuming the superior is not involved. Except where legally prescribed, communication of such problems to authorities or individuals not employed or engaged by the organization is not considered appropriate.
- Clarify relevant concepts by confidential discussion with an objective advisor (e.g., IMA Ethics Consulting Service) to obtain an understanding of possible courses of action.
- Consult your own attorney as to legal obligations and rights concerning the ethical conflict.
- If the ethical conflict still exists after exhausting all levels of internal review, there may be no other recourse on significant matters than to resign from the organization and to submit an informative memorandum to an appropriate representative of the organization. After resignation, depending on the nature of the ethical conflict, it may also be appropriate to notify other parties.

Source: Standards of Ethical Conduct for Practitioners of Management Accounting and Financial Management, Statement No. 1C (Revised), (Montvale, NJ: Institute of Management Accountants, April 30, 1997).

Review Problem

The solution to the review problem is found on page 37. To maximize your learning, you should make a serious attempt to develop a written solution to the review problem before looking at the solution. If there are errors in your solution, you should then attempt to determine their causes.

Classifying Cost Drivers
Classify each of the following as a structural, organizational, or activity cost driver.

a. Meals served to airplane passengers.
b. General Motors' decision to start manufacturing the Saturn®, a totally new automobile in completely new facilities.
c. Zenith's decision to sell its computer operations and focus on the core television business.
d. Number of tax returns filed electronically by H&R Block.
e. Number of passenger cars in a Via train.
f. Coor's decision to expand its market area east from the Rocky Mountains.
g. Boeing's decision to invite airlines to assist in designing the model 777 airplane.
h. DaimlerChrysler's decision to use cross-disciplinary teams to design the Neon® automobile.
i. A hospital's decision to establish review committees to evaluate the appropriateness and effectiveness of medical procedures with the goal of improving patient care.
j. Harley-Davidson's efforts to restructure production procedures to reduce inventories and machine setup times.

Key Terms

Activity (p. 17)
Activity costing (p. 22)
Activity cost drivers (p. 19)
Balance sheet (p. 5)
Controlling (p. 15)
Cost driver (p. 17)
Cost driver analysis (p. 7)
Ethics (p. 24)
Financial accounting (p. 5)
For-profit organization (p. 8)
Goal (p. 8)
Income statement (p. 5)
Management accounting (p. 6)
Mission (p. 8)

Not-for-profit organization (p. 8)
Organization chart (p. 14)
Organizational cost drivers (p. 19)
Organizing (p. 13)
Outcomes assessment (p. 22)
Performance measurement (p. 22)
Planning (p. 13)
Statement of cash flows (p. 5)
Strategic cost management (p. 7)
Strategic position (p. 9)
Strategic position analysis (p. 7)
Strategy (p. 8)
Structural cost drivers (p. 17)
Value chain analysis (p. 7)

Review Questions

1. Contrast financial and management accounting on the basis of user orientation, purpose of information, level of aggregation, length of time period, orientation toward past or future, conformance to external standards, and emphasis on objective data.

2. What three themes are a part of strategic cost management?
3. Distinguish between a mission and a goal.
4. Describe the three strategic positions that Porter views as leading to business success.
5. Distinguish between how management accounting would support the strategy of cost leadership and the strategy of product differentiation.
6. Why are the phases planning, organizing, and controlling referred to as a *continuous cycle?*
7. Identify three advances that have fostered the move away from isolated national economic systems toward an interdependent global economy.
8. What are the three interrelated dimensions of today's competition?
9. Differentiate among structural, organizational, and activity cost drivers.
10. What is the link between performing activities and incurring costs?
11. How have the cost drivers and total cost functions of many organizations changed during the twentieth century?
12. Briefly describe employee empowerment and the role of activity costing in employee empowerment.
13. Describe how pressures to have desirable short-run outcomes can lead to ethical dilemmas.

Exercises

1-1
Matching

Match the following terms with the best descriptions. Each description is used only once.

Terms

1. Ethics
2. Mission
3. Controlling
4. Goal
5. Not-for-profit organization
6. Quality
7. Balance sheet
8. Income statement
9. Organizational cost driver
10. Financial accounting
11. Activity cost driver
12. Strategic cost driver
13. Management accounting
14. Resources
15. Product differentiation

Description

a. Designing components so they are easily assembled
b. The Starlight Foundation raising money to grant wishes for terminally ill children
c. Prepared as of a point in time
d. Accounting for external users
e. Increase year 2005 sales by 10 percent over year 2004 sales
f. Shows the results of operations for a period of time
g. Packing an order for shipment
h. Deciding to build a factory away from a highway but near a railroad
i. The degree to which a new television meets a buyer's expectations
j. Used internally to make decisions
k. Consumed by activities
l. The propriety of taking some action
m. Reduces customer price sensitivity
n. Basic purpose toward which activities are directed
o. Comparing the budget with the actual results

1-2
Financial and Management Accounting

Indicate whether each phrase is more descriptive of financial accounting or management accounting.

a. May be subjective
b. Often used to state corporate goals
c. Typically prepared quarterly or annually
d. May measure time or customer satisfaction
e. Future oriented
f. Subject to cost-benefit analysis
g. Keeps records of assets and liabilities
h. Highly aggregated statements
i. Must conform to external standards
j. Special-purpose reports
k. Decision-making tool
l. Income statement, balance sheet, and statement of cash flows

1-3
Financial and Management Accounting

Assume Michelle Jones has just been promoted to product manager at Procter & Gamble. Although she is an accomplished sales representative and well versed in market research, her accounting background is limited to reviewing her paycheck, balancing her checkbook, filing income tax returns, and reviewing the company's annual income statement and balance sheet. She commented that while the financial statements are no doubt useful to investors, she just doesn't see how accounting can help her be a good product manager.

Required:
Based on her remarks, it is apparent that Michelle's view of accounting is limited to financial accounting. Explain some of the important differences between financial and management accounting and suggest some ways management accounting can help Michelle be a better product manager.

1-4
Missions, Goals, and Strategies

Identify each of the following as a mission, goal, or strategy.

a. Budget time for study, sleep, and relaxation
b. Provide shelter for the homeless
c. Provide an above-average return to investors
d. Protect the public
e. Locate fire stations so that the average response time is less than five minutes
f. Overlap police patrols so that there are always police cars on major thoroughfares
g. Achieve a 12 percent market share
h. Lower prices and costs
i. Select the most scenic route to drive between Las Vegas and Denver
j. Graduate from college

1-5
Line and Staff Organization

Presented are the names of some departments often found in a merchandising organization.

a. Maintenance   d. Payroll
b. Home Furnishings   e. Human Resources
c. Store Manager   f. Advertising

Required:
Identify each as a line or a staff department.

1–6
Line and Staff
Organization

Presented are the names of some departments often found in a manufacturing organization.

a. Manager, Plant 2   d. Controller
b. Design Engineering   e. Property Accounting
c. President   f. Sales Manager, District 1

Required:
Identify each as a line or a staff department.

1–7
Developing an
Organization Chart

Develop an organization chart for a three-outlet bakery chain with a central baking operation and deliveries every few hours. Assume the business is incorporated and that the president has a single staff assistant. Also assume that the delivery truck driver reports to the bakery manager.

1–8
Classifying Cost
Drivers

Classify each of the following as structural, organizational, or activity cost drivers.

a. Oneida Silversmiths reorganizes production facilities from a layout in which all similar types of machines are grouped together to one in which a set of machines is designated for the production of a particular product and that set of machines is grouped together.
b. A cable television company decides to start offering telephone service.
c. Xerox Corporation decides to stop making personal computers.
d. Canon decides to start making high-volume photocopy equipment to compete head-to-head with Xerox.
e. The number of meals a cafeteria serves.
f. The number of miles a taxi drives.
g. A company eliminates the position of supervisor and has each work group elect a team leader.
h. Toyota empowers employees to halt production if a quality problem is identified.
i. The number of tons of grain a ship loads.
j. Crossgate Mall decides to build space for 80 additional stores.

1–9
Classifying Cost
Drivers

Mesa Construction managers provide design and construction management services for various commercial construction projects. Senior managers are trying to apply cost driver concepts to their firm to better understand Mesa's costs.

Required:
Classify each of the following actions or decisions as structural, organizational, or activity cost drivers.

a. The decision to be a leader in computer-assisted design services.
b. The decision to allow staff architects to follow a specific project through to completion.
c. The daily process of inspecting the progress on various construction projects.
d. The process of conducting extensive client interviews to assess the exact needs for Mesa services.
e. The decision to expand the market area by establishing an office in another state.
f. The decision to begin building projects with Mesa staff rather than relying on subcontractors.
g. The process of receiving approval from government authorities along with appropriate permits for each project.
h. The decision to organize the workforce into project teams.
i. The decision to build a new headquarters facility with areas for design and administration as well as storage and maintenance of construction equipment.
j. The process of grading building sites and preparing forms for foundations.

1-10
Identifying Monetary and Nonmonetary Performance Measures

Identify possible monetary and nonmonetary performance measures for each of the following situations. One nonmonetary measure should relate to quality, and one should relate to time.

a. Central University wishes to evaluate the success of last year's graduating class.
b. Cook County Hospital wishes to evaluate the performance of its emergency room.
c. L.L. Bean wishes to evaluate the performance of its telephone order–filling operations.
d. Hilton Hotels wishes to evaluate the performance of registration activities at one of its hotels.
e. United Parcel Service wishes to evaluate the success of its operations in Knoxville.

1-11
Identifying Monetary and Nonmonetary Performance Measures

Identify possible monetary and nonmonetary performance measures for each of the following situations. One nonmonetary measure should relate to quality, and one should relate to time.

a. AOL's evaluation of the performance of its Internet service in Huntsville.
b. Time Warner Cable's evaluation of the performance of new customer cable installations in Rochester.
c. Dell Computer's evaluation of the performance of its logistical arrangements for delivering computers to residential customers.
d. Amazon.com's evaluation of the performance of its Web site.
e. Eastern University's evaluation of the success of its freshman admissions activities.

1-12
Identifying Information Needs of Different Managers

Jerry Damson operates a number of auto dealerships for Acura and Honda. Identify possible monetary and nonmonetary performance measures for each of the following situations. One nonmonetary measure should relate to quality, and one should relate to time.

a. An individual sales associate.
b. The sales manager of a single dealership.
c. The general manager of a particular dealership.
d. The corporate chief financial officer.
e. The president of the corporation.

Discussion Questions and Cases

1-13
Goals and Strategies

a. What is your instructor's goal for students in this course? What strategies has he or she developed to achieve this goal?
b. What is your goal in this course? What strategies will help you achieve this goal?
c. What is your goal for this semester or term? What strategies will help you achieve this goal?
d. What is your employment goal? What strategies will help you achieve this goal?

1-14
Product Differentiation

You are the owner of Louie Lobster's Limited. You have no trouble catching lobsters, but you have difficulty in selling all that you catch. The problem is that all lobsters from all vendors look the same. You do catch high-quality lobsters, but you need to be able to tell your customers that your lobsters are better than those sold by other vendors.

Required:
a. What are some possible ways of distinguishing your lobsters from those of other vendors?
b. Explain the possible results of this differentiation.

1-15 (Appendix) Applying Ethical Standards for Management Accountants

Assume you are a recently hired management accountant and that you intend to follow the Institute of Management Accountants' Standards of Ethical Conduct. Indicate the ethical standard applicable to each of the following situations and determine the appropriate initial course of action.

a. Late Thursday afternoon you learn that your company has received a large government contract that will have a significant impact on future earnings. The award is to be publicly announced by the government agency on Friday afternoon. That evening at a family dinner, your brother-in-law, a stock broker, asks if this would be a good time to buy stock in the company you work for.

b. You are aware that your company has obsolete inventory recorded at cost in its accounting records. Disposing of this inventory or writing it down to its fair market value would significantly reduce reported earnings for the current period. While speaking with your firm's independent external auditor, you learn that your immediate supervisor recently told the auditor that the company has no obsolete or slow-moving inventory.

c. Prior to accepting your current position at a manufacturing organization, you spent four years in public accounting where your primary duties involved tax planning. While you believe your firm's accounting system does a good job of providing the information for compliance with external reporting and income tax requirements, you have become increasingly concerned about negative comments from internal decision makers concerning the usefulness of the accounting information. To date, you have not spent much time reading relevant professional journals or attending any professional continuing education programs. You are concerned that your supervisor will recognize your lack of expertise in cost accounting.

d. One of your first jobs with your new employer was assisting with the preparation of the budget for the coming year. Based on a predicted 20 percent increase in sales volume during the Christmas season, the budget for the early part of the year calls for large expenditures financed by borrowing that is to be repaid after the Christmas sales. The final meeting of the budget preparation committee was this morning. After having lunch with several other new employees in marketing, you come away with a concern that the sales forecast is unrealistic. The budget is to be forwarded to corporate headquarters for final approval tomorrow.

1-16 (Appendix) Ethics and Revenue Recognition

John is in charge of recording sales for a department of a retail firm. His supervisor, Mark, is evaluated based on year-end profits. This has been an especially bad year for the firm, and sales are lower than expected. However, Mark wants to show the highest possible profits for the year. Mark has discreetly asked John to record sales that occur on the first few days of next year as if they had happened in the current year. Doing this would increase revenues and thus make profits higher. John knows that he should record sales in their proper periods, but his evaluation from Mark will determine whether he gets a raise. In addition, if John does not do what Mark asks, he may be fired. However, if John does what Mark asks, he could be fired if his actions are detected.

Required:
Using the code of professional ethics presented in the appendix to Chapter 1 as a guide, what should John do?

1-17 Ethics and "Short-Term Borrowing"

Ethel, a secretary, is in charge of petty cash for a local law firm. Normally, about $200 is kept in the petty cash box. When Ethel is short on cash and needs some for lunch or to pay her babysitter, she sometimes takes a few dollars from the box. Since she is in charge of the box, nobody knows that she takes the money, and she always replaces it within a few days.

Required:

a. Is Ethel's behavior ethical?

b. Assume that Ethel has recently had major problems meeting her bills. She also is in charge of purchasing supplies for the office from petty cash. Last week when she needed $5 for the babysitter, she falsified a voucher for the amount of $5. Is this behavior ethical?

1-18
Ethics and Travel
Reimbursement

Scott takes many business trips throughout the year. All of his expenses are paid by his company. Last week he traveled to Rio De Janeiro, Brazil, and stayed there on business for five days. He is allowed a maximum of $28 per day for food and $100 per day for lodging. To his surprise, the food and accommodations in Brazil were much less than he expected. Being upset about traveling last week and having to sacrifice tickets he'd purchased to a Red Sox baseball game, he decided to inflate his expenses a bit. He increased his lodging expense from $50 per day to $75 per day and his food purchased from $10 per day to $20 per day. Therefore, for the five-day trip, he overstated his expenses by $175 total. After all, the allowance was higher than the amount he spent.

Required:

Assume that the company would never find out that he had actually spent less. Are Scott's actions ethical? Are they acceptable?

1-19 (Appendix)
Applying Ethical
Standards in
Various Professional
Positions

Many organizations have developed ethical standards for their respective professions. Using the code of professional ethics presented in the appendix to Chapter 1 as a model for the given profession, indicate the ethical standard(s) applicable to each of the following situations and determine the appropriate initial course of action.

a. You are the manager of product development for a rapidly growing telecommunications company. You and your spouse have just been invited to join a former college roommate, who is now a stock analyst, for an all-expense-paid ski vacation. Your friend explains that you will be staying at a condominium owned by her firm and that she won the rights to a fully paid vacation for four in a firm contest based on her performance as a stock analyst. "Besides," she added at the end of her invitation, "you might give me the insight needed to win another vacation next year."

b. You are the chief environmental engineer at a facility located in a small town. After a careful evaluation of plant facilities and a recently enacted law, you inform the plant manager that the plant will not be able to meet new emissions standards without an expenditure of $5 million. The plant manager is concerned that because of the low profitability of plant operations, this new information might lead to a decision to close the plant, causing significant disruption of the local economy. Consequently, he reports to corporate headquarters that the changes needed to meet the new emissions requirements would be minimal.

1-20
Ethics and False
Claims Act

In 1986, the U.S. Government passed the Federal False Claims Act to encourage persons to bring forward evidence of fraudulent charges on government contracts. Under the provisions of the Act, whistle-blowers receive up to 25 percent of any money recovered as a result of evidence they bring forth. To date, the largest settlement under the terms of the Act was a $7.5 million reward to a former employee of a defense contractor who filed a suit after leaving his former employer to accept a position as a price analyst for the Department of Defense.

Required:

Evaluate the likely impact of the Federal False Claims Act on corporations doing business with the U.S. government. Do you believe the Act is a good idea?

1–21
Expected Values
of Questionable
Decisions

The members of the jury had to make a decision in a lawsuit brought by the State of Alabama against Exxon Mobile. The suit revolved around natural-gas wells that Exxon drilled in state-owned waters. After signing several leases obligating Exxon to share revenues with Alabama, company officials started questioning the terms of the agreement that prohibited deducting several types of processing costs before paying the state royalties.

During the course of the trial, a memo by an in-house attorney of Exxon Mobile came to light. The memo noted that Royal Dutch/Shell, which had signed a similar lease, interpreted it "in the same manner as the state." The memo then presented arguments the company might use to claim the deduction, estimated the probability of the arguments being successful (less than 50 percent), and proceeded to consider whether Exxon should obey the law using a cost-benefit analysis. According to the memo, "If we adopt anything beyond a 'safe' approach, we should anticipate a quick audit and subsequent litigation." The memo also observed that "our exposure is 12 percent interest on underpayments calculated from the due date, and the cost of litigation."

Deducting the questionable costs did, indeed, result in an audit and a lawsuit.*

Required

If you were a member of the jury, what would you do? Why?

*Mike France, "When Big Oil Gets Too Slick," *Business Week*, April 9, 2001, p. 70.

1–22
Management
Decisions Affecting
Cost Drivers

An avid bicycle rider, you have decided to use an inheritance to start a new business to sell and repair bicycles. Two college friends have already accepted offers to work for you.

Required:
a. What is the mission of your new business?
b. Suggest a strategic positioning goal you might strive for to compete with area hardware and discount stores that sell bicycles.
c. Identify two items that might be long-range goals.
d. Identify two items that might be goals for the coming year.
e. Mention two decisions that will be structural cost drivers.
f. Mention two decisions that will be organizational cost drivers.
g. Identify two activity cost drivers.

1–23
Success Factors
and Performance
Measurement

Three years ago, Vincent Chow completed his college degree. The economy was in a depressed state at the time, and Vincent managed to get an offer of only $20,000 per year as a bookkeeper. In addition to its relatively low pay, this job had limited advancement potential.

Since Vincent was an enterprising and ambitious young man, he started a business of his own. He was convinced that because of changing lifestyles, a drive-through coffee establishment would be profitable. He was able to obtain backing from his parents to open such an establishment close to the industrial park area in town. Vincent named his business The Cappuccino Express and decided to sell only two types of coffee: cappuccino and decaffeinated.

As Vincent had expected, The Cappuccino Express was very well received. Within three years, Vincent had added another outlet north of town. He left the day-to-day management of each site to a manager and turned his attention toward overseeing the entire enterprise. He also hired an assistant to do the record keeping and other selected chores.

Required:

a. Develop an organization chart for The Cappuccino Express.

b. What factors can be expected to have a major impact on the success of The Cappuccino Express?

c. What major tasks must Vincent undertake in managing The Cappuccino Express?

d. What are the major costs of operating The Cappuccino Express?

e. Vincent would like to monitor the performance of each site manager. What measure(s) of performance should he use?

f. If you suggested more than one measure, which of these should Vincent select if he could use only one?

g. Suppose that last year, the original site had yielded total revenues of $146,000, total costs of $120,000, and hence, a profit of $26,000. Vincent had judged this profit performance to be satisfactory. For the coming year, Vincent expects that due to factors such as increased name recognition and demographic changes, the total revenues will increase by 20 percent to $175,200. What amount of profit should he expect from the site? Discuss the issues involved in developing an estimate of profit.

Source: Based on Chee W. Chow, "Instructional Case: Vincent's Cappuccino Express—A Teaching Case to Help Students Master Basic Cost Terms and Concepts Through Interactive Learning," *Issues in Accounting Education,* Spring 1995, pp. 173–190. Reprinted with permission.

Solution to Review Problem

a. Activity cost driver
b. Structural cost driver
c. Structural cost driver
d. Activity cost driver
e. Activity cost driver
f. Structural cost driver
g. Organizational cost driver
h. Organizational cost driver
i. Organizational cost driver
j. Organizational cost driver

ACTIVITY COST ANALYSIS AND PLANNING

After completing this chapter, you should be able to:

LEARNING OBJECTIVE 1   Determine basic patterns of how costs respond to changes in unit-level activity cost drivers.

LEARNING OBJECTIVE 2   Develop a linear cost estimating equation based on unit-level activity cost drivers.

LEARNING OBJECTIVE 3   Discuss problems encountered in cost estimation.

LEARNING OBJECTIVE 4   Describe and develop alternative classification schemes for activity cost drivers.

LEARNING OBJECTIVE 5   Develop cost estimates and cost predictions based on unit- and nonunit-level activity cost drivers.

LEARNING OBJECTIVE 6   Explain and illustrate possible errors when cost estimates or predictions are based solely on unit-level activity cost drivers in multiple product or service organizations.

MANAGERS AND COSTS

Along with decisions about markets, products, and operating policies, managers must focus on cost issues to build profitable firms. Decisions about costs often arise from an ongoing and detailed knowledge of both the firm's cost structure and management's competitive strategy. Cost issues faced by managers of major airlines, low-cost airlines, and regional airlines exemplify the interrelationship between ongoing competitive strategy and cost management issues.

Major airlines such as United, American, Delta, and Northwest compete on a variety of full-service attributes such as convenient scheduling, varying classes of service, frequent flyer programs, and airport executive clubs. Although the elimination or restructuring of frequent flyer programs and executive clubs could lower operating costs, these programs represent important customer services. Managers at these airlines usually must look elsewhere to find targets for cost reduction. At United, the increase in fuel costs during 2001 prompted a change in asset management strategy. United management had planned to phase out the use of older 727, 747, and DC-10 aircraft over several years. These planes, however, are both fuel and labor intensive, and in the current environment, the airline could lower its operating cost by replacing those planes ahead of the original schedule. The reduction in air travel following terrorist attacks on September 11, 2001, accelerated plans to retire older aircraft and delayed plans to acquire new aircraft.

Using a different competitive strategy, managers of airlines such as Southwest, Frontier, and Jet Blue rely on a cost leadership approach that emphasizes different cost categories than do the full-service airlines. Since Southwest, Frontier, and Jet Blue already have lower costs due to their "no-frills" approach to air travel, managers at these firms must emphasize different avenues of cost management. At these airlines, managers focus on such cost-reducing strategies as using regional airports where costs are lower, building the fleet with only one type of aircraft to lower maintenance costs, arranging hedges on fuel contracts, and flying with higher load factors—a higher percentage of filled seats.

Managers at regional airlines such as SkyWest, Mesa Air, and Comair face a different cost challenge—the introduction of the regional jet. Made by firms such as Bombardier, Embraer, and Fairchild-Dornier, these planes are about half the size of regular commercial passenger jets. Carrying between 40 and 70 passengers, these planes are well suited to the medium-distance, low-density routes flown by regional carriers. The regional jets—or RJs—typically fly faster and provide more comfort than the turboprop planes that have traditionally dominated the fleets of regional airlines. The RJs add flexibility to air travel by providing more point-to-point flights and permitting passengers to bypass congested hub airports. A significant issue for managers of regional airlines, however, is the RJs' cost. While a turboprop plane might cost about $14 million, an RJ costs about $21 million. The turboprop is more fuel efficient on shorter trips while the RJ uses less fuel on trips of 400 miles or more. The cost per seat mile for the turboprop plane ranges from $2.16 to $2.85 while the RJ per seat mile costs are $2.79 to $3.34. Although some of the regional carriers have collective marketing and operating agreements with major airlines and have received financial assistance to improve their fleets, managers at all regional carriers must analyze the impact of these potential higher costs on the cost structure of their organizations.

In each case, managers at these three types of airlines rely on specific cost analysis to contribute to their firm's profitability. Although the firms all compete in the same industry, each group operates in a different market segment with a different competitive strategy. Because of these differences in both segment and strategy, the specific approaches to cost analysis differ. The common theme, however, is that a detailed knowledge of cost behavior is an important key to success.

Source: Based on: "Small is Beautiful," *The Economist*, March 20, 2001, p. 65; "Business Focus: United Airlines Speeds Its Plans to Retire Gas-Guzzling Planes," *The Wall Street Journal—Interactive Edition*, June 4, 2001; Michael Arndt, "A Simple and Elegant Flight Plan," *Business Week*, June 11, 2001, p. 118; Martha Brannagan and Melanie Trottman, "Southwest Air Tops Profit Forecasts, Benefits from Robust Flight Demand," *The Wall Street Journal—Interactive Edition*, October 18, 2000; Nicholas Stein, "Regional Jets Join the Jet Set," *Forbes*, September, 14, 2000, pp. 287–290; Alex Taylor III, "Little Jets Are Huge," *Fortune*, September 4, 2000, pp. 275–282.

The purpose of this chapter is to introduce concepts concerning activity cost drivers and the behavior of activity costs and to examine methods used to develop models representing how costs respond to changes in one or more activity cost drivers. Having done this, we will be able to develop and use activity cost driver concepts to assist in planning and controlling activities and the resulting costs.

The chapter begins by considering how costs respond to changes in a single activity cost driver. We then examine methods used to develop cost estimating equations and predict future costs. To lay the foundation for twenty-first century cost management, we consider classification schemes that aid in analyzing cost behavior when there are numerous activity cost drivers. The chapter culminates with a cost model that uses a hierarchy of activity cost drivers to estimate the cost of multiple products or services.

<table>
<tr><td>Learning Objective 1</td><td></td></tr>
</table>

UNIT-LEVEL APPROACH TO COST BEHAVIOR ANALYSIS

Cost behavior concerns how costs respond to changes in an activity cost driver. Cost behavior analysis has traditionally used units of product or service as the cost-driving activity. When multiple products or services are involved, the units are sometimes restated in terms of sales dollars. Because units of final output are used as the cost driver, the traditional approach is identified as the **unit-level approach** to cost behavior analysis. Using the unit-level approach, the cost analyst assumes that changes in costs are best explained by changes in the number of units or sales dollars of products or services provided for customers.

While the unit-level approach is appropriate in many circumstances, it may not capture the full richness of activity cost drivers in complex organizations, especially those with multiple products that have variations in such factors as production volume and complexity. Nevertheless, its relative simplicity provides a foundation for the study of more advanced methods of analyzing cost behavior, and it is useful in many situations involving a single product or service. Therefore, we begin our study of cost behavior using the unit-level approach. We then examine frequently used nonunit cost drivers and the possible errors that occur when the analysis of cost behavior is inappropriately limited to unit level drivers.

FOUR BASIC COST BEHAVIOR PATTERNS

Although there are an unlimited number of ways that costs can respond to changes in activity cost drivers, as a starting point it is useful to classify cost behavior into four categories: variable, fixed, mixed, and step. Graphs of each are presented in Exhibit 2–1. Observe that total cost (the dependent variable) is measured on the vertical axis, and total activity for some time period of interest (the independent variable) is measured on the horizontal axis.

1. **Variable costs** represent an identical amount for each incremental unit of activity. Their total amount increases as activity increases, equaling zero dollars when activity is zero and increasing at a constant amount per unit of activity. The higher the variable cost per unit of activity, the steeper the slope of the line representing total cost. With the number of pizzas served as the unit-level cost driver for Pizza Hut restaurants, the cost of food is an example of a variable cost.
2. **Fixed costs** are unrelated to unit-level activity. With a unit-level cost driver as the independent variable, fixed costs are a constant amount per period of time. Hence, a line representing total fixed costs is flat with a slope (incline) of zero. With the number of pizzas sold as the unit-level cost driver, annual depreciation, property taxes, and property insurance are examples of fixed costs. While fixed costs may respond to structural and organizational cost drivers over time, they do not respond to short-run changes in unit-level activity cost drivers.
3. **Mixed costs** (sometimes called **semivariable costs**) contain a fixed and a variable cost element. Total mixed costs are positive (like fixed costs) when activity is zero, and they increase in a linear fashion (like total variable costs) as activity increases. With the number of pizzas sold as the unit-level cost driver, the cost of electric power is an example of a mixed cost. Some electricity is required to provide basic lighting, while additional electricity is required to prepare food as the number of pizzas served increases.

EXHIBIT 2-1

IMPORTANT TOTAL COST BEHAVIOR PATTERNS

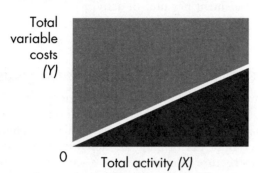

Total variable costs (Y) / Total activity (X)

Total variable costs increase in proportion to increases in unit-level cost drivers.

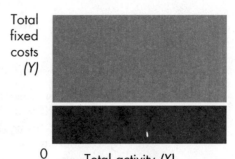

Total fixed costs (Y) / Total activity (X)

Total fixed costs do not respond to changes in unit-level cost drivers within a period.

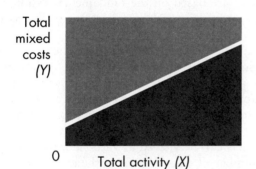

Total mixed costs (Y) / Total activity (X)

Total mixed costs contain fixed and variable cost elements. They increase but not in direct proportion to increases in unit-level cost drivers.

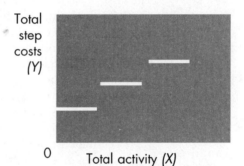

Total step costs (Y) / Total activity (X)

Total step costs are constant over a range of activity for a unit-level cost driver but move to a different amount at different ranges.

4. **Step costs** are constant within a narrow range of activity but shift to a higher level when activity exceeds the range. Total step costs increase in a steplike fashion as activity increases. With the number of pizzas served as the unit-level cost driver, employee wages is an example of a step cost. Up to a certain number of pizzas, only a small staff needs to be on duty. Beyond that number, additional employees are needed for quality service and so forth.

The relationship between total cost (Y axis) and total activity (X axis) for the four cost behavior patterns is mathematically expressed as follows:

$$\text{Variable cost: } Y = bX$$

where

b = the variable cost per unit, sometimes referred to as the slope of the cost function.

$$\text{Fixed cost: } Y = a$$

where

a = total fixed costs. Because fixed costs do not change with activity, the slope of the fixed cost function is zero.

$$\text{Mixed cost: } Y = a + bX$$

where

$$a = \text{total fixed cost element}$$
$$b = \text{variable cost element per unit of activity.}$$
$$\text{Step costs: } Y = a_i$$

where

$$a_i = \text{the step cost within a specific range of activity, identified by the subscript } i.$$

As Exhibit 1–5 on page 21 illustrated, the total cost function of many organizations has shifted toward more fixed costs and fewer variable costs, making it increasingly important for organizations to manage their fixed costs. Some organizations have done this by outsourcing activities rather than performing the activities internally. This avoids the many fixed costs of infrastructure in exchange for a variable cost per unit of activity. What's Happening 2–1 considers how an alliance between the United States Postal Service and Fexeral Express (FedEx) helps keep down the cost of postage.

OTHER FACTORS AFFECTING COST BEHAVIOR PATTERNS

The cost behavior patterns presented are based on the fundamental assumption that a unit of final output is the primary cost driver. The implications of this assumption are examined later in this chapter.

Another important assumption is that the time period is too short to incorporate changes in strategic cost drivers such as the scale of operations. Although this assumption is useful for short-range planning, for the purpose of developing plans for extended time periods, it is more appropriate to consider possible variations in one or more strategic cost drivers. When this is done, many costs previously classified as fixed are better classified as variable.

Even the cost of depreciable assets can be viewed as variable if the time period is long enough. Assuming that the number of pizzas served is the cost driver, for a single month the depreciation on all Pizza Hut restaurants in the world is a fixed cost. Over several years, if sales are strong, a strategic decision will be made to open additional restaurants; if sales are weak, strategic decisions will likely be made to close some restaurants. Hence, over a multiple-year period, the number of restaurants varies with sales volume, making depreciation appear as a variable cost with sales revenue as a unit-level activity cost driver.

2-1   WHAT'S HAPPENING?

USPS–FedEx Alliance Changes USPS Cost Structure

"The Postal Service delivers Main Street, and FedEx provides an air fleet," stated Postmaster General William Henderson, announcing an alliance between the United States Postal Service (USPS) and FedEx. Under the terms of the alliance, FedEx transports express mail, priority mail, and some first-class mail on its fleet of over 650 aircraft. The projected costs to the USPS are approximately $6.3 billion over the seven-year contract period. FedEx will also locate overnight service collection boxes at selected post offices across the United States.

Henderson predicts the USPS will save a billion dollars in transportation costs over the life of the contract. The most significant aspect of the alliance, however, is that it moves the USPS from a fixed-cost transportation network toward a variable cost network. "This is a unique opportunity to turn some fixed costs into variable costs," said Gene Del Polito, president of the Association for Postal Commerce in Arlington, Virginia. "It is using someone else's fixed costs." Frederick Smith, chairman, president, and chief executive officer of FedEx added that the system allows "the Postal Service to grow unconstrained without having to put in big [transportation] networks."

Source: "USPS-FedEx Alliance Could Save $1 Billion in Transportation Costs," *Federal Times*, January 15, 2001, p. 4.

TOTAL COST FUNCTION FOR AN ORGANIZATION OR BUSINESS SEGMENT

To obtain a general understanding of an organization, to compare the cost structures of different organizations, or to perform preliminary planning activities, managers are often interested in how total costs respond to a single measure of overall activity, such as units sold or sales revenue. This overview may be useful, but presenting all costs as a function of a single cost driver (typically unit level) is seldom accurate enough to support decisions concerning products, services, or activities. Doing so implies that all of an organization's costs can be manipulated by changing a single cost driver. This is seldom true.

In developing a total cost function, the independent variable usually represents some unit-level measure of the goods or services provided customers, such as total student credit hours in a university, total sales revenue in a store, total guest-days in a hotel, or total units manufactured in a factory. The resulting cost function is illustrated in Exhibit 2–2.

The resulting equation for total costs is:

$$Y = a + bX$$

where

Y = total costs

a = vertical axis intercept (an approximation of fixed costs)

b = slope (an approximation of variable costs per unit of X)

X = value of independent variable

RELEVANT RANGE FOR COST FUNCTIONS

The use of straight lines in accounting models of cost behavior assumes a linear relationship between cost and activity with each additional unit of activity accompanied by a uniform increment in total cost. Accountants identify this uniform increment as the *variable cost of one unit.*

Economic models show a nonlinear relationship between cost and activity with each incremental unit of activity being accompanied by a varying increment in total cost. Economists identify the varying increment in total cost as the **marginal cost** *of one unit.*

EXHIBIT 2–2

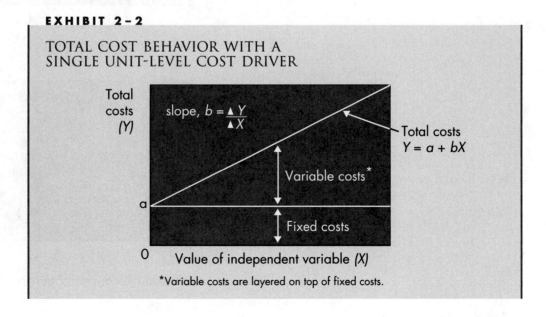

TOTAL COST BEHAVIOR WITH A
SINGLE UNIT-LEVEL COST DRIVER

*Variable costs are layered on top of fixed costs.

It is useful to relate marginal costs to the following three levels of activity:

1. *Below the activity range for which the facility was designed,* the existence of excess capacity results in relatively high marginal costs. Having extra time, employees complete assignments at a leisurely pace, increasing the time and the cost to produce each unit above what it would be if employees were more pressed to complete work. Frequent starting and stopping of equipment may also add to costs.
2. *Within the activity range for which the facility was designed,* activities take place under optimal circumstances and marginal costs are relatively low.
3. *Above the activity range for which the facility was designed,* the existence of capacity constraints again results in relatively high marginal costs. Near capacity, employees may be paid overtime wages, less experienced employees may be used, regular equipment may operate less efficiently, and old equipment with high energy requirements may be placed in service.

Based on marginal cost concepts, the economists' short-run total cost function is illustrated in the first graph in Exhibit 2–3. The vertical axis intercept represents capacity costs. Corresponding to the high marginal costs at low levels of activity, the initial slope is quite steep. In the normal activity range, where marginal costs are relatively low, the slope becomes less steep. Then, corresponding to high marginal costs above the normal activity range, the slope of the economists' total cost function increases again.

EXHIBIT 2–3

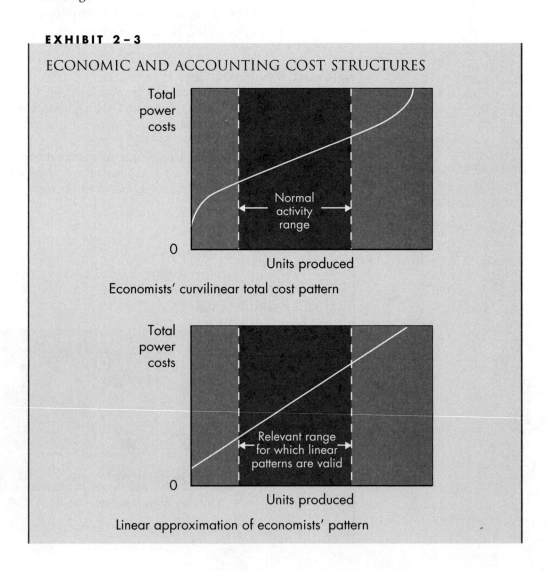

ECONOMIC AND ACCOUNTING COST STRUCTURES

Economists' curvilinear total cost pattern

Linear approximation of economists' pattern

If the economists' total cost curve is valid, how can we reasonably approximate it with a straight line? The answer to this question is in the notion of a *relevant range*. A linear pattern may be a poor approximation of the economists' curvilinear pattern over the entire range of possible activity, but a linear pattern as illustrated in the bottom graph in Exhibit 2–3 is often sufficiently accurate within the range of probable operations. The range of activity within which a linear cost function is valid is called the **relevant range**. Linear estimates of cost behavior are valid only within the relevant range. Extreme care must be exercised when making comments about cost behavior outside the relevant range.

OTHER COST BEHAVIOR PATTERNS

Although we have considered the most frequently used cost behavior patterns, remember that there are numerous ways that costs can respond to changes in activity. Avoid the temptation to automatically assume that the cost in question conforms to one of the patterns discussed in this chapter. Think through each situation and then select a behavior pattern that seems logical and fits the known facts. Additional cost behavior patterns are considered in the assignment material and subsequent chapters.

Particular care needs to be taken with the vertical axis. So far, all graphs have placed *total* costs on the vertical axis. Miscommunication is likely if one party is thinking in terms of *total* costs while the other is thinking in terms of *variable* or *average* costs. Consider the following cost function:

$$\text{Total costs} = \$3,000 + \$5X$$

where

$$X = \text{customers served}$$

The total, variable, and average costs at various levels of activity are computed here and graphed in Exhibit 2–4. Note that as the number of customers served increases, total costs increase, the variable costs of each unit remain constant, and the average cost decreases because fixed costs are spread over a larger number of units. Because division by zero is not possible, the average cost line is not extended to the vertical axis intercept, representing zero customers.

Customers Served	Total Costs	Average Cost*	Variable Costs per Customer
100	$3,500	$35.00	$5.00
200	4,000	20.00	5.00
300	4,500	15.00	5.00
400	5,000	12.50	5.00
500	5,500	11.00	5.00

*Total costs/customers served

To predict total costs for the coming period, management will use the first graph in Exhibit 2–4. To determine the minimum price required to avoid a loss on each additional customer served, management is interested in the variable costs per customer, yet if a manager inquired as to the cost of serving a customer, a financial accountant would probably provide average cost information, as illustrated in the third graph in Exhibit 2–4. The specific average cost would likely be a function of the number of customers served during the most recent accounting period.

Errors can occur if last period's average costs, perhaps based on a volume of 500 customers, were used to predict total costs for a future period when the anticipated volume was some other amount, say 300 units. Using average costs, the predicted total costs of 300 units are $3,300 ($11 × 300). In fact, using the proper total cost function, a more accurate prediction of total costs is $4,500 [$3,000 + ($5 × 300)]. The

EXHIBIT 2–4

TOTAL, VARIABLE, AND AVERAGE COSTS

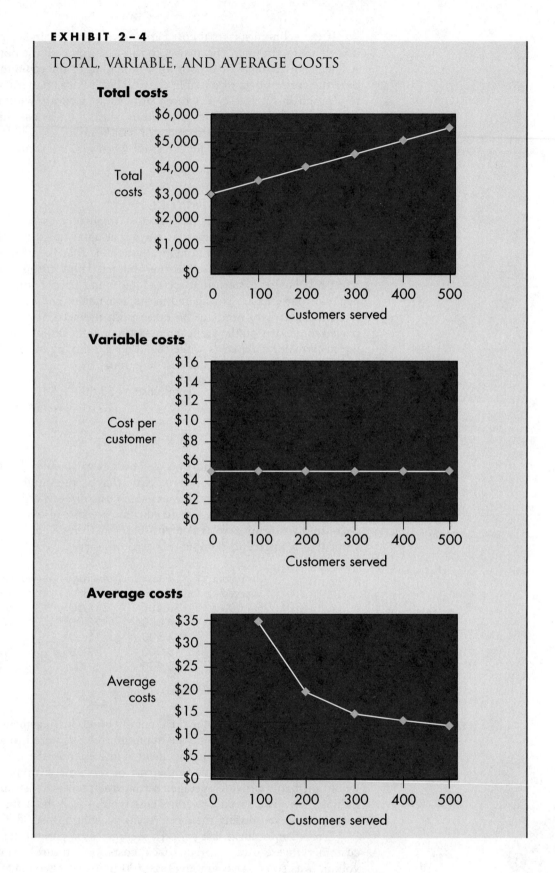

prediction error could cause a number of problems. If management budgeted $3,300 to pay bills and the bills actually totaled $4,500, the company might have to curtail activities or borrow under unfavorable terms to avoid running out of cash.

COMMITTED AND DISCRETIONARY FIXED COSTS

Fixed costs are often classified as *committed* or *discretionary*, depending on their immediate impact on the organization if management attempts to change them. **Committed fixed costs,** sometimes identified as **capacity costs,** are required to maintain the current service or production capacity or to fill previous legal commitments. Examples of committed fixed costs include depreciation, property taxes, rent, and interest on bonds.

Committed fixed costs are often the result of structural decisions about the size and nature of an organization. For example, many years ago the management of the Santa Fe Railroad made decisions concerning what communities the railroad would serve. Track was laid on the basis of those decisions, and the Santa Fe Railroad now pays property taxes each year on the railroad's miles of track. These property taxes could be reduced by disposing of track. However, reducing track would also diminish the Santa Fe's capacity to serve.

Discretionary fixed costs, sometimes called **managed fixed costs,** are set at a fixed amount each period at the discretion of management. It is possible to reduce discretionary fixed costs without reducing production or service capacity in the short term. Typical discretionary fixed costs include advertising, charitable contributions, employee training, and research and development.

Expenditures for discretionary fixed costs are frequently regarded as investments in the future. Research and development, for example, is undertaken to develop new or improved products that can be profitably produced and sold in future periods. During periods of financial well-being, organizations may make large expenditures on discretionary cost items. Conversely, during periods of financial stress, organizations likely reduce discretionary expenditures before reducing capacity costs. Unfortunately, fluctuations in the funding of discretionary fixed costs may reduce the effectiveness of long-range programs. A high-quality research staff may be difficult to reassemble if key personnel are laid off. Even the contemplation of layoffs may reduce the staff's effectiveness. In all periods, discretionary costs are subject to debate and are likely to be changed in the budgeting process.

LEARNING OBJECTIVE 2

COST ESTIMATION WITH UNIT-LEVEL COST DRIVERS

Cost estimation, the determination of the relationship between activity and cost, is an important part of cost management. In this section, we will develop equations for the relationship between total costs and one or more unit-level cost drivers. In a subsequent section, we will consider the implications of nonunit-level cost drivers on cost estimation.

To properly estimate the relationship between activity and cost, you must be familiar with basic cost behavior patterns and cost estimating techniques. Costs known to have a variable or a fixed pattern are readily estimated by interviews or by analyzing available records. From these methods, sales commission per sales dollar, a variable cost, might be determined to be 15 percent of sales. In a similar manner, annual property taxes might be determined by consulting tax documents.

Mixed (semivariable) costs, which contain fixed and variable cost elements, are more difficult to estimate. According to a basic rule of algebra, two equations are needed to determine two unknowns. Following this rule, at least two observations are needed to determine the variable and fixed elements of a mixed cost.

HIGH-LOW COST ESTIMATION

The most straightforward approach to determining the variable and fixed elements of mixed costs is to use the **high-low method of cost estimation.** This method utilizes data from two time periods, a *representative* high activity period and a *representative* low activity period, to estimate fixed and variable costs. Assuming identical fixed costs in both periods, any difference in total costs between these two periods is due entirely to variable costs. The variable costs per unit are found by dividing the difference in total costs by the difference in total activity:

$$\frac{\text{Variable costs}}{\text{per unit}} = \frac{\text{Difference in total costs}}{\text{Difference in activity}}$$

Once variable costs are determined, fixed costs, which are identical in both periods, are computed by subtracting the total variable costs of either the high or the low activity period from the corresponding total costs.

$$\text{Fixed costs} = \text{Total costs} - \text{Variable costs}$$

Assume a mail-order company wants to develop a monthly cost function for its packaging department and that the number of shipments is believed to be the primary cost driver. The following observations are available for the first four months of 2004.

		Number of Shipments	Packaging Costs
Low activity period	January	6,000	$17,000
	February	9,000	26,000
High activity period	March	12,000	32,000
	April	10,000	20,000

Equations for total costs for the packaging department in January and March (the periods of lowest and highest activity) follow:

$$\text{January—}\$17,000 = a + b \ (6,000 \text{ shipments})$$
$$\text{March—}\$32,000 = a + b \ (12,000 \text{ shipments})$$

where

$$a = \text{fixed costs per month}$$
$$b = \text{variable costs per shipment}$$

Solving for the estimated variable costs:

$$b = \frac{\text{Difference in total costs}}{\text{Difference in activity}}$$
$$b = \frac{\$32,000 - \$17,000}{12,000 - 6,000}$$
$$= \$2.50$$

Next, the estimated monthly fixed costs are determined by substituting the $2.50 variable costs per unit in *either* the January or March total cost equation:

$$a = \text{Total costs} - \text{Variable costs}$$
$$\text{January—}\$17,000 = a + (\$2.50 \text{ per shipment} \times 6,000 \text{ shipments})$$
$$a = \$17,000 - (\$2.50 \text{ per shipment} \times 6,000 \text{ shipments})$$
$$= \$2,000$$

or

$$\text{March—}\$32,000 = a + (\$2.50 \text{ per shipment} \times 12,000 \text{ shipments})$$
$$a = \$32,000 - (\$2.50 \text{ per shipment} \times 12,000 \text{ shipments})$$
$$= \$2,000$$

EXHIBIT 2-5

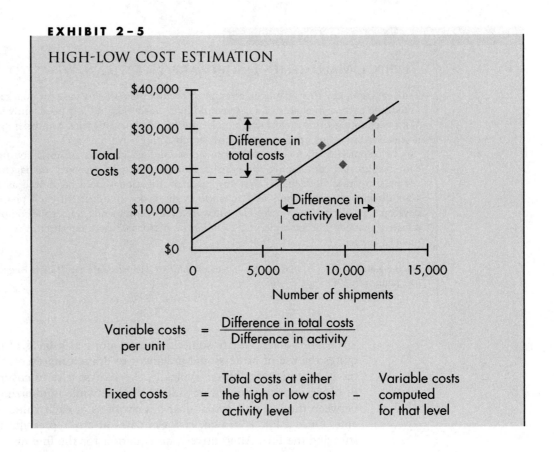

HIGH-LOW COST ESTIMATION

$$\text{Variable costs per unit} = \frac{\text{Difference in total costs}}{\text{Difference in activity}}$$

Fixed costs = Total costs at either the high or low cost activity level − Variable costs computed for that level

The cost estimating equation for total packaging department costs is

$$Y = \$2,000 + \$2.50X$$

where

$$X = \text{number of shipments}$$
$$Y = \text{total costs for the packing department}$$

The concepts underlying the high-low method of cost estimation are illustrated in Exhibit 2–5.

Cost prediction, the forecasting of future costs, is a common purpose of cost estimation. What's Happening 2–2 examines why and how law firms are engaging in cost prediction. Previously developed estimates of cost behavior are often the starting point in predicting future costs. Continuing the mail-order example, 5,000 shipments are budgeted for June 2004, the predicted June 2004 packaging department costs are $14,500 [$2,000 + ($2.50 per shipment × 5,000 shipments)].

SCATTER DIAGRAMS

A **scatter diagram** is a graph of past activity and cost data, with individual observations represented by dots. Plotting historical cost data on a scatter diagram is a useful approach to cost estimation, especially when used in conjunction with other cost-estimating techniques. As illustrated in Exhibit 2–6, a scatter diagram helps in selecting high and low activity levels representative of normal operating conditions. The periods of highest or lowest activity may not be representative because of the cost of overtime, the use of less efficient equipment, strikes, and so forth. If the goal is to develop an equation to predict costs under normal operating conditions, then the equation should be based on observations of normal operating conditions. A scatter diagram is also useful in determining whether costs can be reasonably approximated by a straight line.

PROJECT MANAGEMENT SOFTWARE HELPS LAW FIRMS TO PREDICT COSTS

Ten years ago, law firms made no attempt to predict the cost of a case for a large corporate client. When asked, the partner in charge of a case would likely respond, "It all depends on what the other side does." With accounting firms now doing almost everything short of courtroom briefings, and promising to do it cheaper, law firms are facing new cost-based competitive pressures.

In response to such competitive pressures, Glidden Partners, a Texas law firm, has devoted significant resources to developing software intended for litigation project management. "The theory," according to Craig Glidden, "is that any piece of litigation should be viewed as a self-contained project with distinct phases." The software outlines the tasks and costs of each phase, allowing the firm to develop a budget for each case. The software even recommends ways to accomplish each task in a cost-effective manner. For example, if a task can be performed by a paralegal, the software will not recommend a lawyer.

Source: Kimberly Reeves, "Project Management Software Helps Assure the Price Is Right," *Houston Business Journal,* January 9, 1998, pp. 25–26.

Scatter diagrams are sometimes used alone as a basis of cost estimation. This requires the use of professional judgment to draw a representative straight line through the plot of historical data. Typically, the analyst tries to ensure that an equal number of observations are on either side of the line while minimizing the vertical differences between the line and actual cost observations at each value of the independent variable. Once a line is drawn, cost estimates at any representative volume are made by studying the line. Alternatively, an equation for the line may be developed by applying the high-low method to any two points on the line.

LEAST-SQUARES REGRESSION ANALYSIS

Least-squares regression analysis uses a mathematical technique to fit a cost-estimating equation to the observed data. The technique mathematically accomplishes what the analyst does visually with a scatter diagram. The least-squares technique creates an equation that minimizes the sum of the vertical squared differences between the estimated

EXHIBIT 2-6

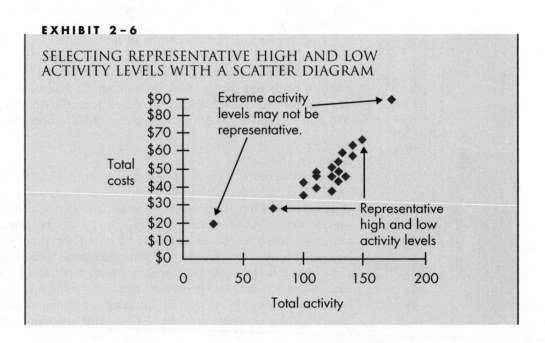

SELECTING REPRESENTATIVE HIGH AND LOW
ACTIVITY LEVELS WITH A SCATTER DIAGRAM

and the actual costs at each observation. Each of these differences is an estimating error. Using the packaging department example, the least-squares criterion is illustrated in Exhibit 2–7. Estimated values of total monthly packaging costs are represented by the straight line, and the actual values of total monthly packaging costs are represented by the dots. For each dot, such as the one at a volume of 10,000 shipments, the line is fit to minimize the vertical squared differences.

Values of *a* and *b* can be manually calculated using a set of equations developed by mathematicians or by using spreadsheet software packages such as Microsoft Excel®. Many calculators also have built-in functions to compute these coefficients. In any case, the least-squares equation for monthly packaging costs is:

$$Y = \$3,400 + \$2.20X$$

Using the least-squares equation, the predicted June 2004 packaging department costs with 5,000 budgeted shipments are $14,400 [$3,400 + ($2.20 per shipment × 5,000 shipments)]. Recall that the high-low method predicted June 2004 costs of $14,500. Although this difference is small, you might wonder which prediction is more reliable.

Advantage of Least-Squares Analysis. Mathematicians regard least-squares regression analysis as superior to both the high-low and the scatter diagram methods. It uses all available data, rather than just two observations, and does not rely on subjective judgment in drawing a line. Statistical measures are also available to determine how well a least-squares equation fits the historical data. These measures are often contained in the output of spreadsheet software packages. A typical output, obtained using Excel®, is presented in the chapter appendix. This appendix also contains brief descriptions of each item of output.

In addition to the vertical axis intercept and the slope, we also focus our attention on the coefficient of determination. The **coefficient of determination** is a measure of the percent of variation in the dependent variable (such as total packaging department costs) that is explained by variations in the independent variable (such as

EXHIBIT 2–7

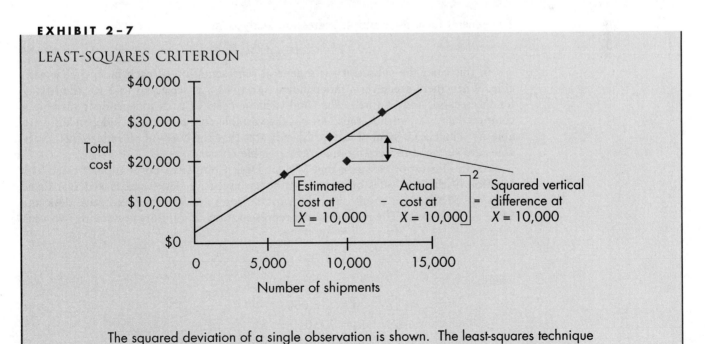

LEAST-SQUARES CRITERION

The squared deviation of a single observation is shown. The least-squares technique minimizes the sum of all squared vertical deviations between individual observations and the cost-estimating line.

total shipments). Statisticians often refer to the coefficient of determination as R-squared and represent it as R^2.

The coefficient of determination can have values between zero and one, with values close to zero suggesting that the equation is not very useful and values close to one indicating that the equation explains most of the variation in the dependent variable. When choosing between two cost-estimating equations, the one with the higher coefficient of determination is generally preferred. The coefficient of determination for the packaging department cost estimation equation, determined using least-squares regression analysis, is 0.68. This means that 68 percent of the variation in packaging department costs is explained by the number of shipments.

People, Not Models, Are Responsible. Although computers make least-squares regression easy to use, the generated output should not merely be accepted as correct. Statistics and other mathematical techniques are tools to help people make decisions. People, not mathematical models, are responsible for decisions. Judgment should always be exercised when considering the validity of the least-squares approach, the solution, and the data. If the objective is to predict future costs under normal operating conditions, observations reflecting abnormal operating conditions should be deleted. Also examine the cost behavior pattern to determine whether it is linear. Scatter diagrams assist in both of these judgments. Finally, the results should make sense. When a large number of possible relationships between cost and activity are examined, it is possible to have a high R-squared purely by chance. Even though the relationship has a high R-squared, if it "doesn't make sense" there is probably something wrong.

Simple and Multiple Regression. Least-squares regression analysis is identified as "simple regression analysis" when there is only one independent variable and as "multiple regression analysis" when there are two or more independent variables. The general form for simple regression analysis is:

$$Y = a + bX$$

The general form for multiple regression analysis is:

$$Y = a + \Sigma b_i X_i$$

In this case, the subscript i is a general representation of each independent variable. When there are several independent variables, i is set equal to 1 for the first, 2 for the second, and so forth. The total variable costs of each independent variable is computed as $b_i X_i$, with b_i representing the variable cost per unit of independent variable X_i. The Greek symbol sigma, Σ, indicates that the costs of all independent variables are summed in determining total variable costs.

As an illustration, assume that Walnut Desk Company's costs are expressed as a function of the unit sales of its two products: executive desks and task desks. Fixed costs are $18,000 per month and the variable costs are $250 per executive desk and $120 per task desk. The mathematical representation of monthly costs with two variables is:

$$Y = a + b_1 X_1 + b_2 X_2$$

where

$$a = \$18,000$$
$$b_1 = \$250$$
$$b_2 = \$120$$
$$X_1 = \text{unit sales of executive desks}$$
$$X_2 = \text{unit sales of task desks}$$

During a month when 105 executive desks and 200 task desks are sold, Walnut Desk Company's estimated total costs are:

$$Y = \$18,000 + \$250(105) + \$120(200)$$
$$= \$68,250$$

In addition to estimating costs, multiple regression analysis can be used to determine the effect of individual product features on the market value of a product or service. Research Shows 2–1 reports a study that estimated the impact of mature trees on the selling price of single-family homes.

LEARNING OBJECTIVE 3

ADDITIONAL ISSUES IN COST ESTIMATION

We have mentioned several items to be wary of when developing cost estimating equations:

- Data that are not based on normal operating conditions.
- Nonlinear relationships between total costs and activity.
- Obtaining a high R-squared purely by chance.

Additional items of concern include:

- Changes in technology or prices.
- Matching activity and cost within each observation.
- Identifying activity cost drivers.

CHANGES IN TECHNOLOGY AND PRICES

Changes in technology and prices make cost estimation and prediction difficult. When telephone companies changed from using human operators to using automated switching equipment to place long-distance telephone calls, cost estimates based on the use of human operators were of little or no value in predicting future costs. Care must be taken to make sure that data used in developing cost estimates are based on the existing technology. When this is not possible, professional judgment is required to make appropriate adjustments.

2–1   **RESEARCH SHOWS**

REGRESSION ANALYSIS PROVES BIG TREES ARE WORTH COOL CASH

While most real estate professionals believe that, all else being equal, homes with mature trees (defined as having a diameter of nine inches or more) are preferred to homes without mature trees, it is difficult to estimate the value of mature trees. The Council of Tree and Landscape Appraisers recommends a cost-based approach for the valuation of trees. While this is possible for small trees, it is difficult to value mature trees.

To better determine the market value of mature trees, Dombrow, Jonathan, Mauricio, and Sirmans used multiple regression analysis to analyze the impact of mature trees on the selling prices of homes in Baton Rouge, Louisiana. Independent variables included the size and age of the house, the presence of other house amenities such as a garage, porch, or fireplace, days on the market, location, and the presence of mature trees. Their study revealed that the presence of mature trees increased the selling price of a home by 1.856 percent. The researchers conclude that an appraiser "would be supported in adding approximately 2 percent to the value of a single-family house that has mature trees."

Source: Jonathan Dombrow, Mauricio Rodriguez, and C. F. Sirmans, "The Market Value of Mature Trees in Single-Family Housing Markets," *Appraisal Journal,* January 2000, p. 39.

Only data reflecting a single price level should be used in cost estimation and prediction. If prices have remained stable in the past but then uniformly increase by 20 percent, cost-estimating equations based on data from previous periods will not accurately predict future costs. In this case, all that is required is a 20 percent increase in the prediction. Unfortunately, adjustments for price changes are seldom this simple. The prices of various cost elements are likely to change at different rates and at different times. Furthermore, there are probably several different price levels included in the past data used to develop cost-estimating equations. Old data should always be used cautiously. If data from different price levels are used, an attempt should be made to restate them to a single price level.

MATCHING ACTIVITY AND COSTS

The development of accurate cost-estimating equations requires the matching of the activity to related costs within each observation. This accuracy is often difficult to achieve because of the time lag between an activity and the recording of the cost of resources consumed by the activity. Current activities may consume electricity, but the electric bill won't be received and recorded until next month. Driving an automobile may require routine maintenance for items such as lubrication and oil, but the auto may be driven several weeks or even months before the maintenance is required. Consequently, daily, weekly, and perhaps even monthly observations of miles driven and maintenance costs are unlikely to match the costs of oil and lubrication with the cost-driving activity, miles driven.

In general, the shorter the time period, the higher the probability of error in matching costs and activity. The cost analyst must carefully review the data base to verify that activity and cost are matched within each observation. If matching problems are found, it may be possible to adjust the data (perhaps by moving the cost of electricity from one observation to another). Under other circumstances, it may be necessary to use longer periods to match costs and activity.

IDENTIFYING ACTIVITY COST DRIVERS

Identifying the appropriate activity cost driver for a particular cost requires judgment and professional experience. In general, the cost driver should have a logical, causal relationship with costs. In many cases, the identity of the most appropriate activity cost driver, such as miles driven for the cost of automobile gasoline, is apparent. In other situations, where different activity cost drivers might be used, scatter diagrams and statistical measures, such as the coefficient of determination, are helpful in selecting the activity cost driver that best explains past variations in cost. When scatter diagrams are used, the analyst can study the dispersion of observations around the cost-estimating line. In general, a small dispersion is preferred. If regression analysis is used, the analyst considers the coefficient of determination. In general, a higher coefficient of determination is preferred. Of course, the relationship between the activity cost driver and the cost must seem logical, and the activity data must be available.

LEARNING OBJECTIVE 4

ALTERNATIVE COST DRIVER CLASSIFICATION SCHEMES

So far we have examined cost behavior and cost estimation using only a unit-level approach, which assumes changes in costs are best explained by changes in the number of units of product or service provided customers. This approach may have worked for Carnegie Steel Company at the turn of the twentieth century, but it is inappropriate for multiproduct organizations, such as General Electric, at the turn of the twenty-first century. The unit-level approach becomes increasingly inaccurate as a basis for analyzing cost behavior, as organizations change from the following:

- Labor-based to automated manufacturing,
- A limited number of related products to multiple products, with variations in product volume and complexity (and related costs), and
- A set of similar customers to a diverse set of customers.

Exhibit 1–5 on page 21 illustrates how cost structures changed during the twentieth century. Exhibit 2–8 takes a closer look at the composition of total manufacturing costs between the years 1900 and 2000, illustrating changes of the percentage of manufacturing costs for three major cost categories.

1. **Direct materials,** the cost of primary raw materials converted into finished goods, have increased slightly as organizations purchase components they formerly fabricated. The word "direct" is used to indicate costs that are easily or directly traced to a finished product or service.
2. **Direct labor,** the wages earned by production employees for the time they spend converting raw materials into finished products, has decreased significantly as employees spend less time physically working on products and more time supporting automated production activities.
3. **Manufacturing overhead,** which includes all manufacturing costs other than direct materials and direct labor, has increased significantly due to automation, product diversity, and product complexity.

These changes in the composition of manufacturing costs have implications for the behavior of total costs and the responsiveness of costs to changes in unit-level cost drivers. Because direct materials and direct labor vary directly with the number of units, they are easy to measure. In the past, when manufacturing overhead was relatively small, it was possible to ignore overhead and assume unit of product or service was the primary cost driver. This is no longer true. Units of final product is no longer an adequate explanation of changes in manufacturing overhead.

The past tendency to ignore overhead, while focusing on direct materials and direct labor, led one researcher to identify overhead causing activities as "the hidden

EXHIBIT 2–8

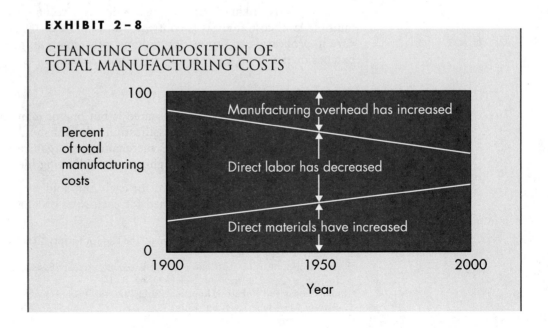

CHANGING COMPOSITION OF
TOTAL MANUFACTURING COSTS

Percent of total manufacturing costs

100

Manufacturing overhead has increased

Direct labor has decreased

Direct materials have increased

0

1900   1950   2000

Year

factory."[1] The growth in overhead has also been likened to "The Blob," a 1960s science fiction movie in which a fast-growing substance from outer space threatened to engulf an entire town.

To better understand "the hidden factory" and control "the blob," several researchers have developed frameworks for categorizing cost-driving activities. The significant feature of these frameworks is the inclusion of nonunit cost drivers. Depending on the characteristics of a particular organization, as well as management's information needs, there are an almost unlimited number of cost driver classification schemes. We consider two frequently applied cost driver classification schemes: one based on a manufacturing cost hierarchy and a second based on a customer cost hierarchy. We also illustrate variations of each.

Manufacturing Cost Hierarchy

The most well-known framework, developed by Cooper[2] and Cooper and Kaplan[3] for manufacturing situations, classifies activities into the following four categories.

1. A **unit-level activity** is performed *for each unit* of product produced. Oneida Silversmiths manufactures high-quality eating utensils. In the production of forks, the stamping of each fork into the prescribed shape is an example of a unit-level cost driver.
2. A **batch-level activity** is performed *for each batch* of product produced. At Oneida Silversmiths, a batch is a number of identical units (such as a fork of a specific design) produced at the same time. Batch-level activities include setting up the machines to stamp each fork in an identical manner, moving the entire batch between work stations (i.e., molding, stamping, and finishing), and inspecting the first unit in the batch to verify that the machines are set up correctly.
3. A **product-level activity** is performed *to support* the production of *each different type of product*. At Oneida Silversmiths, product-level activities for a specific pattern of fork include initially designing the fork, producing and maintaining the mold for the fork, and determining manufacturing operations for the fork.
4. A **facility-level activity** is performed *to maintain* general manufacturing capabilities. At Oneida Silversmiths, facility-level activities include plant management, building maintenance, property taxes, and electricity required to sustain the building.

Several additional examples of the costs driven by activities at each level are presented in Exhibit 2–9.

The relative richness of the single unit level volume-based cost analysis and the multiple level cost analysis is contrasted in Exhibit 2–10. Note that while some costs vary in proportion to production volume, others vary in proportion to the number of batches or the diversity of products manufactured.

Customer Cost Hierarchy

The manufacturing hierarchy presented is but one of many possible ways of classifying activities and their costs. Classification schemes should be designed to fit the organization and meet user needs. A merchandising organization or the sales division of a manufacturing organization might use the following hierarchy.

1. *Unit-level activity*—performed for each unit sold.
2. **Order-level activity**—performed for each sales order.

[1]Jeffrey G. Miller and Thomas E. Vollmann, "The Hidden Factory," *Harvard Business Review,* September–October 1985, pp. 142–150.

[2]Robin Cooper, "Cost Classification in Unit-Based and Activity-Based Manufacturing Cost Systems," *The Journal of Cost Management,* Fall 1990, pp. 4–14.

[3]Robin Cooper and Robert S. Kaplan, "Profit Priorities from Activity-Based Costing," *Harvard Business Review,* May–June 1991, pp. 130–135.

EXHIBIT 2-9
HIERARCHY OF ACTIVITY COSTS

Activity Level	Reason for Activity	Examples of Activity Cost
1. Unit level	Performed for each unit of product produced or sold	• Cost of raw materials • Cost of inserting a component • Utilities cost of operating equipment • Some costs of packaging • Sales commissions
2. Batch level	Performed for each batch of product produced or sold	• Cost of processing sales order • Cost of issuing and tracking work order • Cost of equipment setup • Cost of moving batch between work-stations • Cost of inspection (assuming same number of units inspected in each batch)
3. Product level	Performed to support each different product that can be produced	• Cost of product development • Cost of product marketing such as advertising • Cost of specialized equipment • Cost of maintaining specialized equipment
4. Facility level	Performed to maintain general manufacturing capabilities	• Cost of maintaining general facilities such as buildings and grounds • Cost of nonspecialized equipment • Cost of maintaining nonspecialized equipment • Cost of real property taxes • Cost of general advertising • Cost of general administration such as the plant manager's salary

EXHIBIT 2-10
CHANGING BASIS FOR THE ANALYSIS OF COST BEHAVIOR

Volume-Based Unit-Level Analysis	Activity-Based Multiple-Level Analysis
Variable—only one type of variable cost driver is considered: Unit level	**Variable**—many types of variable cost drivers are considered, including: Unit level **Batch level** **Product level**
Fixed—costs that do not vary with the number of units	**Fixed**—costs that do not respond to changes in variable cost drivers are considered: **Facility level**

3. **Customer-level activity**—performed to obtain or maintain each customer.
4. *Facility-level activity*—performed to maintain the general marketing function

This classification scheme could assist in answering questions concerning the cost of individual orders or individual customers.

If an organization sells to distinct market segments (for profit, not for profit, and government), the cost hierarchy might be modified as follows:

1. *Unit-level activity*
2. *Order-level activity*
3. *Customer-level activity*
4. **Market segment-level activity**—performed to obtain or maintain operations in a market segment.
5. *Facility-level activity*

The market segment–level activities and the related costs would differ with each market segment. This classification scheme could assist in answering questions concerning the profitability of each market segment.

Finally, an organization that completes unique projects for different market segments (such as buildings for IBM and the U.S. Department of Defense) might use the following hierarchy to determine the profitability of each market segment:

1. **Project-level activity**—an activity performed to support the completion of each project.
2. *Market segment–level activity*
3. *Facility-level activity*

The possibilities are endless. The important point, as stated by Foster and Gupta,[4] is that both the cost hierarchy and the costs included in the hierarchy be tailored to meet the specific circumstances of an organization and the interests of management. What's Happening 2–3 considers actions at USAir to reduce product level cost drivers.

2-3   WHAT'S HAPPENING?

USAir Plans to Replace Aircraft to Simplify Its Fleet and Reduce Costs

USAir Group Inc. purchased 120 new aircraft with a list price of $5.3 billion from Airbus Industrie. The primary goal of the acquisition was to reduce the types of aircraft in USAir's fleet from nine to four. The fleet, while not old, had been called a "hodgepodge." This diversity, similar to having an unnecessary number of product-level cost drivers, raises costs for pilot training, maintenance, and spare parts inventory while limiting scheduling flexibility.

Industry experts note that reducing the number of aircraft types allows USAir to get more hours out of its planes and pilots. The resulting increase in efficiency and reduction in costs was important as USAir faced increased competition from low-cost competitors, such as Southwest Airlines.

Source: "USAir Weighs Ordering Up to 120 Jets to Simplify Its Fleet and Reduce Costs," *The Wall Street Journal,* October 14, 1996, pp. A2, A5.

---

[4]George Foster and Mahendra Gupta, "Marketing Cost Management and Management Accounting," *Journal of Management Accounting Research,* 6, Fall 1994, pp. 43–77.

COST ESTIMATION WITH UNIT AND NONUNIT COST DRIVERS

To accurately analyze costs in situations where there are multiple cost drivers, the cost-estimating equation should include an independent variable for each cost driver. Using a manufacturing cost hierarchy, a revised total cost equation for a manufacturing organization with a *single* product might appear as follows:

$$Y = a + b_1X_1 + b_2X_2 + b_3X_3$$

where

Y = total costs for a period

a = facility-level costs that do not vary with units, batches, or products

X_1 = unit-level cost drivers, where the subscript $_1$ refers to the unit level

b_1 = variable cost per unit

X_2 = batch-level cost drivers, where the subscript $_2$ refers to the batch level

b_2 = variable cost per batch

X_3 = product-level cost drivers, where the subscript $_3$ refers to the product level

b_3 = product costs that do not vary with the number of units or batches

Assume that Pace Company, which manufactures only Product A, has developed the following cost information:

	Unit-Level Costs		Batch-Level Costs		Product-Level Costs	Facility-Level Costs (PER MONTH)	
Product A	Materials	$ 8	Setup	$300	Advertising $20,000	Maintenance	$10,000
	Labor	2	Movement	50		Rent	3,000
	Total	$10	Total	$350		Administrative salaries	4,000
						Total	$17,000

During May, Pace produced 2,000 units of Product A in 5 batches of 400 units. The costs for May are as follows:

Y = $17,000 + ($10 × 2,000 units) + ($350 × 5 batches)

$$+ ($20,000 × 1 \text{ for Product A})$$

Y = $58,750

Expanding the model to incorporate multiple products, a revised total cost equation for a manufacturing organization with *two or more* products might appear as follows:

$$Y = a + \Sigma b_{1i}X_{1i} + \Sigma b_{2i}X_{2i} + \Sigma b_{3i}X_{3i}$$

where the subscript $_i$ refers to a specific product, such as Product A, and the Greek symbol sigma, Σ, indicates that the costs of each product at each level must be summed to determine total costs at that level.

To illustrate a multiple product situation, assume that Pace adds Product B in June. The revised activity cost structure is as follows:

	Unit-Level Costs		Batch-Level Costs		Product-Level Costs	Facility-Level Costs (PER MONTH)
Product A	Materials	$ 8	Setup	$300	Advertising $20,000	
	Labor	2	Movement	50		
	Total	$10	Total	$350		

	Unit-Level Costs		Batch-Level Costs		Product-Level Costs		PER MONTH Facility-Level Costs
Product B	Materials	$12	Setup	$300	Advertising $15,000		
	Labor	5	Movement	50			
	Total	$17	Total	$350			

Maintenance	$10,000
Rent	3,000
Administrative salaries	4,000
Total	$17,000

The facility costs are placed on a separate row to indicate their independence from either product.

During June, Pace produced 2,000 units of Product A in 5 batches of 400 units and 10,000 units of Product B in 10 batches of 1,000 units. Total costs at each activity level and total predicted costs for the month are as follows:

Unit: $\quad \Sigma b_{1i}X_{1i} = (\$10 \times 2,000) + (\$17 \times 10,000)$
$\quad\quad\quad = \$190,000$

Batch: $\quad \Sigma b_{2i}X_{2i} = (\$350 \times 5) + (\$350 \times 10)$
$\quad\quad\quad = \$5,250$

Product: $\quad \Sigma b_{3i}X_{3i} = (\$20,000 \times 1 \text{ for Product A}) + (\$15,000 \times 1 \text{ for Product B})$
$\quad\quad\quad = \$35,000$

Facility: $\quad a = \$17,000$

Total: $\quad Y = \$17,000 + \$190,000 + \$5,250 + \$35,000$
$\quad\quad\quad = \$247,250$

LEARNING OBJECTIVE 6

ERRORS WITH THE UNIT-LEVEL APPROACH

When cost estimation is limited to the volume-based unit-level approach, while actual costs follow an activity cost hierarchy, there is a high probability of significant errors in cost estimation and cost prediction. Such errors may lead management to believe that some products cost less and some products cost more than they really do. Based on such a belief, management might discontinue products that are, in fact, profitable or emphasize the production of products that are, in fact, unprofitable. To illustrate how these errors may occur, we consider three examples.

1. The first example uses the high-low method to develop a cost-estimating equation for Pace. The resulting unit-level equation is then used to predict costs for a subsequent month. The predicted costs are then compared to the costs as determined using a multi-level-approach.
2. The second example illustrates the implication of variations in batch size on cost estimation.
3. The third example examines the implication of product complexity and the associated product level costs on cost estimation.

INACCURATE COST PREDICTIONS

During July, Pace produced 3,200 units of Product A in 4 batches of 800 units and 10,000 units of Product B in 10 batches of 1,000. With no changes in activity costs, the total costs for the month were $258,900. As an exercise, you should verify this amount to ensure your understanding of the total cost equation with a hierarchy of activity cost.

By developing a detailed example, a complete analysis of cost drivers is presented to illustrate the shortcomings of the simple unit-level approach that contains only one independent variable. As a baseline, we will use our previous computations of June and July costs.

Following the single variable approach to developing a cost-estimating equation, the June and July costs are analyzed using the high-low method:

	Production	**Total Cost**
June costs	12,000 (2,000 + 10,000) units	$247,250
July costs	13,200 (3,200 + 10,000) units	$258,900

$$b = (\$258,900 - \$247,250)/(13,200 - 12,000)$$
$$= \$9.708$$
$$a = \$247,250 - (\$9.708 \times 12,000 \text{ total units})$$
$$= \$130,754$$
$$Y = \$130,754 + \$9.708X$$

where

$$X = \text{total production}$$

Using this equation for August, when management anticipates producing 1,500 units of Product A in five batches and 13,000 units of Product B in thirteen batches, the predicted costs are $271,520.

$$Y = \$130,754 + \$9.708(1,500 \text{ units of A} + 13,000 \text{ units of B})$$
$$= \$271,520$$

But, if we perform a complete analysis of activities and activity costs, the predicted costs for August are $294,300:

Unit: $\Sigma b_{1i}X_{1i} = (\$10 \times 1,500 \text{ units of A}) + (\$17 \times 13,000 \text{ units of B})$
$$= \$236,000$$

Batch: $\Sigma b_{2i}X_{2i} = (\$350 \times 5 \text{ batches of A}) + (\$350 \times 13 \text{ batches of B})$
$$= \$6,300$$

Product: $\Sigma b_{1i}X_{1i} = (\$20,000 \times 1 \text{ for Product A}) + (\$15,000 \times 1 \text{ for Product B})$
$$= \$35,000$$

Facility: $\Sigma b_{4i}X_{4i} = 1(\$10,000) + 1(\$3,000) + 1(\$4,000)$
$$= \$17,000$$

Total $Y = \$236,000 + \$6,300 + \$35,000 + \$17,000$
$$= \$294,300$$

In this example, the use of a single independent variable for cost prediction produced a difference of ($22,780), [$271,520 unit level prediction − $294,300 activity-hierarchy prediction]. Changes in the mix of unit- and batch-level cost drivers resulted in a difference of more than $20,000 when cost estimates were based on a single independent variable.

INACCURATE ASSIGNMENT OF BATCH LEVEL COSTS

Let us focus our attention on an example that involves only unit- and batch-level costs. Assume a company produces two products, C and D. Both have identical monthly production volumes of 50,000 units, with identical costs of $1 per unit and $20,000 per batch. The only difference is in batch size, 50,000 units for Product C and 5,000 units for Product D.

	Product C	Product D
Monthly production (units)	50,000	50,000
Batch size (units)	50,000	5,000
Batches per month	1	10

The resulting total costs per month using a unit-level analysis are as follows:

Total: $Y = [\$1 \times (50{,}000C + 50{,}000D) \text{ units}] + [\$20{,}000 \times (1C + 10D) \text{ batches}]$
$= \$320{,}000$

Based on a single unit-level volume-based analysis, the average unit cost is \$3.20 (\$320,000/100,000 units).

If Products C and D are analyzed separately, their total and average unit costs are as follows:

	Product C	Product D
Unit level costs:		
C: \$1 × 50,000	\$50,000.00	
D: \$1 × 50,000		\$ 50,000.00
Batch level costs:		
C: \$20,000 × 1	20,000.00	
D: \$20,000 × 10		200,000.00
Total costs	\$70,000.00	\$250,000.00
Units	÷50,000.00	÷ 50,000.00
Average unit cost	\$ 1.40	\$ 5.00

The separate multi-level analysis of Products C and D gives explicit consideration to batch-level costs, ensuring they are assigned to the correct product. The unit-level analysis does not explicitly consider batch-level costs in determining final product costs. Instead, batch-level costs are averaged over all units of both products. The result, made clear in the example because of identical unit and batch costs, is that volume-based unit-level analysis:

- Underestimates the cost of products produced in batches containing a small number of units, and
- Overestimates the cost of products produced in batches containing a large number of units.

	Product C Large Batches	Product D Small Batches
Volume-based unit-level cost	\$3.20	\$3.20
Multi-level cost	1.40	5.00

These relationships are illustrated in Exhibit 2–11. The situation illustrated in this example can be extended to high-volume products (such as standard windows) produced in large batches and low-volume products (such as custom windows) produced in small batches. If costs were analyzed using only unit-level drivers, the high-volume products would be assigned too many costs and the low-volume products would be assigned too few costs.

It is apparent that cost-estimating errors can have severe economic consequences to individuals and organizations of all sizes. Research Shows 2–2 reports on a study that demonstrates how Medicare subsidizes private health insurers by using a single cost driver for determining reimbursable hospital inpatient costs.

INACCURATE ASSIGNMENT OF PRODUCT-LEVEL COSTS

We could easily develop a similar example for two products with identical unit-level costs and unit volume, but with different product-level costs that are caused by differences in

EXHIBIT 2-11

COST ESTIMATION ERRORS WITH UNIT-LEVEL ANALYSIS IN MULTIPLE PRODUCT/ SERVICE ORGANIZATIONS RELATED TO VARIATIONS IN BATCH SIZE

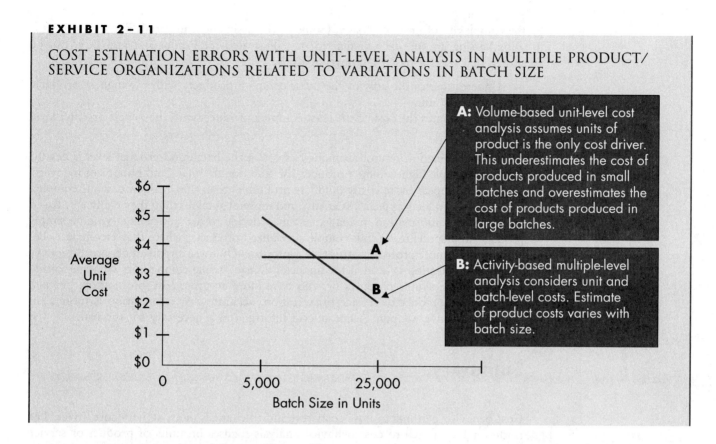

A: Volume-based unit-level cost analysis assumes units of product is the only cost driver. This underestimates the cost of products produced in small batches and overestimates the cost of products produced in large batches.

B: Activity-based multiple-level analysis considers unit and batch-level costs. Estimate of product costs varies with batch size.

2-2   RESEARCH SHOWS

USE OF A SINGLE COST DRIVER HAS MEDICARE SUBSIDIZING PRIVATE HEALTH INSURERS

Hwang and Kirby observed that "hospitals must annually complete a Medicare Cost Report to be eligible for government reimbursement for services rendered to Medicare patients. This cost information is used in determining values of Medicare reimbursement parameters. This same cost information is also often used as the basis for determining the charges for privately insured patients. For inpatient care costs, Medicare reporting requires that all operating costs pertaining to patient care are allocated to patients based only on the number of patient-days. Thus Medicare cost reporting does not take account explicitly of the possibility of multiple cost drivers."

Hwang and Kirby noted that patient care costs can be attributed to at least two cost drivers: (1) the number of days a patient spends in the hospital and (2) the number of inpatients admitted. Patient-day costs include such "hotel" costs as meals, laundry, and basic nursing care, while admission costs include costs related to taking patients' histories, preparing patients for surgery, intensively tending patients immediately following surgery, housekeeping costs related to preparing rooms for new patients, and administrative costs related to medical coding and billing. Patient-day is a unit cost driver, and admission is a batch cost driver.

Hwang and Kirby compared the results of current Medicare reimbursement procedures, which are based on a single unit-level cost driver (patient-days) with the results that would be obtained if Medicare reimbursements were based on two cost drivers: a unit-level driver (patient-days) and a batch-level driver (number of admissions). Contrary to the general wisdom that often suggests that Medicare payments do not cover hospital costs, the results suggest that Medicare is potentially overcharged for hospital patient care by between $66 million and $1.98 billion per year! The explanation is simple when the underlying data are analyzed. Medicare patients tend to be older and have a much longer average length of hospitalization than private insurance patients. Because Medicare reimbursements consider only patient-days, Medicare is charged for a disproportionately large share of the costs of admitting patients.

Source: Yuhchang Hwang and Alison J. Kirby, "Distorted Medicare Reimbursements: The Effect of Cost Accounting Choices," *Journal of Management Accounting Research*, 6, Fall 1994, pp. 128–143.

the complexity of product design. (Some of the assignment materials illustrate this situation.) Using an approach similar to that illustrated for Products C and D, it can be shown that volume-based unit-level analysis:

- Underestimates the cost of the most complex products with the highest product-level costs, and
- Overestimates the cost of the least complex products with the lowest product-level costs.

The combination of cost-estimating errors at the batch and product level is deadly. Relatively simple high-volume products, the traditional "bread and butter" of many organizations, appear more costly (and less profitable) than they really are, while complex low-volume products appear less costly (and more profitable) than they really are. Based on this faulty information, management may decide to get out of high-volume simple products and specialize in low-volume specialized products, where they erroneously believe there are more profit opportunities. Unfortunately, these opportunities are illusionary and the organization is headed for financial disaster, while competitors who specialized in high-volume simple products or who have more accurate cost information, prosper. In a multiple product or service organization, accurate cost information is more than just a competitive weapon. Accurate cost information is necessary for survival.

Summary

Cost behavior pertains to how costs respond to changes in an activity cost driver. The traditional approach to cost behavior analysis focuses on units of product or service as the cost driving activity and has four basic cost behavior patterns—those for variable, fixed, mixed, and step costs.

Cost estimation, the determination of the relationship between activity and cost, is an important part of cost management. Although we focused on the high-low method of cost estimation, we also considered scatter diagrams and least-squares regression analysis. Scatter diagrams are especially useful in selecting representative high- and low-activity levels. Least-squares regression analysis applies a mathematical technique to fit a cost-estimating equation to the observed data. It also provides information on how well the equation explains changes in the dependent variable.

The traditional unit-level approach to cost estimation assumes that changes in costs are best explained by changes in the number of units of products or services. In multiple product or service environments, this approach may underestimate the cost of complex products (or services) produced in small volumes while overestimating the cost of relatively simple products (or services) produced in large volumes.

To better understand and estimate the cost of the many activities performed to serve customers, a number of frameworks for analyzing activity cost drivers are available. The most widely discussed framework, developed for manufacturing situations, classifies activities as unit level, batch level, product level, or facility level. Depending on the characteristics of a particular organization, as well as management's information needs, there are an almost unlimited number of additional cost driver classification schemes.

Appendix

LEAST-SQUARES REGRESSION ANALYSIS USING A COMPUTER SPREADSHEET

This appendix presents the detail underlying the least-squares regression analysis illustration on pages 50 through 52.

First, paired observations of the number of shipments and shipping costs are entered on an Excel spreadsheet. The X and Y labels are provided to assist in identifying the independent and dependent variables.

X	Y
6000	17000
9000	26000
12000	32000
10000	20000

Next, "Tools," "Data Analysis," and "Regression" are selected on the menu. Once in the regression submenu, enter the range of the independent value X, the dependent value Y, and a cell to serve as the upper left corner of the solution area (called the "output range"). The following information taken from the output range is limited to items under discussion in this text.

SUMMARY OUTPUT

Regression Statistics

R Square	0.683616
Standard Error	4582.576
Observations	4

	Coefficients	Standard Error
Intercept	3400	
X Variable 1	2.2	1.058301

The following is a brief explanation of each regression output, starting with the key items of interest in the lower left corner of the output range.

Coefficient of Intercept—the value of *a*. Within the range of normal operations, the monthly fixed costs of operating the packaging department are estimated as $3,400.

Coefficient of X Variable 1—the value of *b*. Within the range of normal observations, this is $2.20 per package. When there are two independent variables, the second is identified in the output as "X Variable 2," and so forth.

R-Squared (coefficient of determination)—a measure of the percent of variation in the dependent variable (such as total cost) that is explained by variations in the independent variable (such as total shipments) when the least-squares estimation equation is used. Statisticians often refer to the coefficient of determination as *R-squared* and represent it as R^2. The coefficient of determination can take on values between zero and one, with values close to zero suggesting that the equation is not very useful and values close to one indicating that the equation explains a large percent of the variation in the dependent variable. In this case, 68.3616 percent of the variation in monthly packaging department costs is explained by the variation in the number of shipments.

Standard Error (also called the standard error of the Y estimate)—a measure of the dispersion of actual values around the cost-estimating equation. If a value of Y is computed using the estimating equation, using the statistical concept of a normal distribution, mathematicians have determined a 68 percent probability that the true value of Y will be equal to the computed value ± the standard error of the Y estimate. If we were interested in costs for a month with 10,000 shipments, the estimated value is $25,400 ($3,400 + $2.20[10,000]), and there is a 68 percent probability that the actual value of Y is between $25,400 ± $4,583.576.

Observations—simply the number of paired X and Y values used in computations.

Standard Error of X Variable 1—a measure of the dispersion of actual values of the X coefficient around the computed value. Mathematicians have determined that under certain circumstances, there is a 68 percent probability that the true value of X will be equal to the computed value ± the standard error of the X coefficient. This is useful if we are particularly interested in estimating the variable cost per shipment. There is a 68 percent probability that the actual value of b, the variable cost, is between $2.20 ± $1.058301.

Review Problems

The solutions to the review problems are found on pages 81–82. To maximize your learning, you should make a serious attempt to develop written solutions to the review problems before looking at the solutions. If there are errors in your solutions, you should then attempt to determine their causes.

2–1
Identifying Cost Behavior Patterns

Identify each of the following cost behavior patterns as variable, fixed committed, fixed discretionary, mixed, or step.

a. Total cost of bakery products used at a McDonald's restaurant when the number of meals served is the activity driver.
b. Total cost of operating a health clinic when the number of patients served is the cost driver.
c. Total property taxes for a Monroe Muffler Shop when the number of vehicles serviced is the cost driver.
d. Total cost of motherboards used by Apple Computer when the number of computers manufactured and shipped is the cost driver.
e. Total cost of secretarial services at a university with each secretary handling the needs of ten faculty members and where part-time secretarial help is not available. The number of faculty is the cost driver.
f. Total advertising costs for International Business Machines (IBM) when sales revenue is the cost driver.
g. Automobile rental costs at Alamo in Orlando, Florida, when there is no mileage charge. The cost driver is the number of miles driven.
h. Automobile rental cost at Hertz in Dallas, Texas, which has a base charge plus a mileage charge. The cost driver is the number of miles driven.
i. Salaries paid to personnel while conducting on-campus employment interviews at Champion International. Number of on-campus interviews is the cost driver.
j. The cost of contributions to educational institutions by Xerox Corporation. The number of employees hired is the cost driver.

2–2
Estimating Cost Behavior and Predicting Future Costs

Dan's Submarine Sandwich Shop reported the following results for April and May:

	April	May
Unit sales	2,100	2,700
Cost of food sold	$1,575	$2,025
Wages and salaries	1,525	1,675
Rent on building	1,500	1,500
Depreciation on equipment	200	200
Utilities	710	770
Supplies	225	255
Miscellaneous	113	131
Total	$5,848	$6,556

Required:
a. Identify each cost as being fixed, variable, or mixed.
b. Using the high-low method, develop an equation for the cost of food, wages and salaries, rent on building, and total monthly costs.

c. Predict total costs for monthly volumes of 1,000 and 2,000 units.
d. Predict the average cost per unit at monthly volumes of 1,000 and 2,000 units and explain why the average costs differ at these two volumes.

Key Terms

Batch-level activity (p. 56)
Capacity costs (p. 47)
Coefficient of determination (R^2) (p. 51)
Committed fixed costs (p. 47)
Cost behavior (p. 40)
Cost estimation (p. 47)
Cost prediction (p. 49)
Customer-level activity (p. 58)
Direct labor (p. 55)
Direct materials (p. 55)
Discretionary fixed costs (p. 47)
Facility-level activity (p. 56)
Fixed costs (p. 40)
High-low method of cost estimation (p. 48)
Least-squares regression analysis (p. 50)

Managed fixed costs (p. 47)
Manufacturing overhead (p. 55)
Marginal cost (p. 43)
Market segment-level activity (p. 58)
Mixed costs (p. 40)
Order-level activity (p. 56)
Product-level activity (p. 56)
Project-level activity (p. 58)
Relevant range (p. 45)
Scatter diagram (p. 49)
Semivariable costs (p. 40)
Step costs (p. 41)
Unit-level activity (p. 56)
Unit-level approach (p. 40)
Variable costs (p. 40)

Review Questions

1. Briefly describe variable, fixed, mixed, and step costs and indicate how the total cost function of each changes as activity increases within a time period.
2. Why is presenting all costs of an organization as a function of a single independent variable, although useful in obtaining a general understanding of cost behavior, not accurate enough to make specific decisions concerning products, services, or activities?
3. Describe the economists' short-run total cost function and identify the range within which a linear pattern is a reasonable approximation of total costs.
4. How are variable and fixed costs determined using the high-low method of cost estimation?
5. Distinguish between cost estimation and cost prediction.
6. Why is a scatter diagram helpful when used in conjunction with other methods of cost estimation?
7. Identify two advantages of least-squares regression analysis as a cost estimation technique.
8. Why is it important to match activity and costs within a single observation? When is this matching problem most likely to exist?
9. During the past century, how have direct materials, direct labor, and manufacturing overhead changed as a portion of total manufacturing costs? What is the implication of the change in manufacturing overhead for cost estimation?
10. Distinguish between the unit-, batch-, product-, and facility-level activities of a manufacturing organization.
11. What cost estimation errors are likely to occur if a company that has products produced both in large and small batches uses unit-level cost estimation?
12. What cost estimation errors are likely to occur if a company that has both complex products with high product-level costs and simple products with low product-level costs uses unit level cost estimation?

Exercises

2–1
Classifying Cost Behavior

Classify the total costs of each of the following as variable, fixed, mixed, or step. Sales volume is the cost driver.

a. Pulpwood in a papermill
b. Salaries of two supervisors
c. Real estate taxes
d. Salaries of quality inspectors when each inspector can evaluate a maximum of 1,000 units per day
e. Wages paid to production employees for the time spent working on products
f. Electric power in a factory
g. Raw materials used in production
h. Automobiles rented on the basis of a fixed charge per day plus an additional charge per mile driven
i. Sales commissions
j. Depreciation on office equipment

2–2
Classifying Cost Behavior

Classify the total costs of each of the following as variable, fixed, mixed, or step.

a. Maintenance costs at a college
b. Property taxes on a building
c. Rent on a photocopy machine charged as a fixed amount per month plus an additional charge per copy
d. Cost of goods sold in a bookstore
e. Salaries paid to temporary instructors in a college as the number of course sessions varies
f. Lumber used by a house construction company
g. The costs of operating a research department
h. The cost of hiring a dance band for three hours
i. Laser printer paper for a department printer
j. Electric power in a restaurant

2–3
Classifying Cost Behavior

For each of the following situations, select the most appropriate cost behavior pattern (as shown in the illustrations on the next page) where the lines represent the cost behavior pattern, the vertical axis represents costs, the horizontal axis represents total volume, and the dots represent actual costs. Each pattern may be used more than once.

a. Variable costs per unit
b. Total mixed costs
c. Total fixed costs
d. Average fixed costs per unit
e. Total current manufacturing costs
f. Average variable costs
g. Total costs when employees are paid $10 per hour for the first 40 hours worked each week and $15 for each additional hour.
h. Total costs when employees are paid $10 per hour and guaranteed a minimum weekly wage of $200.
i. Total costs when a consultant is paid $50 per hour with a maximum fee of $1,000.
j. Total variable costs
k. Total costs for salaries of social workers where each social worker can handle a maximum of 20 cases
l. A water bill where a flat fee of $800 is charged for the first 100,000 gallons and additional water costs $0.005 per gallon

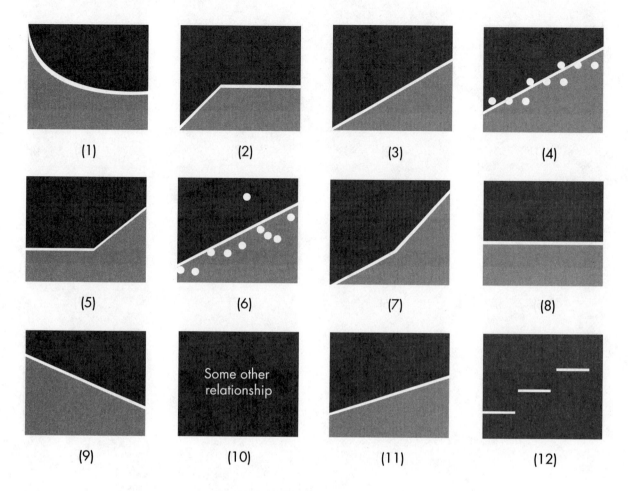

(1) (2) (3) (4)

(5) (6) (7) (8)

(9) (10) Some other relationship (11) (12)

m. Total variable costs properly used to estimate step costs
n. Total materials costs
o. Rent on exhibit space at a convention

**2-4
Classifying Cost
Behavior**

For each of the following situations, select the most appropriate cost behavior pattern (as shown in the illustrations on the next page) where the lines represent the cost behavior pattern, the vertical axis represents total costs, the horizontal axis represents total volume, and the dots represent actual costs. Each pattern may be used more than once.

a. A cellular telephone bill when a flat fee is charged for the first 20 minutes of use per month and additional use costs $0.25 per minute
b. Total selling and administrative costs
c. Total labor costs when employees are paid per unit produced
d. Total overtime premium paid production employees
e. Average total cost per unit
f. Salaries of supervisors when each one can supervise a maximum of 10 employees
g. Total idle time costs when employees are paid for a minimum 40-hour week
h. Materials costs per unit
i. A good linear approximation of actual costs
j. Electric power consumption in a restaurant
k. Total costs when high volumes of production require the use of overtime and obsolete equipment
l. Total sales commissions
m. A linear cost estimation valid only within the relevant range

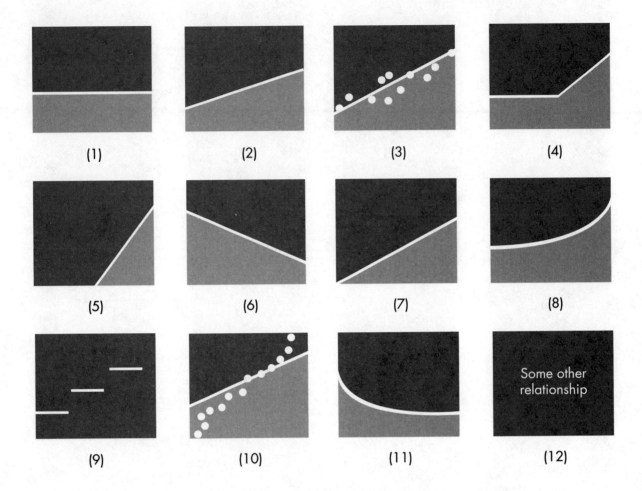

(1)   (2)   (3)   (4)

(5)   (6)   (7)   (8)

(9)   (10)   (11)   (12)

Some other
relationship

2-5
Classifying
Discretionary and
Committed Fixed
Costs

Identify each of the following costs as discretionary or committed.

a. Depreciation on equipment used to produce widgets
b. Annual property taxes for Barb's Bridal Shop
c. Cost of television commercials for Allhere Department Store
d. Cost of the local Methodist church's charitable donation to The Starlight Foundation
e. After a new computer system is installed, the costs of training the employees
f. Annual rent Betty must pay to operate her bakery
g. Cost of research done by federal agencies to find a cure for cancer

2-6
Computing Average
Unit Costs

The total monthly operating costs of El Rancho Chili To Go are:

$$\$5,000 + \$0.40X$$

where

$$X = \text{servings of chili}$$

Required:
a. Determine the average cost per serving at each of the following monthly volumes: 10, 100, 200, 400, 800.
b. Determine the monthly volume at which the average cost per serving is $0.50.

2-7
Automatic versus
Manual Processing

Fast Photo Company operates a 60-minute film development and print service. The current service, which relies extensively on manual operations, has monthly operating costs of $5,000 plus $2 per roll of film developed and printed. Management is evaluating the desirability of acquiring a machine that will automatically develop film and make prints. If the machine is acquired, the monthly fixed costs will increase to $23,000; the variable costs of developing and printing a roll of film will decline to $1.40.

Required:
a. Determine the total costs of developing and printing 20,000 and 50,000 rolls per month:
   1. With the current process.
   2. With the automatic process.
b. Determine the monthly volume at which the automatic process becomes preferable to the manual process.

2–8
Automatic versus Manual Processing

Kopy Kat Photocopy Service processes 1,000,000 photocopies per month at its midtown service center. Approximately 60 percent of the photocopies require collating. Collating is currently performed by high school and college students who are paid $7.50 per hour. Each student collates an average of 5,000 copies per hour.

Management is contemplating the lease of an automatic collating machine that has a monthly capacity of 5,000,000 photocopies, with lease and operating costs totaling $1,450, plus $0.05 per 1,000 units collated.

Required:
a. Determine the total costs of collating 500,000 and 1,500,000 per month:
   1. With student help.
   2. With the collating machine.
b. Determine the monthly volume at which the automatic process becomes preferable to the manual process.
c. Should Kopy Kat lease the automatic collating machine at this time?

2–9
High-Low Cost Estimation

Art's Delivery Company has the following information available about fleet miles and operating costs:

Year	Miles	Operating Costs
2003	556,000	$165,880
2004	684,000	195,320

Required:
Use the high-low method to develop a cost-estimating equation for total annual operating costs.

2–10
Scatter Diagrams and High-Low Cost Estimation

Information on the number of sales orders received and order-processing costs is presented.

Month	Sales Orders	Order-Processing Costs
1	3,000	$40,000
2	1,500	28,000
3	4,000	65,000
4	2,800	39,000
5	2,300	32,000
6	1,000	20,000
7	2,000	30,000

Required:
a. Use information from the high- and low-volume months to develop a cost-estimating equation for monthly order-processing costs.

(continued)

b. Plot the data on a scatter diagram. Using the information from representative high- and low-volume months, develop a cost-estimating equation for monthly production costs.

c. What factors might have caused the difference in the equations developed for requirements (a) and (b)?

2–11
Scatter Diagrams and High-Low Cost Estimation

From April 1 through October 31, Central County Highway Department hires temporary employees to mow and clean the right of way along county roads. The County Road Commissioner has asked you to help her in determining the variable labor cost of mowing and cleaning a mile of road. The following information is available regarding 2001 operations:

Month	Miles Mowed and Cleaned	Labor Costs
April	350	$7,500
May	300	7,000
June	400	8,500
July	250	5,000
August	375	8,000
September ...	200	4,500
October	100	4,300

Required:

a. Use the information from the high- and low-volume months to develop a cost-estimating equation for monthly labor costs.

b. Plot the data on a scatter diagram. Using the information from representative high- and low-volume months, develop a cost-estimating equation for monthly labor costs.

c. What factors might have caused the difference in the equations developed for requirements (a) and (b)?

d. Adjust the equation developed in requirement (b) to incorporate the effect of an anticipated 7 percent increase in wages.

2–12
Cost Behavior Analysis in a Restaurant: High-Low Cost Estimation

Pizza House Restaurant has the following information available regarding costs at representative levels of monthly sales:

	MONTHLY SALES IN UNITS		
	5,000	8,000	10,000
Cost of food sold	$ 5,250	$ 8,400	$10,500
Wages and fringe benefits	4,250	4,400	4,500
Fees paid delivery help	1,250	2,000	2,500
Rent on building	1,200	1,200	1,200
Depreciation on equipment	300	300	300
Utilities	500	560	600
Supplies (soap, floor wax, etc.)	150	180	200
Administrative costs	1,300	1,300	1,300
Total	$14,200	$18,340	$21,100

Required:

a. Identify each cost as being variable, fixed, or mixed.

b. Use the high-low method to develop a schedule identifying the amount of each cost that is fixed per month or variable per unit. Total the amounts under each category to develop an equation for total monthly costs.

c. Predict total costs for a monthly sales volume of 9,500 units.

**2-13
Developing an
Equation from
Average Costs**

The Dog House is a pet hotel located on the outskirts of town. In March, when dog-days (occupancy) were at an annual low of 500, the average cost per dog-day was $18.50. In July, when dog-days were at a capacity level of 3,100, the average cost per dog-day was $5.50.

Required:

a. Develop an equation for monthly operating costs.
b. Determine the average cost per dog-day at an annual volume of 24,000 dog-days.

**2-14
Selecting an
Independent
Variable: Scatter
Diagrams**

Valley Production Company produces backpacks that are sold to sporting goods stores throughout the Rocky Mountains. Presented is information on production costs and inventory changes for five recent months:

	January	February	March	April	May
Finished goods inventory in units:					
Beginning	30,000	40,000	50,000	30,000	60,000
Manufactured	60,000	90,000	80,000	90,000	100,000
Available	90,000	130,000	130,000	120,000	160,000
Sold	(50,000)	(80,000)	(100,000)	(60,000)	(120,000)
Ending	40,000	50,000	30,000	60,000	40,000
Manufacturing costs	$300,000	$500,000	$450,000	$450,000	$550,000

Required:

a. With the aid of scatter diagrams, determine whether units sold or units manufactured is a better predictor of manufacturing costs.
b. Prepare an explanation for your answer to requirement (a).
c. Which independent variable, units sold or units manufactured, should be a better predictor of selling costs? Why?

**2-15
Selecting a Basis
for Predicting
Shipping Expenses:
Requires
Spreadsheet
Program**

Tyson Company assembles and sells computer boards in western Pennsylvania. In an effort to improve the planning and control of shipping expenses, management is trying to determine which of three variables—units shipped, weight shipped, or sales value of units shipped—has the closest relationship with shipping expenses. The following information is available:

Month	Units Shipped	Weight Shipped (lbs.)	Sales Value of Units Shipped	Shipping Expenses
May	3,000	6,200	$50,000	$2,500
June	5,000	8,000	55,000	3,500
July	4,000	8,100	40,000	3,000
August	7,000	10,000	57,000	5,000
September	6,000	7,000	70,000	4,000
October	4,500	8,000	80,000	3,800

Required:

a. With the aid of a spreadsheet program, determine whether units shipped, weight shipped, or sales value of units shipped has the closest relationship with shipping expenses.
b. Using the independent variable that appears to have the closest relationship to shipping expenses, develop a cost-estimating equation for total monthly shipping expenses.
c. Use the equation developed in requirement (b) to predict total shipping expenses in a month when 5,000 units, weighing 7,000 lbs., with a total sales value of $57,000 are shipped.

Problems

2–16 **Analyzing** **Spreadsheet** **Regression Data**	The manager of Jones Petro is analyzing the relationship between operating costs, the dependent variable, and gallons of gasoline sold, the independent variable. Analyzing data for several months with a spreadsheet software package and a personal computer, she obtained the following results:

Regression Output:	
Constant	2700
Std Err of Y Est	650.489
R Squared	0.624956
No. of Observations	10
Degrees of Freedom	8
X Coefficient	1.21
Std Err or Coef.	0.558301

Required

a. How many months were included in the analysis?
b. What percent of the variation in the dependent variable is explained by the cost-estimating equation?
c. Predict total operating costs for a month in which 20,000 gallons are sold.
d. Mention some questions you would like answered before using the prediction developed in requirement (c).

2–17 **High-Low and** **Scatter Diagrams** **with Implications** **for Regression**	Dippie Donut Shop produces and sells donuts at each of its restaurants. Presented is monthly cost and sales information for one of Dippie's restaurants.

Month	Sales (Dozens)	Total Costs
January . .	8,000	$9,000
February .	6,000	7,000
March . . .	4,000	5,000
April	2,000	4,500
May	5,000	6,500
June	5,000	5,500

Required

a. Using the high-low method, develop a cost-estimating equation for Dippie Donut Shop
b. 1. Plot the equation developed in requirement (a).
   2. Using the same graph, develop a scatter diagram of all observations for Dippie Donut Shop and draw a representative cost-estimating equation on the following graph. Be sure to label the high-low and scatter diagram lines.
c. Which is a better predictor of future costs? Why?
d. If you decided to develop a cost-estimating equation using least squares regression analysis, should you include all the observations? Why or why not?
e. Mention two reasons that the least-squares regression is superior to the high-low and scatter diagram methods of cost estimation.

2–18 **Distortion of Batch** **and Product Level** **Cost Drivers**	Monte Sano Company manufactures a variety of high-volume and low-volume products to customer demand. Presented is information on 2004 manufacturing overhead and activity cost drivers.

Level	Total Cost	Units of Cost Driver
Unit	$500,000	20,000 machine hours
Batch	100,000	1,000 customer orders
Product	200,000	50 products

Product X1 required 1,000 machine hours to fill 10 customer orders for a total of 8,000 units.

Required:

a. Assuming all manufacturing overhead is estimated and predicted on the basis of machine hours (a single unit-level cost driver), determine the predicted total overhead costs to produce the 8,000 units of product X1.

b. Assuming manufacturing overhead is estimated and predicted using separate rates for machine hours, customer orders, and products (a multiple-level cost hierarchy), determine the predicted total overhead costs to produce the 8,000 units of product X1.

c. Analyze the error in predicting manufacturing overhead using machine hours. Indicate whether the use of machine hours results in overpredicting or underpredicting the costs to produce 8,000 units of product X1.

d. Determine the error in the prediction of X1 batch-level costs resulting from the use of machine hours. Indicate whether the use of machine hours results in overpredicting or underpredicting the batch-level costs of product X1.

e. Determine the error in the prediction of X1 product-level costs resulting from the use of machine hours. Indicate whether the use of machine hours results in overpredicting or underpredicting the product-level costs of product X1.

2-19
Unit and Batch Level Cost Drivers

Fried Mania, a fast-food restaurant, serves fried chicken, fried fish, and French fries. The managers have estimated the costs of a batch of fried chicken for Fried Mania's all-you-can-eat Friday Fried Fiesta. Each batch must be 100 pieces. The chicken is pre-cut by the chain headquarters and sent to the stores in 10-piece bags. Each bag costs $3. Preparing a batch of 100 pieces of chicken with Fried Mania's special coating takes one employee two hours. The current wage rate is $6 per hour. Another cost driver is the cost of putting fresh oil into the fryers. New oil, costing $5, is used for each batch.

Required:

a. Determine the cost of preparing one batch of 100 pieces.

b. If management projects that it will sell 300 pieces of fried chicken, determine the total unit and batch costs.

c. If management estimates the sales to be 350 pieces, determine the total costs.

d. How much will the batch costs increase if the government raises the minimum wage to $8 per hour?

e. If management decided to reduce the number of pieces in a batch to 50, determine the cost of preparing 350 pieces. Assume that the batch would take half as long to prepare, and management wants to replace the oil after 50 pieces are cooked.

f. Refer to your solutions to requirements (c) and (e). Would management be wise to reduce the batch size to 50?

2-20
Hierarchy of Activity Costs

Dolls Incorporated manufactures and sells two products: the Amanda Doll (A) and the Betsy Star Doll (B). The firm's activities have been analyzed and placed into a hierarchy of activity costs. Information on activity cost drivers and costs per unit of cost driver at each activity level is presented:

	Unit-Level Costs		Batch-Level Costs		Product-Level Costs	Facility-Level Costs
					PER MONTH	
Product A	Materials	$3	Setup	$100	Advertising $10,000	
	Conversion	1	Movement	25		
	Total	$4	Total	$125		
Product B	Materials	$5	Setup	$150	Advertising $15,000	
	Labor	2	Movement	25		
	Total	$7	Total	$175		

Maintenance	$ 5,000
Rent	3,000
Administrative salaries	7,000
Total	$15,000

During August 2000, Dolls Incorporated produced 10,000 units of Product A and 5,000 units of Product B.

During September of 2000, Dolls Incorporated produced 15,000 units of Product A and 10,000 units of Product B. Production increased because the marketing staff had underestimated sales for the holiday season.

Each batch of Product A and each batch of Product B contain 1,000 units.

Required:
a. Determine the total costs for each activity level and the total predicted costs for August.
b. Determine the total costs for each activity level and the total predicted costs for September.

**2–21
Analysis of
Distortions Resulting
from the Exclusive
Use of Unit-Level
Activity Cost
Drivers:
Batch-Level Costs**

Volume-based unit-level analysis underestimates the cost of products produced in batches containing a small number of units and overestimates the cost of products produced in batches containing a large number of units.

Information on unit-, batch-, and product-level costs for Products A, B, and C is presented.

	Product A	Product B	Product C
Unit-level cost per unit	$10	$10	$10
Batch-level cost per batch	$500	$500	$500
Product-level cost	$10,000	$10,000	$10,000
Annual production	?	?	?
Batch size	?	?	?

Assume there are no facility-level costs.

Required:
Complete this table in a manner that will allow you to illustrate the stated concept. Specific answers will vary depending on the numbers selected. Relationships, not specific numbers, are important. Read all requirements before starting.

a. Complete the table for annual production and batch size to develop an example illustrating the stated concept.
b. Determine the average cost per unit assuming the number of units of production is the only driver for all costs. Because unit-level costs are identical and all other costs are assumed to be a function of the number of units, the average cost is the same for all three products.

c. Determine the average unit cost of each product using the manufacturing cost hierarchy and assuming we separately account for the costs of each product.

d. Which product has the lowest unit cost in (c)? Why is this product's cost lower in (c) than in (b)?

2-22
Analysis of Distortions Resulting from the Exclusive Use of Unit-Level Activity Cost Drivers: Product-Level Costs

Volume-based unit-level analysis underestimates the cost of the most complex products with the highest product-level costs and overestimates the cost of the least complex products with the lowest product-level costs.

Information on unit-, batch-, and product-level costs for products A, B, and C is presented.

	Product A	Product B	Product C
Unit-level cost per unit	$20	$20	$20
Batch-level cost per batch	$400	$400	$400
Product-level cost	?	?	?
Annual production	?	?	?
Batch size	100	100	100

Required:

Complete this table in a manner that will allow you to illustrate the stated concept. Specific answers will vary depending on the numbers selected. Relationships, not specific numbers, are important. Read all requirements before starting.

a. Complete the table for annual product-level costs and annual production to develop an example illustrating the concept presented here.

b. Determine the average cost per unit assuming the number of units of production is the only driver for all costs. Because unit-level costs are identical and all other costs are assumed to be a function of the number of units, the average cost is the same for all three products.

c. Determine the average unit cost of each product using the manufacturing cost hierarchy and assuming we separately account for the costs of each product.

d. Which product has the lowest unit cost in (c)? Why is this product's cost lower in (c) than in (b)?

Discussion Questions

2-23
Negative Fixed Costs

"This is crazy!" exclaimed the production supervisor as he reviewed the work of his new assistant. "You and that computer are telling me that my fixed costs are negative! Tell me, how did you get these negative fixed costs, and what am I supposed to do with them?"

Required:

Explain to the supervisor the meaning of the negative "fixed costs" and what can be done with them.

2-24
Significance of High R-Squared

Oliver Morris had always been suspicious of "newfangled mathematical stuff," and the most recent suggestion of his new assistant merely confirmed his belief that schools are putting a lot of useless junk in students' heads. It seems that after an extensive analysis of historical data, the assistant suggested that the number of pounds of scrap was the best basis for predicting manufacturing overhead.

In response to Mr. Morris's rage, the slightly intimidated assistant indicated that of the 35 equations he tried, pounds of scrap had the highest coefficient of determination with manufacturing overhead.

Required:

Comment on Morris's reaction. Is it justified? Is it likely that the number of pounds of scrap is a good basis for predicting manufacturing overhead? Is it a feasible basis for predicting manufacturing overhead?

2-25
Estimating Machine Repair Costs

In an attempt to determine the best basis for predicting machine repair costs, the production supervisor accumulated daily information on these costs and production over a one-month period. Applying simple regression analysis to the data, she obtained the following estimating equation:

$$Y = \$800 - \$2.601X$$

where

$$Y = \text{total daily machine repair costs}$$
$$X = \text{daily production in units}$$

Because of the negative relationship between repair costs and production, she was somewhat skeptical of the results, even though the R-squared was a respectable 0.765.

Required:
a. What is the most likely explanation of the negative variable costs?
b. Suggest an alternative procedure for estimating machine repair costs that might prove more useful.

2-26
Ethical Problem Uncovered by Cost Estimation

Mighty Mall Management Company owns and provides management services for several shopping centers. After five years with the company, Mike Moyer was recently promoted to the position of manager of X-Town, an 18-store mall on the outskirts of a downtown area. When he accepted the assignment, Mike was told that he would hold the position for only a couple of years because X-Town would likely be torn down to make way for a new sports stadium. Mike was also told that if he did well in this assignment, he would be in line for heading one of Mighty Mall's new 200-store operations that were currently in the planning stage.

While reviewing X-Town's financial records for the past few years, Mike observed that last year's oil consumption was up by 8 percent, even though the number of heating degree days was down by 4 percent. Somewhat curious, Mike uncovered the following information:

- X-Town is heated by forced-air oil heat. The furnace is five years old and has been well maintained.
- Fuel oil is kept in four 5,000-gallon underground oil tanks. The oil tanks were installed in 1968.
- Replacing the tanks would cost $80,000. If pollution was found, cleanup costs could go as high as $2,000,000, depending on how much oil had leaked into the ground and how far it had traveled.
- Replacing the tanks would also add more congestion to X-Town's parking situation.

Required:
What should Mike do?

2-27
Activity Cost Drivers and Cost Estimation

The Blue Ridge Ice Cream Company produces ten varieties of ice creams in large vats, several thousand gallons at a time. The ice cream is distributed to several categories of customers. Some ice cream is packaged in large containers and sold to college and university food services. Some is packaged in half-gallon or small containers and sold through wholesale distributors to grocery stores. Finally, some is packaged in a variety of individual servings and sold directly to the public from trucks owned and operated by Blue Ridge.

Management has always assumed that costs fluctuated with the volume of ice cream, and cost-estimating equations have been based on the following cost function:

Estimated costs = Fixed costs + Variable costs per gallon × Production in gallons

Lately, however, this equation has not been a very accurate predictor of total costs. At the same time, management has noticed that the volumes and varieties of ice cream sold through the three distinct distribution channels have fluctuated from month to month.

Required:

a. What *relevant* major assumption is inherent in the cost-estimating equation currently used by Blue Ridge?
b. Why might Blue Ridge wish to develop a cost-estimating equation that recognizes the hierarchy of activity costs? Explain.
c. Develop the general form of a more accurate cost-estimating equation for Blue Ridge. Clearly label and explain all elements of the equation, and provide specific examples of costs for each element.

2-28
Multiple Regression Analysis for a Special Decision: Requires Spreadsheet Program

For billing purposes, Central City Health Clinic classifies its services into one of four major procedures, X1 through X4. A local business has proposed that Central City provide health services to its employees and their families at the following set rates per procedure:

X1	$ 45
X2	90
X3	60
X4	105

Because these rates are significantly below the current rates charged for these services, management has asked for detailed cost information on each procedure.

The following information is available for the most recent 12 months.

Month	Total Cost	NUMBER OF PROCEDURES X1	X2	X3	X4
1	$23,000	30	100	205	75
2	25,000	38	120	180	90
3	27,000	50	80	140	150
4	19,000	20	90	120	100

Month	Total Cost	NUMBER OF PROCEDURES X1	X2	X3	X4
5	$20,000	67	50	160	80
6	27,000	90	75	210	105
7	25,500	20	110	190	110
8	21,500	15	120	175	80
9	26,000	60	85	125	140
10	22,000	20	90	100	140
11	22,800	20	70	150	130
12	26,500	72	60	200	120

Required:

a. Use multiple regression analysis to determine the unit cost of each procedure. How much variation in monthly cost is explained by your cost-estimating equation?
b. Evaluate the rates proposed by the local business. Assuming Central City has

excess capacity and no employees of the local business currently patronize the clinic, what are your recommendations regarding the proposal?

c. Evaluate the rates proposed by the local business. Assuming Central City is operating at capacity and would have to turn current customers away if it agrees to provide health services to the local business, what are your recommendations regarding the proposal?

2-29
Cost Estimation,
Interpretation, and
Analysis: Requires
Spreadsheet
Program

Carolina Table Company produces two styles of tables, dining room and kitchen. Presented is monthly information on production volume and manufacturing costs:

Period	Total Manufacturing Costs	Total Tables Produced	Dining Room Tables Produced	Kitchen Tables Produced
June 2003	$31,100	250	50	200
July	33,925	205	105	100
August	40,420	285	105	180
September	26,495	210	40	170
October	28,080	175	75	100
November	35,050	210	110	100
December	35,245	245	90	155
January 2004	31,550	250	50	200
February	31,490	220	70	150
March	29,650	180	80	100
April	65,200	315	180	135
May	39,955	280	105	175
June	34,695	255	75	180
July	36,920	235	110	125
August	30,815	195	85	110
September	40,290	260	120	140
October	35,805	250	90	160
November	38,400	270	100	170
December	25,100	165	60	105

Required:

a. Use the high-low method to develop a cost-estimating equation for total manufacturing costs. Interpret the meaning of the "fixed" costs and comment on the results.

b. Use the chart feature of a spreadsheet to develop a scatter graph of total manufacturing costs and total units produced. Use the graph to identify any unusual observations.

c. Excluding any unusual observations, use the high-low method to develop a cost-estimating equation for total manufacturing costs. Comment on the results, comparing them with the results in requirement (a).

d. Use simple regression anyalsis to develop a cost-estimating equation for total manufacturing costs. What advantages does simple regression analysis have in comparison with the high-low method of cost estimation? Why must analysts carefully evaluate the date used in simple regression analysis?

e. A customer has offered to purchase 50 dining room tables for $180 per table. Management has asked your advice regarding the desirability of accepting the offer. What advice do you have for management? Additional analysis is required.

2-30
Simple and Multiple
Regression:
Requires Spread-
sheet Program

Wanda Sable is employed by a mail-order distributor and reconditions used tuner/amplifiers, tape decks, and compact disk (CD) players. Wanda is paid $12 per hour, plus an extra $6 per hour for work in excess of 40 hours per week.

The distributor just announced plans to outsource all reconditioning work. Because the distributor is pleased with the quality of Wanda's work, she has been asked to enter into a long-term contract to recondition used CD players at a rate of $30 per player, plus all parts. The distributor also offered to provide all necessary equipment at a rate of $200 per month. She has been informed that she should plan on reconditioning as many CD players as she can handle, up to a maximum of 20 CD players per week.

Wanda has room in her basement to set up a work area, but she is unsure of the economics of accepting the contract, as opposed to working for a local Radio Stuff store at $8 per hour.

Data related to the time spent and the number of units of each type of electronic equipment Wanda has reconditioned in recent weeks is as follows:

Week	Tuner Amplifiers	Tape Decks	Compact Disk (CD) Players	Total Units	Total Hours
1	4	5	5	14	40
2	0	7	6	13	42
3	4	3	7	14	40
4	0	2	12	14	46
5	11	6	4	21	48
6	5	8	3	16	44
7	5	8	3	16	44
8	5	6	5	16	43
9	2	6	10	18	53
10	8	4	6	18	46
Total				160	446

Required:

Assuming she wants to work an average of 40 hours per week, what should Wanda do?

Solutions to Review Problems

2-1 a. Variable cost
   b. Mixed cost
   c. Committed fixed cost
   d. Variable cost
   e. Step cost
   f. Discretionary fixed cost
   g. Fixed cost (Without knowing the purpose of renting the car, the cost cannot be classified as committed or discretionary.)
   h. Mixed cost
   i. Step cost
   j. Discretionary fixed cost

2-2 a. Fixed costs are easily identified. They are the same at each activity level. Variable and mixed costs are determined by dividing the total costs for an item at two activity levels by the corresponding units of activity. The quotients of the variable cost items will be identical at both activity levels. The quotients of the mixed costs will differ, being lower at the higher activity level because the fixed costs are being spread over a larger number of units.

Cost	Behavior
Cost of food sold	Variable
Wages and salaries	Mixed
Rent on building	Fixed

Cost	Behavior
Depreciation on equipment	Fixed
Utilities	Mixed
Supplies	Mixed
Miscellaneous	Mixed

b. The cost of food sold was classified as a variable cost. Hence, the cost of food may be determined by dividing the total costs at either observation by the corresponding number of units.

$$b = \frac{\$1,575 \text{ total variable costs}}{2,100 \text{ units}}$$

$$= \$0.75X$$

Wages and salaries were previously classified as a mixed cost. Hence, the cost of wages and salaries is determined using the high-low method.

$$b = \frac{\$1,675 - \$1,525}{2,700 - 2,100}$$

$$= 0.25X$$

$$a = \$1,525 \text{ total cost} - (\$0.25 \times 2,100) \text{ variable cost}$$

$$= \$1,000$$

Rent on building was classified as a fixed cost.

$$a = \$1,500$$

Total monthly costs most likely follow a mixed cost behavior pattern. Hence, they can be determined using the high-low method.

$$b = \frac{\$6,556 - \$5,848}{2,700 - 2,100}$$

$$= \$1.18X$$

$$a = \$5,848 - (\$1.18 \times 2,100)$$

$$= \$3,370$$

$$\text{Total costs} = \$3,370 + \$1.18X$$

where

$$X = \text{unit sales}$$

c. and d.

Volume	Total Costs	Average Cost per Unit
1,000	$3,370 + ($1.18 × 1,000) = $4,550	$4,550/1,000 = $4.55
2,000	$3,370 + ($1.18 × 2,000) = $5,730	$5,730/2,000 = $2.865

The average costs differ at 1,000 and 2,000 units because the fixed costs are being spread over a different number of units. The larger the number of units, the smaller the average fixed cost per unit.

PROFITABILITY ANALYSIS AND PLANNING

After completing this chapter, you should be able to:

LEARNING OBJECTIVE 1   Discuss the uses and limitations of traditional cost-volume-profit analysis.

LEARNING OBJECTIVE 2   Prepare and contrast contribution and functional income statements.

LEARNING OBJECTIVE 3   Use cost-volume-profit analysis to find a break-even point and for preliminary profit planning with and without income taxes.

LEARNING OBJECTIVE 4   Analyze the profitability of a multiple-product firm with a constant sales mix.

LEARNING OBJECTIVE 5   Use operating leverage to analyze the opportunities for profit and the risks of loss.

LEARNING OBJECTIVE 6   Analyze the profitability of organizations that operate with unit and nonunit cost drivers.

COST STRUCTURE AND PROFITABILITY

Following the economic expansion and increasing profitability of the late 1990s, the slowing of commercial activity and technology investments in the early 2000s radically altered the income projections of many technology-oriented firms. These economic changes and their resulting impact demonstrate a valuable managerial lesson about the impact of cost structure on profitability.

During the expansion of the late 1990s, managers at firms such as Inktomi, Microsoft, Yahoo, Cisco, Amazon, and Webvan spent heavily on new product development. These investments financed projects such as software development, new computer hardware technologies, Internet marketing and Web site development, and fulfillment capacity such as automated warehouses. The investments generated both significant productive and service capacity and cost structures dominated by high fixed costs. These costs resulted from both the need to maintain the technology supporting existing systems and the investment necessary to develop the next generation of hardware and software. In an expanding market, managers take advantage of these fixed costs to generate profitable growth since adding additional customers does not add significant additional costs. In this environment, a cost structure dominated by fixed costs appears to be a smart managerial choice. In an unstable or declining economy, however, a high fixed-cost approach leads to very different results.

Just as adding new customers does not significantly increase costs with a high fixed-cost approach, reducing the number of customers does not lower costs very much. As sales declined at Inktomi—a developer of software to manage Web content—profits fell from $1 million in the first quarter of 2000 to ($58) million in the first quarter of 2001. Yahoo's revenue fell 42 percent, but its costs barely dropped. Income fell from $87 million in the last quarter of 2000 to ($33) million in the first quarter of 2001. These cost structures dominated by high fixed costs proved quite profitable during expansion but caused the rapid deterioration of profits when the firms were hit by declining sales.

The online grocer Webvan is an even more dramatic example of this relationship between fixed costs, volume, and profitability. With $1 billion of financing, Webvan's well-respected management team embarked on a strategy that included the development of highly automated warehouses to service customers. These high fixed-cost fulfillment centers held the promise of substantial profitability but only if Webvan could reach a high customer volume level. Other online grocery firms adopted strategies requiring less technology and more labor in the fulfillment process. Since these labor costs were variable rather than fixed, rival firms would break even at about 40 percent of the customer volume that Webvan required to achieve breakeven. Although Webvan supporters correctly stated that the firm would be much more profitable than its rivals once the firm had covered its costs, operations never reached that volume level. When Webvan ceased operations after exhausting its financing, an observer commented that while demand does exist for an online, home-delivery grocery business, management must use great care in deciding the business model and cost structure that will meet the demand profitably in a business that traditionally generates a 1 percent net profit margin.

Although high fixed costs can lead to significant profits in the right circumstances, the recent experiences of these firms illustrate that these cost structures have some inherent risks as well. The relationships among the possible cost structures, potential volumes, and opportunities for profit provide a conceptual basis for profitability analysis and planning.

Source: Peter Elstrom, "The End of Fuzzy Math," *Business Week,* December 11, 2000, p. EB100; Linda Himelstein, "Webvan Left the Basics on the Shelf," *Business Week,* July 23, 2001, p. 43; and Greg Ip, "As Profits Swoon, Companies Blame a Market Change in Cost Structure," *The Wall Street Journal,* Interactive Edition, May 16, 2001.

The purpose of this chapter is to introduce basic approaches to profitability analysis and planning. We begin with an approach that considers only unit-level cost drivers and conclude by incorporating nonunit cost drivers. We will consider single-, multiple-product, and service organizations, income taxes, and the effect of cost structure on the relationship between profit potential and the risk of loss.

LEARNING OBJECTIVE 1   **PROFITABILITY ANALYSIS WITH UNIT COST DRIVERS**

Profitability analysis involves examining the relationships between revenues, costs, and profits. Performing profitability analysis requires an understanding of selling prices and the behavior of activity cost drivers.[1] Profitability analysis is widely used in the economic evaluation of existing or proposed products or services. Typically, it is performed before decisions are finalized in an operating budget for a future period.

Paralleling our examination of cost behavior, we will examine two approaches to profitability analysis.

1. A unit-level approach based on the assumption that units sold or sales dollars is the only activity cost driver.
2. A cost hierarchy approach that incorporates nonunit as well as unit-level activity cost drivers.

The traditional approach to profitability analysis, which considers only unit-level activity cost drivers, is identified as **cost-volume-profit (CVP) analysis.** It is a technique used to examine the relationships among the total volume of some independent variable, total costs, total revenues, and profits during a time period (typically a month or year). With CVP analysis, volume refers to a single unit-level activity cost driver, such as unit sales, that is assumed to correlate with changes in revenues, costs, and profits.

Cost-volume-profit analysis is useful in the early stages of planning because it provides an easily understood framework for discussing planning issues and organizing relevant data. CVP analysis is widely used by for-profit as well as not-for-profit organizations. It is equally applicable to service, merchandising, and manufacturing firms. In for-profit organizations, CVP analysis is used to answer such questions as these: How many photocopies must the College Avenue Copy Service produce to earn a profit of $80,000? At what dollar sales volume will Burger King's total revenues and total costs be equal? What profit will General Electric earn at an annual sales volume of $30 billion? What will happen to the profit of Duff's Smorgasbord if there is a 20 percent increase in the cost of food and a 10 percent increase in the selling price of meals? Research Shows 3–1 indicates how the concepts discussed in this and other chapters are important to the success of new businesses.

In not-for-profit organizations, CVP analysis is used to establish service levels, plan fund-raising activities, and determine funding requirements. How many meals can the downtown Salvation Army serve with an annual budget of $600,000? How many tickets must be sold for the benefit concert to raise $20,000? Given the current

---

3-1   **RESEARCH SHOWS**

WANT TO FINANCE A NEW BUSINESS?

Approximately 80 percent of all new businesses fail in the first five years. A major reason for their failure is the lack of equity financing. To obtain finances for a new business, it is necessary to show how the business will make a profit. Five simple steps to help convince cautious investors to risk funds in a new business include these:

1. Projecting start-up costs and operating budgets.
2. Providing projected income statements.
3. Creating a cash flow statement.
4. Determining the business's break-even point.
5. Developing Plan "B."

The last step is particularly important. Plan "B" includes "what if" statements offering solutions to potential problems.

Source: "Five Simple Steps to Help Your Business Build Financial Success," *Hudson Valley Business Journal,* January 19, 1998, p. 20.

---

[1]*Activity cost driver* is often referred to as *cost driver* when the context makes it clear we are discussing activity (rather than structural or organizational) cost drivers.

cost structure, current tuition rates, and projected enrollments, how much money must City University raise from other sources?

ASSUMPTIONS

CVP analysis is subject to a number of assumptions. Although these assumptions do not negate the usefulness of CVP models, especially for a single product or service, they do suggest the need for further analysis before plans are finalized. Among the more important assumptions are these:

1. *All costs are classified as fixed or variable with unit level activity cost drivers.* This assumption is most reasonable when analyzing the profitability of a specific event (such as concert) or the profitability of an organization that produces a single product or service on a continuous basis.
2. *The total cost function is linear within the relevant range.* This assumption may be valid within a relevant range of normal operations, but over the entire range of possible activity, changes in efficiency are likely to result in a curvilinear cost function.
3. *The total revenue function is linear within the relevant range.* Unit selling prices are assumed constant over the range of possible volumes. This implies a purely competitive market for final products or services. In some economic models in which demand responds to price changes, the revenue function is curvilinear. In these situations, the linear approximation is accurate only within a limited range of activity.
4. *The analysis is for a single product, or the sales mix of multiple products is constant.* The **sales mix** refers to the relative portion of unit or dollar sales derived from each product or service. If products have different selling prices and costs, changes in the mix will affect CVP model results.
5. *There is only one activity cost driver—unit or dollar sales volume.* The traditional unit-level approach of CVP analysis does not consider other types of cost drivers (batch, product, customer, and so forth). As we have seen in Chapter 2, this is a very limiting assumption, especially in complex organizations with multiple products. Under such circumstances, it is seldom possible to represent the multitude of factors that drive costs for an entire organization with a single cost driver.

When applied to a single product (such as pounds of potato chips), service (such as the number of pages printed), or event (such as the number of tickets sold to a concert), it may be reasonable to assume the single independent variable is the cost driver. The total costs associated with the single product, service, or event during a specific time period are often determined by this single activity cost driver.

Although cost-volume-profit analysis is often used to understand the overall operations of an organization or business segment, accuracy decreases as the scope of operations being analyzed increases. After introducing profitability analysis with only a single unit-level cost driver, we will expand our discussion of profitability analysis to include multiple unit-level cost drivers and, finally, a hierarchy of cost drivers.

THE PROFIT FORMULA

The profit associated with a product, service, or event is equal to the difference between total revenues and total costs.

$$\pi = R - Y$$

where

$$\pi = \text{Profit}$$
$$R = \text{Total revenues}$$
$$Y = \text{Total costs}$$

The revenues are a function of the unit sales volume and the unit selling price, while total costs for a time period are a function of the fixed costs per period and the variable costs of unit sales.

$$R = pX$$
$$Y = a + bX$$

where

p = Unit selling price
a = Fixed costs
b = Unit variable costs
X = Unit sales

The equation for profit can be expanded to include the details of the total revenue and total cost equations.

$$\pi = pX - (a + bX)$$

Given information on the selling price, fixed costs per period, and variable costs per unit, this formula is used to predict profit at any specified activity level. Consider the following example.

Benchmark Paper Company's only product is high-quality photocopy paper that it manufactures and sells to wholesale distributors at $8.00 per carton. Following modern inventory minimization techniques, Benchmark does not maintain inventories of raw materials or finished goods. Instead, newly purchased raw materials are delivered directly to the factory, and finished goods are loaded directly onto trucks for shipment. Benchmark's variable and fixed costs are detailed here.

1. The term **direct materials** refers to the cost of the primary raw materials converted into finished goods. Because the consumption of raw materials increases as the quantity of goods produced increases, *direct materials represents a variable cost.* Benchmark's raw materials consist primarily of paper purchased in large rolls and packing supplies such as boxes. Benchmark also treats the costs of purchasing, receiving, and inspecting raw materials as part of the cost of direct materials. All together, these costs total $1.00 per carton of finished product.

2. **Direct labor** refers to wages earned by production employees for the time they spend working on the conversion of raw materials into finished goods. Based on Benchmark's manufacturing procedures, *direct labor represents a variable cost.* These costs are $0.25 per carton.

3. **Variable manufacturing overhead** includes all other variable costs associated with converting raw materials into finished goods. Benchmark's variable manufacturing overhead costs include the costs of lubricants for cutting and packaging machines, electricity to operate these machines, and the cost to move materials between receiving and shipping docks and the cutting and packaging machines. These costs equal $1.25 per carton.

4. **Variable selling and administrative costs** include all variable costs other than those directly associated with converting raw materials into finished goods. At Benchmark, these costs include sales commissions, transportation of finished goods to wholesale distributors, and the cost of processing the receipt and disbursement of cash. These costs amount to $0.50 per carton.

5. **Fixed manufacturing overhead** includes all fixed costs associated with converting raw materials into finished goods. Benchmark's fixed manufacturing costs include the depreciation, property taxes, and insurance on buildings and machines used for manufacturing, the salaries of manufacturing supervisors, and the fixed portion of electricity used to light the factory. These costs total $5,000.00 per month.

6. **Fixed selling and administrative costs** include all fixed costs other than those directly associated with converting raw materials into finished goods. These costs include the salaries of Benchmark's president and many other staff personnel such as accounting and marketing. Also included are depreciation, property taxes, insurance on facilities used for administrative purposes, and any related utilities costs. These costs equal $10,000.00 per month.

Benchmark's variable and fixed costs are summarized here.

Variable Costs per Carton			Fixed Costs per Month	
Manufacturing:..........			Manufacturing overhead ...	$ 5,000.00
Direct materials	$1.00		Selling and administrative ..	10,000.00
Direct labor	0.25		Total...............	$15,000.00
Manufacturing overhead ..	1.25	$2.50		
Selling and administrative...		0.50		
Total		$3.00		

The cost estimation techniques discussed in Chapter 2 would probably be used to determine many detailed costs. Least-squares regression, for example, might be used to determine the variable and monthly fixed amount of electricity used in manufacturing. Benchmark manufactures and sells a single product on a continuous basis with all sales to distributors under standing contracts. Therefore, it is reasonable to assume that in the short run, Benchmark's total monthly cost function responds to a single cost driver, cartons sold. Combining all this information, Benchmark's profit equation is:

$$Profit = \$8.00X - (\$15,000.00 + \$3.00X)$$

where

$$X = cartons\ sold$$

Using this equation, Benchmark's profit at a volume of 5,400 units is $12,000.00 [($8.00 × 5,400) − {$15,000.00 + ($3.00 × 5,400)}].

LEARNING OBJECTIVE 2

CONTRIBUTION AND FUNCTIONAL INCOME STATEMENTS

To provide more detailed information on anticipated or actual financial results at a particular sales volume, a contribution income statement is often prepared. Benchmark's contribution income statement for a volume of 5,400 units is presented in Exhibit 3–1. Note that in a **contribution income statement,** costs are classified according to behavior as variable or fixed, and the **contribution margin** (the difference between total revenues and total variable costs) that goes toward covering fixed costs and providing a profit is emphasized.

EXHIBIT 3–1

CONTRIBUTION INCOME STATEMENT

Benchmark Paper Company
Contribution Income Statement
For a Monthly Volume of 5,400 Cartons

Sales (5,400 × $8.00).....................		$43,200
Less variable costs:		
Direct materials (5,400 × $1.00).................	$ 5,400	
Direct labor (5,400 × $0.25)	1,350	
Manufacturing overhead (5,400 × $1.25)	6,750	
Selling and administrative (5,400 × $0.50)	2,700	(16,200)
Contribution margin		$27,000
Less fixed costs:		
Manufacturing overhead.......................	$ 5,000	
Selling and administrative....................	10,000	(15,000)
Profit		$12,000

EXHIBIT 3-2

FUNCTIONAL INCOME STATEMENT

Benchmark Paper Company
Functional Income Statement
For a Monthly Volume of 5,400 Cartons

Sales (5,400 × $8.00)		$43,200
Less cost of goods sold:		
Direct materials (5,400 × $1.00)	$ 5,400	
Direct labor (5,400 × $0.25)	1,350	
Variable manufacturing overhead (5,400 × $1.25).	6,750	
Fixed manufacturing overhead	5,000	(18,500)
Gross margin		$24,700
Less other expenses:		
Variable selling and administrative (5,400 × $0.50).	$ 2,700	
Fixed selling and administrative	10,000	(12,700)
Profit.		$12,000

Contrast the contribution income statement in Exhibit 3–1 with the income statement in Exhibit 3–2. This statement is called a **functional income statement** because costs are classified according to function (rather than behavior), such as manufacturing, selling, and administrative. This is the type of income statement typically included in corporate annual reports. Although detailed computations of the cost of goods sold and selling and administrative expense are shown in Exhibit 3–2, in reality, it is unlikely that each functional cost would be further classified by cost behavior.

An obvious problem with a functional income statement is the difficulty of relating it to the profit formula in which costs are classified according to behavior rather than function. The relationship between sales volume, costs, and profits is not readily apparent in a functional income statement. Consequently, we emphasize contribution income statements because they provide better information to internal decision makers.

While the contribution income statement (shown in Exhibit 3–1) presents information on total sales revenue, total variable costs, and so forth, it is sometimes useful to present information on a per-unit or portion of sales basis.

	Total	Per Unit	Ratio to Sales
Sales (5,400 units)	$43,200	$8	1.000
Variable costs	(16,200)	(3)	(0.375)
Contribution margin	$27,000	$5	0.625
Fixed costs	(15,000)		
Profit	$12,000		

The per-unit information assists in short-range planning. The **unit contribution margin** is the difference between the unit selling price and the unit variable costs. It is the amount, $5.00 in this case, that each unit contributes toward covering fixed costs and earning a profit.

The contribution margin is widely used in **sensitivity analysis** (the study of the responsiveness of a model to changes in one or more of its independent variables). Benchmark's income statement is an economic model of the firm, and the unit contribution margin indicates how sensitive Benchmark's income model is to changes in unit sales. If, for example, sales increase by 100 cartons per month, the increase in profit is readily determined by multiplying the 100-carton increase in sales by the $5 unit contribution margin:

100 (carton sales increase) × $5 (unit contribution margin) = $500 (profit increase)

There is no increase in fixed costs, so the new profit level becomes $12,500 ($12,000 + $500) per month.

When expressed as a ratio to sales, the contribution margin is identified as the **contribution margin ratio.** It is the portion of each dollar of sales revenue contributed toward covering fixed costs and earning a profit. In the abbreviated income statement presented above, the portion of each dollar of sales revenue contributed toward covering fixed costs and earning a profit is $0.625 ($27,000 ÷ $43,200). This is Benchmark's contribution margin ratio. If sales revenue increases by $800 per month, the increase in profits is computed as follows:

$800 (sales increase) × 0.625 (contribution margin ratio) = $500 (profit increase)

The contribution margin ratio is especially useful in situations involving several products or when unit sales information is not available.

BREAK-EVEN POINT AND PROFIT PLANNING

LEARNING OBJECTIVE 3

The **break-even point** occurs at the unit or dollar sales volume at which total revenues equal total costs. The break-even point is of great interest to management. Until break-even sales are reached, the product, service, event, or business segment of interest operates at a loss. Beyond this point, increasing levels of profits are achieved. Consequently, management is always interested in the break-even point of a current or planned activity. Also, management often wants to know the **margin of safety,** the amount by which actual or planned sales exceed the break-even point. Other questions of interest include the probability of exceeding the break-even sales volume and the effect of some proposed change on the break-even point.

FINDING THE BREAK-EVEN POINT

In determining the break-even point, the equation for total revenues is set equal to the equation for total costs and solved for the break-even unit sales volume. Using the general equations for total revenues and total costs, the following results are obtained. Setting total revenues equal to total costs:

$$\text{Total revenues} = \text{Total costs}$$
$$pX = a + bX$$

Solving for the break-even sales volume:

$$pX - bX = a$$
$$(p - b)X = a$$
$$X = a/(p - b)$$

In words:

$$\frac{\text{Break-even}}{\text{unit sales}} = \frac{\text{Fixed costs}}{\text{Selling price per unit} - \text{Variable costs per unit}}$$

Because the denominator is the unit contribution margin, the break-even point is also computed by dividing the fixed costs by the unit contribution margin:

$$\frac{\text{Break-even}}{\text{unit sales}} = \frac{\text{Fixed costs}}{\text{Unit contribution margin}}$$

With a $5 unit contribution margin and fixed costs of $15,000 per month, Benchmark's break-even point is 3,000 units per month ($15,000 ÷ $5). Stated another way, at a $5 per-unit contribution margin, 3,000 units of contribution are required to cover $15,000 of fixed costs. As a self-test, determine the margin of safety and the expected profit for a monthly sales volume of 5,400 units. The answer is given in the footnote.[2]

PROFIT PLANNING

Establishing profit objectives is an important part of planning in for-profit organizations. Profit objectives are stated in many ways. They can be set as a percentage of last year's profits, as a percentage of total assets at the start of the current year, or as a percentage of owners' equity. They might be based on a profit trend, or they might be expressed as a percentage of sales. The economic outlook for the firm's products as well as anticipated changes in products, costs, and technology are also considered in establishing profit objectives.

Before incorporating profit plans into a detailed budget, it is useful to obtain some preliminary information on the feasibility of those plans. Cost-volume-profit analysis is one way of doing this. By manipulating cost-volume-profit relationships, management can determine the sales volume corresponding to a desired profit. Management might then evaluate the feasibility of this sales volume. If the profit plans are feasible, a complete budget might be developed for this activity level. The required sales volume might be infeasible because of market conditions or because the required volume exceeds production or service capacity, in which case management must lower its profit objective or consider other ways of achieving it. Alternatively, the required sales volume might be less than management believes the firm is capable of selling, in which case management might raise its profit objective.

Assume that Benchmark's management desires to know the unit sales volume required to achieve a monthly profit of $18,000. Using the profit formula, the required unit sales volume is determined by setting profits equal to $18,000 and solving for X, the unit sales volume.

$$\text{Profit} = \text{Total revenues} - \text{Total costs}$$
$$\$18,000 = \$8X - (\$15,000 + \$3X)$$

Solving for X

$$\$8X - \$3X = \$15,000 + \$18,000$$
$$X = (\$15,000 + \$18,000) \div \$5$$
$$= 6,600 \text{ units}$$

The total contribution must now cover the desired profit as well as the fixed costs. Hence, the target sales volume required to achieve a desired profit is computed as the fixed costs plus the desired profit, all divided by the unit contribution margin.

$$\frac{\text{Target}}{\text{unit sales}} = \frac{\text{Fixed costs} + \text{Desired profit}}{\text{Unit contribution margin}}$$

What's Happening 3–1 considers CVP analysis for *The American,* a small newspaper whose strategic position focuses on a market niche. In contrast, What's Happening 3–2 considers CVP analysis for Hewlett-Packard, a large manufacturer whose strategic position for personal computers focuses on cost leadership.

CVP GRAPH

A **cost-volume-profit graph** illustrates the relationships among activity volume, total revenues, total costs, and profits. Its usefulness comes from highlighting the break-even point and depicting revenue, cost, and profit relationships over a range of activity. This representation allows management to view the relative amount of important variables at any graphed volume. Benchmark's monthly CVP graph is presented in

---

[2]The margin of safety would be 2,400 units (5,400 anticipated sales − 3,000 break-even sales), and profit would be $12,000 (2,400 unit margin of safety × $5 per unit contribution margin).

HIGH-TECH CAPABILITIES AND A MARKET NICHE STRATEGY CONTRIBUTE TO A LOW BREAK-EVEN POINT

The American, a Sunday-only newspaper for overseas Americans, operates with a 12-person staff, 12 personal computers, and used furniture in low-cost facilities on Long Island. Once composed, the 40-page paper is electronically sent to Frankfurt, Germany, where it is printed and distributed. At a relatively high price of $4, *The American* obtains most of its revenue from subscriptions rather than advertising.

The American succeeds by publishing on the one day of the week the Paris-based *International Herald Tribune* does not. While the *Herald's* worldwide daily circulation is 190,000, the *American's* Sunday circulation is just over 20,000.

"We're the beneficiaries of the on-line revolution," observed newspaper founder Hersh Kestin. Given the size of the *Herald's* market and *The American's* 14,000-copy, break-even point, "this was a no-brainer," says Kestin.

Source: Jerry Useem, "American Hopes to Conquer World—From Long Island," *Inc.*, December 1996, p. 23.

Exhibit 3–3. Total revenues and total costs are measured on the vertical axis, with unit sales measured on the horizontal axis. Separate lines are drawn for total variable costs, total costs, and total revenues. The vertical distance between the total revenue and the total cost lines depicts the amount of profit or loss at a given volume. Losses occur when total revenues are less than total costs; profits occur when total revenues exceed total costs.

The total contribution margin is shown by the difference between the total revenue and the total variable cost lines. Observe that as unit sales increase, the contribution margin first goes to cover the fixed costs. Beyond the break-even point, any additional contribution margin provides a profit.

PROFIT-VOLUME GRAPH

In cost-volume-profit graphs, profits are represented by the difference between total revenues and total costs. When management is primarily interested in the impact of changes in sales volume on profits and less interested in the related revenues and costs, a **profit-volume graph** is sometimes used. A profit-volume graph illustrates the rela-

HEWLETT-PACKARD BANKS ON HIGH VOLUME AND LOW PRICE FOR THIRD WORLD PROFITS

"The wealthiest 1 billion people in the world are pretty well served by IT companies," says Lyle Hurst, director of the year-old Hewlett-Packard (HP) program, world e-inclusion. "We're targeting the next 4 billion."

The goal of world e-inclusion is for HP to be the leader in triggering and satisfying a Third World demand for simple and economical computer products. HP already derives 60 percent of its sales overseas, and it plans to build on these beachheads to develop what may be the greatest marketing frontier of the coming decades.

With worldwide operations and a low selling price, the HP strategy combines high fixed costs and a low contribution margin, leading to a high break-even point. While the final payoff is unclear, one HP official observed, "You don't get a harvest until you start planting."

Source: Pete Engardio and Geri Smith, "Hewlett-Packard," *Business Week,* August 27, 2001, p. 137.

EXHIBIT 3-3

TYPICAL COST-VOLUME-PROFIT GRAPH

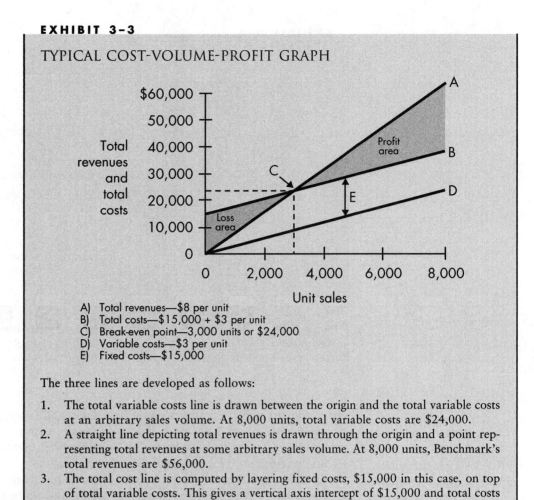

A) Total revenues—$8 per unit
B) Total costs—$15,000 + $3 per unit
C) Break-even point—3,000 units or $24,000
D) Variable costs—$3 per unit
E) Fixed costs—$15,000

The three lines are developed as follows:

1. The total variable costs line is drawn between the origin and the total variable costs at an arbitrary sales volume. At 8,000 units, total variable costs are $24,000.

2. A straight line depicting total revenues is drawn through the origin and a point representing total revenues at some arbitrary sales volume. At 8,000 units, Benchmark's total revenues are $56,000.

3. The total cost line is computed by layering fixed costs, $15,000 in this case, on top of total variable costs. This gives a vertical axis intercept of $15,000 and total costs of $39,000 at 8,000 units.

tionship between volume and profits; it does not show revenues and costs. Profits are read directly from a profit-volume graph, rather than being computed as the difference between total revenues and total costs. Profit-volume graphs are developed by plotting either unit sales or total revenues on the horizontal axis.

Benchmark's monthly profit-volume graph, is presented in Exhibit 3–4. Profit or loss is measured on the vertical axis, and volume (total revenues) is measured on the horizontal axis, which intersects the vertical axis at zero profit. A single line, representing total profit, is drawn intersecting the vertical axis at zero sales volume with a loss equal to the fixed costs. The profit line crosses the horizontal axis at the break-even sales volume. The profit or loss at any volume is depicted by the vertical difference between the profit line and the horizontal axis. Note that the slope of the profit line is determined by the contribution margin. The greater the contribution margin ratio or the unit contribution margin, the steeper the slope of the profit line.

THE IMPACT OF INCOME TAXES

Income taxes are imposed on individuals and for-profit organizations by units of government. The amount of an individual's or organization's income tax is determined by laws that specify the calculation of taxable income (the income subject to tax) and the calculation of the amount of tax on taxable income. Income taxes are computed as a percentage of taxable income, with increases in taxable income usually subject to progressively higher tax rates. The laws governing the computation of taxable income

EXHIBIT 3-4

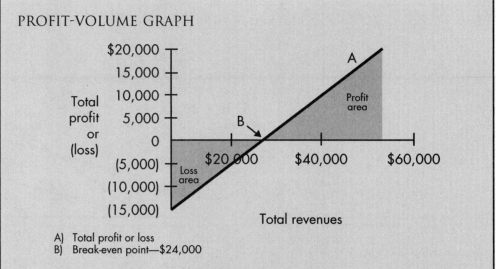

PROFIT-VOLUME GRAPH

A) Total profit or loss
B) Break-even point—$24,000

The profit line is drawn by determining and plotting profit or loss at two different volumes and then drawing a straight line through the plotted values. Perhaps the easiest values to select are the loss at a volume of zero (with a loss equal to the fixed costs) and the volume at which the profit line crosses the horizontal axis (this is the break-even volume).

differ in many ways from the accounting principles and standards that guide the computation of accounting income. This is especially true concerning the timing of the recognition of revenues and expenses. Consequently, taxable income and accounting income are seldom the same in the short run.

In the early stages of profit planning, income taxes are sometimes incorporated in CVP models by assuming that taxable income and accounting income are identical and that the tax rate is constant. Although these assumptions are seldom true, they are useful for assisting management in developing an early prediction of the sales volume required to earn a desired after-tax profit. Once management has developed a general plan, this early prediction should be refined with the advice of tax experts.

Assuming taxes are imposed at a constant rate per dollar of before-tax profit, income taxes are computed as before-tax profit multiplied by the tax rate. After-tax profit is equal to before-tax profit minus income taxes.

$$\text{After-tax profit} = \text{Before-tax profit} - (\text{Before-tax profit} \times \text{Tax rate})$$

After-tax profit can also be expressed as before-tax profit times 1 minus the tax rate.

$$\text{After-tax profit} = \text{Before-tax profit} \times (1 - \text{Tax rate})$$

This formula can be rearranged to isolate before-tax profit as follows:

$$\text{Before-tax profit} = \frac{\text{After-tax profit}}{(1 - \text{Tax rate})}$$

Since all costs and revenues in the profit formula are expressed on a before-tax basis, the most straightforward way of determining the unit sales volume required to earn a desired after-tax profit is to:

1. Determine the required before-tax profit.
2. Substitute the required before-tax profit into the profit formula.
3. Solve for the required unit sales volume.

Assume that Benchmark is subject to a 40 percent tax rate and that management desires to earn an after-tax profit of $18,000 for November 2004. The required before-tax profit is $30,000 ($18,000 ÷ [1 − 0.40]), and the unit sales volume required to earn this profit is 9,000 units ([$15,000 + $30,000] ÷ $5).

Income taxes increase the sales volume required to earn a desired after-tax profit. A 40 percent tax rate increased the sales volume required for Benchmark to earn a profit of $18,000 from 6,600 to 9,000 units. These amounts are verified in Exhibit 3–5.

Another way to remember the computation of before-tax profit is shown on the right side of Exhibit 3–5. The before-tax profit represents 100 percent of the pie, with 40 percent going to income taxes and 60 percent remaining after taxes. Working back from the remaining 60 percent ($18,000), we can easily determine the 100 percent (before-tax profit) by dividing after-tax profit by 0.60.

LEARNING OBJECTIVE 4

MULTIPLE-PRODUCT COST-VOLUME-PROFIT ANALYSIS

Unit cost information may not be available or appropriate when analyzing cost-volume-profit relationships of multiple-product firms. In this case, assuming the sales mix is constant, the contribution margin ratio (the portion of each sales dollar contributed toward covering fixed costs and earning a profit) may be used to determine the break-even dollar sales volume or the dollar sales volume required to achieve a desired profit. Treating a dollar of sales revenue as a unit, the break-even point in dollars is computed as fixed costs divided by the contribution margin ratio (the portion number of cents from each dollar of revenue contributed to covering fixed costs and providing a profit).

$$\text{Dollar break-even point} = \frac{\text{Fixed costs}}{\text{Contribution margin ratio}}$$

If unit selling price and cost information were not available, Benchmark's dollar break-even point could be computed as $24,000 ($15,000 ÷ 0.625).

Corresponding computations can be made to find the dollar sales volume required to achieve a desired profit.

EXHIBIT 3–5

CONTRIBUTION INCOME STATEMENT WITH INCOME TAXES

Benchmark Paper Company
Contribution Income Statement
Planned for the Month of November 2004

Sales (9,000 × $8.00).		$72,000	
Less variable costs:			
Direct materials (9,000 × $1.00).	$ 9,000		
Direct labor (9,000 × $0.25)	2,250		
Manufacturing overhead (9,000 × $1.25)	11,250		
Selling and administrative (9,000 × $0.50)	4,500	(27,000)	
Contribution margin		$45,000	
Less fixed costs:			
Manufacturing overhead.	$ 5,000		
Selling and administrative.	10,000	(15,000)	
Before-tax profit.		$30,000	100%
Income taxes ($30,000 × 0.40).		(12,000)	(40)%
After-tax profit.		$18,000	60%

$$\text{Target dollar sales volume} = \frac{\text{Fixed costs} + \text{Desired profit}}{\text{Contribution margin ratio}}$$

To achieve a desired profit of $12,000, Benchmark needs sales of $43,200 ([$15,000 + $12,000] ÷ 0.625).

These relationships can be graphed by placing sales dollars, rather than unit sales, on the horizontal axis. The slope of the variable and total cost lines, identified as the **variable cost ratio**, presents variable costs as a portion of sales revenue. It indicates the number of cents from each sales dollar required to pay variable costs. What's Happening 3–3 demonstrates how CVP information can be developed from the published financial statements of a multiple-product firm. The effect of changes in the sales mix of multiple-product firms is considered in the appendix to this chapter.

LEARNING OBJECTIVE 5   **OPERATING LEVERAGE**

Operating leverage refers to the extent that an organization's costs are fixed. The **degree of operating leverage** is computed as the contribution margin divided by before-tax profit.

$$\text{Degree of operating leverage} = \frac{\text{Contribution margin}}{\text{Before-tax profit}}$$

3–3   WHAT'S HAPPENING?

DETERMINING CVP RELATIONSHIPS BY ANALYZING PUBLISHED FINANCIAL STATEMENTS

Condensed data from the United Parcel Service, Inc., 1998 and 1999 income statements (in millions) are presented here.

	1999	1998
Revenues	$27,052	$24,788
Operating expenses	(23,147)	(21,785)
Operating income	$ 3,905	$ 3,003

We can determine United Parcel Services (UPS) cost-volume profit relationships for UPS by applying the high-low method of cost estimation to this data. First, we determine the variable costs as a portion of each sales dollar.

$$\text{Variable cost ratio} = \frac{\$23,147 - \$21,785}{\$27,052 - \$24,788} = 0.60159$$

Next, annual fixed costs are determined subtracting the variable costs for either period (the product of revenues and the variable cost ratio) from the corresponding total costs.

$$\text{Annual fixed costs} = \$23,146 - (\$27,146 \times 0.60159) = \underline{\$6,815.24}$$

The contribution margin ratio is 1 minus the variable cost ratio.

$$\text{Contribution margin ratio} = 1 - 0.60159 = \underline{0.39841}$$

The break-even point for UPS is $17,250.52 million ($6,872.78 ÷ 0.39841).

Applying these concepts to 2000 revenues of $29,771, we obtain an expected operating income of $4,988. UPS's actual 2000 income was $4,512, and error of $476, or 10 percent. The analysis worked for UPS because of its stable sales mix and cost structure.

Source: UPS 2000 annual report.

The rationale underlying this computation is that as fixed costs are substituted for variable costs, the contribution margin as a percentage of income before taxes increases. Hence, a high degree of operating leverage signals the existence of a high portion of fixed costs. As noted in Chapter 1 and illustrated in Exhibit 1–5 (p. 21), the shift from labor-based to automated activities has resulted in a decrease in variable costs and an increase in fixed costs, producing an increase in operating leverage.

Operating leverage is a measure of risk and opportunity. Other things being equal, the higher the degree of operating leverage, the greater the opportunity for profit with increases in sales. Conversely, a higher degree of operating leverage also magnifies the risk of large losses with a decrease in sales.

	Operating Leverage	
	High	Low
Profit opportunity with sales increase	High	Low
Risk of loss with sales decrease	High	Low

Research Shows 3–2 considers the importance of reducing financial leverage during periods of economic stress.

Assume that Benchmark Paper Company competes with High-Fixed Paper Company. Information for both companies at a monthly volume of 4,000 units is as follows:

	Benchmark	High-Fixed
Unit selling price.	$ 8.00	$ 8.00
Unit variable costs.	(3.00)	(1.50)
Unit contribution margin	$ 5.00	$ 6.50
Unit sales	× 4,000	× 4,000
Contribution margin.	$20,000	$26,000
Fixed costs	(15,000)	(21,000)
Before-tax profit	$ 5,000	$ 5,000
Contribution margin.	$20,000	$26,000
Before-tax profit	÷ 5,000	÷ 5,000
Degree of operating leverage.	4.0	5.2

Although both companies have identical before-tax profits at a sales volume of 4,000 units, High-Fixed has a higher degree of operating leverage and its profits will vary more with changes in sales volume.

If sales increase by 12.5 percent, from 4,000 to 4,500 units, the percentage of increase in each firm's profits may be computed as the percent change in sales multiplied by the degree of operating leverage.

3-2   RESEARCH SHOWS

To Avoid Financial Crisis, Lower Operating Leverage or Debt

Bankruptcy expert Dr. Gerald Buccino and his business associate, Kraig McKinley, recommend that companies facing sales declines take proactive measures to reduce their operating leverage and the associated risks. If the erosion in market size is permanent, firms must reduce facilities and equipment, and the reductions must be permanent. What's more, to reduce the associated risk of insolvency, firms with high operating leverage should not rely heavily on borrowed funds to acquire fixed assets.

Source: Gerald P. Buccino and Kraig S. McKinley, "The Importance of Operating Leverage in a Turnaround," *Secured Lender*, September/October, 1997, pp. 64–66.

	Benchmark	High-Fixed
Increase in sales	12.5%	12.5%
Degree of operating leverage	× 4.0	× 5.2
Increase in profits	50.0%	65.0%

We can verify this by multiplying each firm's unit contribution margin by the increase in unit sales.

	Benchmark	High-Fixed
Unit contribution margin	$ 5.00	$ 6.50
Unit change in sales	× 500	× 500
Change in profit	$2,500	$3,250
Percent increase from $5,000 profit.	50%	65%

Management is interested in measures of operating leverage to determine how sensitive profits are to changes in sales. Risk-adverse managers will strive to maintain a lower operating leverage, even if this results in some loss of profits. One way to reduce operating leverage is to use more direct labor and less automated equipment. Another way is to contract outside organizations to perform tasks that could be done internally. This approach to reducing operating leverage is further considered in Chapter 4, where we examine the external acquisition of goods and services. Of course, while operating leverage is a useful analytic tool, long-run success comes from keeping the overall level of costs down, while providing customers with the products or services they want at competitive prices.

LEARNING OBJECTIVE 6 # PROFITABILITY ANALYSIS WITH UNIT AND NONUNIT COST DRIVERS

A major limitation of cost-volume-profit analysis and the related contribution income statement is the exclusive use of unit-level activity cost drivers. Even when multiple products are considered, the CVP approach either restates volume in terms of an average unit or in terms of a dollar of sales volume. Additionally, CVP analysis does not consider other categories of cost drivers. As we saw in Chapter 2, when cost estimation is limited to unit-level cost drivers while actual costs follow an activity cost hierarchy, there is a high probability of significant errors in cost estimation and cost prediction.

We will now expand profitability analysis to incorporate nonunit cost drivers. While the addition of multiple levels of cost drivers makes it difficult to develop graphical relationships (illustrating the impact of cost driver changes on revenues, costs, and profits), it is possible to modify the traditional contribution income statement to incorporate a hierarchy of cost drivers. As we shall see, the expanded framework is not only more accurate, but it also encourages management to ask a number of important questions concerning costs and profitability.

MULTI-LEVEL CONTRIBUTION INCOME STATEMENT

To illustrate the use of profitability analysis with unit and nonunit cost drivers, consider General Distribution, a multiple-product merchandising organization with the following cost hierarchy:

Unit-level activities:
    Cost of goods sold . . . . $0.80 per sales dollar[3]
Order-level activities:
    Cost of processing order . . . . $20 per order

---

[3]Eighty cents of each sales dollar is required for the cost of goods sold.

Customer-level activities:
Mail, phone, sales visits,
recordkeeping, and so forth . . . . . $200 per customer per year
Facility-level costs:
Depreciation, manager salaries,
insurance, and so forth . . . . $120,000 per year

Assume that General Distribution, which is subject to a 40 percent income tax rate, has the following plans for the year 2004:

Sales $3,000,000
Number of sales orders 3,200
Number of customers 400

While General Distribution plans could be summarized in a functional income statement, we have previously considered the limitations of such statements for management. Contribution income statements are preferred because they correspond to the cost classification scheme used in CVP analysis. In this case, General Distribution's cost structure (unit level, order level, customer level, and facility level) does not correspond to the classification scheme used in traditional contribution income statements (variable and fixed). The problem occurs because traditional contribution income statements consider only unit-level cost drivers. When a larger set of unit and nonunit cost drivers is used for cost analysis, an expanded contribution income statement should be used for profitability analysis.

A multi-level contribution income statement for General Distribution is presented in Exhibit 3–6. Note that costs are separated using a cost hierarchy and that there are several contribution margins, one for each level of costs that responds to a short-run change in activity. In the case of General Distribution, the contribution margins are at the unit level, order level, and customer level. Because the facility-level costs do not vary with short-run variations in activity, the final customer-level contribution goes to cover facility-level costs and to provide for a profit. If a company had a different activity cost hierarchy, it would use a different set of contribution margins.

EXHIBIT 3-6

MULTI-LEVEL CONTRIBUTION INCOME STATEMENT WITH INCOME TAXES

General Distribution
Multi-Level Contribution Income Statement
For the Year 2004

Sales	$3,000,000
Less unit-level costs:	
Cost of goods sold ($3,000,000 × 0.80)	(2,400,000)
Unit-level contribution margin	$ 600,000
Less order-level costs:	
Cost of processing order (3,200 orders × $20)	(64,000)
Order-level contribution margin	$ 536,000
Less customer-level costs:	
Mail, phone, sales visits, recordkeeping, and so forth	
(400 customers × $200)	(80,000)
Customer-level contribution margin	$ 456,000
Less facility-level costs:	
Depreciation, manager salaries, insurance, etc.	(120,000)
Before-tax profit	$ 336,000
Income taxes ($336,000 × 0.40)	(134,400)
After-tax profit	$ 201,600

A number of additional questions of interest to management can be formulated and answered using the multi-level hierarchy. Consider the following examples:

- Holding the number of sales orders and customers constant, what is the break-even dollar sales volume? The answer is found by treating all other costs as fixed and dividing the total nonunit-level costs by the contribution margin ratio. Here the contribution margin ratio indicates how many cents of each sales dollar is available for profits and costs above the unit level.

$$\text{Unit-level break-even point in dollars with no changes in other costs} = \frac{\text{Current order- + Current customer- + Facility-level costs} \quad \text{level costs} \quad \text{level costs}}{\text{Contribution margin ratio}}$$

$$= (\$64{,}000 + \$80{,}000 + \$120{,}000) \div (1 - 0.80)$$

$$= \$1{,}320{,}000$$

- What order size is required to break even on an individual order? Answering this question might help management to evaluate the desirability of establishing a minimum order size. To break even, each order must have a unit-level contribution equal to the order-level costs. Any additional contribution is used to cover customer- and facility-level costs and provide for a profit.

$$\text{Break-even order size} = \$20 \div (1 - 0.80)$$

$$= \$100$$

- What sales volume is required to break even on an average customer? Answering this question might help management to evaluate the desirability of retaining certain customers. Based on the preceding information, an average customer places 8 orders per year (3,200 orders ÷ 400 customers). With costs of $20 per order and $200 per customer, the sales to an average customer must generate an annual contribution of $360 ([$20 × 8] + $200). Hence, the break-even level for an average customer is $1,800 ($360 ÷ [1 − 0.80]). Management might consider discontinuing relations with customers with annual purchases of less than this amount. Alternatively, they might inquire as to whether such customers could be served in a less costly manner.

The concepts of multi-level break-even analysis and profitability analysis are finding increasing use as companies such as Federal Express, US West, and Bank of America strive to identify profitable and unprofitable customers. At FedEx, customers are sometimes rated as "the good, the bad, and the ugly." FedEx strives to retain the "good" profitable customers, turn the "bad" into profitable customers, and ignore the "ugly" who seem unlikely to become profitable. What's Happening 3–4 describes

3–4   WHAT'S HAPPENING?

STANDARD LIFE ASSURANCE ANALYZES DATA AND FINDS MANY UNPROFITABLE CUSTOMERS

When it comes to sales, the traditional assumption is the more, the better. The same is true of big advertising campaigns. But executives at Standard Life Assurance, Europe's largest mutual life insurance company, were surprised to learn that a large advertising campaign was causing the company to load up on customers who held little or no profit potential.

It seems that the direct mail campaign was encouraging elderly couples and stay-at-home mothers to sign up for costly home visits by sales agents. Revenues were up, but the sales were to customers who, according to Graham Wilson (Standard's database and statistics manager), "loved to sit down and have a cup of tea with someone." These customers typically bought only one small policy.

Source: Paul C. Judge, "What've You Done for Us Lately?" *Business Week,* September 14, 1998, pp. 140–146.

the surprising results of a customer profitability analysis performed by Standard Life Assurance.

VARIATIONS IN MULTI-LEVEL CONTRIBUTION INCOME STATEMENTS

As noted in Chapter 2, classification schemes should be designed to fit the organization and user needs. In Chapter 2, when analyzing the costs of a manufacturing company, we used a manufacturing cost hierarchy. While formatting issues may at times seem mundane and routine, format is important because the way information is presented encourages certain types of questions while discouraging others. Hence, management accountants must inquire as to user needs before developing management accounting reports, just as users of management accounting information should be knowledgeable enough to request appropriate information and know whether the information they are receiving is the information they need. With computers to reduce computational drudgery and to provide a wealth of available data, the most important issues involve identifying the important questions and presenting information to address those questions.

In the case of General Distribution, we used a customer cost hierarchy with information presented in a single column. A multiple-column format may also be useful for presenting and analyzing information. Assume that General Distribution's management believes that the differences between the government and private sector markets are such that these markets could be better served with separate marketing activities. They would have two market segments, one for the government sector and one for the private sector, giving the following cost hierarchy:

1. Unit-level activities
2. Order-level activities
3. Customer-level activities
4. Market segment activities
5. Facility-level activities

One possible way of presenting General Distribution's 2005 multi-level income statement with two market segments is shown in Exhibit 3–7. The details underlying the development of this statement are not presented. In developing the statement, we assume the mix of units sold, their cost structure, and the costs of processing an order are unchanged. Finally, we present new market segment costs and assume that the addition of the segments allows for some reduction in previous facility-level costs.

The information in the total column is all that is required for a multi-level contribution income statement. The information in the two detailed columns for the government and private segments may, however, prove useful in analyzing the profitability of each. Observe that the facility-level costs, incurred for the benefit of both segments, are not assigned to specific segments. Depending on the nature of the goods sold, it may be possible to further analyze the profitability of each product (or type of product) sold in each market segment. The profitability analysis of business segments is more closely examined in Chapter 12.

Summary

Profitability analysis involves examining the relationships between revenues, costs, and profits. Cost-volume-profit analysis, a traditional approach to profitability analysis, considers only unit-level activity cost drivers. In CVP analysis, "volume" refers to a

EXHIBIT 3-7

MULTI-LEVEL CONTRIBUTION INCOME STATEMENT WITH MARKET SEGMENTS AND INCOME TAXES

General Distribution
Multi-Level Contribution Income Statement
For the Year 2005

	Government Segment	Private Segment	Total
Sales	$1,500,000	$2,000,000	$3,500,000
Less unit-level costs:			
Cost of goods sold (0.80)	(1,200,000)	(1,600,000)	(2,800,000)
Unit-level contribution margin	$ 300,000	$ 400,000	$ 700,000
Less order-level costs:			
Cost of processing order (1,000 × $20; 3,000 × $20)	(20,000)	(60,000)	(80,000)
Order-level contribution margin	$ 280,000	$ 340,000	$ 620,000
Less customer-level costs:			
Mail, phone, sales visits, recordkeeping, and so forth (150 × $200, 300 × $200)	(30,000)	(60,000)	(90,000)
Customer-level contribution margin	$ 250,000	$ 280,000	$ 530,000
Less market segment-level costs	(80,000)	(20,000)	(100,000)
Market segment-level contribution	$ 170,000	$ 260,000	$ 430,000
Less facility-level costs:			
Depreciation, manager salaries, insurance, etc.			(90,000)
Before-tax profit			$ 340,000
Income taxes ($340,000 × 0.40)			(136,000)
After-tax profit			$ 204,000

single unit-level cost driver, such as units sold, that is assumed to correlate with changes in revenues, costs, and profits. Because cost-volume-profit analysis provides a framework for discussing planning issues and organizing relevant data, it is widely used in the early stages of planning. To enhance their usefulness, cost-volume-profit relationships are summarized in graphs or in contribution income statements that classify costs according to behavior (variable or fixed) and emphasize the contribution margin that goes toward covering fixed costs and providing a profit.

When applied to a single product, service, or event when a single cost driver drives costs, the use of a single independent variable appears reasonable. Although CVP analysis is often used to develop an understanding of the overall operations of an organization or business segment, accuracy decreases as the scope of operations being analyzed increases.

A major limitation of cost-volume-profit analysis and the related contribution income statement is the use of a single unit-level activity cost driver. Even when multiple products are considered, the CVP approach restates volume either in terms of an average unit or in terms of a dollar of sales volume. This limitation can be addressed with a multi-level contribution income statement that includes unit and nonunit cost drivers. A multi-level contribution income statement has several measures of contribution, one for each level of costs that contributes to a higher level of costs and profits.

In developing multi-level contribution income statements, it is important to remember that cost classification schemes should be designed to fit the organization and user needs. While formatting issues may at times seem mundane and routine, format is important because the way information is presented encourages certain types of questions while discouraging others.

Appendix

SALES MIX ANALYSIS

As noted earlier, *sales mix* refers to the relative portion of unit or dollar sales that are derived from each product. One of the limiting assumptions of the basic cost-volume-profit model is that the analysis is for a single product or the sales mix is constant. When the sales mix is constant, managers of multiple-product organizations can use the average unit contribution margin, or the average contribution margin ratio, to determine the break-even point or the sales volume required for a desired profit. Often, however, management is interested in the effect of a change in the sales mix rather than a change in the sales volume at a constant mix. In this situation, it is necessary to determine either the average unit contribution margin or the average contribution margin ratio for each alternative mix.

Unit Sales Analysis

Assume the Eagle Card Company sells two kinds of greeting cards, regular and deluxe. At a 1:1 (one-to-one) unit sales mix in which Eagle sells one box of regular cards for every box of deluxe cards, the following revenue and cost information is available:

	Regular Box	Deluxe Box	Average Box*
Unit selling price	$4	$12	$8
Unit variable costs	(3)	(3)	(3)
Unit contribution margin	$1	$ 9	$5
Fixed costs per month			$15,000

*At a 1:1 sales mix, the average unit contribution margin is $5[($1 × 1 unit) + ($9 × 1 unit) ÷ 2 units].

At a 1:1 mix, Eagle's current monthly break-even sales volume is 3,000 units ($15,000 ÷ $5), consisting of 1,500 boxes of regular cards and 1,500 boxes of deluxe cards. The top line in Exhibit 3–8 represents the current sales mix. Management wants

EXHIBIT 3-8

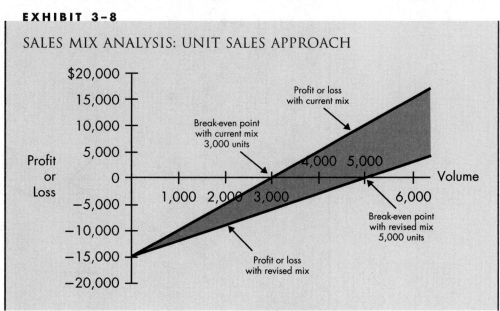

SALES MIX ANALYSIS: UNIT SALES APPROACH

to know the break-even sales volume if the unit sales mix became 3:1; that is, on average, a sale of 4 units contains 3 regular units and 1 deluxe unit. With no changes in the selling prices or variable costs of individual products, the contribution margin becomes $3 [($1 × 3 units) + ($9 × 1 unit) ÷ 4 units], and the revised break-even sales volume is 5,000 units ($15,000 ÷ $3). The revised break-even sales volume includes 3,750 regular cards [5,000 × ¾] and 1,250 deluxe cards [5,000 × ¼].

The bottom line in Exhibit 3–8 represents the revised sales mix. Because a greater portion of the revised mix consists of lower contribution margin regular cards, the shift in the mix increases the break-even point.

Sales Dollar Analysis

The proceeding analysis focused on units and the unit contribution margin. An alternative approach focuses on sales dollars and the contribution margin ratio. Following this approach, the sales mix is expressed in terms of sales dollars.

Eagle's current sales dollars are 25 percent from regular cards and 75 percent from deluxe cards. The following display indicates the contribution margin ratios at the current sales mix and monthly volume of 5,400 units.

	Regular	Deluxe	Total
Unit sales	2,700	2,700	
Selling price	$4.00	$12.00	
Sales	$10,800	$32,400	$43,200
Variable costs	− 8,100	− 8,100	−16,200
Contribution margin	$ 2,700	$24,300	$27,000
Contribution margin ratio	0.25	0.75	0.625

With monthly fixed costs of $15,000, Eagle's current break-even sales volume is $24,000 ($15,000 ÷ 0.65), consisting of $6,000 from regular cards ($24,000 × 0.25) and $18,000 from Deluxe cards ($24,000 × 0.75). The top line in Exhibit 3–9 illustrates the current sales mix.

Management wants to know the break-even sales volume if the unit sales mix became 70 percent regular and 30 percent deluxe. With no changes in the selling prices or variable costs of individual products, the contribution margin ratio becomes 0.40

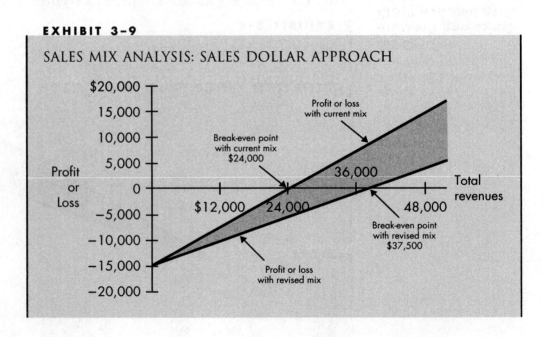

EXHIBIT 3–9

SALES MIX ANALYSIS: SALES DOLLAR APPROACH

[(0.25 × 0.70) + (0.75 × 0.30)], and the revised break-even sales volume is $37,500 ($15,000 ÷ 0.40). The revised break-even sales volume includes $26,250 from regular cards ($37,500 × 0.70) and $11,250 from deluxe cards (37,500 × 0.30).

The bottom line in Exhibit 3–9 represents the revised sales mix. Because a greater portion of the revised mix consists of lower contribution ratio regular cards, the shift in the mix increases the break-even point.

Sales mix analysis is important in multiple-product or service organizations. Management is just as concerned with the mix of products as with the total unit or dollar sales volume. A shift in the sales mix can have a significant impact on the bottom line. Profits may decline, even when sales increase, if the mix shifts toward products or services with lower unit margins. Conversely, profits may increase, even when sales decline, if the mix shifts toward products or services with higher unit margins. Other things being equal, managers of for-profit organizations strive to increase sales of high-margin products or services.

Review Problem

The solution to the review problem is found on pages 120 and 121. To maximize your learning, you should make a serious attempt to develop a written solution to the review problem before looking at the solution. If there are errors in your solution, you should then attempt to determine their causes.

COST-VOLUME-PROFIT ANALYSIS

Memorabilia Cup Company produces keepsake 16-ounce beverage containers for educational institutions. Memorabilia sells the cups for $40 per box of 50 containers. Variable and fixed costs are as follows:

Variable Costs per Box		
Manufacturing:		
Direct materials	$15	
Direct labor	3	
Manufacturing overhead . . .	10	$28
Selling and administrative		2
Total		$30

Fixed Costs per Month	
Manufacturing overhead	$15,000
Selling and administrative	10,000
Total	$25,000

In September 2004, Memorabilia produced and sold 3,000 boxes of beverage containers.

Required:
a. Prepare a contribution income statement for September 2004.
b. Prepare a cost-volume-profit graph with unit sales as the independent variable. Label the revenue line, total costs line, fixed costs line, loss area, profit area, and break-even point. The recommended scale for the horizontal axis is 0 to 5,000 units, and the recommended scale for the vertical axis is $0 to $200,000.
c. Determine Memorabilia's unit contribution margin and contribution margin ratio.
d. Determine Memorabilia's monthly break-even point in units.
e. Determine the monthly dollar sales required for a monthly profit of $5,000 (ignoring taxes).
f. Assuming Memorabilia is subject to a 40 percent income tax, determine the monthly unit sales required to produce a monthly after-tax profit of $4,500.

Key Terms

Break-even point (p. 90)
Contribution income statement (p. 88)
Contribution margin (p. 88)
Contribution margin ratio (p. 90)
Cost-volume-profit (CVP) analysis (p. 85)
Cost-volume-profit graph (p. 91)
Degree of operating leverage (p. 96)
Direct labor (p. 87)
Direct materials (p. 87)
Fixed manufacturing overhead (p. 87)
Fixed selling and administrative costs
  (p. 87)

Functional income statement (p. 89)
Margin of safety (p. 90)
Operating leverage (p. 96)
Profitability analysis (p. 84)
Profit-volume graph (p. 92)
Sales mix (p. 86)
Sensitivity analysis (p. 89)
Unit contribution margin (p. 89)
Variable cost ratio (p. 96)
Variable manufacturing overhead (p. 87)
Variable selling and administrative costs
  (p. 87)

Review Questions

1. What is cost-volume-profit analysis and when is it particularly useful?
2. Identify the important assumptions that underlie cost-volume-profit analysis.
3. When is it most reasonable to use a single independent variable in cost-volume-profit analysis?
4. Distinguish between a contribution and a functional income statement.
5. What is the unit contribution margin? How is it used in computing the unit break-even point?
6. What is the contribution margin ratio and when is it most useful?
7. How is the determination of the break-even point affected by incorporating a desired profit?
8. How does a profit-volume graph differ from a cost-volume-profit graph? When is a profit-volume graph most likely to be used?
9. What impact do income taxes have on the sales volume required to earn a desired after-tax profit?
10. How are profit opportunities and the risk of losses affected by operating leverage?
11. What is the distinguishing feature of a multi-level contribution income statement?
12. Using a manufacturing cost hierarchy, how is the batch-level break-even point determined?

Exercises

3-1
Contribution Income Statement and Cost-Volume-Profit Graph

Alberta Company produces a product that is sold for $50 per unit. Variable and fixed costs follow.

Variable Costs per Unit				Fixed Costs per Month	
Manufacturing:				Manufacturing overhead	$40,000
Direct materials	$ 8			Selling and administrative	20,000
Direct labor	12			Total	$60,000
Factory overhead	10	$30			
Selling and administrative		5			
Total		$35			

The company produced and sold 6,000 units during May 2004. There were no beginning or ending inventories.

Required:
a. Prepare a contribution income statement for May.
b. Prepare a cost-volume-profit graph. Label the horizontal axis in units with a maximum value of 8,000. Label the vertical axis in dollars with a maximum value of $350,000. Draw a vertical line on the graph for the current (6,000) unit sales level, and label total variable costs, total fixed costs, and total profits at 6,000 units.

3-2
Multiple-Product Profitability Analysis

Hair Tops provides cuts, perms, and hair-styling services. Annual fixed costs are $120,000, and variable costs are 25 percent of sales revenue. Last year's revenues totaled $200,000.

Required:
a. Determine Hair Tops' break-even point in sales dollars.
b. Determine last year's margin of safety in sales dollars.
c. Determine the sales volume required for an annual profit of $60,000.

3-3
Contribution Margin Concepts

The following information is taken from the 2004 records of Duke Art Shop.

	Fixed	Variable	
Sales			$800,000
Costs:			
Goods sold		$300,000	
Labor	$160,000	60,000	
Supplies	2,000	5,000	
Utilities	12,000	3,000	
Rent	24,000	—	
Advertising	6,000	2,000	
Miscellaneous	6,000	10,000	
Total costs	$210,000	$380,000	(590,000)
Net income			$210,000

Required:
a. Determine the annual break-even dollar sales volume.
b. Determine the current margin of safety in dollars.
c. Prepare a cost-volume-profit graph for Duke Art Shop. Label both axes in dollars with maximum values of $1,000,000. Draw a vertical line on the graph for the current ($800,000) sales level, and label total variable costs, total fixed costs, and total profits at $800,000 sales.
d. What is the annual break-even dollar sales volume if management makes a decision that increases fixed costs by $52,500?

3-4
Cost-Volume-Profit Graph: Identification and Sensitivity Analysis

A typical cost-volume-profit graph is presented below.

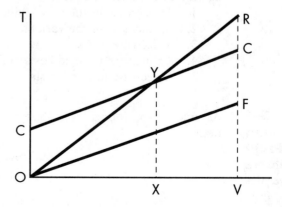

Required:

a. Identify each of the following:
1. Line OF
2. Line OR
3. Line CC
4. The difference between lines OF and OV
5. The difference between lines CC and OF
6. The difference between lines CC and OV
7. The difference between lines OR and OF
8. Point X
9. Area CYO
10. Area RCY

b. Indicate the effect of each of the following independent events on lines CC, OR, and the break-even point:
1. A decrease in fixed costs
2. An increase in unit selling price
3. An increase in the variable costs per unit
4. An increase in fixed costs and a decrease in the unit selling price
5. A decrease in fixed costs and a decrease in the unit variable costs

3-5
Profit-Volume
Graph: Identification
and Sensitivity
Analysis

A typical profit-volume graph follows.

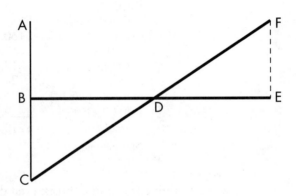

Required:

a. Identify each of the following:
1. Area *BDC*
2. Area *DEF*
3. Point *D*
4. Line *AC*
5. Line *BC*
6. Line *EF*

b. Indicate the effect of each of the following on line *CF* and the break-even point:
1. An increase in the unit selling price
2. An increase in the variable costs per unit
3. A decrease in fixed costs
4. An increase in fixed costs and a decrease in the unit selling price
5. A decrease in fixed costs and an increase in the variable costs per unit

3-6
Preparing
Cost-Volume-Profit
and Profit-Volume
Graphs

Assume a Papa John's Pizza shop has the following monthly revenue and cost functions:

$$\text{Total revenues} = \$6.00X$$
$$\text{Total costs} = \$9,000 + \$1.50X$$

Required:
a. Prepare a graph (similar to that in Exhibit 3–3) illustrating Papa John's cost-volume-profit relationships. The vertical axis should range from $0 to $18,000, in increments of $3,000. The horizontal axis should range from 0 units to 3,000 units, in increments of 1,000 units.
b. Prepare a graph (similar to that in Exhibit 3–4) illustrating Papa John's profit-volume relationships. The horizontal axis should range from 0 units to 3,000 units, in increments of 1,000 units.
c. When is it most appropriate to use a profit-volume graph?

3–7
Preparing Cost-Volume-Profit and Profit-Volume Graphs

Happy Hawkers is a hot dog concession operation at five baseball stadiums. It sells hot dogs, with all the fixings, for $3.50 each. Variable costs are $3.20 per hot dog, and fixed operating costs are $150,000 per year.

Required:
a. Determine the annual break-even point in hot dogs.
b. Prepare a cost-volume-profit graph for Happy Hawkers. Use a format that emphasizes the contribution margin. The vertical axis should vary between $0 and $3,500,000 in increments of $500,000. The horizontal axis should vary between 0 hot dogs and 1,000,000 hot dogs, in increments of 250,000 hot dogs. Label the graph in thousands.
c. Prepare a profit-volume graph for Happy Hawkers. The vertical axis should vary between $(200,000) and $200,000 in increments of $100,000. The horizontal axis should vary as described in requirement (b). Label the graph in thousands.
d. Evaluate the profit-volume graph. In what ways is it superior and in what ways is it inferior to the traditional cost-volume-profit graph?

3–8
Multiple Product Planning with Taxes

In the year 2003, Fenwick Processing Company had the following contribution income statement:

Fenwick Processing Company
Contribution Income Statement
For the Year 2003

Sales		$950,000
Variable costs:		
Cost of goods sold	$420,000	
Selling and administrative	150,000	(570,000)
Contribution margin		$380,000
Fixed costs:		
Factory overhead	$110,000	
Selling and administrative	80,000	(190,000)
Before-tax profit		$190,000
Income taxes (36%)		(68,400)
After-tax profit		$121,600

Required:
a. Determine the annual break-even point in sales dollars.
b. Determine the annual margin of safety in sales dollars.
c. What is the break-even point in sales dollars if management makes a decision that increases fixed costs by $50,000?
d. What dollar sales volume is required to provide an after-tax net income of $200,000? Assume fixed costs are $190,000.
e. Prepare an abbreviated contribution income statement to verify that the solution to requirement (d) will provide the desired after-tax income.

3–9
Not-for-Profit
Applications

Determine the solution to each of the following independent cases:

a. Lakeside College has annual fixed operating costs of $5,000,000 and variable operating costs of $1,000 per student. Tuition is $4,000 per student for the coming academic year, with a projected enrollment of 1,500 students. Expected revenues from endowments and federal and state grants total $250,000. Determine the amount Lakeside must obtain from other sources.

b. The Lakeside College Student Association is planning a fall concert. Expected costs (renting a hall, hiring a band, etc.) are $30,000. Assuming 5,000 people attend the concert, determine the break-even price per ticket. How much will the association lose if this price is charged and only 4,250 tickets are sold?

c. City Hospital has a contract with the city to provide indigent health care on an outpatient basis for $25 per visit. The patient will pay $5 of this amount, with the city paying the balance ($20). Determine the amount the city will pay if the hospital has 10,000 patient visits.

d. A civic organization is engaged in a fund-raising program. On Civic Sunday, it will sell newspapers at $1.25 each. The organization will pay $0.75 for each newspaper. Costs of the necessary permits, signs, and so forth are $500. Determine the amount the organization will raise if it sells 5,000 newspapers.

e. Christmas for the Needy is a civic organization that provides Christmas presents to disadvantaged children. The annual costs of this activity are $5,000, plus $10 per present. Determine the number of presents the organization can provide with $20,000.

3–10
Alternative
Production
Procedures and
Operating Leverage

Assume Paper Mate is planning to introduce a new executive pen that can be manufactured using either a capital-intensive method or a labor-intensive method. The predicted manufacturing costs for each method are as follows:

	Capital Intensive	Labor Intensive
Direct materials per unit	$ 5.00	$ 5.60
Direct labor per unit	$10.00	$11.20
Variable manufacturing overhead per unit	$ 4.00	$ 5.80
Fixed manufacturing overhead per year	$2,440,000.00	$1,320,000.00

Paper Mate's market research department has recommended an introductory unit sales price of $35. The incremental selling costs are predicted to be $500,000 per year, plus $2 per unit sold.

Required:

a. Determine the annual break-even point in units if Paper Mate uses the:
   1. Capital-intensive manufacturing method.
   2. Labor-intensive manufacturing method.

b. Determine the annual unit volume at which Paper Mate is indifferent between the two manufacturing methods.

c. Management wants to know more about the effect of each alternative on operating leverage.
   1. Explain operating leverage and the relationship between operating leverage and the volatility of earnings.
   2. Compute operating leverage for each alternative at a volume of 250,000 units.
   3. Which alternative has the higher operating leverage? Why?

3–11
Contribution Income
Statement and
Operating Leverage

Alabama Berry Basket harvests early-season strawberries for shipment throughout the eastern United States in late March. The strawberry farm is maintained by a permanent staff of 10 employees and seasonal workers who pick and pack the strawberries. The strawberries are sold in crates containing 100 individually packaged one-quart containers. Affixed to each one-quart container is the distinctive Alabama Berry Basket logo inviting buyers to "Enjoy the berry best strawberries in the world!" The selling price is $90 per crate, variable costs are $80 per crate, and fixed costs are $275,000 per year. In the year 2004, Alabama Berry Basket sold 40,000 crates.

Required:

a. Prepare a contribution income statement for the year ended December 31, 2004.
b. Determine Alabama Berry Basket's 2004 operating leverage.
c. Calculate the percentage change in profits if sales decrease by 10 percent.
d. Management is considering the purchase of several berry-picking machines. This will increase annual fixed costs to $375,000 and reduce variable costs to $77.50 per crate. Calculate the effect of this acquisition on operating leverage and explain any change.

3–12
Customer-Level
Planning

Bop-Inn operates a number of convenience stores in small cities. An analysis of operating costs, customer sales, and customer patronage reveals the following:

Fixed costs per store	$80,000.00/year
Variable cost ratio	0.80
Average sale per customer visit	$15.00
Average customer visits per week	1.50
Customers as portion of city population	0.04

Required:

Determine the city population required for a single Bop-Inn to earn an annual profit of $40,000.

3–13
Multiple-Level
Break-Even Analysis

Manufacturing Associates provides marketing services for a number of small manufacturing firms. Manufacturing Associates receives a commission of 10 percent of sales. Operating costs are as follows:

Unit-level costs	$0.02 per sales dollar
Sales-level costs	$200 per sales order
Customer-level costs	$500 per customer per year
Facility-level costs	$60,000 per year

Required:

a. Determine the minimum order size in sales dollars for Manufacturing Associates to break even on an order.
b. Assuming an average customer places four orders per year, determine the minimum annual sales required to break even on a customer.
c. What would be the average order size in (b)?
d. Assuming Manufacturing Associates currently serves 100 customers, with each placing an average of four orders per year, determine the minimum annual sales required to break even.
e. What would be the average order size in (d)?
f. Explain the differences in the answers to (a), (c), and (e).

3–14
Multiple Product
Break-Even Analysis
(Appendix)

Presented is information for Triangle Company's three products.

	A	B	C
Unit selling price	$5	$7	$6
Unit variable costs	(4)	(5)	(3)
Unit contribution margin	$1	$2	$3

With monthly fixed costs of $90,000, Triangle sells two units of A for each unit of B and three units of B for each unit of C.

Required:
Determine the unit sales of product A at the monthly break-even point.

3-15
Multiple Product
Break-Even Analysis
(Appendix)

Bob's Tax Service prepares tax returns for low to middle-income taxpayers. Bob's service operates January 2 through April 15 at a counter in a local department store. All jobs are classified into one of three categories: standard, multiform, and complex. The following is information for last year.

	Standard	Multiform	Complex
Billing rate	$50	$125	$250
Average variable costs	(30)	(75)	(150)
Average contribution margin	$20	$ 50	$100
Number of returns prepared	1,750	500	250

Also last year, the fixed cost of rent, utilities, and so forth were $30,000.

Required:
a. Determine Bob's break-even dollar sales volume.
b. Determine Bob's margin of safety in sales dollars.
c. Prepare a profit-volume graph for Bob's Tax Service.

Problems

3-16
Cost-Volume-Profit
Relationships:
Missing Data

Required:
Supply the missing data in each independent case.

	Case 1	Case 2	Case 3	Case 4
Unit sales	1,000	800	?	?
Sales revenue	$20,000	?	?	$60,000
Variable cost per unit	$10	$1	$12	?
Contribution margin	?	$800	?	?
Fixed costs	$8,000	?	$80,000	?
Net income	?	$400	?	?
Unit contribution margin	?	?	?	$15
Break-even point (units)	?	?	4,000	2,000
Margin of safety (units)	?	?	300	1,000

3-17
Cost-Volume-Profit
Relationships:
Missing Data

Required:
Supply the missing data in each independent case.

	Case 1	Case 2	Case 3	Case 4
Sales revenue	$100,000	$80,000	?	?
Contribution margin	$60,000	?	$20,000	?
Fixed costs	$30,000	?	?	?
Net income	?	$15,000	$10,000	?
Variable cost ratio	?	0.25	?	0.20
Contribution margin ratio	?	?	0.40	?
Break-even point (dollars)	?	?	?	$25,000
Margin of safety (dollars)	?	?	?	$15,000

**3–18
Profit Planning with
Taxes**

Brown Manufacturing Company produces a product that it sells for $35 per unit. Variable and fixed costs follow.

Variable Costs per Unit		Fixed Costs per Year	
Manufacturing	$18	Manufacturing	$ 80,000
Selling and administrative	7	Selling and administrative	30,000
Total	$25	Total	$110,000

Last year, Brown manufactured and sold 20,000 units to obtain an after-tax profit of $49,500.

Required:
a. Determine the tax rate Brown paid last year.
b. What unit sales volume is required to provide an after-tax profit of $88,000?
c. If Brown reduces the unit variable cost by $2.50 and increases fixed manufacturing costs by $20,000, what unit sales volume is required to provide an after-tax profit of $88,000?
d. What assumptions are made about taxable income and tax rates in requirements (a) through (c)?

**3–19
High-Low Cost
Estimation and
Profit Planning**

Comparative 2003 and 2004 income statements for Montana Products Inc. follow:

**Montana Products Inc.
Comparative Income Statements
For the Years Ending December 31, 2003 and 2004**

	2003	2004
Unit sales	5,000	8,000
Sales revenue	$65,000	$104,000
Expenses	(75,000)	(90,000)
Profit (loss)	$(10,000)	$ 14,000

Required:
a. Determine the break-even point in units.
b. Determine the unit sales volume required to earn a profit of $10,000.

**3–20
CVP Analysis and
Special Decisions**

Sweet Grove Citrus Company buys a variety of citrus fruit from growers and then processes the fruit into a product line of fresh fruit, juices, and fruit flavorings. The most recent year's sales revenue was $4,200,000. Variable costs were 60 percent of sales and fixed costs totaled $1,300,000.

Sweet Grove is evaluating several alternatives designed to enhance profitability.

• One staff member has proposed that Sweet Grove purchase more automated processing equipment. This strategy would increase fixed costs by $300,000 but decrease variable costs to 54 percent of sales.

• Another staff member has suggested that Sweet Grove rely more on outsourcing for fruit processing. This would reduce fixed costs by $300,000 but increase variable costs to 65 percent of sales.

Required:
Please assist Sweet Grove management by answering the following questions.

a. What is the current break-even point in sales dollars?
b. Assuming an income tax rate of 34 percent, what dollar sales volume is currently required to obtain an after-tax profit of $500,000?
c. In the absence of income taxes, at what sales volume will both alternatives (automation and outsourcing) provide the same profit?
d. Briefly describe one strength and one weakness of both the automation and the outsourcing alternatives.

**3–21
Break-Even Analysis
in a Not-for-Profit
Organization**

Melford Hospital operates a general hospital but rents space to separately owned entities rendering specialized services such as pediatrics and psychiatry. Melford charges each separate entity for patients' services (meals and laundry) and for administrative services (billings and collections). Space and bed rentals are fixed charges for the year, based on bed capacity rented to each entity.

Melford charged the following costs to Pediatrics for the year ended June 30, 2004:

	Patient Services (Variable)	Bed Capacity (Fixed)
Dietary	$600,000	
Janitorial		$70,000
Laundry	300,000	
Laboratory	450,000	
Pharmacy	350,000	
Repairs and maintenance		30,000
General and administrative		1,300,000
Rent		1,500,000
Billings and collections	300,000	
Total	$2,000,000	$2,900,000

In addition to these charges from Melford Hospital, Pediatrics incurred the following personnel costs:

	Annual Salaries*
Supervising nurses	$100,000
Nurses	200,000
Assistants	180,000
Total	$480,000

These salaries are fixed within the ranges of annual patient-days considered in this problem.

During the year ended June 30, 2004, Pediatrics charged each patient $300 per day, had a capacity of 60 beds, and had revenues of $6,000,000 for 365 days. Pediatrics operated at 100 percent capacity on 90 days during this period. It is estimated that during these 90 days, the demand exceeded 80 beds. (Pediatrics' capacity is 60 beds.) Melford has 20 additional beds available for rent for the year ending June 30, 2005. This additional rental would proportionately increase Pediatrics' annual fixed charges based on bed capacity.

Required:

a. Calculate the minimum number of patient-days required for Pediatrics to break even for the year ending June 30, 2005, if the additional beds are not rented. Patient demand is unknown, but assume that revenue per patient-day, cost per patient-day, cost per bed, and salary rates for the year ending June 30, 2005, remain the same as for the year ended June 30, 2004.

b. Assume Pediatrics rents the extra 20-bed capacity from Melford. Determine the net increase or decrease in earnings by preparing a schedule of increases in revenues and costs for the year ending June 30, 2005. Assume that patient demand, revenue per patient-day, cost per patient-day, cost per bed, and salary rates remain the same as for the year ended June 30, 2004.

(CPA adapted)

**3–22
Cost-Volume-Profit
Analysis of
Alternative Products**

Siberian Ski Company recently expanded its manufacturing capacity to allow production of up to 15,000 pairs of the Mountaineering or the Touring models of cross-country skis. The sales department assures management that it can sell between 9,000 and 13,000 of either product this year. Because the models are very similar, Siberian Ski will produce only one of the two models.

The Accounting Department compiled the following information:

	MODEL	
	Mountaineering	**Touring**
Selling price per unit	$88.00	$80.00
Variable costs per unit	$52.80	$52.80

Fixed costs will total $369,600 if the Mountaineering model is produced but only $316,800 if the Touring model is produced. Siberian Ski Company is subject to a 40 percent income tax rate.

Required:

a. Determine the contribution margin ratio of the Touring model.
b. If Siberian Ski Company desires an after-tax profit of $24,000, how many pairs of Touring model skis will the company have to sell? (Round answer to the nearest unit.)
c. Determine the unit sales volume at which Siberian Ski Company would make the same before-tax profit or loss regardless of the ski model it decides to produce. Also determine the resulting before-tax profit or loss.
d. Determine the dollar sales volume at which Siberian Ski Company would make the same before-tax profit or loss regardless of the ski model it decides to produce. Also determine the resulting before-tax profit or loss. (*Hint:* Work with contribution margin ratios.)
e. What action should Siberian Ski Company take if the annual sales of either model were guaranteed to be at least 12,000 pairs? Why?
f. Determine how much the unit variable costs of the Touring model would have to change before both models would have the same break-even point in units. (Round calculations to the nearest cent.)
g. Determine the new unit break-even point of the Touring model if its variable costs per unit decrease by 10 percent and its fixed costs increase by 10 percent. (Round answer to nearest unit.)

(CMA adapted)

3–23
CVP Analysis Using Published Financial Statements

Condensed data from the 1999 and 2000 financial statements (in millions) of Delta Air Lines and Southwest Airlines follow.

Delta Air Lines*	2000	1999
Revenues	$16,741	$14,883
Operating expenses	(15,104)	(13,566)
Operating profit	$ 1,637	$ 1,317
Southwest Airlines*		
Revenues	$5,649.560	$4,735.587
Operating expenses	(4,628.415)	(3,954.001)
Operating profit	$1,021.145	$ 781.586

Data came from 2000 annual reports of Delta Air Lines and Southwest Airlines.

Required:

a. Develop a cost-estimating equation for annual operating expenses for each company.
b. Determine the break-even point for each airline.
c. Using Southwest Airlines cost structure, predict Southwest's profits at Delta's 2000 volume of revenues.
d. Evaluate the results in requirement (c).

3-24
Multiple-Product Profitability Analysis, Project Profitability Analysis

University Bookstore sells new college textbooks at the publishers' suggested retail prices. It then pays the publishers an amount equal to 75 percent of the suggested retail price. The store's other variable costs average 5 percent of sales revenue and annual fixed costs amount to $300,000.

Required:
a. Determine the bookstore's annual break-even point in sales dollars.
b. Assuming an average textbook has a suggested retail price of $60, determine the bookstore's annual break-even point in units.
c. University Bookstore is planning to add used book sales to its operations. A typical used book costs the store 25 percent of the suggested retail price of a new book. The bookstore plans to sell used books for 75 percent of the suggested retail price of a new book. What is the effect on bookstore profitability of shifting sales toward more used and fewer new textbooks?
d. College Publishing Produces and sells new textbooks to college and university bookstores. Typical project-level costs total $260,000 for a new textbook. Unit-level production and distribution costs amount to 20 percent of the net amount the publisher receives from the bookstores. Textbook authors are paid a royalty of 15 percent of the net amount received from the bookstores. Determine the dollar sales volume required for College Publishing to break even on a new textbook.
e. For a project with predicted sales of 15,000 new books at $60 each, determine:
   1. The bookstores' unit level contribution.
   2. The publisher's project level contribution.
   3. The author's royalties.

3-25
Multiple-Product Profitability Analysis

Hearth Manufacturing Company produces two models of wood-burning stoves, Cozy Kitchen and All-House. Presented is sales information for the year 2004.

	Cozy Kitchen	All-House	Total
Units manufactured and sold	1,000	1,500	2,500
Sales revenue	$300,000	$750,000	$1,050,000
Variable costs	(200,000)	(450,000)	(650,000)
Contribution margin	$100,000	$300,000	$ 400,000
Fixed costs			(240,000)
Before-tax profit			$ 160,000
Income taxes (40 percent)			(64,000)
After-tax profit			$ 96,000

Required:
a. Determine the current break-even point in sales dollars.
b. With the current product mix and break-even point, determine the average unit contribution margin and unit sales.
c. Sales representatives believe that the total sales will increase to 3,000 units, with the sales mix likely shifting to 80 percent Cozy Kitchen and 20 percent All-House over the next few years. Evaluate the desirability of this projection.

3-26
Multi-Level Profitability Analysis

AccuMeter manufactures and sells its only product (Z1) in lot sizes of 500 units. Because of this approach, lot (batch)-level costs are regarded as variable for CVP analysis. Presented is sales and cost information for the year 2004:

Sales revenue (50,000 units at $40)	$2,000,000
Direct materials (50,000 units at $10)	500,000
Processing (50,000 units at $15)	750,000
Setup (100 lots at $2,000)	200,000
Batch movement (100 lots at $400)	40,000

Order filling (100 lots at $200)	$ 20,000
Fixed factory overhead	800,000
Fixed selling and administrative	300,000

Required:
a. Prepare a traditional contribution income statement in good form.
b. Prepare a multi-level contribution income statement in good form. (*Hint:* First determine the appropriate cost hierarchy.)
c. What is the current contribution per lot (batch) of 500 units?
d. Management is contemplating introducing a limited number of specialty products. One product would sell for $60 per unit and have direct materials costs of $12 per unit. All other costs and all production and sales procedures will remain unchanged. What lot (batch) size is required for a contribution of $700 per lot?

3-27
Multiple Product
Break-Even Analysis
(Appendix)

Currently, Corner Lunch Counter sells only Super Burgers for $2.50 each. During a typical month, the Counter reports a profit of $9,000 with sales of $50,000 and fixed costs of $21,000. Management is considering the introduction of a new Super Chicken Sandwich that will sell for $3 and have variable costs of $1.80. The addition of the Super Chicken Sandwich will require hiring additional personnel and renting additional equipment. These actions will increase monthly fixed costs by $7,760.

In the short run, management predicts that Super Chicken sales will average 10,000 sandwiches per month. However, almost all short-run sales of Super Chickens will come from regular customers who switch from Super Burgers to Super Chickens. Consequently, management predicts monthly sales of Super Burgers will decline by 10,000 units to $25,000.

In the long run, management predicts that Super Chicken sales will increase to 15,000 sandwiches per month and that Super Burger sales will increase to 30,000 burgers per month.

Required:
a. Determine each of the following:
  1. The current monthly break-even point in sales dollars.
  2. The short-run monthly profit and break-even point in sales dollars subsequent to the introduction of Super Chickens.
  3. The long-run monthly profit and break-even point in sales dollars subsequent to the introduction of Super Chickens.
b. Based on your analysis, what are your recommendations?

Discussion Questions and Cases

3-28
Ethics and Pressure
to Improve Profit
Plans

Art Conroy is the assistant controller of New City Muffler, Inc., a subsidiary of New City Automotive, which manufactures tail pipes, mufflers, and catalytic converters at several plants throughout North America. Because of pressure for lower selling prices, New City Muffler has had disappointing financial performance in recent years. Indeed, Conroy is aware of rumblings from corporate headquarters threatening to close the plant.

One of Conroy's responsibilities is to present the plant's financial plans for the coming year to the corporate officers and board of directors. In preparing for the presentation, Conroy was intrigued to note that the focal point of the budget presentation was a profit-volume graph projecting an increase in profits and a reduction in the break-even point.

Curious as to how the improvement would be accomplished, Conroy ultimately spoke with Paula Mitchell, the plant manager. Mitchell indicated that a planned increase in productivity would reduce variable costs and increase the contribution margin ratio.

When asked how the productivity increase would be accomplished, Mitchell made a vague reference to increasing the speed of the assembly line. Conroy commented that speeding up the assembly line could lead to labor problems because the speed of the line was set by union contract. Mitchell responded that she was afraid that if the speedup were opened to negotiation, the union would make a big "stink" that could result in the plant being closed. She indicated that the speedup was the "only way to save the plant, our jobs, and the jobs of all plant employees." Besides, she did not believe employees would notice a 2 or 3 percent increase in speed. Mitchell concluded the meeting observing, "You need to emphasize the results we will accomplish next year, not the details of how we will accomplish those results. Top management does not want to be bored with details. If we accomplish what we propose in the budget, we will be in for a big bonus."

Required:
What advice do you have for Art Conroy?

3-29
CVP Analysis with Changing Cost Structure

Homestead Telephone was formed in the 1940s to bring telephone services to remote areas of the U.S. Midwest. The early equipment was quite primitive by today's standards. All calls were handled manually by operators, and all customers were on party lines. By the 1970s, however, all customers were on private lines, and mechanical switching devices handled routine local and long distance calls. Operators remained available for directory assistance, credit card calls, and emergencies.

In the 1990s Homestead Telephone added local Internet connections as an optional service to its regular customers. It also established an optional cellular service, identified as the Home Ranger.

Required:
a. Using a unit-level analysis, develop a graph with two lines, representing Homestead Telephones' cost structure (1) in the 1940s and (2) in the late 1990s. Be sure to label the axis and lines.
b. With sales revenue as the independent variable, what is the likely impact of the changed cost structure on Homestead Telephone's (1) contribution margin percent and (2) break-even point?
c. Would a hierarchical analysis of costs be more appropriate for Homestead Telephone than a unit-level analysis of costs? Why or why not?

3-30
Cost Estimation, CVP Analysis, and Hierarchy of Activity Costs

Presented are the 2003 and 2004 functional income statements of Regional Distribution, Inc.:

Regional Distribution, Inc.
Functional Income Statements
For the Years Ending December 31, 2003 and 2004

	2003		2004	
Sales		$5,520,000		$5,000,000
Expenses:				
Cost of goods sold	$4,140,000		$3,750,000	
Shipping	215,400		200,000	
Sales order processing	52,500		50,000	
Customer relations	120,000		100,000	
Depreciation	80,000		80,000	
Administrative	250,000	(4,857,900)	250,000	(4,430,000)
Before-tax profit		$ 662,100		$ 570,000
Income taxes (40%)		(264,840)		(228,000)
After-tax profit		$ 397,260		$ 342,000

Required:

a. Determine Regional Distribution's break-even point in sales dollars.

b. What dollar sales volume is required to earn an after-tax profit of $480,000?

c. Assuming budgeted 2005 sales of $6,000,000, prepare a 2005 contribution income statement.

d. In an effort to increase sales volume, Regional Distribution has been increasing its customer base. Management is concerned about the profitability of small orders and customers who place only one or two orders per year. Should Regional Distribution specify a minimum order size? If so, what should it be? What annual volume is necessary to continue serving customers who place only one or two orders each year?

The following additional information is available to aid in these decisions:

	2003	2004
Operating statistics:		
Total customers	240	200
Number of orders	2,100	2,000

Activity cost driver information:

- The cost of goods sold is 75 percent of sales.
- Shipping expenses are 2 percent of sales plus $50 per order.
- Sales order processing is driven by the number of sales orders.
- Customer relations is driven by the number of customers.
- Depreciation and administration are facility-level costs.

e. Reevaluate your answer to requirement (a). Under what circumstances would your previous answer be correct?

f. Assume management's $6,000,000 sales forecast for 2005 is based on 340 total customers with 2,750 total orders. Using activity cost hierarchy concepts, prepare a multi-level contribution income statement for 2005. (*Hint:* Use unit, order, customer, and facility levels.) Explain any difference in the after-tax profit obtained here and in requirement (c).

John Shank Case Recommendation

California Products Company

This short case considers contribution analysis, the optimal product mix, and business profitability. It is set in the context of a company manufacturing three products with three machines. Coverage of the case requires consideration of absorption and variable costing in a straightforward manner. Although these topics are not formally considered until Chapter 8, perceptive students should grasp the basics when reading the case. Students are cautioned to avoid assuming short Shank cases are "easy" or expecting to complete them in a short period of time. These cases, like the "real world" they represent, are often unstructured and lack complete information. The challenge is to provide structure and recommend a decision in the face of uncertainty.

Solution To Review Problem

Cost-Volume-Profit Analysis

a.

Memorabilia Cup Company
Contribution Income Statement
For the Month of September 2004

Sales (3,000 × $40)		$120,000
Less variable costs:		
Direct materials (3,000 × $15)	$45,000	
Direct labor (3,000 × $3)	9,000	
Manufacturing overhead (3,000 × $10)	30,000	
Selling and administrative (3,000 × $2)	6,000	(90,000)
Contribution margin		$ 30,000
Less fixed costs:		
Manufacturing overhead	$15,000	
Selling and administrative	10,000	(25,000)
Profit		$ 5,000

b.

c.

Selling price	$40 per unit
Variable costs	(30) per unit
Contribution margin . .	$10 per unit

$$\text{Contribution margin ratio} = \frac{\text{Unit contribution margin}}{\text{Unit selling price}}$$

$$= \$10 \div \$40$$

$$= 0.25$$

d.

$$\text{Break-even point} = \frac{\text{Fixed costs}}{\text{Unit contribution margin}}$$

$$= \$25,000 \div \$10$$

$$= 2,500 \text{ units}$$

e.

$$\text{Required dollar sales} = \frac{\text{Fixed costs} + \text{Desired profit}}{\text{Contribution margin ratio}}$$

$$= (\$25,000 + \$5,000) \div 0.25$$

$$= \$120,000$$

f. Desired before-tax profit $= \dfrac{\text{Desired after-tax profit}}{1.0 - \text{Tax rate}}$

$= \$4,500 \div (1 - 0.40)$

$= \$7,500$

Required unit sales $= \dfrac{\text{Fixed costs} + \text{Desired before-tax profit}}{\text{Unit contribution margin}}$

$= (\$25,000 + 7,500) \div \$10$

$= 3,250 \text{ units}$

CONTRIBUTION ANALYSIS FOR DECISION MAKING

After completing this chapter, you should be able to:

LEARNING OBJECTIVE 1   Differentiate between relevant and irrelevant revenues and costs.

LEARNING OBJECTIVE 2   Organize relevant costs in a manner that clearly indicates how they differ under separate decision alternatives.

LEARNING OBJECTIVE 3   Discuss issues involved in predicting relevant costs.

LEARNING OBJECTIVE 4   Apply differential analysis to evaluate a variety of decision alternatives, including whether to make multiple changes in plans; to accept a special order; to make, buy, or outsource a product or service; or to sell a product or process it further.

LEARNING OBJECTIVE 5   Determine how to allocate limited resources for the purpose of maximizing short-run profit.

PERSPECTIVES ON OUTSOURCING

The process of contracting with other firms to obtain necessary goods and services—currently called outsourcing—*emerged as a key management strategy of the 1990s. Through outsourcing decisions, managers intend to take advantage of specialization, better focus their attention on core activities, decrease costs, and increase flexibility. Cunningham Car Company and StarTek illustrate outsourcing from the perspectives of the purchaser and provider of outsourcing services.*

Noted Detroit automobile executive Bob Lutz discussed both the product and the operating strategy for Cunningham Car Company early in 2001. The Cunningham C-7 is designed to be the first super-exclusive American sports car in decades. Cunningham managers plan to sell each car for about $250,000 with volumes between 400 and 1,000 units per year. In addition to the 500-horsepower engine and sports car styling, the Cunningham will differ from other autos in one other major way—a Cunningham C-7 will be the product of a comprehensive outsourcing effort. Auto manufacturers have traditionally outsourced the manufacture of many of the finished car's components, but the automobile firm itself were responsible for many other parts as well as final assembly. Managers at Cunningham want to outsource the entire production process with one subcontractor acting as *the final assembler of the car. Cunningham will own no fabrication or assembly plants but will be a virtual manufacturer.*

Providing outsourcing services to other firms, StarTek has annual revenues of $200 million. StarTek packs and ships products for Microsoft, provides technical support for customers of AOLTime Warner, and maintains AT&T's communications system. The activity level of a firm like StarTek, however, completely depends on the sales of clients' products and services. Since contract work for Microsoft provides 42 percent of StarTek revenue, any drop in Microsoft sales directly impacts StarTek. In response to recent declines in technology-related sales, StarTek managers expanded the breadth of business activities in which the firm participates. In an attempt to maintain the firm's revenues, managers have invested in a Web retailer and discussed other related ventures. Facing a decline in the firm's core business of providing outsourcing services, StarTek management stated they will consider "anything that's intelligent and represents a chance to enhance the value of the company."

Sources: "Ghost Cars, Ghost Brands," *Forbes,* April 30, 2001, pp. 106–12; Michael Selz, "StarTek Expands Beyond Its Core Services As Falling Demand Halts Financial Growth," *The Wall Street Journal, Interactive Edition,* June 26, 2001; and David Welch, "Bob Lutz: The First Virtual Carmaker," *Business Week,* June 18, 2001, pp. 66, 70.

Like many competitive concepts, outsourcing can be successful, but managers must carefully weigh both the strengths and limitations of this strategy. **The purpose of this chapter is to examine approaches to identifying and analyzing revenue and cost information for specific decisions, such as the decision to outsource.** Our emphasis is on identifying **relevant costs** (future costs that differ among competing decision alternatives) and distinguishing relevant costs from **irrelevant costs** that do not differ among competing decision alternatives. We will consider a number of frequently encountered decisions: to make multiple changes in profit plans, to accept or reject a special order, to acquire a component or service internally or externally, to sell a product or process it further, and how to best use limited capacity. These decision situations are not exhaustive; they only illustrate relevant cost concepts. Once you understand these concepts, you may apply them to a variety of decisions.

To better focus on relevant cost concepts, the emphasis in this chapter is on decisions that involve an analysis only of activity cost drivers. In subsequent chapters we emphasize decisions affecting structural and organizational cost drivers. Although our focus in this chapter is on profit maximization, keep in mind that decisions should not be based solely on this criterion, especially maximizing profit in the short run. Decision makers must consider the implications decisions have on long-run profit, as well as legal, ethical, social, and other nonquantitative factors. These factors may lead management to select a course of action other than that selected by financial information alone.

LEARNING OBJECTIVE 1

IDENTIFYING RELEVANT COSTS

For a specific decision, the key to differential cost analysis is first to identify the relevant costs (and revenues) and then to organize them in a manner that clearly indicates how they differ under each alternative. Consider the following equipment replacement decision.

Ace Welding Company manufactures frames for Mountain and Touring bicycles. Mountain bicycle frames have a unit selling price of $20, and Touring bicycle frames have a unit selling price of $15. Annual production and sales total 10,000 Mountain bicycle frames and 11,000 Touring bicycle frames. Each product is manufactured with separate equipment in a shared building. Activity cost information is as follows:

	Mountain	Touring	Common
Unit level:			
Direct materials	$3.00 per unit	$2.50 per unit	
Conversion	5.00 per unit	3.50 per unit	
Selling and distribution	1.00 per unit	0.75 per unit	
Batch level:			
Inspection and adjustment	$500 per batch (1,000 units)	$400 per batch (1,000 units)	
Product level:			
Depreciation on welding machines	$15,000 per year	$12,000 per year	
Machine maintenance	$200 per month	$500 per six months	
Advertising	$5,000 per year	$4,500 per year	
Facility level:			
Administrative salaries			$65,000 per year
Building operations			23,000 per year
Building rent			24,000 per year

In the unit level costs listed above, **conversion costs** include all costs (direct labor and variable manufacturing overhead) required to convert raw materials into finished goods. In a two-dimensional graph with total units produced on the horizontal axis and total costs on the vertical axis:

- Total unit activity costs follow a variable cost function (they increase in direct proportion to increases in activity),
- Total batch activity costs follow a step cost function (they are fixed over a range of activity but change between different activity range levels), and
- Total product and total facility activity costs follow fixed cost functions (once plans are set for a time period, they do not vary with changes in activity levels).

The Model I welding machine used in the manufacture of Mountain bicycle frames is two years old and has a remaining useful life of four years. Its purchase price was $90,000 (new), and it has an estimated salvage value of zero dollars at the end of its useful life. Its current book value (original cost less accumulated depreciation) is $60,000, but its current disposal value is only $35,000.

Management is evaluating the desirability of replacing the Model I welding machine with a new Model II welding machine. The new machine costs $80,000, has a useful life of four years, and a predicted salvage value of zero dollars at the end of its useful life. Although the new machine has the same production capacity as the old machine, its predicted operating costs are lower because it consumes less electricity. Furthermore, because of a computer control system, the Model II machine allows production of twice as many units between inspections and adjustments, and the cost of inspections and adjustments is lower. Finally, the Model II machine requires only annual, rather than monthly, overhauls. Hence, machine maintenance costs are lower. The new conversion, inspection and adjustment, and machine maintenance costs are predicted to be as follows:

Conversion costs	$4.00 per unit
Inspection and adjustment	$300 per batch (2,000 units)
Machine maintenance	$200 per year

All other costs and all revenues remain unchanged.

The decision alternatives are to keep the old Model I welding machine or to replace it with a new Model II welding machine. An analysis of how costs and revenues differ under each alternative assists management in making the best choice. Although the clearest presentation is one that contains only those costs and revenues that differ, the first objective of this chapter is to study the distinction between relevant and irrelevant items. To help accomplish this objective, a complete analysis of all costs and revenues under each alternative is presented in Exhibit 4–1. After evaluating the relevance of each item, we develop a more focused analysis of relevant costs.

The first thing to notice about Exhibit 4–1 is that many costs and revenues are the same under each alternative. These items are not relevant to the replacement decision. The only relevant items are those that have an entry in the Difference column. For emphasis, the relevant costs are in bold.

FUTURE REVENUES MAY BE RELEVANT

Revenues, which are inflows of resources from the sale of goods and services,[1] are relevant if they differ between alternatives. In this example, revenues are not relevant because they are identical under each alternative. They would be relevant if the new machine had greater capacity that would be used or if management intended to change the selling price should it acquire the new machine.

The keep-or-replace decision facing Ace's management might be called a **cost reduction proposal** because it is based on the assumption that the organization is committed to an activity and that management desires to minimize the cost of activities. Here, the two alternatives are either to continue operating with the old machine or to replace it with a new machine.

Although this approach is appropriate for many activities, managers of for-profit organizations should remember that they have another alternative—discontinue operations. To simplify the analysis, managers normally do not consider the alternative to discontinue when operations appear to be profitable. However, if there is any doubt about an operation's profitability, this alternative should be considered. Because revenues will change if an operation is discontinued, revenues are relevant whenever this alternative is considered.

OUTLAY COSTS MAY BE RELEVANT

Outlay costs are costs that require future expenditures of cash or other resources. Outlay costs that differ under the decision alternatives at hand are relevant; outlay costs that do not differ are irrelevant. Ace Welding Company's relevant and irrelevant outlay costs for the equipment replacement decision follow.

Relevant Outlay Costs	**Irrelevant Outlay Costs**
Mountain frame conversion costs	Mountain frame direct materials
Mountain frame inspection and adjustment costs	Mountain frame selling and distribution
Cost of new Model II machine	Mountain frame advertising
Mountain frame machine maintenance	Touring frame outlay costs
	Facility-level outlay costs

Because unit-level costs are variable and respond to changes in the level of activity, they are relevant when decision alternatives have different activity levels or different costs per unit of activity. Unit-level costs are not relevant when decision alternatives have the same activity level and the same cost per unit of activity. In this

---

[1]The $35,000 disposal value of the Model I machine is an inflow of resources. However, *revenues* refer to resources from the sale of goods and services the organization is established to provide to customers in the normal course of business. We include the sale of the Model I machine under a separate category, disposal and salvage values.

EXHIBIT 4-1

COMPLETE ANALYSIS OF ALL COSTS AND REVENUES

	COMPLETE ANALYSIS OF FOUR-YEAR TOTALS		
	(1) Replace with New Model II Machine	(2) Keep Old Model I Machine	(1) − (2) Difference (effect of replacement on income)
Sales:			
Mountain (10,000 units × $20 × 4 years)	$ 800,000	$ 800,000	
Touring (11,000 units × $15 × 4 years)	660,000	660,000	
Total	$ 1,460,000	$ 1,460,000	
Direct materials:			
Mountain (10,000 units × $3 × 4 years)	$ 120,000	$ 120,000	
Touring (11,000 units × $2.50 × 4 years)	110,000	110,000	
Conversion:			
Mountain, Model I (10,000 units × $5 × 4 years)		**200,000**	
Mountain, Model II (10,000 units × $4 × 4 years)	**160,000**		**$40,000**
Touring (11,000 units × $3.50 × 4 years)	154,000	154,000	
Selling and distribution:			
Mountain (10,000 units × $1 × 4 years)	40,000	40,000	
Touring (11,000 units × $0.75 × 4 years)	33,000	33,000	
Inspection and adjustment:			
Mountain, Model I (10* setups × $500 × 4 years)		**20,000**	
Mountain, Model II (5* setups × $300 × 4 years)	**6,000**		**14,000**
Touring (11† setups × $400 × 4 years)	17,600	17,600	
Depreciation, write-off, or disposal:			
Mountain, Model I, depreciation ($15,000 × 4 years) or write-off ($60,000 book value)	60,000	60,000	
Touring, depreciation on welding machine ($12,000 × 4 years)	48,000	48,000	
Mountain, Model I, disposal value	**(35,000)**		**35,000**
Cost of Model II	**80,000**		**(80,000)**
Machine maintenance:			
Mountain, Model I ($200 × 12 months × 4 years)		**9,600**	
Mountain, Model II ($200 × 4 years)	**800**		**8,800**
Touring ($500 × 2 per year × 4 years)	4,000	4,000	
Advertising:			
Mountain ($5,000 × 4 years)	20,000	20,000	
Touring ($4,500 × 4 years)	18,000	18,000	
Administrative salaries ($65,000 × 4 years)	260,000	260,000	
Building operations ($23,000 × 4 years)	92,000	92,000	
Building rent ($24,000 × 4 years)	96,000	96,000	
Total costs	(1,284,400)	(1,302,200)	
Profit	$ 175,600	$ 157,800	$17,800

*Model I: 10,000 units ÷ 1,000 units per batch
 Model II: 10,000 units ÷ 2,000 units per batch
†11,000 units ÷ 1,000 units per batch

example, while the level of activity was unchanged, there were changes in unit-level activity costs. The Mountain frame conversion costs are relevant because they are $5 per unit for Model I and $4 per unit for Model II.

Batch-level activity costs are also relevant when decision alternatives have a different number of batches or different costs per batch. In this example, there were changes in both the number of batches and in the inspection and adjustment costs per batch for the Mountain bicycle frames.

For the organization as a whole, product-level activity costs are relevant if decision alternatives involve a different number of products or different costs per product. In this example, although there was no change in the number of products, there was a change in Mountain frame product-level costs for machine maintenance. There was also a product-level cash outlay to acquire the new Model II machine.

In the short run, facility-level activity costs do not change in direct response to the number of units, batches, or products. Facility-level costs are relevant, however, if management is contemplating an action that affects the ability or method of performing facility-level activities. In this example, no changes are being considered for facility-level activities. If, however, both Mountain and Touring bicycle frames were produced using the same machines and management was contemplating replacing these common machines, facility-level costs would be involved in the replacement decision.

When a change involves several products, outlay costs associated with all involved products may be relevant. In this example, the machinery replacement decision affects the production of Mountain bicycle frames only. Hence, all unit, batch, and product outlay costs for Touring bicycle frames are irrelevant. Although including them in the analysis does not change the bottom line in Exhibit 4–1, their inclusion may distract attention from the relevant costs and revenues.

SUNK COSTS ARE NEVER RELEVANT

Sunk costs result from past decisions that cannot be changed. Suppose you purchased a car for $15,000 five years ago. Today you must decide whether to purchase another car or have major maintenance performed on your current car. In making this decision, the purchase price of your current car is a sunk cost.

Although the relevance of outlay costs is determined by the decision at hand, sunk costs (aside from possible tax consequences) are never relevant. The cost of the Model I machine is a sunk cost, not a future cost. This cost, and the related depreciation, results from the past decision to acquire the old machine. Even though all the outlay costs discussed earlier would be relevant to a decision to continue or discontinue operations, the sunk cost of the Model I machine is not relevant even to this decision.

If management elects to keep the old machine, its book value will be depreciated over its remaining useful life of four years. However, if management elects to replace the old machine, its book value will be written off when it is replaced. You can see the irrelevance of the Model I machine's sunk cost in Exhibit 4–1, where the $60,000 does not differ between decision alternatives. Even if management elects to discontinue operations, the book value of the old machine must be written off in the accounting records.

SUNK COSTS MAY CAUSE ETHICAL DILEMMAS

Although the book value of the old machine has no economic significance, the accounting treatment of past costs may make it psychologically difficult for managers to regard them as irrelevant. If management replaces the old machine, a $25,000 accounting loss will be recorded in the year of replacement:

Book value	$60,000
Disposal value	(35,000)
Loss on disposal	$25,000

The possibility of recording an accounting loss may place managers in an ethical dilemma. Although an action may be desirable from the long-run viewpoint of the organization, in the short run, choosing the action may result in an accounting loss. Fearing the loss will lead superiors to question his or her judgment, a manager might prefer to use the old machine (with lower total profits over the four-year period) as opposed to replacing it and being forced to record a loss on disposal. Although this action may now avoid raising troublesome questions, the cumulative effect of many decisions of this nature will be harmful to the organization's long-run economic health.

From an economic viewpoint, the analysis should focus on future costs and revenues that differ. The decision should not be influenced by sunk costs. Although there is no easy solution to this behavioral and ethical problem, managers and management accountants should be aware of its potential impact.

DISPOSAL AND SALVAGE VALUES MAY BE RELEVANT

Ace Welding Company's revenues (inflows of resources from operations) from the sale of Mountain and Touring bicycle frames were discussed earlier. The sale of fixed assets is also a source of resources. Because the sale of fixed assets is a nonoperating item, cash inflows obtained from these sales are discussed separately.

The disposal value of the Model I welding machine is a relevant cash inflow. It is obtained only if the replacement alternative is selected. Any salvage value available at the end of the useful life of either machine is also relevant. A loss on disposal may have a favorable tax impact if the loss can be offset against taxable gains or taxable income. In this case, although the book value of the old asset remains irrelevant, the expected tax reduction *would* be relevant.

LEARNING OBJECTIVE 2

PERFORMING DIFFERENTIAL ANALYSIS OF RELEVANT COSTS

Differential cost analysis is an approach to the analysis of relevant costs that focuses on the costs that differ under alternative actions. A differential analysis of relevant costs for Ace Welding Company's equipment replacement decision is presented in Exhibit 4–2. Replacement provides a net advantage of $17,800 over the life of both machines.[2]

Assuming the organization is committed to providing a particular product or service, a differential analysis of relevant costs (as shown in Exhibit 4–2) is preferred to a complete analysis of all costs and revenues (as shown in Exhibit 4–1) for a number of reasons:

- A differential analysis focuses on only those items that differ, providing a clearer picture of the impact of the decision at hand. Management is less apt to be confused by this analysis than by one that combines relevant and irrelevant items.
- A differential analysis contains fewer items, making it easier and quicker to prepare.
- A differential analysis can help to simplify complex situations (such as those encountered by multiple-product or multiple-plant firms), when it is difficult to develop complete firmwide statements to analyze all decision alternatives.

Before preparing a differential analysis, it is always desirable to reassess the organization's commitment to a product or service. This helps avoid "throwing good money after bad." If Ace Welding Company currently had large annual losses, acquiring the Model II machine would merely reduce total losses over the next four years by $17,800. In this case, discontinuing operations (a third alternative) should be considered.

---

[2]Our current objectives are first to distinguish between relevant and irrelevant costs and then to demonstrate the advantages of analyzing only relevant costs. An analysis of long-term projects should also consider the time value of money (further discussed in Chapter 10).

EXHIBIT 4-2

DIFFERENTIAL ANALYSIS OF RELEVANT COSTS

	DIFFERENTIAL ANALYSIS OF FOUR-YEAR TOTALS		
	(1) Replace with New Model II Machine	(2) Keep Old Model I Machine	(1) − (2) Difference (effect of replacement on income)
Conversion:			
Mountain, Model I (10,000 units × $5 × 4 years)		$200,000	
Mountain, Model II (10,000 units × $4 × 4 years)	$160,000		$40,000
Inspection and adjustment:			
Mountain, Model I (10* setups × $500 × 4 years)		20,000	
Mountain, Model II (5* setups × $300 × 4 years)	6,000		14,000
Machine maintenance:			
Mountain, Model I ($200 × 12 months × 4 years)		9,600	
Mountain, Model II ($200 × 4 years)	800		8,800
Disposal of Model I	(35,000)		35,000
Cost of Model II	80,000		(80,000)
Total costs	$211,800	$229,600	$17,800
Advantage of replacement	$17,800		

*Model I: 10,000 units ÷ 1,000 units per batch
  Model II: 10,000 units ÷ 2,000 units per batch

An advantage of a complete analysis of costs and revenues (see Exhibit 4–1) is that it does disclose overall profitability, thereby helping management assess the desirability of continuing operations. Unfortunately, the complete analysis does not distinguish between the profitability of the Mountain and the Touring bicycle frames. However, segment analysis, which concerns the analysis of the profitability of a business segment such as a product or service, could be used to separately determine the profitability of the Mountain and the Touring frames. (Segment analysis is considered in Chapter 13.) For now, the key point to remember is that a differential analysis assumes a commitment to a product or service. When this commitment is justified, differential analysis is an efficient analytical tool. When this commitment is not justified, a more thorough approach, such as a complete analysis of all costs and revenues or a segment analysis, is required.

LEARNING OBJECTIVE 3

PREDICTING RELEVANT COSTS

Information on relevant costs is almost always given in textbook examples and problems. In these cases, the task is to distinguish between relevant and irrelevant costs and to properly classify the relevant costs. In practice, the analyst has the difficult job of obtaining the relevant cost information. This is a very time-consuming process that requires questioning, observing, and analyzing. Obviously, an understanding of relevant cost concepts is a prerequisite to obtaining relevant cost information. Simply stated, the analyst must know what to look for. This knowledge helps guide the search for the few pieces of relevant information contained in voluminous sets of data.

Predicting relevant costs may involve an examination of past cost trends. If one of the alternatives under consideration is to continue operations as in the past, the techniques discussed in Chapter 2 can be used to estimate past costs and to develop predictions of future costs. The predicted operating costs of the Model I welding machine would be developed in this manner.

It is more difficult to predict costs when technology changes. The substitution of the Model II for the Model I welding machine is an example of a technological change. Ace Welding Company's historical information is of limited value in predicting the operating costs of the new Model II machine. Cost predictions for the Model II machine must be deduced from information obtained from the manufacturer, trade associations, publications, and engineers employed by Ace. Management should carefully evaluate the credibility of this information.

A **cost prediction error** is the difference between a predicted future cost and the actual amount of the cost when, or if, it is incurred. Because cost predictions may be inaccurate, management should determine how sensitive a decision is to prediction errors. This would include, for example, determining how much a prediction could change before affecting the decision.

Ace Welding Company's new machine has a net advantage of $17,800 over its four-year life; hence, cost predictions could increase by $17,800 before affecting the decision. Given the size of the relevant operating costs, a $17,800 prediction error seems unlikely. If the net advantage of the new machine were smaller, say $5,000, management might want to consider the likelihood of a $5,000 prediction error.

LEARNING OBJECTIVE 4

APPLYING DIFFERENTIAL ANALYSIS

Differential analysis is used to provide information for a variety of planning and decision-making situations. This section illustrates some of the more frequently encountered applications of differential analysis. To focus on differential analysis concepts and avoid the complexities introduced by a hierarchy of cost drivers, we will use a simple example involving the production of one product on a continuous basis with all output sold to a single chain of discount stores. Because of continuous production, there are no batch-level costs. Also, with only one product and one customer, there is no need to distinguish among product, customer, or facility costs. From the viewpoint of our single-product, single-customer firm, all costs can be classified as either (1) unit-level costs that vary with units produced and sold or (2) facility-level costs that are fixed in the short run.

MULTIPLE CHANGES IN PROFIT PLANS

Mind Trek, Limited, located in Lancaster, England, manufactures an electronic game sold to distributors for £22 per unit (a pound sterling, represented by the symbol £, is the basic unit of currency of the United Kingdom[3]). Variable costs per unit and fixed costs per month are as follows:

Variable Costs per Unit		Fixed Costs per Month	
Direct materials	£ 5	Manufacturing overhead	£30,000
Direct labor	3	Selling and administrative	15,000
Manufacturing overhead	2	Total	£45,000
Selling	2		
Total	£12		

The unit contribution margin (UCM) is £10 (£22 selling price − £12 variable costs). Mind Trek's contribution income statement for April 2004 is presented in

---

[3]Although the United Kingdom is a member of the European Union, it has elected to retain its own currency.

Exhibit 4–3. The April 2004 operations are typical. Monthly production and sales average 5,000 units, and monthly profits average £5,000.

Management wants to know the effect the following three mutually exclusive alternatives would have on monthly profits.

1. Increasing the monthly advertising budget by £4,000, which should result in a 1,000-unit increase in monthly sales.
2. Increasing the selling price by £3, which should result in a 2,000-unit decrease in monthly sales.
3. Decreasing the selling price by £2, which should result in a 2,000-unit increase in monthly sales. However, because of capacity constraints, the last 1,000 units would be produced during overtime with the direct labor costs increasing by £1 per unit.

It is possible to develop contribution income statements for each alternative and then determine the profit impact of the proposed change by comparing the new income with the current income. A more direct approach is to use differential analysis and focus on only those items that differ under each alternative.

Alternative 1:
Profit increase from increased sales
(1,000 additional unit sales × £10 UCM) £10,000
Profit decrease from increased advertising expenditures . . . . (4,000)
Increase in monthly profit . . . . £ 6,000

Alternative 2:
Profit decrease from reduced sales if there were no
changes in prices or costs
(2,000 lost unit sales × £10 UCM) . . . . £(20,000)
Profit increase from increased selling price
[(5,000 current unit sales − 2,000 lost unit sales)
× £3 increase in unit selling price] 9,000
Decrease in monthly profit . . . . £(11,000)

Alternative 3:
Profit increase from increased sales if there were no
changes in prices or costs
(2,000 increased unit sales × £10 UCM) £20,000
Profit decrease from reduced selling price of all units
[(5,000 current unit sales + 2,000 additional unit sales)
× £2 decrease in unit selling price] . . . . (14,000)
Profit decrease from increased direct labor costs of
the last 1,000 units
(1,000 units × £1 increase in unit labor costs) . . . . (1,000)
Increase in monthly profit . . . . £ 5,000

Alternative 2 is undesirable because it would result in a decrease in monthly profit. Because Alternative 1 results in a larger increase in monthly profit, it is preferred to Alternative 3.

SPECIAL ORDERS

Assume a Brazilian distributor offered to place a special, one-time order for 1,000 units at a reduced price of £12 per unit. The Brazilian distributor will contract for a common carrier to handle all packing and transportation. There are no other order-level costs. Mind Trek has sufficient production capacity to produce the additional units without reducing sales to the discount chain. Management desires to know the profit impact of accepting the order. The following analysis focuses on those costs and revenues that will differ if the order is accepted.

EXHIBIT 4-3

CONTRIBUTION INCOME STATEMENT

Mind Trek, Limited
Contribution Income Statement
For the Month of April 2004

Sales (5,000 units × £22)		£110,000
Less variable costs:		
Direct materials (5,000 units × £5)	£25,000	
Direct labor (5,000 units × £3)	15,000	
Manufacturing overhead (5,000 units × £2)	10,000	
Selling and administrative (5,000 units × £2)	10,000	(60,000)
Contribution margin		£ 50,000
Less fixed costs:		
Manufacturing overhead	£30,000	
Selling and administrative	15,000	(45,000)
Profit		£ 5,000

Increase in revenues (1,000 units × £12)		£12,000
Increase in costs:		
Direct materials (1,000 units × £5)	£5,000	
Direct labor (1,000 units × £3)	3,000	
Variable manufacturing overhead (1,000 units × £2)	2,000	(10,000)
Increase in profits		£ 2,000

Accepting the special order will result in a profit increase of £2,000.

If management were unaware of relevant cost concepts, it might be tempted to compare the special order price to average unit cost information developed from accounting reports. Based on Mind Trek's April 2004 contribution income statement in Exhibit 4–3, the average cost of all manufacturing, selling, and administrative expenses was £21 per unit.

Variable costs:	
Direct materials (5,000 units × £5)	£ 25,000
Direct labor (5,000 units × £3)	15,000
Manufacturing overhead (5,000 units × £2)	10,000
Selling and administrative (5,000 units × £2)	10,000
Fixed costs:	
Manufacturing overhead	30,000
Selling and administrative	15,000
Total costs	£105,000
Unit production and sales	÷ 5,000
Average unit cost	£ 21

Comparing the special order price of £12 per unit to the average unit cost of £21, management might conclude the order would result in a loss of £9 per unit.

It is apparent that the £21 figure encompasses variable costs of £12 per unit (including irrelevant selling and administrative costs of £2 per unit) and irrelevant fixed costs of £45,000 spread over 5,000 units. But remember, management may not have detailed cost information. To obtain appropriate information for decision-making purposes, management must ask its accounting staff for the specific information needed. Different configurations of cost information are provided for different purposes. In the absence of special instructions, the accounting staff might supply some average cost information.

Importance of Time Span. The special order is a one-time order for 1,000 units that will use current excess capacity. Because no special setups or equipment are required to produce the order, it is appropriate to consider only variable costs in computing the order's profitability.

But what if the Brazilian distributor wanted Mind Trek to sign a multiyear contract to provide 1,000 units per month at £12 each? Under these circumstances, management would be well advised to reject the contract because there is a high probability that cost increases would make the order unprofitable in later years. At the very least, management should insist that a cost escalation clause be added to the purchase agreement, specifying that the selling price would increase to cover any cost increases and detailing the cost computation.

Of more concern is the variable nature of all long-run costs. Given adequate time, management must replace fixed assets and may adjust both the number of machines as well as the size of machines used in the manufacturing process. Accordingly, *in the long run, all costs (including costs classified as fixed in a given period) are relevant.* To remain in business in the long run, Mind Trek must replace equipment, pay property taxes, pay administrative salaries, and so forth. Consequently, management should consider *all costs* (fixed and variable, manufacturing and nonmanufacturing) in evaluating a long-term contract.

Full costs include all costs, regardless of their behavior pattern or activity level. The average full cost per unit is sometimes used to approximate long-run variable costs. If accepting a long-term contract increases the monthly production and sales volume to 6,000 units, the average full cost per unit will be £19.5 (nineteen and one-half pounds).

Direct materials	£ 5.0
Direct labor	3.0
Variable manufacturing overhead	2.0
Variable selling and administrative	2.0
Fixed manufacturing overhead (£30,000/6,000 units)	5.0
Fixed selling and administrative (£15,000/6,000 units)	2.5
Average full cost per unit	£19.5

If the Brazilian distributor agrees to separately pay all variable selling and administrative expenses associated with the contract, the estimated long-run variable costs are £17.5 per unit (£19.5 − £2). Many managers would say this is the minimum acceptable selling price, especially if the order extends over a long period of time.

Relevance of Opportunity Costs. An **opportunity cost** is the net cash inflow that could be obtained if the resources committed to one action were used in the most desirable other alternative. Because Mind Trek has excess productive capacity, no opportunity cost is associated with accepting the Brazilian distributor's one-time order. There is no alternative use of the productive capacity in the short run, so there is no opportunity cost.

But what if Mind Trek were operating at capacity? In this case, accepting the special order would require reducing regular sales.[4] With an alternative use of the production capacity, an opportunity cost is associated with its use to fill the special order.

Each unit sold to the Brazilian distributor could otherwise generate a £10 contribution from regular customers. Accepting the special order would cause Mind Trek

---

[4]To simplify the illustration, assume overtime production is not possible.

to incur an opportunity cost of £10,000, the net benefit of the most desirable alternative action, selling to regular customers.

Lost sales to regular customers (units)	1,000
Regular unit contribution margin	× £10
Opportunity cost of accepting special order	£10,000

Because this opportunity cost exceeds the £2,000 contribution derived from the special order, management should reject the special order. Accepting the order will reduce profits by £8,000 (£2,000 contribution − £10,000 opportunity cost).

Qualitative Considerations. Although an analysis of cost and revenue information may indicate that a special order would be profitable in the short run, management might still reject the order because of qualitative considerations. Any concerns regarding the order's impact on regular customers might lead management to reject the order even if there is excess capacity. If the order involves a special low price, regular customers might demand a similar price reduction and threaten to take their business elsewhere. Alternatively, management might accept the special order while operating at capacity if they believed there were long-term benefits associated with penetrating a new market. Legal factors must also be considered if the special order is from a buyer who competes with regular customers. These legal factors are discussed in conjunction with the pricing decision in Chapter 9.

INTERNAL OR EXTERNAL ACQUISITION OF COMPONENTS OR SERVICES (OUTSOURCING)

Organizations often have external opportunities to acquire services or components of products they manufacture rather than providing the service or manufacturing the component internally. The external acquisition of services or components is called **outsourcing.** There are three major reasons for outsourcing: (1) to focus on the key aspects of the business by outsourcing noncore activities, (2) to improve the quality of support activities, and (3) to better control costs. The first two points are considered in What's Happening 4–1, which examines the benefits Med Resorts International obtained by outsourcing accounts receivable and collections. Addressing the third point, Kenneth D. Tuchman, CEO of TeleTech Holdings (which handles customer service calls for companies such at AT&T), notes that "we show companies how to turn fixed costs into variable costs."[5]

On college campuses, Marriott and ARA Food operate many university dining halls, and Barnes & Noble manages many university bookstores. Some organizations are even outsourcing employees. SCP Enterprises of Ann Arbor Michigan, for example, fired all 65 employees and had them rehired by a professional employer organization that is now responsible for handling all payroll and employee benefit issues and complying with employment laws. Edward Gudeman, president of National Human Resource Committee, Inc., a professional employer organization, observed that "employer regulations are becoming more complex and costly. It's our job to stay up with all that, and we do."[6]

Suppose a Canadian manufacturer offers a one-year contract to supply Mind Trek with an electronic component at a cost of £2 per unit. Mind Trek is now faced with the decision to continue to make the electronic component internally or to buy the component from the Canadian company. This is often called a *make or buy* decision. An analysis of the materials and operations required to manufacture the component

---

[5]John A. Byrne, "Has Outsourcing Gone Too Far?" *Business Week*, April 1, 1996, pp. 26–28.
[6]Rick Haglund (Newhouse News Service), "More Companies Are Farming Out Payrolls," *Huntsville Times*, January 4, 1997, pp. A21, A24.

THE SURPRISING BENEFITS OF OUTSOURCING

Med Resorts sells vacation programs in the leisure-time industry. Paralleling the growth in revenues, the Contract Services Department staff (responsible for billing, collecting, and maintaining accounts receivable records) had grown to 12 employees by the time Med Resorts made the decision to outsource this function. Outsourcing provided several expected benefits, including improved cash flows, reductions in the age of accounts receivable, and related cost reductions of $75,000 per year. Interestingly, Med Resorts reported a number of unexpected benefits.

- Management no longer had to worry that invoices were not sent out on time.
- Because of a higher capacity, the external service provider eliminated delays in processing transactions during peak periods. This improved cash flows and provided more accurate customer records.
- The vendor's state-of-the-art system and experienced staff was able to inexpensively develop specialized reports.
- Med Resorts no longer needed to invest in software and hardware for billing and collections, nor in related employee training.
- The improved performance of the accounts receivable portfolio and the investor contacts provided by the vendor enabled Med Resorts to obtain more favorable financing.
- Med Resorts reduced the "hassles" that occasionally arise when dissatisfied customers refuse to pay their bills.

Source: Kathleen A. Cormier, "Outsourcing Accounts Receivable and Other Serendipitus Benefits," *Management Accounting,* September 1996, pp. 16–18.

internally reveals that if Mind Trek accepts the offer, it will be able to reduce the following:

- Materials costs by 10 percent per unit.
- Direct labor and variable factory overhead costs by 20 percent per unit.
- Fixed manufacturing overhead by £20,000 per year.

A differential analysis of Mind Trek's make or buy decision is presented in Exhibit 4–4. Continuing to make the component has a net advantage of £10,000.

EXHIBIT 4-4

DIFFERENTIAL ANALYSIS OF MAKE OR BUY DECISION

	(1) Cost to Make	(2) Cost to Buy	(1) − (2) Difference (effect of buying on income)
Cost to buy (£2 × 60,000* units)		£120,000	£(120,000)
Cost to make:			
Direct materials (£5 × 0.10 × 60,000 units)	£ 30,000		30,000
Direct labor (£3 × 0.20 × 60,000 units)	36,000		36,000
Variable manufacturing overhead (£2 × 0.20 × 60,000 units)	24,000		24,000
Fixed manufacturing overhead	20,000		20,000
Total	£110,000	£120,000	£ (10,000)
Advantage of making	£10,000		

5,000 units per month × 12 months

135

But what if the space currently used to manufacture the electronic component can be rented to a third party for £40,000 per year? In this case, the production capacity has an alternative use, and the net cash flow from this alternative use is an opportunity cost of making the component. Treating the rent Mind Trek will not receive if it continues to make the component as an opportunity cost, the analysis in Exhibit 4–5 indicates that buying now has a net advantage of £30,000.

Even if outsourcing appears financially advantageous in the short run, management should not decide to outsource before considering a variety of qualitative factors. Is the outside supplier interested in developing a long-term relationship or merely attempting to use some temporarily idle capacity? If so, what will happen at the end of the contract period? What impact would a decision to outsource have on the morale of Mind Trek's employees? Will Mind Trek have to rehire laid-off employees after the contract expires? Will the outside supplier meet delivery schedules? Does the supplied part meet Mind Trek's quality standards? Will it continue to meet them? Organizations often manufacture products or provide services they can obtain elsewhere in order to control quality, to have an assured supply source, to avoid dealing with a potential competitor, or to maintain a core competency.

The movement toward outsourcing has grown to include many units of government, where elected officials have concluded that a profit motive in a competitive environment often leads to higher quality at lower costs. Consider the following examples:

- California Private Transportation Co. is building toll roads.
- BFI provides waste collection and disposal services for many communities.
- Rural/Metro is contracting to run fire departments and provide medical services.
- Corrections Corporation of America and Wackenhut build, finance, and operate jails.[7]

EXHIBIT 4-5

DIFFERENTIAL ANALYSIS OF MAKE OR BUY DECISION WITH OPPORTUNITY TO RENT FACILITIES

	(1) Cost to Make	(2) Cost to Buy	(1) – (2) Difference (effect of buying on income)
Cost to buy (£2 × 60,000* units)		£120,000	£(120,000)
Cost to make:			
Direct materials (£5 × 0.10 × 60,000 units)	£ 30,000		30,000
Direct labor (£3 × 0.20 × 60,000 units)	36,000		36,000
Variable manufacturing overhead (£2 × 0.20 × 60,000 units)	24,000		24,000
Fixed manufacturing overhead	20,000		20,000
Opportunity cost of lost rent income	40,000		40,000
Total	£150,000	£120,000	£ 30,000
Advantage of buying	£30,000		

*5,000 units per month × 12 months

[7]Gail DeGeorge and Julia Flynn, "Go Directly to Jail," *Business Week*, December 15, 1997, pp. 139–42.

According to Mark Liebner, chief financial officer of Rural/Metro, his company provides better service at a fraction of the cost of traditional government-run services by focusing on the bottom line. He cites Scottsdale, Arizona, where fire losses have declined 84 percent since 1985, as an example. Some politicians have even proposed that package carriers, such as Federal Express and United Parcel Service, should be allowed to compete with the U.S. Postal Service in delivering first-class mail. Experts have estimated that the increased competition would reduce the cost of first-class mail by 25 percent.[8]

SELL OR PROCESS FURTHER

When a product is salable at various stages of completion, management must determine the product's most advantageous selling point. As each stage is completed, management must determine whether to sell the product then or to process it further. We will consider two types of sell or process further decisions: (1) for a single product and (2) for joint products.

Single Product Decisions. Assume that Boston Rocking Company manufactures rocking chairs from precut and shaped wood. Although the chairs are salable once they are assembled, Boston Rocking sands and paints all chairs before they are sold. Management wishes to know if this is the optimal selling point.

A complete listing of unit costs and revenues for the alternative selling points is as follows:

	PER CHAIR		
	Sell after Assembly	Sell after Painting	Difference (effect of painting on income)
Selling price	$40	$75	$35
Assembly costs	(25)	(25)	
Sanding and painting costs		(12)	(12)
Contribution margin	$15	$38	$23
Advantage of painting		$23	

The sanding and painting operation has an additional contribution of $23 per unit. The chairs should be sold after they are painted.

Note that the assembly costs are the same under both alternatives. This illustrates that *all costs incurred prior to the decision point are irrelevant.* Given the existence of an assembled chair, the decision alternatives are to sell it now or to process it further. A differential analysis for the decision to sell or process further should include only revenues and the incremental costs of further processing.

Increase in revenues:		
Sell after painting	$75	
Sell after assembly	(40)	$35
Additional costs of sanding and painting		(12)
Advantage of sanding and painting		$23

The identical solution is obtained if the selling price without further processing is treated as an opportunity cost.

---

[8]Eric Schine, Richard S. Dunham, and Christopher Farrell, "America's New Watchword: If It Moves, Privatize It," *Business Week,* December 12, 1994, p. 39.

Revenues after painting		$75
Additional costs of sanding and painting	$12	
Opportunity cost of not selling after assembly	40	(52)
Advantage of sanding and painting		$23

By processing a chair further, Boston Rocking has forgone the opportunity to receive $40 from its sale. Since the chair is already made, this $40 is the net cash inflow from the most desirable alternative; it is the opportunity cost of painting.

Joint Product Decisions. Two or more products simultaneously produced by a single process from a common set of inputs are called **joint products.** Joint products are often found in basic industries that process natural raw materials such as dairy, chemical, meat, petroleum, and wood products. In the petroleum industry, crude oil is refined into fuel oil, gasoline, kerosene, lubricating oil, and other products.

The point in the process where the joint products become separately identifiable is called the **split-off point.** Materials and conversion costs incurred prior to the split-off point are called **joint costs.** For external reporting purposes, a number of techniques are used to allocate joint costs among joint products. We will not discuss these techniques here (interested students should consult a cost accounting textbook), except to note that none of the methods provide information useful for determining what to do with a joint product once it is produced. Because joint costs are incurred prior to the decision point, they are sunk costs. Consequently, *joint costs are irrelevant to a decision to sell a joint product or to process it further.* The only relevant factors are the alternative costs and revenues subsequent to the split-off point.

LEARNING OBJECTIVE 5

BEST USE OF LIMITED RESOURCES

No doubt, *you* have experienced time as a limiting or constraining resource. With two exams the day after tomorrow and a paper due next week, your problem is how to allocate limited study time. The solution depends on your objectives, your current status (grades, knowledge, skill levels, and so forth), and the available time. Given this information, you devise a work plan to best meet your objectives.

Managers must also decide how to best use limited resources to accomplish organizational goals. A supermarket may lose sales because limited shelf space prevents stocking all available brands of soft drinks. A manufacturer may lose sales because limited machine hours or labor hours prevent filling all orders. Managers of for-profit organizations will likely find the problems of capacity constraints less troublesome than the problems of excess capacity; nonetheless, these problems are real. What's Happening 4–2 is an illustration of the efforts organizations will make to overcome production delays or to provide additional capacity as quickly as possible.

If the limited resource is not a core business activity, such as manufacturing computer chips at Intel, it may be appropriate to acquire additional units of the limited resource externally. For example, many organizations have a small legal staff to handle routine activities; if the internal staff becomes fully committed, the organization seeks outside legal counsel. The external acquisition of such resources was discussed previously.

The long-run solution to the problem of limited resources to perform core activities may be to expand capacity. However, this is usually not feasible in the short run. Economic models suggest that another solution is to reduce demand by increasing the price. Again, this may not be desirable. The supermarket, for example, may want to maintain competitive prices. The manufacturer might want to maintain a long-run price to retain customer goodwill, to avoid attracting competitors, or to prevent accusations of "price gouging."

FROM GUNS TO DIESELS TO PEPSI: RUSSIAN-BUILT MILITARY AIRCRAFT BECOMES A CAPITALIST TOOL

The Russian Antonov 124, built to move military cargo, burns 3.3 tons of fuel to taxi on a runway. Some of its engines need replacement after 1,000 hours (as opposed to the 8,000 to 10,000 hours before maintenance is required on a jet engine manufactured in the West). It has a crew of 19 so emergency repairs can be made promptly. It can be rented for approximately $11,000 per flying hour. Compared to a Boeing 747-400 cargo jet, this plane is a gas-guzzling clunker. Yet this relic of the Cold War is an important tool of capitalists trying to compete on the basis of time.

The secret to the Antonov's success is not high technology. It is massive capacity and raw power. At 330,639 pounds, its maximum payload is almost 70,000 pounds more than a Lockheed C-5B. Plus, with a cargo tunnel 14 feet high, 20 feet wide, and 134 feet long, the Antonov can handle cargo that won't fit into a Boeing 747-400.

When production delays jeopardized General Motors Corporation's sale of locomotives to an Irish railroad, an Antonov carried a 240,000-pound locomotive across the Atlantic. When Pepsi wanted to get an Italian-manufactured bottling line to Mexico as soon as possible, Pepsi's management called upon an Antonov. This allowed a new 1,200-cans-a-minute line to begin operations one month sooner than would have been possible if the next feasible method of transportation, a cargo ship, were used.

Source: Douglas Lavin, "The Mighty Antonov Is the Only Way to Fly Your Locomotive," *The Wall Street Journal,* December 29, 1994, pp. 1, 4.

SINGLE CONSTRAINT

The allocation of limited resources should be made only after a careful consideration of many qualitative factors. The following rule provides a useful starting point in making short-run decisions of how to best use limited resources: *To achieve short-run profit maximization, a for-profit organization should allocate limited resources in a manner that maximizes the contribution per unit of the limited resource.* The application of this rule is illustrated in the following example.

Delta Manufacturing Company produces three products: A, B, and C. A limitation of 120 machine hours per week for machine Z1 prevents Delta from meeting the sales demand for these products. Product information is as follows:

	A	B	C
Unit selling price	$100	$80	$50
Unit variable costs	(90)	(50)	(25)
Unit contribution margin	$ 10	$30	$25
Machine hours per unit	2	2	1

Product A has the highest selling price and Product B has the highest unit contribution margin. Product C is shown here to have the highest contribution per Z1 machine hour.

	A	B	C
Unit contribution margin	$10	$30	$25
Machine hours per unit	÷ 2	÷ 2	÷ 1
Contribution per machine hour	$ 5	$15	$25

Following the rule of maximizing the contribution per unit of a constraining factor, Delta should use its limited machine hours to produce Product C. As shown in the following analysis, any other plan would result in lower profits:

	A	B	C
	Highest Selling Price	**Highest Contribution per Unit**	**Highest Contribution per Unit of Constraining Factor**
Machine hours available	120	120	120
Machine hours per unit	÷ 2	÷ 2	÷ 1
Weekly production in units	60	60	120
Unit contribution margin	× $10	× $30	× $25
Total weekly contribution margin	$600	$1,800	$3,000

Despite this analysis, management may decide to produce some units of A or B or both to satisfy the requests of some "good" customers or to offer a full product line. However, such decisions sacrifice short-run profits. Each machine hour used to produce A or B has an opportunity cost of $25, the net cash flow from using that hour to produce a unit of C, the most desirable alternative. Producing all A, for example, results in an opportunity cost of $3,000 (120 units of C × $25). The net disadvantage of producing all A is $2,400:

Contribution from A	$ 600
Opportunity cost of not producing C	(3,000)
Net disadvantage of producing A	$(2,400)

The opportunity cost of producing all C is $1,800. This is the net cash flow from the most desirable other alternative, producing B. However, when compared to producing B, producing C has a net advantage of $1,200:

Contribution from C	$ 3,000
Opportunity cost of not producing B	(1,800)
Net advantage of producing C	$ 1,200

When there is a single constraint, it is very often related to time. However, as noted in Research Shows 4–1, space is often the single most important constraint in the retail industry.

4–1   RESEARCH SHOWS

FOR COOL PROFITS, STOCK MORE ICE CREAM

Food stores have traditionally determined the gross profit (selling price less cost of goods sold) of individual products. With limited space, they often determine each product's gross profit per square foot of aisle-facing shelf space per store per week. While a useful guide, such an analysis is incomplete in that it fails to consider operating costs, such as unloading, storing, refrigeration, and so forth.

Activity-based costing has, for the first time, provided retail management a tool to accurately determine the contribution margin of individual products and to evaluate the contribution margin per square foot of facing, per store per week. Using this new technique, a recent study of frozen foods at more than 250 grocery stores found that the overall contribution margin was $1.67 per square foot of facing per week. The contribution margins ranged from a low of $1.23 for dry goods to $2.19 for refrigerated foods and $2.32 for frozen foods. The most profitable product was ice cream, which yielded a cool contribution of $5.85 per square foot per week. With space as the constraining resource, the study concluded that ice cream is "underspaced."

Source: Warren Thayer, "ABCs of Ice Cream Profitability," *Frozen Food Age*, March 1997, pp. 7–10.

MULTIPLE CONSTRAINTS

Now assume the weekly demand for C is only 80 units although the company is capable of producing 120 units of C each week. In this case, the production capacity of machine Z1 should first be used to satisfy the demand for Product C, with any remaining capacity going to produce Product B, which has the next highest contribution per unit of constraining factor. This allocation will provide a total weekly contribution of $2,600.

Available hours	120
Required for C (80 units × 1 machine hour)	(80)
Hours available for B	40
Machine hours per unit	÷ 2
Production of B in units	20
Unit contribution margin of B	× $30
Contribution from B	$ 600
Contribution from C ($25 per unit × 80 units)	2,000
Total weekly contribution margin	$2,600

When an organization has alternative uses for several limited resources, the optimal use of those resources cannot be determined using the rule for short-run profit maximization. In these situations, techniques such as linear programming (see Appendix A to this chapter) may be used to assist in determining the optimal mix of products or services.

Our discussion was also based on the assumption that all costs are classified as fixed or variable. When there are batch- and product-level costs, the optimal allocation of one or more limited resources must be determined using integer programming, as illustrated in Appendix B to this chapter.

THEORY OF CONSTRAINTS

Recognizing the importance of managing constraints, Dr. Eliyah Goldratt developed what he refers to as the "theory of constraints." The **theory of constraints** states that every process has a bottleneck (constraining resource) and that production cannot take place faster than it is processed through that bottleneck. The goal of the theory of constraints is to maximize **throughput** (defined as sales revenue minus direct materials costs) in a constrained environment.[9] The theory has several implications for management.

- Management should identify the bottleneck. This is often difficult when several different products are produced in a facility containing many different production activities. One approach is to walk around and observe where inventory is building up in front of work stations. The bottleneck will likely have the largest piles of work that have been waiting for the longest time.
- Management should schedule production to maximize the efficient use of the bottleneck resource. Efficiently using the bottleneck resource might necessitate inspecting all units before they reach the bottleneck rather than after the units are completed. The bottleneck resource is too valuable to waste on units that may already be defective.
- Management should schedule production to avoid a buildup of inventory. Reducing inventory lowers the cost of inventory investments and the cost of carrying inventory. It also assists in improving quality by making it easier to identify quality problems that might otherwise be hidden in large piles of inventory. Reducing

[9]*The Goal,* by Eliyah M. Goldratt and Jeff Cox, presents the concepts underlying the theory of constraints in the form of a novel. (See the suggested readings.) Goldratt has developed a scheduling system, called Optimum Production Technology, to schedule production in a manner that maximizes throughput in organizations that have internal bottlenecks.

inventory will require a change in the attitude of managers who like to see machines and people constantly working. To avoid a buildup of inventory in front of the bottleneck, it may be necessary for people and equipment to remain idle until the bottleneck resource calls for additional input.

- Management should work to eliminate the bottleneck, perhaps by increasing the capacity of the bottleneck resource, redesigning products so they can be produced with less use of the bottleneck resource, rescheduling production procedures to substitute nonbottleneck resources, or outsourcing work performed by bottleneck resources.

The theory of constraints has implications for management accounting performance reports. Keeping people and equipment working on production full-time is often a goal of management. To support this goal, management accounting performance reports have traditionally highlighted underutilization as an unfavorable variance.[10] This has encouraged managers to have people and equipment producing inventory, even if the inventory is not needed or cannot be further processed because of bottlenecks. The theory of constraints suggests that it is better to have nonbottleneck resources idle than it is to have them fully utilized. To support the theory of constraints, performance reports should:

- Measure the utilization of bottleneck resources
- Measure factory throughput
- Not encourage the full utilization of nonbottleneck resources
- Discourage the buildup of excess inventory

While the theory of constraints is *similar* to our general rule for how to best use limited resources, it emphasizes throughput (selling price minus direct materials) rather than contribution (selling price minus variable costs) in allocating the limited resource. The exclusion of direct labor and variable manufacturing overhead yields larger unit contribution margins, and it may affect resource allocations based on throughput rankings. The result will likely be a reduction in profits from those that could be achieved using our general rule for how to allocate limited resources.

It is easy to develop a textbook example demonstrating the weaknesses of this incomplete measure of contribution, and it is easy to envision situations in which the theory of constraints will produce a significant improvement in performance, even if optimal performance is not attained. Consider a situation in which management is finding it difficult to meet sales orders and the only cost information available is that used for financial reporting. Management needs a place to start in its efforts to control operations in a manner that will enhance profits. The determination of direct materials costs is relatively easy. Under these circumstances, a simple and incomplete measurement of the unit contribution margin (computed as selling price less direct materials) may be a useful and pragmatic starting point in managing production constraints. What's Happening 4–3 illustrates how a small business utilized the theory of constraints to improve profit planning.

Summary

A number of decision-making situations were presented in this chapter, including whether to accept or reject a special order, to make or buy a product or service, to sell a product or to process it further, and how to best use limited resources. When evaluating alternative actions such as these, managers should focus on the decision at hand. They should evaluate only those costs and revenues that differ under each alternative.

---

[10]This issue is examined in Chapter 12, Appendix B.

THEORY OF CONSTRAINTS HELPS SMALL BUSINESS CATCH PROFITS

Daufel Enterprises is a small business that produces high-quality, hand-tied fishing flies from feathers, fur, and synthetics placed on a hook and seamed with thread. By its very nature, producing hand-tied fishing flies is labor intensive, and recruiting qualified personnel is difficult. Because of product quality and the popularity of fly-fishing, Daufel was operating at capacity, and management was wrestling with tough decisions regarding the use of limited resources.

In the past, Daufel charged the same price, $12.00 per dozen, for all five of its flies: Hare's Ear, Pheasant Tail, Compara Dun, Thorax Dun, and Woolly Bugger. A detailed analysis revealed differences in materials costs, ranging from $1.95 for a dozen Compara Duns to $3.09 for a dozen Thorax Duns. With labor time as the limiting factor, management determined the time required to produce a dozen of each type of fly and computed the throughput per labor hour.

The results revealed a surprisingly wide variation in throughput, with the throughput of Pheasant Tail $29.30 per labor hour and of Thorax Duns $14.85 per hour. Although management decided to keep all five products for the benefit of having a complete product line, they used the throughput cost analysis to (1) shift some production toward more profitable products and (2) increase prices on less profitable products. Within market-pricing constraints, Daufel's strategy is to increase prices on selected products so that the throughput per labor hour on all products is close to $29.30.

Source: J. Gregory Bushong, John C. Talbot, and John F. Burke, "An Application of the Theory of Constraints," *The CPA Journal*, April 1999, p. 53.

Relevant costs include all future costs that differ under each alternative, sometimes including an opportunity cost. An outlay cost requires a future expenditure. When resources are limited, the initiation of one action requires management to forgo competing alternative actions. The net cash inflow from the most desirable other alternative is the opportunity cost of the action selected.

Irrelevant costs, which include sunk costs and certain other outlay costs, do not differ among competing alternatives. Sunk costs are historical costs resulting from past decisions. There is nothing management can do to change the total amount of these costs. All outlay costs are relevant to *some* decisions, such as the decision to continue or discontinue operations, but not all outlay costs are relevant to *all* decisions. Outlay costs that do not differ under decision alternatives are not relevant to that decision. A summary classification of relevant and irrelevant costs is presented in Exhibit 4–6.

Although this chapter has focused on profit maximization, decisions should not be based solely on this basis, especially in the short run. The long-run profit, legal, ethical, and social implications of decisions must always be recognized.

EXHIBIT 4–6

SUMMARY CLASSIFICATION OF RELEVANT AND IRRELEVANT COSTS

RELEVANT COSTS		IRRELEVANT COSTS	
Future costs that differ among competing alternatives		Costs that do not differ among competing alternatives	
Opportunity Costs	**Outlay Costs**	**Costs**	**Sunk Costs**
Net cash flow from the best alternative	Future costs requiring future expenditures that differ	Future costs requiring future expenditures that do not differ	A historical cost resulting from a past decision

Appendix A

Relevant Cost Information for Quantitative Models such as Linear Programming

A **model** is a simplified representation of some real-world phenomenon. Models are used to learn about related phenomenon and to quickly and inexpensively determine the effect of some proposed action. Museums contain educational models of buildings, spaceships, prehistoric animals, and ecosystems. Airframe manufacturers study the aerodynamics of model planes in wind tunnels. Airplane pilots learn how to control their craft using flight simulators. These are all examples of **physical models,** scaled-down versions or replicas of physical reality.

Managers and other decision makers also use **quantitative models** that are simply sets of mathematical relationships. These models can be further classified into **descriptive models** that merely specify the relationships between a series of independent and dependent variables, and **optimizing models** that suggest a specific choice between decision alternatives. Cost-volume-profit relationships, contribution income statements, and operating budgets are all descriptive models. CVP models do not suggest an optimal action, but they help managers understand how profits respond to changes in volume, selling price, or costs.

The purpose of this appendix is to discuss the proper use of accounting data in linear programming, a widely used optimizing model. While linear programming is not an accounting model per se, accounting data are frequently used in linear programming. Consequently, the accuracy and relevance of accounting data are critical to the proper use of linear programming models.

Quantitative Models as Decision Aids

Quantitative models, especially optimizing models, are often criticized as being overly simplistic, unrealistic, and prone to "make" incorrect decisions. It is true that models are a simplified representation of reality, but this is also one of their strengths. The use of a model helps decision makers focus on the few variables that are most critical to a decision. Furthermore, the assumptions that underlie a model can be specified and evaluated.

All quantitative models, descriptive and optimizing, *assist* in decision making. People cannot relinquish their decision-making responsibility to models that are merely intended to be decision support systems. In the final analysis, *people, not models, make decisions.* Managers must carefully evaluate the data used in the model, the assumptions underlying the model, and the output of the model. If everything appears satisfactory, a manager may decide to implement the action suggested by an optimizing model. If the responsible person suspects faulty data, an erroneous assumption, or changed circumstances that invalidate the model, the suggested action should not be implemented. Instead, the manager should undertake further analysis or make a decision based on professional judgment.

Linear Programming

Linear programming is an optimizing model used to assist managers in making decisions under constrained conditions when linear relationships exist among all variables. The constraints can represent limited resources (such as labor hours, machine hours, raw materials, or financial resources), limited consumer demand, or required physical characteristics of the final product (such as a minimum percentage of protein or a maximum percentage of fat).

Linear programming may be applied to a variety of business decisions, including product mix, raw materials mix, production scheduling, transportation scheduling, and cash management. The objective in linear programming is to determine the action that will maximize profits or minimize costs.

Although the concepts underlying linear programming are straightforward, solving linear programming problems can be tedious. Fortunately, with the availability of computers and modeling software, a manager need not be concerned about the details of the solution technique. The manager should, of course, have a general understanding of how the solution is determined (the model's assumptions) and be able to evaluate both the data used and the suggested solution.

Assumptions and Uses of Accounting Data. As its name implies, the most critical linear programming assumption is that linear relationships exist among all variables. This is possible only when costs are analyzed using a unit cost approach in which, from the viewpoint of individual units of product, all costs are classified as variable or fixed. (This restriction is relaxed in Appendix B, where integer programming is introduced.) The total contribution from the sale of Products X and Y, for example, must be of the form $aX + bY$, where a is the unit contribution of Product X and b is the unit contribution of Product Y. Curvilinear relationships are not allowed.

Another assumption of linear programming is that fractional solutions are permitted. (Again, this restriction is relaxed somewhat with the material in Appendix B.) The suggested solution to a linear programming problem might, for example, specify the production and sale of 25.2 units of X and 32.7 units of Y. When these assumptions are not valid, the manager might elect to use other models. Alternatively, if it seems appropriate, the manager might use professional judgment to adjust the suggested linear programming solution. The production of X and Y might be rounded *down* to 25 and 32 units. In linear programming, resource constraints prevent upward rounding. Hence, while 32.7 would normally be rounded up to 33, in linear programming, we can round down only to 32.

Every linear programming model includes an **objective function,** or goal to be maximized or minimized. Accounting data are often used in the objective function. For now, we assume that all costs are either variable at the unit level or fixed at the facility level. In Appendix B, we will subsequently consider how to incorporate an activity cost hierarchy into linear programming models.

With only unit-level cost drivers, *if the objective is to maximize profits, the coefficients of the variables in the objective function should be unit contribution margins.* If the objective is to minimize costs, the coefficients should be unit variable costs. The total contribution margin or variable costs of each product will vary in proportion to changes in volume. Profit and cost measures that include an allocation of fixed costs do not vary in direct proportion to changes in production and should not be used in the objective function.

Graphic Analysis of Product Mix Decisions. We use graphic analysis to illustrate the solution of linear programming problems. Although graphic analysis can be used only to solve problems containing two variables, it provides the general understanding necessary to evaluate more complex problems containing three or more variables. The following steps are involved in graphic analysis:

1. *Develop an equation for the objective function*, indicating how each variable affects the profit maximization or cost minimization goal.
2. *Develop an equation for each constraint*, indicating how each variable affects the total use of the constraint.
3. *Graph the constraints.*
4. *Identify the feasible solutions* that are bounded by the constraints.
5. *Determine the optimal solution* that maximizes or minimizes the value of the objective function.

Assume the Martin Company produces two products, A and B, in two departments, Assembly and Finishing. Product A has a unit contribution margin of $50, and

Product B has a unit contribution margin of $40. There are no batch- or product-level costs. Facility-level costs are $400 per week. The demand for each product exceeds Martin's capacity to produce. Production information is as follows:

	LABOR HOURS PER UNIT		Total Labor Hours Available per Week
	A	B	
Assembly Department	20	20	600
Finishing Department	20	10	400

Martin can obtain raw materials sufficient to produce only 25 units of B each week. Management desires the product mix that will maximize the weekly contribution of Products A and B toward fixed costs and profits. Using the five steps in graphic analysis, the problem is solved as follows:

1. *Objective function.* The objective is to maximize the total weekly contribution of Products A and B. Given information on the unit contribution margin, Martin's objective function is as follows:

$$\text{Maximize } \$50A + \$40B$$

2. *Constraints.* There are constraints for maximum assembly hours, maximum finishing hours, and maximum production of Product B. Because each constraint indicates an upper limit on the use of some resource, the less than or equal to symbol is used in each:

$$20A + 20B \leq 600 \text{ Assembly hours}$$
$$20A + 10B \leq 400 \text{ Finishing hours}$$
$$B \leq 25 \text{ units}$$

The assembly hours constraint indicates that any combination of A and B can be produced, providing it does not require more than 600 assembly hours. The finishing hours constraint indicates that any combination of A and B can be produced, providing it does not require more than 400 finishing hours. Finally, because of raw materials limitations, no more than 25 units of B can be produced.

To be technically precise, two more constraints are added to indicate that negative production is prohibited:

$$A \geq 0$$
$$B \geq 0$$

Hence, the production of A and the production of B must be greater than or equal to zero.

3. *Graph.* One axis must be designated to represent each variable. In Exhibit 4–7, the horizontal axis represents production and sales of Product A, and the vertical axis represents production and sales of Product B. (The products could also have been reversed on the axis.)

The set of all feasible A and B production values is determined by solving each constraint for its maximum A and B values (assuming all production was devoted to that product) and drawing lines on graph paper connecting the maximum value of each product for each constraint. We compute the maximum values of A and B as the maximum amount of each constraint divided by the units of the constraint required to produce a unit of A or a unit of B:

	MAXIMUM VALUES	
	Product A	Product B
Assembly hours	600 ÷ 20 = 30	600 ÷ 20 = 30
Finishing hours	400 ÷ 20 = 20	400 ÷ 10 = 40
Raw materials		25

EXHIBIT 4-7

GRAPHIC APPROACH TO LINEAR PROGRAMMING

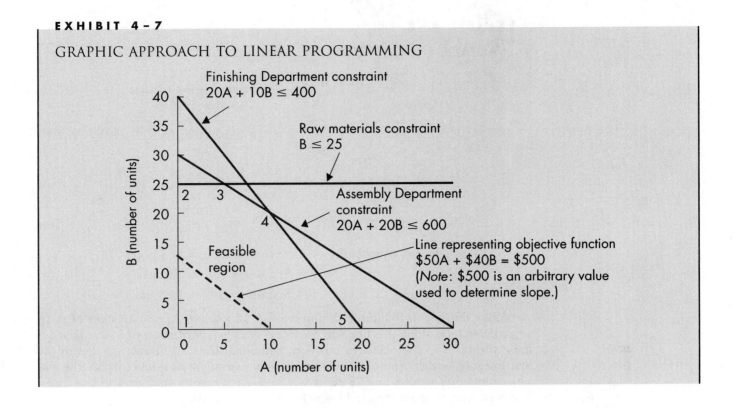

The lines connecting these maximum values are illustrated in Exhibit 4–7. Because the raw materials constraint affects only Product B, it does not intersect the horizontal axis for Product A. Instead, it is drawn parallel to the horizontal axis. The horizontal and vertical axes represent the nonnegativity constraints.

4. *Feasible solutions.* The feasible solutions (possible production volumes and mixes) are within the area between the vertical and horizontal axes and the first set of enclosing lines. In Exhibit 4–7, this is the area enclosed by the solid lines from the points identified as 1, 2, 3, 4, and 5. The firm can produce any of the feasible solutions; however, it is likely that one product mix will provide a higher total contribution than any other mix.

5. *Optimal solution.* In linear programming, the **optimal solution** is the feasible solution that maximizes or minimizes the value of the objective function, depending on management's goal. An important characteristic of linear programming is that if there is a single optimal solution, it is found at a corner point where the lines representing two or more constraints intersect. Knowing this, it is necessary to evaluate only the solutions represented by corner points. In Exhibit 4–7, the five corner points are numbered 1 through 5. The value of the objective function at each corner point is computed in Exhibit 4–8. The maximum optimal solution (represented by corner 4) calls for a solution that will provide a weekly contribution of $1,300. Fixed costs would, of course, be deducted from the contribution to determine profit. With a weekly contribution of $1,300 and fixed costs of $400 per week, the weekly profit is $900 ($1,300 − $400).

The Corner Solution. The reason that the optimal solution is always found at a corner point can be illustrated by drawing a line representing some arbitrary value for the objective function. In the Martin Company case, the end points for an objective function with an arbitrarily selected value of $500 are 10 units of Product A and 12.5 units of Product B. In general, the following equation applies.

EXHIBIT 4-8

EVALUATION OF ALTERNATIVE CORNER SOLUTIONS

	VALUE OF		Value of Objective Function
Corner	A	B	$50A + $40B =
1	0	0	$ 0
2	0	25	1,000
3	5	25	1,250
4	10*	20*	1,300*
5	20	0	1,000

Desired contribution ÷ Unit contribution = End point

For A: $500 ÷ $50 = 10 units

For B: $500 ÷ $40 = 12.5 units

Along this line in Exhibit 4–7, observe that 10 units of A, or 12.5 units of B, or any combination along this line will provide a weekly contribution of $500. To maximize the value of the objective function, additional lines are drawn parallel to the first line, but farther from the origin, until only one point on a line touches the feasible solution. This one unique point will be a corner point (corner 4 in this case). You may wish to draw these additional lines as an exercise.

Solving with Three or More Variables. Although it is possible to solve two-variable problems with the aid of graphic analysis, linear programming problems containing three or more variables must be solved by a mathematical solution technique known as the **simplex method.** The mechanics of the simplex method are far from simple, even though the method arrives at a solution by comparing objective function values at multidimensional corner points (just as was done earlier with the graphic approach). To solve the Martin Company's product mix problem, the same set of equations would be used as in the previous illustration. Software packages are available to solve linear programming problems on most computers.

Appendix B

INCORPORATING AN ACTIVITY-COST HIERARCHY WITH THE USE OF INTEGER PROGRAMMING

Two major limitations of linear programming (as noted before) include these:

1. The possibility of fractional solutions, and
2. The assumption that linear relationships exist among all variables.

A variation of linear programming that determines the solution in whole numbers, **integer programming**, overcomes both of these problems. Using integer programming, we can require that the consumption of resources and the final solution be in whole numbers. With a bit of creativity in the development of the objective function and the related constraints, integer programming will also accommodate an activity-cost hierarchy.

Assume the following detailed information is available regarding Products A and B of Martin Company (as introduced in Appendix A):

	Product A	Product B
Unit selling price	$130	$ 80
Unit-level costs	(40)	(20)
Unit-level contribution	$ 90	$ 60
Batch-level costs (per batch)	$100	$100
Maximum batch size (units)	10	10
Product-level costs	$300	$200
Facility-level costs		$400

The batch-level costs are incurred for each batch of product, and the product-level costs are incurred if there is any production and sale of a product. In Appendix A, these costs were assigned to specific products and averaged in with unit-level costs in determining variable costs. An integer programming objective function and the constraints to determine the optimal solution are presented.[11] The variables and constraints are explained here.

The objective function follows:

Maximize $+90A +60B -100BA -100BB - 300PA - 200PB$

Constraints:

(1)	$+20A +20B$			≤ 600 assembly hrs.
(2)	$+20A +10B$			≤ 400 finishing hrs.
(3)	$+ 1B$			≤ 25 units
(4)	$+ 1A$	$- 10BA$		≤ 0 for A batches
(5)	$+ 1B$	$- 10BB$		≤ 0 for B batches
(6)	$+ 1A$		$- 1{,}000PA$	≤ 0 for A product
(7)	$+ 1B$		$-1{,}000PB$	≤ 0 for B product

To be technically precise, additional constraints specifying that A through PB are greater than or equal to zero should be included.

Where

A = Number of units of A

B = Number of units of B

BA = Number of batches of A

BB = Number of batches of B

PA = 1 if A is produced, 0 otherwise

PB = 1 if B is produced, 0 otherwise

Constraints (1), (2), and (3) are the same as in Appendix A. Note that the unit-level contributions are used as coefficients of A and B in the objective function. These are the only positive coefficients. Because they reduce profitability, the coefficients of the batch- and product-level costs are negative. Again, because facility-level costs do not vary, they are excluded from the model and must be subtracted from the value of the objective function to determine profits.

Constraints (4) and (5) and variables BA and BB are for the batch-level costs. Because of the minus signs, the model minimizes the absolute integer values of BA and BB. The objective function coefficients of BA and BB are the setup costs of $100 per batch. The constraint coefficients of BA and BB are based on the maximum number of units in a batch. For example, with no production of A, the left side of (4) is zero

---

[11]Robert Kee, "Integrating Activity-Based Costing with the Theory of Constraints to Enhance Production Related Decision Making," *Accounting Horizons*, December 1995, pp. 48–61. We believe the solution approach presented here is the first demonstration of the applicability of linear or integer programming to a constrained situation involving an activity-cost hierarchy.

and BA is zero. Production of A can vary from one to ten with BA having a value of 1. Eleven to twenty units of A require BA to equal 2, and so forth.

Constraints (6) and (7), along with variables PA and PB, are for the product-level costs. Again, because of the minus signs, the model will minimize the absolute integer values of PA and PB. Because we want the values of PA and PB to be either 0, if the related product is not produced or 1 if the related product is produced, care must be taken in developing constraints (6) and (7) to prevent these variables from taking a higher value. One approach is to select coefficients that, because of other constraints, are known to exceed the possible values of A and B. For example, constraint (1) limits production to a maximum of 30 units of A or B (600 available assembly hours ÷ 20 hours required per unit of either product). Hence, while an arbitrary value of 1,000 was used for PA and PB in (6) and (7), any value larger than 30 could have been used. In constraint (6), production of A can vary from one to 1,000 with PA having a value of 1.

Using integer programming,[12] the results are as follows:

Value of objective function	1,300
Optimal solution:	
A	10
B	20
BA	1
BB	2
PA	1
PB	1

Based on this information, the weekly profit is $900, computed as the product-level contribution ($1,300) minus the facility-level costs ($400).

A multi-product, multiple-level contribution income statement reflecting this information is presented in Exhibit 4–9. It is similar to the multi-level contribution income

EXHIBIT 4–9

MULTI-PRODUCT, MULTI-LEVEL CONTRIBUTION INCOME STATEMENT

Martin Company
Multi-Product, Multi-Level Contribution Income Statement
For a Typical Week Based on the Integer-Programming Optimal Solution

	Product A	Product B	Total
Sales:			
($130 × 10 units)	$1,300		
($80 × 20 units)		$1,600	$2,900
Less unit level costs:			
($40 × 10)	(400)		
($20 × 20)		(400)	(800)
Unit level contribution margin	$ 900	$1,200	$2,100
Batch level costs:			
($100 × 1)	(100)		
($100 × 2)		(200)	(300)
Batch level contribution	$ 800	$1,000	$1,800
Less product level costs	(300)	(200)	(500)
Product level contribution	$ 500	$ 800	$1,300
Less facility level costs			(400)
Profit			$ 900

---

[12]Emmonds Hamilton, A. Dale Flowers, Chandrashekhar M. Khot, and Kamlesh Mathur, *Storm: Personal Version 3.0* (Englewood Cliffs, New Jersey: Prentice Hall, 1992), pp. 78–95.

statement in Exhibit 3–7 except for the detailed information pertaining to Products A and B. Note that the information for individual products concludes at the product-level contribution. The total product-level contribution from each product covers the common facility-level costs and provides for any profit.

Review Problem

The solution to the review problem is found on pages 169–170. To maximize your learning, you should make a serious attempt to develop a written solution to the review problem before looking at the solution. If there are errors in your solution, you should then attempt to determine their causes.

Applications of Differential Analysis

Final Copy Company produces color cartridges for inkjet printers. The cartridges are sold to mail-order distributors for $4.80 each. Manufacturing and other costs are as follows:

Variable Costs per Unit		Fixed Costs per Month	
Direct materials	$2.00	Factory overhead	$15,000
Direct labor	0.20	Selling and administrative	5,000
Factory overhead	0.25	Total	$20,000
Distribution	0.05		
Total	$2.50		

The variable distribution costs are for transportation to mail-order distributors. The current monthly production and sales volume is 15,000. Monthly capacity is 20,000 units.

Required:
Determine the effect of the following independent situations on monthly profits.

a. A $1.50 increase in the unit selling price should result in an 1,800 unit decrease in monthly sales.
b. A $1.80 decrease in the unit selling price should result in a 6,000 unit increase in monthly sales. However, because of capacity constraints, the last 1,000 units would be produced during overtime, when the direct labor costs increase by 50 percent.
c. A New Zealand distributor has proposed to place a special, one-time order for 4,000 units next month at a reduced price of $4.00 per unit. The distributor would pay all transportation costs. There would be additional fixed selling and administrative costs of $500.00
d. An Australian distributor has proposed to place a special, one-time order for 8,000 units at a special price of $4.00 per unit. The distributor would pay all transportation costs. There would be additional fixed selling and administrative costs of $500.00 Assume overtime production is not possible.
e. A Mexican manufacturer has offered a one-year contract to supply ink for the cartridges at a cost of $1.00 per unit. If Final Copy accepts the offer, it will be able to reduce variable manufacturing costs by 40 percent and rent some currently used space for $1,000.00 per month.
f. The cartridges are currently unpackaged; that is, they are sold in bulk. Individual packaging would increase costs by $0.10 per unit. However, the units could then be sold for $5.05.

Key Terms

Conversion costs (p. 124)
Cost prediction error (p. 130)
Cost reduction proposal (p. 125)
Differential cost analysis (p. 128)
Full costs (p. 133)
Irrelevant costs (p. 123)
Joint costs (p. 138)
Joint products (p. 138)
Opportunity cost (p. 133)

Outlay costs (p. 125)
Outsourcing (p. 134)
Relevant costs (p. 123)
Revenues (p. 125)
Split-off point (p. 138)
Sunk costs (p. 127)
Theory of constraints (p. 141)
Throughput (p. 141)

Appendix Key Terms:

Descriptive model (p. 144)
Integer programming (p. 148)
Linear programming (p. 144)
Model (p. 144)
Objective function (p. 145)

Optimal solution (p. 147)
Optimizing model (p. 144)
Physical model (p. 144)
Quantitative model (p. 144)
Simplex method (p. 148)

Review Questions

1. Distinguish between relevant and irrelevant costs.
2. In evaluating a cost reduction proposal, what three alternatives are available to management?
3. When are outlay costs relevant and when are they irrelevant?
4. When are product-level activity costs relevant and when are they irrelevant?
5. Why is a differential analysis of relevant items preferred to a detailed listing of all costs and revenues associated with each alternative?
6. How can cost predictions be made when the acquisition of new equipment results in a technological change?
7. When are opportunity costs relevant to the evaluation of a special order?
8. Identify some important qualitative considerations in evaluating a decision to make or buy a part.
9. In a decision to sell or to process further, of what relevance are costs incurred prior to the decision point? Explain your answer.
10. How should limited resources be used to achieve short-run profit maximization?
11. What should performance reports do in support of the theory of constraints?

Exercises

4–1
Relevant Cost
Terms: Matching

A company that produces three products, M, N, and O, is evaluating a proposal that will result in doubling the production of N and discontinuing the production of O. The facilities currently used to produce O will be devoted to the production of N. Furthermore, additional machinery will be acquired to produce N. The production of M will not be affected. All products have a positive contribution margin.

Required:
Presented are a number of phrases related to the proposal. For each phrase, select the most appropriate cost term. Each term is used only once.

Phrases
1. Increased revenues from the sale of N
2. Increased variable costs of N
3. Property taxes on the new machinery
4. Revenues from the sale of M
5. Cost of the equipment used to produce O
6. Contribution margin of O
7. Variable costs of M
8. Company president's salary

Cost terms
a. Opportunity cost
b. Sunk cost
c. Irrelevant variable outlay cost
d. Irrelevant fixed outlay cost
e. Relevant variable outlay cost
f. Relevant fixed outlay cost
g. Relevant revenues
h. Irrelevant revenues

4-2
Relevant Cost
Terms: Matching

A company that produces and sells 4,000 units per month, with the capacity to produce 5,000 units per month, is evaluating a one-time, special order for 2,000 units from a large chain store. Accepting the order will increase variable manufacturing costs and certain fixed selling and administrative costs. It will also require the company to forgo the sale of 1,000 units to regular customers.

Required:
Presented are a number of statements related to the proposal. For each statement, select the most appropriate cost term. Each term is used only once.

Statements
1. Cost of existing equipment used to produce special order
2. Lost contribution margin from forgone sales to regular customers
3. Increased revenues from special order
4. Variable cost of 4,000 units sold to regular customers
5. Increase in fixed selling and administrative expenses
6. Revenues from 4,000 units sold to regular customers
7. Salary paid to current supervisor who oversees manufacture of special order
8. Increased variable costs of special order

Cost terms
a. Irrelevant variable outlay cost
b. Irrelevant fixed outlay cost
c. Sunk cost
d. Relevant variable outlay cost
e. Relevant fixed outlay cost
f. Opportunity cost
g. Relevant revenues
h. Irrelevant revenues

4-3
Identifying Relevant
Costs and Revenues

The village of Twin Falls operates a hydroelectric plant on the west side of a river that flows through town. The village uses some of this generated electricity to operate a water treatment plant and sells the excess electricity to a local utility. The village council is evaluating two alternative proposals:

- *Proposal 1* calls for replacing the generators used in the plant with more efficient generators that will produce more electricity and have lower operation costs. The salvage value of the old generators is higher than their removal cost.
- *Proposal 2* calls for raising the level of the dam to retain more water for generating power and increasing the force of water flowing through the dam. This will significantly increase the amount of electricity generated by the plant. Operating costs will not be affected.

Required:

Presented are a number of cost and revenue items. Indicate whether each item is relevant or irrelevant to proposals 1 and 2 in the appropriate columns.

	Proposal 1	Proposal 2
1. Cost of new fire engine		
2. Cost of old generators		
3. Cost of new generators		
4. Operating cost of old generators		
5. Operating cost of new generators		
6. Mayor's salary		
7. Depreciation on old generators		
8. Salvage value of old generators		
9. Removal cost of old generators		
10. Cost of raising dam		
11. Maintenance costs of water plant		
12. Revenues from sale of electricity		

4–4
Classifying Relevant and Irrelevant Items

The law firm of Taylor, Taylor, and Tower has been asked to represent a local client. All legal proceedings will be held out of town in Washington, D.C.

Required:

Classify each of the following items on the basis of their relationship to this engagement. Items may have multiple classifications.

	RELEVANT COSTS		IRRELEVANT COSTS	
	Opportunity	Outlay	Outlay	Sunk
1. The case will require three attorneys to stay four nights in a Washington hotel. The predicted hotel bill is $1,200.				
2. Taylor, Taylor, and Tower's professional staff is paid $800 per day for out-of-town assignments.				
3. Last year, depreciation on Taylor, Taylor, and Tower's office was $12,000.				
4. Round-trip transportation to Washington is expected to cost $250 per person.				
5. The firm has recently accepted an engagement that will require partners to spend two weeks in Atlanta. The predicted out-of-pocket costs of this trip are $8,500.				

	RELEVANT COSTS		IRRELEVANT COSTS	
	Opportunity	Outlay	Outlay	Sunk

6. The firm has a maintenance contract on its word processing equipment that will cost $2,200 next year.
7. If the firm accepts the client and sends attorneys to Washington, it will have to decline a conflicting engagement in Hilton Head that would have provided a net cash inflow of $7,200.
8. The firm's variable overhead is $80 per client hour.
9. The firm pays $250 per year for Mr. Tower's subscription to a law journal.
10. Last year the firm paid $3,500 to increase the insulation in its building.

4–5
Relevant Costs for Equipment Replacement Decision

Bone Center paid $50,000 for X-ray equipment four years ago. The equipment was expected to have a useful life of 10 years from the date of acquisition with annual operating costs of $40,000. Technological advances have made the machine purchased four years ago obsolete with a zero salvage value. An improved X-ray device incorporating the new technology is available at an initial cost of $60,000 and annual operating costs of $25,000. The new machine is expected to last only six years before it, too, is obsolete.

Asked by Dr. Bone to analyze the financial aspects of replacing the obsolete but still functional machine, Bone Center's accountant prepared the following analysis:

Six-year savings [($40,000 − $25,000) × 6]	$90,000
Cost of new machine	(60,000)
Undepreciated cost of old machine	(30,000)
Advantage (disadvantage of replacement)	$ 0

After looking over these numbers, Dr. Bone rejected the proposal and told his accountants that this "is a for-profit practice, and we must do better than break even while fixing broken bones. When it comes to equipment, if it isn't broke, don't replace it."

Required:
Perform an analysis of relevant costs to determine whether Dr. Bone made the correct decision.

4–6
Special Order

Better See TV produces wall mounts for television sets. The forecasted income statement for 2004 is as follows:

Better See TV
Budgeted Income Statement
For the Year 2004

Sales ($10 per unit)	$4,000,000
Cost of good sold ($8.00 per unit)	−3,200,000
Gross profit	$ 800,000
Selling expenses ($0.75 per unit)	− 300,000
Net income	$ 500,000

Additional Information

Of the production costs and selling expenses, $1,200,000 and $100,000, respectively, are fixed.

Better See TV received a special order from a hospital supply company offering to buy 50,000 wall mounts for $7.50. If it accepts the order, there will be no additional selling expenses, and there is currently sufficient excess capacity to fill the order. Better See TV's sales manager argues for rejecting the order because "we are not in the business of paying $8 to make a product to sell for $7.50."

Required:

Do you think Better See TV should accept the special order? Explain.

4–7
Special Order

Delta Farms grows vegetables and sells them after processing to local restaurants. The firm's leading product is Salad-in-a-Bag, which is a mixture of green salad ingredients prepared and ready to serve. Delta sells a large bag to restaurants for $20. It calculates the variable cost per bag at $16 (including $1.50 for local delivery). The average cost per bag is $17.50.

Because the vegetables are perishable and Delta is experiencing a large crop, the firm has extra capacity. A representative of a restaurant association in another city has offered to buy fresh salad stock from Delta to augment its regular supply during an upcoming international festival. The restaurant association wants to buy 2,500 bags during the next month for $18 per bag. Delivery to restaurants in the other city will cost Delta $2 per bag.

Delta can meet most of the order with excess capacity but would sacrifice 500 bags of regular sales to fill this special order. Please assist Delta's management by answering the following questions.

Required:

a. Using differential analysis, what is the impact on profits of accepting this special order?

b. What nonquantitative issues should Delta management consider before making a final decision?

c. How would the analysis change if the special order were for 2,500 bags per month for the next five years?

4–8
Special Order

The Produce Patch, a new health-food restaurant situated on a busy highway in Pomona, California, specializes in a chef's salad dinner selling for $6. Daily fixed costs are $1,500, and variable costs are $3 per meal. With a capacity of 800 meals per day, The Produce Patch serves an average of 750 meals each day.

Required:

a. Determine the current average cost per meal.

b. A bus load of 40 Girl Scouts stops on its way home from the San Bernardino National Forest. The leader offers to bring them in if the scouts can all be served a meal for a total of $150. The owner refuses, saying he would lose $1.25 per meal if he accepted this offer. Comment on the owner's reasoning.

c. A local businessman on a break overhears the conversation with the leader and offers the owner a one-year contract to feed 300 of the businessman's employees at a special price of $3.75 per meal. Should the restaurant owner accept this offer? Why or why not?

4–9
Special Order: High-Low Cost Estimation

Quality Belt Company produces seat belts that it sells to North American automobile manufacturers. Although the company has a capacity of 300,000 belts per year, it is currently producing at an annual rate of 180,000 belts.

Quality Belt has received an order from a German manufacturer to purchase 60,000 belts at $9.50 each. Budgeted costs for 180,000 and 240,000 units are as follows:

	180,000 Units	240,000 Units
Manufacturing costs:		
Direct materials	$ 450,000	$ 600,000
Direct labor	315,000	420,000
Factory overhead	1,215,000	1,260,000
Total	$1,980,000	$2,280,000
Selling and administrative	765,000	780,000
Total	$2,745,000	$3,060,000
Costs per unit:		
Manufacturing	$11.00	$ 9.50
Selling and administrative	4.25	3.25
Total	$15.25	$12.75

Sales to North American manufacturers are priced at $20 per unit, but the sales manager believes Quality Belt should aggressively seek the German business even if it results in a loss of $3.25 per unit. She believes obtaining this order would open up several new markets for the company's product. The general manager commented that Quality Belt cannot tighten its belt to absorb the $195,000 loss ($3.25 × 60,000) it would incur if the order is accepted.

Required:
a. Determine the financial implications of accepting the order.
b. How would your analysis differ if Quality Belt were operating at capacity? Determine the advantage or disadvantage of accepting the order under full-capacity circumstances.

4–10
Make or Buy

Assume a division of Hewlett-Packard currently makes 10,000 circuit boards per year used in producing diagnostic electronic instruments at a cost of $32 per board, consisting of variable costs per unit of $24 and fixed costs per unit of $8. Further assume SCI offers to sell Hewlett-Packard the 10,000 circuit boards for $30 each. If Hewlett-Packard accepts this offer, the facilities currently used to make the boards could be rented to one of Hewlett-Packard's suppliers for $45,000. In addition, $5 per unit of the fixed overhead applied to the circuit boards would be totally eliminated.

Required:
What alternative (make or buy) is more desirable and by what amount is it more desirable?

4–11
Make or Buy

Fresh Air Limited manufactures a line of room air fresheners. Management is currently evaluating the possible production of an air freshener for automobiles. Based on an annual volume of 10,000 units, the predicted cost per unit of an auto air freshener follows.

Direct materials	$ 8.00
Direct labor	1.50
Factory overhead	7.00
Total	$16.50

These cost predictions include $50,000 in facility-level fixed factory overhead averaged over 10,000 units.

One of the component parts of the auto air freshener is a battery-operated electric motor. Although Fresh Air does not currently manufacture these motors, the preceding cost predictions are based on the assumption that Fresh Air will assemble such a motor.

Mini Motor Company has offered to supply an assembled battery-operated motor at a cost of $4.00 per unit, with a minimum annual order of 5,000 units. If Fresh Air accepts this offer, it will be able to reduce the variable labor and variable overhead costs of the auto air freshener by 50 percent. The electric motor's components will cost $2.00 if Fresh Air assembles the motors.

Required:
a. Determine whether Fresh Air should make or buy the electric motor.
b. If Fresh Air could otherwise rent the motor-assembly space for $8,000 per year, should it make or buy this component?
c. What additional factors should Fresh Air consider in deciding whether it should make or buy the electric motors?

4-12
Make or Buy

John Rahavy III, M.D., is a general practitioner whose offices are located in the South Falls Professional Building. In the past, Dr. Rahavy has operated his practice with a nurse, a receptionist/secretary, and a part-time bookkeeper. Dr. Rahavy, like many small-town physicians, has billed his patients and their insurance companies from his own office. The part-time bookkeeper, who works 10 hours per week, is employed exclusively for this purpose.

North Falls Physician's Service Center has offered to take over all of Dr. Rahavy's billings and collections for an annual fee of $7,500. If Dr. Rahavy accepts this offer, he will no longer need the bookkeeper. The bookkeeper's wages and fringe benefits amount to $8 per hour, and the bookkeeper works 50 weeks per year. With all the billings and collections done elsewhere, Dr. Rahavy will have two additional hours available per week to see patients. He sees an average of three patients per hour at an average fee of $30 per visit. Dr. Rahavy's practice is expanding, and new patients often have to wait several weeks for an appointment. He has resisted expanding his office hours or working more than 50 weeks per year. Finally, if Dr. Rahavy signs on with the center, he will no longer need to rent a records storage locker in the basement of the Professional Building. The locker rents for $100 per month.

Required:
Determine whether or not Dr. Rahavy should subscribe to the service.

4-13
Sell or Process Further

Finger Lakes Boat Company manufactures sailboat hulls at a cost of $4,200 per unit. The hulls are sold to boat yards for $5,000. Finger Lakes Boat Company is evaluating the desirability of adding masts, sails, and rigging to the hulls prior to sale at an additional cost of $1,500. The completed sailboats could then be sold for $5,800 each.

Required:
Determine whether Finger Lakes should sell sailboat hulls or process them further into complete sailboats. Assume sales volume will not be affected.

4-14
Sell or Process Further

Morristown Chemical Company processes raw material D into joint products E and F. Raw material D costs $5 per liter. It costs $100 to convert 100 liters of D into 60 liters of E and 40 liters of F. Product F can be sold immediately for $5 per liter or processed further into Product G at an additional cost of $4 per liter. Product G can then be sold for $15 per liter.

Required:
Determine whether Product F should be sold or processed further into Product G.

4–15
Limited Resources

Cape Town Manufacturing Company, Ltd., produces three products: X, Y, and Z. A limitation of 200 labor hours per week prevents Cape Town Manufacturing from meeting the sales demand for these products. Product information is as follows:

	X	Y	Z
Unit selling price	$160	$100	$200
Unit variable costs	(100)	(50)	(180)
Unit contribution margin	$ 60	$ 50	$ 20
Labor hours per unit	4	2	4

Required:
a. Determine the weekly contribution from each product when total labor hours are allocated to the product with the highest
   1. Unit selling price.
   2. Unit contribution margin.
   3. Contribution per labor hour.
   (*Hint:* Each situation is independent of the others.)
b. What generalization can be made regarding the allocation of limited resources to achieve short-run profit maximization?
c. Determine the opportunity cost Cape Town Manufacturing will incur if management requires the weekly production of 10 units of X.

4–16
Limited Resources

John Drive, a regional sales representative for Byte Computer Supply Company, has been working more than 80 hours per week calling on a total of 140 regular customers each month. Because of family and health considerations, he has decided to spend no more than 40 hours per week (160 per month) with customers. Unfortunately, this cutback will require John to turn away some of his regular customers or, at least, serve them less frequently than once a month. John has developed the following information to assist him in determining how to best allocate his time:

	CUSTOMER CLASSIFICATION		
	Large Business	Small Business	Individual
Number of customers	10	50	80
Average monthly sales per customer	$2,000	$1,000	$500
Commission percentage	5%	7%	10%
Hours per customer per monthly visit	4.0	2.0	2.5

Required:
a. Develop a monthly plan that indicates the number of customers John should call on in each classification to maximize his monthly sales commissions.
b. Determine the monthly commissions John will earn if he implements this plan.

4–17
Linear
Programming with
Graphic Analysis
(Appendix A)

Menz Company produces two products, X and Y, in one department. Product X has a unit contribution margin of $40, and Product Y has a unit contribution margin of $70. The demand for Product X exceeds Menz's production capacity, which is limited by available labor hours and machine hours. The maximum demand for Product Y is 8 units per week. Product information follows:

	HOURS PER UNIT		Total Hours
	X	Y	Available per Week
Labor	12	18	180
Machine	6	4	60

Management desires the product mix that will maximize the weekly contribution toward fixed costs and profits.

Required:
a. Formulate the objective function and constraints necessary to determine the optimal product mix.
b. Determine the optimal solution and the corresponding value of the objective function with the aid of graphic analysis.

4-18
Linear
Programming with
Graphic Analysis
(Appendix A)

Old Salt Desk Company produces two styles of desks, Captain and Mate, in two departments, Assembly and Finishing. The unit contribution margin for the Captain desks is $200 and for the Mate desks is $150. The demand for Captain desks exceeds Old Salt's production capacity, which is limited by the available hours in each department. The demand for Mate desks is 80 units per month. Production information follows:

	HOURS PER UNIT		Total Hours
	Captain	Mate	Available per Month
Assembly Department	10	10	1,500
Finishing Department	40	20	4,000

Management desires the product mix that will maximize the monthly contribution toward fixed costs and profits.

Required:
a. Formulate the objective function and constraints necessary to determine the optimal product mix.
b. Determine the optimal solution and the corresponding value of the objective function with the aid of graphic analysis.

Problems

4-19
Multiple Changes
in Profit Plans

In an attempt to improve profit performance, Mountainside Company's management is considering a number of alternative actions. An April 2005 contribution income statement for Mountainside Company is presented on the following page.

Mountainside Company
Contribution Income Statement
For the Month of April 2005

Sales (10,000 units × $40)		$ 400,000
Less variable costs:		
Direct materials (10,000 units × $5)	$ 50,000	
Direct labor (10,000 units × $14)	140,000	
Variable factory overhead (10,000 units × $6)	60,000	
Selling and administrative (10,000 units × $5)	50,000	(300,000)
Contribution margin (10,000 units × $10)		$ 100,000
Less fixed costs:		
Factory overhead	$ 50,000	
Selling and administrative	60,000	(110,000)
Net income (loss)		$ (10,000)

Required:
Determine the effect of each of the following independent situations on monthly profit.

a. Purchasing automated assembly equipment, which should reduce direct labor costs by $6 per unit and increase variable overhead costs by $2 per unit and fixed factory overhead by $20,000 per month.

b. Reducing the selling price by $5 per unit. This should increase the monthly sales by 5,000 units. At this higher volume, additional equipment and salaried personnel would be required. This will increase fixed factory overhead by $3,000 per month and fixed selling and administrative costs by $2,500 per month.

c. Buying rather than manufacturing a component of Mountainside's final product. This will increase direct materials costs by $15 per unit. However, direct labor will decline $4 per unit, variable factory overhead will decline $1 per unit, and fixed factory overhead will decline $10,000 per month.

d. Increasing the unit selling price by $3 per unit. This action should result in a 1,000-unit decrease in monthly sales.

e. Combining alternatives (a) and (d).

4–20
Multiple Changes in Profit Plans: Multiple Products

Information on Flamingo Bay's three products follows:

	A	B	C
Unit sales per month	800	1,400	900
Selling price per unit	$ 5.00	$7.50	$4.00
Variable costs per unit	(5.20)	(6.00)	(2.00)
Unit contribution margin	$(0.20)	$1.50	$2.00

Required:
Determine the effect each of the following situations would have on monthly profits. Each situation should be evaluated independently of all others.

a. Product A is discontinued.

b. Product A is discontinued, and the subsequent loss of customers causes sales of Product B to decline by 100 units.

c. The selling price of A is increased to $5.50 with a sales decrease of 200 units.

d. The price of Product B is increased to $8.00 with a resulting sales decrease of 200 units. However, some of these customers shift to Product A; sales of Product A increase by 100 units.

e. Product A is discontinued, and the plant in which A was produced is used to produce D, a new product. Product D has a unit contribution margin of $0.30. Monthly sales of Product D are predicted to be 700 units.

f. The selling price of Product C is increased to $5.00, and the selling price of Product B is decreased to $7.00. Sales of C decline by 200 units, while sales of B increase by 300 units.

4–21
Relevant Costs and Differential Analysis

Third National Bank of Outback paid $50,000 for a check-sorting machine in January 2000. The machine had an estimated life of 10 years and annual operating costs of $40,000, excluding depreciation. Although management is pleased with the machine, recent technological advances have made it obsolete. Consequently, as of January 2004, the machine has a book value of $30,000, a remaining operating life of 6 years, and a salvage value of $0.

The manager of operations is evaluating a proposal to acquire a new Perfect Reader II–Optical Scanning and Sorting Machine. The new machine would cost $60,000 and reduce annual operating costs to $25,000, excluding depreciation. Because of expected technological improvements, the manager believes the new machine will have an economic life of 6 years and no salvage value at the end of that life.

Prior to signing the papers authorizing the acquisition of the new machine, the president of the Third National Bank prepared the following analysis:

Six-year savings [($40,000 − $25,000) × 6 years]	$90,000
Cost of new machine	(60,000)
Loss on disposal of old machine	(30,000)
Advantage (disadvantage) of replacement	$ 0

After looking at these numbers, he rejected the proposal and commented that he was "tired of looking at marginal projects. This bank is in business to make a profit, not to break even. If you want to break even, go work for the government."

Required:
a. Evaluate the president's analysis.
b. Prepare a differential analysis of six-year totals for the old and the new machines.

4–22
Special Order

Thousand Islands Propulsion Company produces a variety of electric trolling motors. Management follows a pricing policy of manufacturing cost plus 60 percent. In response to a request from Northern Sporting Goods, the following price has been developed for an order of 300 Minnow Motors (the smallest motor Thousand Island produces):

Manufacturing costs:	
Direct materials	$10,000
Direct labor	12,000
Factory overhead	18,000
Total	$40,000
Markup (60%)	24,000
Selling price	$64,000

Mr. Bass, the president of Northern Sporting Goods, rejected this price and offered to purchase the 300 Minnow Motors at a price of $44,000. The following additional information is available:

- Thousand Islands has sufficient excess capacity to produce the motors.
- Factory overhead is applied on the basis of direct labor dollars.
- Budgeted factory overhead is $400,000 for the current year. Of this amount, $100,000 is fixed. Of the $18,000 of factory overhead assigned to the Minnow Motors, only $13,500 is driven by the special order; $3,500 is a facility-level cost.
- Selling and administrative expenses are budgeted as follows:

Fixed	$90,000 per year (facility level)
Variable	$20 per unit manufactured and sold

Required:
a. The president of Thousand Islands Propulsion wants to know if he should allow Mr. Bass to have the Minnows for $44,000. Determine the effect on profits of accepting Mr. Bass's offer.
b. Briefly explain why certain costs should be omitted from the analysis in requirement (a).
c. Assume Thousand Islands is operating at capacity and could sell the 300 Minnows at its regular markup.
   1. Determine the opportunity cost of accepting Mr. Bass's offer.
   2. Determine the effect on profits of accepting Mr. Bass's offer.

4–23
Special Order

Every Halloween, Glacier Ice Cream Shop offers a trick-or-treat package of 20 coupons for $3. The coupons are redeemable by children 12 years or under, for a single-scoop cone, with a limit of one coupon per child per visit. Coupon sales average 500 books per year. The printing costs are $60. A single-scoop cone of Glacier ice cream normally sells for $0.60. The variable costs of a single-scoop cone are $0.40.

Required:

a. Determine the loss if all coupons are redeemed without any other effect on sales.
b. Assume all coupons will not be redeemed. With regular sales unaffected, determine the coupon redemption rate at which Glacier will break even on the offer.
c. Assuming regular sales are not affected and one additional single-scoop cone is sold at the regular price each time a coupon is redeemed, determine the coupon redemption rate at which Glacier will break even on the offer.
d. Determine the profit or loss incurred on the offer if the coupon redemption rate is 60 percent and:
   1. One-fourth of the redeemed coupons have no effect on sales.
   2. One-fourth of the redeemed coupons result in additional sales of two single-scoop cones.
   3. One-fourth of the redeemed coupons result in additional sales of three single-scoop cones.
   4. One-fourth of the redeemed coupons come out of regular sales of single-scoop cones.

4–24
Applications of Differential Analysis

The Bird Box produces squirrel-proof bird feeders that it sells to mail-order distributors for $25. Manufacturing and other costs follow:

Variable Costs per Unit		Fixed Costs per Month	
Direct materials	$ 8	Factory overhead	$10,000
Direct labor	7	Selling and administrative	5,000
Factory overhead	2	Total	$15,000
Distribution	3		
Total	$20		

The variable distribution costs are for transportation to mail-order distributors. The current monthly production and sales volume is 5,000 units. Monthly capacity is 6,000 units.

Required:
Determine the effect of each of the following independent situations on monthly profits.

a. A $2.50 increase in the unit selling price should result in a 1,000-unit decrease in monthly sales.
b. A $2.00 decrease in the unit selling price should result in a 2,000-unit increase in monthly sales. However, because of capacity constraints, the last 1,000 units would be produced during overtime with the direct labor costs increasing by 60 percent.
c. A British distributor has proposed to place a special, one-time order for 1,000 units at a reduced price of $20 per unit. The distributor would pay all transportation costs. There would be additional fixed selling and administrative costs of $100.
d. A Dutch distributor has proposed to place a special, one-time order for 2,500 units at a special price of $20 per unit. The distributor would pay all transportation costs. There would be additional fixed selling and administrative costs of $200. Assume overtime production is not possible.

(continued)

e. A Canadian manufacturer has offered a one-year contract to supply a squirrel guard that attaches to the bottom of the feeder at a cost of $4 per unit. If The Bird Box accepts the offer, it will be able to reduce variable manufacturing costs by 10 percent, reduce fixed costs by $500 per month, and rent some currently used space for $900 per month.

f. The bird feeders are currently sold assembled and ready for mounting. Selling the feeders unassembled would reduce costs by $5 per unit and reduce the selling price to only $21.

g. The Bird Box produces a variety of bird feeders. The given information is for an average unit. Determine the variable cost markup required to earn a monthly profit of $20,000.

4-25
Applications of
Differential Analysis

Bushwhack Expeditions offers guided back-country hiking/camping trips in British Columbia. Bushwhack provides a guide and all necessary food and equipment at a fee of $50 per person per day. Bushwhack currently provides an average of 600 guide-days per month in June, July, August, and September. Based on available equipment and staff, maximum capacity is 800 guide-days per month. Monthly variable and fixed operating costs (valued in Canadian dollars) are as follows:

Variable Costs per Guide-Day		Fixed Costs per Month	
Food	$ 5	Equipment rental	$ 5,000
Guide salary	25	Administration	5,000
Supplies	2	Advertising	2,000
Insurance	8	Total	$12,000
Total	$40		

Required:

Determine the effect of each of the following situations on monthly profits. Each situation is to be evaluated independent of all others.

a. A $12 increase in the daily fee should result in a 200-unit decrease in monthly sales.

b. A $5 decrease in the daily fee should result in a 300-unit increase in monthly sales. However, because of capacity constraints, the last 100 guide-days would be provided by subcontracting to another firm at a cost of $46 per guide-day.

c. A French tour agency has proposed to place a special, one-time order for 80 guide-days at a reduced fee of $45 per guide-day. The agency would pay all insurance costs. There would be additional fixed administrative costs of $200.

d. An Italian tour agency has proposed to place a special, one-time order for 300 guide-days next month at a special fee of $45 per guide-day. The agency would pay all insurance costs. There would be additional fixed administrative costs of $200. Assume additional capacity beyond 800 guide-days is not available.

e. An Alberta outdoor supply company has offered to supply all necessary food and camping equipment at $7.50 per guide-day. This eliminates the current food costs and reduces the monthly equipment rental costs to $1,500.

f. Clients must currently carry a backpack and assist in camp activities such as cooking. Bushwhack is considering the addition of mules to carry all food and equipment and the hiring of college students to perform camp activities such as cooking. This will increase variable costs by $10 per guide-day and fixed costs by $1,200 per month. However, 600 full-service guide-days per month could now be sold at $75 each.

g. Bushwhack provides a number of different types of wilderness experiences. The given information is for an average tour. Determine the variable cost markup required to earn a monthly profit of $6,000.

**4-26
Accounting
Inputs to Linear
Programming:
Graphic Analysis
(Appendix A)**

Kyoto Electric produces two video cassette recorders, a manual model and an automatic model that contains an automatic timer. Although demand for the automatic model is only 75 units per month, Kyoto has been unable to satisfy the demand for the lower-priced manual model.

The following information is available from the accounting records:

	Manual	Automatic
Unit selling price	$200	$329
Unit manufacturing costs:		
Direct materials	$105	$190
Conversion costs:		
Department 1	24	24
Department 2	45	90
Total	$174	$304

The per-unit conversion costs include direct labor, variable overhead, and fixed overhead. The fixed factory overhead is driven by facility rather than by unit-level activity. In Department 1, conversion costs are assigned at the rate of $20 per hour. Fifty percent is for variable costs, and fifty percent is for fixed costs. A total of 180 hours is available each month in Department 1. In Department 2, conversion costs are assigned at the rate of $30 per hour. Eighty percent is for variable costs, and twenty percent is for fixed costs. A total of 300 hours is available each month in Department 2. The fixed overhead rates, as a portion of total conversion costs, are based on the full utilization of production capacity. The following additional information is available:

- Variable selling and administrative expenses are $10 per unit (for both products).
- Fixed selling and administrative expenses are $1,200 per month.

Required:
a. Formulate the objective function and the constraints necessary to determine the optimal monthly production mix.
b. Determine the optimal solution and the corresponding value of the objective function with the aid of graphic analysis.
c. Determine Kyoto Electric's expected monthly profit.

**4-27
Formulating
Objective Function
(Appendix A)**

A processing department of East Orange Chemical Company can vary the production mix of two products, Compound B1 and Compound B2. Because of the high demand for these products, a chemical engineer has been requested to determine the optimal monthly volumes of each product. The engineer has formulated all constraints needed to determine the optimal mix with the aid of linear programming and has asked you to assist in developing the objective function coefficients. The engineer has provided you the following production information:

	PER TWO-LITER BOTTLE*	
	Compound B1	Compound B2
Raw materials:		
C25	1 liter	2 liters
D80	3 liters	1 liter
MA5	—	1 liter
Bottles	1	1
Direct labor	0.4 hours	0.6 hours

The difference between total inputs and outputs is due to shrinkage, waste, and evaporation.

You obtain the following information from an analysis of the accounting records:

Selling prices:
Compound B1 . . . . $12.20/bottle
Compound B2 . . . . 18.00/bottle
Raw materials costs:
C25 . . . . $ 0.80/liter
D80 . . . . 0.40/liter
MA5 . . . . 0.65/liter
Bottles . . . . 0.50 each
Direct labor rate . . . . $ 9.00/hour
Monthly factory overhead: $20,000 + 0.40 direct labor dollars
Monthly selling and administrative costs: $15,000 + 0.25 sales revenue

Required:
Formulate the objective function necessary to determine the optimal monthly production in bottles.

4–28
Activity Cost Hierarchy and Integer Programming (Appendix B)

Davis Company produces two products with the following contribution and cost information:

	Product A	Product B
Unit contribution margin	$5	$3
Batch-level costs	$ 2,000	$ 1,000
Product-level costs	$20,000	$12,000
Facility-level costs (per month)		$30,000

Production is limited by constraints for raw materials, assembly hours, finishing hours, and batch size. With 20,000 units of raw materials available each month, each unit of A requires two units of materials and each unit of B requires one unit of materials. With 500 monthly assembly hours available, each unit of A requires 0.02 hour and each unit of B requires 0.01 hour. Of the 500 finishing hours available each month, each unit of A requires 0.02 hour and each unit of B requires 0.02 hour. Finally, the production process is such that each batch size is limited to a maximum of 2,000 units of A and 10,000 units of B.

Required:
a. Formulate the objective function and the constraints necessary to determine the optimal product mix using integer programming.
b. If integer programming software is available, determine the optimal solution, the value of the objective function, and the monthly profit.

Discussion Questions

4–29
Continue or Discontinue

Peachtree Eye Clinic primarily performs three medical procedures: cataract removal, corneal implants, and keratotomy. At the end of the first quarter of this year, Dr. Hartsfield, president of Peachtree, expressed grave concern about the cataract sector because it had reported a loss of $10,000. He rationalized that "since the cataract market is losing $10,000, and the overall practice is making $40,000, if we eliminate the cataract market, our total profits will increase to $50,000."

Required:
a. Is the president's analysis correct?
b. Will total profits increase if the cataract section is dropped?
c. Is it possible total profits will decline?

4-30
Ethics of
Frequent-Flyer
Mile Incentives

In an attempt to attract and retain loyal customers, many organizations offer frequent-flyer miles. Consider the following examples:

- Airlines offer frequent-flyer miles, sometimes with a minimum of 500 or 750 miles per flight segment.
- Major automobile rental agencies award frequent-flyer mile credits on cooperating airlines.
- Many hotel chains award frequent-flyer mile credits on cooperating airlines, sometimes at the rate of 1,000 miles per night.
- A few credit cards have even joined in, offering frequent-flyer miles on cooperating selected airlines at the rate of one mile per dollar charged.

In exchange for accumulated frequent-flyer miles, airlines offer free tickets, free upgrades, and membership in airport clubs. Cooperating hotels offer free lodging for the exchange of frequent-flyer miles.

Frequent-flyer programs are structured so that frequent-flyer miles can accrue only to the traveler. Hence, organizations paying for employee travel cannot accumulate frequent-flyer miles as an asset. Some frequent-flyer programs are structured so that travelers can reassign their unused frequent-flyer miles to a charitable purpose sponsored by the airline. The charity can then pool these miles to accomplish its goals.

Required:

a. Discuss the potential impact of frequent-flyer incentive programs on the travel costs of organizations.
b. Discuss why the programs are structured so that organizations paying for employee travel cannot accumulate frequent-flyer miles.
c. Discuss the ethics of frequent-flyer programs. Are there any circumstances when taking advantage of frequent-flyer incentives is clearly ethical or clearly unethical? Are the administrators of frequent-flyer programs encouraging unethical behavior by not allowing organizations that pay for employee travel to accumulate frequent-flyer miles?

4-31
Ethics of Markups
on Service Charges

Resellers of a variety of products (such as computers) often perform marketing services for manufacturers. In billing manufacturers, there is some question about the ethics and legality of adding a markup to the out-of-pocket cost of marketing services. Consider the following statements by executives in manufacturing and reselling organizations:[13]

- Paul Thomas, a marketing executive for Apple (a major computer manufacturer), said that Apple allows "no scope for profit-making on any Apple [marketing] program."
- Robert Sutis, in-house counsel for Hewlett-Packard (a major manufacturer of computer printers), noted that H-P bases marketing reimbursements on "claim forms that have documentation attached," such as "invoices or tear sheets or other paperwork."
- Curtis J. Scheel, a vice president of MicroAge, Inc. (a computer reseller), commented that to the extent that a company charges more than it spends, it does so to offset costs of running its marketing operations. He added that if vendors discovered that marketing money was going to the bottom line, "they might stop funding."

Susan Thompson just accepted a position with Digital Distributors (DD), a regional computer wholesale company, as the new marketing director. In reviewing company records, she determined that DD was charging manufacturers much more than

---

[13]Raju Narisetti, "Intelligent Electronics Made Much of Its Profit at Suppliers Expense," *The Wall Street Journal,* December 6, 1994, pp. A1, A17.

it spent on marketing activities. Big Pear Computing, for example, was charged $2.9 million in 2001 for advertising, but only $1.5 million was recorded as advertising expenses on Big Pear's account.

The cumulative effect of these markups was very significant to DD's overall profitability. After asking a few questions and analyzing some data with a spreadsheet program, Susan determined that in 2001 marketing took in $15 million more from charges to manufacturers than it spent for all marketing operations. Meanwhile, DD's profit after taxes was $24 million.

Concerned about the situation, Susan spoke with Mike Murdstone, DD's controller. He immediately commented that DD had done nothing wrong. Mike observed that DD sends invoices to vendors with a simple statement, such as, "For marketing services, $235,000." Mike continued with the following advice: "We do not claim to bill for only actual outlay costs. If manufacturers feel we are overcharging, they could do business with someone else. In the meantime, I recommend you not kill the goose that lays the golden egg."

Required:
Discuss the ethics and legality of DD's billing practices for marketing services. What advice do you have for Susan?

4–32
Traditional Accounting and Throughput Accounting Linear Programming (Appendix A)

Smile Camera Company manufactures two popular cameras, Little Smile and Big Smile. Recent increases in demand have pushed Smile Camera to the limits of its production capacity. The president is a former engineer who knows that linear programming can be used to determine the optimal product mix. However, he needs your assistance in formulating the objective function coefficients and in determining the profit implications of the optimal solution.

The following information is available from the accounting records:

	Little Smile	Big Smile
Unit selling price	$150	$220
Unit manufacturing costs:		
Direct materials	$ 38	$ 54
Direct labor	30	30
Factory overhead	48	80
Total	$116	$164

Production employees are paid $10 per direct labor hour with a total of 450 direct labor hours available each month. Factory overhead is assigned to units manufactured at the rate of $16 per machine hour. Of the overhead rate, 75 percent is for variable costs, and 25 percent is for fixed costs. Although the fixed factory overhead is averaged over units produced for financial accounting purposes, it is driven by facility-level activities rather than by unit-level activities. A total of 750 machine hours is available each month. The factory overhead rate is based on the full utilization of 750 machine hours each month. The following additional information is available:

- Because of insufficient raw materials, only 100 Big Smile cameras can be produced each month.
- Variable selling and administrative expenses are $6 per unit of either product.
- Fixed selling and administrative expenses are $2,300 per month.

Required:
a. Formulate the objective function and constraints necessary to determine the optimal monthly production mix.

b. Determine the optimal solution and the corresponding value of the objective function with the aid of graphic analysis.

c. Determine Smile Camera Company's expected monthly profit. (*Hint:* Determine the fixed factory overhead assigned to each unit at 750 machine hours and then determine monthly fixed factory overhead.)

d. How would the solutions for (a) through (c) differ using throughput accounting concepts presented as part of the theory of constraints?

e. Evaluate the solution obtained in (d).

John Shank Case Recommendation

Reichard Maschinen   This short case considers incremental costs, sunk costs, full costs, opportunity costs, and product profitability. It is set in Western Europe in 1974, just after the Arab oil shocks of 1972–73. The case concerns decisions faced by the management of the Grinding Machines Division of Reichard Maschinen.

Initron Corporation   This case considers decision analysis with joint costs. It is set in 1974 in a Boston-based "hi-tech" firm manufacturing solid state electronic components that were early prototypes for modern integrated circuits. Coverage of the case requires consideration of the relevance of joint cost allocations.

Solution to Review Problem

Unit selling price	$4.80
Unit variable costs	(2.50)
Unit contribution margin	$2.30

a. Profit decrease from reduced sales if there were no
changes in prices or costs (1,800 units × $2.30) . . . $ (4,140)
Profit increase from increase in selling price
[(15,000 units − 1,800 units) × $1.50]   19,800
Increase in monthly profit . . . . $ 15,660

b. Profit increase from increased sales if there were no
changes in prices or costs (6,000 units × $2.30) . . . $ 13,800
Profit decrease from reduced selling price of all units
[(15,000 units + 6,000 units) × $1.80] . . . .   (37,800)
Profit decrease from increased direct labor costs for the
last 1,000 units [1,000 units × ($0.20 × 0.50)] . . .   (100)
Decrease in monthly profit . . . . $(24,100)

c. Increase in revenues (4,000 units × $4.00) . . . . $ 16,000
Increase in costs:
Direct materials (4,000 units × $2.00) . . . . $ 8,000
Direct labor (4,000 units × $0.20)   800
Factory overhead (4,000 units × $0.25)   1,000
Selling and administrative   500   (10,300)
Increase in profits . . . . $ 5,700

(continued)

d. Increase in revenues (8,000 units × $4.00) . . . . $ 32,000
   Increase in costs:
     Direct materials (8,000 units × $2.00) $16,000
     Direct labor (8,000 units × $0.20)   1,600
     Factory overhead (8,000 units × $0.25)   2,000
     Selling and administrative   500
     Opportunity cost of lost regular sales
       [(15,000 units + 8,000 units −
       20,000 unit capacity) × $2.30]   6,900   (27,000)
   Increase in profits . . . . $ 5,000

e.

	Cost to Make	Cost to Buy	Difference (effect of buying on income)
Cost to buy (15,000 units × $1.00)		$15,000	$(15,000)
Cost to make:			
Direct materials			
(15,000 units × $2.00 × 0.40)	$12,000		12,000
Direct labor			
(15,000 units × $0.20 × 0.40)	1,200		1,200
Factory overhead			
(15,000 units × $0.25 × 0.40)	1,500		1,500
Opportunity cost	1,000		1,000
Totals	$15,700	$15,000	$ 700

   Advantage of buying $700

f. Increase in revenues:
     Package individually (15,000 units × $5.05) $75,750
     Sell in bulk (15,000 units × $4.80) . . . . (72,000) $3,750
   Additional packaging costs (15,000 units × $0.10) . . .   (1,500)
   Advantage of individual packaging $2,250

VALUE CHAIN ANALYSIS AND ACTIVITY-BASED MANAGEMENT

After completing this chapter, you should be able to:

LEARNING OBJECTIVE 1   Describe strategic cost management.

LEARNING OBJECTIVE 2   Discuss the importance of the value chain approach to analyzing decision alternatives.

LEARNING OBJECTIVE 3   Analyze an organization's internal value chain, dividing it into processes and activities.

LEARNING OBJECTIVE 4   Explain how process management can help improve organizational performance.

LEARNING OBJECTIVE 5   Determine the costs of individual activities and the activity costs associated with various cost objectives.

LEARNING OBJECTIVE 6   Explain how activity-based costing is used as a basis for activity-based management.

RETHINKING THE REVOLUTION IN AUTOMOBILE RETAILING

The set of processes involved in producing and distributing a particular good or service—the value chain*—often involves many different business organizations. In the automobile business, parts suppliers, assemblers, dealers, insurers, and financial institutions must all coordinate their efforts to provide customers with automobile transportation. For many decades, independent dealers operating as exclusive franchises dominated the retail step of the value chain. Throughout the 1990s, however, this distribution process underwent significant changes.*

In the mid-1990s, several firms outside the auto industry, such as Republic Industries and Circuit City, entered the auto retailing market with a competitive strategy that other firms had already brought to general merchandise, hardware and home improvement products, office supplies, and consumer electronics. This "superstore concept" emphasized large inventories, customer-friendly service, no-haggle pricing, and money-back guarantees. Deciding that the auto distribution process could be accomplished with much less cost and total investment, managers at Republic's AutoNation began consolidating auto distribution by acquiring *independent dealers in new and used car sales, rental car agencies, and auto re-conditioning firms. The objective of these actions was to participate profitably in every transaction involving a car throughout its life cycle. Although both Auto-Nation and rival CarMax grew quite rapidly, applying this merchandising concept to auto distribution did not necessarily prove profitable. In 1998, CarMax lost $23.5 million on sales of $1.5 billion. Although AutoNation did generate income, the firm's growth in income did not match the growth in sales. Between 1998 and 1999, AutoNation's sales grew by 54 percent (from $13 billion to $20 billion) while income grew by only 30 percent (from $356 million to $463 million). These results did not reflect the efficiencies anticipated by AutoNation managers.*

As one observer of this distribution revolution stated, the concept is 10 percent but execution is the other 90 percent. Effective execution proved difficult, and these firms encountered some major challenges. The large size of the individual stores—sometimes up to 80,000 square feet—led to high fixed costs and unrealistic break-even sales volume targets. The large choices of models, colors, and option packages resulted in inventory control problems associated with having the right car at the right place at the right time. Many used cars were obtained from affiliated rental car companies, but customers were not attracted to the bland models typically released from rental fleets. Customers who said they preferred no-haggle prices often commented that these prices were too high. Finally, these super stores also lost customers to Internet firms such as autobytel.com and Autoweb.com.

Managers at AutoNation and CarMax met these challenges by merging new and used car sales locations; developing a hub-and-spoke concept for car reconditioning; altering the sales commission formula to encourage sales volume; using the Internet to help customers find the model, color, and features at a guaranteed price; and enlisting sports celebrities' endorsements.

Observers comment that the automobile distribution system has many diverse components including new cars, used cars, parts, and service. The experiences of managers at AutoNation and CarMax demonstrate that executives must understand these distribution processes to effectively manage components of the value chain.

Source: Arthur Cummins, "Used Cars Are Tough Sell for Automobile Superstores," *The Wall Street Journal,* March 31, 1998, pp. B1, B14; Peter Spiegel, "Car Crash," *Forbes,* May 17, 1999, pp. 130–31; Alex Taylor III, "Car Wars: Wayne Huizenga vs. Everybody," *Fortune,* June 9, 1997, pp. 92–96; Alex Taylor III, "Would You Buy a Car from This Man?" *Fortune,* October 25, 1999, pp. 165–70; David Welch, "AutoNation's Driver Takes a Sharp Turn," *Business Week,* March 13, 2000, pp. 70, 74.

The purpose of this chapter is to broaden your analytic viewpoint (from that of the contribution margin for a narrowly defined decision alternative) to encompass the place of an organization in a much larger value chain, such as that for automobiles, stretching from basic resources to final consumers. First, we consider the elements of strategic planning and strategic cost management. We continue by examining the value chain and considering the advantages of taking a value chain perspective to decision making. We then illustrate how major links in an organization's internal value chain may be broken into processes and activities. Including cost information in our analysis, we determine the costs of individual activities. Finally, we illustrate the accumulation of activity costs to determine the cost of products, projects, and services across an organization's internal value chain.

LEARNING OBJECTIVE 1   ELEMENTS OF STRATEGIC COST MANAGEMENT

An organization's *mission* is the basic purpose toward which its activities are directed. Based on its mission, management sets a number of long- and short-range goals. Management also develops a **strategic plan** to serve as a guideline or framework for making specific medium-range and short-run decisions. Deciding to achieve a market position of cost leadership (discussed in Chapter 1) might be part of an organization's strategic plan. In this case, management is less concerned with designing innovative new products or services than with the process changes needed for cost reductions. With an alternative strategy of product differentiation, management must balance the concern for low cost against the need to develop and introduce distinctive products on a timely basis. Whatever an organization's strategic plan, management needs cost information and an appropriate cost-evaluation framework to achieve its goals.

In this chapter, we introduce strategic cost management as a framework for incorporating cost information into decisions made in support of an organization's strategic plan. **Strategic cost management** is defined as making decisions concerning specific cost drivers within the context of an organization's business strategy, its internal value chain, and its place in a larger value chain stretching from the development and use of resources to the final consumers. Strategic cost management has a long-run orientation, focusing on structural cost drivers (such as the location and size of a hospital) or on organizational cost drivers (such as designing processes for billing credit card customers). It also has the following three key elements:

1. The organization's *strategic plan*, which strategic cost management is designed to support.
2. The *value chain*, which is the set of value-producing activities stretching from basic raw materials to the final consumer.
3. *Activity-based management* (ABM), which concerns the identification and selection of activities to maximize the value of activities while minimizing their cost from the viewpoint of the final customer.

Strategic planning (the first key element) was introduced in Chapter 1. The final two key elements of strategic cost management, the value chain and activity-based management, are introduced in this chapter.

LEARNING OBJECTIVE 2   THE IMPORTANCE OF THE VALUE CHAIN IN DECISION ANALYSIS

The **value chain** for a product or service is the set of value-producing activities that stretches from basic raw materials to the final consumer. Each product or service has a distinct value chain, and all entities along the value chain depend on the final customer's perception of the value and cost of a product or service. It is the final customer who ultimately pays all costs and provides all profits to all organizations along the entire value chain. Consequently, *the goal of every organization should be to maximize the value while minimizing the cost of a product or service to final customers.*

The value chain provides a viewpoint that encompasses all activities performed to deliver products and services to final customers. Depending on the needs of management, value chains are developed at varying levels of detail. Developing a value chain from the perspective of the final consumer requires working backward from the end product or service to the basic raw materials entering into the product or service. Developing a value chain from the viewpoint of an organization that is in the middle of a value chain requires working forward (downstream) to the final consumer and backward (upstream) to the source of raw materials.

Exhibit 5–1 presents the value chain for the paperboard cartons used to package beverages, such as Coca-Cola, Pepsi, or Budweiser products. The value chain is presented

EXHIBIT 5-1

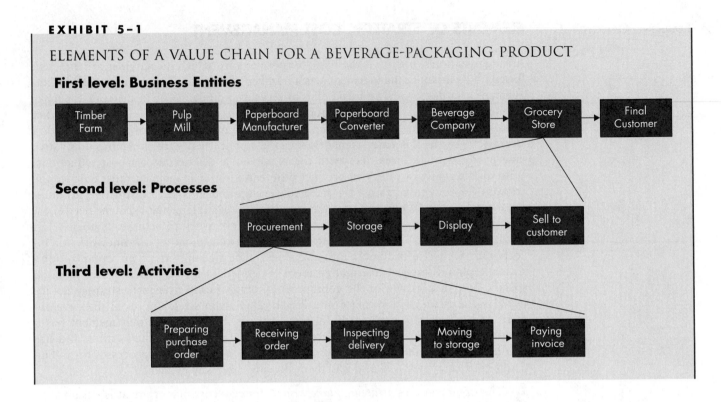

at three levels, with each successive level containing additional details. The first level depicts the various business entities in the value chain:

- Timber farms grow the pulp wood (usually pine) used as the basic input into producing paper products. Some large paper companies, such as Boise Cascade and Georgia Pacific, harvest much of their pulp wood from timber lands that they manage. Other companies, including Riverwood International, which is a leading producer of paperboard for the beverage industry, do not manage their own timber lands, but purchase pulp for their mills on the open market through pulp intermediaries.
- Pulp mills produce the kraft (unbleached) paper used to produce the paperboard. Some of the smaller paperboard manufacturers purchase the kraft paper product from pulp mills; Riverwood International, however, owns its own paper mills that produce paper for its paperboard production facilities.
- Paperboard manufacturers perform a laminating process of coating paperboard material used to produce beverage packages. The paperboard consists of two layers of paper product plus three layers of coating that gives the top surface a high gloss finish that is water resistent and suitable for multi-color printing. Riverwood International is a manufacturer of paperboard for the beverage industry that is marketed under the name of Aqua-Kote.
- The paperboard converter uses manufactured paperboard to print and produce the completed beverage packaging product, such as the cartons used to package the Coca-Cola Classic 12-pack.
- Beverage distributors, such as Coca-Cola Enterprises and Anheuser-Busch, purchase the completed paperboard packages from Riverwood International to package their many different brands in various package sizes and shapes.
- Grocery and convenience stores, such as Safeway and 7-11, display and sell beverages packaged in the paperboard containers.
- The final customer purchases beverages packaged in paperboard packages and uses the packages to carry the beverages and to store them until consumed. The packages not only perform a transport and storage function but also serve as an advertising medium for the beverage company. The beverage company's advertising

on the paperboard packages is intended to entice customers to purchase the beverage company's product and to help create a sense of satisfaction for the customer.

To better understand how business entities within the chain add value and incur costs, management might further refine the value chain into **processes,** collections of related activities intended to achieve a common purpose. The second level in Exhibit 5–1 represents major processes concerning the procurement and sale of Coca-Cola products by a grocery store. To simplify our illustration, we show only the processes for the grocery store related to the purchase and sale of Coca-Cola products packaged in paperboard packages. These processes include procuring Coca-Cola products from the bottling company, storing and displaying the product, and selling the product to the final consumer.

An **activity** is a unit of work. In the third level of Exhibit 5–1, the grocery store process to procure Coca-Cola products is further analyzed as these activities:

- *Placing* a purchase order for Coca-Cola products packaged in paper board packages.
- *Receiving* delivery of the Coca-Cola products in paperboard packages.
- *Inspecting* the delivery to make sure it corresponds with the purchase order and to verify that the products are in good condition.
- *Storing* Coca-Cola products in paperboard packages until needed for display.
- *Paying* for the Coca-Cola products purchased after the invoice arrives from the bottler.

Notice that each of the activities involved in procuring product from a vendor is described by a word ending with *ing*. This suggests that most work activities involve action.

USEFULNESS OF A VALUE CHAIN PERSPECTIVE

The goal of maximizing final customer value while minimizing final customer cost leads organizations to examine *internal* and *external links* in the value chain rather than the departments, processes, or activities independently. From a value chain perspective, it is total cost across the entire value chain, not the cost of individual businesses, departments, processes, or activities that is most important.

The Value Chain Perspective Fosters Supplier-Buyer Partnerships. In the past, relationships between suppliers and buyers were often adversarial. Contact between suppliers and buyers was solely through the selling and purchasing departments. Suppliers attempted merely to meet purchasing contract specifications at the lowest possible cost. Buyers encouraged competition among suppliers with the primary—and often single—goal of obtaining the lowest purchase price.

Exploiting cost reduction and value-enhancing opportunities in the value chain has led many buyers and suppliers to view each other as partners rather than as adversaries. Buyers have reduced the number of suppliers they deal with, often developing long-term partnerships with a single supplier. Once they establish mutual trust, both proceed to share detailed information on internal operations and help each other solve problems. Partners work closely to examine mutual opportunities by studying their common value chain. Supplier engineers might determine that a minor relaxation in buyer specifications would significantly reduce supplier manufacturing costs with only minor increases in subsequent buyer processing costs. Working together, they determine how best to modify processes to reduce overall costs and share increased profits.

Companies such as Hewlett-Packard and Ford now involve suppliers in design, development, and manufacturing decisions. Motorola has even developed a survey asking suppliers to assess Motorola as a buyer. Among other questions, the survey asks sellers to evaluate Motorola's performance in helping suppliers to identify major cost drivers and to increase their profitability. These questions clearly represent the concerns of a partner rather than those of an adversary. What's Happening 5–1 describes

VALUE CHAIN PERSPECTIVE LEADS TO VIRTUAL INTEGRATION OF DELL COMPUTERS' SUPPLIERS AND CUSTOMERS

Dell Computers uses technology and information to integrate the processes of suppliers, manufacturers, and users along the PC value chain. Company founder Michael Dell believes this allows Dell to achieve new levels of efficiency, productivity, and profitability. Furthermore, he believes the resulting value chain responds to the market like a single, "virtually integrated" corporation that will become the organizational model of the information age.

Working with suppliers of computer components, Dell coordinates deliveries to its factories so that components arrive as needed on the shop floor, rather than being delivered to a warehouse for unloading, inspection, storage, removal from storage, and so forth. This requires the continuous sharing of information and schedules.

Sony Corporation supplies monitors for Dell computers. However, the monitors are not delivered to Dell for inspection and matching with the computers before shipment to customers. Instead, Airborne Express or UPS pairs packages containing computers with those containing monitors and delivers them together to customers.

Dell works closely to enhance the value of its product and to help reduce the costs of corporate customers, such as Eastman Chemical and Boeing. Eastman requires highly specialized software on its PCs. Loading this software on individual machines after delivery was costing Eastman more than $200 per machine. Dell set up a special Ethernet to load the software on all Eastman PCs during assembly for an extra charge of $15 to $20.

Dell has 30 employees permanently stationed at Boeing, which has more than 100,000 Dell PCs. "We look more like Boeing's PC department," observed Michael Dell, who noted that Dell is intimately involved in planning Boeing's PC needs and network.

Source: Joan Magretta, "The Power of Virtual Integration: An Interview with Dell Computers' Michael Dell," *Harvard Business Review,* April–May 1998, pp. 73–83.

how Dell Computers has molded partnerships with upstream suppliers and downstream customers into what company founder Michael Dell identifies as "virtual integration."

On a smaller scale, the grocery store in Exhibit 5–1 should examine its external links. It may be willing to pay more for Coca-Cola products if the distributors cooperate to help reduce costs:

- Making more frequent deliveries in small lots would enable the store to reduce storage costs.
- Being reponsible for maintaining and changing the product displays would relieve the store of having their workers be responsible for these tasks.
- Streamlining ordering and payment procedures would enable the store to reduce bookkeeping costs.

If partnership arrangements with upstream suppliers enable the grocery store to reduce its total costs, the store can enhance or maintain its competitive position by reducing prices charged to its consumers. Remember that competitors are also striving to reduce costs and enhance their competitive position. Hence, failing to strive for improvements will likely result in reduced sales and profits.

Value Chain Perspective Fosters Focus on Core Competencies. Using value chain concepts, relationships with suppliers often begin to represent an extended family, allowing companies to focus on core competencies; this capability provides a distinct competitive advantage. This has led to the type of super-outsourcing discussed in the opening scenario to Chapter 4, where Cunningham Car Company contemplates outsourcing *all* manufacturing functions.

Although Cunningham remains an extreme case, a new breed of contract manufacturers, such as Solectron Corporation of Milpitas, California, and SCI Systems Inc. of Huntsville, Alabama, have emerged in recent years. These organizations manufacture products for other companies, ranging from Hewlett-Packard printers to Xerox photocopy machines, with such close partnership arrangements that they behave like a single company. This allows Hewlett-Packard and Xerox to focus on marketing and product development while Solectron and SCI Systems focus on efficient, low-cost manufacturing.

Interestingly, because their facilities are available to all innovators with the necessary financing, the emergence of contract manufacturers may speed innovation. Michael Dell (see What's Happening 5–1) attributes much of Dell Computers' rapid growth and profitability to virtual integration with suppliers. **Virtual integration** is the use of information technology and partnership concepts to allow two or more entities along a value chain to act as if they were a single economic entity. According to Michael Dell, "If we had to build our own factories for every single component of the system, growing at 57 percent per year would not be possible. I would spend 57 percent of my time interviewing prospective vice presidents because the company would not have 15,000 employees but 80,000."

Value Chain Perspective Focuses on Processes, Not Departments. Because processes often cross the boundaries of departments within an organization, studying processes helps managers understand how activities in one department are linked to (and can drive) activities and costs in other departments. While the focus in cost control is typically on department budgets and costs, the value chain perspective suggests that cost management might be more effective through a focus on processes.

It is difficult to control costs by focusing on a department when processes require activities in several departments. Looking at departments, upper-level managers are tempted to implement across-the-board cuts in department budgets. Unfortunately, across-the-board cuts are often counterproductive in the long run. They may lead to frustration on the part of employees who still have the same workload to perform with fewer resources. Unless there is excess capacity, pressure to perform the same amount of work with fewer resources may lead to reduced quality and service that will harm competitive position and put additional pressure on costs.

In fact, using departments, rather than processes and activities, as the focal point of cost reduction may motivate actions that increase rather than reduce overall costs. A production department might reduce its total batch-level costs (such as machine setup) by significantly increasing batch size (the number of units produced each time machines are set up for a particular product). This might reduce the production department's costs, but the increase in batch size will increase handling and storage costs elsewhere in the organization.

Looking at the activities within a process, management might determine that certain activities could be combined, eliminated, or replaced by lower cost alternatives. *As a long-run approach to profit-enhancing cost reductions, it is better to eliminate or reduce activities that drive costs than to merely cut budgets.*

Value chain analysis often leads managers to increase the budgets of departments performing activities found early in the internal value chain and to reduce the budgets of departments performing activities late in the internal value chain. Spending more to design a product that is easy to manufacture may reduce subsequent manufacturing costs, and spending more on employee training might reduce the cost of rework or response to customer complaints.

VALUE-ADDED AND VALUE CHAIN PERSPECTIVES

The value chain perspective is often contrasted with a value-added perspective. Under a value-added perspective, decision makers consider only the cost of resources to their organization and the selling price of products or services to their immediate customers. Using a value-added perspective, the goal is to maximize the value added (the difference between the selling price and costs) by the organization. To do this, the value-added perspective focuses primarily on internal activities and costs. Under a value chain perspective, the goal is to maximize value and minimize cost to final customers, often by developing linkages or partnerships with suppliers and customers.

Although initial efforts to enhance competitiveness might start with a value-added perspective, it is important to expand to a value chain perspective. World-class competitors utilize both a value-added and a value chain perspective. These firms always keep the final customer in mind and recognize that the profitability of each entity in the value chain depends on the overall value and cost of the products and services delivered to final customers.

Note that the value-added perspective is the foundation of the make or buy (outsourcing) decision considered in Chapter 4. The key differences between the partnering decisions considered here and the make or buy decision in Chapter 4 concern time frame, perspective, and attitude. The make or buy decision is a stand-alone decision, often in the short run, that does not view vendors and customers as partners. In contrast, characteristics of the value chain perspective are as follows:

- Comprehensive.
- Focused on the final customers.
- Strategic.
- Basis for partnerships between vendors and customers.

Enhancing or maintaining a competitive position requires an understanding of the entire system used to develop and deliver value to final customers, including interactions among organizations along the value chain. All organizations in the value chain are in business together and should work together as partners rather than as adversaries.

DISAGGREGATING AN ENTITY LEVEL LINK INTO INTERNAL PROCESSES AND ACTIVITIES

Developing a diagram of a value chain is a subjective art rather than an objective science. The specific elements included in the diagram vary with the analyst's perceptions.

Before considering the procedures used to develop an internal value chain, it is important to understand the relationship between cost drivers and the value chain. Cost drivers, the factors that influence costs, were previously classified into three major categories: structural, organizational, and activity. Although the most obvious cost drivers are activities that consume costly resources, the specific activities used to serve customer needs are determined by previous structural and organizational decisions.

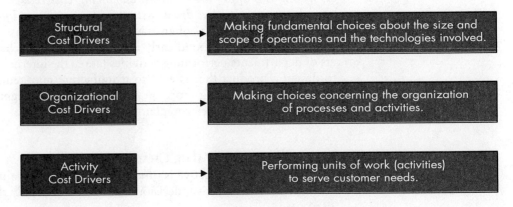

Consider the grocery store in Exhibit 5–1. Structural cost drivers would include decisions affecting the following items:

- *Goals* (to enter the grocery store business),
- *Location* (freestanding buildings or part of strip mall),
- *Scale* (size and number of stores),
- *Scope* (vertical integration through ownership of food-processing subsidiary),
- *Technology* (bar code scanning at cash registers linked to computers for inventory control and reordering), and
- *Complexity* (number and type of products offered for sale).

Organizational cost drivers would include decisions affecting these areas:

- *Organization of processes* (purchase orders placed by the manager of the beverages department or all orders placed by the assistant managers),
- *Layout efficiency* (relative locations of unloading dock, storage, and display cases),
- *Product configuration* (emphasis on more health-related beverages, such as juices and energy drinks),
- *Exploitation of linkages in the value chain* (the development of partnerships with suppliers and customers),
- *Work force involvement* (empowering employees to make decisions and to participate in the continuous improvement of the organization), and
- *Attitudes toward total quality management* (continuously striving to deliver a product that maximizes value for and minimizes the costs to final customers).

Exhibit 5–2 contains an overview of structural, organizational, and activity cost drivers. The activity cost drivers in the lower portion of Exhibit 5–2 are matched with possible ways of measuring the volume of the activity. The performance of each activity, such as verifying that a shipment received at the unloading dock is the result of a legitimate order, consumes resources. In this case the resource is the receiving clerk's time.

Exhibit 5–3 contains a "generic" internal value chain. It is *generic* in the sense that it represents the major internal processes of virtually any organization. In addition to processes directly related to serving customer needs, such as inbound logistics and operations, Exhibit 5–3 recognizes the existence of supporting processes such as accounting, design, finance, human resources, and maintenance.

Representative activities of supporting processes include the following:

1. Accounting
   - Processing employee paychecks.
   - Developing budgets.
   - Determining activity costs.
   - Verifying the existence of recorded assets.

2. Design
   - Developing specifications for products or services delivered to customers.
   - Developing specifications for procedures to produce products or services.

3. Finance
   - Signing checks.
   - Obtaining financial resources.

4. Human resources
   - Recruiting employees.
   - Hiring employees.
   - Training employees.

5. Maintenance
   - Repairing equipment.
   - Cleaning buildings.

EXHIBIT 5-2

COST DRIVERS AND ACTIVITIES

Structural Cost Drivers—determining activities available to respond to customer needs.
Mission and goals (decision to enter the grocery store business)
Location (freestanding stores or mall location)
Scale (horizontal integration for the number of stores and the size of each store)
Scope (vertical integration through ownership of wholesale distributors)
Technology (bar code scanning at cash registers linked to computers for inventory control and reordering)
Complexity (number and type of products offered for sale)

Organizational Cost Drivers—selecting activities used to respond to customer needs.
Work force involvement (participation, empowerment, commitment)
Total quality management (attitudes and achievements concerning quality)
Plant layout efficiency (efficiency of plant layout)
Product configuration (effectiveness and efficiency of design)
Exploitation of linkages in value chain (partnerships with suppliers and customers)

Activity Cost Drivers—performing units of work (activities) to serve customer needs.
Activities (within procurement process for Coca-Cola at a grocery store)

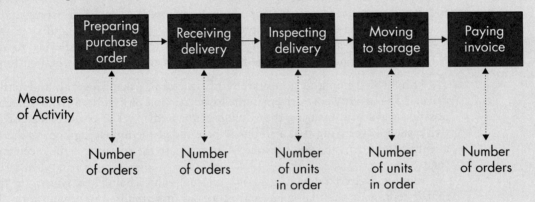

The generic internal value chain is a useful starting point in identifying major processes. It is equally applicable to service and manufacturing, profit, not-for-profit, and government organizations. Consider the following examples of activities that are part of the inbound logistics (purchasing and receiving) and operations processes in various organizations.

Organization	Type of Organization	Inbound Logistics	Operations
McDonald's	Service, for-profit	Ordering food from suppliers	Preparing food
Internal Revenue Service	Service, government	Receiving tax returns electronically	Transferring data to IRS database
Mitsubishi Electronics	Manufacturing, for profit	Receiving TV components	Assembling TV components
University of California	Service, not for profit	Unloading office supplies	Teaching courses

We could easily extend the examples to include illustrations of outbound logistics and service, as well as marketing and sales. At McDonald's, outbound logistics would simply involve handing the order to a customer, and service would include keeping eating areas clean. At Mitsubishi, outbound logistics would include all activities required to physically move finished televisions from the factory to customers, and service would include an information telephone service to assist customers with the setup of various product options.

EXHIBIT 5-3

GENERIC INTERNAL PROCESSES
(GROUPED INTO GENERIC PROCESSES OF THE INTERNAL VALUE CHAIN)

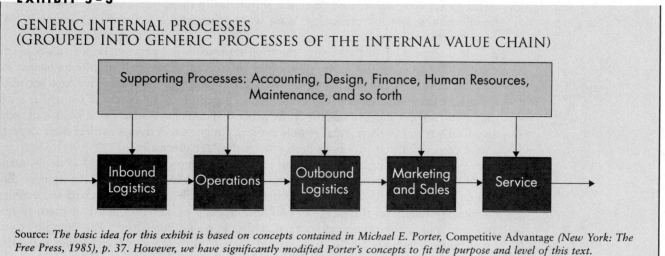

Source: *The basic idea for this exhibit is based on concepts contained in Michael E. Porter,* Competitive Advantage *(New York: The Free Press, 1985), p. 37. However, we have significantly modified Porter's concepts to fit the purpose and level of this text.*

PROCESS MAP

Once the major processes performed to serve customer needs have been identified, the next step is to determine the activities involved in each process. The best ideas will fail if they are not implemented correctly. Designing and managing processes is a key, and often neglected, element of success. One of the jobs of management is to organize work. Among other things, organizing involves determining and properly sequencing the activities that must be included in a process. While the development of an activity list may be straightforward when the entire process occurs within a single department, it is less apparent when a process cuts across organizational units. In all but the simplest situations, developing a process map is a useful tool for identifying activities and their relationships.

A **process map,** or **process flowchart,** is a schematic overview of all the activities within a process. Each major activity is represented by a rectangle on the map, with the arrows indicating the flow of activities. The activities are typically organized from left to right and/or top to bottom. The diamonds represent decisions, with two or more output lines for alternative actions. Like a road map, a process map indicates how to get from point A (input) to point B (output) and all the communities (activities) along the way. The activities level of Exhibit 5–1 contains a simple process map for procurement. Consider the following example for the decision to accept or reject a shipment of goods based on the existence of a purchase order.

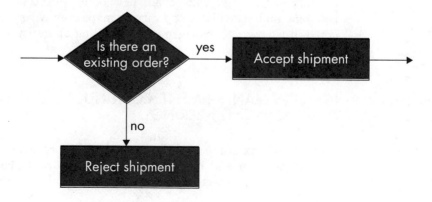

When a process involves activities in several departments, vertical lines are drawn on the map to distinguish between the activities performed in each department. Additional symbols for activities in a process map are similar to those used in flowcharts (discussed in information systems textbooks). Many word processing and spreadsheet programs contain flowchart symbols.

It is important to make sure the map represents the process as it actually exists rather than as it should exist. Developing an accurate map requires the assistance of personnel involved in the process. When developing a process map, it often becomes apparent that while each person involved in a process is an expert in his or her own specialty, no one understands the entire process. This is particularly true when a process involves several departments. People typically focus on activities within their department rather than on processes across the entire organization.

While identifying and describing activities is time consuming and difficult, standardized activity dictionaries are now available for many processes.[1] An **activity dictionary** is a list of processes and related activities. The use of a standardized activity dictionary facilitates the identification and labeling of activities and consistent terminology. Standard terminology, in turn, assists in cost management. For example, most standardized activity dictionaries would include the activity of inspecting materials and products to ensure conformance with quality standards.

Determining the appropriate level of detail is a matter of professional judgement. Although the process map should be comprehensive enough to include all significant activities, it may be counterproductive to identify every single task or action as a separate activity. For the activity *placing a purchase order,* the detailed tasks might start as follows:

Activity: Placing a Purchase Order

This level of detail is analogous to writing lines of code for a computer program. While the manager responsible for purchasing may find these details useful, their inclusion in a higher-level overview makes it difficult to understand and manage a process. Consequently, our development of a process map for the procurement process shows *placing the purchase order* as a single activity.

Of course, the number of activities and the level of detail included in a model should be a function of the purpose of the model. If management wanted to specifically evaluate and improve the activity *placing a purchase order*, it would be appropriate to examine individual tasks.

Like developing a value chain, developing a process map is more art than science. Different analysts will develop varying maps even when studying the same process. As noted in Chapter 1, management accounting allows subjective data when subjective information is relevant.

LEARNING OBJECTIVE 4

PROCESS MANAGEMENT, CONTINUOUS IMPROVEMENT, AND PROCESS REENGINEERING

Understanding a company's processes through process mapping is the launching pad for improvement and redesign of those processes. In **continuous improvement,** an organization's employees constantly evaluate products, services, and processes seeking

---

[1]For further information on activity dictionaries, see Robert S. Kaplan and Robin Cooper, *Cost and Effect: Using Integrated Cost Systems to Drive Profitability and Performance* (Boston: Harvard Business School Press, 1998), pp. 85–88, 108–10.

ways to do better. The Beiersdorf, Inc., plant in Cincinnati was very close to being closed when it launched improvement programs that changed its fate, helping it instead to become one of the nation's best plants. In just three years the plant achieved the impressive results of reducing production time by 78 percent, reducing total inventory by 53 percent, and in a recent year having only 16 consumer complaints related to the 6.8 million units manufactured during the year.[2] What's Happening 5–2 discusses how the video and video service management group at a global telecommunications company used process mapping to improve its processes.

Some companies have the goal of drastically reducing costs or radically improving quality or service. In such situations, it may be necessary to reinvent a process rather than to simply improve it. **Process reengineering** is the fundamental redesign of a process to serve internal or external customers. While continuous improvement focuses on improving existing processes, reengineering reinvents a process. The goal in process reengineering is to drastically reduce costs or to radically improve quality or service. Process reengineering starts with a blank sheet of paper and determines how the process should be performed under ideal circumstances. Consider what happened at Phoenix Designs.

Phoenix Designs, Inc., sells custom-designed furniture through independent dealers. Formerly, sales representatives gathered information regarding customer needs and forwarded it to the design studio. Employees then designed the furniture and sent the designs to the appropriate sales representative for review with the customer. After receiving requested changes from the customer, the process of finalizing the design and

---

5-2   WHAT'S HAPPENING?

GLOBAL TELECOMMUNICATIONS FIRM USES PROCESS MAPPING WITH DRAMATIC RESULTS

The Video and Video Service Management Group ("The Group") is an internal communications group of a multibillion-dollar global telecommunications company that is responsible for all internal voice and video communications within the company. These tasks range from handling simple changes in individual phone lines up to major installations of internal call centers. The Group also manages the internal help desk for all corporate communications needs.

An internal survey showed that one-third of The Group's internal customers rated its services as "fair to poor." It immediately responded by assigning a project team that drew up an "as-is" process map from the internal customers' perspective. This process map included more than 600 steps categorized according to process times, work volumes, and activity type.

After analyzing the process map, the project team discovered that employees used about 30 percent of the process time setting up or moving work around. They spent another 55 percent checking for or fixing failures. Only 15 percent of what was going on in the process was actually related to what the customer wanted: inexpensive communications support provided quickly and accurately.

By analyzing and separating the steps based on level of complexity, the team concluded that it could discard two-thirds of the moves and steps. Since many of the rework steps were related to incorrect billing of services returned to The Group, it was determined that changing billing practices could eliminate most of the billing-related rework activities.

Through the use of process mapping and continuous improvement concepts, the project team believed that the improved process could in 15 months cut failures by 50 percent and moves and setups by 67 percent, as well as expanding value-added activities to 35 percent, all while freeing up 25 percent in excess capacity. The projected annual net benefit was $2.8 million. The process mapping and analysis tools used by The Group became a catalyst for change by helping convince the participants of the need for change and the likely benefits.

Source: Jeffery P. Selander and Kelvin F. Cross, "Process Redesign: Is It Worth It?" *Management Accounting,* January 1999, p. 40.

---

[2]Peter Strozniak, "The Comeback Plant," *Industry Week,* October 18, 1999, p. 42.

obtaining a sales contract took up to six weeks. Rather than attempting to improve this process, Phoenix Designs reengineered it, providing sales representatives with personal computers and special software. The sales representatives are now able to design the furniture at the customer's office. The results are a greatly reduced time span from developing a final design to obtaining a sales contract, a 1,000 percent increase in dealer sales, and a 27 percent increase in income.[3]

The concepts of continuous improvement and process reengineering have been prominent in management circles for almost two decades, but they have become more powerful concepts for improving process performance with the advent of activity-based costing. In the early stages of implementing a process improvement program, it is often important to justify the program with cost savings. Information on the cost of alternative activities may assist in determining the best way to perform a process. Developing cost information for current activities is illustrated in the next section of this chapter.

LEARNING OBJECTIVE 5

ACTIVITY-BASED COSTING

A **cost objective** is any object to which costs are assigned. In management accounting, the selection of cost objectives and the subsequent cost assignments are made to assist in internal decision making. Consequently, the selection of a cost objective depends on the decision at hand. Possible cost objectives include processes, products, projects, services, and customers. Activity-based costing is used to develop cost information for the following (and other) purposes in which management might be interested:

- The cost of processing a purchase order to assist in continuous improvement.
- The cost of a product or service to determine the profitability of the product or service.
- The cost of alternative long-distance telephone carriers (MCI versus Sprint versus AT&T) to identify the carrier with the best combination of quality, service, and cost.

Activity-based costing (ABC) involves determining the cost of activities and tracing their costs to cost objectives on the basis of the cost objective's utilization of units of activity. ABC concepts were introduced in Chapter 2 when we considered the hierarchy of activity costs. We used activity cost information in Chapter 3 for contribution analysis and in Chapter 4 for an equipment replacement decision. Having introduced the value chain, processes within the value chain, and activities within processes, we are now ready to consider the assignment of costs to activities and the determination of the cost per unit of activity.

The concepts underlying ABC can be summarized in the following two statements and illustrations:

1. Activities performed to fill customer needs consume resources that cost money.

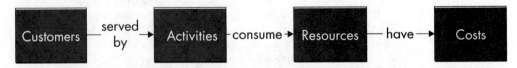

2. The cost of resources consumed by activities should be assigned to cost objectives on the basis of the units of activity consumed by the cost objective.

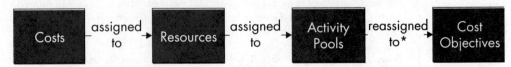

Based on units of activity utilized by the cost objective.

---

[3]Marshall Romney, "Business Process Reengineering," *The CPA Journal,* October 1994, pp. 30–31.

The cost objective is typically a product or service provided to a customer. Depending on the information needs of decision makers, the cost objective might be the customer.

Two-Stage Model

The most widely used approach to activity-based costing involves the use of a two-stage model. In the first stage, costs are assigned to activities. In the second stage, costs are reassigned from activities to cost objectives on the basis of the cost objective's use of activities. Operationalizing the two-stage model requires the following:

1. Identifying activities.
2. Assigning costs to activities.
3. Determining the basis (activity cost driver) for assigning the cost of activities to cost objectives.
4. Determining the cost per unit of activity.
5. Reassigning costs from the activity to the cost objective on the basis of the cost objective's volume of consumption of activities.

Identifying Activities. To simplify the illustration of ABC concepts, the example involves two processes: (1) inbound logistics and (2) operations in a manufacturing organization. We assume that the purpose is to determine the total cost and profitability of jobs completed. The review problem in this chapter continues the example with the addition of activity costs for outbound logistics, marketing and sales, and service. The following example combined with the review problem illustrates the use of activity-based costing across an organization's entire internal value chain.

Assume that Detroit Metal Shop produces custom metal parts in response to customer job orders. Inbound logistics are handled by the Purchasing Department, whose activities include placing the purchase orders for raw materials used in specific jobs and receiving the raw materials. Operations are handled in the Machining and Finishing departments. The Machining Department activities include setup, performed once for each job, and conversion, which is a function of the time (work) required to complete machine operations on the job. Conversion activities are performed automatically by machines once the machines have been set up. In the Finishing Department, the metal parts are polished by hand and packed. Detroit's inbound logistics and operations activities are summarized as follows:

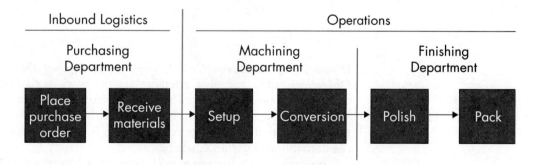

Assigning Costs to Activities. Because accounting systems are typically designed to assign costs to departments, additional analysis is required to determine the cost of activities performed in each department. The assignment of costs to activities may be based on objective data, perhaps from job descriptions or engineering time studies. Cost assignments are just as likely to be based on subjective estimates obtained from interviews and questionnaires. The costs and benefits of increasingly accurate cost assignments must be considered. Although it may be possible to have employees keep detailed logs of how they spend their time, keeping such a log is very time consuming and costly. Consequently, in assigning costs to activities, the analyst will often settle for approximately correct information.

An analysis of available records and interviews with Purchasing Department personnel reveals the following:

- The total costs of operating the Purchasing Department during a month amount to $45,000 (when the department is operating at its practical capacity of 200 purchase orders for $800,000 of direct materials). Salaries and wages of $33,000 and other costs of $12,000 are included in the $45,000.
- Three purchasing agents are involved in contacting suppliers and processing purchase orders. Each purchase order receives identical attention, regardless of its dollar value. Purchasing agents earn an average of $4,000 per month.
- Five receiving employees are involved in unloading, unpacking, and inspecting incoming goods. During interviews, the receiving employees indicated that approximately 20 percent of their time is spent verifying the specific requirements for each order and 80 percent of their time is spent on factors related to the dollar amount of each order. Receiving employees are paid $3,000 per month.
- The department supervisor indicated that his time is equally divided among each of the eight purchasing agents and receiving room employees. The supervisor is paid $6,000 per month.
- Other costs of the Purchasing Department are related to space. Ignoring the space of the supervisor's office, the purchase order-processing activity uses approximately 15 percent of the department's space, and the receiving area uses the remaining 85 percent.

Monthly costs of the Purchasing Department activities are as follows:

	Placing Purchase Orders	Receiving Materials
Salaries:		
Purchasing agents ($4,000 × 3 agents)	$12,000	
Receiving room employees ($3,000 × 5 employees)		$15,000
Supervisor		
($6,000 × 0.375 time with purchasing agents)	2,250	
($6,000 × 0.625 time with receiving employees)		3,750
Other costs:		
($12,000 × 0.15 purchasing space)	1,800	
($12,000 × 0.85 receiving space)		10,200
Total	$16,050	$28,950

Determining the Basis (Cost Driver) for Assigning the Cost of Activities to Cost Objectives. The basis for assigning activity costs to cost objectives can be identified from direct observation, from interviews, from questionnaires, from statistical analysis, and from logical analysis. Interviews with Detroit Metal Shop's purchasing agents reveal that the number of purchase orders is the best basis for assigning the costs of the activity *placing purchase orders.*

Interviews with receiving employees reveal that the activity *receiving materials* has two important subactivities: (1) verifying the purchase order and (2) unloading, unpacking, and inspecting. It is determined that the number of purchase orders is the best basis for assigning the costs of the activity *verifying purchase orders* and that the dollar amount of purchase orders is the best basis for assigning the costs of the activity *unloading/unpacking/inspecting.*[4]

---

[4]If data from several periods were available, multiple regression analysis might be used to determine the cost per purchase order and the cost per dollar amount.

This refinement of data is an inherent part of a subjective procedure intended to provide relevant information for management decisions. Reanalyzing the Purchasing Department costs, we now have three major activities with the following activity costs:

	Placing Purchase Orders	Verifying Purchase Orders	Unloading/ Unpacking/ Inspecting
Salaries:			
Purchasing agent ($4,000 × 3 agents)	$12,000		
Receiving room employees			
($3,000 × 5 employees × 0.20 verifying time)		$3,000	
($3,000 × 5 employees × 0.80 unloading/unpacking/inspecting time)			$12,000
Supervisor:			
($6,000 × 0.375 time with purchasing agents)	2,250		
($6,000 × 0.625 time with receiving employees × 0.20 verifying time)		750	
($6,000 × 0.625 time with receiving employees × 0.80 unloading/unpacking/inspecting time)			3,000
Other costs*:			
($12,000 × 0.15 purchasing space)	1,800		
($12,000 × 0.85 receiving space)			10,200
Total	$16,050	$3,750	$25,200

Because the purchase order is verified before the delivery trucks are unloaded, the space devoted to this activity is assumed to be insignificant.

Note that the number of purchase orders is the cost driver used for assigning the cost of two activities, "placing purchase orders" and "verifying purchase orders." To minimize computations, when the costing purpose is to determine the cost of a product or service, some analysts recommend combining activities that have the same basis of cost assignment. However, if the purpose of the analysis is to improve the process, it is better to separately track activities and costs, even if two or more activities have the same cost driver.

Determining the Cost per Unit of Activity.   After the cost of activities and the activity cost drivers have been identified, the determination of the cost per unit of cost driver is straightforward:

Cost per unit of activity cost driver = Cost of activity ÷ Units of cost driver

For Detroit Metal Shop, the cost per unit of activity follows:

	Placing Purchase Orders	Verifying Purchase Orders	Unloading/ Unpacking/ Inspecting
Total cost of activity	$16,050	$3,750	$ 25,200
Units of cost driver	÷ 200 orders	÷ 200 orders	÷$800,000 dollar value
Cost per unit of activity	$ 80.25 per order	$18.75 per order	0.0315 per dollar

Assigning Activity Costs to Cost Objectives.   Once the cost per unit of activity is found, the activity costs are assigned to the cost objectives based on the number of units of activity performed for the cost objective. Detroit Metal Shop's management wishes to know the total costs of each job. The cost of direct materials is an important element of the final cost of each job. Assume that Job 102 requires two purchase orders for direct materials, in the amounts of $5,000 and $3,500, respectively.

An activity-based cost system treats these two purchases as cost objectives, assigning costs as follows:

	Purchase Order 1	Purchase Order 2	Total
Direct materials costs	$5,000.00	$3,500.00	$8,500.00
Activity costs:			
Placing purchase order	$ 80.25	$ 80.25	$ 160.50
Verifying purchase order	18.75	18.75	37.50
Unloading/unpacking/inspecting			
($5,000 × 0.0315)	157.50		
($3,500 × 0.0315)		110.25	267.75
Total	256.50	209.25	465.75
Total costs assigned to cost objective	$5,256.50	$3,709.25	$8,965.75

The relationships between the Purchasing Department, the three activities performed in the department, and the purchase orders are illustrated below. In the hierarchy of activity costs, the costs of placing the purchase order and verifying the purchase order are batch-level costs, and the costs of unloading, unpacking, and inspecting are unit-level costs.

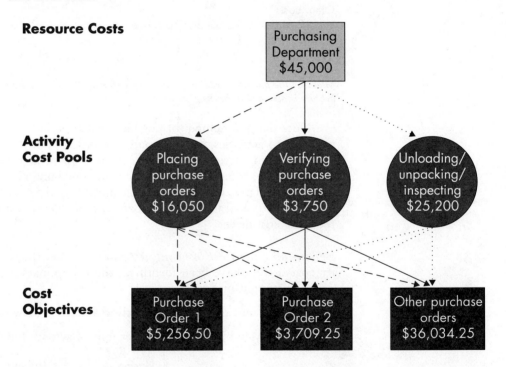

Continuing with the Detroit Metal Shop example, assume that procedures similar to those discussed for the Purchasing Department activities were used to determine the following activity costs in the Machining and Finishing departments:

Machining Department:
Setup .... $250 per job
Conversion .... 100 per machine hour
Finishing Department:
Polish .... $ 50 per labor hour
Pack .... 5 per kilogram

If Job 102 requires 35 machine hours in the Machining Department and 20 labor hours in the Finishing Department and has a final weight of 450 kilograms, the costs assigned to this cost objective for operations processes total $7,000.

Job 102

Activity costs:
Machining Department:

Setup	$ 250
Conversion ($100 × 35 machine hours)	3,500

Finishing Department:

Polish ($50 × 20 labor hours)	1,000
Pack ($5 × 450 kilograms)	2,250
Total costs assigned to cost objective	$7,000

The relationships among the Machining and Finishing departments, the four activities performed, and Job 102 are illustrated by the following diagram:

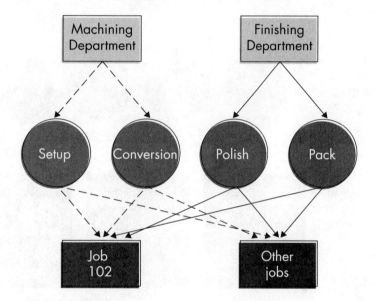

The costs assigned to Job 102 through the end of inbound logistics and operations total $15,965.75.

Direct materials:		
Order 1	$5,000.00	
Order 2	3,500.00	$ 8,500.00
Inbound logistics:		
Placing purchase order	$ 160.50	
Verifying purchase order	37.50	
Unloading/unpacking/inspecting	267.75	465.75
Operations:		
Setup	$ 250.00	
Conversion	3,500.00	
Polish	1,000.00	
Pack	2,250.00	7,000.00
Total costs assigned to Job 102		$15,965.75

A generalized version of the two-stage activity-based costing model is presented in Exhibit 5–4. The arrows represent cost reassignments. Note the following:

- Resource costs are any costs incurred for goods or services for the benefit of one or more cost objectives.
- Resource costs include costs that are directly traceable to cost objectives, such as direct materials, and costs that are not traced directly to cost objectives, such as

EXHIBIT 5-4

TWO-STAGE ACTIVITY-BASED COSTING MODEL

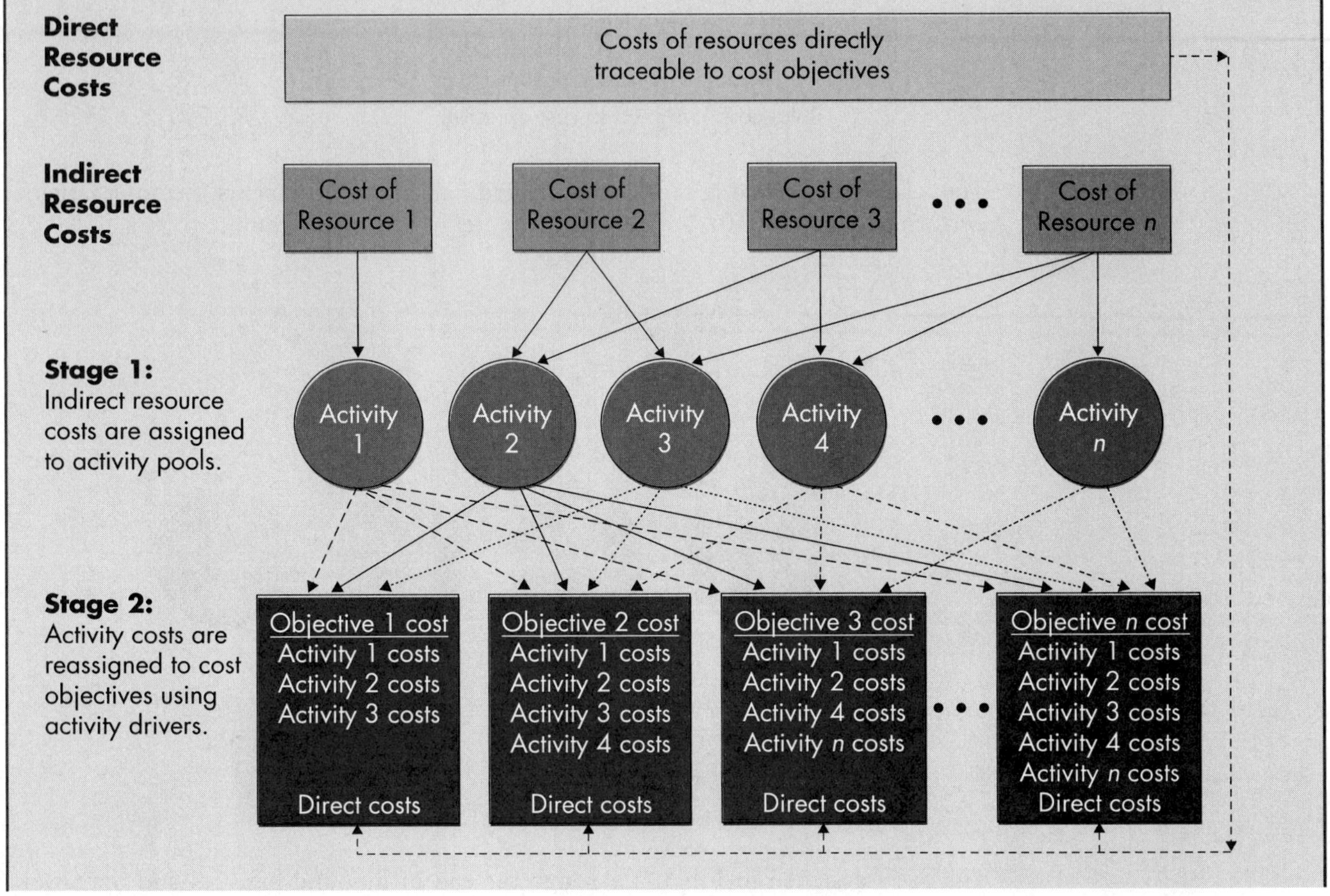

incidental materials and supplies or supervisory labor in a department that makes several different products.

- In accounting systems, cost of resources that can be traced to a specific cost objective are typically assigned directly to the cost objective. Therefore, they are not assigned to cost objectives through the ABC system.

- In accounting systems, the costs of resources that cannot be traced directly to a specific cost objective are typically assigned to temporary resource accounts (usually referred to as *overhead accounts*). These costs are assigned to cost objectives through the ABC system.

- In Stage 1 of the two-stage ABC model, the indirect costs assigned to temporary resource accounts are reassigned to activity pools. In Stage 2, these activity pools are reassigned to cost objectives.

- Individual resource categories may be associated with one or more activity pools, and a given activity pool is usually associated with one or more resource categories. For example, supervisory labor may be associated with both the setup and inspection activity cost pools. Furthermore, setup costs would include labor and supplies as well as other indirect resource costs.

ADDITIONAL CONSIDERATIONS

Activity-based costing is a relatively new approach to cost assignment. However, because of its ability to provide a more detailed and relevant analysis of costs for internal decision making, ABC is gaining recognition as being superior to cost assignment systems traditionally used for financial reporting.[5]

Because activity-based costing is not guided by financial accounting requirements, there is wide variation in the components of ABC systems. One size does not fit all. Each ABC system is designed to fit the needs and circumstances of a particular organization. These characteristics make the implementation of ABC systems time consuming and expensive. Consequently, many organizations develop ABC cost information on an irregular basis to assist with strategic decisions such as analyzing the profitability of products or services. Some organizations only develop ABC data for processes that management deems critical for success such as manufacturing or marketing and sales.

ABC Information Assists in Decisions. ABC information assists in evaluating product, service, and customer profitability. Management may determine that a customer is more profitable than originally thought, in which case, it should make extra efforts to retain the customer. Alternatively, management might determine that a product, though previously thought to be profitable, is highly unprofitable. In this case, management might want to consider discontinuing the product, encouraging customers to purchase substitutes, raising prices, or undertaking cost reducing process improvements. What's Happening 5–3 describes product profitability information provided by an ABC system at Alcoa, Inc.

Activity-Based Costs Are Strategic. Some analysts argue that activity-based costs would be more useful for short-range decision making if separate rates were developed for variable costs that changed with the volume of activity and for fixed costs that do not change with the volume of activity. Others respond that activity-based costing is intended to assist in making long-term structural and organizational

---

5-3   WHAT'S HAPPENING

ALCOA INSTALLS ABC SYSTEM TO REDUCE COSTS

Facing a downturn in its aviation sector in early 1999, managers of Alcoa, Inc., turned to activity-based costing as a means of determining how much of its overhead was being used to make each product. Since its Cleveland plant had so few products, measuring the amount of overhead for each product and, hence, each product's profitability was important so good decisions could be made about which products to keep. The plant's business analyst, Jeffrey Weeks, said that with complex processes, varied output, and long production cycles, "We had to make sure that we could make money on our products."

Alcoa used ABC to capture indirect costs such as those for setups, quality control, and packing and shipping. Using proprietary software to generate its ABC costs, Alcoa is in a position to make smarter decisions. Not only is it using the results of the ABC study to make decisions such as which line of business to pursue and which assets to sell, but also it is using the data "to rejigger its prices."

Source: Hugh Filmann, "Manufacturing Masters Its ABCs," *Business Week,* August 7, 2000, pp. 86–89.

---

[5] "ABC Beats Old-Style Costing, Survey Finds," *Accounting Today,* June 6, 1994, p. 14; "More Companies Turn to ABC," *Journal of Accountancy,* July 1994, p. 14; and Kip R. Krumwiede, "ABC: Why It's Tried and How It Succeeds," *Management Accounting,* April 1998, pp. 32–38.

decisions rather than day-to-day short-range decisions and that all costs are variable in the long run. One danger of separating fixed and variable costs in a model for strategic planning is that decision makers may be left believing that variable costs are more important than fixed costs because fixed costs cannot be controlled in the near term. Such an attitude leads to continual growth of fixed costs and a feeling of helplessness on the part of managers. ABC is intended to help reassert control over so-called fixed costs, which increased dramatically during the twentieth century.

The long-range cost perspective of ABC contrasts with the extreme short-run viewpoint of costs in the theory of constraints. In the illustration developed previously in this chapter, materials, inbound logistics, and operations costs totaling $15,965.75 were assigned to Job 102. The review problem for this chapter adds additional activity-based costs for outbound logistics, marketing and sales, and service to Job 102. Throughput accounting, on the other hand, would assign only the direct materials costs of $8,500 to Job 102 and regard all other costs as fixed. Traditional product costing systems used for financial reporting (discussed in Chapters 6–8) would give yet another cost.

Activity-Based Costs Should Be Based on Practical Capacity.

With most costs (other than direct materials) fixed in the short run, the number of units of the activity cost driver has a major impact on the cost per unit of activity.

$$\text{Cost per unit of activity} = \frac{\text{Cost of activity}}{\text{Units of activity cost driver}}$$

When initially implementing ABC, organizations frequently use the actual cost of an activity and the actual number of units of an activity. However, to avoid variations in cost assignments that result solely from capacity utilization, activity costs should be developed using practical capacity. **Practical capacity** is the maximum possible activity while allowing for normal repairs and maintenance.

Practical capacity produces lower costs than actual activity or average activity. The resulting cost assignments are a better indication of what costs would be if capacity and utilization were in balance. For an organization to be a world-class competitor, management must strive to balance capacity and utilization. With the competition accomplishing this, few customers are willing to pay for excess capacity. In the accounting records, unassigned costs resulting from the underutilization of capacity can be identified as an idle capacity variance. The existence and the magnitude of the variance are clear signals to management that excess capacity exists.

Measuring the Performance of Activities and Processes.

The use of management accounting information to develop performance reports for departments and functional areas, such as marketing, manufacturing, and administration, is considered in Chapter 12. Those performance reports are developed in a relatively straightforward manner from the accounting records.

ABC can be used to develop financial performance reports for processes or activities. Returning to our example of Detroit Metal Shop, assume that the total budget for the activity placing purchase orders is $16,050 for the month and that the activity cost per order is $80.25 at a practical capacity of 200 orders. Now assume that during the month of July, the actual cost of this activity was $15,500 and that 180 orders were placed.

Actual activity costs were less than budgeted activity costs, producing a $550 ($16,050 − $15,500) favorable (F) activity cost variance. Because there were only 180 orders, the costs assigned to cost objectives amounted to $14,445 ($80.25 × 180), and the idle capacity variance was $1,605 ($16,050 − $14,445) unfavorable (U). These two variances are summarized as follows:

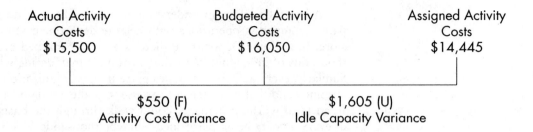

Actual Activity Costs	Budgeted Activity Costs	Assigned Activity Costs
$15,500	$16,050	$14,445

$550 (F)	$1,605 (U)
Activity Cost Variance	Idle Capacity Variance

The activity cost variance indicates that actual activity costs were less than the budgeted activity costs. Management might try to find out why this is so. Perhaps it is possible and appropriate to plan on similar cost reductions in future budgets. The idle capacity variance is a reminder of the existence of excess capacity.

Number of Cost Drivers. Determining when to stop is a major issue in developing ABC models. While increasing the number of activity cost drivers will increase accuracy, there comes a point where the marginal improvements from expanding the model are more than offset by the additional costs. Trying for too much accuracy is a widely recognized reason for failure in attempts to implement ABC systems. A survey revealed that 30 percent of the organizations using ABC had between 20 and 30 activities in their models.[6] In the final analysis, the determination of the number of activities is based on the professional judgment of the people developing the ABC model.

Multiple-Stage ABC Models. We have presented the widely discussed and utilized two-stage ABC model. The literature contains discussions of even more sophisticated multiple-stage models some of whose costs are reassigned from one activity to another before being assigned to final cost objectives. Although multiple-stage models more accurately trace the cost of activities in supporting departments to final cost objectives, few multistage ABC models are encountered in practice, and a discussion of such models is beyond the scope of this text.

LEARNING OBJECTIVE 6

ACTIVITY-BASED MANAGEMENT—THE REAL POWER OF ABC

Activity-based costing has been highly touted as a technique for improving the measurement of the cost and profitability of products, customers, and other cost objectives. In the early development of ABC, it was discovered that a by-product of accurately measuring the cost of cost objectives using ABC is that management invariably gains a much better understanding of the processes and activities that are used to create those cost objectives. Although ABC could be justified on the basis of its value as a tool in helping produce more accurate cost measurements for various cost objectives, its greatest potential value may be in its (originally unintended) by-products. The access to ABC data enables managers to engage in **activity-based management (ABM),** defined as the identification and selection of activities to maximize the value of the activities while minimizing their cost from the perspective of the final consumer. In other words, ABM is concerned with how to efficiently and effectively manage activities and processes to provide value to the final consumer.

Defining processes and identifying key activities helps management better understand the business and to evaluate whether activities being performed add value to the customer. ABM focuses managerial attention on what is most important among the activities performed to create value for customers.

---

[6]"Activity-Based Costing," *Management Accounting Issue Paper 3* (Hamilton, Ontario: The Society of Management Accountants of Canada, 1993), p. 18.

A helpful analogy in understanding what ABC can do for a company is to compare a company's operations with a large department store, such as a Home Depot store. In a Home Depot store there is a clearly marked price on each of the tens of thousands of individual items that customers may decide whether or not to purchase. Similarly, every activity that takes place in any organization has a cost that can be determined and that management can use to make a judgment about the activity's value. In an ideal world, a manager could walk through the business and evaluate the cost of every activity being performed—maybe thousands of different activities—and then decide which ones are worth the cost and which ones are not adding value. Since generating ABC data has a cost, management must decide which ABC data are likely to be useful and cost beneficial.

REDUCING NON-VALUE-ADDED ACTIVITIES: A GOAL OF CONTINUOUS IMPROVEMENT

One way to *start* improving processes is to classify each activity as value-added or non-value-added and then determine how to minimize non-value-added activities. A **value-added activity** adds value to a product or service from the viewpoint of the customer. A **non-value-added activity** does not add value to a product or service from the viewpoint of the customer.

Because non-value-added activities take time and require the use of costly resources, both continuous improvement and process reengineering seek to minimize non-value-added activities. As noted in Exhibit 5–5, the four classic examples of non-value-added activities within a manufacturing process are movement, waiting, setup, and inspection.

The movement of product between workstations in a factory or the movement of patient records between offices in a hospital increases costs without independently adding value. The movement merely facilitates adding value after the product has been delivered to the next work station. Many manufacturing organizations are rearranging the layout of equipment to minimize product movement. The introduction of the electronic filing of tax returns has allowed the Internal Revenue Service to eliminate some physical movement without rearranging workstations. Likewise, many colleges use electronic registration to minimize student movement.

Setup involves preparing to do work. Gathering your book, calculator, paper, and pencil prior to starting homework is an example of setup. Fifteen minutes spent trying to locate your calculator is a non-value-added activity. Keeping your calculator in the top drawer of your desk will reduce nonproductive setup time prior to doing homework.

Inspection involves determining whether goods or services meet quality standards. If processes can be established to ensure a job is done right the first time, every time, inspection can be eliminated.

Examining non-value-added activities for possible areas of waste is a useful starting point that may yield savings in time and money. It is seldom possible to eliminate all non-value-added activities because the way value-added activities are performed

EXHIBIT 5–5

NON-VALUE-ADDED ACTIVITIES WITHIN A MANUFACTURING PROCESS

- Movement—time spent for transfer between workstations where value-added activities are performed.
- Waiting—time spent between value-added activities.
- Setup—time spent preparing to perform a value-added activity.
- Inspection—time spent verifying that a value-added activity was done correctly.

may impact the need for non-value-added activities, such as inspection. However, a change in a value-added activity that enhances product quality would reduce the need for inspection. In an ideal situation with 100 percent efficiency, we would not have to set up equipment, move goods, and so forth. In reality, these tasks are necessary even if they do not directly add to customer value.

Once the easy changes have been made, attention must be turned to the more difficult task of reducing the cost of value-added activities. In manufacturing organizations, engineers with an understanding of cost management concepts typically take the lead in efforts to improve value-added activities. Engineers at Maytag, for example, determined that manufacturing a washing machine agitator using a gas-assisted molding process reduced the time of this value-added activity by 38 percent, cut part weight by 12 percent, and increased product quality (measured as conformance to part specifications).[7]

THE ABC/ABM CROSS

Raffish and Tourney[8] created the following graphic to illustrate two ways to look at the components of activity-based costing: the ABC/cost assignment view and the ABM/process management view. Because it has the shape of a cross, they refer to it as the *ABC Cross*. More appropriately, it could be called the *ABC/ABM cross*.

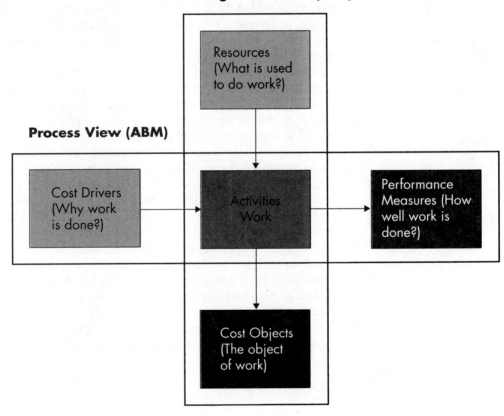

[7]Joseph Ogando, "Gas-Assisted Molding Proves Its Worth," *Plastics Technology,* July 1997, p. 29.
[8]The original ABC Cross concept was published in 1991 in *The CAM-I Glossary of Activity-Based Management*, edited by Norm Raffish and Peter B.B. Turney. Variations of the ABC Cross have been published in *An ABC Manager's Primer* by Gary Cokins, Alan Stratton, and Jack Helbling (Homewood, Illinois: Irwin Professional Publishing, 1993); and *Cost and Effect*, by Robert S. Kaplan and Robin Cooper (Boston: Harvard Business School Press, 1998).

The vertical "costing" view of the ABC/ABM Cross focuses on the cost of individual activities that produce the various cost objects and how much activity cost was incurred to produce a given cost objective. The ABC view is primarily concerned with the accurate measurement of cost objectives, not with how effective or efficient the company was in producing the cost objective.

On the other hand, the horizontal "process" view of the ABC/ABM Cross analyzes and evaluates the cost of each activity as well as the individual elements of the cost of each activity. It is not enough to know that a unit of finished product cost $25 or that a machine setup used in producing a batch of product cost $400. If we believe $400 is too high a cost of a setup procedure, then we need to know what the cost components of setups are so we can decide whether to try to lower the cost or to redesign the process to produce a lower setup cost. When management knows the cost of an activity (value added or not), or better still, its detailed cost components, it can make a better informed decision on how to manage that activity. This clearly shifts the focus from the cost objects to processes and activities and how best to manage them, which is the essence of activity-based management.

MISSION-DRIVEN PROCESSES AND ACTIVITIES

World-class organizations today are able to compete in the global marketplace on the dimensions of quality, cost, and service because they have a well-defined strategy aimed at achieving a higher-level organizational mission. An alternative to the value-added/non-value-added dichotomy for classifying activities is to evaluate their contribution to the achievement of the organization's mission. In this sense, mission-driven activities might be described as adding value, and non-mission-driven activities might be described as not adding value.

Activities associated with improving a company's quality programs if its mission is to be the high-quality producer in the industry are examples of mission-driven activities. At Maytag, for instance, the company's whole strategic image has been focused on producing the highest-quality appliances. Quality enhancement programs aimed at supporting this objective could be described as mission-driven activities.

As companies launch activity-based management programs, they usually find multiple criteria, or attributes, for evaluating their processes and activities. We have discussed two: value-added versus non-value-added and mission-driven versus non-mission driven. Other dimensions on which companies may evaluate their processes and activities include social responsibility, environmental effectiveness, total quality enhancement, and business process improvement. Identifying the activities that relate to each dimension and measuring their activity costs help management to assess how well it is performing on each of these dimensions. In addition, once activity costs have been generated for a company's key activities, these costs can be compared, or benchmarked, with comparable activity costs throughout the company, as well as with other companies, as a basis for evaluating performance. Some of the many ways that managers can benefit from ABC/ABM are summarized in a case study of six companies discussed in Research Shows 5–1.

Summary

Strategic cost management involves making decisions concerning specific cost drivers within the context of an organization's business strategy, its internal value chain, and its position in a larger value chain stretching from basic resources to final consumers. The goal of every organization should be to maximize the value and minimize the cost of a product or service to final customers. Recognition of this goal leads to an examination of internal processes and the development of partnership links with upstream suppliers and downstream customers in the value chain.

5-1   RESEARCH SHOWS

STUDY SHOWS THAT ABC SYSTEMS PROVIDE VALUABLE INFORMATION TO MANAGERS

Case studies of six companies across the insurance, banking, packaging, and manufacturing sectors, all of which had experience in using activity-based costing for a minimum of two years, provide useful insight into how companies are benefiting from the implementation of ABC systems and the adoption of ABM. Managers in the six companies advocated using in-house staff, as opposed to consultants, to implement the system so that staff could solve any problems that arose during the implementation phase. Managers also expressed strong support for the ABC system and indicated that they believed that management accountants wanted to help them improve their performance. Managers in the six case studies made extensive use of the ABC information, including these:

- Increased awareness and understanding of overhead costs.
- Better overhead cost control.
- Increased awareness of activities in the overhead area.
- Improved management of overhead resources.
- Better assessment of proposals (including capital investment proposals).
- Redesign of business processes.
- Improved communications among managers, between managers and accountants, and between managers and both suppliers and customers.

Managers used terms such as *relevant, accurate, reliable,* and *understandable* to describe their perceptions of the information produced by their ABC systems. A strong message conveyed by the participants in the study was that "it's how you use the activity-based information that matters." They also indicated that implementing an ABC system may be "a longer road to getting it right than anticipated" but "the rewards of getting it right far outweigh those anticipated."

Source: John Innes and Gweneth Norris, *The Use of Activity-Based Information: A Managerial Perspective* (London: Chartered Institute of Management Accountants, 1997), pp. 1–56.

To better understand how an economic entity adds value and incurs costs, management might further refine the value chain into processes. Studying processes that cross over departmental boundaries helps managers to understand how activities in one department drive activities and costs in another department. Once the major processes performed to serve customer needs have been identified, the next step is to determine the activities and the activity costs involved in each process.

Activity-based costing involves determining the cost of activities and tracing their costs to cost objectives on the basis of the cost objective's utilization of units of activity. ABC is based on the premise that customer needs are the immediate cause of the performance of activities that consume resources that cost money. Consequently, the cost of resources consumed by activities should be assigned to cost objectives on the basis of their consumption of activities.

This chapter and the accompanying review problem consider activity-based costing across an organization's entire internal value chain. The use for activity-based costing for the narrower purpose of inventory valuation is examined further in Chapter 7.

Review Problem

The solution to the review problem is found on page 220. To maximize your learning, you should make a serious attempt to develop a written solution to the review problem before looking at the solution. If there are errors in your solution, you should then attempt to determine their causes.

Activity-Based Costing

In this chapter, the Detroit Metal Shop example concerned the processes for inbound logistics and operations. Direct materials and activity costs for inbound logistics and operations were assigned to Job 102 as follows:

Direct materials:		
Order 1	$5,000.00	
Order 2	3,500.00	$ 8,500.00
Inbound logistics:		
Placing purchase orders ($80.25 × 2 orders)	$ 160.50	
Verifying purchase orders ($18.75 × 2 orders)	37.50	
Unloading/unpacking/inspecting ($8,500 × 0.0315)	267.75	465.75
Operations:		
Setup ($250 × 1 setup)	$ 250.00	
Conversion ($100 × 35 machine hours)	3,500.00	
Polish ($50 × 20 labor hours)	1,000.00	
Pack ($5 × 450 kilograms)	2,250.00	7,000.00
Total costs assigned to Job 102 through operations		$15,965.75

This review problem concerns outbound logistics, marketing and sales, and service. When combined with the example from the chapter, you will have completed an illustration of activity-based costing across an organization's entire internal value chain.

After studying the activities, costs, and measures of activity cost drivers for each of these processes, you have obtained the following information:

- Outbound logistics is handled by an independent trucking service that charges $10 per pickup, $10 per delivery, and $0.50 per kilogram of weight.
- Marketing and sales employees are paid an annual salary and no commission. Their primary activities relate to maintaining customer relationships, assisting customers in developing specifications and taking orders, and providing subsequent service. The annual costs of maintaining a customer are $1,000 per customer. Each visit to develop specifications, take an order, or provide subsequent service costs an average of $175.
- Detroit Metal Shop does not have a separate service staff. Marketing and sales employees perform all service activities.

Job 102 was produced in response to an order from Orleans Company. Developing the order specifications and taking the order for Job 102 required three site visits to Orleans' headquarters. The order contains parts for delivery to two separate facilities operated by Orleans. Subsequent to delivery, Detroit representatives made one visit to an Orleans facility to offer technical advice. The final selling price of Job 102 was $20,000.

Required:
a. Using appropriate measures of activity, assign all remaining activity costs that can be specifically identified with Job 102.
b. Identify any costs that are not specifically related to Job 102.
c. Determine the profitability of Job 102 by developing a statement that shows sales revenue and summarizes costs in each of five generic processes.
d. Assuming Job 102 is the only order received this year from the Orleans Company, determine the current-year profitability of relationships with the Orleans Company.
e. Classify each activity cost driver included in the textbook example of Detroit Metal Shop and the related review problem as unit, batch, or customer.

Key Terms

Activity (p. 175)
Activity-based costing (ABC) (p. 184)
Activity-based management (ABM) (p. 193)
Activity dictionary (p. 182)
Continuous improvement (p. 182)
Cost objective (p. 184)
Non-value-added activity (p. 194)
Practical capacity (p. 192)

Process (p. 175)
Process map (or process flowchart) (p. 181)
Process reengineering (p. 183)
Strategic cost management (p. 173)
Strategic plan (p. 173)
Value-added activity (p. 194)
Value chain (p. 173)
Virtual integration (p. 177)

Review Questions

1. What are the key elements of strategic cost management?
2. What is the relationship among a value chain, processes, and activities?
3. What should be the goal of every organization along a value chain?
4. What is wrong with across-the-board budget cuts as a means to cost reduction?
5. Distinguish between the value-added and the value chain perspective.
6. Why should the people who perform activities be involved in developing process maps?
7. Distinguish between continuous improvement and process reengineering.
8. Why do both continuous improvement and process reengineering seek to eliminate non-value-added activities?
9. Summarize the concepts underlying activity-based costing in two sentences.
10. What steps are required to operationalize the two-stage activity-based costing model?
11. Why do some analysts prefer not to develop separate fixed and variable rates in activity-based costing?
12. Why should activity-based costs be based on practical capacity?
13. Explain the two perspectives illustrated by the ABC/ABM Cross.
14. Define and discuss the term *mission-driven activities*.

Exercises

**5–1
Activities and
Cost Drivers**

For each of the following activities, select the most appropriate cost driver. Each cost driver may be used only once.

Activity	**Cost Driver**
1. Pay vendors	a. Number of different kinds of raw materials
2. Evaluate vendors	b. Number of classes offered
3. Inspect raw materials	c. Number of tables
4. Plan for purchases of raw materials	d. Number of employees
5. Packaging	e. Number of operating hours
6. Supervision	f. Number of units of raw materials received
7. Employee training	g. Number of moves
8. Clean tables	h. Number of vendors
9. Machine maintenance	i. Number of checks issued
10. Move patients to and from surgery	j. Number of customer orders

**5–2
Matching Terms
and Descriptions**

Match the following terms with the best description of each term. Each description may be used only once.

Term	Description
1. Activity-cost variance	a. Worth or usefulness
2. Process	b. A unit of work
3. Process reengineering	c. Selection of activities to maximize value while minimizing cost
4. Non-value-added activity	d. Has a goal of radical improvement
5. Value chain	e. A decision to pursue vertical integration
6. Activity-based management	f. Element of a value chain
7. Upstream	g. Assigned directly to cost objectives
8. Direct materials	h. Is frequently accomplished using a two-stage model
9. Value	i. A criterion for classifying activities
10. Structural cost driver	j. Entities between the one being analyzed and sources of raw materials
11. Process map	k. Actual activity costs minus budgeted activity costs
12. Activity-based costing	l. A decision to have all quality inspection performed by independent quality specialists
13. Organizational cost driver	m. Something to be minimized
14. Mission-based activities	n. Set of value-producing processes and activities
15. Activity	o. Useful starting point in continuous improvement

**5–3
Developing a Value
Chain from the
Perspective of the
Final Customer**

Prepare a value chain for bottled orange juice that was purchased for personal consumption at an on-campus cafeteria.

**5–4
Developing a Value
Chain: Upstream
and Downstream
Entities**

Prepare a value chain for a firm that produces cotton T-shirts. Clearly identify upstream and downstream entities in the value chain.

**5–5
Classifying Activities
Using the Generic
Internal Value
Chain: Aluminum
Cable Manufacturer**

Using the generic internal value chain shown in Exhibit 5–3 (page 181), classify each of the following activities of an aluminum cable manufacturer as inbound logistics, operations, outbound logistics, marketing and sales, service, or support.

a. Advertising in a construction magazine
b. Inspecting incoming aluminum ingots
c. Placing bar codes on coils of finished products
d. Borrowing money to finance a build up of inventory
e. Hiring new employees
f. Heating aluminum ingots
g. Drawing wire from aluminum ingots
h. Coiling wire
i. Visiting a customer to determine the cause of cable breakage
j. Filing tax returns

5-6
Classifying Activities Using the Generic Internal Value Chain: Cable TV Company

Using the generic internal value chain shown in Exhibit 5-3 (page 181), classify each of the following activities of a cable television company as inbound logistics, operations, outbound logistics, marketing and sales, service, or support.

a. Installing cable in the apartment of a new customer
b. Repairing cable after a windstorm
c. Mailing brochures to prospective customers
d. Discussing a rate increase with members of a regulatory agency
e. Selling shares of stock in the company
f. Monitoring the quality of reception at the company's satellite downlink
g. Preparing financial statements
h. Visiting a customer to determine the cause of poor-quality television reception
i. Traveling to a conference to learn about technological changes affecting the industry
j. Inspecting television cables for wear

5-7
Classifying Activities as Value-Added or Non-Value-Added in a Manufacturing Firm

Classify each of the following activities in a manufacturing firm as value-added or non-value-added.

a. Receiving order to manufacture a product for Big Value Hardware Stores
b. Scheduling production of order for Big Value Hardware Stores
c. Placing order for necessary raw materials
d. Unloading raw materials
e. Paying for raw materials
f. Moving raw materials to Grinding Department
g. Setting up grinding machinery to work on raw materials
h. Grinding raw materials
i. Placing partially finished product in storage area to await further work
j. Maintaining storage area for partially finished product
k. Removing partially finished product from storage area
l. Moving partially finished product to Assembly Department
m. Completing production in Assembly Department
n. Moving finished product to Shipping Department
o. Packing finished product in display cases for shipment to Big Value Hardware Stores
p. Loading packed display cases on truck
q. Sending invoice to Big Value Hardware Stores
r. Receiving payment of invoice from Big Value Hardware Stores
s. Depositing payment in checking account

5-8
Classifying Activities as Value-Added or Non-Value-Added at a Physician's Office

Classify each of the following activities in a physician's office as value-added or non-value-added.

a. Patient phones and appointment is scheduled.
b. Patient checks in with receptionist and is placed on waiting list.
c. Patient goes to waiting room.
d. Large waiting room is furnished, stocked with magazines, cleaned, and heated.
e Patient is placed in one of several examining rooms.
f. Patient's file is obtained and placed outside door.
g. Physician reviews file.
h. Physician interviews patient.
i. Physician examines patient.
j. Physician advises patient.
k. Physician dictates notes to be transcribed for patient's file.
l. Patient returns to receptionist to complete billing information and schedule any further appointments.

5-9
Developing a List of Activities for Baggage Handling at an Airport

As part of a continuous improvement program, you have been asked to determine the activities involved in the baggage-handling process of a major airline at one of the airline's hubs. Prior to conducting observations and interviews, you decide that a list of possible activities would help you to better observe key activities and ask meaningful questions.

Required:
For incoming aircraft only, develop a sequential list of baggage-handling activities. Your list should contain between 8 and 10 activities.

5-10
Developing a Process Map

The complex procedure of manufacturing cars includes the attachment of tires to the car. A brief description of this process is presented here.

Following a predetermined schedule, subcontractors deliver tires and rims directly to the assembly area. In the assembly area, the tires are attached to the rim, inflated, and balanced. Next, a set of four tires and rims is bolted to each car, and a tire and rim are secured in the trunk of the car. Finally, the five tires and rims are inspected. If the set passes inspection, the car moves to the next manufacturing operation. If one or more tires or rims fails inspection, the faulty ones are replaced and reinspected.

Required:
Develop a process map from the information given.

5-11
Stage 1 ABC at a College: Assigning Costs to Activities

An economics professor at Western College devotes 60 percent of her time to teaching, 20 percent of her time to research and writing, and 20 percent of her time to service activities such as committee work and student advising. The professor teaches two semesters per year. During each semester, she teaches two sections of an introductory economics course (with a maximum enrollment of 80 students each) and one section of a graduate economics course (with a maximum enrollment of 30 students). Including course preparation, classroom instruction, and appointments with students, each course requires an equal amount of time. The economics professor is paid $58,000 per year.

Required:
Determine the activity cost of instruction per student in both the introductory and the graduate economics courses.

5-12
Stage 1 ABC for a Machine Shop: Assigning Costs to Activities

As the chief engineer of a small machine shop, Barry Tanner refers to himself as a "jack-of-all-trades." When an order for a new product comes in, Barry must do the following:

1. Design the product to meet customer requirements.
2. Prepare a bill of materials (a list of materials required to produce the product).
3. Prepare an operations list (a sequential list of the steps involved in manufacturing the product).

Each time the foundry manufactures a batch of the product, Barry must perform these activities:

1. Schedule the job.
2. Supervise the setup of machines that will work on the job.
3. Inspect the first unit produced to verify that it meets specifications.

Barry supervises the production employees who perform the actual work on individual units of product. He is also responsible for employee training, ensuring that production facilities are in proper operating condition, and attending professional meetings. Barry's estimates of time spent on each of these activities last year are as follows:

Designing product 15%
Preparing bills of materials 5
Preparing operations lists 10
Scheduling jobs 18
Supervising setups 5
Inspecting first units 2
Supervising production 20
Training employees 15
Maintaining facility 7
Attending professional meetings 3

Required:
Assuming Barry Tanner's salary is $80,000 per year, determine the dollar amount of his salary assigned to unit-, batch-, product-, and facility-level activities.

5-13
Stage 2 ABC for a Wholesale Company: Reassigning Costs to Cost Objectives

Information is presented on the activity costs of Boston Wholesale Company:

Activity	Activity Cost
Customer relations	$200.00 per customer per month
Selling	0.06 per sales dollar
Accounting	5.00 per order
Warehousing	0.50 per unit shipped
Packing	0.25 per unit shipped
Shipping	0.10 per pound shipped

The following information pertains to Boston Wholesale Company's activities in Vermont for the month of March 2004:

Sales orders	235
Sales revenue	$122,200
Cost of goods sold	$73,320
Customers	25
Units shipped	4,700
Pounds shipped	70,500

Required:
Determine the profitability of sales in Vermont for March 2004.

5-14
Stage 2 ABC for Manufacturing: Reassigning Costs to Cost Objectives

Regency Products has developed the following activity cost information for its manufacturing activities:

Activity	Activity Cost
Machine setup	$50.00 per batch
Movement	10.00 per batch per move
	0.10 per pound
Drilling	3.00 per hole
Welding	4.00 per inch
Shaping	25.00 per hour
Assembly	15.00 per hour
Inspection	2.00 per unit

Filling an order for a batch of 60 fireplace inserts that weighed 150 pounds each required the following:

1. Three batch moves
2. Two sets of inspections
3. Drilling five holes in each unit
4. Completing 80 inches of welds on each unit
5. Thirty minutes of shaping for each unit
6. One hour of assembly per unit

Required:
Determine the activity cost of converting the raw materials into 60 fireplace inserts.

5-15
Two-Stage ABC for Manufacturing

Midwest Foundry, a large manufacturer of heavy equipment components, has determined the following activity cost pools and cost driver levels for the year:

Activity Cost Pool	Activity Cost	Activity Cost Driver
Machine setup	$600,000	12,000 setup hours
Material handling	120,000	2,000 tons of materials
Machine operation	500,000	10,000 machine hours

The following data are for the production of single batches of two products, J26 Cams and Z43 Shafts:

	J26 Cams	Z43 Shafts
Units produced	500	300
Machine hours	3	5
Direct labor hours	200	400
Direct labor cost	$5,000	$10,000
Direct materials cost	$25,000	$18,000
Tons of materials	12.5	9
Setup hours	3	7

Required:
Determine the batch and unit costs of J26 Cams and Z43 Shafts using ABC.

5-16
Two-Stage ABC for Manufacturing

Assume Duron Company, a large paint manufacturer, has determined the following activity cost pools and cost driver levels for the latest period:

Activity Cost Pool	Activity Cost	Activity Cost Driver
Machine setup	$900,000	3,000 setup hours
Material handling	820,000	5,000 tons of materials
Machine operation	200,000	20,000 machine hours

The following data are for the production of single batches of two products, Mirlite and Subdue:

	Mirlite	Subdue
Gallons produced	50,000	30,000
Direct labor hours	400	250
Machine hours	800	250
Direct labor cost	$10,000	$7,500
Direct materials cost	$350,000	$150,000
Setup hours	15	12
Material moves	50	35

Required:
Determine the batch and costs per gallon of Mirlite and Subdue using ABC.

5-17
Two-Stage ABC for Manufacturing

Marrison Company has determined its activity cost pools and cost drivers to be the following:

Cost pools:

Setup	$ 45,000
Material handling	12,800
Machine operation	240,000
Packing	60,000
Total indirect manufacturing costs	$357,800

Cost drivers:

Setups	300
Material moves	640
Machine hours	20,000
Packing orders	1,200

One product made by Marrison, metal casements, used the following activities during the period:

Setups	20
Material moves	80
Machine hours	1,900
Packing orders	150

Required:
a. Calculate the cost per unit of activity for each activity cost pool.
b. Calculate the manufacturing overhead cost per metal casement manufactured, assuming 500 units were produced.
c. Comment on the adequacy of Marrison's costing system.

5-18
Activity Cost Variance Analysis for a University

The instructional budget for Central City Evening University indicates that $5,000 is budgeted for teaching an evening class in general psychology. The Psychology Department has determined that the maximum class size for an evening class in general psychology is 40 students. Last semester, when 35 students enrolled in this evening class, the related instructional costs amounted to $5,200.

Required:

a. Determine the activity cost variance and the idle capacity variance.
b. Discuss the implications of each variance.

Problems

5-19
Unit-Level and Multiple-Level Costing with Decision Implications

Digital Calculator Company manufactures two types of hand calculators, the Custom Scientist and the Consumer. The Custom Scientist is made to order in small batches. The Consumer is produced in large batches for sale in discount stores. Presented is information regarding February 2004 manufacturing costs and activities:

	Custom Scientist	Consumer
Units	5,000	25,000
Batches	50	10
Batch moves between work stations	250	20
Direct materials	$25,000	$75,000
Direct labor	8,400	19,000
Total prime costs	$33,400	$94,000

Manufacturing overhead:

Activity	Cost	Cost Driver
Materials acquisition and inspection	$20,000	Direct materials cost
Materials movement	10,800	Batch moves between work stations
Scheduling	24,000	Number of batches
Total	$54,800	

Required:

a. Determine the (1) total and (2) unit cost of manufacturing the Custom Scientist and the Consumer during February, assuming manufacturing overhead is assigned on the basis of direct labor dollars.

b. Determine the (1) total and (2) unit cost of manufacturing the Custom Scientist and the Consumer during February, assuming manufacturing overhead is assigned using activity-based costing.

c. Comment on the differences between the solutions to requirements (a) and (b). Which method is more accurate? Assuming the selling prices of each product are set by competitive market conditions, what error might management make if all manufacturing overhead costs are assigned on the basis of direct labor dollars?

5-20
Two-Stage ABC for Manufacturing with ABC Variances

Hendricks Manufacturing has developed the following activity cost pool information for its 2004 manufacturing activities:

Activity	Budgeted Activity Cost	Activity Cost Driver at Practical Capacity
Purchasing and materials handling	$675,000	900,000 kilograms
Setup	700,000	1,400 setups
Machine operations	960,000	12,000 hours
First unit inspection	50,000	800 batches
Packaging	250,000	312,500 units

Actual 2004 production information is as follows:

	Standard Product A	Standard Product B	Specialty Products
Units	150,000	100,000	50,000
Batches	100	80	600
Setups*	300	160	900
Machine operations	6,000	3,000	2,000
Kilograms of raw materials	400,000	300,000	200,000
Direct materials costs	$900,000	$600,000	$800,000

Some products require setups on two or more machines.

Required:

a. Determine the unit cost of each product.

b. Explain why the unit cost of the specialty products is so much higher than the unit cost of Standard Product A or Standard Product B.

c. Determine the total idle capacity variance for 2004.

d. What arguments can be made in favor of basing activity costs on practical capacity rather than on actual activity?

5–21
Unit-Level and Multiple-Level Costing Assignment with Decision Implications

Mobar, Inc., produces three products in a single production department. For years, Mobar produced a single type of electric motor, the Standard A but last year added two new specialty products, Deluxe B and Special C. These new products have relatively low annual sales and are produced in relatively short production runs. However, Deluxe B and particularly Special C have proven to be so profitable that management is contemplating becoming a specialty producer of short-run products. The marketing manager observed that it made sense to move into areas where there is little foreign competition and where Mobar's ability to respond quickly to customer needs can be exploited.

The production supervisor is opposed to this action, arguing that the profits of Deluxe B and Special C are deceptive. You have been called to perform a special study of the profitability of each product and you quickly obtain the following information:

	UNIT DATA	
	Selling Price	Direct Costs
Standard A	$35	$20
Deluxe B	50	30
Special C	65	40

After discussions with the production supervisor, you determine that Mobar uses highly automated equipment that has fast unit cycle times but relatively slow setup times. Also, the setups are expensive because they require the work of a supervisor and several highly trained production employees. Once set up, however, the machines operate with little attention. This information leads you to question Mobar's procedure of reassigning production costs on the basis of units produced.

Additional discussions with production personnel and a statistical analysis of historical data reveal the following information pertaining to the production last year and the actual behavior of Mobar's manufacturing overhead costs.

	Total Units	Job/Batch Size (Units)	Setup Time per Job	Production Time per Unit
Standard A	40,000	5,000	5 hours	0.10 hour
Deluxe B	10,000	500	10 hours	0.20 hour
Special C	5,000	100	5 hours	0.10 hour

Manufacturing overhead costs:

Setup	$200 per hour × 490 hours =	$ 98,000
Operations	100 per hour × 6,500 hours =	650,000
Total		$748,000

Required:

a. Determine each product's gross profit per unit when manufacturing overhead is assigned on the basis of (1) units produced and (2) operating time.
b. Based on this analysis, what conclusion is management likely to reach about relative profitability?
c. Determine the gross profit per unit when manufacturing overhead is assigned on the basis of the activities that drive overhead costs.
d. Based on the analysis in requirement (c), what conclusion is management likely to reach about relative profitability?

5–22
Unit-Level and Multiple-Level Costing Assignment: Evaluation of Costing Errors

For many years, Underwood Motor Company has been using direct labor hours as the basis for allocating factory overhead to its two product lines, gasoline engines and diesel engines. As the company has moved toward a more automated assembly process, the company controller has suggested that direct labor hours are no longer an appropriate basis for reassigning costs to the products. Accordingly, she has engaged in a detailed study of factory overhead cost drivers with the factory engineers and is suggesting a revision in the costing system that will better reflect activity-based costing. She is proposing that three cost pools and allocation bases be used: one pool for labor-related costs that will be assigned based on direct labor hours, another pool for machine maintenance and support based on machine hours, and the final one for space costs assigned on the basis of the number of hours the assembly line is set up to run the respective products. The following data have been collected for the most recent month of production activity:

	Direct Labor Hours	Machine Hours	Assembly Hours	Units Produced
Gasoline engines	20,000	2,000	320	1,000
Diesel engines	10,000	8,000	80	500
Total	30,000	10,000	400	1,500

Factory overhead costs:
Indirect labor-related costs	$750,000
Indirect machine-related costs	300,000
Indirect space-related costs	150,000

Required:

a. Under the old system of indirect cost allocation, how much factory overhead cost would be allocated to each gasoline and diesel engine produced during the month?

b. Under the new system of indirect cost assignment, how much factory overhead cost would be allocated to each gasoline and diesel engine produced during the month?

c. Assuming the new system is more accurate than the old system, which product has been assigned too much cost (cross-subsidizing the cost of the other) and by how much?

d. What are the implications of cross-subsidization for product costing, product pricing, product sales, and firm profitability?

e. Does the proposed new system constitute an activity-based costing system, or is it just a unit-level system with more cost pools? Explain.

**5-23
ABC—A Service
Application**

Cumberland Village is a senior living community that offers a full range of services including independent living, assisted living, and skilled nursing care. The assisted living division provides residential space, meals, and medical services (MS) to its residents. The current costing system adds the cost of all of these services (space, meals, and MS) and divides by total resident days to get a cost per resident day for each month. Recognizing that MS tends to vary significantly among the residents, Cumberland's accountant recommended that an ABC system be designed to calculate more accurately the cost of MS provided to residents. She decided that residents should be classified into four categories (A, B, C, D) based on the level of services received, with group A representing the lowest level of service and D representing the highest level of service. Two cost drivers being considered for measuring MS costs are number of assistance calls and number of assistant contacts. A contact is registered each time an assistance professional provides medical services or aid to a resident. The accountant has gathered the following data for the most recent annual period:

Resident Classification	Annual Resident Days	Annual Assistance Hours	Number of Assistance Contacts
A	8,760	15,000	60,000
B	6,570	20,000	52,000
C	4,380	22,500	52,000
D	2,190	32,500	52,000
	21,900	90,000	216,000

Other data:

Total cost of medical services for the period $2,625,000
Total cost of meals and residential space $3,000,000

Required (round all answers to the nearest dollar):

a. Determine the ABC cost of a resident day for each category of residents using assistance hours as the cost driver.

b. Determine the ABC cost of a resident day for each category of residents using assistance contacts as the cost driver.

c. Which cost driver do you think provides the more accurate measure of the cost per day for a Cumberland resident?

**5-24
Activity-Based
Costing Application**

Aristocrat Tableware manufactures quality place settings (knives, forks, spoons). Presented is information regarding predicted annual manufacturing overhead costs at capacity:

Activity Level	Predicted Cost	Cost Driver	Units of Driver at Capacity
Unit:			
Purchasing costs	$ 18,000	Direct materials cost	$1,000,000
Inspection	30,000	Units of final product	240,000
Batch level:			
Setups	300,000	Number of setups	3,000
Moves	180,000	Number of moves	18,000
Scheduling	30,000	Number of jobs (batches)	500
Product level:			
Maintain molds, bills of materials, & operations lists	20,000	Number of products	20
Facility level:			
Depreciation	432,000	Unit processing steps	2,880,000*
Total	$1,010,000		

Total units of final product times the average number of processing steps per product

In 2004 Aristocrat produced 12,000 units of the Plutocrat line in two jobs. Direct costs of these two jobs were materials costs of $30,000 and direct labor costs of $5,000. The following information is available regarding overhead activities:

Jobs (batches) 2
Units of final product 12,000
Direct materials $30,000
Setups 24
Moves 72
Unit processing steps 144,000

Required:

a. Determine the total and average unit manufacturing cost of the Plutocrat line during 2004 using activity-based costing.

b. Determine the maximum possible cost savings from producing the total annual requirements for the Plutocrat line in one job instead of two jobs. Mention at least one other factor that should be considered before a decision is made to do this.

c. Why is capacity rather than actual activity preferred as a basis for determining the activity costs of a product or service?

**5-25
ABC Costing for a
Service Organization**

Mid-Atlantic Mortgage Company is a full-service residential mortgage company in the Baltimore area that operates in a very competitive market. The manager, Richard Sissom, is concerned about operating costs associated with processing mortgage applications and has decided to install an ABC costing system to help him get a handle on costs. Although labor hours seems to be the primary driver of the cost of processing a new mortgage, the labor cost for the different activities involved in processing new loans varies widely. The Accounting Department has provided the following data for the company's five major cost pools for 2005:

Activity Cost Pools		Activity Drivers	
Taking customer applications	$ 300,000	Time—assistant managers	12,000 hours
Conducting credit investigations	450,000	Time—credit managers	16,500 hours
Underwriting	500,000	Time—Underwriting Department	10,000 hours
Preparing loan packages	200,000	Time—Processing Department	10,000 hours
Closing loans	600,000	Time—Legal Department hours	6,000 hours
	$2,050,000		54,500 hours

During 2005, Mid-Atlantic processed and issued 5,000 new mortgages, two of which are summarized here with regard to activities used to process the mortgages:

	Loan 5066	Loan 5429
Application processing hours	1.50	2.75
Credit investigating hours	4.00	3.00
Underwriting hours	2.00	5.00
Processing hours	3.50	3.00
Legal processing hours	1.50	1.50
Total hours	12.50	15.25

Required:

a. Determine the cost per unit of activity for each activity cost pool.
b. Determine the cost of processing loans 5066 and 5429.
c. Determine the cost of preparing loans 5066 and 5429 assuming that an average cost per hour for all activities is used.
d. Compare and discuss your answers to requirements (b) and (c).

5-26
Value-Added Analysis and Organizational Changes in Manufacturing Procedures

Assume that Lazyboy Chair Company manufactures three styles of office chairs in batches of 100 units. Last year, Lazyboy manufactured and sold 10,000 Task chairs, 5,000 Desk chairs, and 4,000 Executive chairs. The direct materials and manufacturing activity costs per batch of each product are as follows:

	Task Chair	Desk Chair	Executive Chair
Direct materials	$1,500	$1,700	$2,500
Molding Department:			
Setup	400	500	600
Operations	500	600	800
Movement to Fabric Department*	100	100	100
Fabric Department:			
Setup	150	175	190
Operations	600	800	1,000
Movement to Assembly Department*	100	100	100
Assembly Department operations	500	750	1,000
Movement to Packing Department*	100	100	100
Packing Department operations	300	400	500
Total	$4,250	$5,225	$6,890

*$1 per unit

Required:

a. For each product, determine the total of the value-added activities and the total of the non-value-added activities per batch.

b. For each product, determine the materials cost, value-added activity costs, non-value-added activity costs, and total cost per chair.

c. Determine the annual savings from an increased batch size to 500 units. Mention some factors that should be considered before increasing the batch size.

d. Lazyboy's management is contemplating rearranging the manufacturing facilities to allow each product to be manufactured on a separate assembly line. This would virtually eliminate setup and movement activities. It would, however, require renting some specialized high-volume equipment. Determine the annual cost savings that should be considered in evaluating the desirability of the change in manufacturing procedures.

5-27
Determining Activity
Costs and the
Activity Cost
Hierarchy

Pedal Power, Inc., a new company, is owned and operated by Percilla Snyder and Jane Cummings, two young bicycle enthusiasts. To form the company, Percilla gave up a job paying $48,000 per year, and Jane gave up a job paying $52,000 per year.

Pedal Power's only product is a small electric motor that provides supplementary power for bicycling up hills. In 2004, Pedal Power produced and sold 600 units at a selling price of $300 each. The direct materials costs for this product are as follows:

Electric motor	$ 75
Battery holder	10
Switch and wire ...	15
Total	$100

Other materials costs include these:

Instructional brochure (included with motor)	$0.25
Display package (one motor per package)	3.00
Shipping box (10 display packages per box)	5.00

UPS or Federal Express picks up the shipping boxes and delivers them to customers for an average cost of $8.50 per box.

Percilla devotes her time to four activities and Jane devotes her time to three activities. The activities and the time breakdowns follow:

Percilla:
Ordering raw materials (lots of 100 units)	15%
Unpacking and inspecting raw materials	5%
Assembly	65%
Developing product	15%

Jane:
Packaging:
Individual display packages	15%
Shipping boxes	10%
Marketing and sales	60%
Keeping records	15%

Other 2004 operating costs were:

Telephone used for marketing	$ 900
Rent and utilities for space used for unpacking/inspecting, assembling, and packing	6,000
Miscellaneous costs	5,000

Approximately 25 percent of the space is used for unpacking and inspecting, 50 percent is used for assembly, and 25 percent is used for packaging (15 percent into display packages and 10 percent into shipping boxes). The joint nature of the miscellaneous costs makes it impractical to assign them to specific activities.

Required:

a. Identify all major activities performed by Pedal Power and classify them into the six generic processes identified in Exhibit 5–3 (page 181).

b. Assuming Percilla and Jane want a personal income equal to the opportunity cost they incurred in giving up their former jobs, prepare a detailed analysis of 2004 costs. Determine the total unit, batch, product, and facility level costs for 2004.

c. Determine Pedal Power 2004 income.

d. What factors would make it difficult to perform a traditional cost-volume-profit analysis for Pedal Power?

5–28
Using Activity Cost Data: Value-Added and Non-Value-Added Activities

Morvis Inc. has developed the following activity cost data for its purchasing and manufacturing activities:

Activity	Activity Cost
Prepare purchase order and receiving report	$20.00 per order
Unpack and inspect incoming goods	$0.50 per unit purchased
Raw materials inventory carrying cost	1% of invoice cost
Issue raw materials	$14.00 per type of item/batch
Move to a workstation, inspection station, or to finished goods	$1.50 per unit in batch
In-process inventory carrying cost*	$0.50 per unit in batch/day
Assembly/labor activities	$25.00 per hour
Perform quality inspection	$0.50 per inspection
Set up Machine A	$50.00 per batch
Operate Machine A	$40.00 per hour
Set up Machine B	$60.00 per batch
Operate Machine B	$42.00 per hour
Set up Machine C	$55.00 per batch
Operate Machine C	$30.00 per hour

Applicable to all units, regardless of whether they are being worked on or are awaiting work

Management is contemplating the production of a new product, G57, and desires to know the average annual unit cost at an annual production volume of 10,000 units (10 batches of 1,000 units).

Purchasing, engineering, and production scheduling have developed the following information for an annual volume of 10,000 units:

Raw Material	Annual Requirements	Order Quantity	Orders per Year	Unit Price
D34	20,000	5,000	4	$ 5.00
G77	30,000	10,000	3	0.50
H65	10,000	1,000	10	20.00

Production requirements per batch of 1,000 units are as follows:

Raw materials:
D34 .... 2,000 units
G77 .... 3,000 units
H65 .... 1,000 units

Machine activities:

A	100 hours
B	50 hours
C	50 hours
Labor	60 hours
Quality inspections	2 per unit

All raw materials required for the batch will be issued at the start of production. The machines will be set up before production on the batch begins, and units will be moved directly from one operation to the next as each is ready. This will reduce work-in-process inventories as much as possible. Inspections take place at an inspection station containing sophisticated equipment. The average cycle time for a unit from start to finish is estimated to be three days.

Required:

a. Use activity cost data to determine the total annual and average unit cost of product G57. Round computations to the nearest cent.

b. At a recent seminar, a discussion leader proposed these theories: all materials movement, inspection, and carrying activities are non-value-added and conversion costs related to materials movement, inspection, and carrying inventory are wasted, therefore management should strive to eliminate the activities that cause them. Break total conversion costs into the categories of value added and non-value added.

Discussion Questions and Cases

**5-29
ABC/ABM
Discussion
Questions**

The following questions relate to activity-based costing and activity-based management.

a. Suppose that Dell Computer has been using a traditional costing system but has decided to adopt ABC with the expectation that it would produce more accurate product cost calculations. To management's surprise, the new ABC costs were not significantly different from the old product costs using traditional costing methods. Does this mean that Dell does not stand to benefit from using ABC and should abandon it if it is less costly to use the old costing methods? Discuss.

b. IT Corporation is a hypothetical company that makes only one product, a high-speed computer processor chip sold only to one customer, an Asian laptop computer manufacturer. IT has a single plant that is highly automated with the latest production technology. Is IT a candidate for using an ABC system? Would an ABC system be expected to produce different unit product cost calculations than a traditional system? What are the possible benefits of using ABC at IT other than possible improvements in the accuracy of cost data?

c. Assume that Dell Computer's ABC system includes two activity pools (product warranty costs and procurement costs) that have the same cost driver (number of parts). Is there any advantage to maintaining separate cost pools for these two activities, or should they be combined into a single cost pool since they have the same cost driver?

d. Even though ABC usually assigns direct costs associated with a particular cost objective directly to the cost objective, are there situations in which it might be advantageous from an ABM perspective to assign some direct costs to an activity pool and then reassign them to the cost objective? Is it possible that in some contexts, ABC and ABM perspectives may conflict with each other?

5-30
Value Chain, ABC, and ABM— Discussion Case with Internet Research

GE Mortgage Insurance Company (GEMIC) was an early adopter of ABC and ABM concepts. It is a service company that provides mortgage insurance services for financial institutions and their customers (borrowers). (*Hint:* You may need to do some research on the Internet into the business of GEMIC [http://www.gemortgageinsurance.com/general/index.htm] and/or the mortgage insurance industry before attempting to answer the following questions.) GEMIC's experience was so successful that it went outside its internal value chain to encourage some of its banking customers to adopt ABC/ABM concepts into their business practices.

a. Describe the general steps in the GEMIC internal value chain that are probably involved in providing mortgage insurance products to its customers. Who is the end user of GEMIC's services? Is it the bank or mortgage company that issues a loan, or is it the customer of the bank or mortgage company that borrows money from the bank or mortgage company? Explain.
b. Describe the external value chain for the services that GEMIC provides.
c. What are some of the cost objectives for which ABC might be used to calculate costs at GEMIC?
d. What ABM benefits might GEMIC gain from adopting ABC?
e. How could GEMIC benefit from encouraging its customers to adopt ABC/ABM methods?

5-31
Cycle Efficiency

Cycle time is the total time required to complete a manufacturing process. It is computed as the sum of five time elements:

$$\text{Cycle} = \text{Set up} + \text{Process} + \text{Move} + \text{Wait} + \text{Inspect}$$

Of the five elements of cycle time, only process time adds value from the perspective of final customers. This leads to the following measure of cycle efficiency:

$$\text{Cycle efficiency} = \frac{\text{Processing time}}{\text{Cycle time}}$$

Required:
a. What would the computed amount of cycle efficiency equal if non-value-added activities were completely eliminated?
b. Should the failure to eliminate all non-value-added activities be considered in evaluating the performance of management? Why or why not?
c. If cycle time consisted only of processing time, would this mean that no further reduction in cycle time is possible?
d. Why might management select a low-speed rather than a high-speed machine to perform a manufacturing activity?
e. Assume management can manufacture a product using one of three processes. Cycle time and cost information on each process are as follows:

	ALTERNATIVE A		ALTERNATIVE B		ALTERNATIVE C	
	Time (min.)	Cost	Time (min.)	Cost	Time (min.)	Cost
Set up	30	$ 90	35	$ 100	5	$ 200
Process	300	600	500	650	100	800
Move	50	75	50	75	20	60
Wait	180	90	180	90	30	60
Inspect	30	120	30	120	10	40
Total	590	$975	795	$1,035	165	$1,160

Which alternative would be preferred if management's performance was based on

1. Minimizing cycle time?
2. Minimizing manufacturing costs?
3. Maximizing cycle efficiency?

5-32
Is Marketing a Value-Added Activity?

Custom Office Furniture designs and manufactures office furniture to meet customer specifications. Bill Martinez, senior marketing manager for Custom Office Furniture, was pleased to attend a manufacturing seminar focusing on process reengineering. In attending the seminar with Carl Janaro, Custom Office Furniture's chief production engineer, and Susan Brafman, the firm's production cost accountant, Bill believed he would gather useful insights into emerging topics that would make him a better member of the corporate team.

As he listened to the seminar leader's opening comments, Bill began to wonder if attending the program was a good idea. According to the seminar leader, "The only value-added activity in a manufacturing organization is the physical transformation of raw materials into a final product that meets customer wants." Throughout the seminar, the focus continued to be on eliminating paperwork, movement, waiting, and checking and on seeking the least-cost method of transforming raw materials into finished goods.

Riding home, Carl and Susan engaged in a detailed conversation about the ideal way to manufacture office furniture at the lowest possible costs. Finally, the moment Bill feared arrived. Carl commented that one sure-fire way of reducing costs at Custom Office Furniture would be to eliminate all marketing activities and install an 800 number directly to production scheduling.

Required:

Respond to Carl's comment and explain how marketing adds value to the customers of Custom Office Furniture.

5-33
Across-the-Board Budget Cuts

Midstate Pipe manufactures plumbing supplies used primarily in the construction of new houses. Recent increases in interest rates have led to a decline in the purchase and construction of new houses, placing financial pressure on Midstate Pipe. To maintain profits, management has announced a hiring freeze and an across-the-board cut of 15 percent in all department budgets.

Required:

Discuss the potential consequences of Midstate Pipe's approach to solving its financial problems. Recommend an alternative approach to reducing costs that might avoid many of these undesirable consequences and explain why this alternative approach is better.

5-34
The Cost and Ethics of Unlimited Returns[9]

Is it possible to have too much emphasis on pleasing final customers? Many manufacturers of consumer electronics argue that the answer is yes.

"There is an escalation of problems with returns, and it is frightening," says Jerry Kalov, president of Cobra Electronic Corp. "I think of this as a problem of consumer ethics and retailer ethics." Mr. Kalov and others are unhappy with the product return policies of discount retail stores such as that of Kmart Corp. Kmart's policy guarantees a full refund, no questions asked, any time a product is returned, no matter how long since the date of purchase.

Return policies such as Kmart's have resulted in televisions being returned the Monday after a Superbowl, camcorders being returned shortly after a wedding, and radar detectors being returned after a long trip. Mr. Kalov says Cobra even received a two-year-old cordless telephone (that had obviously been chewed by a dog) from a retailer who gave the customer a complete refund.

Robert Shaw, president of International Jensen, estimates that "bogus returns" lower his company's profits by 25 percent. Mr. Shaw believes that only 15 percent of the products returned to International Jensen are defective.

---

[9]Timothy L. O'Brien, "Unjustified Returns Plague Electronics Makers," *The Wall Street Journal*, September 26, 1994, pp. B1, B2.

In an attempt to reduce returns, many small companies are opening customer assistance phone numbers to supply the kind of technical expertise that is not available from sales personnel at discount stores. But, according to one expert, the cost of customer assistance services will ultimately be passed along to customers in the form of higher prices.

Required:

a. Does an unlimited return policy such as Kmart's pose an ethical problem? Is it unethical to buy a product with the intention of returning it? Is it unethical to return a product that has been subject to abuse?

b. Over an extended period of time, what are the likely consequences of unlimited returns on small manufacturers, small retail stores, large manufacturers, discount superstores, and customers?

5-35
Ethical Issues with
Supplier-Buyer
Partnerships

John Snyder was excited to learn of his appointment as Central Electronics Corporation's new vendor sales representative to Household Appliance, Inc. For the past four years, Central Electronics has supplied all of the electric switches used in Household's washers and dryers. As Central Electronics' vendor sales representative, John Snyder's job involves the following tasks.

1. Working with Household engineers to design electric switches that can be manufactured to meet cost and quality requirements.
2. Assisting Household in resolving any problems related to electric switches.
3. Monitoring the inventory levels of electric switches at Household and placing orders for additional switches when appropriate.

This appointment will require John to move to Bonn, Germany, for two years. Although John has mixed feelings about the move, he is familiar with the success of the program in improving Central Electronics' financial performance. He is also very much aware of the fact that the two previous vendor sales representatives received promotions at the end of their appointments.

As John toured the Household factory in Bonn with his predecessor, Janet Smith, his excitement turned to concern. It became apparent that Central Electronics had not been supplying Household with the best available switches at the lowest possible costs. Although the switches were adequate, they were more likely to wear out after five or six years of use than would switches currently on the market (and being used by Household's competitors). Furthermore, when the switches in transit by ship from North America to Europe were counted, it also appeared that the inventory level of electric switches would soon be more than enough to satisfy Household's needs for the next four months.

Required:
If you were John, what would you do?

5-36
Activity-Based
Costing in a Service
Organization

Springfield National Bank has ten automatic teller machines spread throughout the city maintained by the Automatic Teller Department. You have been assigned the task of determining the cost of operating each machine. Management will use the information you develop, along with other information pertaining to the volume and type of transactions at each machine, to evaluate the desirability of continuing to operate each machine and/or changing security arrangements for a particular machine.

The Automatic Teller Department consists of a total of six employees: a supervisor, a head cashier, two associate cashiers, and two maintenance personnel. The associate cashiers make between two and four daily trips to each machine to collect and replenish cash and to replenish supplies, deposit tickets, and so forth. Each machine contains a small computer that automatically summarizes and reports transactions to the head cashier. The head cashier reconciles the activities of the two associate cashiers to the computerized reports. The supervisor, who does not handle cash, reviews the reconciliation. When an automatic teller's computer, a customer, or a cashier reports a problem, the two maintenance employees and one cashier are dispatched immediately. The cashier removes all cash and transaction records, and the maintenance employees repair the machine.

Maintenance employees spend all of their time on maintenance-related activities. The associate cashiers spend approximately 50 percent of their time on maintenance-related activities and 50 percent on daily trips. The head cashier's time is divided, with 75 percent directly related to daily trips to each machine and 25 percent related to supervising cashiers on maintenance calls. The supervisor devotes 20 percent of the time to daily trips to each machine and 80 percent to the equal supervision of each employee.

Cost information for a recent month is as follows:

Salaries:	
Supervisor	$ 3,000
Head cashier	2,000
Other ($1,800 each)	7,200
Lease and operating costs:	
Cashiers' service vehicle	1,200
Maintenance service vehicle	1,400
Office rent and utilities	2,300
Machine lease, space rent, and utilities ($1,500 each)	15,000
Total	$32,100

Related monthly activity information for the month is as follows:

Machine	Routine Trips	Maintenance Hours
1	30	5
2	90	17
3	60	15
4	60	30
5	120	15
6	30	10
7	90	25
8	120	5
9	60	20
10	60	18
Total	720	160

Additional information follows:

- The office is centrally located with approximately equal travel time to each machine.
- Maintenance hours include travel time.
- The cashiers' service vehicle is used exclusively for routine visits.
- The office space is divided equally between the supervisor and the head cashier.

Required:

a. Determine the monthly operating costs of machines 7 and 8 when cost assignments are based on the number of machines.

b. Determine the activity cost of a routine trip and a maintenance hour for the month given. Round answers to the nearest cent.

c. Determine the operating costs assigned and reassigned to machines 7 and 8 when activity-based costing is used.

5-37
Unit-Level and
Multiple-Level Cost
Assignments
with Decision
Implications[10]

CarryAll Company produces briefcases from leather, fabric, and synthetic materials in a single production department. The basic product is a standard briefcase made from leather and lined with fabric. CarryAll has a good reputation in the market because the standard briefcase is a high-quality item that has been produced for many years.

Last year, the company decided to expand its product line and produce specialty briefcases for special orders. These briefcases differ from the standard in that they vary in size, contain both leather and synthetic materials, and are imprinted with the buyer's logo (the standard briefcase is simply imprinted with the CarryAll name in small letters). The decision to use some synthetic materials in the briefcase was made to hold down the materials cost. To reduce the labor costs per unit, most of the cutting and stitching on the specialty briefcases is done by automated machines, which are used to a much lesser degree in the production of the standard briefcases. Because of these changes in the design and production of the specialty briefcases, CarryAll management believed that they would cost less to produce than the standard briefcases. However, because they are specialty items, they were priced slightly higher; standards are priced at $30 and specialty briefcases at $32.

After reviewing last month's results of operations, CarryAll's president became concerned about the profitability of the two product lines because the standard briefcase showed a loss while the specialty briefcase showed a greater profit margin than expected. The president is wondering whether the company should drop the standard briefcase and focus entirely on specialty items. The cost data for last month's operations as reported to the president are as follows:

	Standard	Specialty
Units produced	10,000	2,500
Direct materials:		
Leather (1 sq. yd. × $15.00; ½ sq. yd. × $15.00)	$15.00	$ 7.50
Fabric (1 sq. yd. × $5.00; 1 sq. yd. × $5.00)	5.00	5.00
Synthetic		5.00
Total materials	$20.00	$17.50
Direct labor (½ hr. × $12.00; ¼ hr. × $12.00)	6.00	3.00
Manufacturing overhead (½ hr. × $8.98; ¼ hr. × $8.98)	4.49	2.25
Cost per unit	$30.49	$22.75

Factory overhead is applied on the basis of direct labor hours. The rate of $8.98 per direct labor hour was calculated by dividing the total overhead ($50,500) by the direct labor hours (5,625). As shown in the table, the cost of a standard briefcase is $0.49 higher than its $30 sales price; the specialty briefcase has a cost of only $22.75, for a gross profit per unit of $9.25. The problem with these costs is that they do not accurately reflect the activities involved in manufacturing each product. Determining the costs using ABC should provide better product costing data to help gauge the actual profitability of each product line.

The manufacturing overhead costs must be analyzed to determine the activities driving the costs. Assume that the following costs and cost drivers have been identified:

- The Purchasing Department's cost is $6,000. The major activity driving these costs is the number of purchase orders processed. During the month, the Purchasing Department prepared the following number of purchase orders for the materials indicated:

    Leather 20
    Fabric 30
    Synthetic material 50

---

[10]The CarryAll Company case, prepared by Professors Harold Roth and Imogene Posey, was originally published in the *Management Accounting Campus Report*. It is reproduced with permission of the Institute of Management Accountants.

- The cost of receiving and inspecting materials is $7,500. These costs are driven by the number of deliveries. During the month, the following number of deliveries were made:

  Leather 30
  Fabric 40
  Synthetic material 80

- Production line setup cost is $10,000. Setup activities involve changing the machines to produce the different types of briefcases. Each setup for production of the standard briefcases requires one hour; each setup for specialty briefcases requires two hours. Standard briefcases are produced in batches of 200, and specialty briefcases are produced in batches of 25. During the last month, there were 50 setups for the standard item and 100 setups for the specialty item.

- The cost of inspecting finished goods is $8,000. All briefcases are inspected to ensure that quality standards are met. However, the final inspection of standard briefcases takes very little time because the employees identify and correct quality problems as they do the hand cutting and stitching. A survey of the personnel responsible for inspecting the final products showed that 150 hours were spent on standard briefcases and 250 hours on specialty briefcases during the month.

- Equipment-related costs are $6,000. Equipment-related costs include repairs, depreciation, and utilities. Management has determined that a logical basis for assigning these costs to products is machine hours. A standard briefcase requires $1/2$ hour of machine time, and a specialty briefcase requires two hours. Thus, during the last month, 5,000 hours of machine time relate to the standard line and 5,000 hours relate to the specialty line.

- Plant-related costs are $13,000. These costs include property taxes, insurance, administration, and others. For the purpose of determining average unit costs, they are to be assigned to products using machine hours.

Required:

a. Using activity-based costing concepts, what overhead costs should be assigned to the two products?

b. What is the unit cost of each product using activity-based costing concepts?

c. Reevaluate the president's concern about the profitability of the two product lines.

John Shank Case Recommendation

Allied Office Products

This is a moderately short case that is set in the business forms business in 1992 in a company that augments its "commodity" products with value-added distribution and logistics services. The subject of the case is customer profitability analysis using activity-based costing, activity-based management, and strategic cost management. It illustrates how activity-based costing can be an effective tool for evaluating customer pricing and profitability.

Chalice Wines

This rather lengthy case is set in 1993 in California's Sonoma Valley, home of many wine millionaires. The primary thrust of the case is value chain analysis and activity-based costing. It requires the student to calculate ABC cost for a vintage of a particular wine variety and to conduct a value chain analysis including several profitability calculations for each link in the value chain. It challenges the students to consider issues regarding the value chain for one particular product as well as the implications for the business as a whole.

Solution to Review Problem

a. Additional costs of Job 102:

Outbound logistics:

Pickup ($10 × 1 pickup)	$ 10.00	
Deliveries ($10 × 2 deliveries)	20.00	
Weight ($0.50 × 450 kilograms)	225.00	$255.00

Marketing and sales:

Site visit ($175 × 3 visits)		525.00

Service:

Site visit ($175 × 1 visit)		175.00
Total remaining costs assigned to Job 102		$955.00

b. The annual costs of maintaining customer relations are not specifically driven by Job 102.

c. Profitability of Job 102:

Selling price		$20,000.00
Costs:		
Direct materials	$8,500.00	
Inbound logistics	465.75	
Operations	7,000.00	
Outbound logistics	255.00	
Marketing and sales	525.00	
Service	175.00	(16,920.75)
Profit		$ 3,079.25

d. Profitability of relationship with Orleans Company:

Profit on Job 102	$3,079.25
Annual costs to maintain customer	(1,000.00)
Profitability of customer	$2,079.25

e. Classification of costs:

Placing purchase order	Batch
Verifying purchase order	Batch
Unloading/unpacking/inspecting	Unit
Setup	Batch
Conversion	Unit
Polish	Unit
Pack	Unit
Pickup	Batch
Delivery	Batch
Weight	Unit
Maintain customer	Customer
Marketing site visit	Batch or unit (Arguments can be made for either.)
Service site visit	Batch or unit (Arguments can be made for either.)

PRODUCT COSTING AND THE MANUFACTURING ENVIRONMENT

After completing this chapter, you should be able to:

LEARNING OBJECTIVE 1   Understand the inventory requirements and the related inventory measurement issues of service, merchandising, and manufacturing organizations.

LEARNING OBJECTIVE 2   Explain the basic conceptual framework of inventory costing for financial reporting.

LEARNING OBJECTIVE 3   Describe the manufacturing environment as it relates to product costing systems.

LEARNING OBJECTIVE 4   Explain the operation of a basic job costing system.

LEARNING OBJECTIVE 5   Explain the operation of a basic process costing system.

DIFFERENT FIRMS, DIFFERENT MANUFACTURING ENVIRONMENTS

Financial reporting is the process of preparing a firm's financial statements—the income statement, the balance sheet, and the statement of cash flows—in accordance with generally accepted accounting principles (GAAP). GAAP requires that companies producing products maintain systematic procedures to measure the cost of products sold and the cost of ending inventory at the end of each period. These financial reporting concepts include some fundamental techniques and prototype approaches that managers can apply to a variety of manufacturing settings and specific products. The circumstances of USG Corporation, Navistar Corporation, and Roto Zip Corporation present very different environments in which both the cost of products sold and ending inventory costs must be determined.

USG Corporation makes the Sheetrock brand of wallboard—also called dry-wall—and has one-third of the wallboard market that sells 27 billion square foot per year. The 4-foot by 8-foot sheets of Sheetrock command a 10 percent premium price over competitors because of their ease of handling. To maintain this premium edge, the firm spends $20 million on research and development each *year. In 2000, USG earned $285 million on sales of $3.7 billion. As leading manufacturers of what industry analysts consider a classic commodity product, USG managers have improved efficiency in their five production plants to develop a significant cost advantage over their competition. USG produces wallboard at about $50 per 1,000 square feet; the competition's cost is closer to $80 for the same quantity.*

Navistar Corporation manufactures heavy-duty trucks, and its large, long haul trucks—commonly called 18-wheelers—represent 30 percent of the firm's sales. In this extremely cyclical market, Navistar competes with Paccar and Freightliner—a division of DaimlerChrysler. In 2000, the firm earned $159 million on sales of $8.5 billion. Each unit sold by one of these competitors can cost $100,000 and include many custom options to meet the needs of both fleet owners and individual owner-operators. To develop a competitive edge in this market, Navistar managers have focused on production efficiency. This emphasis has paid off with Navistar recording a 17 percent gross margin percentage compared with 12 to 13 percent for rival Paccar. (Gross margin percentage represents the portion of each sales dollar remaining after the cost of the product has been deducted.)

Begun in 1974 as a home-based business with $20,000 of startup capital, Roto Zip Corporation manufactures a unique power jigsaw that cuts easily through tile, aluminum, wood, Plexiglas, and other common building materials. In 2000, the firm shipped about 10,000 units per day to buyers such as Sears, Home Depot, Lowe's and Ace Hardware. Sales grew from $9 million in 1996 to an estimated $250 million in 2000. The privately held firm does not disclose its income. Depending on the specific model, Roto Zip's revenue per unit ranges from $60 to $200. In the early 2000s, Roto Zip managers plan to add precision drills and mini-table saws to the firm's product line.

Although they are all manufacturers, these three firms represent very different environments in which to measure costs. The volumes and products range from several hundred million units of an inexpensive commodity to millions of precision products to thousands of highly customized, very expensive items. Although the specific accounting techniques and approaches may differ somewhat among these three firms, the intent of these accounting efforts is the same. Each product costing system must accumulate and assign the costs of the direct and indirect activities involved in the manufacturing of the firm's products.

Sources: Brandon Copple, "Runaway Rig," Forbes, April 2, 2001, pp. 68–70; Stephanie Fitch, "The Gypsum King," Forbes, February 5, 2001, pp. 68–70; and Kemp Powers, "Upward Spiral," Forbes, August 8, 2001, pp. 104–105.

The purpose of this chapter is to provide an overview of product costing systems and a framework for understanding costs in a production environment. We also examine aspects of the manufacturing environment that may affect product costing systems and discuss costing issues related to the production of physical products versus the production of services.

INVENTORY COSTS IN VARIOUS TYPES OF ORGANIZATIONS

Organizations may be classified generally as service, merchandising, or manufacturing organizations. **Service organizations** perform work for others. Included in this category are Bank of America, Supercuts hair salons, The Shriners Children's Hospitals,

Pizza Hut restaurants, United Artists movie theaters, Consolidated Edison electric utility, the City of New York, CSX Railroad, and Delta Air Lines. **Merchandising organizations** buy and sell goods and include companies such as Safeway grocery stores, L. L. Bean, Ace Hardware, and Wal-Mart. **Manufacturing organizations** process raw materials into finished products for sale to others and include General Motors, Birmingham Steel, and Compaq Computer.

In general, service organizations have a low percentage of their total assets invested in inventory, which usually consists only of the supplies needed to facilitate their operations. In contrast, merchandising organizations usually have a high percentage of their total assets invested in inventory. Their most significant inventory investment is merchandise purchased for resale, but they also have supplies inventories. Wal-Mart, the world's largest retailer, reported $21.4 billion in inventories in its 2001 financial statements, representing 22 percent of its total assets.

Manufacturing organizations, like merchandisers, often have a high percentage of their total assets invested in inventories. However, rather than just one major inventory category, manufacturing organizations typically have three: raw materials, work-in-process, and finished goods. **Raw materials inventories** contain the physical ingredients and components that will be converted by machines and/or human labor into a finished product. **Work-in-process inventories** are the partially completed goods that are in the process of being converted into a finished product. **Finished goods inventories** are the completely manufactured products held for sale to customers. At the end of 2000, General Motors reported the following inventories:

Materials, work-in-process, and supplies	$ 5.6 billion
Finished goods	7.3
Total	$12.9 billion

Manufacturing organizations also have supplies inventories used to facilitate production and selling and administrative activities. Exhibit 6–1 illustrates the flow of inventory costs in service, merchandising, and manufacturing organizations. Note that in all three types of organizations, the financial accounting system initially records the costs of inventories as assets; when they are eventually consumed or sold, inventory costs become expenses.

The formalized inventory costing systems in use today were developed in the late eighteenth and early nineteenth centuries (as large manufacturing companies began to emerge both in Europe and America) to provide accountants with the necessary information for preparing company financial statements. Before the balance sheet and income statement could be prepared, accountants needed to know both the cost of inventory on hand at the end of the year and the cost of inventory sold during the year.

As large, industrialized companies emerged, the need for outside capital grew. This need has been satisfied by lenders (such as banks) and equity markets that developed to allow businesses to raise large amounts of capital by selling ownership rights in their companies to investors. Throughout this evolution, inventory has played an important role in the financial reporting process. Inventory valuations are often the basis for loans to companies, and stock prices are influenced by profits (which are directly affected by the cost of inventory sold).

Product cost information is crucial to business success. Managers use it to evaluate product profitability (since price minus cost equals profit) and organizational performance (since lower costs mean higher profit and higher profit means a better performance). It also affects the product mix as managers strive to replace low-profit products with high-profit products. Unreliable cost information can lead to disastrous results such as noncompetitive pricing of goods and services, wrong conclusions about performance, and bad decisions regarding product mix.

Although they were first developed in manufacturing organizations, costing systems are becoming increasingly important to service organizations. Whereas the term *product* was once used only to indicate a physical product, it has taken on a much

EXHIBIT 6-1

INVENTORY COSTS IN VARIOUS ORGANIZATIONS

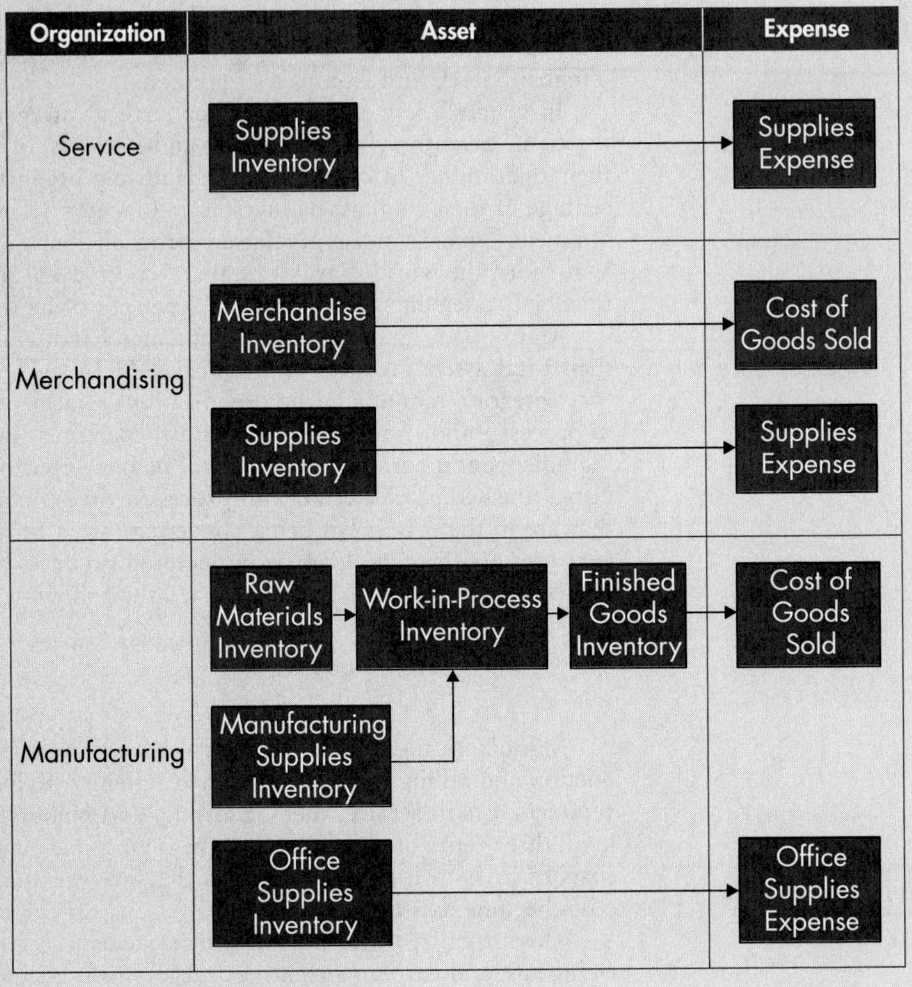

Organization	Asset	Expense
Service	Supplies Inventory →	→ Supplies Expense
Merchandising	Merchandise Inventory ——————	Cost of Goods Sold
	Supplies Inventory ——————	→ Supplies Expense
Manufacturing	Raw Materials Inventory → Work-in-Process Inventory → Finished Goods Inventory →	Cost of Goods Sold
	Manufacturing Supplies Inventory	
	Office Supplies Inventory ————————	→ Office Supplies Expense

broader meaning to include both physical products and services. In many cases, it is now difficult to determine whether a company is primarily a producer of goods or services. Is McDonald's producing food products or providing a service?

All organizations need information about the cost of their goods and services. Besides being used for preparing external financial reports, this information also aids in good decision making on a day-to-day basis that ultimately leads to a strong and progressively improving balance sheet and income statement. The profit motive and the need to produce favorable financial statements are closely linked with the need for managers to have reliable and timely cost information. Throughout the book we discuss various costing systems, pointing out strengths and weaknesses of these systems in meeting management's information needs.

LEARNING OBJECTIVE 2   **INVENTORY COSTS FOR FINANCIAL REPORTING**

Financial reporting for manufacturing organizations makes an important distinction between the cost of *producing* products and the cost of all other activities such as selling and administration. In general, inventory values for financial reporting purposes include only the costs of producing products. Costs related to *selling* inventories (such as marketing, distribution, customer service, and so forth) are all important for managerial decision-making purposes, but they are specifically excluded from product costs in the corporate financial statements.

PRODUCT COSTS AND PERIOD COSTS

For financial reporting, all costs incurred in the *manufacturing* of products are called **product costs;** these costs are carried in the accounts as an asset (inventory) until the product is sold, at which time they are recognized as an expense (cost of goods sold). Product costs include the costs of raw materials, plant employee salaries and wages, and all other *manufacturing* costs incurred to transform raw materials into finished products. Expired costs (other than those related to manufacturing inventory) are called **period costs** and are recognized as expenses when incurred. Period costs include the president's salary, sales commissions, advertising costs, and all other *nonmanufacturing* costs. Product and period costs are illustrated in Exhibit 6–2.

EXHIBIT 6–2

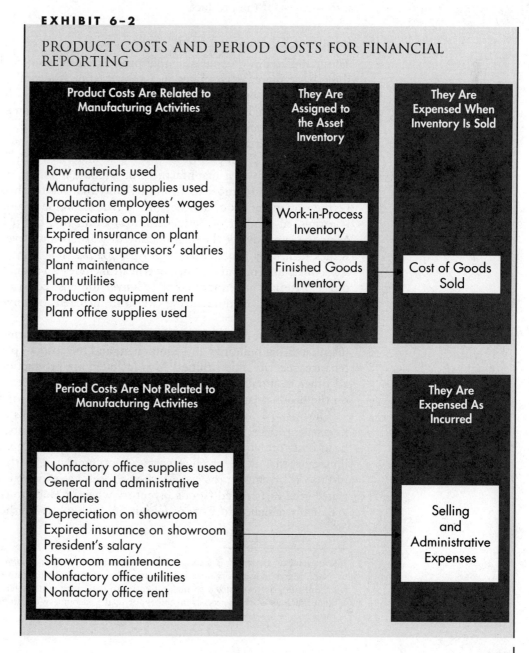

PRODUCT COSTS AND PERIOD COSTS FOR FINANCIAL REPORTING

Product Costs Are Related to Manufacturing Activities	They Are Assigned to the Asset Inventory	They Are Expensed When Inventory Is Sold
Raw materials used Manufacturing supplies used Production employees' wages Depreciation on plant Expired insurance on plant Production supervisors' salaries Plant maintenance Plant utilities Production equipment rent Plant office supplies used	Work-in-Process Inventory Finished Goods Inventory	Cost of Goods Sold

Period Costs Are Not Related to Manufacturing Activities	They Are Expensed As Incurred
Nonfactory office supplies used General and administrative salaries Depreciation on showroom Expired insurance on showroom President's salary Showroom maintenance Nonfactory office utilities Nonfactory office rent	Selling and Administrative Expenses

Costs such as research and development, marketing, distribution, and customer service are important for strategic and value chain analyses; however, since these costs are not incurred in the production process, they are not product costs for *financial reporting purposes*. For *internal managerial purposes*, accountants and managers often use the term *product costing* to embrace all costs incurred in connection with a product or service throughout the value chain.

To summarize, in the *product cost* versus *period cost* framework of *financial reporting*, costs are classified based on whether or not they are related to the manufacturing process. If they are related to the manufacturing process, they are product costs; otherwise, they are period costs. In this framework, costs that seem very similar may be treated quite differently. For example, note in Exhibit 6–2 that the expired cost of insurance on the *plant* is a *product cost*, but the expired cost of insurance on the *showroom* is a *period cost*. The reason is that the plant is used in manufacturing, but the showroom is not. This method of accounting for inventory that assigns all manufacturing costs to inventory is sometimes referred to as the **absorption cost** (or **full absorption cost**) method because all manufacturing costs are said to be fully absorbed into the cost of the product.

THREE COMPONENTS OF PRODUCT COSTS

The manufacture of even a simple product, such as a small wooden table, requires three basic ingredients: materials (wood), labor (the skill of a worker), and production facilities (a building to work in, a saw, and other tools). Corresponding to these three basic ingredients of any product are three basic categories of product costs: direct materials, direct labor, and manufacturing overhead.

Direct materials are the costs of the primary raw materials that are converted into finished goods. Examples of primary raw materials include iron ore to a steel mill, coiled aluminum to a manufacturer of aluminum siding, cow's milk to a dairy, logs to a sawmill, and lumber to a builder. Note that the finished product of one firm may be the raw materials of another firm down the value chain. For example, rolled steel is a finished product of Bethlehem Steel Company, but it is the raw material of the Maytag Company for the manufacture of washers and dryers. **Direct labor** consists of wages earned by *production employees for the time they actually spend working on a product*, and **manufacturing overhead** includes all manufacturing costs other than direct materials and direct labor.[1] **Conversion cost** consists of the combined costs of direct labor and manufacturing overhead incurred to convert raw materials into finished goods.

Examples of manufacturing overhead are manufacturing supplies, depreciation on manufacturing buildings and equipment, and the costs of plant taxes, insurance, maintenance, security, and utilities. Also included are production supervisors' salaries and all other manufacturing-related labor costs for employees who do not work directly on the product (such as maintenance, security, and janitorial personnel).

Just as raw materials, labor, and production facilities are combined to produce a finished product, direct materials costs, direct labor costs, and manufacturing overhead costs are accumulated to obtain the total cost of goods produced. Exhibit 6–3 illustrates that these product costs are accumulated in the general ledger in Work-in-Process Inventory[2] (or just Work-in-Process) as production takes place and then are transferred to Finished Goods Inventory when production is completed. Product costs are finally assigned to Cost of Goods Sold when the finished goods are sold.

---

[1] Manufacturing overhead is also called *factory overhead*, *burden*, *manufacturing burden*, and just *overhead*. Merchandising organizations occasionally refer to administrative costs as *overhead*.

[2] Account titles are capitalized to make it easier to determine when reference is being made to a physical item, such as work-in-process inventory, or to the account, Work-in-Process Inventory, in which costs assigned to the work-in-process inventory are accumulated.

EXHIBIT 6-3

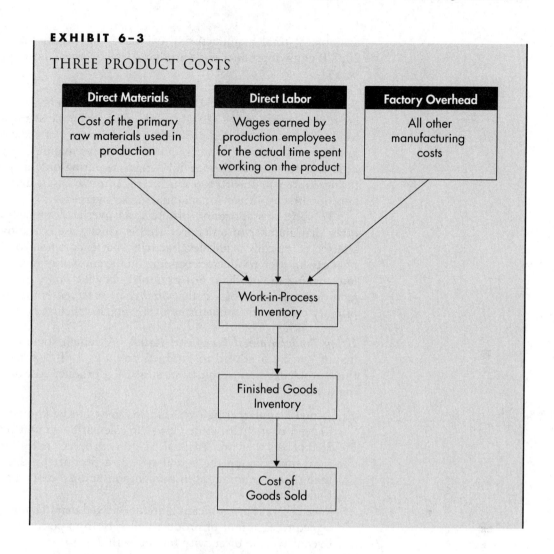

THREE PRODUCT COSTS

Direct Materials	Direct Labor	Factory Overhead
Cost of the primary raw materials used in production	Wages earned by production employees for the actual time spent working on the product	All other manufacturing costs

Work-in-Process Inventory

Finished Goods Inventory

Cost of Goods Sold

A CLOSER LOOK AT MANUFACTURING OVERHEAD

Possibly the biggest challenge in measuring the cost of a product is determining the amount of overhead incurred to produce it. Direct materials cost is driven by the number of raw materials units used; hence, its cost is simply the number of units of raw materials used multiplied by the related cost per unit. Direct labor cost is driven by the number of directly traceable labor hours worked on the product; so its cost is the number of direct labor hours used times the appropriate rate per hour. But what about manufacturing overhead? Manufacturing overhead often consists of dozens of different cost elements, potentially with many different cost drivers. Electricity cost is based on kilowatt-hours and water cost on gallons used; depreciation is usually measured in years of service and insurance in premium dollars per thousand dollars of coverage; and supervisors' salaries are a fixed amount per month.

Historically, accountants have believed that, even when possible, it is not cost effective to try to separately measure the cost incurred for each manufacturing overhead item to produce a unit of finished product. Instead of identifying separate cost drivers for each individual cost component in manufacturing overhead, all overhead costs for a department or plant are frequently placed in a cost pool and a single unit-level cost driver is used to assign (or apply) overhead to products.

If a company produced only one product, it would be simple to apply overhead to the units produced because it would merely involve dividing total manufacturing overhead cost incurred by the number of units produced to get a cost per unit. For example, if total manufacturing overhead costs were $100,000 for a period when 20,000 units of product were produced, the overhead cost applied to each unit would be $5.

Selecting a Basis (or Cost Driver) for Applying Overhead. When multiple products are manufactured in the same facilities, using a simple average of manufacturing overhead cost per unit seldom provides a good estimate of the overhead costs incurred to produce each product. Units requiring extensive manufacturing activity will have too little cost assigned to them, while others requiring only a small amount of manufacturing effort will absorb too much cost. In these cases, units of production is not an appropriate cost driver for manufacturing overhead.

To solve this allocation problem, an overhead application base (or cost driver) other than number of units produced is usually used. The overhead application base selected is typically a unit-level activity that is common to all products but varies in quantity for each product, depending on the amount of manufacturing effort that went into making the product. For example, *machine hours* may be used to apply manufacturing overhead costs if the *number of machine hours used* is believed to be the primary cause of manufacturing overhead cost incurred.

Using Predetermined Overhead Rates. Although some organizations assign actual manufacturing overhead to products at the end of each period (normally a month), three problems often result from measuring product cost using "actual" manufacturing overhead costs:

1. Actual manufacturing overhead cost may not be known until days or weeks after the end of the period, delaying the calculation of unit product cost.
2. Some costs that are seasonal, such as property taxes, are not incurred each period, thus making the actual cost of a product produced in one month greater than that of another, even though nonseasonal costs may have been identical for both months.
3. When there is a significant amount of fixed manufacturing overhead, the costs assigned to each unit of product will vary from period to period, depending on the overall volume of activity for the period.

To overcome these problems, most firms use a **predetermined manufacturing overhead rate** to assign manufacturing overhead costs to products. A predetermined rate is established at the start of each year by dividing the predicted overhead costs for the year by the *predicted volume of activity in the overhead base* for the year. A predetermined manufacturing overhead rate based on direct labor hours is computed as follows:

$$\text{Predetermined manufacturing overhead rate per direct labor hour} = \frac{\text{Predicted total manufacturing overhead cost for the year}}{\text{Predicted total direct labor hours for the year}}$$

If management believed machine hours had a greater influence on the consumption of overhead, the denominator would change to predicted machine hours.

Using a predetermined manufacturing overhead rate based on direct labor hours, we compute the assignment of overhead to Work-in-Process Inventory as follows:

$$\begin{array}{l}\text{Manufacturing} \\ \text{overhead assigned to} \\ \text{Work-in-Process Inventory}\end{array} = \begin{array}{l}\text{Actual} \\ \text{direct labor} \\ \text{hours}\end{array} \times \begin{array}{l}\text{Predetermined manufacturing} \\ \text{overhead rate per} \\ \text{direct labor hour}\end{array}$$

To illustrate, late in 2004, Harmon Manufacturing Company predicted a 2005 activity level of 25,000 direct labor hours with manufacturing overhead totaling $187,500. Using this information, its 2005 predetermined overhead rate per direct labor hour was computed:

$$\frac{\text{Predetermined}}{\text{overhead rate}} = \frac{\$187,500}{25,000 \text{ direct labor hours}}$$
$$= \$7.50 \text{ per direct labor hour}$$

If 2,000 direct labor hours were used in September 2005, the applied overhead would be $15,000, as shown here:

$$2,000 \times \$7.50 = \$15,000$$

When a predetermined rate is used, monthly variations between actual and applied manufacturing overhead are expected because of the seasonality in costs and the variations in monthly activity. Hence, in some months overhead will be "overapplied" as applied overhead exceeds actual overhead; in other months overhead will be "underapplied" as actual overhead exceeds applied overhead. If the beginning-of-the-year estimates are accurate for annual overhead costs and annual activity in the application base, monthly over- and underapplied amounts during the year should offset each other by the end of the period. During the year, the cumulative balance should be monitored to identify an excessive over- or underapplied balance and to determine whether the estimate of the overhead rate should be revised before year-end. Later in this chapter, we consider methods for accounting for any over- or underapplied manufacturing overhead balance that may exist at the end of the year.

Changing Cost Structures Limit Unit-Level Basis of Overhead Application. By using a single overhead rate, we assume that overhead costs are primarily caused by a single unit-level cost driver. Historically, a single plantwide overhead application rate based on direct labor hours was widely used when direct labor was the predominant cost factor in production and manufacturing overhead costs were driven by the utilization of direct labor.

Technological progress over the past 25 years has caused significant changes in the factors of manufacturing costs, resulting in major shifts in costs in many industries from direct labor to manufacturing overhead. A good example of this shift is the worldwide automobile industry where firms such as DaimlerChrysler, Toyota, and Volvo have spent billions of dollars on robotics and other technologies, thereby reducing the significance of direct labor in the production process. In many cases, these technological changes mean that direct labor hours are no longer an appropriate basis for assigning manufacturing costs to products. In others, these changes mean there is no longer a single cost driver that is appropriate for assigning manufacturing overhead to products.

Although some companies continue to use a single (actual or predetermined) manufacturing overhead rate because it is convenient, many companies no longer use this approach. Instead, they have adopted multiple overhead rates based on either major departments or activities within the organization.

ABC AND INVENTORY COSTS FOR FINANCIAL REPORTING

Activity-based costing was introduced in Chapter 5 where the final cost of Job 102 (see the solution to the Chapter 5 review problem on page 220) was detailed as shown at the top of the following page.

Although the entire $16,920.75 is associated with Job 102, for financial reporting purposes, only the costs of purchasing the raw materials and converting the raw materials into a finished product are classified as product costs. Assuming the job is delivered to the buyer, these costs are shown on the income statement as part of the cost of goods sold in the amount of $15,965.75 ($8,500.00 + $465.75 + $7,000.00). The costs of outbound logistics, marketing and sales, and service are then classified as period costs and shown on the income statement as general and administrative expenses totaling $955 ($255 + $525 + $175).

Direct materials:		
Order 1	$5,000.00	
Order 2	3,500.00	$ 8,500.00
Inbound logistics:		
Placing purchase orders ($80.25 × 2 orders)	$ 160.50	
Verifying purchase orders ($18.75 × 2 orders)	37.50	
Unloading/unpacking/inspecting ($8,500 × 0.0315)	267.75	465.75
Operations:		
Setup ($250 × 1 setup)	$ 250.00	
Conversion ($100 × 35 machine hours)	3,500.00	
Polish ($50 × 20 labor hours)	1,000.00	
Pack ($5 × 450 kilograms)	2,250.00	7,000.00
Outbound logistics:		
Pickup ($10 × 1 pickup)	$ 10.00	
Delivery ($10 × 2 deliveries)	20.00	
Weight ($0.50 × 450 kilograms)	225.00	255.00
Marketing and sales:		
Site visit ($175 × 3 visits)		525.00
Service:		
Site visit ($175 × 1 visit)		175.00
Total		$16,920.75

Because activity-based costing information is primarily intended to assist internal decision making, it should not be constrained by the financial reporting distinction between product and period costs. Depending on the information needs of management, activity-based costing information may be developed for any part or all of the internal value chain. If activity-based costing information is developed for the entire internal value chain (as in Chapter 5 and the accompanying review problem) and management desires to use this information for financial reporting, it is necessary to reorganize the ABC information into the financial reporting classifications of product and period costs.

As can be determined from the illustration in Chapter 5, the development of ABC information requires many subjective judgments, and the implementation of ABC requires a detailed understanding of an organization's activities and the corresponding development of activity-cost information. These factors make it apparent that although ABC is a very useful management tool, it is not always cost effective to develop formal ABC systems for financial reporting. Financial reporting requires objective data, a clear audit trail, and the consistent treatment of a large number of transactions. Many organizations find it preferable to utilize simpler systems for financial reporting. These simpler financial reporting systems often serve most of management's needs for internal information, or the information routinely produced can be modified to provide relevant information. When this is done, managers must take extra care to make sure they are obtaining relevant cost information for internal decision making.

LEARNING OBJECTIVE 3

THE MANUFACTURING ENVIRONMENT

Manufacturing personnel need to know the specific products to produce on specific machines on a daily or even hourly basis. The detailed scheduling of products on machines is performed by production scheduling personnel. Exactly how production is scheduled depends on whether process manufacturing or job production is used and whether production is in response to a specific customer sales order or for the company's inventory in anticipation of future sales.

In **process manufacturing**, production is on a continuous basis; a production facility may be devoted exclusively to one product or to a set of closely related products. Companies where you would likely find a process manufacturing environment include Exxon Mobil and Bowater Incorporated (which makes rolled paper for the printing of daily newspapers such as the *Chicago Tribune*). Process manufacturing is discussed later in this chapter.

In **job production**, also called **job order production**, products are manufactured in single units or in batches of identical units. Of course, the products included in different jobs may vary considerably. Examples of single-unit jobs are found at Hallco Builders, a builder of custom-designed homes; Metric Constructors Inc., which builds skyscrapers; and Riverwood International, which designs, produces, and installs packaging systems for food processors. Examples of multiple-unit jobs are found at Hartmarx, a clothing manufacturer; Steelcase Furniture Company, a large producer of office furnishings; and Intermet Corporation, a foundry company that makes parts for the automobile industry.

In a job production environment, when a customer's order is received, the marketing department forwards the order to production scheduling, where employees determine when and how the product is to be produced. Important scheduling considerations include the overall workload, raw materials availability, specific equipment or labor requirements, and the delivery date(s) of the finished product.

Important staff groups involved in production planning and control include engineering, scheduling, expediting, quality control, and accounting. Engineering is primarily concerned with determining how a product should be produced. Based on an engineering analysis and cost data, engineering personnel develop manufacturing specifications for each product. These manufacturing specifications are often summarized in two important documents: a bill of materials and an operations list. Each product's **bill of materials** specifies the kinds and quantities of raw materials required for one unit of product. The **operations list** (sometimes called an **activities list**) specifies the manufacturing operations and related times required for one unit or batch of product. The operations list should also include information on any machine setup time, movements between work areas, and other scheduled activities, such as quality inspections.

Scheduling personnel prepare a production order for each job. The **production order** contains a job's unique identification number and specifies such details as the quantity to be produced, raw materials requirements, manufacturing operations and other activities to be performed, and perhaps even the time when each manufacturing operation should be performed. In preparing a production order, scheduling personnel use the product's bill of materials and operations list to determine the materials, operations, and manufacturing times required for the job.

A **job cost sheet** is a document used to accumulate the costs for a specific job. The job cost sheet serves as the basic record for recording actual progress on the job. As production takes place, the materials, labor, and machine resources utilized are recorded on the job cost sheet along with the related costs. When a job is completed, the final cost of the job is determined by totalling the costs on the sheet. See What's Happening 6–1 for a discussion of a new software product that supports job costing in the construction industry.

PRODUCTION FILES AND RECORDS

A **file** is simply a collection of related records, and a **record** is a related set of alphabetic and/or numeric data items. Both records and files may be maintained electronically on a computer or manually in a paper-based system. Important files in any product cost system include files of inventory records for raw materials, work-in-process, and finished goods, as well as files for the bills of materials and operations lists. Sample records from a manual system for raw materials, finished goods, the bill of materials, and an operations list are illustrated in Exhibit 6–4.

6-1   WHAT'S HAPPENING?

COMPUTEREASE® SOFTWARE SUPPORTS JOB COSTING FOR CONTRACTORS

One of the challenges of maintaining job cost systems with detailed cost sheets is capturing cost data in a timely manner. ComputerEase provides job costing systems software for the construction industry that enables job managers to automatically update and calculate job costs to date, projected job costs and profits, percentage of completion, and other information vital to completing jobs on budget. To provide greater timeliness, the software developer has created FieldEase, a linked program for handheld computers that allows users to enter information into the office system by modem. One user of FieldEase said, "We were working pretty much the old-fashioned way, with faxes and time cards, and we always had the feeling our foremen were trying to remember what they had been doing earlier in the week." The software developer noted that "foremen are picking it up more quickly than we expected. They're using it for time and materials because they can immediately get feedback on their job."

Source: Tom Sawyer, "Taking the Back Office to the Jobsite," *Engineering News Report*, May 7, 2001, p. 27; and http://www.construction-software.com.

EXHIBIT 6-4

BASIC PRODUCTION RECORDS

Raw Materials Inventory Record

Part No. ....   Description ....

| | Purchased | | | Issued | | | Balance | | |
Date	Units	Unit Cost	Total Cost	Units	Unit Cost	Total Cost	Units	Unit Cost	Total Cost

Finished Goods Inventory Record

Product No. ....   Description ....

| | Received from factory | | | Sold | | | Balance | | |
Date	Units	Unit Cost	Total Cost	Units	Unit Cost	Total Cost	Units	Unit Cost	Total Cost

Bill of Materials
Raw Materials Requirements per Unit of Product

Product No. ....   Description ....

Part Number	Description	Quantity per Unit

Operations List
Production Operations and Times per Unit of Product

Product No. ....   Description ....

Department Number	Operation Description	Machine/Labor Requirements	Setup Time	Operating Time

Certain files in the cost system provide the necessary detail for amounts maintained in total in the general ledger. For example, the raw materials inventory file contains separate records for each type of raw materials, indicating increases, decreases, and the available balance for both units and costs. Every time there is a change in the Raw Materials Inventory general ledger account, there must be an equal change in one or more individual inventory records. Therefore, at any given time, the total of the balances for all raw materials inventory records should equal the balance in the Raw Materials Inventory general ledger account. Because of this relationship between the raw materials inventory file and Raw Materials Inventory in the general ledger, Raw Materials Inventory is called a *control account* and the raw materials file of detailed records is called a *subsidiary ledger*. Other general ledger accounts related to the product cost system that have subsidiary files of records are Work-in-Process, Finished Goods Inventory, and Cost of Goods Sold.

Each product has a record in the bill of materials and the operations list (activity list) files indicating the resources required for one unit of the product. These files do not have related general ledger accounts; hence, they are not subsidiary ledgers.

Other records required to operate a job cost system include production orders, job cost sheets, materials requisition forms, and work tickets. These records are illustrated in Exhibit 6–5. Production orders and job cost sheets were previously discussed. The job number assigned in the production order is also recorded on the job cost sheet. The production order serves as authorization for production supervisors to obtain materials from the storeroom and to issue work orders to production employees.

A **materials requisition form** indicates the type and quantity of each raw material issued to the factory. This form is used to record the transfer of responsibility for materials and to record materials changes on raw materials and job cost sheet records. The materials requisition form has a field to record the job number; the job cost sheet has a field to record the requisition number. If a question arises regarding the issuance of materials, the requisition number and job number provide a trail for tracing the destination and the source of the materials. The materials requisition form also identifies the materials warehouse employee who issued the materials and the production employee who received them.

A **work ticket** is used to record the time a job spends in a specific manufacturing operation. Each manufacturing operation performed on a job is documented by a work ticket. The completed work tickets for a job should correspond to the operations specified on the job's production order. Time information on the work tickets is used by production scheduling or expediting personnel to determine whether the job is on schedule. When production times are multiplied by appropriate rates in the lower portion, the work ticket is used to assign costs to the job.

A manufacturing operation may involve a single employee, a group of employees, a machine, or even heating, cooling, or aging processes. When the operation involves a single employee, the rate recorded on the work ticket is simply the employee's wage rate. When it involves a group of employees, the rate is composed of the wage rates of all employees in the group. When the work involves a machine operation, the rate includes a charge for machine time, as well as the time of any machine operators. Other operations, such as heating, cooling, or aging, will also have a rate for each unit of time.

IMPACT OF COMPUTERS ON MANUFACTURING

Significant changes are taking place in production planning and control procedures. Perhaps the most significant changes involve the increasing use of computers for scheduling, monitoring, and costing. Just a few years ago, the files and records illustrated in Exhibits 6–4 and 6–5 were maintained manually, making data collection and analysis costly and time consuming. Even with centralized data processing, the original transactions were still manually recorded on materials requisitions or work tickets and

EXHIBIT 6-5

JOB COST SYSTEM RECORDS

Production Order

Job No. _____   Start Date _____

Product No. _____   Description _____   Quantity _____

Raw Materials

Part Number	Description	Total Quantity

Operation

Department Number	Operation Description	Labor/Machine Requirements	Start Time	Stop Time	Total Time

Authorized by _____   Date _____

Job Cost Sheet

Job No. _____   Start Date _____

Product No. _____   Description _____   Quantity _____

Raw Materials Cost

Date	Department Number	Requisition Number	Description	Total Cost

Conversion Costs: Direct Labor or Machine

Date	Department Number	Work Ticket Number	Description	Total Time	Total Cost

Applied Overhead

Date	Department Number	Basis of Application	Total Cost

Total Cost of Job   ═══════

Unit Cost   ═══════

Materials Requisition Form

Requisition No. _____   Job No. _____   Department _____   Date _____

Part Number	Description	Total Quantity	Unit Cost	Total Cost

Issued by _____   Received by _____

Work Ticket

Work Ticket No. _____   Date _____

Department _____   Job No. _____

Time Started _____   Time Completed _____

Employee/Machine Operator _____

Office Use		
Total Time _____	Rate _____	Total Cost _____

then entered into the computer. Today, computer terminals are often spread throughout the factory. As each operation on a job is started and completed, the job's status is entered into the computer.

Many firms have implemented bar coding and **automatic identification systems (AIS)** that allow inventory and production information to be entered into a computer without writing or keying. Laser scanners connected to a computer database "read" bar codes attached to production orders, materials, machines, or employee badges. The bar codes may be read as materials pass by a fixed laser scanner, or they may be read by a handheld scanner such as those used at major retailers, Macy's and Home Depot for example. In this environment, managers keep information at whatever level of detail they wish. Production supervisors have the capability to continuously monitor inventory levels, the status of personnel and machines, the location of jobs in the plant, the on-time status of jobs, and the costs assigned to jobs. Exception reports are easily developed to alert appropriate personnel when operations are not proceeding according to schedule.

In addition to being used to monitor production and to rapidly process data, computers aid in designing new products, controlling machine operations, and automating machine setups. **Computer-aided design (CAD)** involves the use of computers to design products. Using high-resolution computer monitors with graphics software, custom products can be rapidly designed. Engineering drawings for the product, as well as a bill of materials and an operations list, are developed when needed.

Computer-aided manufacturing (CAM) involves the use of computers to control machine operations. Although few firms have operations that are completely controlled by computers, many have "islands of automation" for some operations existing alongside more traditional labor- and machine-intensive manufacturing techniques. See What's Happening 6–2 for an example of how computers are used in the movement of materials and products.

Flexible manufacturing systems (FMS) are an extension of computer-aided manufacturing techniques through a series of manufacturing operations. These operations include the automatic movement of units between operations and the automatic and rapid setup of machines to produce each product. An FMS virtually eliminates all direct labor in the manufacturing process.

Computer-integrated manufacturing (CIM) is the ultimate extension of the CAD, CAM, and FMS concepts to a completely automated, computer-controlled factory. Production with CIM is self-operating once a product has been designed and the decision to produce has been made. In the advanced stages, factories utilizing flexible manufacturing systems and computer-integrated manufacturing are sometimes referred

---

6–2   WHAT'S HAPPENING?

A LIGHTS-OUT WAREHOUSE IMPROVES PRODUCT DELIVERY TIME AT SOUTH-WESTERN PUBLISHING

Before publishing this text, the authors were invited to South-Western Publishing Company's corporate headquarters in Cincinnati to meet the editorial staff. During the visit, we were given a tour of South-Western's facilities, including the warehouse and order-filling departments. One of the most fascinating aspects of the tour was the "lights-out" warehouse where textbooks are stored on pallets held by steel racks about 20 to 30 feet tall. A totally automated, computer-controlled system stores and retrieves books from the warehouse without the intervention of human hands. When South-Western received the order for this book from a bookstore, equipment was electronically directed to go to the appropriate location in the warehouse, retrieve the correct number of boxes of this text, and deliver them to the Shipping Department for addressing and delivery. This illustrates how many companies are using computer-controlled equipment to improve the manufacturing, storage, and movement of products.

to as *lights-out factories* because they can be operated in the dark and without people. Obviously, CIM represents a point on a continuum that begins with paper, pencil, and hand tools.

The attractions of these computer-based monitoring, design, and production techniques are lower production times, higher-quality products, and lower product costs. With lower production times, a firm obtains a competitive advantage by being able to fill customers' orders quickly, thereby providing better service. Lower production times also reduce the need for inventories that provide for variability in the demand for products or components since unexpected demand can be filled quickly. Lower inventories result in lower holding costs for spoilage, theft, warehousing, and obsolescence. High quality arises from better design, rapid identification of defects, and correction of the cause of defects before large numbers of defective units are produced. Hence, both speed and quality improvements make it possible to reduce production costs. These lower costs mean greater profits at a given price or an increased ability to compete on the basis of price.

LEARNING OBJECTIVE 4

JOB COSTING FOR PRODUCTS AND SERVICES

Exhibit 6–6 shows how inventory costs in a manufacturing organization flow in a logical pattern through the financial accounting system. Pay particular attention to the major inventory accounts (Raw Materials, Work-in-Process, and Finished Goods Inventory), Manufacturing Overhead, and the flow of costs through the inventory accounts. Each of the numbered items, representing a cost flow affecting an inventory account or Manufacturing Overhead, is explained here:

1. The costs of purchased raw materials and manufacturing supplies are recorded in Raw Materials and Manufacturing Supplies, respectively. An increase in Accounts Payable typically offsets these increases.
2. As primary raw materials are requisitioned (using a materials requisition form) to the factory, direct materials costs are transferred from Raw Materials to Work-in-Process.
3. Direct labor costs are assigned to Work-in-Process on the basis of the time devoted to processing raw materials. Indirect labor costs associated with production employees are initially assigned to Manufacturing Overhead.
4.–6. Other production related costs are also assigned to Manufacturing Overhead. Other Payables represents the incurrence of a variety of costs such as repairs and maintenance, utilities, and property taxes.
7. Costs assigned to Manufacturing Overhead are periodically reassigned (applied) to Work-in-Process, preferably with the use of a predetermined overhead rate such as direct labor hours, machine hours, or some other cost assignment base.
8. When products are completed, their accumulated product costs are totaled on a job cost sheet and transferred from Work-in-Process to Finished Goods Inventory.
9. When the completed products are sold, their costs are transferred from Finished Goods Inventory to Cost of Goods Sold.

A possible pattern of cost flows for a factory containing only machine-intensive manufacturing operations is shown in Exhibit 6–7. The major difference between Exhibits 6–6 and 6–7 is the combining of direct labor and manufacturing overhead into a single conversion cost pool. This is illustrated by comparing item (3) in the two exhibits. With all labor costs flowing into the conversion cost pool, the cost assignment rate used for item (7) in Exhibit 6–7 includes direct labor and manufacturing overhead. Another difference is the basis for cost assignment. Although manufacturing overhead in a labor-intensive operation is most often applied on the basis of direct labor hours or dollars, it is more appropriate to apply conversion costs in a machine-intensive operation on the basis of machine hours.

EXHIBIT 6-6

BASIC MANUFACTURING COST FLOWS

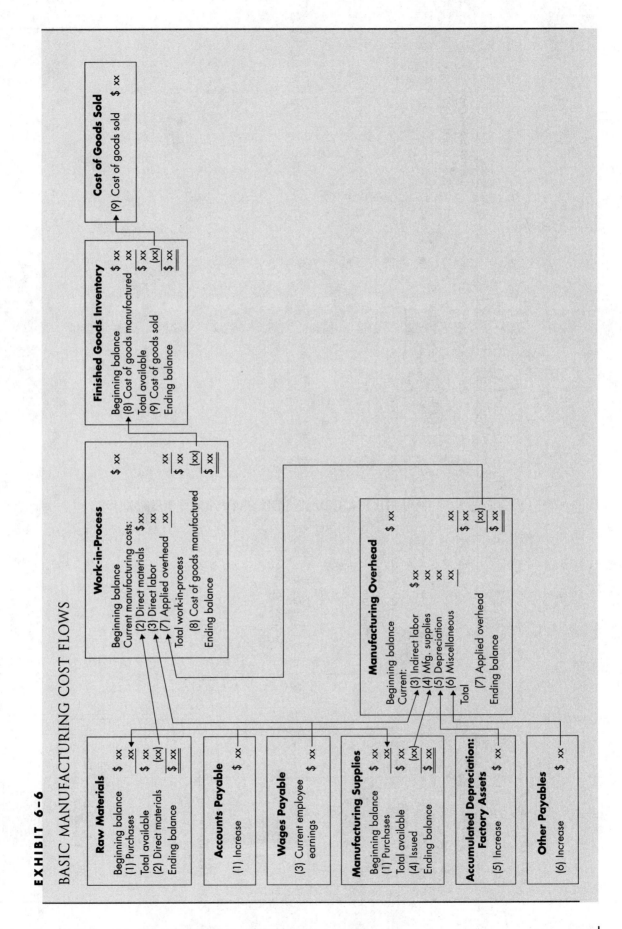

EXHIBIT 6-7

BASIC MANUFACTURING COST FLOWS FOR A MACHINE-INTENSIVE OPERATION

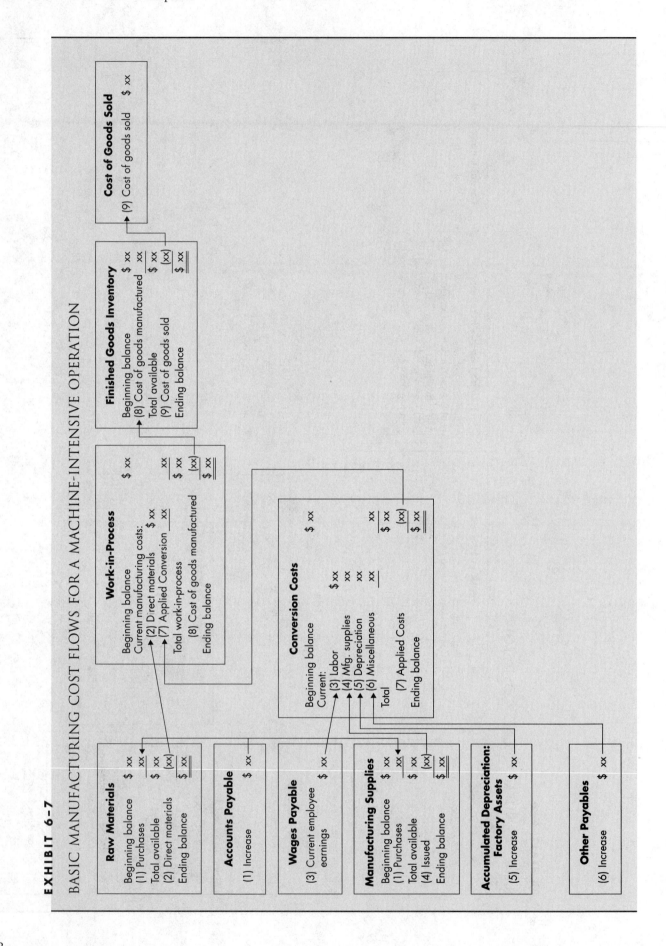

JOB COSTING ILLUSTRATED

Even though data can be processed using manual or computerized systems, data processing procedures are best illustrated within the context of a paper-based manual system. Fox Brothers, Inc., manufactures a line of wool sports jackets for men and women. Because there are significant differences in materials costs and a need to carefully control inventories, detailed records are kept concerning the raw materials assigned to specific jobs. Raw materials consist of different styles of wool fabric, interfacing fabric, liner fabric, and button sets.

Total inventory accounts at the beginning of August 2001 included Raw Materials, $36,100; Work-in-Process, $109,900; and Finished Goods, $75,000. In addition, there were manufacturing supplies of $1,600, consisting of various items such as thread, needles, shears, and machine lubricant. The August 1 balance in Manufacturing Overhead was $0.

RAW MATERIALS

Description	Quantity	Unit Cost	Total Cost
Wool fabric W09	3,000 yards	$ 7	$21,000
Wool fabric W12	500 yards	12	6,000
Interfacing	1,500 yards	1	1,500
Liner	2,000 yards	3	6,000
Buttons	400 sets	4	1,600
Total			$36,100

MANUFACTURING SUPPLIES

Item	Total Cost
Various	$1,600

WORK-IN-PROCESS

Job	Total Cost
425	$ 58,600
426	51,300
Total	$109,900

FINISHED GOODS INVENTORY

Job	Total Cost
424	$75,000

To illustrate manufacturing cost flows in a job cost system, Exhibit 6–8 presents summary manufacturing cost flows for Fox Brothers, Inc., for August 2004. In reality, there would be a number of entries for each type of transaction. Each cost assignment is supported by documented information that is recorded in subsidiary cost

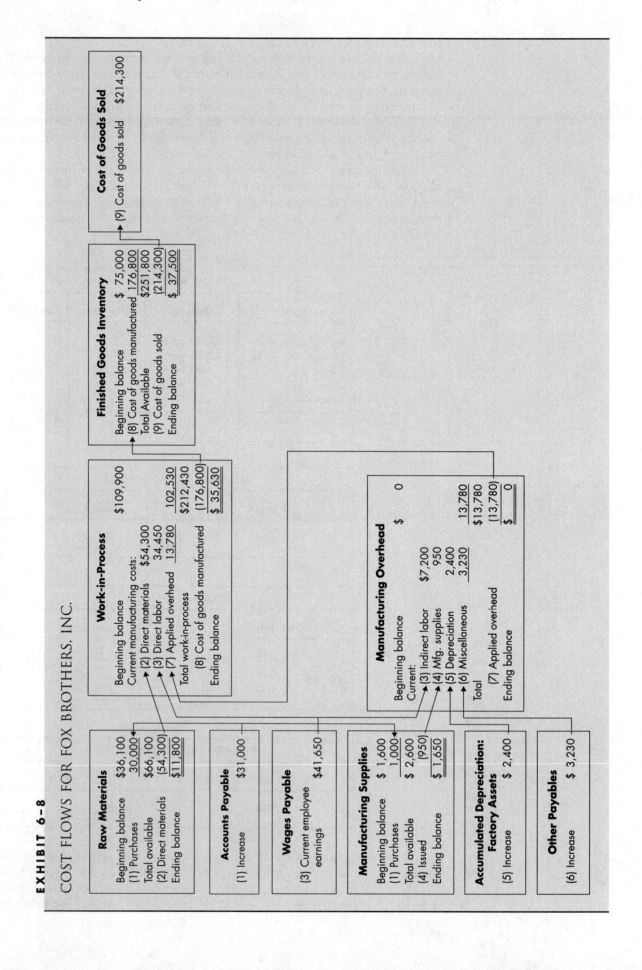

EXHIBIT 6-8

COST FLOWS FOR FOX BROTHERS, INC.

system records. The supporting cost system records for each entry in Exhibit 6–8 are discussed here, and journal entries for these transactions are included in the appendix to this chapter.

1. Raw materials and manufacturing supplies are purchased on account. The vendor's invoice totals $31,000, including $1,000 of manufacturing supplies and $30,000 of raw materials. The cost of the raw materials must be assigned to specific raw materials inventory records:

Wool fabric W12	1,000 yards × $12 =	$12,000
Liner	2,000 yards × $3 =	6,000
Buttons	3,000 sets × $4 =	12,000
Total		$30,000

2. Materials needed to complete Jobs 425 and 426 are requisitioned. Two new jobs, 427 and 428, were also started and direct materials were requisitioned for them. These actions require the following:
   a. Preparing production orders and job cost sheets for Jobs 427 and 428.
   b. Preparing a materials requisition for the issuance of materials for each job.
   c. Recording the issuance of raw materials on raw materials inventory records and job cost sheets.

	Job 425	Job 426	Job 427	Job 428	Total
Buttons:					
1,200 sets × $4	$4,800				$ 4,800
900 sets × $4		$3,600			3,600
500 sets × $4			$ 2,000		2,000
Wool fabric W09:					
2,400 yds. × $7				$16,800	16,800
Wool fabric W12:					
1,500 yds. × $12			18,000		18,000
Interfacing:					
500 yds. × $1			500		500
800 yds. × $1				800	800
Liner:					
1,000 yds. × $3			3,000		3,000
1,600 yds × $3				4,800	4,800
Total	$4,800	$3,600	$23,500	$22,400	$54,300

3. The August payroll liability was $41,650, including $34,450 for direct labor and $7,200 for indirect labor. Assigning direct labor costs requires the following two steps:
   a. Preparing the work tickets.
   b. Assigning direct labor costs to jobs.
   c. Assigning indirect labor to Manufacturing Overhead.

	Job 425	Job 426	Job 427	Job 428	Total
Labor hours	600	900	1,000	945	
Labor rate	× $10	× $10	× $10	× $10	
Total	$6,000	$9,000	$10,000	$9,450	$34,450

Note: The $7,200 of indirect labor costs is assigned to products as part of applied overhead.

4.–6. In addition to indirect labor, Fox Brothers incurred the following manufacturing overhead costs:

Manufacturing Supplies . . . . $ 950
Accumulated Depreciation—Factory Assets 2,400
Miscellaneous (Other Payables) 3,230

7. Manufacturing overhead is applied to jobs using a predetermined rate of $4 per direct labor hour. Assignments to individual jobs are as follows:

	Job 425	**Job 426**	**Job 427**	**Job 428**	**Total**
Labor hours Labor rate	600 × $4	900 × $4	1,000 × $4	945 × $4	
Total	$2,400	$3,600	$4,000	$3,780	$13,780

8. Jobs 425, 426, and 427 are completed. Properly accounting for the cost of the completed jobs requires the following:
  a. Completing job cost sheets to determine the total cost of the finished jobs.

	Job 425	**Job 426**	**Job 427**	**Total**
Beginning balance	$58,600	$51,300	$ 0	$109,900
Current costs:				
Direct materials (entry 2)	4,800	3,600	23,500	31,900
Direct labor (entry 3)	6,000	9,000	10,000	25,000
Applied overhead (entry 7)	2,400	3,600	4,000	10,000
Total	$71,800	$67,500	$37,500	$176,800

  b. Transferring costs from Work-in-Process to Finished Goods Inventory and placing job cost sheets for the completed jobs in the finished goods subsidiary file.
  c. Performing any additional analysis desired for the completed jobs, such as determining unit costs.

	Job 425	**Job 426**	**Job 427**
Total cost of job Units in job	$71,800 ÷ 1,200	$67,500 ÷ 900	$37,500 ÷ 500
Unit cost	$ 59.83	$ 75.00	$ 75.00

9. Jobs 424, 425, and 426 are delivered to customers for a sales price of $400,000. Determining the costs transferred from Finished Goods Inventory to Cost of Goods Sold requires summing the total cost of jobs sold. When the entire job is sold, the related job cost sheets are also transferred from the finished goods subsidiary file to a file for jobs completed and shipped.

Job 424 . . . . . $ 75,000
Job 425 71,800
Job 426 67,500
Total $214,300

At this point we can determine the gross profit on completed jobs:

Sales	$400,000
Cost of goods sold	(214,300)
Gross profit	$185,700

If inventory was produced in anticipation of future sales rather than in response to specific customer orders, it is likely that not all units in a job will be sold at the same time. In this case, the unit cost information is used to determine the amount transferred from Finished Goods Inventory to Cost of Goods Sold.

Exhibit 6–9 shows the cost system records supporting the ending balances in the major inventory accounts and Cost of Goods Sold. Note the importance of the job cost sheets for determining cost transfers affecting Work-in-Process and Finished Goods Inventory. The job cost assets are also used in determining the ending balances of these accounts.

Fox Brothers' product costing system is probably adequate for determining the cost for each job for purposes of valuing ending inventories and cost of goods sold in its external financial statements. It recognizes the differences in materials costs by carefully tracking each type of material as a separate cost pool. Because all direct labor employees are paid the same rate, it is necessary to maintain only one labor cost pool. Although there are three distinct operations in making sports coats (cutting, sewing, and finishing), the various styles of coats likely require the same proportionate times on each operation. Hence, with only one plantwide manufacturing overhead cost pool applied on the basis of direct labor hours, individual product costs are reasonably accurate.

Although the Fox Brothers' costing system may be adequate for inventory costing for financial statement purposes, the data it routinely generates do not provide management with information required for many management decisions. To evaluate product or customer profitability, management needs additional information concerning marketing, distributing, selling, and customer service costs, which are not included in the product cost system. Also, the cost system does not provide information for decisions concerning individual operations, such as cutting. A comparison of budgeted and planned cutting hours may be useful in evaluating the cutting operation. The system also does not provide the detailed information required for special decisions such as subcontracting cutting operations rather than performing them internally. To answer these questions, Fox Brothers' accountants should perform a special cost study to obtain activity-cost information. In spite of these limitations, this system may be adequate for the purposes it was designed; management might continue to operate the current system if the costs of improving and modifying the cost system exceed the perceived benefits.

In recent years, computer software producers, such as SAP, Oracle, and People-Soft have added activity-based costing modules to their enterprisewide systems. **Enterprise Resource Planning (ERP) systems** are enterprisewide management information systems that provide organizations an integrated set of operating, financial, and management systems. These systems have evolved over the last 30 years from materials planning and manufacturing planning systems to include applications for virtually all enterprise functions. Companies that have ERP systems with ABC modules no longer have to conduct special studies to generate ABC data but can produce them routinely. They also have the option of integrating ABC into their financial reporting. Consequently, as more and more companies implement ERP systems with ABC capabilities, it is likely that they will use ABC not only for managerial decision purposes but also for financial reporting. What's Happening 6–3 provides another example of how advances in technology are influencing costing models in the commercial printing industry.

EXHIBIT 6-9

SUBSIDIARY RECORD DETAILS FOR ENDING BALANCES IN MAJOR INVENTORY
ACCOUNTS AND COST OF GOODS SOLD

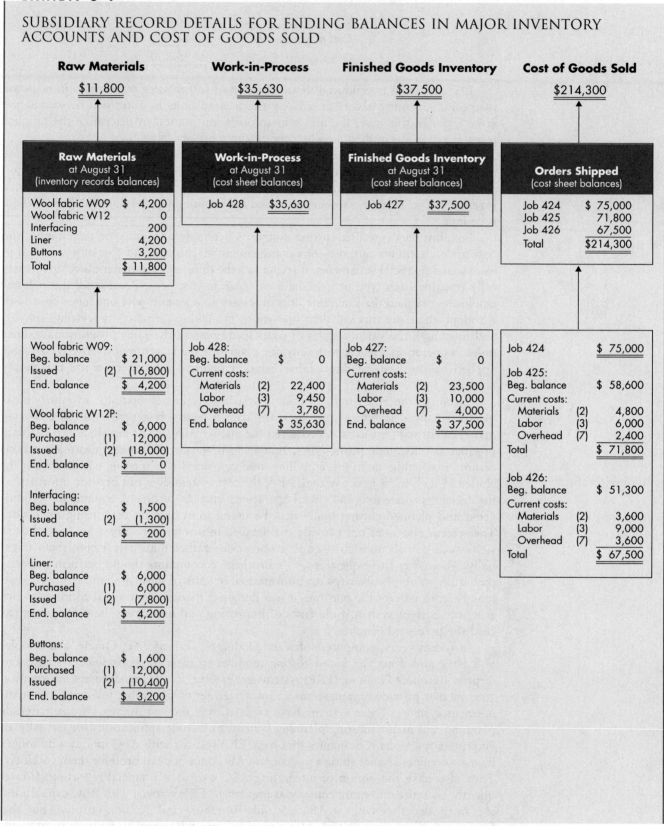

Raw Materials	Work-in-Process	Finished Goods Inventory	Cost of Goods Sold
$11,800	$35,630	$37,500	$214,300

Raw Materials
at August 31
(inventory records balances)

Wool fabric W09	$ 4,200
Wool fabric W12	0
Interfacing	200
Liner	4,200
Buttons	3,200
Total	$ 11,800

Work-in-Process
at August 31
(cost sheet balances)

Job 428	$35,630

Finished Goods Inventory
at August 31
(cost sheet balances)

Job 427	$37,500

Orders Shipped
(cost sheet balances)

Job 424	$ 75,000
Job 425	71,800
Job 426	67,500
Total	$214,300

Wool fabric W09:

Beg. balance		$ 21,000
Issued	(2)	(16,800)
End. balance		$ 4,200

Wool fabric W12P:

Beg. balance		$ 6,000
Purchased	(1)	12,000
Issued	(2)	(18,000)
End. balance		$ 0

Interfacing:

Beg. balance		$ 1,500
Issued	(2)	(1,300)
End. balance		$ 200

Liner:

Beg. balance		$ 6,000
Purchased	(1)	6,000
Issued	(2)	(7,800)
End. balance		$ 4,200

Buttons:

Beg. balance		$ 1,600
Purchased	(1)	12,000
Issued	(2)	(10,400)
End. balance		$ 3,200

Job 428:

Beg. balance		$ 0
Current costs:		
Materials	(2)	22,400
Labor	(3)	9,450
Overhead	(7)	3,780
End. balance		$ 35,630

Job 427:

Beg. balance		$ 0
Current costs:		
Materials	(2)	23,500
Labor	(3)	10,000
Overhead	(7)	4,000
End. balance		$ 37,500

Job 424 | | $ 75,000

Job 425:

Beg. balance		$ 58,600
Current costs:		
Materials	(2)	4,800
Labor	(3)	6,000
Overhead	(7)	2,400
Total		$ 71,800

Job 426:

Beg. balance		$ 51,300
Current costs:		
Materials	(2)	3,600
Labor	(3)	9,000
Overhead	(7)	3,600
Total		$ 67,500

E-COMMERCE REVEALS WEAKNESSES IN THE JOB COST BUSINESS MODEL

The printing industry has long been one of the classic examples of job cost accounting. One can readily visualize the large envelope on which is printed the job cost sheet, which follows each printing job through the various processes. The time and materials records are placed in the envelope, and at the completion of the job, all costs are added and then a markup is applied to determine what the customer should pay for the job. The job cost envelope represents the cost accounting system. The problem with a job-focused business model is that it tends to overlook the efficiency of the processes that go into completing the job.

The traditional business model for commercial printers began to change with the rising popularity of the fax machine when print customers began spewing out requests for print quotes, which led to increased competition and narrower margins. Roger Dickeson, writing in the printing industry magazine, *Printing Impressions*, stated, "Now that broadband is upon us, digital everything is sweeping in like a tsunami. The separations, proofs, layouts, graphics, mail lists, photos, quote requests, orders, invoices, changes, corrections and supply chains are increasingly digital each day." He went on to say that in this environment, "the old job cost model is obsolete; it served us poorly anyway. The old king is dead. Long live the new king: Statistical Print Production Management (SPPM)."

SPPM is a process model that offers improved decision support as well as better harmonization with general ledger costs. It is a variant of activity-based costing that recognizes that any activity consuming time or materials in the print process that does not result in value-added product in the hands of a customer is a loss. Changeovers, stops, trashed materials, waiting, and idle time are misuse and nonuse; they are process loss that must not be hidden away in job envelopes. They must be openly measured and managed. As a supplement to traditional job costing, SPPM is providing valuable decision support information for managers in an increasingly competitive industry.

Source: Roger V. Dickeson, "Goodbye Job Cost Accountancy," *Printing Impressions*, January 2001, pp. 67–68.

STATEMENT OF COST OF GOODS MANUFACTURED

The income statement for a merchandising organization, which purchases products ready to sell, normally includes the following calculation of cost of goods sold:

```
Sales .................................... $X,XXX
Less cost of goods sold:
    Beginning inventory  ............... $XXXX
    Plus purchases ....................   XXXX
    Goods available for sale ...........  $XXXX
    Less ending inventory ............... (XXXX)
Cost of goods sold ........................   (X,XXX)
Gross profit .............................  $X,XXX
Less selling and administrative expenses ...........  (X,XXX)
Net income  ..............................  $X,XXX
```

Manufacturing organizations modify only one line of this income statement format, changing Purchases to Cost of goods manufactured. Since a manufacturer acquires finished goods from the factory, its cost of finished goods completed is the total cost transferred from Work-in-Process to Finished Goods Inventory during the period.

For internal reporting purposes, most companies prepare a separate **statement of cost of goods manufactured,** which summarizes the cost of goods completed and transferred into Finished Goods Inventory during the period. A statement of cost of goods manufactured and an income statement for Fox Brothers, Inc., are presented in Exhibit 6–10 for August 2004.

EXHIBIT 6-10

STATEMENT OF COST OF GOODS MANUFACTURED AND INCOME STATEMENT FOR FOX BROTHERS, INC.

Fox Brothers, Inc.
Statement of Cost of Goods Manufactured
For the Month Ending August 31, 2004

Current manufacturing costs:			
Cost of materials placed in production:			
Raw materials, 8/1/04	$36,100		
Purchases	30,000		
Total available	$66,100		
Raw materials, 8/31/04	(11,800)	$ 54,300	
Direct labor		34,450	
Manufacturing overhead		13,780	$102,530
Work-in-process, 8/1/04			109,900
Total costs in process			$212,430
Work-in-process, 8/31/04			(35,630)
Cost of goods manufactured			$176,800

Fox Brothers, Inc.
Income Statement
For the Month Ending August 31, 2004

Sales		$400,000
Cost of goods sold:		
Finished goods inventory, 8/1/04	$ 75,000	
Cost of goods manufactured	176,800	
Total goods available for sale	$251,800	
Finished goods inventory, 8/31/04	(37,500)	214,300
Gross profit		$185,700
Selling and administrative expenses*		(90,000)
Net income		$ 95,700

Selling and administrative expenses for Fox Brothers are assumed to be $90,000.

OVERAPPLIED AND UNDERAPPLIED OVERHEAD

In the Fox Brothers' example, assume that the predetermined manufacturing overhead rate of $4 per direct labor hour was based on predicted manufacturing overhead for the year of $100,000 and predicted direct labor hours of 25,000. Assume further that it was determined that the company actually incurred $100,000 in manufacturing overhead during the year and that actual direct labor hours for the year were 25,000, resulting in applied overhead of $100,000 (25,000 hours × $4). The activity in Manufacturing Overhead is summarized as follows:

Manufacturing Overhead	
Beginning balance	$ 0
Actual overhead	100,000
Total	$100,000
Applied overhead	(100,000)
Ending balance	$ 0

With identical amounts of actual and applied overhead, the ending balance in Manufacturing Overhead is zero. However, if either the actual overhead cost or the actual level of the production activity base differed from its predicted value, there would be a balance in Manufacturing Overhead representing overapplied or underapplied overhead.

Assume, for example, that the prediction of 25,000 direct labor hours was correct but that actual overhead cost was $105,000. In this case, Manufacturing Overhead shows a $5,000 positive balance, representing underapplied manufacturing overhead:

Manufacturing Overhead

Beginning balance	$ 0
Actual overhead	105,000
Total	$105,000
Applied overhead	(100,000)
Ending balance	$ 5,000*

Underapplied, actual exceeds applied.

If actual manufacturing overhead were only $98,000, Manufacturing Overhead would be overapplied and show a $2,000 negative balance.

If the *prediction* of total manufacturing overhead cost is not accurate, there will be an underapplied or overapplied balance in Manufacturing Overhead at the end of the year. A similar result occurs when the *predicted* activity level used in computing the predetermined rate differs from the actual activity level. It is not uncommon for such differences to occur. Predictions are exactly that—predictions.

Month-to-month balances in Manufacturing Overhead are usually allowed to accumulate during the year. In the absence of evidence to the contrary, it is assumed that such differences result from seasonal variations in production or costs or both. However, any year-end balance in Manufacturing Overhead must be eliminated.

Theoretically, the disposition of any year-end balance in Manufacturing Overhead should be accomplished in a manner that adjusts every account to what its balance would have been if an actual, rather than a predetermined, overhead rate were used. This involves adjusting the ending balances in Work-in-Process, Finished Goods Inventory, and Cost of Goods Sold. Procedures to do this are examined in cost accounting textbooks.

In most situations, the simple procedure of treating the remaining overhead as an adjustment to Cost of Goods Sold may be used. Unless there are large ending balances in inventories and a large year-end balance in Manufacturing Overhead, this simple procedure produces acceptable results. Underapplied overhead indicates that the assigned costs are less than the actual costs, understating Cost of Goods Sold. Hence, disposing of an underapplied balance in Manufacturing Overhead increases the balance in Cost of Goods Sold.

Manufacturing Overhead

Beginning balance	$ 0
Actual overhead	105,000
Total	$105,000
Applied overhead	(100,000)
Ending balance	$ 5,000* ──▶ Increase Cost of Goods Sold

Underapplied, actual exceeds applied.

Conversely, overapplied overhead indicates that the assigned costs are more than the actual costs, overstating Cost of Goods Sold. Hence, disposing of an overapplied balance in Manufacturing Overhead decreases Cost of Goods Sold.

JOB COSTING IN SERVICE ORGANIZATIONS

Service costing, the assignment of costs to services performed, uses job costing concepts to determine the cost of filling customer service orders in organizations such as automobile repair shops, charter airlines, CPA firms, hospitals, and law firms. Many of these organizations bill clients on the basis of resources consumed. Consequently, they maintain detailed records for billing purposes. On the invoice sent to the client, the organization itemizes any materials consumed on the job at a selling price per unit, the labor hours worked on the job at a billing rate per hour, and the time special facilities were used at a billing rate per unit of time. Employees with different capabilities and experience often have different billing rates. In a CPA firm, for example, a partner or a senior manager has a higher billing rate than a staff accountant.

The prices and rates must be high enough to cover costs not assigned to specific jobs and to provide for a profit. To evaluate the contribution to common costs and profit from a job, a comparison must be made between the price charged the customer and the actual cost of the job. This is easily done when the actual cost of resources itemized on the customer's invoice is presented on a job cost sheet. A CPA firm, for example, should accumulate the actual hardware and software costs of an accounting system installed for a client, along with the actual wages earned by employees while working on the job and any related travel costs. Comparing the total of these costs with the price charged, the client indicates the total contribution of the job to common costs and profit.

Although service organizations may identify costs with individual jobs for management accounting purposes, there is considerable variation in the way job cost information is presented in financial statements. Some organizations report the cost of jobs completed in their income statements using an account such as Cost of Services Provided. They use procedures similar to those outlined in Exhibits 6–6 and 6–7; the only major change involves replacing Cost of Goods Sold with Cost of Services Provided.

More often, however, service organizations do not formally establish detailed procedures to trace the flow of service costs. Instead, service job costs are left in their original cost categories such as materials expense, salaries and wages expense, travel expense, and so forth. Because all service costs are typically regarded as expenses rather than product costs, either procedure is acceptable for financial reporting. Regardless of the formal treatment of service costs in financial accounting records and statements, the managers of a well-run service organization have a need for information regarding job cost and contribution. What's Happening 6–4 discusses how one hospital used product cost information to improve managerial decisions.

6–4 WHAT'S HAPPENING?

THOMAS JEFFERSON UNIVERSITY HOSPITAL USES A COST ACCOUNTING SYSTEM TO EVALUATE THE FINANCIAL IMPACT OF NEW TREATMENTS

Thomas Jefferson University Hospital (TJUH) uses its "costing" system to determine the relative costs of different treatments for a given illness. In effect, the system is a job cost system with each patient being a separate job. One objective of the system is to evaluate the financial impact and the clinical impact of new treatments simultaneously. For example, TJUH used the system to evaluate the cost of using a new pharmaceutical product, Zofran, developed to prevent severe episodes of nausea and vomiting associated with cancer chemotherapy treatments. Chemotherapy patients were divided into three different groups (job cost categories) for the study: those who received Zofran therapy, those who received traditional therapy to prevent nausea and vomiting, and those who received both.

The results showed that even though Zofran was a more expensive drug, it did not cost more to use because patients using it had shorter hospital stays. As health care cost containment pressures increase, the need for this type of cost analysis will become more critical; good cost accounting systems can help hospitals produce more reliable cost data for these studies.

Source: Carly E. Carpenter, Linda C. Weitzel, Nelda E. Johnson, and David B. Nash, "Cost Accounting Supports Clinical Evaluations," *Healthcare Financial Management*, April 1994, pp. 40–45.

All preceding examples of service costing involve situations in which the order is filled in response to a specific customer request. Job order costing can also be used to determine the cost of making services available even when the names of specific customers are not known in advance and the service is being provided on a speculative basis. A regularly scheduled airline flight, for example, could be regarded as a job. Management is interested in knowing the cost of the job in order to determine its profitability. This is but another example of the versatility of job order costing.

LEARNING OBJECTIVE 5   ## PROCESS COSTING

A job costing system works well when products are made one at time (building houses) or in batches of identical items (making blue jeans). However, if products are produced in a continuous manufacturing environment, where production does not have a distinct beginning and ending (refining fossil fuels such as gasoline or diesel), companies usually use a process costing system.

In job costing, the unit cost is the total cost of the "job" divided by the units produced in the job. Costs are accumulated for each job on a job cost sheet, and those costs remain in Work-in-Process until the job is completed, regardless of how long the job is in progress. A multiple-unit job is not considered completed until all units in the job are finished. The cost is not determined until the job is completed, which will not necessarily coincide with the end of an accounting period. Large jobs (such as construction products) and jobs started near the end of the period frequently overlap two or more accounting periods.

In process costing, the cost of a single unit is equal to the total product costs assigned to a "process" or "department" during the accounting period (frequently a month) divided by the number of units produced. Since goods in the beginning and ending work-in-process inventory are only partially processed during the period, it is necessary to determine the total production for the period in terms of the equivalent number of completed units. For example, if 300 units were started and completed through 40 percent of the process during the period, then the equivalent of 120 fully completed units (300 units × 0.40) were produced. The average cost per unit is computed as total product costs divided by the number of equivalent units produced.

A good example of a process costing environment involving continuous production is the soft drink bottling process. At Coca-Cola's bottling facility in Atlanta, more than 2,000 twelve-ounce cans of Coca-Cola are produced per minute in a continuous process. The process adds the ingredients (concentrate syrup, water, sweetener, and the carbonation agent) at various points in the process and blends the ingredients in the can. At the end of the process, the cans are automatically wrapped in either 6-pack or 12-pack sizes. For another example, see What's Happening 6–5 for a discussion of the process costing environment at a large Japanese chemicals producer.

In a job cost system, job cost sheets are used to collect cost information for each and every job. In a process costing system, cost accumulation requires fewer records because each department's production is treated as the only job worked on during the period. In a department that has just one manufacturing process, process costing is particularly straightforward because the Work-in-Process account is, in effect, the departmental cost record. If a department has more than one manufacturing process, separate records should be maintained for each process.

THE COST OF PRODUCTION REPORT

To illustrate process costing procedures, consider Micro Systems Co., which manufactures memory chips for microcomputers in a one-step process using sophisticated

PROCESS COSTING IN A JAPANESE DYESTUFFS PLANT

Nippon Kayaku is a large industrial company in Japan that produces a wide range of products, including industrial explosives, pharmaceuticals, agrochemicals, sophisticated products (resins, flame retardants, etc.) and dyestuffs. Nippon Kayaku's dyestuff division produces dyes that are particularly targeted to the polyester and cotton-blended textiles market.

The Fukuyama plant manufactures about 600 products for the sophisticated products and dyestuffs divisions, some of which are produced in continuous processes and others in batches. The costing system accumulates costs separately for the more than 1,000 processes, and product costs are determined for a particular product merely by adding the unit costs of the processes used to make that product. For example, the cost of the dyestuff product, Kayaset, consists of the costs of five processes: condensation, filtration, drying, grinding, and packaging. Nippon Kayaku uses these product costs for inventory valuation purposes and for managerial decision-making purposes.

Source: Robin Cooper, "Nippon Kayaku," *Harvard Business School Case #9-195-068*, pp. 1–7.

machinery. Each finished unit requires one unit of raw materials added at the beginning of the manufacturing process. The production and cost data for the month of July 2004 for Micro Systems are as follows:

July Production Data

Units in process, beginning of period (75% converted)	4,000
Units started	36,000
Completed and transferred to finished goods	35,000
Units in process, end of period (20% converted)	5,000

July Cost Data

Beginning work-in-process:		
Materials costs		$ 16,000
Conversion costs		9,000
Total		$ 25,000
Current manufacturing costs:		
Direct materials (36,000 × $4)		$144,000
Conversion costs:		
Direct labor	$62,200	
Manufacturing overhead applied	46,700	108,900
Total		$252,900

Developing a cost of production report is a useful way of organizing and accounting for costs in a process costing environment. A **cost of production report,** which summarizes unit and cost data for each department or process for each period, consists of the following sections:

- Summary of units in process.
- Equivalent units.
- Total cost to be accounted for and cost per equivalent unit.
- Accounting for total costs.

The cost of production report for Micro Systems Co. is shown in Exhibit 6–11, and its four sections are discussed here.

EXHIBIT 6-11

COST OF PRODUCTION REPORT FOR PROCESS COSTING SYSTEM

Micro Systems Co.
Cost of Production Report
For the Month Ending July 31, 2004

Summary of units in process:

Beginning	4,000
Units started	36,000
In process	40,000
Completed	(35,000)
Ending	5,000

Equivalent units in process:	Materials	Conversion
Units completed	35,000	35,000
Plus equivalent units in ending inventory . .	5,000	1,000*
Equivalent units in process	40,000	36,000

Total cost to be accounted for and cost per equivalent units in process:	Materials	Conversion	Total
Beginning work-in-process	$ 16,000	$ 9,000	$ 25,000
Current cost	144,000	108,900**	252,900
Total cost in process	$160,000	$117,900	$277,900
Equivalent units in process	÷ 40,000	÷ 36,000	
Cost per equivalent unit in process	$ 4.00	$ 3.275	$ 7.275

Accounting for total costs:

Transferred out (35,000 × $7.275)		$254,625
Ending work-in-process:		
Materials (5,000 × $4.00)	$20,000	
Conversion (1,000 × $3.275)	3,275	23,275
Total cost accounted for		$277,900

5,000 units, 20% converted
**Includes direct labor of $62,200 and applied manufacturing overhead of $46,700*

Summary of Units in Process. This section of the cost of production report provides a summary of all units in the department during the period—both from an input and an output perspective—regardless of their stage of completion. From an input perspective, total units in process during the period consisted of the following:

- Units in process at the beginning of the period, plus
- Units started during the period.

From an output perspective, these units in process during the period were either

- Completed and transferred out of the department, or
- Still on hand at the end of the period.

In the summary of units in process, all units are treated as the same, regardless of the amount of processing that took place on them during the period. The objective here is to account for all discrete units of product in process at any time during the period. In the summary of units in process in Exhibit 6–11, 40,000 individual units were in process, including 4,000 partially completed units in the beginning inventory and 36,000 new units started during the month. During the period, 35,000 units were completed, and the remaining 5,000 were still in process at the end of the month.

Equivalent Units in Process.   This section of the report translates the number of units in process during the period into equivalent completed units of production. The term **equivalent completed units** refers to the number of completed units that is equal, in terms of production effort, to a given number of partially completed units. For example, 80 units for which 50 percent of the expected total processing cost has been incurred is the equivalent of 40 completed units (80 × 0.50).

Frequently, direct materials costs are incurred largely, if not entirely, at the beginning of the process, whereas direct labor and manufacturing overhead costs are added throughout the production process. If direct labor and manufacturing costs are added to the process simultaneously, it is common to treat them jointly as conversion costs. Micro Systems Co. adds all materials at the beginning of the process; all conversion costs are added evenly throughout the process. Therefore, separate computations are made for equivalent units of materials and equivalent units of conversion. Although the department worked on 40,000 units during the period, the total number of equivalent units in process with respect to conversion costs was only 36,000 units, consisting of 35,000 finished units plus 1,000 equivalent units in ending inventory (5,000 units 20 percent converted). Because all materials are added at the start of the process, 40,000 equivalent units (35,000 finished and 5,000 in process) were in process with respect to materials costs.

Total Cost to Be Accounted for and Cost per Equivalent Unit in Process.   This section of the report summarizes total costs in Work-in-Process during the period and calculates the cost per equivalent unit for materials, conversion, and in total. Total cost consists of the beginning Work-in-Process balance (if any) plus current costs incurred. For Micro Systems, the total cost to be accounted for during July was $277,900, consisting of $25,000 in Work-in-Process at the beginning of the period plus current costs of $252,900 incurred in July. Notice in Exhibit 6–11 that these amounts are broken down between materials costs and conversion costs.

To compute cost per equivalent unit, divide total cost in process by the equivalent units in process. This is done separately for materials cost and conversion cost. The total cost per equivalent unit is the sum of the unit costs for materials and conversion. Because the number of equivalent units in process was different for materials and conversion, it is not possible to get the total cost per unit by dividing total costs of $277,900 by some equivalent unit amount.

Accounting for Total Costs.   This section shows the disposition of the total costs in process during the period divided between units completed (and sent to finished goods) and units still in process at the end of the period. As noted in the previous section, total cost in process is $277,900 and each equivalent unit in process has $4.00 of materials cost and $3.275 of conversion costs for a total of $7.275.

The first step in assigning total costs is to calculate the cost of units transferred out by multiplying the units completed during the period by the total cost per unit (35,000 units × $7.275). This assigns $254,625 of the total cost to units transferred out, leaving $23,275 ($277,900 − $254,625) to be assigned to ending Work-in-Process. To verify that $23,275 is the correct amount of cost remaining in ending Work-in-Process, the materials and conversion costs in ending Work-in-Process are calculated separately. Recall that the 5,000 units in process at the end of the period are 100 percent completed with materials costs, but only 20 percent completed with conversion costs. Therefore, in ending Work-in-Process, the materials cost component is $20,000 (5,000 × 1.00 × $4.00), the conversion cost component is $3,275 (5,000 × 0.20 × $3.275), and the total cost of ending Work-in-Process is $23,275 ($20,000 + $3,275).

The cost of production report summarizes manufacturing costs assigned to Work-in-Process during the period and provides information for determining the transfer of costs from Work-in-Process to Finished Goods Inventory. The supporting documents are similar to those previously illustrated for job costing, except that the single cost of production report replaces all the job cost sheets that flow through a department or process. The flow of costs through Work-in-Process is as follows:

Work-in-Process

Beginning balance		$ 25,000
Current manufacturing costs:		
Direct materials	$144,000	
Direct labor	62,200	
Applied overhead	46,700	252,900
Total		$277,900
Cost of goods manufactured		(254,625)
Ending balance		$ 23,275

The reduction in Work-in-Process for the units completed during the period is determined in the cost of production report (see Exhibit 6–11). This amount is transferred to Finished Goods Inventory. The $23,275 ending balance in Work-in-Process is also determined in the cost of production report as the amount assigned to units in ending Work-in-Process.

WEIGHTED AVERAGE AND FIRST-IN, FIRST-OUT PROCESS COSTING

Because the costs of materials, labor, and overhead are constantly changing, unit costs are seldom exactly the same from period to period. Hence, if a unit is manufactured partially in one period and partially in the following period, its actual cost is seldom equal to the unit cost of units produced in either period.

In the cost of production report in Exhibit 6–11, we made no attempt to account separately for the completed units that came from beginning inventory and those that were started during the current period. The method illustrated in Exhibit 6–11 is called the **weighted average method,** and it simply spreads the combined beginning inventory cost and current manufacturing costs (for materials, labor, and overhead) over the units completed and those in ending inventory on an average basis. For example, the total cost in process for conversion ($117,900) included both beginning inventory cost and current costs; the 36,000 equivalent units in process for conversion included both units from beginning inventory and units started during the current period. Hence, the average cost per unit of $3.275 (or $117,900 ÷ 36,000) is a weighted average cost of the partially completed units in beginning inventory (prior period costs) and units started during the current period. It is not a precise cost per unit for the current period's production activity but an average cost that includes the cost of partially completed units in beginning inventory carried over from the previous period.

An alternative, more precise process costing method is the **first-in, first-out (FIFO) method.** It accounts for unit costs of beginning inventory units separately from those started during the current period. Under this method, the first costs incurred each period are assumed to have been used to complete the unfinished units carried over from the previous period. Hence, the cost of the beginning inventory is partially based on the prior period's unit costs and partially based on the current period's unit costs.

If unit costs are changing significantly from period to period and beginning inventories are large in relation to total production for the period, the FIFO method is more accurate. However, with the current trend toward smaller inventories, the additional effort and cost of the FIFO method may not be justified. Detailed coverage of the FIFO method is included in cost accounting textbooks.

PROCESS COSTING IN SERVICE ORGANIZATIONS

There are many applications of process costing for service organizations. Process costing in service organizations is similar to that in manufacturing organizations, the primary purpose being to assign costs to cost objectives. Generally, the use of process costing techniques for service organizations is easier than for manufacturing organizations because the raw materials element is not necessary. The applications for the labor and overhead costs are similar, if not identical, to those of a manufacturing firm.

Process costing for services is similar to job costing for batches in that an average cost for similar or identical services is determined. There are important differences, though, between batch and process costing. In a batch environment, a discrete group of services is identified, but in a process environment, services are performed on a continuous basis. Batch costing accumulates the cost for a specific group of services as the batch moves through the various activities that make up the service. Process service costing measures the average cost of identical or similar services performed each period (each month) in a department. An example of batch service costing is determining the cost of registering a student at your college during the fall term registration period; an example of process service costing is determining the cost each month of processing a check by a bank. If continuously performed services involved multiple processes, the total cost of the service would be the sum of the costs for each process.

There are several important considerations before using process costing in service organizations. One difficulty in many service situations is defining the appropriate cost objective. For manufacturing applications, the normal cost objective is a physical item. Because most service applications do not involve physical inventory, the selection of the cost objective becomes a major management decision. Is the cost objective a general activity (check processing in a bank), a specific activity (sorting only letters, as opposed to letters and packages), or a mission activity (total patient care in a hospital as opposed to individual patients)?

General activities should be used when the service process is identical for all processing even though some of the items processed may be different. A bank processes many types of checks (personal, business, cashiers, and travelers), but all checks go through the same chain of activities. Specific activity cost objectives should be used when the items processed take different activity paths. Although the mail center processes all mail via the same processes (receiving, sorting, bundling, etc.), the specific activities may differ. Letters can be sorted and handled by machine, but packages must be sorted and grouped by hand.

Using mission activity as the cost objective is another approach to applying process costing to service situations. Rather than tracking the cost of each service rendered per unit or batch (a job processing approach), a company can assign costs over a longer period of time to another reasonable objective, for example, all patient care. At the end of a period, costs assigned to patient care are divided by the total number of patient-days during the period to obtain the cost per patient-day. This approach assumes that all processed units (patients) receive approximately the same activity (patient care); therefore, the average cost per unit (patient-day) is sufficient for evaluation purposes.

After it is determined that process costing would be appropriate for a service activity, the actual decision to use it is generally contingent on two important factors about the items being evaluated. First, is average cost per unit acceptable as an input item to the decision process? For some activities, the answer is obvious. For instance, tracking the actual cost of processing each check through a bank would probably not be as useful as determining the average cost of processing checks for a given period;

therefore, average cost is acceptable. For other activities, the answer is more difficult to determine. Should the decision model include average cost per patient-day or actual cost per individual patient?

The second issue relates to the benefits versus the costs of the resulting information. Normally, it is easier to track and record the cost of an activity or process than it is to track and record the cost of each individual item in the activity. Often actual cost tracking is impossible for practical reasons (the actual cost of processing a check through a banking system, for example). Although process costing will not work in every situation, it has many applications in service organizations. As illustrated in this text, there are many possibilities for applying either job or process costing to activities in service organizations.

Summary

Product costing involves determining the cost of goods and/or services as they flow through the production process. A primary purpose of the product costing system is to assign costs in the financial statements. Cost information developed for financial reporting may be useful for other purposes, as long as the user understands the assumptions underlying the cost data and makes any necessary modifications to suit the purpose at hand.

For financial reporting, costs are differentiated into product or period costs. Product costs are related to manufacturing a product; period costs are related to non-manufacturing activities such as selling and general administration. In the financial statements, product costs are carried as an asset until the product is sold, but period costs are deducted as an expense as they are incurred.

The two most widely used product costing methods are job costing and process costing. Job costing is particularly useful when a company produces a variety of products in discrete batches, as illustrated for the production of garments. It is also well suited when each job is a single, unique product such as in constructing commercial buildings. Process costing is used primarily in situations in which a continuous process produces homogeneous products such as petroleum or newsprint paper.

The primary objective of both job and process costing is to identify all product costs, direct materials, direct labor, and overhead, and assign them systematically and equitably to jobs or departments. Once product costs are assigned to jobs or departments, they follow the physical inventory through Work-in-Process and Finished Goods Inventory to Cost of Goods Sold.

Although product costing concepts were initially developed for physical products, these concepts are also used by service organizations. In these organizations the primary purpose is to provide information useful to managers as opposed to aiding financial reporting. The major issues in designing the cost system in a service environment still relate to identifying direct costs (frequently labor) and determining how to assign overhead costs to the units of service. The key to developing a good cost system is in tailoring the system to the characteristics of the production environment and to the needs of management.

Appendix

JOURNAL ENTRIES FOR RECORDING PRODUCT COSTS

Understanding how financial accountants record transactions in the accounting records is not essential for understanding product cost concepts; however, students who plan on accounting careers will want to understand not only the concepts of product costs but also the procedures for implementing product costs into the accounting system. Although the details of such systems are discussed in cost accounting classes, the journal entries for recording product cost flows are provided here for the nine transactions recorded in the Fox Brothers job cost illustration discussed in this chapter.

1. Raw Materials	31,000	
Manufacturing Supplies	1,000	
Accounts Payable		32,000

To record the purchase of raw materials and manufacturing supplies.

2. Work-in-Process	54,300	
Raw Materials		54,300

To record the requisition and issuance of raw materials to the factory.

3. Work-in-Process	34,450	
Manufacturing Overhead	7,200	
Wages Payable		41,650

To record direct labor and indirect labor costs for the month.

4. Manufacturing Overhead	950	
Manufacturing Supplies		950

To record the issuance of manufacturing supplies to the factory.

5. Manufacturing Overhead	2,400	
Accumulated Depreciation—		
Factory Assets		2,400

To record depreciation for the month on factory assets.

6. Manufacturing Overhead	3,230	
Other Payables		3,230

To record miscellaneous overhead costs incurred.

7. Work-in-Process	13,780	
Manufacturing Overhead		13,780

To record the application of manufacturing overhead to jobs.

8. Finished Goods Inventory   176,800
    Work-in-Process   176,800

To record the cost for jobs completed and transferred to finished goods inventory during the month.

9. Cost of Goods Sold   214,300
    Finished Goods Inventory   214,300

To record the cost of jobs delivered to customers during the month.

Review Problem

The solution to the review problem is found on pages 276–277. To maximize your learning, you should make a serious attempt to develop a written solution to the review problem before looking at the solution. If there are errors in your solution, you should then attempt to determine their causes.

Job Costing and Statement of Cost of Goods Manufactured

Tri-Star Printing Company prints sales fliers for retail and mail-order companies. Production costs are accounted for using a job cost system. At the beginning of June 2004, raw materials inventories totaled $7,000; manufacturing supplies amounted to $800; two jobs were in process—Job 225 with assigned costs of $13,750, and Job 226 with assigned costs of $1,800—and there were no finished goods inventories. There was no underapplied or overapplied manufacturing overhead on June 1. The following information summarized June manufacturing activities:

- Purchased raw materials costing $40,000 on account.
- Purchased manufacturing supplies costing $9,000 on account.
- Requisitioned materials needed to complete Job 226. Started two new jobs, 227 and 228, and requisitioned direct materials for them as follows:

> Job 226 . . . . . $ 2,600
> Job 227 18,000
> Job 228 14,400
> Total $35,000

- Incurred June salaries and wages as follows:

> Job 225 (500 hours × $10 per hour) . . . . . . $ 5,000
> Job 226 (1,500 hours × $10 per hour) 15,000
> Job 227 (2,050 hours × $10 per hour) 20,500
> Job 228 (800 hours × $10 per hour) 8,000
> Total direct labor $48,500
> Indirect labor 5,000
> Total $53,500

- Used manufacturing supplies costing $5,500.
- Recognized depreciation on factory fixed assets of $5,000.
- Incurred miscellaneous factory overhead cost of $10,750 on account.
- Applied factory overhead at the rate of $5 per direct labor hour.
- Completed Jobs 225, 226, and 227.
- Delivered Jobs 225 and 226 to customers.

Required:

a. Prepare a diagram summarizing the flow of costs through all manufacturing accounts, Finished Goods Inventory, and Cost of Goods Sold. (*Hint:* Prepare cost sheets for the completed jobs.)

b. Show the job cost details to support the June 30, 2004, balance in Work-in-Process.

c. Prepare a statement of cost of goods manufactured for June 2004.

Key Terms

Absorption cost (p. 226)
Activities list (p. 231)
Automatic identification systems (AIS) (p. 235)
Bill of materials (p. 231)
Computer-aided design (CAD) (p. 235)
Computer-aided manufacturing (CAM) (p. 235)
Computer-integrated manufacturing (CIM) (p. 235)
Conversion cost (p. 226)
Cost of production report (p. 250)
Direct labor (p. 226)
Direct materials (p. 226)
Enterprise Resource Planning (ERP) systems (p. 243)
Equivalent completed units (p. 252)
File (p. 231)
Financial reporting (p. 221)
Finished goods inventories (p. 223)
First-in, first-out (FIFO) method (p. 253)
Flexible manufacturing systems (FMS) (p. 235)

Full absorption cost (p. 226)
Job cost sheet (p. 231)
Job order production (p. 231)
Job production (p. 231)
Manufacturing organizations (p. 223)
Manufacturing overhead (p. 226)
Materials requisition form (p. 233)
Merchandising organizations (p. 223)
Operations list (p. 231)
Period costs (p. 225)
Predetermined manufacturing overhead rate (p. 228)
Process manufacturing (p. 231)
Product costs (p. 225)
Production order (p. 231)
Raw materials inventories (p. 223)
Record (p. 231)
Service costing (p. 247)
Service organizations (p. 222)
Statement of cost of goods manufactured (p. 245)
Weighted average method (p. 253)
Work-in-process inventories (p. 223)
Work ticket (p. 233)

Review Questions

1. Distinguish among service, merchandising, and manufacturing organizations on the basis of the importance and complexity of inventory cost measurement.
2. Distinguish between product costing and service costing.
3. When is depreciation a product cost? When is depreciation a period cost?
4. What are the three major product cost elements?
5. How are predetermined overhead rates developed? Why are they widely used?
6. Briefly distinguish between process manufacturing and job order production. Provide examples of products typically produced under each system.
7. Briefly describe the role of engineering personnel and production scheduling personnel in the production planning process.
8. Identify the primary records involved in the operation of a job cost system.
9. Describe the flow of costs through the accounting system of a labor-intensive manufacturing organization.
10. Identify two reasons that a service organization should maintain detailed job cost information.

11. What are the four major elements of a cost of production report?
12. What are equivalent completed units?
13. Under what conditions will equivalent units in process be different for materials and conversion costs?

Exercises

6-1
Classification of Product and Period Costs

Classify the following costs incurred by an automobile manufacturer as product costs or period costs. Also classify the product costs as direct materials or conversion costs.

a. Salaries of legal staff
b. Automobile window glass
c. Depreciation on word processor in president's office
d. Plant fire department
e. Automobile tires
f. Automobile bumpers
g. Wages paid assembly line maintenance workers
h. Salary of corporate controller
i. Automobile engines
j. Subsidy of plant cafeteria
k. Wages paid assembly line production workers
l. National sales meeting in Detroit
m. Overtime premium paid assembly line workers
n. Advertising on national television
o. Depreciation on assembly line

6-2
Analyzing Activity in Inventory Accounts

Selected data concerning operations of Berry Manufacturing Company for the past fiscal year follow:

Raw materials used	$290,000
Total manufacturing costs charged to production during the year (includes raw materials, direct labor, and manufacturing overhead applied at a rate of 60 percent of direct labor costs)	681,000
Cost of goods available for sale	826,000
Selling and general expenses	30,000

	INVENTORIES	
	Beginning	**Ending**
Raw materials	$70,000	$ 80,000
Work-in-process	85,000	30,000
Finished goods	90,000	110,000

Required:
Determine each of the following:

a. Cost of raw materials purchased
b. Direct labor costs charged to production
c. Cost of goods manufactured
d. Cost of goods sold

6-3
Statements: Cost of Goods Manufactured and Income

Information from the records of the Jackson Manufacturing Company for August 2004 follows:

Sales	$205,000
Selling and administrative expenses	83,000
Purchases of raw materials	20,000
Direct labor	15,000
Manufacturing overhead	32,000

INVENTORIES		
	August 1	August 31
Raw materials	$ 7,000	$ 5,000
Work-in-process	14,000	11,000
Finished goods	15,000	19,000

Required:

Prepare a statement of cost of goods manufactured and an income statement for August 2004.

6-4
Statement of Cost of Goods Manufactured from Percent Relationships

Information about NuWay Products Company for the year ending December 31, 2004, follows:

- Sales equal $400,000.
- Direct materials used total $64,000.
- Manufacturing overhead is 150 percent of direct labor dollars.
- The beginning inventory of finished goods is 20 percent of the cost of goods sold.
- The ending inventory of finished goods is twice the beginning inventory.
- The gross profit is 20 percent of sales.
- There is no beginning or ending work-in-process.

Required:

Prepare a statement of cost of goods manufactured for 2004. (*Hint:* Prepare an analysis of changes in Finished Goods Inventory.)

6-5
Income Statement and Statement of Cost of Goods Manufactured from Percent Relationships

Information about the Piedmont Fabricating Company for the year ending December 31, 2004, is as follows:

Sales	$350,000
Net income	5,000
Ending inventories:	
Raw materials	18,000
Work-in-process	8,000
Finished goods	67,000

Inventory changes include:

- Ending raw materials is twice beginning raw materials.
- Ending work-in-process is one-third larger than beginning work-in-process.
- Finished goods inventory increased by $15,000 during the year.
- Selling and administrative expenses are five times net income.
- Prime costs (direct materials and direct labor) are 60 percent of manufacturing costs.
- Conversion costs are 80 percent of manufacturing costs.

Required:

Prepare a statement of cost of goods manufactured and an income statement for 2004. (*Hint:* Set up the statement formats and start the solution from known information.)

6-6
Developing and Using a Predetermined Overhead Rate

Assume that the following predictions were made for 2005 for one of the plants of Milliken & Company:

Total manufacturing overhead for the year	$38,000,000
Total machine hours for the year	2,000,000

Actual results for February 2005 were as follows:

Manufacturing overhead	$5,520,000
Machine hours	310,000

Required:
a. Determine the 2005 predetermined overhead rate per machine hour.
b. Using the predetermined overhead rate per machine hour, determine the manufacturing overhead applied to Work-in-Process during February.
c. As of February 1, actual overhead was underapplied by $400,000. Determine the cumulative amount of any overapplied or underapplied overhead at the end of February.

6–7
Developing and Using a Predetermined Overhead Rate: High-Low Cost Estimation

For years, Simko Parts Company has used an actual plantwide overhead rate and based its prices on cost plus a markup of 25 percent. Recently the marketing manager, Jan Barton, and the production manager, Susan Young, confronted the controller with a common problem.

The marketing manager expressed a concern that Simko's prices seem to vary widely throughout the year. According to Barton, "It seems irrational to charge higher prices when business is bad and lower prices when business is good. While we get a lot of business during high-volume months because we charge less than our competitors, it is a waste of time to even call on customers during low-volume months because we are raising prices while our competitors are lowering them."

Young also believed that it was "folly to be so pushed that we have to pay overtime in some months and then lay employees off in others." She commented, "While there are natural variations in customer demand, the accounting system seems to amplify this variation."

Required:
a. Evaluate the arguments presented by Barton and Young. What suggestions do you have for improving the accounting and pricing procedures?
b. Assume that the Simko Parts Company had the following total manufacturing overhead costs and direct labor hours in 2004 and 2005:

	2004	2005
Total manufacturing overhead	$200,000	$237,500
Direct labor hours	20,000	27,500

Use the high-low method to develop a cost estimating equation for total manufacturing overhead.
c. Develop a predetermined rate for 2006, assuming 25,000 direct labor hours are budgeted for 2006.
d. Assume that the actual level of activity in 2006 was 30,000 direct labor hours and that the total 2006 manufacturing overhead was $240,000. Determine the underapplied or overapplied manufacturing overhead at the end of 2006.
e. Describe two ways of handling any underapplied or overapplied manufacturing overhead at the end of the year.

6–8
Manufacturing Cost Flows with Machine Hours Allocation

On November 1, 2004, Torque Manufacturing Company's beginning balances in manufacturing accounts and finished goods inventory were as follows:

Raw Materials	$ 7,000
Manufacturing Supplies	500
Work-in-Process	5,000
Manufacturing Overhead	0
Finished Goods	20,000

During November, Torque Manufacturing completed the following manufacturing transactions:

• Purchased raw materials costing $60,000 and manufacturing supplies costing $3,000 on account.

- Requisitioned raw materials costing $40,000 to the factory.
- Incurred direct labor costs of $27,000 and indirect labor costs of $4,800.
- Used manufacturing supplies costing $3,000.
- Recorded manufacturing depreciation of $15,000.
- Miscellaneous payables for manufacturing overhead totaled $3,600.
- Applied manufacturing overhead, based on 2,250 machine hours, at a predetermined rate of $10 per machine hour.
- Completed jobs costing $85,000.
- Finished goods costing $96,000 were sold.

Required:

Prepare a diagram summarizing the flow of costs through all manufacturing accounts, Finished Goods Inventory, and Cost of Goods Sold.

6-9
Recording Cost Flows—Journal Entries (Appendix)

Refer to Exercise 6–8.

Required:

Prepare the general journal entries to record each of the manufacturing transactions of Torque Manufacturing Company for the month of November.

6-10
Manufacturing Cost Flows with Labor Hours Allocation

On June 1, 2004, Fitzgerald Manufacturing Company's Manufacturing Overhead and Finished Goods Inventory account balances were as follows:

Raw Materials	$ 8,000
Manufacturing Supplies	100
Work-in-Process	4,000
Manufacturing Overhead	(400) overapplied
Finished Goods	20,000

During June, Fitzgerald Manufacturing completed the following manufacturing transactions:

- Purchased raw materials costing $24,000 and manufacturing supplies costing $2,000 on account.
- Requisitioned raw materials costing $28,000 to the factory.
- Recorded manufacturing payroll for the month of 2,200 hours of direct labor and 400 hours of indirect labor, both at $11 per hour.
- Used manufacturing supplies costing $800.
- Recorded manufacturing depreciation of $12,000.
- Recognized miscellaneous payables for manufacturing overhead of $2,800.
- Applied manufacturing overhead at a predetermined rate of $8 per direct labor hour.
- Completed jobs costing $72,000.
- Sold finished goods costing $81,500.

Required:

Prepare a diagram summarizing the flow of costs through all manufacturing accounts, Finished Goods Inventory, and Cost of Goods Sold.

6-11
Recording Cost Flows—Journal Entries (Appendix)

Refer to Exercise 6–10.

Required:

Prepare general journal entries to record each of the manufacturing transactions of Fitzgerald Manufacturing Company for the month of June.

6-12
Service Cost Flows

Video Marketing, Ltd., produces television advertisements for businesses that are marketing products in the western provinces of Canada. To achieve cost control, Video Marketing uses a job cost system similar to that found in a manufacturing organization. It uses some different account titles:

Account	Replaces
Videos-in-Process	Work-in-Process
Production Supplies Inventory	Manufacturing Supplies Inventory
Cost of Videos Completed	Cost of Goods Sold
Accumulated Depreciation, Studio Assets	Accumulated Depreciation, Factory Assets
Studio Overhead	Manufacturing Overhead

Video Marketing does not maintain Raw Materials or Finished Goods Inventory accounts. Materials, such as props needed for videos, are purchased as needed from outside sources and charged directly to Videos-in-Process and the appropriate job. Videos are delivered directly to clients upon completion. The October 1, 2004, balances were as follows:

Video Supplies	$ 275
Videos-in-Process	1,000
Studio Overhead	(250) overapplied

During October, Video Marketing completed the following production transactions:

- Purchased production supplies costing $1,500 on account.
- Purchased materials for specific jobs costing $27,000 on account.
- Incurred direct labor costs of $65,000 and indirect labor costs of $3,200.
- Used production supplies costing $850.
- Recorded studio depreciation of $3,000.
- Incurred miscellaneous payables for studio overhead of $1,800.
- Applied studio overhead at a predetermined rate of $18 per studio hour, with 480 studio hours.
- Completed jobs costing $97,000 and delivered them directly to clients.

Required:
Prepare a diagram summarizing the flow of costs through all service accounts and Cost of Videos Completed.

6-13
Recording Cost Flows—Journal Entries (Appendix)

Refer to Exercise 6–12.

Required:
Prepare general journal entries to record each of the production transactions of Video Marketing Company for the month of October.

6-14
Manufacturing Accounts: Missing Data

Selected data from manufacturing accounts are presented:

Raw materials:	
Beginning balance	$ 7,000
Purchases	?
Direct materials	?
Ending balance	12,000
Work-in-process:	
Beginning balance	?
Direct materials	?
Direct labor	?
Applied manufacturing overhead	75,000
Cost of goods manufactured	?
Ending balance	24,000

Finished goods inventory:
Beginning balance . . . . $ 0
Cost of goods manufactured . . . . ?
Cost of goods sold 110,000
Ending balance 20,000

Additional information follows:

- Ending Work-in-Process is three times as large as beginning Work-in-Process.
- Manufacturing overhead is applied at 150 percent of direct materials.

Required:
Determine each of the following amounts:

a. Purchases
b. Direct materials
c. Beginning work-in-process
d. Direct labor
e. Cost of goods manufactured

6-15
Construction Accounts: Missing Data

Selected data for the accounts of a construction company are presented:

Raw materials:
Beginning balance . . . . $ 4,000
Purchases 80,000
Direct materials . . . . ?
Ending balance 9,000
Contracts-in-process:
Beginning balance 12,000
Direct materials . . . . ?
Direct labor . . . . ?
Applied construction overhead . . . . . . ?
Cost of completed contracts . . . . ?
Ending balance . . . . ?

Additional information follows:

- Ending Contracts-in-Process equals one-half beginning Contracts-in-Process.
- Conversion costs amount to two-thirds of the total current construction costs.
- Construction overhead is applied at 50 percent of direct labor dollars.

Required:
Determine each of the following amounts:

a. Direct materials
b. Direct labor
c. Applied construction overhead
d. Ending contracts-in-process
e. Cost of completed contracts

6-16
Job Order Costing and Process Costing Applications

For each of the following manufacturing situations, indicate whether job order or process costing is more appropriate and why.

a. Peanut butter manufacturer
b. Chemical plant that produces household cleaners
c. Shoe manufacturer
d. Modular home builder
e. Company that makes windshields for automobile manufacturers

6-17
Job Order Costing and Process Costing Applications

For each of the following situations, indicate whether job order or process costing is more appropriate and why.

a. Building contractor for residential dwellings
b. Manufacturer of nylon yarn that sells to fabric-making textile companies
c. Clothing manufacturer that makes suits in several different fabrics, colors, styles, and sizes
d. Hosiery mill that manufactures a one-size-fits-all product
e. Vehicle battery manufacturer that has just received an order for 400,000 identical batteries to be delivered as completed over the next 12 months

6-18
Process Costing

Kingston Manufacturing Company makes a single product that is produced on a continuous basis in one department. All materials are added at the beginning of production. The total cost per equivalent unit in process in March 2004 was $4.60, consisting of $3.00 for materials and $1.60 for conversion. During the month, 8,000 units of product were transferred to finished goods inventory; on March 31, 4,000 units were in process, 10 percent converted. Kingston uses weighted average costing.

Required:

a. Determine the cost of goods transferred to finished goods inventory.
b. Determine the cost of the ending work-in-process inventory.
c. What was the total cost of the beginning work-in-process inventory plus the current manufacturing costs?

6-19
Cost of Production Report: No Beginning Inventories

Fisk Paper Company produces newsprint paper through a special recycling process using scrap paper products. Production and cost data for October 2004, the first month of operations for the company's new Augusta plant, follow:

Units of product started in process during October	90,000 tons
Units completed and transferred to finished goods	75,000 tons
Machine hours operated	10,000
Direct materials costs incurred	$486,000
Direct labor costs incurred	$190,530

Raw materials are added at the beginning of the process for each unit of product produced, and labor and manufacturing overhead are added evenly throughout the manufacturing process. Manufacturing overhead is applied to Work-in-Process at the rate of $24 per machine hour. Units in process at the end of the period were 65 percent converted.

Required:
Prepare a cost of production report for Fisk Paper Company for October.

6-20
Cost of Production Report: No Beginning Inventories

Rodeway Paving Products Company manufactures asphalt paving materials for highway construction through a one-step process in which all materials are added at the beginning of the process. During October 2004, Rodeway accumulated the following data in its process costing system:

Production data:	
Work-in-process, 10/1/04	0 tons
Raw materials transferred to processing	25,000 tons
Work-in-process, 10/31/04 (75% converted)	5,000 tons
Cost data:	
Raw materials transferred to processing	$600,000
Conversion costs:	
Direct labor cost incurred	$38,000
Manufacturing overhead applied	?

Manufacturing overhead is applied at the rate of $2 per equivalent unit (ton) processed.

Required:
Prepare a cost of production report for October 2004.

Problems

6-21
Statements: Cost of Goods Manufactured and Income

Following is information from the records of the Saskatchewan Company for July 2004.

Purchases:

Raw materials	$ 80,000
Manufacturing supplies	3,500
Office supplies	1,200
Sales	425,700
Administrative salaries	12,000
Direct labor	117,500
Production employees' fringe benefits*	4,000
Sales commissions	50,000
Production supervisors' salaries	7,200
Plant depreciation	14,000
Office depreciation	20,000
Plant maintenance	10,000
Plant utilities	35,000
Office utilities	8,000
Office maintenance	2,000
Production equipment rent	6,000
Office equipment rent	1,300

*Classified as manufacturing overhead

Inventories:

	July 1	July 31
Raw materials	$17,000	$25,000
Manufacturing supplies	1,500	3,000
Office supplies	600	1,000
Work-in-process	51,000	40,000
Finished goods	35,000	27,100

Required:
Prepare a statement of cost of goods manufactured and an income statement. Actual overhead costs are assigned to products.

6-22
Correcting Erroneous Statements: Cost of Goods Manufactured and Income

Two reports prepared by the former accountant of Columbus Manufacturing Corporation are presented:

Columbus Manufacturing Corporation
Statement of Cost of Goods Manufactured and Income
For the Month Ending December 31, 2004

Sales		$200,000
Less direct materials		(40,000)
Gross profit		$160,000
Less other expenses:		
Cost of goods sold (computed below)	$89,000	
Office supplies	500	
Manufacturing utilities	2,000	
Office utilities	500	(92,000)
Net income		$ 68,000

Columbus Manufacturing Corporation
Statement of Cost of Goods Sold
For the Month Ending December 31, 2004

Finished goods inventory, 12/1/04			$30,000
Work-in-process, 12/1/04			6,000
Total			$36,000
Current manufacturing costs:			
Salaries and wages:			
Direct labor	$10,000		
Other manufacturing	4,000		
Sales	8,000		
Administrative	6,000	$28,000	
Other:			
Manufacturing supplies	$ 3,000		
Manufacturing depreciation	7,000		
Insurance on showroom	2,000		
Miscellaneous manufacturing overhead	13,000	25,000	53,000
Total work-in-process			$89,000
Work-in-process, 12/31/04			(0)
Cost of goods sold			$89,000

Additional information follows:

- The December 31 finished goods inventory was $4,000.
- Dividends of $20,000 were declared and paid during December.
- All amounts except those specifically computed in the presented statements are correct.

Required:

Prepare a statement of cost of goods manufactured and an income statement in good form.

6–23
Account
Interrelationships:
Missing Data

Supply the missing data in each independent case.

	Case 1	Case 2	Case 3	Case 4
Sales	$55,000	$?	$?	$?
Raw materials, beginning	10,000	13,000	?	5,000
Purchases	?	13,000	2,500	31,700
Raw materials, ending	8,000	?	500	6,200
Direct materials	?	20,000	2,000	?
Direct labor	20,000	25,000	6,000	?
Manufacturing overhead	10,000	8,000	?	29,200
Current manufacturing costs	55,000	?	12,000	?
Work-in-process, beginning	?	8,000	8,000	5,300
Work-in-process, ending	5,000	7,000	?	4,000
Cost of goods manufactured	55,000	?	19,000	82,000
Finished goods, beginning	?	6,000	1,500	8,000
Finished goods, ending	25,000	?	500	10,000
Cost of goods sold	?	55,000	?	?
Gross profit	10,000	9,000	?	10,500
Other expenses	13,000	?	4,000	3,500
Net income (loss)	?	(4,000)	2,000	?

6-24
Statements: Cost of Goods Manufactured and Income with Predetermined Overhead and Labor Cost Classifications

Information pertaining to Calloway, Inc., for April 2004 is presented.

Sales	$200,000
Purchases:	
Raw materials	35,000
Manufacturing supplies	800
Office supplies	500
Salaries (including fringe benefits):	
Administrative	6,000
Production supervisors	3,600
Sales	15,000
Depreciation:	
Plant and machinery	8,000
Office and office equipment	4,000
Utilities:	
Plant	5,250
Office	890

Inventories:

	April 1	April 30
Raw materials	$5,000	$3,500
Manufacturing supplies	1,000	1,100
Office supplies	900	800
Work-in-process	2,000	2,300
Finished goods	8,000	9,000

Additional information follows:

- Manufacturing overhead is applied to products at 80 percent of direct labor dollars.
- Employee base wages are $12 per hour.
- Employee fringe benefits amount to 40 percent of the base wage rate. They are classified as manufacturing overhead.
- During April, production employees worked 5,600 hours, including 4,800 regular hours and 200 overtime hours spent working on products. There were 600 indirect labor hours.
- Employees are paid a 50 percent overtime premium. Any overtime premium is treated as manufacturing overhead.

Required:
a. Prepare a statement of cost of goods manufactured and an income statement.
b. Determine underapplied or overapplied overhead for April.
c. Recompute direct labor and actual manufacturing overhead assuming employee fringe benefits for direct labor hours are classified as direct labor.

6-25
Actual and Predetermined Overhead Rates

Elliott's Engines, which builds high performance auto engines for race cars, started operations on January 1, 2004. During the month, the following events occurred:

- Materials costing $8,000 were purchased on account.
- Direct materials costing $3,000 were placed in process.
- A total of 400 direct labor hours was charged to individual jobs at a rate of $15 per hour.
- Overhead costs for the month of January were as follows:

Depreciation on building and equipment	$ 500
Indirect labor	1,500
Utilities	600
Property taxes on building	650
Insurance on building	550

- On January 31, only one job (A06) was in process with materials costs of $600, direct labor charges of $300 for 30 direct labor hours, and applied overhead.
- The building and equipment were purchased before operations began and the insurance was prepaid. All other costs will be paid during the following month.

Note: Predetermined overhead rates are used throughout the chapter. An alternative is to accumulate actual overhead costs for the period in Manufacturing Overhead and apply actual costs at the close of the period to all jobs in process during the period.

Required:
a. Assuming Elliott's Engines assigned actual monthly overhead costs to jobs on the basis of actual monthly direct labor hours, prepare an analysis of Work-in-Process for the month of January.
b. Assuming Elliott's Engines uses a predetermined overhead rate of $10 per direct labor hour, prepare an analysis of Work-in-Process for the month of January. Describe the appropriate treatment of any overapplied or underapplied overhead for the month of January.
c. Review the overhead items and classify each as fixed or variable in relation to direct labor hours. Next, predict the actual overhead rates for months when 200 and 1,000 direct labor hours are used. Assuming jobs similar to A06 were in process at the end of each month, determine the costs assigned to these jobs. (*Hint:* Determine a variable overhead rate.)
d. Why do you suppose predetermined overhead rates are preferred to actual overhead rates?

6-26
Job Costing with Predetermined Overhead Rate

Steelcase, Inc. manufactures desks, chairs, file cabinets, and similar office products in batches for speculative inventories. Assume that Steelcase's production costs are accounted for using a job cost system. At the beginning of April 2001, raw materials inventories totaled $8,500,000, manufacturing supplies amounted to $1,200,000 and finished goods inventories totaled $6,000,000. Two jobs were in process: Job 522 with assigned costs of $5,640,000 and Job 523 with assigned costs of $2,400,000. The following information summarizes April manufacturing activities:

- Purchased raw materials costing $25,000,000 on account.
- Purchased manufacturing supplies costing $3,000,000 on account.
- Requisitioned materials needed to complete Job 523. Started two new jobs, 524 and 525, and requisitioned direct materials for them.

Direct materials:		
Job 523	....	$ 3,400,000
Job 524	....	12,500,000
Job 525	....	9,600,000
Total	......	$25,500,000

- Recorded April salaries and wages as follows:

Direct labor:	
Job 522 (300,000 hours × $12 per hour)	$ 3,600,000
Job 523 (800,000 hours × $12 per hour)	9,600,000
Job 524 (1,200,000 hours × $12 per hour)	14,400,000
Job 525 (1,000,000 hours × $12 per hour)	12,000,000
Total direct labor	$39,600,000
Indirect labor	6,400,000
Total	$46,000,000

- Used manufacturing supplies costing $2,250,000.
- Recognized depreciation on factory fixed assets of $4,000,000.

- Incurred miscellaneous manufacturing overhead costs of $5,500,000 on account.
- Applied manufacturing overhead at the rate of $6 per direct labor hour.
- Completed Jobs 522, 523, and 524.

Required:
Prepare a complete analysis of all activity in Work-in-Process. Be sure to show the beginning and ending balances, all increases and decreases, and label each item. Support information on decreases with job cost sheets.

6-27
Job Costing with Predetermined Overhead Rate

Surecut Mower Company manufactures a variety of gasoline-powered mowers for discount hardware and department stores. Surecut uses a job cost system and treats each customer's order as a separate job.

The primary mower components (motors, chassis, and wheels) are purchased from three different suppliers under long-term contracts that call for the direct delivery of raw materials to the production floor as needed. When a customer's order is received, a raw materials purchase order is electronically placed with suppliers. The purchase order specifies the scheduled date that production is to begin as the delivery date for motors and chassis; the scheduled date production is to be completed is specified as the delivery date for the wheels. As a consequence, there are no raw materials inventories; raw materials are charged directly to Work-in-Process upon receipt.

Upon completion, goods are shipped directly to customers rather than transferred to finished goods inventory.

At the beginning of July 2001, Surecut had the following work-in-process inventories:

Job 365	$20,000
Job 366	16,500
Job 367	15,000
Job 368	9,000
Total	$60,500

During July, the following activities took place:

- Started Jobs 369, 370, and 371.
- Ordered and received the following raw materials for specified jobs:

Job	Motors	Chassis	Wheels	Total
366	$ 0	$ 0	$ 800	$ 800
367	0	0	1,200	1,200
368	0	0	1,600	1,600
369	12,000	4,000	1,000	17,000
370	9,000	3,500	900	13,400
371	8,500	3,800	0	12,300
Total	$29,500	$11,300	$5,500	$46,300

- Incurred July manufacturing payroll summarized here:

Direct labor:	
Job 365	$ 500
Job 366	3,200
Job 367	3,400
Job 368	4,160
Job 369	1,300
Job 370	2,620
Job 371	2,000
Total	$17,180
Indirect labor	3,436
Total	$20,616

- Incurred additional manufacturing overhead costs for July:

Manufacturing supplies purchased on account and used	$ 2,800
Depreciation on factory fixed assets	6,000
Miscellaneous payables	5,100
Total	$13,900

- Applied manufacturing overhead using a predetermined rate based on predicted annual overhead of $180,000 and predicted annual direct labor of $200,000.
- Completed and shipped Jobs 365 through 370.

Required:

Prepare a complete analysis of all activity in Work-in-Process. Be sure to show the beginning and ending balances, all increases and decreases, and label each item. Support information on decreases with job cost sheets.

6–28
Weighted Average Process Costing

Forsythe Processing Company manufactures one product on a continuous basis in two departments, Processing and Finishing. All materials are added at the beginning of work on the product in the Processing Department. During December 2004, the following events occurred in the Processing Department:

Units started	16,000 units
Units completed and transferred to Finishing Department	15,000 units

Costs assigned to processing:
Raw materials (one unit of raw materials for each unit of product started)	$142,000
Manufacturing supplies used	18,000
Direct labor costs incurred	51,000
Supervisors' salaries	12,000
Other production labor costs	14,000
Depreciation on equipment	6,000
Other production costs	18,000

Additional information follows:

- Forsythe uses weighted average costing and applies manufacturing overhead to Work-in-Process at the rate of 100 percent of direct labor cost.
- Ending inventory in the Processing Department consists of 3,000 units that are one-third converted.
- Beginning inventory contained 2,000 units, one-half converted, with a cost of $27,300 ($17,300 for materials and $10,000 for conversion).

Required:

a. Prepare a cost of production report for the Processing Department for December.
b. Prepare an analysis of all changes in Work-in-Process.

6–29
Weighted Average Process Costing

Plains Peanut Butter, Inc., processes its only product, 12-ounce jars of peanut butter, in a single process and uses weighted average process costing to account for inventory costs. All materials are added at the beginning of production. The following inventory, production, and cost data are provided for June 2004:

Production data:
Beginning inventory (25% converted)	210,000 units
Units started	650,000 units
Ending inventory (50% converted)	180,000 units

Manufacturing costs:
  Beginning inventory in process:
    Materials cost $146,000
    Conversion cost 88,000
  Raw materials cost added at beginning of process 739,800
  Direct labor cost incurred 410,000
  Manufacturing overhead applied 333,600

Required:

a. Prepare a cost of production report for June.
b. Prepare a statement of cost of goods manufactured for June.

Discussion Questions and Cases

6-30
Cost Data for Financial Reporting, Cost-Volume-Profit Analysis, and Sell or Process Further Decisions

White Pines Furniture Company manufactures a single product, unassembled and un-painted wooden chairs, sold through direct mail. Presented are a statement of cost of goods manufactured and an income statement for 2004, when 8,000 units were man-ufactured and sold. Beginning and ending inventories were each 1,000 units of fin-ished goods.

White Pines Furniture Company
Statement of Cost of Goods Manufactured
For the Year Ending December 31, 2004

Current manufacturing costs:
  Cost of materials placed in production $120,000
  Direct labor 40,000
  Manufacturing overhead:
    Variable $24,000
    Fixed 30,000   54,000 $214,000

Work-in-process, 1/1/04 0

Total costs in process $214,000
Work-in-process, 12/31/04 . . . . (0)

Cost of goods manufactured $214,000

White Pines Furniture Company
Income Statement
For the Year Ending December 31, 2004

Sales (8,000 units × $60) $480,000
Cost of goods sold:
  Finished goods, 1/1/04 (1,000 units × $26.75) . . . . $ 26,750
  Cost of goods manufactured 214,000

  Total goods available for sale $240,750
  Finished goods, 12/31/04 (1,000 units × $26.75) . . . . . (26,750)   (214,000)

Gross profit $266,000
Selling and administrative expenses:
  Variable . . . . $ 80,000
  Fixed 40,000   (120,000)

Net income $146,000

Required:

You may need to review the material presented in Chapters 2, 3, and 4 of this text in order to complete this answer.

a. Determine White Pines' annual break-even point in units.
b. Determine the annual sales volume required to obtain an annual profit of $160,000.

c. Explain why the unit cost used in determining the break-even point and the sales volume required to achieve a desired profit differs from the unit cost of goods sold and the unit cost of the ending inventory used for financial reporting.

d. What type of income statement would be more useful to management in making decisions? Why?

e. Management is contemplating assembling and painting the chairs for sale through outdoor furniture stores rather than selling the unassembled and unpainted chairs by direct mail. At an annual volume of 8,000 units, this will increase manufacturing costs by $160,000 while reducing selling and administrative costs by $20,000. Including a 40 percent markup on White Pines' selling price, the outdoor furniture stores will list the chairs for $112 each. Should White Pines finish the chairs or continue selling them by direct mail? Why?

f. Assuming White Pines finishes the chairs, for financial reporting purposes, what unit cost should it assign to any ending inventory of finished goods?

g. Explain why the inventory value used in requirement (f) differs from the costs used in requirement (e).

6–31
Cost Data for
Financial Reporting
and Special Order
Decisions

Friendly Greeting Card Company produces a full range of greeting cards sold through pharmacies and department stores. Each card is designed by independent artists. A production master is then prepared for each design. The production master has an indefinite life. Product designs for popular cards are deemed to be valuable assets. If a card sells well, many batches of the design will be manufactured over a period of years. Hence, Friendly Greeting maintains an inventory of production masters so that cards may be periodically reissued.

Cards are produced in batches that may vary in sizes of 1,000 units. An average batch consists of approximately 10,000 cards. Producing a batch requires placing the production master on the printing press, setting the press for the appropriate paper size, and making other adjustments for colors and so forth.

Presented are facility-, product-, batch-, and unit-level cost information:

Product design and production master per new card	$ 1,500.00
Batch setup (typically per 10,000 cards)	150.00
Materials per 1,000 cards	100.00
Conversion per 1,000 cards	80.00
Shipping:	
Per batch	20.00
Per card	0.01
Selling and administrative:	
Companywide	200,000.00
Per product design marketed	500.00

Information from previous year:

Product designs and masters prepared for new cards	90
Product designs marketed	120
Batches manufactured	500
Cards manufactured and sold	5,000,000

Required:
You may need to review the material presented in Chapters 2 and 3 of this text in order to complete this answer.

a. Describe how you would determine the cost of goods sold and the value of any ending inventory for financial reporting purposes. (No computations are required.)

b. You have just received an inquiry from Mall-Mart department stores to develop and manufacture 20 special designs for sale exclusively in Mall-Mart stores. The cards would be sold for $1.50 each, and Mall-Mart would pay Friendly Greeting

$0.40 per card. The initial order is for 20,000 cards of each design. If the cards sell well, Mall-Mart plans to place additional orders for these and other designs. Because of the preestablished sales relationship, no marketing costs would be associated with the cards sold to Mall-Mart. How would you evaluate the desirability of the Mall-Mart proposal?

c. Explain any differences between the costs considered in your answer to requirement (a) and the costs considered in your answer to requirement (b).

6-32
Continue or
Discontinue:
Plantwide
Overhead
with Unit and Batch
Level Cost Drivers

Cobera Electronics is the producer of the once popular "Good Buddy" citizens band (CB) radio. Although Cobera Electronics was one of the early producers of CB radios, in recent years, the profitability of CB radios has declined because of market saturation and foreign competition. To fully utilize its production capacity, Cobera has started producing a variety of special-order consumer electronic appliances. This additional business necessitated a change in the firm's accounting system.

When a single product was produced on a continuous basis, product costs were computed by dividing current manufacturing costs by the number of units produced. With the expansion of activities to include products made to customer specifications, Cobera instituted a job cost system. The system assigns actual direct materials costs to each job. Because production operations make extensive use of machine assembly operations, direct labor and overhead costs are combined into a single conversion rate per machine hour.

Last year, Cobera produced 100,000 Good Buddy CB radios and 250 other jobs to customer order. These additional jobs averaged 200 units each. Unit selling price and cost information for last year is presented:

	Good Buddy CB Radio		Other Products
Selling price	$90.00		$125.00
Manufacturing costs:			
Direct materials	$60.00	$60.00	
Conversion	25.20	50.40	
Total	(85.20)		(110.40)
Gross profit	$ 4.80		$ 14.60
Selling and distribution costs	(2.00)		(2.00)
Profit	$ 2.80		$ 12.60

David Wallace, the president, is concerned about the declining profitability of CB radios in comparison with specialty products. He is considering a proposal to discontinue the production of CB radios to specialize in other products. Even though the other products have a relatively low volume and require additional selling and manufacturing effort, they are more profitable due to the premium prices they command.

Prior to finalizing his recommendation, Mr. Wallace asked you to take a final look at the situation and prepare a written report by noon tomorrow. You eagerly talk with personnel in sales, accounting, and production where you acquire the following additional information:

- CB radios require 0.1 machine hour each; the custom products will require an average of 0.2 machine hour each.
- All products are produced using similar types of equipment that have similar original costs and hourly operating costs.
- To avoid excess finished goods inventory levels, CB radios are produced in 10 equal-sized batches throughout the year rather than in one batch of 100,000 units. Each of the 250 other jobs is manufactured in a separate batch.
- Regardless of the product or the length of the production run, machine setup time is approximately 20 machine hours per batch. The cost of machine setup is treated as manufacturing overhead.

- Variable operating costs are the same per unit of time, regardless of whether machines are operating or being set up.
- Conversion costs are assigned to jobs on the basis of machine hours.
- Last year's selling and distribution costs for CB radios included a fixed element of $50,000 and a variable element of $0.50 per unit.
- Selling and distribution costs for the other products average $800 per order.
- In preparing the analysis of product profitability, selling and administrative costs were placed in a single cost pool and assigned on the basis of units sold.

Required:

You may need to review the material in Chapters 2–5 of this text in order to complete this case. Determine the actual unit profitability of CB radios and the other products, and prepare a report recommending whether or not the production of CB radios should be discontinued.

6-33
**Continue or
Discontinue:
Plantwide
Overhead
with Labor- and
Machine-Intensive
Operations**

When Dartmouth Products started operation five years ago, its only product was a radar detector known as the Bear Detector. The production system was simple, with Bear Detectors manually assembled from purchased components. With no ending work-in-process inventories, unit costs were calculated once a month by dividing current manufacturing costs by units produced.

Last year, Dartmouth Products began to manufacture a second product, codenamed the Lion Tamer. The production of Lion Tamers involves both machine-intensive fabrication and assembly.

The introduction of the second product necessitated a change in the firm's simple accounting system. Dartmouth Products now separately assigns direct material and direct labor costs to each product using information contained on materials requisitions and work tickets. Manufacturing overhead is accumulated in a single cost pool and assigned on the basis of direct labor hours, which is common to both products.

Presented are last year's financial results by product:

	Bear Detector		Lion Tamer
Sales:			
Units	5,000		2,000
Dollars	$ 500,000		$ 300,000
Cost of goods sold:			
Direct materials	$100,000	$60,000	
Direct labor	150,000	45,000	
Applied overhead	270,000	81,000	
Total	(520,000)		(186,000)
Gross profit	$ (20,000)		$ 114,000

Management is concerned about the mixed nature of last year's financial performance. It appears that the Lion Tamer is a roaring success. The only competition, the Nittney Company, has been selling a competing product for considerably more than Dartmouth's Lion Tamer; this company is in financial difficulty and is likely to file for bankruptcy. The management of Dartmouth Products attributes the Lion Tamer's success to excellent production management.

Management is concerned, however, about the future of the Bear Detector and is likely to discontinue that product unless its profitability can be improved. You have been asked to help with this decision and have obtained the following information:

- The labor rate is $15 per hour.
- Dartmouth has two separate production operations, fabrication and assembly. Bear Detectors undergo only assembly operations and require 2.0 assembly hours

per unit. Lion Tamers undergo both fabrication and assembly and require 1.0 fabrication hour and 0.5 assembly hour per unit.

- The annual Fabricating Department cost function is:

$$200,000 + \$5 \text{ (labor hours)}$$

- The annual Assembly Department overhead cost function is:

$$20,000 + \$11 \text{ (labor hours)}$$

Required:

You may need to review the material in Chapters 2–5 of this text in order to complete this case. Evaluate the profitability of Dartmouth's two products and make any recommendations you believe appropriate.

Solution to Review Problem

a. See page 277 for diagram.
b. Job 228:

Direct materials	$14,400
Direct labor	8,000
Applied manufacturing overhead (800 × $5)	4,000
Total	$26,400

c.

Tri-Star Printing Company
Statement of Cost of Goods Manufactured
For the Month Ending June 30, 2004

Current manufacturing costs:			
Cost of materials placed in production:			
Raw materials, 6/1/04	$ 7,000		
Purchases	40,000		
Total available	$47,000		
Raw materials, 6/30/04	(12,000)	$35,000	
Direct labor		48,500	
Manufacturing overhead applied		24,250	$107,750
Work-in-process, 6/1/04			15,550
Total costs in process			$123,300
Work-in-process, 6/30/04			(26,400)
Cost of goods manufactured			$ 96,900

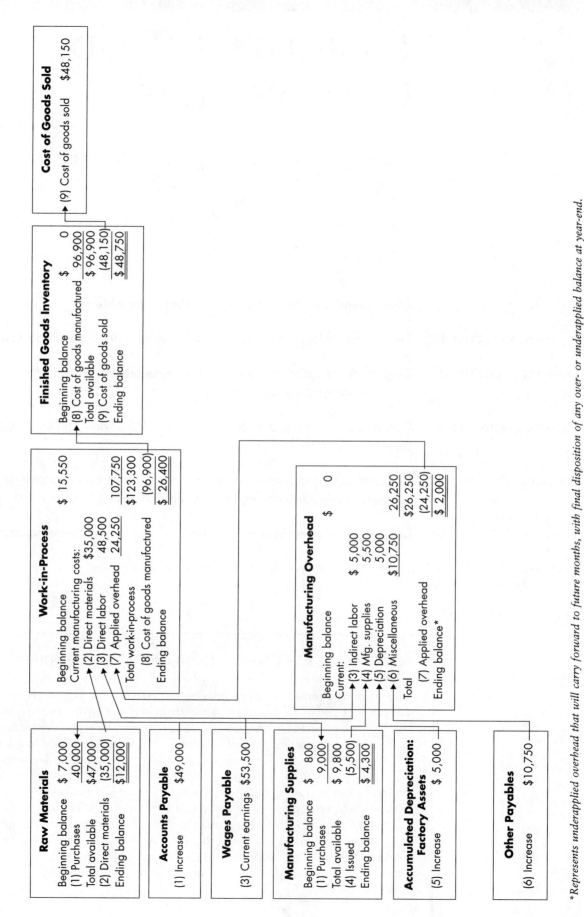

Cost of Goods Sold

(9) Cost of goods sold $48,150

Finished Goods Inventory

Beginning balance	$ 0
(8) Cost of goods manufactured	96,900
Total available	$ 96,900
(9) Cost of goods sold	(48,150)
Ending balance	$ 48,750

Work-in-Process

Beginning balance		$ 15,550
Current manufacturing costs:		
(2) Direct materials	$35,000	
(3) Direct labor	48,500	
(7) Applied overhead	24,250	107,750
Total work-in-process		$123,300
(8) Cost of goods manufactured		(96,900)
Ending balance		$ 26,400

Manufacturing Overhead

Beginning balance		$ 0
Current:		
(3) Indirect labor	$ 5,000	
(4) Mfg. supplies	5,500	
(5) Depreciation	5,000	
(6) Miscellaneous	10,750	
Total		26,250
(7) Applied overhead		$26,250
		(24,250)
Ending balance*		$ 2,000

Raw Materials

Beginning balance	$ 7,000
(1) Purchases	40,000
Total available	$47,000
(2) Direct materials	(35,000)
Ending balance	$12,000

Accounts Payable

| (1) Increase | $49,000 |

Wages Payable

| (3) Current earnings | $53,500 |

Manufacturing Supplies

Beginning balance	$ 800
(1) Purchases	9,000
Total available	$ 9,800
(4) Issued	(5,500)
Ending balance	$ 4,300

Accumulated Depreciation: Factory Assets

| (5) Increase | $ 5,000 |

Other Payables

| (6) Increase | $10,750 |

*Represents underapplied overhead that will carry forward to future months, with final disposition of any over- or underapplied balance at year-end.

DESIGNING PRODUCT COST SYSTEMS

After completing this chapter, you should be able to:

LEARNING OBJECTIVE 1   Define and explain the primary elements of an indirect cost allocation system.

LEARNING OBJECTIVE 2   Describe the process of allocating service department costs, including the treatment of interdepartment services.

LEARNING OBJECTIVE 3   Compare and contrast activity-based costing (ABC) and traditional organization-based costing (OBC).

LEARNING OBJECTIVE 4   Calculate overhead rates under three methods on the product costing continuum using plantwide, department, or activity-based rates.

LEARNING OBJECTIVE 5   Discuss the issues associated with implementing an activity-based costing system.

LEARNING OBJECTIVE 6   Explain the uses and evolution of activity-based costing.

MEASURING, ASSIGNING, AND CONTROLLING INDIRECT COSTS

In a globally competitive environment, the effective management of all costs is a hallmark of sound management. Sometimes indirect costs are the most challenging to manage. Direct items such as direct materials and direct labor in manufacturing firms or only direct labor in service firms can be traced to a job, product, or other unit of work. The other costs necessary to carry on business—the indirect costs—are not so easily traced to specific units or projects. In addition, these indirect costs, including both manufacturing overhead costs and general administration costs, have increased from about 8 percent of sales in the 1920s to about 32 percent in the 1990s. A cost category that was once small is now a much larger component of a firm's overall costs. The circumstances of three diverse firms— SRAM Corporation, Oshkosh Truck Corporation, and Enviro-Recovery Corporation—demonstrate the managerial challenges of measuring and controlling indirect costs.

SRAM makes bicycle components such as gear shifts, brakes, and handlebars. With a Chicago headquarters office that includes an indoor test track, the firm had an estimated $120 million in sales during 1999. In the early 1990s, SRAM pioneered the handgrip gear shift mechanism that allows bicycle riders to change gears without taking their hands off the handgrips. To stay a step ahead of competitors such as Shimano, SRAM management recently introduced a series of new products including SmartBars and SparcDrive. SmartBars are handlebars that allow a rider to quickly adjust the height and reach. SparcDrive is a small electric motor that provides an extra boost to riders when they travel uphill. Both products have been designed for the "comfort rider" segment of the bicycle market.

With 1999 sales of about $1.2 billion, Oshkosh Truck Corporation specializes in fire, concrete-mixing, garbage, and military trucks. Military trucks make up 17 percent of sales, fire engines 27 percent, and concrete and garbage trucks 56 percent. Using contemporary manufacturing techniques, Oshkosh can produce a fire truck in 28 days rather than the 50 days it formerly took. As a result, the firm has saved 1.5 acres of floor space that once held inventory. Along with this increased response time, Oshkosh offers fire departments more than 19,000 different options that can customize a rig for the needs of any fire department.

Enviro-Recovery Corporation pulls up old logs from the bottom of Lake Superior and mills them for restoration projects, musical instruments, and antique furniture. With sales of about $1 million in 1999, the firm can provide custom orders of 16-inch board width rarely available in modern lumber. Demand for these older pine, oak, and maple planks and beams has increased as more dealers begin to stock environmentally friendly lumber.

At first glance, the relationship between these firms and the indirect cost question might not be apparent. These three firms do have two common characteristics, however, that make their indirect cost assignment questions interesting. First, they have some common, indirect costs that they must assign to their products. The costs of the indoor test track, truck production floor, and mill and drying kiln represent common costs that must be distributed to products. Second, each firm's product line includes a group of similar but not identical products. The various bicycle components, fire truck options, and sizes and species of logs likely mean that these different products consume differing amounts of their respective firm's common costs. These two characteristics require that the management of these three companies carefully consider the common cost assignment process in the design of their product costing systems.

Source: David Armstrong, "A Stick in the Spokes," *Forbes,* March 5, 2001, pp. 148–49; Tom Post, "Waterlogged," *Forbes,* March 6, 2000, pp. 132–34; Thomas A. Stewart, "Yikes! Deadwood Is Coming Back," *Fortune,* August 18, 1997, pp. 221–22; and Mark Tatge, "Red Bodies, Black Ink," *Forbes,* March 18, 2000, pp. 114–15.

The purpose of this chapter is to explore the nature of indirect costs and the frequently used approaches to assigning indirect costs to products or services. We begin by considering the relationship between indirect costs and cost objectives such as products or services. Next, we introduce some of the traditional organization-based approaches for assigning indirect costs to cost objectives, noting the strengths and weaknesses of each. We then compare and contrast organization-based and activity-based approaches to cost assignment.

A significant portion of this chapter is devoted to a comprehensive example of cost assignment that illustrates the increased accuracy obtained as we progress from the simplest organization-based approach to the newer activity-based approaches. The chapter concludes with a discussion of issues involved in implementing activity-based costing.

ALLOCATING INDIRECT COSTS

To manage costs, you must be able to measure them. Hence, a major theme of this book is cost measurement, which involves determining the costs appropriately assigned to or associated with a particular cost objective. Costs are generally assignable to a particular cost objective if they were incurred for its benefit or if the costs were caused by the existence of that cost objective. For a shipping department, the wages of the department's employees, clearly, are department costs. They can be directly traced to, or associated with, the shipping department, and they are incurred for the direct benefit of that department.

On the other hand, the cost of electricity was incurred for the common benefit of all occupants of the building. Hence, it is an indirect cost, or **common cost,** for all the departments occupying the building. Other indirect costs that benefited the shipping department include those for security, maintenance of the grounds and parking areas, and cleaning supplies. But what about the cost of operating the payroll department, the computer processing department, or the legal department? Should some of these costs be allocated to the shipping department if it receives services or benefits from these departments? What about the president's salary? Since the president is responsible for the whole company, should this cost be allocated to all departments in the company? What about the cost of operating the company airplane? Should this cost be combined with the president's salary (since the president is the primary user of the plane) and be allocated to all departments?

These are just a few examples of the many difficult questions concerning the allocation of indirect costs. To provide some structure for the discussion of these and other questions, it is necessary to examine the three basic elements of any indirect cost allocation system:

- Cost objectives
- Cost pools
- Allocation bases

COST OBJECTIVES

As noted previously, a **cost objective** is anything to which costs are assigned. Although the most traditional cost objectives are departments, products, or services, managers' needs for cost information are quite varied. A cost objective can be anything for which management desires cost information. Examples of useful cost objectives include (1) the cost of moving materials between work stations (used in evaluating the desirability of rearranging equipment), (2) the cost of inspecting incoming raw materials and returning raw materials that do not meet quality specifications (used in rating vendors and negotiating with them), and (3) the firmwide cost of long distance telephone service (used to evaluate the desirability of switching carriers and/or subscribing to wide-area telephone service).

COST POOLS

A **cost pool** is a collection of related costs, such as manufacturing overhead, that is assigned to one or more cost objectives. It is not feasible in many situations to assign each item of cost separately. Instead, several similar costs are combined into a cost pool, and the entire pool is allocated as a single item. Indirect costs are often pooled along organization lines, such as costs for the payroll department, computing center, or maintenance department. All building-related costs, or other closely related costs, are also frequently pooled. Sometimes these functional cost pools are referred to as *departments* even though they are not real departments. For example, all building-related costs (depreciation, insurance, repairs, etc.) are often pooled together to form building department costs, which are then allocated to the various users of the building.

The key consideration in establishing cost pools is that the items pooled together should be relatively homogeneous and have a logical cause-and-effect relationship to the allocation base. For instance, a building cost pool would include all costs related to the maintenance and operation of the building and might be allocated on the basis of square footage occupied. The costs in this pool, such as insurance, property taxes, and depreciation, have a logical cause-and-effect relationship to the amount of square footage provided. As the square footage increases, these costs are usually expected to increase.

ALLOCATION BASES

The **cost allocation base** is the factor, or characteristic, common to the cost objectives that determines how much of the cost pool is assigned to each cost objective. The allocation base is the link between cost objective and cost pool. For example, labor-related costs may be allocated according to some measure (or estimate) of the labor time devoted to the various cost objectives. Depreciation and other building-related costs are often allocated on the basis of square footage occupied. Other examples of indirect costs and frequently used allocation bases include the following:

Indirect Cost Category	Allocation Base
Employee health services	Number of employees or visits
Personnel	Number of employees or new hires
Maintenance and repairs	Number of repair orders or service hours
Purchasing	Number of orders placed
Warehouse	Amount of square footage used or value of materials stored

The most important consideration in selecting an allocation base is ensuring that a logical association exists between the base selected and the costs incurred. For instance, it is logical to allocate personnel department costs according to the number of employees because the function of the personnel department is to provide employee-related services to the various departments. Thus, personnel costs are incurred as these services are provided. It follows that departments with a large number of employees should receive a larger allocation of personnel department costs than departments with fewer employees.

Selecting allocation bases may not always be simple and straightforward. For example, it might be necessary when allocating building costs to differentiate between various areas of the building. Some areas of the building could be more costly to operate than other areas, or some space, because of its preferred location within the building might be more valuable. For the allocation of indirect costs to be fair, these types of differences should be reflected in the choice of the allocation base, as illustrated in What's Happening 7–1 for Bellcore.

PRODUCTION AND SERVICE DEPARTMENT COSTS

In product costing, all manufacturing costs (direct and indirect) ultimately must be assigned to products. Some companies accumulate all overhead costs for an entire plant in a single overhead cost pool and then allocate (reassign) those costs to products using a plantwide overhead rate based on direct labor hours, machine hours, or some other basis. This is sometimes referred to as the "peanut butter" approach that spreads all overhead costs evenly among products based on a general volume-based cost driver without any effort to differentiate among products. This approach results in an accurate product cost measurement if the plant manufactures only one product. However, when a plant utilizes multiple processes to make two or more products, it might be desirable to accumulate overhead costs by production departments to capture the unique overhead cost characteristics of the various production processes. In such cases, product costs are calculated using multiple department overhead rates reflecting the amount of work done on the products in each department.

BELLCORE CORRECTS UNFAIR SERVICE COST ALLOCATIONS

Bellcore (which stands for Bell Communications Research) is a joint venture organization that provides scientific and engineering research services to several regional telephone companies in the United States. Bellcore was set up to provide services on a cost charge-back basis to seven regional companies. It was necessary for all support costs incurred at Bellcore to be assigned, along with direct costs, to the services performed by Bellcore engineers and scientists for the various telephone companies. This created a classic support service cost allocation problem.

Cost cross-subsidization was strictly forbidden at Bellcore, making it even more important to have equitable bases for allocating support function costs to the primary operating departments. A problem emerged almost immediately after Bellcore's establishment, when the service and operating departments were allocated unusually large costs for support services such as Graphics, Secretarial/Clerical, and Technical Publications. Feeling that support service costs were being unfairly allocated, some managers declined to use such services, either forgoing them entirely or going outside Bellcore to less expensive vendors.

The problem of unfair support service cost allocations was discovered to be caused by inappropriate cost allocation bases. For example, Landlord (or Building) Services costs were being assigned based on square footage without regard to the nature of the space occupied; this caused Secretarial/Clerical to be assigned the same square footage cost for very basic building space as was charged to the Applied Research Department, which had much more technically sophisticated space. In effect, Secretarial/Clerical was subsidizing Applied Research. A thorough study of the cost allocation system at Bellcore resulted in significant changes in the allocation of support services costs, causing the allocations for some services to decrease and others to increase.

Source: Edward J. Kovac and Henry P. Troy, "Getting the Transfer Prices Right: What Bellcore Did," *Harvard Business Review*, September–October 1989, pp. 148–54.

For example, assume that Mitsubishi Company has a plant that produces both DVD players and VCRs, each of which requires work in two production departments (A and B) but not in the same proportions. Department A is a highly automated department that uses robotics; Department B relies more heavily on manual procedures. DVDs are produced 70 percent in Department A and 30 percent in Department B, and VCRs are produced 40 percent in Department A and 60 percent in Department B. This is a situation in which more accurate product cost measurements are likely to result from using department overhead rates than using a plantwide overhead rate.

In addition to multiple *production* departments, many companies have several production *support* departments such as maintenance, facilities, engineering, and administration. These departments, which provide support services to production and/or other support departments, are called **service departments**. Typically, service department costs are allocated (reassigned) to the production (and/or other service) departments that utilize their services. Production department overhead rates, therefore, include the overhead costs incurred directly by the department plus any allocated service department costs. A **direct department cost** is a cost assigned directly to a department (production or service) when it is incurred; an **indirect department cost** is a cost assigned to a department as a result of an indirect allocation, or reassignment, from another department or cost objective.

LEARNING OBJECTIVE 2   ## SERVICE DEPARTMENT COST ALLOCATION

Service departments (maintenance, administration, security, etc.) provide a wide range of support functions, primarily for one or more production departments. These departments, which are considered essential elements in the overall manufacturing process, do not work directly on the "product" but provide auxiliary support to the producing departments. In addition to providing support for the various producing departments, some service departments also provide services to *other service departments*. For example, the payroll and personnel departments may provide services to all departments, and maintenance may provide services to the producing departments as well as to the medical center and food services. Services provided by one service department to other service departments are called **interdepartment services.**

To illustrate service department cost allocations, consider the Manufacturing Division of Krown Drink Company, which has two producing departments, three service departments, and two products. The service departments and their respective service functions and cost allocation bases are as follows:

Department	Service Functions	Allocation Base
Support Services	Receiving and inventory control	Total amount of department capital investment
Engineering Resources	Production setup and engineering and testing	Number of employees
Building and Grounds	Machinery maintenance and depreciation	Amount of square footage occupied

Difficulty in choosing an allocation base for service department costs is not uncommon. For example, Krown Drink may have readily determined the appropriate allocation bases for the Engineering Resources and the Building and Grounds Departments but may have found the choice for Support Services to be less clear. Perhaps after conducting correlation studies, the most equitable base for allocating Support Services costs to other departments was determined to be total capital investment in the departments because they included expensive computer-tracking equipment, both manual and automated forklifts, and other material moving equipment.

Direct department costs and allocation base information used to illustrate Krown Drink's July service department cost allocations are summarized as follows:

	Direct Department Costs	Number of Employees		Amount of Square Footage Occupied		Total Amount of Department Capital Investment	
Service departments:							
Support Services	$ 27,000	15	15%	4,000	8%	—	—
Engineering Resources	20,000	—	—	2,000	4	$ 45,000	8%
Building and Grounds	10,000	5	5	—	—	50,000	9
Producing departments:							
Mixing	40,000*	24	24	11,000	22	180,000	33
Bottling	90,000*	56	56	33,000	66	270,000	50
	$187,000	100	100%	50,000	100%	$545,000	100%

*Direct department overhead

Note that the preceding information omitted the amount of capital investment in the Support Services Department, the number of employees in the Engineering Resources Department, and the amount of square footage used by the Building and Grounds Department. These data were omitted because a department normally does not allocate costs to itself; it allocates costs only to the departments it serves. The three methods commonly used for service department cost allocations—direct, step, and linear algebra—are discussed here.

DIRECT METHOD

The **direct method** allocates all service department costs based only on the amount of services provided to the producing departments. Exhibit 7–1 shows the flow of costs using the direct method. Note that all arrows depicting the cost flows extend directly

EXHIBIT 7–1

FLOW OF COSTS—DIRECT METHOD

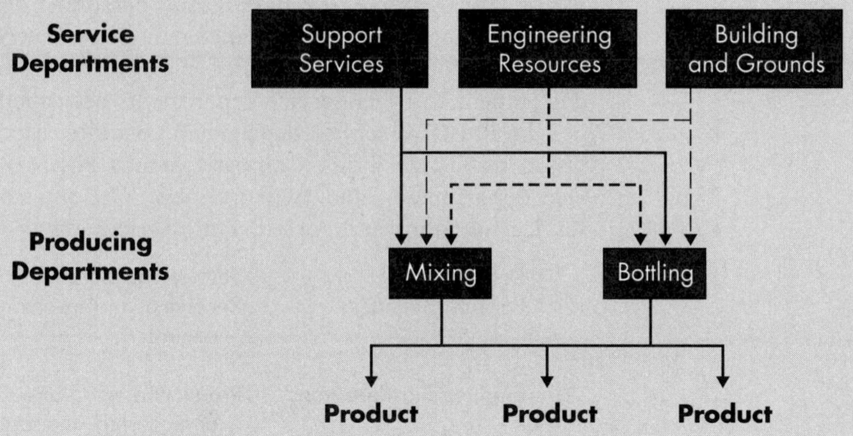

from service departments to producing departments; there are no cost allocations between the service departments.

Exhibit 7–2 shows the service department cost allocations for the direct method. Notice the allocation base used to allocate Engineering Resources costs; only the employees in the producing departments are considered in computing the allocation percentages—24 in Mixing and 56 in Bottling, for a total of 80 employees in the allocation base. Thirty percent (24 ÷ 80) of the producing department employees work in Mixing; therefore, 30 percent of Engineering Resources costs are allocated to Mixing. Applying the same reasoning, 70 percent of Engineering Resources costs are allocated to Bottling. Similar logic is followed in computing the cost allocations for Building and Grounds and Support Services.

The cost allocation summary at the bottom of Exhibit 7–2 shows that all service department costs have been allocated, decreasing the service department costs to zero and increasing the producing department overhead balances by the amounts of the respective allocations. Also note that total costs are not affected by the allocations; the total of $187,000 was merely redistributed so that all costs are reassigned to the producing departments. Total department overhead costs of the producing departments after allocation of service costs are $59,300 for Mixing and $127,700 for Bottling.

The advantage of the direct method of allocating service department costs is that it is easy and convenient to use (see What's Happening 7–2). Its primary disadvantage is that it does not recognize the costs for interdepartment services provided by one service department to another. Instead, any costs incurred to provide services to other service departments are passed directly to the producing departments. The step method improves on the allocation procedure by redirecting some of the costs to other service departments before they are finally allocated to the production departments.

STEP METHOD

The **step method** gives partial recognition of interdepartmental services by using a methodology that allocates the service departments costs *sequentially* both to the remaining service departments and the producing departments. Any indirect costs allocated to a service department in this process are added to that department's direct costs to determine the total costs for allocation to the remaining departments. All service department costs will be applied to the production departments and ultimately to the products.

EXHIBIT 7-2

SERVICE DEPARTMENT COST ALLOCATIONS—DIRECT METHOD

	Total	Mixing	Bottling
Support Services Department:			
Allocation base (capital investment)	$450,000	$180,000	$270,000
Percent of total base	100%	40%	60%
Cost allocations	$27,000	$10,800	$16,200
Engineering Resources Department:			
Allocation base (number of employees)	80	24	56
Percent of total base	100%	30%	70%
Cost allocations	$20,000	$6,000	$14,000
Building and Grounds Department:			
Allocation base (square footage occupied)	44,000	11,000	33,000
Percent of total base	100%	25%	75%
Cost allocations	$10,000	$2,500	$7,500

COST ALLOCATION SUMMARY

	Support Services	Engineering Resources	Building and Grounds	Mixing	Bottling	Total
Department cost before allocations	$27,000	$20,000	$10,000	$40,000	$ 90,000	$187,000
Cost allocations:						
Support Services	(27,000)			10,800	16,200	—
Engineering Resources		(20,000)		6,000	14,000	—
Building and Grounds			(10,000)	2,500	7,500	—
Department costs after allocations	$ 0	$ 0	$ 0	$59,300	$127,700	$187,000

COST ALLOCATIONS FOR SERVICES IN A UNIVERSITY

A typical case of service department cost allocation using the direct method can be found in many large colleges and universities. The producing departments of a university are its academic departments and professional schools; its support service departments are those such as student services (which includes housing, dining, and student life activities), facilities management (which is responsible for the physical campus), academic support (such as libraries and computer centers), and administration (such as the president's office, fund-raising activities, and the legal department). Commonly used bases for allocating these service department costs are the number of students for student services and academic support, square footage of space occupied for facilities management, and total revenues for administration.

The allocation of these support service costs are often major budget line items in the operating budgets for deans and department heads. These costs greatly affect the amount of money left for direct operating needs such as faculty salaries, research support, and professional development. Hence, it is important that the cost allocation method be perceived as fair and appropriate by those whose budgets are charged with these allocated costs. Using the direct allocation method might be appropriate in allocating some university service costs, such as student services; it would probably not be appropriate in allocating others, such as computer services, which are used by both the academic departments and the other service departments.

To illustrate the problem that may result from using the direct method, assume that Ramso Company has two service departments, S1 and S2, and two producing departments, P1 and P2, that provide services as follows:

	RECEIVER OF SERVICES			
Provider of Services	S1	S2	P1	P2
S1	0%	0%	70%	30%
S2	50%	0%	25%	25%

If the direct method is used to allocate service department costs to the producing departments, S2 total costs will be allocated equally to the producing departments because they use the same amount of S2 services (25 percent each). Is this an equitable allocation of S2 costs? S2 actually provides half of its services to the other service department (S1), which, in turn, provides the majority of its services to P1. Assume that S2 has total direct department costs of $100,000. If the direct method is used to allocate service department costs, the entire $100,000 will be divided equally among the two producing departments, each being allocated $50,000, with no allocation to S1.

	S1	S2	P1	P2
Direct allocation of S2 to P1 and P2	$0	$(100,000)	$50,000	$50,000

Consider the following alternative allocation of the $100,000 of S2 costs that takes into account interdepartment services. First, 25 percent, or $25,000, is allocated to each of the producing departments, and 50 percent, or $50,000, is allocated to S1. Next, the $50,000 allocated to S1 from S2 is reallocated to the producing departments in proportion to the amount of services provided to them by S1: 70 percent and 30 percent, respectively. In this scenario, the $100,000 of S2 costs is ultimately allocated $60,000 to P1 and $40,000 to P2 as follows:

	S1	S2	P1	P2
Step 1:				
Allocate S2 costs to S1, P1, and P2	$50,000	$(100,000)	$25,000	$25,000
Step 2:				
Reallocate S1 costs to P1 and P2	(50,000)	0	35,000	15,000
Total allocation of S2 costs via step method	$ 0	$ 0	$60,000	$40,000

This calculation shows only the ultimate allocation of S2 costs. Of course, any S1 direct department costs would also have to be allocated to P1 and P2 on a 70/30 basis. If interdepartmental services are ignored, P1 is allocated only $50,000 of S2 costs; by considering interdepartment services, P1 is allocated $60,000. Certainly, a more accurate measure of both the direct and indirect services received by P1 from S2 is $60,000, not $50,000.

As long as all producing departments use approximately the same percentage of services of each service department, the direct method provides a reasonably accurate cost assignment. In this example, the percentages of services used by the producing departments were quite different: 70 percent and 30 percent for S1, and 50 percent and 50 percent for S2. In such situations, the direct method can result in significantly different allocations.

The step method is illustrated graphically in Exhibit 7–3 for the Krown Drink Company. Notice the sequence of the allocations: Engineering Resources, Support Services, and Building and Grounds.

When using the step method, the sequence of allocation is typically based on the relative percentage of services provided to other service departments, with the largest provider of interdepartment services allocated first and the smallest provider of interdepartment services allocated last. For Krown Drink, Engineering Resources is allocated first because, of the three service departments, it provides the largest percentage (20 percent) of its services to other service departments: 15 percent to Support Services and 5 percent to Building and Grounds (see original data on page 283). Building and Grounds is allocated last because it provides the least amount (12 percent) of its services to other service departments: 8 percent to Support Services and 4 percent to Engineering Resources. The service department cost allocations for Krown Drink using the step method are shown in Exhibit 7–4.

EXHIBIT 7–3

FLOW OF COSTS—STEP METHOD

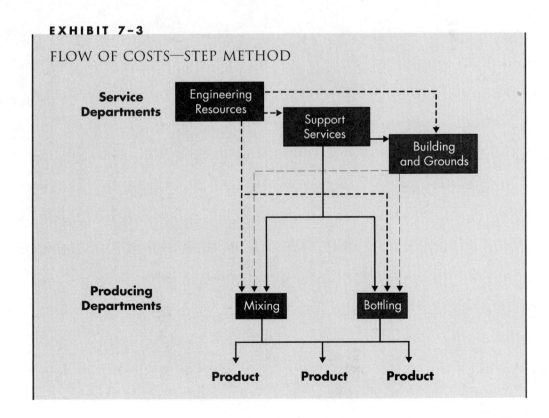

EXHIBIT 7-4

SERVICE DEPARTMENT COST ALLOCATIONS—STEP METHOD

	Total	Support Services	Building and Grounds	Mixing	Bottling
Engineering Resources Department:					
Allocation base (number of employees)	100	15	5	24	56
Percent of total base	100%	15%	5%	24%	56%
Cost allocations	$20,000	$3,000	$1,000	$4,800	$11,200
Support Services Department:					
Allocation base (capital investment)	$500,000		$50,000	$180,000	$270,000
Percent of total base	100%		10%	36%	54%
Cost allocations	$30,000*		$3,000	$10,800	$16,200
Building and Grounds Department:					
Allocation base (square footage occupied)	44,000			11,000	33,000
Percent of total base	100%			25%	75%
Cost allocations	$14,000**			$3,500	$10,500

COST ALLOCATION SUMMARY:

	Engineering Resources	Support Services	Building and Grounds	Mixing	Bottling	Total
Department cost before allocations	$20,000	$27,000	$10,000	$40,000	$ 90,000	$187,000
Cost allocations:						
Engineering Resources	(20,000)	3,000	1,000	4,800	11,200	—
Support Services		(30,000)*	3,000	10,800	16,200	—
Building and Grounds			(14,000)**	3,500	10,500	—
Department costs after allocations	$ 0	$ 0	$ 0	$59,100	$127,900	$187,000

LINEAR ALGEBRA (RECIPROCAL) METHOD

The disadvantage of the step method is that it provides only partial recognition of interdepartment services. For Krown Drink, the step method recognizes Engineering Resources services provided to the other two service departments; however, no services received by Engineering Resources from the other two departments are recognized. Similarly, services from Support Services to Building and Grounds are recognized, but not the reverse. To achieve the most mathematically accurate service department cost allocation, there should be full recognition of services between service departments as well as between service and producing departments. This requires using the linear algebra method, sometimes called the *reciprocal method*. The **linear algebra (reciprocal) method** uses a series of linear algebraic equations, which are solved simultaneously, to allocate service department costs both interdepartmentally and to the producing departments. This method is illustrated graphically in Exhibit 7–5 for a company that has two service departments and two producing departments. Notice that the cost allocation arrows run from each service department to the other service department as well as to the producing departments. Mathematical illustrations are provided in the Appendix to this chapter; however, the method is easily solved using computer spreadsheets. Whether a company should use the direct method, step method, or linear algebra method depends on the extensiveness of interdepartment services and how evenly services are used by the producing departments.

DUAL RATES

When pooling costs for subsequent reassignment or allocation, it may be useful to provide separate pools for fixed costs and variable costs. This will result in cost allocations that more accurately reflect the factors that drive costs. The capacity provided most often drives fixed costs, whereas some type of actual activity usually drives variable costs. Dual rates involve establishing separate bases for allocating fixed and variable costs. Fixed costs are typically allocated based on capacity provided, while variable costs are typically allocated based on actual activity used. Dual rates may be used for one or all service departments, depending on the size and nature of the costs in each service department. They may also be used in conjunction with the direct, step, or linear algebra methods.

It is important to remember the relationship between capacity and cost when selecting the allocation method. Total variable costs change as activity changes. Fixed

EXHIBIT 7-5

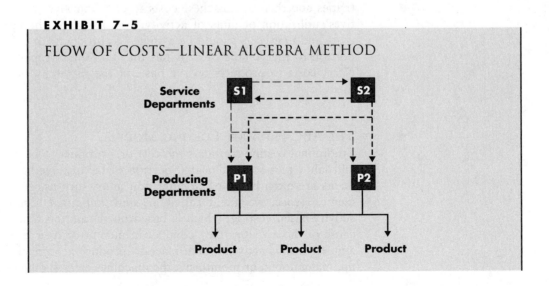

FLOW OF COSTS—LINEAR ALGEBRA METHOD

costs, however, are the same whether the activity is at or below capacity. Fixed costs should usually be allocated based on the relative capacity provided the benefiting department, while variable costs should be allocated on the basis of actual usage. The allocation methods and bases also may be different for variable and fixed cost.

Fixed costs based on capacity provided eliminates the possibility that the amount of the cost allocation to one department is affected by the level of services utilized by other departments. When fixed service department costs are allocated based on the capacity provided to the user department, managers of the user departments are charged for that capacity whether they use it or not, and their use of services has no effect on the amount of costs allocated to other departments. A benefit of this allocation system is that it reduces the temptation for managers to avoid or delay services to minimize fixed cost allocations to their departments. Dual rates are examined in more detail in most cost accounting texts.

ABC PRODUCT COSTING

The manufacturing overhead cost pool has sometimes been referred to as a "blob" of common costs. The constant growth of costs classified as overhead has forced accountants to search for increasingly detailed methods to analyze these costs. If overhead costs are low in comparison with other costs and if factories produce few products in large production runs, the use of a single plantwide overhead rate may be adequate. However, as the amount of overhead costs continues to grow, as manufacturing facilities produce a wider variety of products, and as competition intensifies, the inadequacies of a single plantwide overhead rate become evident. These conditions shift attention to ways to improve overhead rates and the reassignment of service department costs. One method often used to improve product costing is to adopt multiple department overhead rates, as discussed earlier in this chapter.

Fortunately, advances in information technology and the declining costs of computerized information systems have facilitated the development and maintenance of increasingly detailed databases. These and other factors (such as declining inventory levels that make product costing less significant for financial reporting) have led to the emergence and continuing development of activity-based costing. What's Happening 7–3 includes a summary of how a New England soap company with 5,000 different products used ABC to manage costs and profits.

As discussed previously, activity-based costing involves determining the cost of activities and then tracing these costs to cost objectives on the basis of the cost objectives' utilization of units of activity. It is based on the premise that activities drive costs and that costs should be assigned to products (or other cost objectives) in proportion to the volume of activities they consume. Applied to product costing, ABC traces costs to products on the basis of the hierarchy of activities used to produce them.

THE ABC PRODUCT COSTING MODEL

Traditional costing considers the cost of a product to be its direct costs for materials and labor plus some allocated portion of factory overhead. Traditional cost assignments are often based on organization units, such as service and production departments. Hence, we might call it *organization-based costing* (*OBC*), as opposed to activity-based costing, which is based on the notion that companies incur costs because of the activities they conduct in pursuit of their goals and objectives. For example, various activities take place to produce a particular product, such as setting up, maintaining, or monitoring the machines to make the product, physically moving

7-3 WHAT'S HAPPENING?

HOW A PRIVATE-LABEL SOAP MANUFACTURER CLEANED UP ITS OPERATIONS WITH ABC

The Original Bradford Soap Works is a manufacturer of 5,000 private-label soap products. The company reached a management decision threshold in the mid-1980s when a combination of the following factors brought the company to a crisis point: an increased variety of products, an increased volume of all product types, new customers with unique service requirements, and full production capacity of the current plant facilities. Within this setting, Bradford undertook the implementation of ABC.

Unlike many companies that experiment with ABC, Bradford did not linger on the fringes of this new technique. Instead, Bradford decided to fully integrate ABC into its financial and management reporting system. It developed an ABC database of cost pools and cost drivers, and then it recast the general ledger to match this database so that the cost estimates being used to make management decisions would correspond to those reflected in the financial reports of operations.

The result was a management accounting system that tracked the job costs of products based on activities used to produce the products. Managers quickly started using the ABC system for bidding new products since it provided them with detailed estimates of activities and expected costs needed to manufacture the proposed products. Bradford's ABC system has provided the company the flexibility to organize data into useful information to "identify products and customers that provide an optimal mix of business to ensure long-term profitability." The new system helped employees identify opportunities for improvement on the plant floor, reinforcing the total quality process. According to the authors, Bradford's ABC system is ". . . helping management stabilize and control profitability, providing it with the funds it needs to grow its soap-making business."

Source: Frances Gammell and C. J. McNair, "Jumping the Growth Threshold Through Activity-Based Cost Management," *Management Accounting,* September 1994, pp. 37–46.

raw materials and work in process, and so forth. Each of these activities has a cost; therefore, the total cost of producing a product using ABC is the sum of the direct materials and direct labor costs of that product, plus the cost of other activities conducted to produce that product.

Before proceeding further, take a few minutes to review the general ABC model illustrated in Exhibit 5–4 on page 190. Recall that two stages are involved in ABC. The first stage includes the assignment of resource costs, such as indirect labor, depreciation, utilities, and so on, to activity cost pools for the key activities identified. The second stage includes the assignment of those activity cost pools to products or other ultimate cost objectives. Notice in Exhibit 5–4 that costs are assigned to activity pools from the various accounts of departments that incurred the costs; hence, the cost in a particular activity pool may have been incurred in one of several different departments. It may be possible to directly assign certain resource costs to a cost objective. The cost of lumber might be directly assigned to a house. Other costs, such as the cost of the contractor's supervisor, may be assigned to various activity pools based on the amount of time the supervisor spends supervising the various activities.

Exhibit 7–6 presents another view of the ABC model that emphasizes product costing. This model is a modification of the general ABC model in Exhibit 5–4. Notice in Exhibit 7–6 that direct product costs, such as direct materials and direct labor, are directly assigned to products and are excluded from the activity cost pools.[1] Only

---

[1] In highly automated companies, direct labor is often small; thus, it is not treated as a direct cost. Instead, it is pooled with related activity costs and allocated to the products.

EXHIBIT 7-6

ABC TWO-STAGE PRODUCT COSTING MODEL

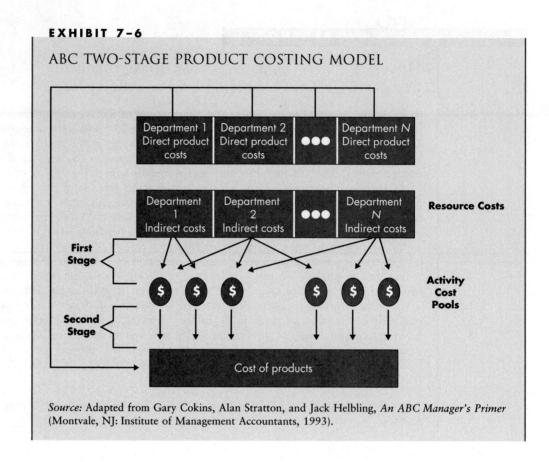

Source: Adapted from Gary Cokins, Alan Stratton, and Jack Helbling, *An ABC Manager's Primer* (Montvale, NJ: Institute of Management Accountants, 1993).

indirect product costs (manufacturing overhead) are assigned to products via activity cost pools.

Probably the most critical step in ABC is identifying cost drivers. The activity cost driver for a particular cost (or cost pool) is the characteristic selected for measuring the quantity of the activity for a particular period of time. For example, if an activity cost pool is established for machine setup, it is necessary to select some basis for measuring the quantity of machine setup activity associated with the costs in the pool. The quantity of setup activity could be measured by the number of different times machines are set up to produce a different product, the amount of time used in completing machine setups, the number of staff working on setups, or some other measure. It is critical that the activity measure used has a logical causal relationship to the costs in the pool and that the quantity of the activity is highly correlated with the amount of cost in the pool. Statistical methods, such as regression analysis and correlation analysis, can be very useful in selecting activity cost drivers.

Once the total cost in the activity pool and the activity cost driver have been determined, the cost per unit of activity is calculated as the total cost divided by the total amount of activity. For example, if total costs assigned to the setup activity pool in July is $100,000 and 200 setups were completed in July, the cost per setup for the month is $500.[2] If during July machines were set up 10 times to make product JX2, the total setup cost that would be assigned to product JX2 would be $5,000 ($500 × 10).

---

[2]This assumes that 200 setups was the total capacity of setups provided by $100,000 of cost. If the activity cost of $100,000 provided more capacity than the 200 setups actually used, there would be an idle capacity variance equal to the cost per setup times the unused setup capacity. The cost associated with idle capacity would normally not be assigned to products. Instead, it would be written off as an operating expense or as cost of goods sold.

ACTIVITY-BASED AND ORGANIZATION-BASED COSTING SYSTEMS COMPARED

Procedurally, ABC is not a new method for assigning costs to cost objectives. For decades traditional costing systems have used a two-stage allocation model (similar to the ABC model) to assign costs to cost pools (such as departments) and subsequently assign those cost pools to products using an allocation base. In many organization-based costing (OBC) systems, overhead is assigned to one or more cost pools based on departments and functional characteristics (e.g., labor-related, machine-related, and space-related costs) and then is reassigned to products using a general allocation base such as direct labor hours or machine hours. ABC is different in that it divides the overall manufacturing operations into processes, which are broken down into activities. ABC accumulates costs in cost pools for the major activities and then assigns the costs of these activities to products or other cost objectives that benefit from these activities. *Conceptually*, ABC is different from OBC because it is a different way of viewing the operations of the company; *procedurally*, it uses a methodology that has been around for a long time.

The challenge in using ABC is specifying the model, that is, determining how many activity pools should be established for a given cost measurement purpose, which costs should be assigned to each activity pool, and the appropriate activity driver for each pool. Specifying the model also includes determining the resource cost drivers for assigning indirect resource costs to the various activity cost pools.

The following three scenarios will help illustrate the differences between activity-based and organization-based costing systems.

1. Using OBC allocation, maintenance department costs are typically allocated to production departments based on the number of repair orders or the number of service hours associated with repairs made in each production department. These costs become a part of the production department overhead rates used for assigning cost to products. Using ABC, the organization would attempt to determine whether maintenance is a key activity that can be associated with products based on an activity cost driver. For instance, in a job cost system, it might be possible to identify the maintenance activity costs associated with each job by measuring the maintenance service hours (the activity driver) used while each job was in production. Alternatively, the resource costs associated with the maintenance department might be assigned to other activity cost pools, such as setup costs, processing costs, and finishing costs, all of which are subsequently assigned to products based on the activity cost drivers for those cost pools.

2. In an OBC allocation system, purchasing department costs may be allocated to production departments based on the dollar value of raw materials issued to each department. Using ABC, the purchasing activity might represent a key activity that is assigned to products using an activity cost driver such as the dollar value of the materials used in producing a given amount of product. Alternatively, if purchasing consists of three key activities (processing, follow-up on purchase orders, and processing receipt of ordered goods), a cost pool for each of these activities is assigned to products using a separate activity cost driver. For example, processing could be assigned using the number of purchase orders as the cost driver, follow-up costs could be assigned based on the number of parts per product, and the cost of processing receipt of goods could be assigned to products based on the dollar value of the raw materials used to make the product.

3. A pure OBC system allocates service department costs first to the producing departments using the direct, step, or linear algebra method. Total overhead costs of the producing departments (*direct department overhead costs* plus allocated *indirect department overhead costs*) are combined and allocated to products using a single cost driver for each department, such as labor hours or machine hours. In its purest form, ABC assigns all overhead costs from both service and production departments to products using ABC. Another possibility is to use ABC to

assign service department costs to production departments, with subsequent assignment of production departments' costs to products, also using ABC. Often companies combine OBC and ABC, making some cost assignments using traditional OBC methods and others using ABC. For example, service department costs (1) are assigned to production departments using ABC, with subsequent allocation of production department costs to products using a single department overhead rate, or (2) are allocated to production departments using a traditional allocation method, with subsequent allocation of production department costs to products using ABC.

Several important conclusions about activity-based costing emerge from the preceding discussion:

- ABC normally uses more cost pools than OBC allocation methods use.
- ABC does not use the established departmental structure for pooling costs unless that structure happens to coincide with key activities for which appropriate activity cost drivers can be determined.
- Although OBC procedures generally attempt to find causal bases for cost allocation, ABC insists even more on the use of causal factors in assigning costs based on activity cost "drivers."
- By definition, ABC assigns costs based on their activity cost drivers, and if cost drivers cannot be identified and measured, ABC cannot be used to assign those costs. In these cases, if full allocation of costs is required (e.g., for financial reporting purposes), a traditional cost allocation approach must be used.
- Implementation of ABC requires an understanding of the production process, the activities that occur in the production process, and the cost drivers that generate the costs of those activities. Hence, a team approach is useful in designing and implementing an ABC system. The team typically includes accountants, engineers, production personnel, and information systems specialists.
- Implementation and operation of ABC requires the use of judgment in identifying key activities, determining which costs should be assigned to each activity cost pool, and identifying the cost drivers for allocating each cost pool. Making these judgments is often based on observation and interviews with personnel involved in the various processes and activities. Resorting to "most common practice" is not acceptable in ABC; each application must be tailored to the specific situation—and that requires using judgement.

LEARNING OBJECTIVE 4

THE PRODUCT COSTING CONTINUUM ILLUSTRATED

APPLYING MANUFACTURING OVERHEAD WITH PLANTWIDE RATES

As illustrated in Exhibit 7–7, if we think of the three approaches to factory overhead cost allocation (plantwide rate, department rates, and ABC rates) in terms of a continuum of complexity and precision, the plantwide rate system is the simplest to apply but provides the least precise allocation of cost; ABC is the most complex system and provides the most precise allocation of costs. For Krown Drink, the first progression is to move from the plantwide rate, Krown's traditional method, to department rates. Assume that the most common element of all products is machine hours in both Mixing and Bottling. Carbonated drink takes 3 machine hours per barrel and Fruit drink takes 2 machine hours per barrel. For July, Krown Drink produced 232 barrels of Carbonated drink and 400 barrels of Fruit drink. If the total manufacturing overhead of $187,000 is divided by total machine hours of 1,496, the plantwide overhead rate will be $125 per hour. This is the simplest method and provides a total cost per unit (barrel) of $610 for Carbonated and $400 for Fruit as shown here.

EXHIBIT 7-7

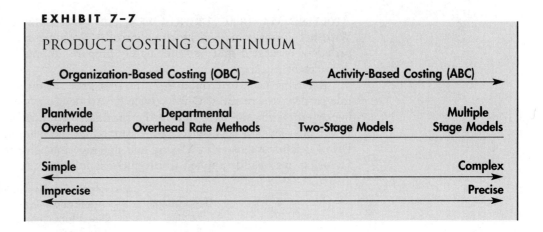

PRODUCT COSTING CONTINUUM

Organization-Based Costing (OBC)   Activity-Based Costing (ABC)

| Plantwide Overhead | Departmental Overhead Rate Methods | Two-Stage Models | Multiple Stage Models |

Simple ——————————————————————————— Complex

Imprecise ——————————————————————— Precise

	UNIT COSTS	
	Carbonated	Fruit
Direct materials	$125	$120
Direct labor	110	30
Manufacturing overhead:		
Carbonated: 3 machine hours × $125	375	
Fruit: 2 machine hours × $125		250
Total unit cost	$610	$400

Recently, competition has become a problem for Krown Drink as new companies have entered the market with competing products, leading to falling sales for Krown. Speculating on the possible causes for the falling sales, Krown's president expressed suspicion that some competitors were engaging in below-cost selling. As a case in point, the president recently received a letter from a long-time customer stating that it will no longer be able to purchase carbonated drinks at Krown's current price of $625 per barrel because of an offer from a competitor to provide the same product for $525 per barrel—which is below Krown's manufacturing cost of $610 per unit. In a staff meeting, the president suggested that Krown might no longer be competitive in the carbonated market and perhaps should shift its emphasis to becoming the leader in the fruit juice market in which the selling price of $500 per unit provides substantial profit margins. The marketing manager for carbonated drinks suggested that before making such a major change in corporate strategy, a study of revenue and cost data for both products should be conducted to see whether possible cost efficiencies could be made to help Krown become more competitive.

In a meeting with the company's executives, the president asked for a candid discussion about Krown's manufacturing and cost control systems compared to those of its competitors. The manufacturing manager assured the president that Krown was "state-of-the-art" in its production processes but raised some concerns about whether Carbonated should have an overhead cost almost equal to that of Fruit. The controller responded that Krown was using plantwide rates for overhead allocation that were very easy to compute given the company's current data collection system. However, he added that some firms in the industry were using different cost allocation methods, such as departmental rates, which recognize differences in department cost structures, and activity-based costing, which focuses on activities rather than departments.

Product cost continuum observation: Note that by using plantwide rates, Krown was at the left end of the cost allocation continuum, which provides easy application but the least precision in allocating overhead costs to products.

APPLYING MANUFACTURING OVERHEAD WITH DEPARTMENT RATES

With her curiosity piqued by the controller's comment about department rates, the president requested that he immediately prepare an analysis of the July results using department rates.

Referring back to Exhibit 7–7, the first progression is to move from a plantwide rate to department rates. Once service department costs are allocated to the producing departments, the next step in the product costing process is to apply those costs to the next level of cost objectives. Assume that the manufacturing process at Krown Drink is labor intensive in Mixing and machine intensive in Bottling and that manufacturing overhead is applied to products as follows:

Department	Manufacturing Overhead Application Base
Mixing	Direct labor hours
Bottling	Machine hours

During the month of July, 500 direct labor hours were worked in Mixing, and Bottling used 800 machine hours. Using the total production department overhead costs calculated by the step method (see Exhibit 7–4), the department manufacturing overhead rates based on actual costs for July are calculated as follows:

Overhead costs per unit for July:

	Mixing	Bottling
Total department manufacturing overhead (direct department costs plus allocated costs)	$59,100	$127,900
Quantity of overhead application base:		
Direct labor hours	÷ 500	
Machine hours		÷ 800
Department manufacturing overhead rates	$118.20	$159.875
	Per direct labor hour	Per machine hour

Total costs per unit for July using department rates:

	UNIT COSTS PER BARREL	
	Carbonated	Fruit
Direct materials	$125	$120
Direct labor	110	30
Manufacturing overhead		
Mixing: 1 labor hr. × $118.20	118*	
0.67 labor hrs. × $118.20		79*
Bottling: 1 machine hr. × $159.875	160*	
1.42 machine hrs. × $159.875		227*
Total costs	$513	$456

*Rounded

Allocating factory overhead costs based on department rates (rather than on a plantwide rate of $125 per machine hour) causes a shift in costs from Carbonated to Fruit drinks because Carbonated's overhead activity is incurred evenly in both Mixing and Bottling (1.00 hour each) while Fruit incurs more of its overhead activity in Bottling (1.42 hours versus 0.67 hour).

Product cost continuum observation: Note that as we move along the cost allocation system continuum from a plantwide rate to department rates, the calculations become more complex, and the cost allocations are more precise measures of actual resources used to produce the respective products because they consider the cost characteristics of the individual departments.

The per-unit costs with multiple allocations are substantially different from the per-unit costs when using plantwide rates and, in fact, show the carbonated beverages to be slightly below the competitor's bid of $525 that was offered by one of Krown's customers.

By creating separate manufacturing overhead cost allocation pools, allocation bases, and overhead application rates for Mixing and Bottling, it is possible to recognize overhead cost differences in various products based on differences in Mixing Department labor hours used and Bottling Department machine hours used for each product. In most multiproduct manufacturing environments, this approach represents a cost system improvement over using a single, plantwide overhead rate, and it reduces the likelihood of cost cross-subsidization. While department overhead rates may improve product costing results for many organizations, and in fact may be satisfactory, this method does not complete the continuum. By implementing activity-based costing concepts, an organization can continue to improve its product costing system.

Although the new cost rates gave the president of Krown Drinks encouragement that Carbonated could be competitive, she was concerned about the accuracy since it gave a cost that was just below the competitive price of $525. She agreed that using department rates is clearly an improvement over using a plantwide rate in situations in which department overhead costs are not the same and in which various products use department activity in the producing departments in disproportionate amounts but wondered whether this is just another way accountants make things turn out the way they want them to. The controller responded that although it was in fact another acceptable way of applying manufacturing costs to products, OBC methods do not consider information about the relationship of products with the activities required to produce the products. In fact, the controller stated that he could provide detailed information about product/activity relationships by using another method known as *activity-based costing*. This was interesting to the president, and she asked for another analysis using activity-based costing for the July operations.

APPLYING MANUFACTURING OVERHEAD WITH ACTIVITY-BASED COSTING

Now that we have used department rates to account for overhead cost, we need to examine how the continuum can be extended with the use of ABC to cost our products. For Krown Drink, we know that Mixing and Bottling, when using the step method, have overhead costs of $59,100 and $127,900, respectively. The overhead rates for each department were determined in the last section as $118.20 and $159.875, respectively, per relevant hour of use. The easiest way to assign these costs to products is by using one base and one rate for all products going through a given process (e.g., mixing). However, different products typically use different amounts of resources from a given process and using the same base and overhead rate for all may be distorting the cost for some or all products.

Before making a final decision on the appropriate strategy, the president asked the controller to examine all costs to see whether ABC calculations were in line with costs based on department overhead rates. The controller determined that the direct department overhead costs in Mixing were driven by labor hours, whereas direct department overhead costs in Bottling were driven by machine hours. He also determined that each component of engineering, support, and building and grounds represents a separate activity cost pool and that these costs should be assigned to the products based on specific cost drivers.

Following the president's request, the controller developed the following detailed analysis of overhead cost data for July's operations:

Overhead Activity	Total Activity Cost	Activity Cost Driver (number of)	Quantity of Activity	Unit Activity Rates
Direct departmental overhead costs:				
Mixing	$ 40,000	Labor hours	500	$ 80.00
Bottling	90,000	Machine hours	800	112.50
Common overhead costs:				
Support Services:				
Receiving	14,000	Purchase orders	100	140.00
Inventory control	13,000	Units produced	632	20.57*
Engineering Resources:				
Production setup	12,000	Production runs	20	600.00
Engineering and testing	8,000	Machine hours	800	10.00
Building and Grounds:				
Maintenance, machines	4,000	Machine hours	800	5.00
Depreciation, machines	6,000	Units produced	632	9.49*
Total	$187,000			

*Rounded

The amounts of activity attributed to Carbonated and Fruit drinks and the factory overhead cost per unit based on ABC costs are as follows:

	CARBONATED		FRUIT	
Activity (cost per unit of driver activity)	Quantity of Activity	Cost of Activity	Quantity of Activity	Cost of Activity
Mixing ($80.00 per labor hour)	232	$18,560	268	$ 21,440
Bottling ($112.50 per machine hour)	174	19,575	626	70,425
Receiving ($140.00 per order)	40	5,600	60	8,400
Inventory control ($20.57 per unit produced)	232	4,772*	400	8,228
Production setup ($600.00 per run)	5	3,000	15	9,000
Engineering and testing ($10.00 per machine hour)	174	1,740	626	6,260
Maintenance, machines ($5.00 per machine hour)	174	870	626	3,130
Depreciation, machines ($9.49 per unit produced)	232	2,202*	400	3,796
Total factory overhead product cost		$56,319		$130,679
Units produced		÷ 232		÷ 400
Factory overhead cost per unit of product*		$ 243*		$ 327*
Direct materials cost per unit of product		125		120
Direct labor cost per unit of product		110		30
Total unit product cost using ABC		$ 478		$ 477

*Rounded

Product cost continuum observation: Notice that ABC is more complex than the previous two systems—plantwide and department rate systems—but provides the most accurate measurement of the costs of activities used in producing Carbonated and Fruit drink products.

After reviewing the costs based on ABC, the president and management team reviewed their strategy for competing with the lower price of the competition and decided what actions to take regarding each product. They agreed that ABC provided a more accurate measurement of overhead costs incurred in the production of the products than either the old system based on a plantwide rate or the alternative system based on department rates. In light of the ABC data, it now appears that Carbonated drinks can be profitable with a margin the president is comfortable with ($525 −

$478 = \$47$). However, ABC changes the perspective of the highly profitable Fruit drink product line. It now has a profit margin of only $23 ($500 − $477) instead of a highly desirable profit margin of $100 ($500 − $400) when plantwide overhead rates were used.

After the meeting, the president announced that a price reduction for Carbonated drink products is in order and that the focus of cost control must now shift to the Fruit drink products. She also endorsed the concept of activity-based costing and encouraged the controller to implement ABC in all areas of the organization.

LIMITATIONS OF KROWN DRINK ABC ILLUSTRATION

Several limitations of the Krown Drink illustration should be mentioned. For the sake of simplicity, the example was limited to manufacturing cost considerations. A complete analysis would also require considerations of nonmanufacturing costs, such as marketing, distribution, and customer service, before a final determination of product profitability could be made. Also, the illustrated costs represent mainly unit- and batch-level costs, with limited product-level (engineering and testing) and facility-level (maintenance and depreciation) costs. Most organizations have additional cost categories that must be considered. Finally, the analysis was based on the assumption that actual capacity was the same as practical capacity. Hence, no idle capacity was involved. Refer to Chapter 5 for a detailed discussion of these issues.

LEARNING OBJECTIVE 5

ABC IMPLEMENTATION ISSUES

The illustration of the cost distortions (and hence, profit distortions) for Krown Drink from using OBC systems, while hypothetical, is not uncommon. Studies have shown that distortions of this type occur regularly in OBC systems in which a significant variation exists in the volume and complexity of products and services produced.[3] OBC systems tend to overcost high-volume, low-complexity products, and they tend to undercost low-volume, high-complexity products. These studies indicate that the typical amount of overcosting is up to 200 percent for high-volume products with low complexity and that the typical undercosting can be more than 1,000 percent for low-volume, highly complex products. In companies with a large number of different products, OBC can show that most products are profitable. After changing to ABC, however, these companies might find that 10 to 15 percent of the products are profitable while the remainder are unprofitable. Adopting ABC often leads to increased profits merely by changing the product mix to minimize the number of unprofitable products.

Most companies initially do not abandon their OBC system and move to a system that uses ABC for management and financial reporting purposes because financial statements must withstand the scrutiny of auditors and tax authorities. This scrutiny typically implies more demands on the cost accounting system for consistency, objectivity, and uniformity than required when the system is used only for management purposes. In addition, ABC systems must be built facility by facility rather than being embedded in a software program that can be used by all facilities within the company.[4] Most companies maintain OBC for external reporting purposes and ABC for pricing and other internal decision-making purposes.

Proponents of ABC believe that management must reassert its authority to control what are often dismissed as "common" or "fixed" costs. ABC attacks the shapeless mass of common costs, decomposing them into smaller, more homogeneous cost

---

[3]Gary Cokins, Alan Stratton, and Jack Helbling, *An ABC Manager's Primer* (Montvale, NJ: Institute of Management Accountants, 1993).

[4]Robert S. Kaplan and Robin Cooper, *Cost and Effect* (Boston: Harvard Business School Press, 1998), p. 105.

pools related to specific activities. ABC also takes a long-term view of fixed costs, and in the long run all costs are variable—that is, fixed costs (such as depreciation) merely represent costs incurred for larger chunks of activity than those paid for on a per unit or per batch basis; when one of these large chunks of activity is completed, another chunk must be purchased. Hence, management must control fixed costs and take action to reduce them when normal periodic activity levels decline. Certainly, difficult problems exist in determining how to treat fixed costs in either an OBC or ABC system, since fixed costs usually represent some amount of capacity of activity that ultimately may or may not be used.

Once an ABC system has been developed for a production facility (including an activities list (sometimes called an activities dictionary), identification of activity cost drivers, and calculation of cost per unit of driver activity), the activity costs of a current or proposed product can be readily determined. In ABC, manufacturing a product is viewed simply as the combination of activities selected to make it; therefore, the activity cost of a product or service is the sum of the costs of those activities. This approach to viewing a product enables management to evaluate the importance of each of the activities consumed in making a product. Possibly some activities can be eliminated or a lower cost activity substituted for a more costly one without reducing the quality or performance of the product. The Coca-Cola Company used ABC to determine that it was less costly—and thus, more profitable—to deliver soft drink concentrate to some fountain drink retailers (such as fast-food restaurants) in nonreturnable, disposable containers rather than in returnable stainless steel containers, which had been standard in the industry for many years. When the final list of activities selected for making a product is determined, ABC data can be used to develop detailed standard costs for various operations conducted in making the product.

Although an ABC system may be complex, it merely mirrors the complexity of an organization's design, manufacturing, and distribution systems. If a firm's products are diverse and its production and distribution procedures complex, the ABC system will also be complex; however, if its products are homogeneous and its production environment relatively simple, its ABC system should also be relatively simple. Even in highly complex manufacturing environments, ABC systems usually have no more than 10 to 20 cost pools. Many ABC experts in practice have observed that creating a large number of activity cost pools for a given costing application normally does not significantly improve cost accuracy above that of a smaller number of cost pools. As with any information system design, the costs of developing and maintaining the system must not exceed its benefits; hence, although adding more activity cost pools may result in some small amount of increased accuracy, it may be so small as not to be cost effective. What's Happening 7–4 provides a list of ten practical tips to remember when implementing an ABC system.

It is important to reiterate that ABC is not just a product costing system used to provide data for external financial reports. If that were its only use, its cost of implementation would seldom be justifiable. ABC's primary benefit is that it provides more accurate cost data for internal decision-making purposes. Companies that sell virtually everything they produce obviously have little or no inventories. Consequently, they do not need a product costing system for external reporting purposes because all manufacturing costs are expensed as cost of goods sold each period. However, even these companies need a good cost system for evaluating product profitability, tracking changes in costs over time, and benchmarking against their competitors.

In addition to using ABC for product costing purposes, other important uses for ABC have also been found. One of the most useful applications for ABC is in evaluating customer costs and distribution channel costs. Other applications include costing administrative functions such as processing accounts receivable or accounts payable; costing the process of hiring and training employees; and costing such menial tasks as processing a letter or copying a document. Any process, function, or activity performed in an organization, whether it is related to production, marketing and sales, finance and accounting, human resources, or even research and development, is

PRACTICAL ADVICE FOR IMPLEMENTING ABC

A partner in KPMG's Performance Improvement Practice offered ten practical lessons he has learned in working with clients to design and install ABC systems:

1. *Capture the attention of top management.* ABC represents a substantial change that must be driven by the support of top management.
2. *Don't shoot the customer.* If ABC reveals that a group of customers is unprofitable, a top priority must be to find a way to meet the needs of the customer, even if it means finding another supplier for the customer.
3. *Decide the form ABC will take.* Will it be a special study, a decision model, or a real-time system?
4. *Supplement the ABC measures creatively when appropriate.* Other measures such as bottleneck accounting and value-added analysis may be needed to supplement ABC before a proper decision can be made.
5. *Be careful in costing bottlenecks that create excess capacity.* Pricing at full capacity cost could result in underpricing with possible end-game results, and pricing at current utilization can lead to a death spiral by overpricing.
6. *Challenge managers who believe their costs are fixed.* In the long run, virtually all costs can be avoided.
7. *Calculate costs top-down and bottom-up.* Costs should be calculated based on both individual activities within a process (bottom-up) and the total process (top-down) as a check back to the accounting system.
8. *Account for the cost of capital.* Although traditional accounting does not consider costs of capital, modern management should allow for these opportunity costs in decision making.
9. *Use multi-functional teams.* Empowered multi-functional teams must be compelled to deal with problems that are critical to the business as a whole.
10. *Do not underestimate the need for managing change.* ABC needs to be led, not managed, and this must be done from the top.

Source: Michael Gering, "Activity-Based Costing Lessons Learned from Implementing ABC," *Management Accounting*, May 1999, pp. 26–27.

a candidate for ABC analysis. In short, almost any cost objective that has more than an insignificant amount of indirect costs can be more effectively measured using ABC. As the demand for increased analysis and accuracy of complex cost systems is sought by managers, there may be a shift toward the multiple-stage models shown in Exhibit 7–7. Like the step and linear algebra methods of service department cost allocation, multiple-stage ABC models recognize that some activities are performed to support the performance of other activities.

LEARNING OBJECTIVE 6   **USES AND EVOLUTION OF ACTIVITY-BASED COSTING**

In theory, ABC costing can be used for any purpose for which traditional OBC costing is used. Some uses for ABC are summarized here:

- *Product or service profitability.* ABC was originally developed to help managers better measure the profitability of products and services they were producing.
- *Pricing.* Although market conditions often have the most influence on prices, it is important, especially for new products, to know the true activity-based cost of a product when setting its price.

- *Managing processes/activities.* One of the most important purposes of ABC (as discussed in Chapter 5) is to use cost information to make better decisions about processes and activities and how to reduce the number of non-value-added activities.
- *Budgeting.* As companies integrate ABC into their enterprisewide information systems, they can use ABC information to improve the process of budgeting costs. Companies without enterprise resource planning (ERP) systems seldom use ABC for budgeting because of the data requirements of generating ABC costs. However, these companies can use ABC for specific elements of the budget (a specific activity or department).
- *Product costing.* As discussed in Chapter 6, most companies that use ABC do not integrate it into their product cost measurements for inventory valuation purposes in their financial statements. However, as companies add ERP systems with ABC modules, the companies can integrate ABC into the financial information system for both internal and external purposes. Companies that do not have an ERP system might use standard product costs (see Chapter 11) based on an ABC analysis for financial accounting purposes.

Research Shows 7–1 presents the results of a recent survey that addresses questions about how extensively companies are implementing ABC and the extent to which they are using the output of their ABC systems.

To understand the evolution of ABC and its applications, the use of the generic model developed by the philosopher Hegel for analyzing the logical development of ideas is helpful. Hegel's model begins with an existing and accepted idea (thesis) that is challenged by an opposing idea (antithesis), which leads to a blending of the original idea and the new idea (synthesis). The traditional costing model (thesis) was developed principally for financial reporting purposes when materials and labor were the dominant cost elements that could readily be traced directly to cost objectives. The technology revolution led to a decline in direct labor and a dramatic increase in overhead costs in most organizations. This led to the development of ABC (antithesis), which uses specific activity drivers as the vehicles for assigning activity costs to cost objectives instead of using generalized volume-based drivers such as direct labor hours or machine hours to assign plantwide or department overhead pools to cost objectives. Today in many companies we see hybrid ABC systems (synthesis) that combine aspects of traditional and pure ABC systems.

Many companies jumped on the ABC bandwagon in the early to mid-1990s only to discover that the data requirements of many ABC systems are overwhelming. Some of these early adopters soon pulled back from their commitment to ABC and returned to traditional costing models. Others recognized that using ABC offered substantial benefits but concluded that it was too expensive or burdensome to apply throughout their organizations, so they modified their traditional systems to contain some elements of ABC. For example, companies may use organization units (departments) as the first stage in their costing models, but within their departments, they have developed cost pools that reflect activities instead of cost functions. Instead of assigning all of a production department's overhead costs directly to products or services based on direct labor hours or machine hours, they assign them in a second stage to the four or five major activities that occur in the department but that various products or services use unevenly. The third stage of the cost model is to assign the activity costs to products or services based on activity cost drivers. This approach reflects a synthesizing of some traditional costing methods with ABC methods to arrive at a cost model that is both cost beneficial and more effective than the traditional OBC model. Today's ABC systems rarely reflect a pure application of the original ABC concept that assigns resource costs to activity pools without regard for departmental cost centers. It is safe to conclude that cost systems of the future will reflect additional evolution as new ideas and technologies emerge.

ABC: WHO IS USING IT AND HOW?

A survey of more than 500 users of ABC completed in late 1999 showed the following uses of ABC information:

Product/service costing	58%
Process analysis	51
Performance management	49
Profitability assessment	38
Value-based management	18

Another question on the survey asked for the number of different locations where ABC models were being used in the company:

1	39%
2 to 3	19
4 to 5	10
6 to 7	6
8 to 10	7
More than 10	14

The frequency of reporting ABC data for products or services was:

Weekly	2%
Monthly	27
Quarterly	40
Yearly	18
As needed	13

The users of ABC information in the survey came from the following industries:

Process manufacturing	15%
Discrete manufacturing	9
Service	24
Consulting	11%
Public sector	40

The respondents described their ABC experience level as follows:

Beginners	42%
Proficient	29
Advanced	21
Cutting edge	8

The survey also investigated the existence of enterprise resource planning (ERP) systems within respondents' organizations and the extent of the integration of those systems with best-of-breed applications, such as ABC. When asked whether ABC systems needed to be integrated with the ERP system, 64 percent said integration is required. Of larger companies (revenues of $500 million to $1 billion), 81 percent considered integration a requirement.

Although this survey was taken at an ABC users conference, it indicates that the demand for ABC information is increasing as managers see the benefits of leveraging ABC information beyond profitability analysis into areas such as budgeting, planning, and performance management. This expanded use of ABC requires continuing improvements in the areas of integration with ERP and data warehousing systems.

Source: Mohand Nair, "Activity-Based Costing: Who's Using It and Why?" *Management Accounting Quarterly,* Spring 2000, pp. 29–33.

Summary

Cost measurement involves assigning costs to cost objectives or reassigning them from one cost objective to another. The cost objective may be a product, department, activity, service, territory, or any other item of interest to management. For various reasons, it is not always possible or feasible to make a direct association between a cost objective and all of its costs. These indirect costs can be associated with a cost objective only by the process of *reassignment*, also called *allocation*.

If a cost objective has numerous indirect costs, it is seldom feasible to allocate them individually. Instead, they are placed into homogeneous groupings of related costs called *cost pools*, which are then reassigned using an allocation base that is common to all cost objectives. A good cost allocation base has a logical cause-and-effect relationship with the costs in the pool.

We examined the relationship between cost pools and cost objectives across a costing continuum, ranging from a single plantwide overhead rate through the use of departmental overhead rates (that require service departmental cost allocations using the direct, step, or linear algebra methods), to activity-based costing. Contrasting OBC (using plantwide and departmental overhead rates) with activity-based costing, we concluded that ABC is the most accurate and complex cost assignment method. Its accuracy is derived from the fact that ABC captures the costs of the activities used to deliver a product or service, whereas OBC is based on more abstract and artificial organization cost groupings. The complexity of an ABC system reflects the complexity of an organization and its products or services. Organizations with a limited number of homogeneous products or services may obtain accurate product or service costs with relatively simple accounting systems. Organizations with a large number of heterogeneous products or services need more complex accounting systems to obtain accurate product or service costs.

APPENDIX

LINEAR ALGEBRA METHOD OF SERVICE DEPARTMENT COST ALLOCATION

The *linear algebra method* reassigns all service department costs simultaneously to service departments and to producing departments. To use this method, a linear algebraic equation is developed for each service and production department. Each equation represents total department costs, that is, direct department costs plus a percentage of service department costs. To illustrate the equations, assume a company has two service departments (S1 and S2) and two producing departments (P1 and P2). The percentage distribution of services follows for each department.

Services Provided from	SERVICES PROVIDED TO				
	S1	S2	P1	P2	Total
S1	—	5%	40%	55%	100%
S2	10%	—	30	60	100

Total direct department costs for the service and producing departments are as follows:

S1	$ 20,000
S2	$ 35,000
P1	$150,000
P2	$ 90,000

The algebraic equations expressing the total costs (direct and reassigned) for each department follow:

$$S1 = 20,000 + 0.10\ S2$$
$$S2 = 35,000 + 0.05\ S1$$
$$P1 = 150,000 + 0.40\ S1 + 0.30\ S2$$
$$P2 = 90,000 + 0.55\ S1 + 0.60\ S2$$

Using the substitution method, these equations are solved as shown.
Substituting S2 into S1:

$$S1 = 20,000 + 0.10(35,000 + 0.05\ S1)$$
$$S1 = 20,000 + 3,500 + 0.005\ S1$$
$$0.995\ S1 = 23,500$$
$$S1 = 23,618$$

Substituting the solution of S1 into S2:

$$S2 = 35,000 + 0.05(23,618)$$
$$S2 = 35,000 + 1,181$$
$$S2 = 36,181$$

Substituting the solutions of S1 and S2 into P1:

$$P1 = 150,000 + 0.40(23,618) + 0.30(36,181)$$
$$P1 = 150,000 + 9,447 + 10,854$$
$$P1 = 170,301$$

Substituting the solutions of S1 and S2 into P2:

$$P2 = 90,000 + 0.55(23,618) + 0.60(36,181)$$
$$P2 = 90,000 + 12,990 + 21,709$$
$$P2 = 124,699$$

How do we interpret these solutions? First, note that the solutions to S1 and S2 consist of two components, their respective direct department costs plus the cost reassigned from the other service department. For example, since the solved value for S1 is $23,618, the reassigned costs from S2 are $3,618, or the difference between the final value assigned to S1 and the S1 direct department costs. In a similar fashion, the solutions to P1 and P2 consist of three components. P1 consists of $150,000 plus $9,447 plus $10,854, and P2 consists of $90,000 plus $12,990 plus $21,709. For each of these producing department variables, the first component represents the department's *direct costs*. The second component represents the reassignment of S1 costs to the producing department, and the third component represents the reassignment of S2 costs to the producing departments.

A summary of all cost reassignments among service departments and producing departments follows.

	S1	S2	P1	P2	Total
Departmental costs before reassignments	$20,000	$35,000	$150,000	$ 90,000	$295,000
S1 reassignment	(23,618)	1,181	9,447	12,990	—
S2 reassignment	3,618	(36,181)	10,854	21,709	—
Departmental costs after reassignments	$ —	$ —	$170,301	$124,699	$295,000

The substitution method of simultaneously solving linear equations is inefficient except in the simplest of situations (such as our example). When more than two service departments provide interdepartmental services, it is necessary to use matrix algebra for solving equations simultaneously. Using matrix algebra would also be very laborious were it not for the aid of computers. With a computer and appropriate software, solving matrix algebra problems is relatively easy. Several spreadsheet software programs contain easy-to-use matrix algebra routines. (A detailed discussion of matrix algebra is beyond the scope of this text.)

Key Terms

Common cost (p. 280)

Cost allocation base (p. 281)

Cost objective (p. 280)

Cost pool (p. 280)

Direct department cost (p. 282)

Direct method (p. 283)

Indirect department cost (p. 282)

Interdepartment services (p. 283)

Linear algebra (reciprocal) method (p. 289)

Service department (p. 282)

Step method (p. 284)

Review Problems

The solutions to the review problems are found on pages 325–328. To maximize your learning, you should make a serious attempt to develop a written solution to the review problem before looking at the solution. If there are errors in your solution, you should then attempt to determine their causes.

1.

Service Department Cost Allocation

Cotswald's Clothiers Inc. is organized into four departments: Women's Apparel, Men's Apparel, Administrative Services, and Facilities Services. The first two departments are the primary producing departments; the last two departments provide services to the producing departments as well as to each other. Top management has decided that, for internal reporting purposes, the cost of service department operations should be allocated to the producing departments.

Administrative Services costs are allocated on the basis of the number of employees, and Facilities Services costs are allocated based on the amount of square footage of floor space occupied. Data pertaining to the cost allocations for February 2004 are as follows:

Department	Direct Department Cost	Number of Employees	Square Footage Occupied
Women's Apparel	$ 60,000	15	15,000
Men's Apparel	50,000	9	7,500
Administrative Services	18,000	3	2,500
Facilities	12,000	2	1,000
Total	$140,000	29	26,000

Required:

a. Determine the amount of service department costs to be allocated to the producing departments under both the *direct method* and the *step method* of service department cost allocation.

b. Discuss the *linear algebra method* of service department cost allocation, explaining circumstances when it should be considered over the direct and step methods.

c. Should Cotswald's Clothier Inc. consider using the linear algebra method?

2.
Plantwide, Department, and Activity-Based Overhead Rates

Slack Corporation has the following predicted indirect costs and cost drivers for 2004 for the given activity cost pools:

	Fabrication Department	Finishing Department	Cost Driver
Maintenance	$ 20,000	$10,000	Machine hours
Materials handling	30,000	15,000	Material moves
Machine setups	70,000	5,000	Machine setups
Inspections	—	25,000	Inspection hours
	$120,000	$55,000	

The following activity predictions were also made for the year:

	Fabrication Department	Finishing Department
Machine hours	10,000	5,000
Materials moves	3,000	1,500
Machine setups	700	50
Inspection hours	—	1,000

It is assumed that the cost per unit of activity for a given activity does not vary between departments.

Slack's president, Charles Slack, is trying to evaluate the company's product mix strategy regarding two of its five product models, ZX300 and SL500. The company has been using a plantwide overhead rate based on machine hours but is considering switching to either department rates or activity-based rates. The production manager has provided the following data for the production of a batch of 100 units for each of these models:

	ZX300	SL500
Direct materials cost	$12,000	$18,000
Direct labor cost	$5,000	$4,000
Machine hours (Fabrication)	500	700
Machine hours (Finishing)	200	100
Materials moves	30	50
Machine setups	5	9
Inspection hours	30	60

Required:

a. Determine the cost of one unit each of ZX300 and SL500, assuming a plantwide overhead rate is used based on total machine hours.

b. Determine the cost of one unit of ZX300 and SL500, assuming department overhead rates are used. Overhead is assigned based on machine hours in both departments.

c. Determine the cost of one unit of ZX300 and SL500, assuming activity-based overhead rates are used for maintenance, materials handling, machine setup, and inspection activities.

d. Comment on the results of these cost calculations.

Review Questions

1. Distinguish between the following terms:
   a. Direct product costs and indirect product costs.
   b. Direct department costs and indirect department costs.
   c. Product costs and period costs.
2. Can any generalized distinctions be made about direct and indirect costs? Explain.

3. Explain the difference between cost assignment and cost allocation. What alternative term can be used to refer to cost allocation?

4. Can a cost item be both a direct cost and an indirect cost? Explain.

5. Why might cost allocations developed for financial reporting or tax purposes not be adequate for other purposes that require the accurate determination of individual product costs?

6. What is a cost objective? Give several examples of cost objectives that may be of interest to managers.

7. Why are cost pools used in allocating direct costs?

8. What is the primary advantage of separately allocating fixed and variable indirect costs?

9. To what extent are interdepartment services recognized under the direct, step, and linear algebra methods of service department cost allocation?

10. Explain the product cost continuum.

11. What is the premise of activity-based costing for product costing purposes?

12. In what ways does ABC differ from traditional product cost assignment?

13. Explain why ABC often reveals existing product cost cross-subsidization problems.

14. How can ABC be used to improve cost analysis other than for product costing? Relate ABC benefits to value chain analysis.

15. Define activity cost pool, activity cost driver, and cost per unit of activity.

16. Name two possible activity cost drivers for each of the following activities: maintenance, materials movement, machine setup, inspection, materials purchases, and customer service.

Exercises

7–1
Allocating Service Department Costs: Allocation Basis Alternatives

Clayton Glassworks has two producing departments, P1 and P2, and one service department, S1. Estimated direct overhead costs per month are as follows:

P1 . . . . . $100,000
P2 200,000
S1 60,000

Other data follow:

	P1	P2
Number of employees	75	25
Production capacity (units)	50,000	30,000
Space occupied (square feet)	2,500	7,500
Five-year average percent of S1's service output used	65%	35%

Required:

a. For each of the following allocation bases, determine the total estimated overhead cost for P1 and P2 after allocating S1 cost to the producing departments.
   1. Number of employees
   2. Production capacity in units
   3. Space occupied
   4. Five-year average percentage of S1 services used
   5. Estimated direct overhead costs. (Round your answer to the nearest dollar.)

b. For each of the five allocation bases, explain the circumstances (including examples) under which each allocation base might be most appropriately used to allocate service department cost in a manufacturing plant such as Clayton Glassworks. Also, discuss the advantages and disadvantages that might result from using each of the allocation bases.

7-2
Indirect Cost Allocation: Direct Method

Springfield Manufacturing Company has two production departments, Melting and Molding. Direct general plant management and plant security costs benefit both production departments. Springfield allocates general plant management costs on the basis of the number of production employees and plant security costs on the basis of space occupied by the production departments.

In November, the following costs were recorded:

Melting Department direct overhead	$125,000
Molding Department direct overhead	300,000
General plant management	90,000
Plant security	35,000

Other pertinent data are provided here.

	Melting	Molding
Number of employees	25	45
Space occupied (square feet)	10,000	40,000
Machine hours	10,000	2,000
Direct labor hours	4,000	20,000

Required:

a. Prepare a schedule allocating general plant management costs and plant security costs to the Melting and Molding Departments.

b. Determine the total departmental overhead costs for the Melting and Molding Departments.

c. Assuming the Melting Department uses machine hours and the Molding Department uses direct labor hours to apply overhead to production, calculate the overhead rate for each production department.

7-3
Plantwide versus Department Allocation (a continuation of 7-2)

Refer to Exercise 7–2 for Springfield Manufacturing Company. In addition to the facts given, assume that Springfield produces a product, Q45, that uses 5 direct labor hours per unit (2 hours in the Melting Department and 3 hours in the Molding Department) and 2 machine hours (1 hour in each department).

Required:

a. Calculate the total overhead cost to produce one unit of Q45 using the department overhead rates calculated in Exercise 7–3.

b. Calculate the manufacturing overhead rate assuming that Springfield uses a single plantwide rate based on direct labor hours to allocate both producing and service department costs to products.

c. Calculate the total overhead cost to produce one unit of Q45 using the plantwide overhead rate.

d. Comment on the cost of one unit of Q45 using departmental overhead rates versus a plantwide overhead rate.

7-4
Interdepartment Services: Step Method

O'Brian's Department Stores allocates the costs of the Personnel and Payroll departments to three retail sales departments, Housewares, Clothing, and Furniture. In addition to providing services to the operating departments, Personnel and Payroll provide services to each other. O'Brian's allocates Personnel Department costs on the basis of the number of employees and Payroll Department costs on the basis of gross payroll. Cost and allocation information for June is as follows:

	Personnel	Payroll	Housewares	Clothing	Furniture
Direct department cost	$6,900	$3,200	$12,200	$20,000	$15,750
Number of employees	5	3	8	15	4
Gross payroll	$6,000	$3,300	$11,200	$17,400	$8,100

Required:

a. Determine the percentage of total Personnel Department services that was provided to the Payroll Department.

b. Determine the percentage of total Payroll Department services that was provided to the Personnel Department.

c. Prepare a schedule showing Personnel Department and Payroll Department cost allocations to the operating departments, assuming O'Brian's uses the step method. (Round calculations to the nearest dollar.)

7–5
Interdepartment Services: Direct Method

Portland Manufacturing Company has five operating departments, two of which are producing departments (P1 and P2) and three of which are service departments (S1, S2, and S3). All costs of the service departments are allocated to the producing departments. The following table shows the distribution of services from the service departments.

Services Provided	SERVICES PROVIDED TO				
From	S1	S2	S3	P1	P2
S1	—	5%	25%	50%	20%
S2	10%	—	5	45	40
S3	15	5	—	20	60

The direct operating costs of the service departments are as follows:

S1	$42,000
S2	80,000
S3	19,000

Required:
Using the direct method, prepare a schedule allocating the service department costs to the producing departments.

7–6
Interdepartment Services: Step Method

Refer to the data in Exercise 7–5. Using the step method, prepare a schedule allocating the service department costs to the producing departments. (Round calculations to the nearest dollar.)

7–7
Interdepartment Services: Linear Algebra Method (Appendix)

Refer to the data in Exercise 7–5. Using the linear algebra method, determine the service department costs that will be simultaneously allocated to other service departments and the production departments. (Note: *This exercise involves three service departments; hence, it requires the use of matrix algebra to determine the simultaneous allocation of costs. Since the coverage of matrix algebra is beyond the scope of this text, this exercise should be assigned only if the students have been previously exposed to matrix algebra concepts and procedures.*)

7–8
Interdepartment Services: Direct and Linear Algebra Methods (Appendix)

Fargo Company's filament plant has two service departments (Administration and Maintenance) and two producing departments (Cutting and Assembling). Service and cost data for these departments follow:

Services Provided from	SERVICES PROVIDED TO			
	Administration	Maintenance	Cutting	Assembling
Administration	—	30%	35%	35%
Maintenance	5%	—	60%	35%
Direct department costs	$235,000	$126,500	$540,000	$360,000

Required:

a. Prepare a schedule reassigning the service department costs to the producing departments using the direct method.

b. Prepare a schedule reassigning the service department costs to the producing departments using the linear algebra method.

c. Explain why the reassignments to the producing departments differ under the direct and linear algebra methods.

7-9
Interdepartment Services: Linear Algebra Method (Appendix)

Hannibal, Inc., has two service departments (S1 and S2) and two producing departments (P1 and P2). The distribution of services provided by the service departments is as follows:

	SERVICES PROVIDED TO			
Services provided from	S1	S2	P1	P2
S1	—	10%	40%	50%
S2	20%	—	55	25

Total direct department costs for each department are as follows:

S1	$ 45,000
S2	30,000
P1	180,000
P2	260,000
Total	$515,000

Required:

a. Set up algebraic equations expressing the total cost for each department reflecting the simultaneous reassignment of service department costs to all departments receiving services.

b. Solve the equations in requirement (a) using the substitution method or any other method that you may have learned for simultaneously solving linear equations, including the use of a computer. (Round calculations to the nearest dollar if the substitution method is used.)

c. How much cost is reassigned between S1 and S2? How much S1 and S2 cost is reassigned to P1 and P2?

7-10
Calculating Manufacturing Overhead Rates

Goldratt Company, accumulated the following data for 2004:

Milling Department manufacturing overhead	$320,000
Finishing Department manufacturing overhead	$100,000
Machine hours used:	
Milling Department	10,000 hours
Finishing Department	2,000 hours
Labor hours used:	
Milling Department	1,000 hours
Finishing Department	1,000 hours

Required:

a. Calculate the plantwide manufacturing overhead rate using machine hours as the allocation base.

b. Calculate the plantwide manufacturing overhead rate using direct labor hours as the allocation base.

c. Calculate department overhead rates using machine hours in Milling and direct labor hours in Finishing as the allocation bases.

d. Calculate department overhead rates using direct labor hours in Milling and machine hours in Finishing as the allocation bases.

e. Which of these allocation systems seems to be the most appropriate? Explain.

7-11
Calculating Activity-Based Costing Overhead Rates

Refer to Exercise 7–10. Assume that manufacturing overhead consisted of the following activities and costs:

Setup (1,000 setup hours)	$100,000
Production scheduling (400 batches)	60,000
Production engineering (60 change orders)	120,000
Supervision (2,000 direct labor hours)	56,000
Machine maintenance (12,000 machine hours)	84,000
Total activity costs	$420,000

The following additional data were provided for Job 845:

Direct materials costs	$7,000
Direct labor cost (5 Milling direct labor hours; 35 Finishing direct labor hours)	$1,000
Setup hours	5 hours
Production scheduling	1 batch
Machine hours used (25 Milling machine hours; 5 Finishing machine hours)	30 hours
Production engineering	3 change orders

Required:

a. Calculate the cost per unit of activity driver for each activity cost category.
b. Calculate the cost of Job 845 using ABC to assign the overhead costs.
c. Calculate the cost of Job 845 using the plantwide overhead rate based on machine hours calculated in the previous exercise.
d. Calculate the cost of Job 845 using the departmental overhead rates calculated in the previous exercise in which the rate for Milling was based on machine hours and the rate for Finishing was based on direct labor hours.
e. What additional cost data will management need for Job 845 to adequately evaluate its price and profitability?

7-12
Activity-Based Costing and Conventional Costs Compared

Chef Grill Company manufactures two types of cooking grills: the Gas Cooker and the Charcoal Smoker. The Cooker is a premium product sold in upscale outdoor shops; the Smoker is sold in major discount stores. Following is information pertaining to the manufacturing costs for the current month.

	Gas Cooker	Charcoal Smoker
Units	1,000	5,000
Number of batches	50	10
Number of batch moves	80	20
Direct materials	$40,000	$100,000
Direct labor	$20,000	$25,000

Manufacturing overhead follows:

Activity	Cost	Cost Driver
Materials acquisition and inspection	$30,000	Amount of direct materials cost
Materials movement	16,200	Number of batch moves
Scheduling	36,000	Number of batches
	$82,200	

Required:

a. Determine the total and per-unit costs of manufacturing the Gas Cooker and Charcoal Smoker for the month, assuming all manufacturing overhead is assigned on the basis of direct labor dollars.
b. Determine the total and per-unit costs of manufacturing the Gas Cooker and Charcoal Smoker for the month, assuming manufacturing overhead is assigned using activity-based costing.

c. Comment on the differences between the solutions to requirements (a) and (b). Which is more accurate? What errors might managers make if all manufacturing overhead costs are assigned on the basis of direct labor dollars?

d. Comment on the adequacy of the preceding data to meet management's needs.

7-13
Traditional Product Costing versus Activity-Based Costing

Assume that Panasonic Company has determined its estimated total manufacturing overhead cost for one of its plants to be $183,000, consisting of the following activity cost pools for the current month:

Activity Centers	Activity Costs	Cost Drivers	Activity Level
Machine setups	$ 30,000	Setup hours	1,500
Materials handling	15,000	Number of moves	300
Machining	120,000	Machine hours	12,000
Maintenance	18,000	Maintenance hours	1,200

Total direct labor hours used during the month were 8,000.

Panasonic produces many different electronic products, including the following two products produced during the current month:

	Model X301	Model Z205
Units produced	1,000	1,000
Direct materials costs	$15,000	$15,000
Direct labor costs	$12,500	$12,500
Direct labor hours	500	500
Setup hours	50	100
Materials moves	25	50
Machine hours	800	800
Maintenance hours	10	40

Required:

a. Calculate the total per-unit cost of each model using direct labor hours to assign manufacturing overhead to products.

b. Calculate the total per-unit cost of each model using activity-based costing to assign manufacturing overhead to products.

c. Comment on the accuracy of the two methods for determining product costs.

7-14
Traditional Product Costing versus Activity-Based Costing

Chestatee Rugged Luggage, Inc., makes backpacks for large sporting goods chains that are sold under the customers' store brand names. The accounting department has identified the following overhead costs and cost drivers for next year:

Overhead Item	Expected Costs	Cost Driver	Maximum Quantity
Setup costs	$ 900,000	Number of setups	7,200
Ordering costs	240,000	Number of orders	60,000
Maintenance	1,200,000	Number of machine hours	96,000
Power	120,000	Number of kilowatt hours	600,000

Total predicted direct labor hours for next year is 60,000.
The following data are for two recently completed jobs:

	Job 201	Job 202
Cost of direct materials	$13,500	$15,000
Cost of direct labor	$18,000	71,250
Number of units completed	1,125	900
Number of direct labor hours	270	330
Number of setups	18	22
Number of orders	24	45
Number of machine hours	540	450
Number of kilowatt hours	270	360

Required:

a. Determine the unit cost for each job using a traditional plantwide overhead rate based on direct labor hours.

b. Determine the unit cost for each job using ABC. (Round answers to two decimal places.)

c. As the manager of Chestatee, is there additional information that you would want to help you evaluate the pricing and profitability of Jobs 201 and 202?

Problems

7-15
Predetermined Overhead Rates with Allocation of Budgeted Service Department Costs: Direct Method

Albany Company applies manufacturing overhead in its two producing departments using a predetermined rate. This rate is based on budgeted machine hours in the Stamping Department and budgeted labor hours in the Fabricating Department. The following data concerning next year's operations have been developed.

	SERVICE DEPARTMENTS		PRODUCING DEPARTMENTS	
	Human Resources	Maintenance and Repairs	Stamping	Fabricating
Budgeted overhead:				
Variable costs:				
Indirect materials	—	$16,000	$200,000	$ 80,000
Indirect labor	$60,000	50,000	140,000	200,000
Miscellaneous	—	—	28,000	30,000
Fixed costs:				
Miscellaneous	20,000	42,000	80,000	120,000
Other data:				
Direct labor hours (capacity)			20,000	30,000
Direct labor hours (budgeted)			14,000	20,000
Machine hours (capacity)			16,000	8,000
Machine hours (budgeted)			12,000	6,000
Number of employees (capacity)			20	30
Number of employees (budgeted)			12	18

Fixed Human Resources costs are allocated to the producing departments based on employee capacity, and variable costs are allocated based on the budgeted number of employees. Fixed Maintenance and Repairs costs are allocated based on machine hour capacity, and variable costs are allocated based on the budgeted number of machine hours.

Required:

a. Prepare a schedule showing the direct allocation of budgeted service department costs to the producing departments.

b. Calculate the predetermined overhead rates for the producing departments.

c. When is it appropriate to use budgeted data versus capacity data in allocating costs? Comment.

7-16
Selecting Cost Allocation Bases and Direct Method Allocations

Minot Company has three producing departments (P1, P2, and P3) for which direct department costs are accumulated. In January, the following indirect costs of operation were incurred.

Plant manager's salary and office expense	$ 4,800
Plant security	1,200
Plant nurse's salary and office expense	1,500
Plant depreciation	2,000
Machine maintenance	2,400
Plant cafeteria cost subsidy	1,200
	$13,100

The following additional data have been collected for the three producing departments:

	P1	P2	P3
Number of employees	10	15	5
Space occupied (square feet)	2,000	5,000	3,000
Direct labor hours	1,600	4,000	750
Machine hours	4,800	8,000	3,200
Number of nurse office visits	20	45	10

Required:

a. Group the indirect cost items into cost pools based on the nature of the costs and their common basis for allocation. Identify the most appropriate allocation basis for each cost pool and determine the total January costs in the pool. (*Hint:* A cost pool may consist of one or more cost items.)

b. Allocate the cost pools directly to the three producing departments using the allocation bases selected in requirement (a).

c. How much indirect cost would be allocated to each producing department if Minot Company were using a plantwide rate based on direct labor hours? Based on machine hours?

d. Comment on the benefits of allocating costs in pools compared with using a plantwide rate.

7-17
Evaluating Allocation Bases and Direct Method Allocations

Cheyenne Company has two service departments, Maintenance and Cafeteria, that serve two producing departments, Mixing and Packaging. The following data have been collected for these departments for the current year:

	Cafeteria	Maintenance	Mixing	Packaging
Direct department costs	$176,000	$112,000	$465,000	$295,000
Number of employees			50	30
Number of meals served			9,000	7,000
Number of maintenance hours used			800	600
Number of maintenance orders			180	170

Required:

a. Using the direct method, allocate the service department costs under the following independent assumptions:
   1. Cafeteria costs are allocated based on the number of employees, and Maintenance costs are allocated based on the number of maintenance hours used.
   2. Cafeteria costs are allocated based on the number of meals served, and Maintenance costs are allocated based on the number of maintenance orders.

b. Comment on the reasonableness of the bases used in the calculations in requirement (a). What considerations should determine which bases to use for allocating Cafeteria and Maintenance costs?

7-18
Cost Reimbursement and Step Allocation Method

Norcross Community Clinic is a not-for-profit outpatient facility that provides medical services to both fee-paying patients and low-income government supported patients. Reimbursement from the government is based on total actual costs of services provided, including both direct costs of patient services and indirect operating costs. Patient services are provided through two producing departments, Medical Services and Ancillary Services (includes X-ray, therapy, etc.). In addition to the direct costs of these departments, the clinic incurs indirect costs in two service departments, Administration and Facilities. Administration costs are allocated based on the number of full-time employees, and Facilities costs are allocated based on space occupied. Costs and related data for the current month are as follows:

	Administration	Facilities	Medical Services	Ancillary Services
Direct costs	$18,000	$4,000	$121,400	$37,200
Number of employees	5	4	12	8
Amount of space occupied (square feet) . .	1,500	—	8,000	2,000
Number of patient visits	—	—	4,000	1,500

Required:

a. Using the step method, prepare a schedule allocating the common service department costs to the producing departments.
b. Determine the amount to be reimbursed from the government for each low-income patient visit.

7-19
Budgeted Service Department Cost Allocation: Pricing a New Product

Trimco Products Company is adding a new diet food concentrate called Body Trim to its line of bodybuilding and exercise products. A plant is being built for manufacturing the new product. Management has decided to price the new product based on a 100 percent markup on total manufacturing costs. A direct cost budget for the new plant projects that direct department costs of $2,100,000 will be incurred in producing an expected normal output of 700,000 pounds of finished product. In addition, indirect costs for Administration and Technical Support will be shared by Body Trim with the two exercise products divisions, Commercial Products and Retail Products. Budgeted annual data to be used in making the allocations are summarized here.

	Administration	Technical Support	Commercial Products	Retail Products	Body Trim
Number of employees	5	5	50	30	20
Amount of technical . . . . . support time (hours)	500	—	1,500	1,250	750

Direct costs are budgeted at $90,000 for the Administration Department and $160,000 for the Technical Support Department.

Required:

a. Using the step method, determine the total direct and indirect costs of Body Trim.
b. Determine the selling price per pound of Body Trim. (Round calculations to the nearest cent.)

7-20
Allocation and Responsibility Accounting

Assume that Timberland Company uses a responsibility accounting system for evaluating its managers, and that abbreviated performance reports for the company's three divisions for the month of March are as presented here (amounts in thousands).

	Total	East	Central	West
Income	$165,000	$60,000	$75,000	$30,000
Less allocated costs:				
Computer Services	(66,000)	(22,000)	(22,000)	(22,000)
Personnel	(72,000)	(28,000)	(32,000)	(12,000)
Division income	$ 27,000	$10,000	$21,000	$ (4,000)

The West Division manager is very disturbed over his performance report and recent rumors that his division may be closed because of its failure to report a profit in recent periods. He believes that the reported profit figures do not fairly present operating results because his division is being unfairly burdened with service department costs. He is particularly concerned over the amount of Computer Services costs charged to his division. He believes that it is inequitable for his division to be charged with one-third of the total cost when it is using only 20 percent of the services. He believes that the Personnel Department's use of the Computer Services Department should also be considered in the cost allocations.

Cost allocations were based on the following distributions of service provided:

		SERVICES RECEIVER			
Services Provider	Personnel	Computer Services	East	Central	West
Computer Services	40%	—	20%	20%	20%
Personnel	—	10%	35	40	15

Required:
a. What method is the company using to allocate Personnel and Computer Services costs?
b. Recompute the cost allocations using the step method. (Round calculations to the nearest dollar.)
c. Revise the performance reports to reflect the cost allocations computed in requirement (b).
d. Comment on the complaint of the West Division's manager.

7–21
Allocating Service Department Costs: Direct and Step Methods; Department and Plantwide Overhead Rates

Assume that Pennington Group, a manufacturer of fine casual outdoor furniture, allocates Human Resources Department costs to the producing departments (Cutting and Welding) based on number of employees; Facilities Department costs are allocated based on the amount of square footage occupied. Direct department costs, labor hours, and square footage data for the four departments for October are as follows:

	Human Resources	Facilities	Cutting	Welding
Direct department overhead costs	$40,000	$120,000	$800,000	$350,000
Number of employees	5	5	35	60
Number of direct labor hours	—	—	8,000	10,000
Amount of square footage	10,000	3,000	100,000	50,000

Assume that two jobs, A1 and A2, were completed during October and that each job had direct materials costs of $1,200. Job A1 used 80 direct labor hours in the Cutting Department and 20 direct labor hours in the Welding Department. Job A2 used 20 direct labor hours in the Cutting Department and 80 direct labor hours in the Welding Department. The direct labor rate is $50 in both departments.

Required:
a. Find the cost of each job using a plantwide rate.
b. Find the cost of each job using department rates with *direct* service department cost allocation.
c. Find the cost of each job using department rates with *step* service department cost allocation.
d. Explain the differences in the costs computed in requirements (a)–(c) for each job. Which costing method is better for product pricing and profitability analysis?

7–22
Allocating Service Department Costs: Linear Algebra Method (Appendix)

Refer to the data in Problem 7–21.

Required:
a. Prepare a schedule showing the service department cost assignments to the production departments using the linear algebra method. (Round to the nearest dollar.)
b. Determine the cost of each job using department rates with linear algebra department cost allocation.
c. Discuss the relative advantages of the direct, step, and linear algebra methods of allocating service department costs.

7–23
Service Department
Cost Allocation:
Direct and Step
Methods

Parker Manufacturing Company has two production departments (Fabrication and Assembly) and three service departments (General Factory Administration, Factory Maintenance, and Factory Cafeteria). The costs of the three service departments are allocated to the production departments on the basis of the number of direct labor hours, amount of square footage occupied, and number of employees, respectively. A summary of costs and other data for each department prior to allocation of service department costs for the year ended June 30, 2004, appears here.

	Fabrication	Assembly	General Factory Administration	Factory Maintenance	Cafeteria
Direct department overhead costs	$1,650,000	$1,850,000	$160,000	$203,200	$240,000
Number of direct labor hours .	562,500	437,500	—	—	—
Number of employees	280	200	12	8	20
Amount of square footage occupied	88,000	72,000	1,750	2,000	4,800

Required:

a. Assuming that Parker elects to distribute service department costs directly to production departments without recognizing interdepartmental services, how much Factory Maintenance Department costs would be allocated to the Fabrication Department?

b. Assuming the same method of allocation as in requirement (a), how much General Factory Administration costs would be allocated to the Assembly Department?

c. Assuming that Parker elects to distribute service department costs to other service departments (starting with the service department with the highest total costs) as well as to the production departments, how much Factory Cafeteria costs would be allocated to Factory Maintenance?

d. Assuming the same method of allocation as in requirement (c), how much Factory Maintenance costs would be allocated to the cafeteria?

(CPA Adapted)

7–24
Product Costing
Continuum

Maron Corporation, a small manufacturer of specialized medical-care equipment, operates a plant with two departments, Forging and Finishing. Each product requires processing in each department. Expected indirect manufacturing costs for 2004 are as follows:

Forging Department	$300,000
Finishing Department	200,000
Total manufacturing overhead	$500,000
Direct labor hours for the year	10,000

An activity-based cost analysis determined that manufacturing overhead was incurred to support the following activities:

Setups (500)	$100,000
Engineering (5,000 hours)	125,000
Materials movement (6,000 movements)	75,000
Quality control inspections (1,000 inspections)	85,000
Machine operation (5,000 hours)	115,000
Total activity costs	$500,000

It was determined when the activity costs were being developed that similar activities that were performed in both departments, such as materials movement, had similar costs in each department; hence, Maron decided that separate departmental activity cost pools were not needed.

One of Maron's most successful products is a patented forceps that is produced in batches of 200. Each batch uses $3,000 of direct materials, all added in the Forging Department, and 25 machine hours in the Forging Department. The manufacturing process is almost totally automated in the Forging Department and depends completely on direct labor in the Finishing Department. Direct labor costs, all incurred in the Finishing Department, are $1,000 per batch for 40 direct labor hours. It was also determined that each batch of forceps requires 5 setups, 15 engineering hours, 50 materials movements, and 25 inspections.

Required:
a. Calculate the product cost per unit for forceps, assuming manufacturing overhead is assigned to products using a plantwide overhead rate based on machine hours.
b. Calculate the product cost per unit for forceps, assuming manufacturing overhead is assigned to products using department overhead rates based on machine hours for Forging and direct labor hours for Finishing.
c. Calculate the product cost per unit for forceps, assuming manufacturing overhead is assigned to products using activity-based overhead rates.
d. Comment on the reasons for the differences in the product costs calculated in requirements (a), (b), and (c).
e. What additional cost information will management need to assess the profitability of forceps?

7-25
Product Costing: Activity-Based Costing and Conventional Cost Allocation

Alpha Company manufactures two products (AA and BB). The overhead costs have been divided into four cost pools that use the following cost drivers:

Product	Number of Orders	Number of Setups	Number of Labor Transactions	Number of Labor Hours
AA	30	10	25	1,000
BB	10	40	35	250
Cost per pool $8,000	$6,500	$1,200	$10,000

Required:
a. Allocate the overhead costs using activity-based costing to products AA and BB.
b. Using conventional costing, allocate the overhead costs based on direct labor hours to products AA and BB.
c. Presented are four arguments against using activity-based costing. Provide an appropriate response to each of these arguments.
   1. Conventional systems will do the job if we change to department overhead rates from a plantwide overhead rate.
   2. A cost system should be kept simple so that it makes sense to managers and production employees.
   3. The market sets prices, so we do not need accurate product cost information.
   4. Our current cost system produces financial statements that conform to generally accepted accounting principles.

7-26
Product Costing: Plantwide Overhead versus Activity-Based Costing

Sconti, Inc., produces machine parts as a contract provider for a large manufacturing company. Sconti produces two particular parts, shafts and gears. The competition is keen among contract producers, and Sconti's top management realizes how vulnerable its market is to cost-cutting competitors. Hence, having a very accurate understanding of costs is important to Sconti's survival.

Sconti's president, Joe Disharoon, has observed that the company's current cost to produce shafts is $21.24, and the current cost to produce gears is $12.62. He indicated to the controller that he suspects some problems with the cost system because Sconti is suddenly experiencing extraordinary competition on shafts, but it seems to have a virtual corner on the gears market. He is even considering dropping the shaft line and converting the company to a one-product manufacturer of gears. He asked the controller to conduct a thorough cost study and to consider whether changes in the cost system are necessary. The controller collected the following data about the company's costs and various manufacturing activities for the most recent month:

	Shafts	Gears
Production units	50,000	10,000
Selling price	$31.86	$24
Overhead per unit (based on direct labor hours)	$12.71	$6.36
Materials and direct labor cost per unit	$8.53	$6.26
Number of production runs	10	20
Number of purchasing and receiving orders processed	40	100
Number of machine hours	12,500	6,000
Number of direct labor hours	25,000	2,500
Number of engineering hours	5,000	5,000
Number of material moves	50	40

The controller was able to summarize the company's total manufacturing overhead into the following pools:

Setup costs	$ 24,000
Machine costs	175,000
Purchasing and receiving costs	210,000
Engineering costs	200,000
Materials handling costs	90,000
Total	$699,000

Required:

a. Calculate Sconti's current plantwide overhead rate based on direct labor hours.

b. Verify Sconti's calculation of overhead cost per unit of $12.71 for shafts and $6.36 for gears.

c. Calculate the manufacturing overhead cost per unit for shafts and gears using activity-based costing, assuming each of the five cost pools represents a separate activity pool. Use the most appropriate activity driver for assigning activity costs to the two products.

d. Comment on Sconti's current cost system and the reason the company is facing fierce competition for shafts but little competition for gears.

7–27
Product Costing: Department versus Activity-Based Costing for Overhead

Advertising Services Company (ASCO), a wholly owned subsidiary of Bell-of-the-South Telecommunications, Inc. (BOST), specializes in providing published and on-line advertising services for the business marketplace. The company monitors its costs based on the cost per column inch of published space printed in the advertising book ("The Peach Pages") and based on the cost per minute of telephone advertising time delivered on "The Peach Line," a computer-based, on-line advertising service. ASCO has one major competitor, Atlantatec, in the teleadvertising market; with increased competition, ASCO has seen a decline in sales of on-line advertising in recent years. ASCO's president, Andrea Remington, believes that predatory pricing by Atlantatec has caused the problem. The following is a recent conversation between Andrea and Jim Tate, director of marketing for ASCO.

Jim: I just received a call from one of our major customers concerning our advertising rates on "The Peach Line" who said that a sales rep from another firm (it had to be Atlantatec) had offered the same service at $1 per minute, which is $1.50 per minute less than our price.

Andrea: It's costing about $1.10 per minute to produce that product. I don't see how they can afford to sell it so cheaply. I'm not convinced that we should meet the price. Perhaps the better strategy is to emphasize producing and selling more published ads, which we're more experienced with and where our margins are high and we have virtually no competition.

Jim: You may be right. Based on a recent survey of our customers, I think we can raise the price significantly for published advertising and still not lose business.

Andrea: That sounds promising; however, before we make a major recommitment to publishing, let's explore other possible explanations. I want to know how our costs compare with our competitors. Maybe we could be more efficient and find a way to earn a good return on teleadvertising.

After this meeting, Andrea and Jim requested an investigation of the production costs and comparative efficiency of producing published versus on-line advertising services. The controller, Joanna Turner, indicated that ASCO's efficiency was comparable to that of its competitors but prepared the following data regarding costs:

	Published Advertising	On-Line Advertising
Estimated number of production units	50,000	10,000,000
Selling price	$1,000	$2.50
Direct product costs	$21,000,000	$5,000,000
Overhead allocation*	$14,000,000	$11,000,000
Overhead per unit	$280	$0.60
Direct costs per unit	$420	$0.50
Number of customers	180,000	25,000
Number of salesperson days	28,000	2,000
Number of art and design hours	35,000	5,000
Number of creative services subcontract hours	100,000	25,000
Number of customer service calls	72,000	8,000

*Based on direct labor costs

Upon examining the data, Andrea decided that she wanted to know more about the overhead costs since they were such a high proportion of total production costs. She was provided the following list of overhead costs and told that they were currently being assigned to products in proportion to direct product costs.

Selling costs	$15,000,000
Visual and Audio Design costs	3,000,000
Creative Services costs	5,000,000
Customer Service costs	2,000,000

Required:

Using the data provided by the controller, prepare analyses to help Andrea and Jim in making their decisions. (*Hint:* Prepare cost calculations for both product lines using ABC to see whether there is any significant difference in their unit costs). Should ASCO switch from the fast-growing, on-line advertising market back into the well-established published advertising market? Does the charge of predatory pricing seem valid? Why are customers likely to be willing to pay a higher price to get published services? Do traditional costing and activity-based costing lead to the same conclusions?

Discussion Questions and Cases

7-28
Whether or Not to Allocate: Selecting Bases for Allocation

Bonn Company recently reorganized its computer and data processing activities. The small installations located within the accounting departments at its plants and subsidiaries have been replaced with a centralized data processing department at corporate headquarters. This department is responsible for the operations of a newly acquired large-scale computer system. The new department has been in operation for two years and has been regularly producing reliable and timely data for the past 12 months. Because the department has focused its activities on converting applications to the new system and producing reports for managers at the plants and subsidiaries, little attention has been devoted to the costs of the department. Now that the department's activities are operating relatively smoothly, company management has requested that the department manager recommend a cost accumulation system to facilitate cost control and the development of suitable rates to charge users for services. For the past two years, the department costs have been recorded in one account. The costs have been allocated to user departments on the basis of computer time used. The following schedule reports the costs and charging rate for 2001.

Salaries and benefits	$ 622,600
Supplies	40,000
Equipment maintenance contract	15,000
Insurance	25,000
Heat and air conditioning	36,000
Electricity	50,000
Equipment and furniture depreciation	285,400
Building improvements depreciation	10,000
Building occupancy and security	39,300
Corporate administrative charges	52,700
Total costs	$1,176,000
Computer hours for user processing	÷ 2,750
Hourly rate ($1,176,000 ÷ 2,750)	$ 428 (rounded)
Use of available computer hours:	
Testing and debugging programs	250
Setup of jobs	500
Processing jobs	2,750
Downtime for maintenance	750
Idle time	742
Total	4,992

The department manager recommends that department costs be accumulated by five activity centers within the department: Systems Analysis, Programming, Data Processing, Computer Operations (processing), and Administration. He then suggests that the costs of Administration should be allocated to the other four activity centers before a separate rate for charging users is developed for each of the first four activities. After reviewing the details of the accounts, the manager made the following observations regarding the charges to the several subsidiary accounts within the department.

1. *Salaries and benefits*—records the salary and benefit costs of all employees in the department.
2. *Supplies*—records magnetic disk costs, paper costs for printers, and a small amount for other miscellaneous costs.
3. *Equipment maintenance contracts*—records charges for maintenance contracts; all equipment is covered by maintenance contracts.
4. *Insurance*—records cost of insurance covering the equipment and furniture.

5. *Heat and air conditioning*—records a charge from the corporate Heating and Air Conditioning Department estimated to be the incremental costs to meet the special needs of the Computer Department.
6. *Electricity*—records the charge for electricity based on a separate meter within the department.
7. *Equipment and furniture depreciation*—records the depreciation for all owned equipment and furniture within the department.
8. *Building improvements depreciation*—records amortization of the depreciation of all building improvements required to provide proper environmental control and electrical service for the computer equipment.
9. *Building occupancy and security*—records the Computer Department's share of the depreciation, maintenance, heat, and security costs of the building; these costs are allocated on the basis of square feet occupied.
10. *Corporate administrative charges*—records the Computer Department's share of the corporate administrative costs; they are allocated on the basis of the number of employees.

Required:

a. State whether or not each of the ten cost items should be allocated to the five activity centers. For each cost item that should be allocated, recommend the basis on which it should be allocated. Justify your conclusion in each case.

b. Assume that the costs of the Computer Operations (processing) activity will be charged to the user departments on the basis of computer hours. Using the given analysis of computer utilization, determine the total number of hours that should be employed to determine the charging rate for Computer Operations (processing). Justify your answer.

(CMA Adapted)

7-29
Cost Allocation and Performance Evaluation

The Village Branch of Citizens and Northern Bank is managed by Ron Short, who has full responsibility for the bank's operations. The Village Branch is treated as a profit center within the company's responsibility accounting system; according to rumors throughout the company, if The Village Branch does not become more profitable, it is likely to be closed. Ron is upset with the corporate accounting department because of the number of different indirect costs that are allocated to his branch each period. He believes that many of these costs provide no direct benefits to his branch and that they are not relevant to an evaluation of his performance or that of The Village Branch. An income statement for The Village Branch for February follows:

Branch revenues		$350,000
Direct branch costs		(295,000)
Branch margin		$ 55,000
Allocated costs:		
Computer operations	$ 4,500	
Personnel	5,000	
Payroll	3,800	
Maintenance	6,000	
Accounting	5,200	
Legal and audit	4,200	
Transportation	9,000	
Administrative overhead	12,000	(49,700)
Branch net income		$ 5,300

An investigation of Mr. Short's complaint by the controller's office provided the following additional information:

- Computer operations costs are billed based on actual CPU and computer connection time used by the branch.

- Personnel and payroll costs, primarily fixed, are allocated to the various operating departments based on the number of employees in each division.
- Maintenance costs are charged to the operating departments based on the standard hours actually worked in each department plus the actual cost of materials and supplies used.
- Accounting costs are allocated based on the number of transactions processed by the computer for each branch.
- Legal and audit costs are allocated based on the total revenues of the operating departments. The Village Branch has been involved in only one lawsuit, which was about five years ago. Mr. Short receives a copy of the company audit report each year but seldom reads it.
- Transportation costs consist primarily of the costs of operating the company helicopter and the company airplane. The helicopter is used to deliver checks to the local clearing center and for local executive transportation; the airplane is used primarily for executive travel out of town. Transportation costs are allocated to the operating departments based on revenues. Mr. Short has never flown in the corporate airplane.
- Administrative overhead consists of all other administrative costs including home office salaries and office expenses. These costs are allocated to the operating departments based on revenues. Mr. Short seldom sees anyone from the home office.

Required:
a. Evaluate each cost allocation to determine whether it seems appropriate to allocate it to the operating divisions. Also evaluate the basis on which each cost is allocated to the operating departments.
b. Prepare a revised income statement for The Village Branch based on your evaluations in requirement (a).
c. Do you agree with Mr. Short's complaint? How do the cost allocations affect the decision to continue or discontinue The Village Branch?

John Shank Case Recommendation

Societé Bonlieu

This case is set in a carpentry shop in Grenoble, France, in 1956 in the midst of the post-WWII construction boom. Although issues in this case are timeless, the case provides an excellent context for applying a modern costing technique for dealing with these issues, namely, activity-based costing. Like most John Shank cases, it has a "strategic" twist in that it challenges the student to evaluate the company's strategy in view of the student's analysis of costs.

Tijuana Bronze Machining

This is a classic cost system design case where a firm using a traditional costing system has one group of products with low profit margins and strong price competition and another group with very comfortable margins and little price competition. This scenario raises the question of whether costs are being properly measured and whether activity-based costing would provide more accurate cost numbers. It is a good case for illustrating the advantages of activity-based costing and the benefits of product profitability analysis.

Solutions to Review Problems

1.
Service Department Cost Allocation

a. *Direct Method*

	Total	Women's	Men's
Administrative Services Department:			
Allocation base (number of employees)	24	15	9
Percent of total base	100%	62.5%	37.5%
Cost allocation	$18,000	$11,250	$6,750
Facilities Services Department:			
Allocation base (square footage)	22,500	15,000	7,500
Percent of total base	100%	66.7%	33.3%
Cost allocation	$12,000	$8,000	$4,000

COST ALLOCATION SUMMARY

	Administrative	Facilities	Women's	Men's	Total
Departmental costs before allocation	$18,000	$12,000	$60,000	$50,000	$140,000
Cost allocations:					
Administrative	(18,000)	—	11,250	6,750	0
Facilities	—	(12,000)	8,000	4,000	0
Departmental costs after allocation	$ 0	$ 0	$79,250	$60,750	$140,000

Step Method

ALLOCATION SEQUENCE

	Administrative	Facilities
Allocation base	Number of employees	Amount of square footage
Total base for other service *and* producing departments (a)	26	25,000
Total base for other service departments (b)	2	2,500
Percent of total services provided to other service departments (b ÷ a)	7.7%	10.0%
Order of allocation	Second	First

STEP ALLOCATIONS

	Total	Administrative	Women's	Men's
Facilities Services Department:				
Allocation base (square footage)	25,000	2,500	15,000	7,500
Percent of total base	100%	10%	60%	30%
Cost allocation	$12,000	$1,200	$ 7,200	$3,600
Administrative Services Department:				
Allocation base (number of employees)	24	—	15	9
Percent of total base	100%	—	62.5%	37.5%
Cost allocation (18,000 + 1,200) . . .	$19,200	—	$12,000	$7,200

Chapter 7

COST ALLOCATION SUMMARY

	Facilities	Administrative	Women's	Men's	Total
Departmental costs before allocation	$12,000	$18,000	$60,000	$50,000	$140,000
Cost allocations:					
Facilities	(12,000)	1,200	7,200	3,600	0
Administrative	—	(19,200)	12,000	7,200	0
Departmental costs after allocations	$ 0	$ 0	$79,200	$60,800	$140,000

  b. Another service department cost allocation method is the *linear algebra method.* This method simultaneously allocates service department costs both to other service departments and to the producing departments. It has an advantage over the *step method* in that it fully recognizes interdepartmental services.

  c. If Cotswald's Clothiers wants the most precise allocation of service department costs to the producing departments, considering both direct services and indirect services, it must use the linear algebra method of service department allocation. As indicated in the Allocation sequence section of the step method in (a), Facilities provides 10 percent of its services to Administrative, and Administrative provides 7.7 percent of its services to Facilities. The step method recognized the Facilities services provided to Administrative, but it did not recognize the Administrative services provided to Facilities.

    In this case, the producing departments are using approximately the same proportion of services from each of the service departments (60.0 percent to 62.5 percent for the Women's Department and 30.0 percent to 37.5 percent for the Men's Department). Hence, using a more precise measure of cost allocation is not likely to produce significantly different results, especially since the interdepartmental services are so close (7.7 percent versus 10.0 percent). Just as the step method allocation results were quite close to the direct method results, the linear method results would likely be quite close to both the direct and step method results. Use of the linear algebra method is not recommended in this case. On the basis of simplicity and convenience, the direct method is probably the best method for Cotswald's to use.

2.
Plantwide,
Department, and
Activity-Based
Overhead Rates

  a. Plantwide overhead rate = Total manufacturing overhead ÷ Total machine hours
= ($120,000 + $55,000) ÷ (10,000 + 5,000)
= $175,000 ÷ (15,000)
= $11.67 per machine hour

	ZX300	SL500
Product costs per unit:		
Direct materials	$12,000	$18,000
Direct labor	5,000	4,000
Manufacturing overhead		
700 machine hours × $11.67	8,169	
800 machine hours × $11.67		9,336
Total cost per batch	$25,169	$31,336
Number of units per batch	÷ 100	÷ 100
Cost per unit	$251.69	$313.36

  b. Departmental overhead rates = Total departmental overhead ÷ Dept. allocation base
Fabricating: = $120,000 ÷ 10,000 machine hours
= $12 per machine hour
Finishing: = $55,000 ÷ 5,000 inspection hours
= $11 per machine hour

	ZX300	SL500
Product costs per unit:		
Direct materials	$12,000	$18,000
Direct labor	5,000	4,000
Manufacturing overhead		
Fabricating Department:		
500 machine hours × $12	6,000	
700 machine hours × $12		8,400
Finishing Department:		
200 machine hours × $11	2,200	
100 machine hours × $11		1,100
Total cost per batch	$25,200	$31,500
Number of units per batch	÷ 100	÷ 100
Cost per unit	$252.00	$315.00

c. Activity-based overhead rates = Activity cost pool ÷ Activity cost driver

Maintenance: = $30,000 ÷ 15,000 machine hours
= $2 per machine hour

Materials handling: = $45,000 ÷ 4,500 materials moves
= $10 per materials move

Machine setups: = $75,000 ÷ 750 setups
= $100 per machine setup

Inspections: = $25,000 ÷ 1,000 inspection hours
= $25 per inspection hour

	ZX300	SL500
Product costs per unit:		
Direct materials	$12,000	$18,000
Direct labor	5,000	4,000
Manufacturing overhead		
Maintenance activity:		
700 machine hours × $2	1,400	
800 machine hours × $2		1,600
Materials handling activity:		
30 materials moves × $10	300	
50 materials moves × $10		500
Machine setups activity:		
5 machine setups × $100	500	
9 machine setups × $100		900
Inspections activity:		
30 inspection hours × $25	750	
60 inspection hours × $25		1,500
Total cost per batch	$19,950	$26,500
Number of units per batch	÷ 100	÷ 100
Cost per unit	$199.50	$265.00

d. The following is a summary of the product costs for ZX300 and SL500 assigning overhead costs based on a plantwide rate, department rates, and activity-based rates:

	ZX300	SL500
Plantwide rate	$251.69	$313.36
Department rates	$252.00	$315.00
Activity rates	$199.50	$265.00

Changing from a plantwide rate to department rates had little effect on unit costs because the department rates per machine hour are very close to the plantwide rate per machine hour. Based on machine hours, both departments have similar cost structures.

When using activity rates, however, the cost of these two products drops dramatically because they use only a small portion (less than 2 percent) of the activities of setup (14 of 750) and materials moves (80 of 4,500). Neither a plantwide rate nor department rates recognize this fact, resulting in a large amount of cost cross-subsizidation of other products by ZX300 and SL500 for these costs. Although this problem did not include cost analysis of the other three products, it clearly shows that they are less profitable and that ZX300 and SL500 are much more profitable than management previously thought.

INVENTORY VALUATION APPROACHES AND JUST-IN-TIME INVENTORY MANAGEMENT

After completing this chapter, you should be able to:

LEARNING OBJECTIVE 1   Explain the primary characteristics of the absorption costing and variable costing inventory valuation methods.

LEARNING OBJECTIVE 2   Prepare absorption costing and variable costing income statements.

LEARNING OBJECTIVE 3   Evaluate the benefits and limitations of variable costing.

LEARNING OBJECTIVE 4   Describe just-in-time (JIT) inventory management and discuss how it is used to reduce raw materials, work-in-process, and finished goods inventories.

LEARNING OBJECTIVE 5   Explain the changes required in performance evaluation and recordkeeping when an organization adopts the JIT approach to inventory management.

INVENTORY MANAGEMENT AND SUPPLY CHAIN EFFICIENCY

As a current asset, a hefty stock of inventory may seem positive to a novice inspecting a firm's balance sheet. From a management or analyst's perspective, inventory is a necessary part of business activity for a merchandiser or manufacturer, but it also generates handling, financing, and holding costs that decrease profits. Distribution lags, variations in consumer tastes, and changes in competition all make managing inventories a real concern for executives. Contemporary examples from the management experiences at Kimberly-Clark and Nokia illustrate the dimensions of the inventory management challenge.

Throughout the decade of the 1990s and into the 2000s, Kimberly-Clark managers increased the coordinating linkages with their large retail customers and successfully lowered costs in the logistical step between manufacturer and merchandiser. As a manufacturer of paper products, Kimberly Clark developed a supply strategy with large customers like Costco that uses information as a competitive weapon. A Kimberly-Clark management team assumed responsibility for maintaining their firm's inventory at individual Costco stores. In exchange for this shift in inventory management responsibility, retailers such as Costco, Wal-Mart, and Target share specific sales information with the manufacturer. Working as a team, an inventory manager, logistics manager, and field sales manager at Kimberly-Clark coordinate the replenishment of Costco's inventory of paper products. Observers now contend that when this process is working well, the manufacturer has a better understanding of the retailer's sinventory that the retailer does. The goal of all these efforts is to keep the inventory as low as possible without risking empty shelves. Costco now stocks a two-week supply of Kimberly-Clark products rather than the one-month supply they maintained under the former inventory management system. In addition, the Kimberly-Clark management team can suggest improvements in packaging and variety that will meet emerging customer needs and interests.

As this circumstance demonstrates, both merchandising and manufacturing inventory management involve many diverse and sometimes complex decisions, and managerial accounting can assist managers as they analyze inventory issues. Two specific managerial accounting issues involving inventories are the impact of inventory valuation on financial statements and the just-in-time approach to inventory management.

Sources: Based on Almar Latour, "A Fire in Albuquerque Sparks Crisis for European Cell-Phone Giants," *The Wall Street Journal (Interactive Edition),* January 29, 2001 and Emily Nelson and Ann Zimmerman, "How Kimberly Clark Keeps Costco in Diapers," *The Wall Street Journal (Interactive Edition),* September 7, 2000.

Inventory management for both merchandising and manufacturing firms involves many diverse and sometimes complex decisions; management accounting can assist managers as they analyze inventory issues. **The purpose of this chapter is to examine two specific management accounting issues involving inventories: the impact of inventory valuation on financial statements and the just-in-time approach to inventory management.**

LEARNING OBJECTIVE 1

INVENTORY VALUATION WITH ABSORPTION AND VARIABLE COSTING

Product costing for inventory valuation is the link between financial and management accounting. Product costing systems determine the cost-based valuation of the manufactured inventories used in making key financial accounting measurements (net income on the income statement and financial position on the balance sheet). On the other hand, as shown in earlier chapters, product costing systems also provide vital information for managers in setting prices, controlling costs, and evaluating management performance. The influence of financial accounting on product costing systems is apparent in the design of traditional job order and process costing systems. These systems reflect the requirement of financial accounting (i.e., generally accepted accounting principles) that all manufacturing costs be included in inventory valuations for external financial reporting purposes. In these systems, all other costs incurred, such as selling, general, and administrative costs, are treated as expenses of the period.

In previous chapters, the discussions of activity-based costing stressed the need for management accounting to develop more extensive and more accurate inventory costing systems that include measurements of all activities throughout the internal value chain of a business—not just manufacturing activities. Hence, for internal decision-making purposes, many companies now augment their traditional costing systems with activity-based systems that encompass selling and distribution activities as well as various administrative functions. Although we emphasize the need for effective costing systems for internal decision making (management accounting), we also recognize the importance of product cost measurements in preparing income statements and balance sheets for either internal or external use (financial accounting).

This chapter presents the two inventory valuation models—absorption costing and variable costing—used in preparing financial statements. Although both models are concerned with financial data reported in the income statement and the balance sheet, only the absorption costing model is permissible for external reporting purposes under generally accepted accounting principles. Variable costing is an alternative to absorption costing only for internal reporting of income and financial position.

Absorption and variable costing methods are similar in that they both treat *nonmanufacturing* costs incurred during the period, such as selling and administration costs, as expenses (period costs). The difference between absorption and variable costing is how they treat *manufacturing* costs. Whereas absorption costing treats both *variable* and *fixed* manufacturing costs as inventoriable product costs, variable costing treats only *variable* manufacturing costs as inventoriable product costs; fixed manufacturing costs are treated as period costs.[1]

BASIC CONCEPTS

One of the theoretical issues in accounting that has generated considerable debate over the past fifty years is how to treat fixed overhead costs in the valuation of inventory. The debate centers around whether fixed overhead, such as machine depreciation, should be considered an *inventoriable product cost* and treated as an asset cost until the inventory is sold, or as a *period cost* and recorded immediately as an operating expense. **Absorption costing** (also called **full costing**) treats fixed manufacturing overhead as a product cost, whereas **variable costing** (also called **direct costing**) treats it as a period cost. Therefore, fixed manufacturing overhead is recorded initially as an asset (inventory) under absorption costing but as an operating expense under variable costing.

Suppose a company leases a manufacturing facility for a fixed amount of $25,000 per month. Absorption costing assigns the $25,000 to the asset, inventory, and spreads it over the units produced in calculating the cost of each unit, whereas variable costing excludes this cost from the inventory cost valuation, recording it immediately as an expense. As illustrated in Exhibit 8–1, the only difference between absorption and variable costing is in the accounting for fixed manufacturing overhead. All other costs are treated the same way under both methods.

Since fixed product costs are eventually recorded as expenses under both variable and absorption costing by the time the inventory is sold, why does it matter whether fixed overhead is treated as a product cost or a period cost? It matters because the way it is treated affects the measurement of income for a particular period as well as the valuation assigned to inventory on the balance sheet at the end of the period. It could also have a behavioral effect on management decisions.

---

[1]The discussion of absorption and variable costing in this chapter is presented from the "unit cost" behavior perspective of fixed and variable costs (see Chapters 2 and 3). Fixed costs are assumed to remain unchanged when unit volume changes; variable costs are assumed to vary in proportion to the change in unit volume.

EXHIBIT 8-1

COMPARISON OF ABSORPTION AND VARIABLE COSTING

Absorption Costing	Variable Costing
Product Costs	
Direct materials	Direct materials
Direct labor	Direct labor
Variable manufacturing overhead	Variable manufacturing overhead
Fixed manufacturing overhead	
Period Costs	
Variable selling and administrative	Variable selling and administrative
Fixed selling and administrative	Fixed selling and administrative
	Fixed manufacturing overhead

INVENTORY VALUATIONS

To illustrate the difference in inventory valuations between absorption and variable costing, consider the following assumed cost data for Nutech Company at a monthly volume of 4,000 units:

Direct materials	$7 per unit
Direct labor	$5 per unit
Variable manufacturing overhead	$4 per unit
Fixed manufacturing overhead	$8,000 per month

To determine the unit cost of inventory using absorption costing, the average fixed overhead cost of $2 per unit is calculated by dividing the monthly fixed manufacturing overhead ($8,000) by the monthly volume (4,000 units). Even though fixed manufacturing overhead is not a variable cost, under absorption costing it is applied to inventory on a per-unit basis, the same as variable costs. At a monthly volume of 4,000 units, Nutech's inventory costs per unit under variable and absorption are as follows:

	COST PER UNIT	
	Variable Costing	Absorption Costing
Direct materials	$ 7	$ 7
Direct labor	5	5
Variable manufacturing overhead	4	4
Fixed manufacturing overhead ($8,000 ÷ 4,000 units)	—	2
Total unit cost	$16	$18

The $2 difference in total unit cost is attributed to the treatment of fixed overhead. The difference in the total inventory valuation on the balance sheet between absorption and variable costing is the number of units in ending inventory times $2. So if 1,000 units are on hand at the end of the month, they are valued at $18,000 if absorption costing is used but at only $16,000 with variable costing.

Note that the $2 fixed cost per unit depends on the assumptions of $8,000 in total fixed overhead cost and 4,000 units of production per month. As illustrated later, if either total fixed overhead cost or the production volume is different, the fixed overhead per unit will change.

LEARNING OBJECTIVE 2

INCOME MEASUREMENT UNDER ABSORPTION AND VARIABLE COSTING

The income statement formats used for variable and absorption costing are not the same. One of the primary benefits of *variable costing* is that it separates costs into variable and fixed costs, making it possible to present the income statement in a *contribution format*. As illustrated in Chapter 3, in a **contribution income statement**, variable costs are subtracted from revenues to calculate contribution margin; fixed costs are then subtracted from contribution margin to calculate profit or net income.[2]

When *absorption costing* is used, the income statement is usually formatted using the *functional format*, which classifies costs based on cost function, such as manufacturing, selling, and administrative. The **functional income statement**, also illustrated in Chapter 3, subtracts manufacturing costs (represented by cost of goods sold) from revenues to calculate gross profit; selling and administrative costs are then subtracted from gross profit to calculate net income. The contribution and functional formats are summarized as follows:

Contribution Format		Functional Format	
Sales	$000	Sales	$000
Less variable expenses:		Less cost of goods sold	(000)
Cost of goods sold	(000)	Gross profit	$000
Selling	(000)	Less operating expenses:	
Administrative	(000)	Selling	(000)
Contribution margin	$000	Administrative	(000)
Less fixed expenses:		Net income	$000
Manufacturing	(000)		
Selling	(000)		
Administrative	(000)		
Net income	$000		

Notice that the contribution format provides information for determining the contribution margin ratio, which is calculated as total contribution margin divided by total sales. It also provides the total amount of fixed costs. These are the primary items of data needed to determine the break-even point and to conduct other cost-volume-profit analysis (see Chapter 3).

Not only is the income statement format usually different for absorption and variable costing methods but also as illustrated in the following examples for Nutech Company, the amount of income reported on the income statement *might* not be the same because of the difference in the treatment of fixed manufacturing overhead. The following additional information is necessary for the Nutech Company examples:

Selling price	$30 per unit
Variable selling and administrative expenses	$3 per unit
Fixed selling and administrative expenses	$10,000 per month

SALES VARY BUT PRODUCTION REMAINS CONSTANT

Nutech has no inventory on June 1. Production remains constant at 4,000 units per month for June, July, and August, while sales are 4,000, 2,500, and 5,500 units, respectively for these months. Therefore, both total production and total sales are 12,000 units for this three-month period. A summary of inventory changes is presented at the top of Exhibit 8–2. Absorption and variable costing income statements for June, July, and August are also presented. Recall that the total manufacturing unit cost is $18

---

[2]We have previously used the word *profit* when discussing cost-volume-profit analysis and introducing the contribution income statement. Because the bottom line in published income statements is identified as *net income*, we will also use this term, especially when discussing formal financial statements.

EXHIBIT 8-2

ABSORPTION AND VARIABLE COSTING INCOME (PRODUCTION CONSTANT)

Nutech Company: Summary of Unit Inventory Changes

	June	July	August
Beginning inventory	0	0	1,500
Production	4,000	4,000	4,000
Total available	4,000	4,000	5,500
Sales	4,000	2,500	5,500
Ending inventory	0	1,500	0

Nutech Company
Absorption Costing Income Statements
For June, July, and August

	(Sales Equal Production) June	(Production Exceeds Sales) July	(Sales Exceed Production) August
Unit sales	4,000	2,500	5,500
Sales ($30 per unit)	$120,000	$75,000	$165,000
Cost of goods sold ($18 per unit)	(72,000)	(45,000)	(99,000)
Gross profit	$ 48,000	$30,000	$ 66,000
Selling and administrative expenses:			
Variable ($3 per unit)	$ 12,000	$ 7,500	$ 16,500
Fixed	10,000	10,000	10,000
Total	(22,000)	(17,500)	(26,500)
Net income	$ 26,000	$12,500	$ 39,500

Nutech Company
Variable Costing Income Statements
For June, July, and August

	June	July	August
Unit sales	4,000	2,500	5,500
Sales ($30 per unit)	$120,000	$75,000	$165,000
Less variable expenses:			
Cost of goods sold ($16 per unit)	$ 64,000	$40,000	$ 88,000
Selling and administrative ($3 per unit)	12,000	7,500	16,500
Total	(76,000)	(47,500)	(104,500)
Contribution margin	$ 44,000	$27,500	$ 60,500
Less fixed expenses:			
Manufacturing overhead	$ 8,000	$ 8,000	$ 8,000
Selling and administrative	10,000	10,000	10,000
Total	(18,000)	(18,000)	(18,000)
Net income	$ 26,000	$ 9,500	$ 42,500

using absorption costing and $16 using variable costing, the $2 differential caused by the difference in accounting for fixed overhead costs.

In June (the first month of operation), when 4,000 units were produced and sold, no units remained in inventory, which means that all fixed manufacturing overhead cost was deducted as an expense during the current period under both methods. Under absorption costing, $8,000 of fixed overhead was deducted as part of cost of goods sold (4,000 units × $2 per unit). Under variable costing, $8,000 was deducted as a period cost from contribution margin. No costs were assigned to ending inventory under either method since all units produced were sold.

In July, the 4,000 units produced exceeded the 2,500 units sold by 1,500 units. Because variable costing treats fixed manufacturing overhead as a period cost, the full $8,000 was deducted in July. Absorption costing assigned $5,000 (2,500 units sold × $2) to cost of goods sold and $3,000 (1,500 units remaining × $2) to ending inventory. Because absorption costing deducted only $5,000 of manufacturing overhead cost on the July income statement while variable costing deducted $8,000, net income was $3,000 more under absorption costing than variable costing. Furthermore, since absorption costing assigned $2 more to each unit produced as a product cost than did variable costing, ending inventory was $3,000 more (1,500 units × $2) under absorption costing than variable costing.

In August, just the opposite of July's situation occurred: sales of 5,500 units exceeded production of 4,000 units by 1,500 units. These extra units came from the beginning inventory left from July. As in the two previous months, variable costing deducted $8,000 for fixed manufacturing overhead as a period cost. Since 5,500 units were sold in August, however, absorption costing deducted $11,000 (5,500 units × $2) for fixed manufacturing overhead. Stated another way, because absorption costing assigned $3,000 more cost to the July ending inventory, when those units were then sold in August, they had $3,000 more cost. Hence, August net income was $3,000 more under variable costing than absorption costing.

What can we conclude from this analysis? As long as the number of units produced equals units sold, the two methods will deduct the same total costs on the income statement. However, net income is higher under absorption costing when production exceeds sales (i.e., in periods when inventories are increasing), and net income is higher under variable costing when sales exceed production (i.e., when inventories are decreasing). This is logical because when inventories increase, absorption costing defers some of the current period's fixed overhead costs in inventories as an asset on the balance sheet. When inventories decrease, however, those costs are moved from the balance sheet and placed on the income statement as an expense. Absorption costing assumes that fixed overhead costs do not expire until the product is sold, whereas variable costing assumes that these costs expire as incurred each period.

SALES REMAIN CONSTANT BUT PRODUCTION VARIES

Assume that Nutech's unit variable and monthly fixed costs remain the same for the months of October, November, and December when 4,000 units per month were sold, but 4,000, 5,000, and 3,200 were produced, respectively, per month. Unlike the previous illustration in which production was constant and fixed manufacturing overhead cost was $2 per unit for absorption costing, this illustration has the following fixed manufacturing overhead costs per unit:

	October	November	December
Fixed manufacturing overhead	$8,000	$8,000	$8,000
Units produced	÷ 4,000	÷ 5,000	÷ 3,200
Fixed cost per unit	$ 2.00	$ 1.60	$ 2.50

As a result, the unit cost of inventory and, consequently, the cost of goods sold will vary each period, even if sales remain constant. Given that variable costs are $16 per unit, the total unit manufacturing costs for these three months under absorption costing are as follows:

	October	November	December
Variable costs per unit	$16.00	$16.00	$16.00
Fixed costs per unit	2.00	1.60	2.50
Total manufacturing cost per unit	$18.00	$17.60	$18.50

Exhibit 8–3 presents Nutech's income statements under absorption and variable costing for October, November, and December. This exhibit also illustrates the following:

EXHIBIT 8-3

ABSORPTION AND VARIABLE COSTING INCOME (SALES CONSTANT)

Nutech Company: Summary of Unit Inventory Changes

	October	November	December
Beginning inventory	0	0	1,000
Production	4,000	5,000	3,200
Total available	4,000	5,000	4,200
Sales	4,000	4,000	4,000
Ending inventory	0	1,000	200

Nutech Company
Absorption Costing Income Statements
For October, November, and December

	(Sales Equal Production) October	(Production Exceeds Sales) November	(Sales Exceed Production) December
Unit sales	4,000	4,000	4,000
Sales ($30 per unit)	$120,000	$120,000	$120,000
Cost of goods sold:			
Beginning inventory	$ 0	$ 0	$ 17,600
Variable manufacturing costs	64,000	80,000	51,200
Fixed manufacturing overhead	8,000	8,000	8,000
Cost of goods available	$ 72,000	$ 88,000	$ 76,800
Less ending inventory*	0	(17,600)	(3,700)
Cost of goods sold	(72,000)	(70,400)	(73,100)
Gross profit	$ 48,000	$ 49,600	$ 46,900
Selling and administrative expenses:			
Variable ($3 per unit)	$ 12,000	$ 12,000	$ 12,000
Fixed	10,000	10,000	10,000
Total	(22,000)	(22,000)	(22,000)
Net income	$ 26,000	$ 27,600	$ 24,900

(Continued)

*November, 1,000 units × $17.60; December, 200 units × $18.50.

EXHIBIT 8-3 *(concluded)*

Nutech Company
Variable Costing Income Statements
For October, November, and December

	October	November	December
Unit sales	4,000	4,000	4,000
Sales ($30 per unit)	$120,000	$120,000	$120,000
Less variable expenses:			
Cost of goods sold ($16 per unit)	$ 64,000	$ 64,000	$ 64,000
Selling and administrative ($3 per unit)	12,000	12,000	12,000
Total	(76,000)	(76,000)	(76,000)
Contribution margin	$ 44,000	$ 44,000	$ 44,000
Less fixed expenses:			
Manufacturing overhead	$ 8,000	$ 8,000	$ 8,000
Selling and administrative	10,000	10,000	10,000
Total	(18,000)	(18,000)	(18,000)
Net income	$ 26,000	$ 26,000	$ 26,000

- When sales and production are equal (October), net income is the same for absorption and variable costing.
- When production exceeds sales (November), net income is higher under the absorption costing method.
- When sales exceed production (December), net income is higher under the variable costing method.

More significantly, this exhibit illustrates that although unit sales are constant and manufacturing cost behavior is unchanged, net income can vary under the absorption method simply by changing the number of units produced.

Sales did not change from October to November, but net income increased by $1,600 merely by increasing the number of units produced. By producing more units and spreading the fixed overhead cost over more units, unit cost decreased from $18.00 to $17.60, thereby increasing net income by $1,600 (4,000 × $0.40 per unit). On the other hand, from November to December, the number of units produced decreased to 3,200 and the total unit cost increased from $17.60 to $18.50, or by $0.90 per unit. Under a first-in, first-out assumption, the 1,000 units in beginning inventory with a cost of $17.60 were sold first, followed by 3,000 of the units produced in December at a cost of $18.50. The other 200 units produced in December remained in ending inventory. Hence, the decrease in net income from November to December was $2,700 (3,000 units × $0.90 per unit).

RECONCILIATION OF INCOME DIFFERENCES

Exhibits 8–2 and 8–3 reveal several important relationships between absorption costing net income and variable costing net income, as well as the way net income responds to changes in sales and production under both methods.

For each period, the income differences between absorption and variable costing can be explained by analyzing the change in inventoried fixed manufacturing overhead under absorption costing net income. In general, the following relationship exists:

Variable   Increase (or minus decrease)   Absorption
costing   + in inventoried fixed   = costing
net income   manufacturing overhead   net income

Using Nutech's November information, the equation would be as follows:

$$\$26,000 + (1,000 \times \$1.60) = \$27,600$$

This equation may be reversed to reconcile absorption costing net income to variable costing net income:

Absorption   Decrease (or minus increase)   Variable
costing   + in inventoried fixed   = costing
net income   manufacturing overhead   net income

For any given time period, regardless of length, if total units produced equals total units sold, net income will be the same for absorption costing and variable costing, all other things being equal. Under absorption costing, all fixed manufacturing overhead is released as a product cost through cost of goods sold when inventory is sold. Under variable costing, all fixed manufacturing overhead is reported as a period cost and expensed in the period incurred. Consequently, over the life of a product, the income differences within periods are offset since they occur only because of the timing of the release of fixed manufacturing overhead to the income statement.

LEARNING OBJECTIVE 3

EVALUATION AND COMPARISON OF ALTERNATIVE APPROACHES TO INVENTORY VALUATION

The central theoretical issue in the variable costing debate is whether or not fixed manufacturing costs add value to products. Proponents of variable costing argue that these costs do not add value to a product. They believe that fixed costs are incurred to provide the capacity to produce during a given period, and these costs expire with the passage of time regardless of whether the related capacity was used. Variable manufacturing costs, on the other hand, are incurred only if production takes place. Consequently, these costs are properly assignable to the units produced.

ARGUMENTS FAVORING VARIABLE COSTING

Proponents of variable costing also argue that inventories have value only to the extent that they avoid the necessity of incurring costs in the future. Having inventory available for sale avoids the necessity of incurring some future variable costs, but the availability of finished goods inventory does not avoid the incurrence of future fixed manufacturing costs. Proponents conclude that inventories should be valued at their variable manufacturing cost, and fixed manufacturing costs should be expensed as incurred.

When considering the financial accounting principle of matching, variable costing has an advantage over absorption costing because it matches revenues with the direct cost of producing those revenues. This causes net income to vary only with sales, not with both sales and production, as is often found in absorption costing. In absorption costing, overproduction especially distorts net income during a period because the excess inventory is assigned fixed costs that would otherwise be assigned to the units produced and sold. Using absorption costing, a company can increase net operating income by simply producing more than it sells.

ARGUMENTS OPPOSING VARIABLE COSTING

Opponents of variable costing argue that fixed manufacturing costs are incurred for only one purpose, namely, to manufacture the product. Because they are incurred to manufacture the product, they should be assigned to the product. It is also argued that in the long run all costs are variable. Consequently, by omitting fixed costs, variable costing understates long-run variable costs and misleads decision makers into underestimating true production costs.

On a pragmatic level, the central arguments for variable costing center around the fact that the use of variable costing facilitates the development of contribution income statements and cost-volume-profit analysis. With costs accumulated on an absorption costing basis, contribution income statements are difficult to develop, and cost-volume-profit analysis becomes very complicated unless production and sales are equal. What's Happening 8–1 shows how FMI Forms Manufacturers used a combination of absorption and variable costing to guide price-bidding decisions.

Proponents of activity-based costing typically do not favor variable costing because ABC is based on the assumption that, in the long run, all costs are variable and that fixed costs should be assigned to products or services to represent long-run variable costs. Hence, inventory valuation using an ABC approach will tend to be closer to absorption costing values than variable costing values. This does not mean that one who advocates ABC for inventory valuation purposes would not recognize the value of classifying costs according to their behavior for analytic purposes. However, by contrasting the activity cost hierarchy with the traditional fixed/variable cost dichotomy (see Exhibit 2–10, page 57), it is apparent that activity-based costing recognizes fewer fixed costs.

As modern manufacturing techniques have led to major reductions in inventory levels in many companies (discussed later in this chapter), the significance of the debate over absorption versus variable costing has declined. If a company has no inventories, all its costs are deducted as expenses (either as operating expenses or cost of goods sold expense) during the current period whether it uses absorption or variable costing. Hence, from an income determination standpoint, it does not matter in such cases whether fixed costs are considered a product or period cost. Despite the

---

8–1   **WHAT'S HAPPENING?**

FMI FORMS MANUFACTURERS COMBINES ABSORPTION COSTING AND VARIABLE COSTING TO GAIN A COMPETITIVE EDGE

FMI Forms Manufacturers, a medium-size, machine-intensive printer of business forms, used a traditional costing system during the 1970s and 1980s. The system was designed to compute the direct costs (primarily paper cost) of each job and apply overhead using a rate based on total direct costs. It became apparent that the total cost measurements produced by this system were not accurate. The inaccuracies were due to overhead not being driven by total direct costs but by factors related to the characteristics of the printing press used and the size of the forms being printed. Hence, the first step in customizing its cost system was for FMI to determine the actual drivers of printing costs.

The critical use of "cost" information at a printing company such as FMI is for bidding jobs. FMI takes a two-pronged approach to bidding. It uses absorption costing for submitting initial bids to make sure that the company receives prices sufficient to cover full costs on an ongoing basis. If initial bids are turned down but allowed to be resubmitted, the company uses direct costing by subtracting all variable costs from the initial bid price to get the total contribution margin reflected in the bid. This total contribution margin is divided by the number of estimated press hours to get the contribution margin per press hour, which is then compared with a minimum acceptable contribution margin per press hour. If the bid margin is above the acceptable minimum, the bid price is lowered; otherwise, it is not adjusted. According to FMI managers, with this new costing system, which combines absorption costing, variable costing, and activity-based costing, "the company is profitable and has increased business in increasingly competitive markets."

Source: Jacci L. Rodgers, S. Mark Comstock, and Karl Pritz, "Customize Your Costing System," *Management Accounting,* May 1993, pp. 134–35.

emergence of inventory management techniques that substantially reduce inventory levels, few companies have been able to *completely* eliminate inventories.

COMPARISON OF ABSORPTION AND VARIABLE COSTING WITH THEORY OF CONSTRAINTS AND ACTIVITY-BASED COSTING MODELS

In earlier chapters, we discussed and illustrated two other inventory valuation models, the theory of constraints (TOC) and full activity-based costing (ABC). These models and absorption and variable costing differ primarily with regard to the cost components included in inventory. TOC considers only the cost of direct materials to be appropriately included in inventory because this model emphasizes maximization of throughput, which is defined as revenues less direct materials costs. Full ABC includes the cost of direct materials and direct labor in inventory, as well as manufacturing overhead, selling, and administration. Full ABC emphasizes overall profitability; hence, it attempts to capture the cost of all activities that were caused by the manufacture, sale, and distribution of the inventory. As we have seen in this chapter, absorption costing, which emphasizes gross profit, and variable costing, which emphasizes contribution margin, fall between the extremes of TOC and full ABC.

Since generally accepted accounting principles require companies to include all manufacturing cost components in inventory, until fairly recently, virtually all companies used a traditional absorption costing approach for preparing external financial statements. In these systems, variable and fixed manufacturing costs are assigned to inventory either through direct assignment (for direct materials and direct labor) or through indirect allocation using a unit-level allocation base such as direct labor hours. With the rise of ABC, some companies now use a system for external reporting in which they assign only the cost of manufacturing activities to inventory. These systems are, in effect, ABC-absorption costing systems because they assign cost based on activity drivers while including all manufacturing costs in inventory. The following table compares inventory cost components using TOC, variable costing, traditional absorption costing, ABC absorption costing, and full ABC approaches:

	Theory of Constraints	Variable Costing	Traditional Absorption Costing	ABC Absorption Costing*	Full ABC†
Emphasis on	Throughput	Contribution margin	Gross profit	Gross profit	Net income

Product cost components	Direct materials	Direct materials
		Direct labor
		Variable manufacturing overhead
			Direct materials
			Direct labor
			Variable manufacturing overhead
			Fixed manufacturing overhead
				Direct materials
				Direct labor
				Manufacturing overhead:
				  Unit level
				  Batch level
				  Product level
				  Facility level
					Direct materials
					Direct labor
					Unit-level costs
					Batch-level costs
					Product-level costs
					Order-level costs
					Customer-level costs
					Market-segment-level costs
					Facility-level costs

*Assigns only manufacturing costs to inventory
†Associates manufacturing and nonmanufacturing costs with inventory

Each of these product costing models has advantages and disadvantages, and they vary depending on the purpose for which the cost valuation is being used. In practice, a firm might use several or all of these five models at different times and for different purposes. For example, a company could at the same time use TOC to evaluate management operating performance, variable costing for making certain types of relevant costing decisions, either traditional or ABC absorption costing for external financial reporting, and full ABC for evaluating product profitability.

LEARNING OBJECTIVE 4 **JUST-IN-TIME INVENTORY MANAGEMENT**

To this point in the chapter, our discussions about inventories have centered around how to measure the cost of products. A related issue is how to manage physical inventory levels. Cost accounting textbooks, as well as operations management textbooks, usually discuss models that have been used for decades to determine the economic order quantities for products given the particular level of inventory a company wants to maintain. Although these models are still relevant in many situations, managing inventory levels has changed dramatically in the last decade as more companies have adopted a value chain approach to management. No longer do most managers consider only their company's strategies, goals, and objectives in deciding the characteristics and quantities of inventory that should be acquired or produced and maintained. A value chain approach to inventory management requires that managers consider their suppliers' and customers' strategies, goals, and objectives as well if they hope to compete successfully in a global marketplace. Computer technology has affected the way inventories are manufactured and handled (using robotics, fully computerized manufacturing and product handling systems, bar code identification systems, etc.), and it is changing the way companies relate to other parties in the value chain. It has spawned worldwide use of new inventory management techniques and processes such as just-in-time (JIT) inventory management. Research Shows 8–1 considers some of the proven benefits of JIT.

Just-in-time (JIT) inventory management is a comprehensive inventory management philosophy that stresses policies, procedures, and attitudes by managers and other workers that result in the efficient production of high-quality goods while maintaining the minimum level of inventories. JIT is often described simply as an inventory model that maintains only the level of inventories required to meet current production and sales requirements, but it is, in reality, much more than that. The key elements of the JIT philosophy include increased coordination throughout the value chain, reduced inventory, reduced production times, increased product quality, and increased employee involvement and empowerment. Approaches to reducing inventories of raw materials, work in process, and finished goods are considered here.

REDUCING INCOMING MATERIALS INVENTORY
The JIT approach to reducing incoming materials includes these elements:

1. Developing long-term relationships with a limited number of vendors.
2. Selecting vendors on the basis of service and material quality, as well as price.

8–1   RESEARCH SHOWS

AN EMPIRICAL STUDY VALIDATES THE POSITIVE EFFECTS OF JIT

Data obtained from 116 plants for AT&T, Boeing, Chrysler, Ford, Hewlett-Packard, and Kodak were used to develop an empirical model to test the effects of reduced inventories (i.e., JIT) and related variables on quality and cost. The authors found positive effects on quality and cost from lowering inventories; they also found that employee training and empowerment and a flexible manufacturing environment are important factors in lowering inventories. The authors concluded from this study that employee training and empowerment, when coupled with a flexible manufacturing environment, help to lower inventories, resulting in a higher level of sophisticated effort by workers, which in turn results in improvements in process reliability, yields, quality, and costs.

Source: A. Amershi, M. Alles, S. Datar, and R. Datar, "Information and Incentive Effects of Inventory in JIT Production," (research paper presented at the annual Conference of the Management Accounting Section of the American Accounting Association, Orlando, Florida, January 1999).

3. Establishing procedures for key employees to order materials for current needs directly from approved vendors.
4. Accepting vendor deliveries directly to the shop floor or department store.

When fully implemented, these steps would minimize or eliminate many materials inventories. Sufficient materials would be on hand to meet only short-term needs, and the materials inventories in the manufacturing setting would be located on the shop floor.

To achieve this reduction, it is apparent that vendors and buyers must work as a team and that key employees must be involved in decision making. The goal of the JIT approach to purchasing is not to shift materials carrying costs to vendors. A close, long-term working relationship between purchasers and vendors should be beneficial to both. Purchasers' scheduling information is provided to vendors so that vendors also can reduce inventories and minimize costs. Vendors are therefore able to manufacture small batches frequently, rather than manufacturing large batches infrequently. What's more, vendors are more confident of future sales.

REDUCING WORK-IN-PROCESS INVENTORY

Reducing **cycle time,** the total time required to complete a process, is the key to reducing work-in-process inventories. In a manufacturing organization, cycle time is composed of the time needed for setup, processing, movement, waiting, and inspection. **Setup time** is the time required to prepare equipment to produce a specific product. **Processing time** is the time spent working on units. **Movement time** is the time units spend moving between work or inspection stations. **Waiting time** is the time units spend in temporary storage waiting to be processed, moved, or inspected. **Inspection time** is the amount of time it takes units to be inspected. Of the five elements of cycle time, only processing time adds value to the product. Efforts to reduce cycle time are appropriate for both continuous and batch production.

Devising means of reducing setup times will directly reduce the cycle time for batch production and thus reduce setup costs. Setup times can also be reduced by shifting from batch to continuous production whenever practical. Rearranging the shop floor to eliminate unnecessary movements of materials can help reduce movement time for both continuous and batch production.

Many companies have created **quality circles,** which are groups of employees involved in production who have the authority, within certain parameters, to address and resolve quality problems as they occur, without seeking management approval. Giving employees more authority and responsibility for quality, including the right to stop production whenever quality problems are noted, can reduce the need for separate inspection time.

In the case of batch production, waiting time can be reduced by better job scheduling. In the case of continuous production, waiting time can be reduced by moving from a materials push to a materials pull approach to production.

Under a traditional **materials push system,** employees work to reduce the pile of inventory building up at their work stations. Workers at each station remove materials from an in-process storage area, complete their operation, and place the output in another in-process storage area. Hence, they *push* the work to the next work station. The emphasis is on production efficiency at each station. In a push system, one of the functions of work-in-process inventory is to help make work stations independent of each other. Inventories are large enough to allow for variations in processing speeds, for discarding defective units without interrupting production, and for machine downtime.

Under a **materials pull system** (often called a **Kanban**[3] **system**), employees at each station work to replenish the inventory used by employees at subsequent stations. The

---

[3] *Kanban,* the Japanese word for *card,* is a system created in Japan that originally used cards to indicate that a department needed additional components.

building of excess inventories is strictly prohibited. When the number of units in inventory reaches a specified limit, work at the station stops until workers at a subsequent station pull a unit from the in-process storage area. Hence, the *pull* of inventory by a subsequent station authorizes production to continue. A pull, or Kanban, system's low inventory levels require a team effort. To avoid idle time, processing speeds must be balanced and equipment must be kept in good repair. Quality problems are identified immediately, and the low inventory levels require immediate correction of quality problems.

To make a pull system work, management must accept the notion that it is better to have employees idle than to have them building excess inventory. A pull system also requires careful planning by management and active participation in decision making by employees. Retail organizations also use pull systems to increase their inventory efficiency as illustrated in What's Happening 8–2.

REDUCING FINISHED GOODS INVENTORY

Finished goods inventory can be reduced by reducing cycle time and by better predicting customer demand for finished units. Lowering cycle times reduces the need for speculative inventories. If finished goods can be replenished quickly, the need diminishes for large inventory levels to satisfy customer needs and to provide for unanticipated fluctuations in customer orders. Anticipating customers' demand for goods can be improved by adopting a value chain approach to inventory management by which the manufacturer or supplier is working as a partner with its customers to meet their inventory needs. This frequently involves having on-line computer access to customers' inventory levels on a real-time basis and being able to synchronize changes in production with changes in customers' inventory levels as they occur.

Sharing this type of information obviously requires an enormous amount of mutual trust between a manufacturer or supplier and its customers, but it is becoming increasingly common among world-class organizations. Research Shows 8–2 illustrates

---

8-2   WHAT'S HAPPENING?

RETAIL COMPANY APPLIES PULL INVENTORY SYSTEM

The ability to maintain low inventory levels is more inherent in some situations than others. Marketing strategies, such as direct marketing of noncritical items (sporting goods, toys, books, vacations, etc.), more often result in inventory reductions than strategies of on site demand where customers select items in person, (typical of food goods and automobiles). Consolidated Stores Corporation, headquartered in Columbus, Ohio, has experienced success through its customer strategy implementation.

Consolidated Stores, primarily known as the parent company of Big Lots, changed its strategy during 2000 to better align its stores with its customers' needs. The focus began with an emphasis on merchandise management. Areas of merchandise mix, pricing, store allocation, and item presentation were first targeted as needing improvement.

After these efforts had begun, the next phase focused on the customer. The stockholder letter stated, "Our ultimate objective is to manage through customer *pull* rather than merchandise *push*." The execution of this objective involves purchasing managers' efforts to search for closeouts to satisfy customer needs rather than to buy closeouts based solely on price. Being one of the nation's largest buyers of closeout merchandise, the company believes that its leverage will allow the managers to be more selective in what they acquire and therefore increase customer satisfaction.

To improve the integration of this approach into the overall inventory system, the company began increasing its emphasis on supply chain management in early 2001. With the investment in the people and system to facilitate the inventory control process, management states, "It is absolutely vital that we manage the flow of this inventory to the best of our ability." The inventory pull system has therefore become a part of another company's efforts to improve its overall management of inventory.

Source: Consolidated Stores Corporation Annual Report 2000.

COORDINATION UP AND DOWN THE SUPPLY CHAIN

Supply chain management involves the integration of an organization's suppliers throughout the planning and operations activities along with a focus on customer needs. This application has not caught on more quickly because managers are reluctant to share critical information with others, and possibly lose their competitive advantage.

Supply chain management is based on the premise that organizational strategies should be designed and managed around customer needs. This includes the downstream activity of minimizing finished goods inventory and the upstream activity of timely raw materials supply. Meeting these demands begins with understanding customer needs and working backward (upstream) to keep the entire process running smoothly. Efficient supply chain management should analyze order data to identify items such as seasonal fluctuations, cyclical trends, product mix, and order volume.

Only after the distribution and production processes have been developed around market demands should materials management be analyzed for improvement. To manage a materials system that can support fast, on-time distribution networks, a company must get outside its boundaries and include suppliers in the production scheduling process. Often known as automatic replenishment programs (ARPs), the value of these materials systems is created by substituting information for inventory to reduce overall stock levels in the distribution channel. A company should evaluate each supplier's willingness to become a team player by offering cost reductions (creating increased value) tied to some type of sharing of the savings generated. Once a supplier becomes a part of the team, management should encourage the supplier's suppliers to commit to building a team throughout the entire supply chain. To make the supply chain efficient, efforts must be made to go beyond product costs to include materials quality control, product design, packaging, materials handling, and other value-added activities.

Source: Noah P. Barsky and Alexander E. Ellinger, "Unleashing the Value in the Supply Chain, *Strategic Finance*, January 2001, pp. 33–37 and Randall J. Cloud, "Supply Chain Management," *Strategic Finance*, August 2000, pp. 29–32.

these efforts with supply chain management. An example of this type of vendor-customer relationship is the relationship between Procter & Gamble, one of the world's largest consumer products companies, and its largest customer, Wal-Mart. By having access to Wal-Mart's computer inventory system, Procter & Gamble is better able to determine and fill Wal-Mart's specific needs for products, such as disposable diapers.

OTHER ASPECTS OF JIT

Although JIT focuses on procedures to reduce inventories, as a philosophy of management, it offers benefits that extend far beyond just cutting inventories. As indicated earlier, a critical element of the JIT "philosophy" is coordination with other organizations up and down the value chain. It also involves training and empowering employees to make decisions that are necessary to correct inventory production and quality problems when they occur. Giving workers a sense that they are important to the firm's success and that they are adding value to the firm is a key aspect of the philosophy. JIT is a "way of life" in many companies, and its importance in today's manufacturing environment can be seen simply by performing an Internet or Lexis-Nexis search of the term "JIT," which produces hundreds of hits.

LEARNING OBJECTIVE 5

PERFORMANCE EVALUATION AND RECORDKEEPING IN A JUST-IN-TIME ENVIRONMENT

Movement toward a JIT inventory philosophy requires changes in performance evaluation procedures and offers opportunities for significant reductions in recordkeeping costs. These changes are considered here.

PERFORMANCE EVALUATION

JIT regards inventory as something to be eliminated. Hence, in a manufacturing organization, inventories are kept as small as possible. Under the JIT ideal, inventories do not exist because vendors deliver raw materials in small batches directly to the shop floor. JIT also strives to minimize work-in-process inventory by minimizing the non-processing elements of cycle time and by having processing times as short as possible. Ideally, setup, waiting, movement, and inspection times do not exist. A new application incorporating the theory of constraints with JIT is discussed in Research Shows 8–3.

Dysfunctional Effects of Traditional Performance Measures. A potential conflict exists between the goals of JIT and those of traditional performance measures applied at the level of the department or cost center. Although JIT emphasizes overall efficiency, many traditional performance measures emphasize local (departmental) cost savings and local (departmental) efficiency. Consider the following traditional performance measures for a purchasing agent and a departmental production supervisor:

- To achieve quantity discounts and favorable prices, a purchasing agent might order excess inventory, thereby increasing subsequent storage, obsolescence, and handling costs.
- To obtain a low price, a purchasing agent might order from a supplier whose goods have not been certified as meeting quality specifications, thereby causing subsequent inspection, rework, and spoilage costs, and perhaps, dissatisfied customers further down the value chain.
- To avoid having idle employees and equipment, a supervisor might refuse to halt production to determine the cause of a quality problem, thereby increasing inspection, rework, and spoilage costs.
- To obtain low fixed costs per unit under absorption costing, a supervisor might produce in excess of current needs (preferably in long production runs), thereby causing subsequent increases in storage, obsolescence, and handling costs.

8-3   RESEARCH SHOWS

NEW JUST-IN-TIME APPLICATION IS BASED ON THEORY OF CONSTRAINTS

One of the major inventory categories of many manufacturing companies is work in process. Because work in process is within the production environment, its flow is important for the efficiency of each succeeding operation. According to the theory of constraints (TOC), every operation generally has a constraint of some kind, whether it be qualified employees, size of building, number of machines, or limited materials. The TOC has three principles for production: increased throughput, decreased operating expenses, and decreased inventory. Drum-buffer-rope (DBR) scheduling is based on TOC and recognizes that companies must deal with constraints to implement a smooth-flowing operation.

In DBR scheduling, the *drum* is the constraint being examined, and the *buffer* is a time buffer used to protect the constraint from disruption. The *rope* controls the scheduling that dictates the release of work (inventory) throughout the system. The schedule is designed to keep all activities coordinated within the constraints.

As an example, assume that machine 3 is the slowest machine in the assembly line. Work performed at Machine 2 is controlled to provide sufficient, but not surplus, work in process for Machine 3. Likewise, if Machine 4 has excess idle time waiting on Machine 3, some of its resources (labor, for example) could be moved to help Machine 3 or at least make its task easier.

By using the TOC to identify the primary constraint(s), management can apply DBR to improve the overall flow of inventory and work processes. Therefore, DBR becomes a type of JIT inventory system with the focus on work-in-process inventory.

Source: Patricia Hull, "Using Drum-Buffer-Rope Scheduling Rather Than Just-in-Time Production," *Management Accounting Quarterly*, Winter 2001, pp. 36–40.

JIT Supportive Performance Measures. In accordance with the goal of eliminating inventory and reducing cycle time to processing time, JIT supportive performance measures emphasize inventory turnover, cycle time, and **cycle efficiency** (the ratio of value-added to nonvalue-added manufacturing activities).

When applied to a specific item of raw materials or finished goods, **inventory turnover** is computed as the annual demand in units divided by the average inventory in units:

$$\text{Inventory turnover} = \frac{\text{Annual demand in units}}{\text{Average inventory in units}}$$

Progress toward the goal of reducing inventory is measured by comparing successive inventory turnover ratios. The higher the inventory turnover, the better.

When stated in dollars, inventory turnover can be used as a measure of the organization's overall success in reducing inventory. This financial measure can be derived directly from a firm's financial statements.

$$\text{Inventory turnover} = \frac{\text{Cost of goods sold}}{\text{Average inventory (in dollars)}}$$

Cycle time is a measure of the total time required to produce one unit of a product:

$$\frac{\text{Cycle}}{\text{time}} = \frac{\text{Setup}}{\text{time}} + \frac{\text{Processing}}{\text{time}} + \frac{\text{Movement}}{\text{time}} + \frac{\text{Waiting}}{\text{time}} + \frac{\text{Inspection}}{\text{time}}$$

Under ideal circumstances, cycle time would consist of only processing time, and processing time would be as low as possible. Only processing time adds value to the product; hence, the time required for all other activities should be driven toward zero. The use of flexible manufacturing systems, properly sequencing jobs, and properly placing tools will minimize setup time. If the shop floor is optimally arranged, workers pass products directly from one workstation to the next. If production is optimally scheduled, inventory will not wait in temporary storage between workstations. If raw materials are of high quality and products are manufactured so that they always conform to specifications, separate inspection activities are not needed.

Cycle efficiency is computed as the ratio of processing time to total cycle time:

$$\text{Cycle efficiency} = \frac{\text{Processing time}}{\text{Cycle time}}$$

The highest cycle efficiency possible is always sought. If all non-value-added activities are eliminated, this ratio equals one.

SIMPLIFIED RECORDKEEPING

Just-in-time inventory allows significant reductions in the number of accounting transactions required for purchasing and production activities. This can result in cost savings for bookkeeping activities and in shifting accounting resources from detailed bookkeeping to the development of more useful activity cost data.

Purchasing. In a traditional accounting system, every purchase results in the generation of several documents. Additional documents are prepared for the issuance of raw materials to the factory. These items are discussed in detail in accounting information systems textbooks, but it is useful to consider them briefly here. They include these documents:

- A *purchase requisition* completed by a computerized inventory control system or an inventory clerk who notes the need to place an order.
- A *purchase order* prepared in the purchasing department.

- A *receiving and inspection report* prepared by receiving room personnel.
- An *invoice* received from the vendor indicating the amount due.
- A *payment voucher* prepared by accounts payable authorizing the preparation of a check.
- A *check* prepared by the cashier.

Tracking inventory takes place as raw materials are issued to production. A *materials requisition* documents the transfer of inventory from the storeroom to the shop floor. In batch processing, appropriate notations are also made on *job cost sheets*.

These documents are required to ensure that purchases and issuances are authorized in accordance with company policy. Detailed documentation is especially important with high inventory levels and when purchases are made from a large number of vendors who compete on the basis of price.

JIT, on the other hand, attempts to minimize inventory levels and stresses long-term relationships with a limited number of vendors who have demonstrated their ability to provide quality raw materials on a timely basis, as well as at a competitive price. Under a JIT inventory system, a company often has standing purchase orders for specified materials from specified vendors at specified prices. Production personnel are authorized to requisition materials directly from authorized vendors, who deliver limited quantities of materials as needed directly to the shop floor. Production personnel verify receipt of the raw materials. Periodically, each vendor sends an invoice for several shipments, which the company acknowledges and pays.

Product Costing. Another advantage of JIT is that it reduces the amount of detailed bookkeeping required for financial accounting purposes. If ending inventories are nonexistent, or so small that the costs assigned to them are insignificant in comparison with the costs assigned to Cost of Goods Sold, it makes little sense to track product costs through several inventory accounts. Instead of using a traditional product cost accounting system (as illustrated in Chapter 6), firms that have implemented JIT often use a backflush approach to accounting for product costs.

Under an extreme version of **backflush costing,** all costs of direct materials, direct labor, and manufacturing overhead are assigned as incurred to Cost of Goods Sold. If there are no inventories on hand at the end of the period, no additional steps are required. However, if there are inventories on hand at year-end, costs are backed out of Cost of Goods Sold and assigned to the appropriate inventory accounts. Other versions of backflush costing use some intermediate accounts to accumulate manufacturing costs but with less detail than found in most traditional product cost accounting systems. For a complete discussion of backflush costing, refer to a cost accounting text.

Also under a JIT inventory approach, many of the distinctions and arguments regarding absorption versus variable costing are moot. If the quantity of inventory is insignificant, it matters little whether inventory cost includes only variable manufacturing costs or both variable and fixed manufacturing costs. Whether absorption or variable costing is used, the total cost assigned to inventory on the balance sheet will be small, and the income reported on the income statement is likely to be about the same amount.

Electronic Data Interchange. JIT inventory systems are frequently facilitated by **electronic data interchange (EDI),** the electronic communication of data between organizations. Using EDI, production personnel enter a materials requisition into a computer terminal and transmit the order by electronic mail to an authorized vendor. This procedure reduces the lead time required to order goods. When the vendor's EDI system is integrated in such a manner that eliminates data reentry, order-processing costs and errors are reduced. Vendor invoices can also be sent using EDI. It is even becoming quite common to pay an invoice using EDI rather than a check.

Standing purchase orders and EDI reduce the number of documents and the amount of data entry involved in purchase transactions. In a traditional system, each purchase order might require a separate materials requisition, purchase order, receiving report, invoice, payment voucher, and check, with multiple copies often required. All the documents and bookkeeping procedures associated with traditional accounting systems cause high order-processing costs. Standing orders with direct delivery to the shop floor and the electronic transmission of purchase orders, invoices, and payments significantly reduce order-processing costs.

Summary

This chapter has focused attention on two topics related to inventories: *valuation* and *management*. The first section of the chapter compared variable costing, which includes only variable manufacturing costs in inventory valuation, with traditional absorption costing, which includes all manufacturing costs (both variable and fixed) in inventory valuation. The second part of the chapter discussed the just-in-time (JIT) philosophy of inventory management.

Although absorption costing is required for external financial and income tax reporting, variable costing usually provides better information internally for management to use in evaluating the consequences of short-run decisions and in planning operations in the short term. Variable costing is superior for short-run analysis primarily because it permits the development of contribution income statements, in which costs are classified by behavior (variable and fixed), to assist management in understanding cost-volume-profit relationships. Most ABC proponents consider all product costs to be variable in the long-run; therefore, an ABC approach to inventory valuation would tend to be more consistent with absorption costing than with variable costing. Variable costing, on the other hand, is closer to the theory of constraints view of inventory that includes only direct materials costs in inventory. From an income measurement standpoint, if a company has insignificant amounts of inventories, it makes little difference whether it uses the absorption costing, variable costing, theory of constraints, or ABC approach to inventory valuation. All product costs will be expenses on the income statement, and very little cost will be capitalized as an asset on the balance sheet.

The chapter discussed the just-in-time approach to inventory management not only as a method for reducing inventories, but as a philosophy that embraces much more than procedures for limiting the scale of raw materials, work-in-process, and finished goods inventories. As a management philosophy, it emphasizes managing from a value-chain perspective and empowering employees to make decisions to ensure high-quality goods and services and to deal quickly with problems that develop at the production level. The chapter also discussed various nonfinancial performance measures that are helpful in a JIT environment.

Review Problem

The solution to the review problem is found on pages 362–363. To maximize your learning, you should make a serious attempt to develop a written solution to the review problem before looking at the solution. If there are errors in your solution, you should then attempt to determine their causes.

Variable and Absorption Costing

Colorado Ski Company completed its first year of operation on December 31, 2004. The company president says she needs financial statements for both management review and external reporting purposes. The controller informs the president that two sets of statements should be provided, one based on absorption costing and the other based on variable costing. Although concerned about the cost of preparing two reports, the president agrees to let the controller go ahead.

During the first year of operations, the company manufactured 50,000 pairs of skis and sold 40,000 pairs at a price of $40. The following additional data are also available:

Direct labor	$200,000
Direct materials	250,000
Variable manufacturing overhead	100,000
Fixed manufacturing overhead	130,000
Variable selling expenses	75,000
Fixed administrative expenses	112,000

Required:

a. Compute the costs of the inventory at the end of the year using absorption costing and variable costing.
b. Prepare income statements for 2004 using both the absorption and variable costing methods.
c. Reconcile the difference in absorption costing and variable costing net incomes in part (b).
d. Explain to the president why both sets of statements are needed.

Key Terms

Absorption costing (p. 331)
Backflush costing (p. 347)
Contribution income statement (p. 333)
Cycle efficiency (p. 346)
Cycle time (p. 342)
Direct costing (p. 331)
Electronic data interchange (EDI) (p. 347)
Full costing (p. 331)
Functional income statement (p. 333)
Inspection time (p. 342)
Inventory turnover (p. 346)

Just-in-time (JIT) inventory management (p. 341)
Kanban system (p. 342)
Materials pull system (p. 342)
Materials push system (p. 342)
Movement time (p. 342)
Processing time (p. 342)
Quality circles (p. 342)
Setup time (p. 342)
Variable costing (p. 331)
Waiting time (p. 342)

Review Questions

1. Can period costs exist under the absorption costing method? If so, give examples.
2. Explain the basic difference between absorption and variable costing.
3. What is the relationship between variable costing and a contribution income statement?
4. Explain how the differences between variable costing and absorption costing net income are reconciled.
5. What are the primary arguments favoring the use of variable costing instead of absorption costing?
6. Compare and contrast the four following inventory valuation models: absorption costing, full activity-based costing, theory of constraints, and variable costing.
7. Explain the concept of just-in-time inventory management.

8. What elements of the JIT approach contribute to reducing materials inventories?
9. Define and identify the elements of cycle time. Which of these elements adds value to the product?
10. Explain briefly how JIT benefits organizations that take a value-chain approach to management.
11. How can electronic data interchange enhance a company's implementation of JIT?
12. It can be said that companies that use JIT are not concerned with the distinctions and arguments regarding variable versus absorption costing. Explain.

Exercises

8–1
Absorption and Variable Costing Inventory Valuation

Automotive Electric Company projects the following costs for 2004.

	Per Unit
Direct materials	$6
Direct labor	8
Variable overhead	2
Fixed overhead ($40,000 for 20,000 units)	2

During May, the company produced 20,000 units but sold only 10,000. Throughout June, it produced and sold 20,000 units. During July, it produced 20,000 units and sold 24,000 units. There was no inventory on May 1.

Required:
Compute the amount of ending inventory and cost of goods sold under absorption and variable costing for each of the three months.

8–2
Absorption and Variable Costing Inventory Valuation

Cisco Systems, Inc., has a highly automated assembly line that uses very little direct labor. Therefore, direct labor is part of variable overhead. For October it incurred the following unit costs:

Direct materials	$200
Variable overhead	150
Fixed overhead	50

The 100 units of beginning inventory for October had an absorption costing value of $38,000 and a variable costing value of $32,000. For October Cisco produced 500 units and sold 540 units.

Required:
Compute the amount of ending inventory under both absorption and variable costing if the FIFO inventory method was used.

8–3
Absorption and Variable Costing Cost of Goods Sold

Use data from Exercise 8–2.

Required:
Compute the Cost of Goods Sold using both the variable and absorption costing methods.

8-4
Absorption and Variable Costing Comparisons: Production Equals Sales

Hammond Catsup Company manufactures and sells 15,000 cases of catsup each quarter. The following data are available for the third quarter of 2004.

Total fixed manufacturing overhead	$30,000
Fixed selling and administrative expenses	10,000
Sales price per case	25
Direct materials per case	12
Direct labor per case	4
Variable manufacturing overhead per case	3

Required:
a. Compute the cost per case under both absorption costing and variable costing.
b. Compute net income under both absorption costing and variable costing.
c. Reconcile any differences in income. Explain.

8-5
Absorption and Variable Costing Income Statements: Production Exceeds Sales

Franklin Company sells its product at a unit price of $11.00. Unit manufacturing costs are direct materials, $2.00; direct labor, $3.00; and variable manufacturing overhead, $1.50. Total fixed manufacturing costs are $30,000 per year. Selling and administrative expenses are $1.00 per unit variable and $10,000 per year fixed. Though 25,000 units were produced during 2001, only 20,000 units were sold. There was no beginning inventory.

Required:
a. Prepare an income statement using absorption costing.
b. Prepare an income statement using variable costing.

8-6
Absorption and Variable Costing Comparisons: Production Exceeds Sales

Daniel Derma Company produces hand lotion, which it sells in bulk to distributors who in turn bottle the product under private labels. The sales price per five-gallon container is $10. The production information for July 2004 is as follows:

Fixed selling and administrative expenses	$20,000
Fixed manufacturing overhead	66,000
Variable manufacturing overhead per container	2
Direct labor costs per hour	12
Direct materials costs per container	1

The average time for direct labor per container is 15 minutes. During July, the company produced 30,000 containers of hand lotion but sold only 28,000. There was no beginning inventory on July 1, 2004.

Required:
a. Compute the cost per container under both absorption and variable costing.
b. Compute net income under both absorption and variable costing.
c. Compute the ending inventories under both absorption and variable costing.

8-7
Absorption and Variable Costing Comparisons: Sales Exceed Production

Goldberg Development sells commercial building lots. During 2004, the company bought 1,000 acres of land for $5,000,000 and divided it into 200 sites of equal size. As the lots are sold, they are cleared at an average cost of $2,500. Storm drains and driveways are then installed at an average cost of $4,000 per site. Selling costs are 10 percent of sales price. Administrative costs are $425,000 per year. The average selling price per site was $80,000 during 2004 when 50 sites were sold.

During 2005, the company purchased and developed another 1,000 acres with all costs remaining constant. Sales totaled 300 sites in 2005 at an average price of $80,000.

Required:
Compute net income for 2004 and 2005 under both absorption costing and variable costing.

8-8
Absorption and Variable Costing Income Statements: Sales Exceed Product

Lamar Corporation was disappointed to find that increased sales volume in 2005 did not result in increased profits. Both variable unit manufacturing costs and total fixed manufacturing costs remained constant from 2004 to 2005 at $10 and $1,000,000, respectively.

In 2004, the company produced 100,000 units and sold 80,000 units at a price of $25 per unit. There was no inventory at the beginning of 2004. In 2005, the company made 70,000 units and sold 90,000 units at a price of $25 per unit. Selling and administrative expenses (all fixed) were $50,000 each year.

Required:

a. Prepare income statements for 2004 and 2005 using the absorption costing method.
b. Prepare income statement for 2004 and 2005 using the variable costing method.
c. Explain why the profit each year varied for the two methods. Show computations.

8-9
Income Statements: Conversion from Absorption to Variable Costing

Greenville Company began operation on January 1, 2004. The 2004 income statement on an absorption costing basis is as follows:

Greenville Company
Absorption Costing Income Statement
For the Year Ended December 31, 2004

Sales (15,000 units)		$450,000
Less cost of goods sold:		
Beginning inventory	$ 0	
Cost of goods manufactured (20,000 units)	280,000	
Ending inventory (5,000 units)	(70,000)	(210,000)
Gross profit		$240,000
Selling and administrative expenses		(40,000)
Net income		$200,000

All selling and administrative expenses are fixed. Manufacturing costs include the following unit costs:

Direct materials	$ 4
Direct labor	5
Variable manufacturing overhead	2
Fixed manufacturing overhead	3
Total	$14

Required:
Prepare a variable costing income statement for 2004.

8-10
Income Statements: Conversion from Variable to Absorption Costing

The variable costing income statement for Sahota Company is as follows:

Sahota Company
Variable Costing Income Statement
For the Year Ended June 30, 2004

Sales (9,000 units × $50)		$450,000
Variable expenses:		
Cost of goods sold (9,000 units × $24)	$216,000	
Selling (10% of sales)	45,000	(261,000)
Contribution margin		$189,000
Fixed expenses:		
Manufacturing overhead	$100,000	
Administrative	45,000	(145,000)
Net income		$ 44,000

Selected 2004 data concerning the operations of the company are as follows:

Beginning inventory	0 units
Units produced	10,000 units
Manufacturing costs:	
Direct materials	$9 per unit
Direct labor	$12 per unit
Variable overhead	$3 per unit

Required:
Prepare an absorption costing income statement for 2004.

8–11
Product Cost under Traditional Absorption Costing, Activity-Based Absorption Costing, Full Activity-Based Costing, Theory of Constraints, and Variable Costing

White-Westinghouse manufacturers laminates for computer memory boards. The company has developed several cost drivers for its operations. For 2004 the following costs are planned for 80,000 units of production. There are no beginning or ending inventories.

Direct materials	$ 80,000
Direct labor	20,000
Variable manufacturing overhead:	
Maintenance	12,000
Inspection	8,000
Operations	40,000
Fixed manufacturing overhead	100,000
Variable selling expenses:	
Packing	24,000
Shipping	36,000
Fixed selling expenses	60,000

Required:
Calculate the approximate cost per unit under each of the following product costing systems.

a. Theory of constraints.
b. Variable costing.
c. Traditional absorption costing.
d. Activity-based absorption costing.
e. Full activity-based costing.

8–12
Product Costs under Traditional Absorption Costing, Activity-Based Absorption Costing, Full Activity-Based Costing, Theory of Constraints, and Variable Costing

Ernst Products Inc., a supplier to the automobile manufacturing industry, produces a single product, an advanced machined drive shaft for high-performance engines. Ernst's activity-based costing system, established primarily for the benefits of managing costs, produced the following product cost data for the month of July. These cost data represent the cost per unit of finished product calculated after activity costs were assigned to products using activity cost drivers.

Direct materials	$45
Direct labor	50
Other manufacturing activity costs:	
Purchasing activity	5
Materials movement	7
Setup	6
Machine operation	15
Inspection	2
Depreciation	4
Supervision	1
Selling and distribution activity costs:	
Packaging	2

Selling and distribution activity costs:
Shipping 6
Customer service 3
Other data:
Total variable overhead $14,000,000
Total fixed overhead $2,000,000
Total direct labor hours 400,000
Production of each unit requires about one direct labor hour

Required:
Calculate the approximate cost per unit under each of the following product costing systems (when appropriate, use direct labor hours to assign manufacturing overhead to inventory):

a. Theory of constraints.
b. Variable costing.
c. Traditional absorption costing.
d. Activity-based absorption costing.
e. Full activity-based costing.

8–13
Just-in-Time
Environment and
Product Costing

Presented is information pertaining to the standard or budgeted unit cost of a product manufactured in a JIT environment at Simko Systems Inc.:

Direct materials $15
Conversion 10
Total $25

All materials are added at the start of the production process. All raw materials purchases and conversion costs are directly assigned to Cost of Goods Sold. At the end of the period, costs are backed out and assigned to Raw Materials in Process (only for materials still in the plant) and Finished Goods Inventory (for materials and conversion costs). Costs assigned to inventories are based on the standard or budgeted cost multiplied by the number of units in inventory. Conversion costs are assigned to inventories only for fully converted units. Since inventory levels tend to be small in this JIT environment, partially completed units are assigned no conversion costs.

Simko had no beginning inventories on August 1, 2004. During the month, it incurred the following manufacturing-related costs:

Purchase of raw materials on account $300,000
Factory wages 125,000
Factory supervision salaries 30,000
Utilities bill for month 17,000
Factory supplies purchased 1,500
Depreciation 9,500

The end-of-month inventory included raw materials in process of 600 units and finished goods of 400 units. One hundred units of raw materials were zero percent converted; the other 500 units averaged 60 percent converted.

Required:
a. Calculate the total cost charged to Cost of Goods Sold during August.
b. Calculate the balances in Raw Materials in Process, Finished Goods Inventory, and Cost of Goods Sold at the end of August.
c. Assuming that August is a typical month, is it likely that using the company's shortcut backflush accounting procedures will produce misleading financial statements? Explain.

8-14
Just-in-Time Inventory Management and Performance Evaluation

Olathe Metal Shop is trying to decide which automated production line to acquire for its new metal furniture process. The two best systems have the following performance characteristics on a per-minute basis:

	System A	System B
Setup time	20	10
Movement time from start to finish	10	15
Waiting time	2	16
Inspection time	5	6
Processing time	40	30
Total time in minutes	77	77

Required:
a. Determine the cycle time for each system.
b. Determine the cycle efficiency for each system.
c. Which system do you recommend and why?

Problems

8-15
Variable Costing Income Statement

For the first three quarters of 2004, Mustang Motor Company has had wide fluctuations in production and sales. Sales volume and the variable cost of production have increased with no increase in the selling price. Variable manufacturing costs per unit were as follows:

	QUARTER		
	First	Second	Third
Direct materials	$1,500	$2,000	$2,500
Direct labor	2,000	2,000	3,000
Variable manufacturing overhead	500	1,000	2,000

The motors sell for $10,000 each. The fixed manufacturing costs were $250,000,000 each quarter. The variable selling and administrative expenses were $600 for each unit sold, and the fixed selling and administrative expenses were $80,000,000 per quarter. Beginning inventory of 20,000 units at the start of the first quarter was recorded at $110,000,000, including $30,000,000 of fixed costs. The company uses the FIFO inventory method. Production and sales data are as follows:

Quarter	Produced	Sold
First	150,000	140,000
Second	160,000	150,000
Third	160,000	170,000

Required:
a. Prepare income statements for each quarter using variable costing.
b. Prepare income statements for each quarter using absorption costing.
c. Reconcile the incomes for each quarter for the two methods.

8-16
Profit Planning with Absorption and Variable Costing

Profit Control Corporation wants to ensure that its profits do not decline in proportion to sales declines. To prevent profits from decreasing, Profit Control plans to increase production above normal capacity. For 2004 and 2005, the following budget information is available:

	2004	2005
Sales volume estimate	500,000 units	400,000 units
Normal production capacity	500,000 units	500,000 units
Planned production	500,000 units	700,000 units
Fixed manufacturing overhead	$1,000,000	$1,000,000
Fixed selling and administrative expenses	$ 100,000	$100,000
Total variable manufacturing costs	$10 per unit	$10 per unit
Sales	$20 per unit	$20 per unit

Required:

a. Prepare pro forma (budget) income statements using absorption costing for 2004 and 2005. (Round computations to the nearest dollar.)
b. Prepare pro forma income statements using variable costing for 2004 and 2005.
c. Can the company actually control profits? Explain.

8-17
Absorption and Variable Costing Income Statements

The operating data for Silver Spoon Company follow.

	2004	2005	2006
Units manufactured	80,000	100,000	80,000
Units sold	70,000	90,000	100,000
Unit selling price	$10	$10	$10
Variable manufacturing costs per unit	$4	$4	$4
Fixed manufacturing cost	$200,000	$250,000	$300,000

There was no inventory on hand on January 1, 2001. The company uses the FIFO method to maintain its inventories. Variable selling expenses are $1.20 per unit, and fixed selling and administrative expenses are $60,000 per year.

Required:

a. Prepare income statements for each year using absorption costing.
b. Prepare income statements for each year using variable costing.
c. Reconcile the income differences for each year for the two methods.

8-18
Absorption Costing and Variable Costing Income Statements with All Fixed Costs

Fixed Rock Company has only fixed costs. It built its building over a pile of rocks and simply sells them when customers visit the plant.

All employees of the plant are paid a fixed annual wage. The company has no material costs and no variable overhead because the rocks came with the land and no processing is needed; the rocks are simply washed in a creek that flows through the property. Costs are estimated for 2004 and 2005 as follows:

Labor	$200,000
Depreciation	50,000
Insurance	20,000
Administration	40,000

Production capacity is 2,000 tons per year with the rocks selling for $200 per ton. Production results for the two years are as follows:

	2004	2005
Tons produced	1,600	2,000
Tons sold	1,500	2,100

Required:

Prepare income statements for each year under both absorption costing and variable costing. Which method is better? Why?

8-19
Absorption and Variable Costing Comparisons

Never Quit Shoe Company is concerned with changing to the variable costing method of inventory valuation for making internal decisions. The absorption costing income statements for January and February follow.

Never Quit Shoe Company
Absorption Costing Income Statements
For January and February 2004

	January	February
Sales (8,000 units)	$160,000	$160,000
Cost of goods sold	(99,200)	(108,800)
Gross profit	$ 60,800	$ 51,200
Selling and administrative expenses	(30,000)	(30,000)
Net income	$ 30,800	$ 21,200

Production data follow.

Production units	10,000	6,000
Variable costs per unit	$10	$10
Fixed overhead costs	$24,000	$24,000

The preceding selling and administrative expenses include variable costs of $1 per unit sold.

Required:
a. Compute the absorption cost per unit manufactured in January and February.
b. Explain why the net income for January was higher than the net income for February when the same number of units was sold in each month.
c. Prepare income statements for both months using variable costing.
d. Reconcile the absorption costing and variable costing net income figures for each month. (Start with variable costing net income.)

8-20
Absorption and Variable Costing Comparisons

Sweet Company manufactures peach jam. Because of bad weather, its peach crop was small. The following data have been gathered for the summer quarter of 2004:

Beginning inventory (cases)	0
Cases produced	10,000
Cases sold	9,600
Sales price per case	$50
Direct materials per case	$7
Direct labor per case	$6
Variable manufacturing overhead per case	$3
Total fixed manufacturing overhead	$400,000
Variable selling and administrative cost per case	$2
Fixed selling and administrative cost	$48,000

Required:
a. Prepare an income statement for the quarter using absorption costing.
b. Prepare an income statement for the quarter using variable costing.
c. What is the value of ending inventory under absorption costing?
d. What is the value of ending inventory under variable costing?
e. Explain the difference in ending inventory under absorption costing and variable costing.

8–21
Absorption and Variable Costing Compared to Activity-Based Costing and Theory of Constraints

Speedo Electronics, a new company, manufactures one product, a specialized electronic component, for a single customer. Presented here is information pertaining to September, its first month of operations:

Variable costs:

Direct materials costs	$200,000
Direct labor	80,000
Variable manufacturing overhead	7,500
Variable selling costs	20,000

Fixed costs:

Fixed manufacturing overhead	$ 21,000
Fixed selling costs	15,000

During the period, 20,000 units were completed. At the end of the period, no inventories were on hand except for 500 completed units that had not yet been delivered to the customer. Each unit sells for $25.

Required:
a. Calculate the approximate cost of a finished unit of product under each of the five inventory costing systems: theory of constraints, variable costing, traditional absorption costing, activity-based absorption costing, and full activity-based costing.
b. Calculate ending inventory, total expenses, and net income under each of the five costing systems.
c. Discuss the primary uses of each of the five inventory costing systems.

8–22
Benefits of Implementing a Just-in-Time Inventory System

Car Parts Inc. distributes replacement parts for various automobile models, competing primarily with the dealers for the major automobile manufacturers. The key to Car Parts' success is having parts in stock when independent mechanics come to one of its retail stores. The firm's controller has become concerned about the escalating costs of maintaining large inventories at each store location. At the beginning of 2004, she decided to test a modified just-in-time inventory system in the Canton, Ohio, store that significantly reduced the number of parts for each inventory item stocked. After one year of experience with the JIT system, the controller assessed the benefits of using JIT and gathered the following data for the Canton store:

• Average inventory declined from $800,000 to $200,000.
• Annual insurance costs declined from $60,000 to $15,000.
• As a result of reduced inventory levels, a 5,000-square-foot warehouse that had been leased for $10,000 per year to store parts was not used at all during the year. Car Parts was able to sublet the space for the year for $2.50 per square foot.
• The employee who staffed the parts warehouse was reassigned to help coordinate the JIT inventory system. His $30,000 salary was charged to the fixed portion of indirect manufacturing costs.
• With the reduction in inventory levels, increases in overnight shipping costs were required to meet customer demands on a timely basis. The estimated overnight shipping premium paid was $5 per part on a total of 5,000 parts. It was also estimated that sales of 3,000 parts were lost due to stockouts.
• In the past, Car Parts store in Canton has had an annual expense of about $30,000 for obsolete inventories. With the implementation of JIT, the current year's expense was only $5,000.
• Car Parts has a cost of capital rate of 15 percent for investments in inventory.

Before deciding to implement the JIT inventory system, the budgeted income statement for the Canton, Ohio, store for 2004 had been projected as follows:

Sales (300,000 parts)		$6,600,000
Cost of goods sold:		
Variable manufacturing costs	$2,850,000	
Fixed manufacturing costs	1,200,000	(4,050,000)
Gross profit		$2,550,000
Selling and administrative expenses:		
Variable	$ 750,000	
Fixed	550,000	(1,300,000)
Operating income		$1,250,000
Interest expense		(160,000)
Income before taxes		$1,090,000

Required:

a. Calculate the savings (loss) before taxes for Car Parts' Canton, Ohio, store related to implementing the JIT inventory system.

b. What factors other than financial considerations should Car Parts consider before deciding whether to implement the JIT inventory system throughout its entire retail organization?

8–23
Just-in-Time
Performance
Evaluation

To control operations, Justa Company makes extensive and exclusive use of financial performance reports for each department. Although all departments have been reporting favorable cost variances in most periods, management is perplexed by the firm's low overall return on investment. You have been asked to look into the matter.

Believing the purchasing department is typical of Justa's operations, you obtained the following information concerning the purchases of parts for a product Justa started producing in 2004:

Year	Purchase Price Variance	Quantity Used (units)	Average Inventory (units)
2004	$ 1,000 F	20,000	4,000
2005	10,000 F	30,000	7,500
2006	12,000 F	30,000	10,000
2007	20,000 U	25,000	6,250
2008	8,000 F	27,000	9,000
2009	9,500 F	29,000	11,600

Required:

a. Compute the inventory turnover for each year. What conclusions can be drawn from a yearly comparison of the purchase price variance and the inventory turnover?

b. Identify problems likely to be caused by evaluating purchasing only on the basis of the purchase price variance.

c. Offer whatever recommendations you believe appropriate.

Discussion Questions and Cases

8–24
Materials Push
and Materials
Pull Systems

Media Storage Inc. produces three models of hard disk drives for personal computers. Each model is produced on a separate assembly line. Production consists of several operations in separate work centers. Because of a high demand for Media's products, management is most interested in high-production volume and operating efficiency. Each work center is evaluated on the basis of its operating efficiency. To avoid idle time caused by defective units, variations in machine times, and machine breakdowns, significant inventories are maintained between each workstation.

At a recent administrative committee meeting, the director of research announced that the firm's engineers have made a dramatic breakthrough in designing a low-cost, read/write optical storage device. Media Storage's president is very enthusiastic, and the vice president of marketing wishes to add an assembly line for optical storage devices as soon as possible. The equipment necessary to manufacture the new product can be purchased and installed in less than 60 days. Unfortunately, all available plant space is currently devoted to the production of hard disk drives, and expansion is not possible at the current plant location. It appears that adding the new product will require dropping a current product, relocating the entire operation, or manufacturing the optical storage devices at a separate location.

The vice president of marketing is opposed to dropping a current product. The vice president of finance is opposed to relocating the entire operation because of financing requirements and the associated financial risks. The vice president of production is opposed to splitting up production activities because of the loss of control and the added costs for various types of overhead.

Required:

Explain how switching to a materials pull (Kanban) system can help solve Media Storage's space problems while improving quality and cycle time. In your answer, be sure to describe how a materials pull system works and the changes required in management's attitude toward inventory and efficiency to make it work.

8-25
Product Costing Using Activity-Based Costing and Just-in-Time: A Value Chain Approach

Wearwell Carpet Company is a small residential carpet manufacturer started by Don Stegall, a longtime engineer and manager in the carpet industry. Stegall began Wearwell in the early 1990s after learning about ABC, JIT, total quality management, and several other manufacturing concepts being used successfully in Japan and other parts of the world. Although it was a small company, he believed that with his many years of experience and by applying these advanced techniques, Wearwell could very quickly become a world-class competitor.

Stegall buys dyed carpet yarns for Wearwell from three different major yarn manufacturers with which he has done business for many years. He chose these companies because of their reputation for producing high-quality products and their state-of-the art research and development departments. He has arranged for two carpet manufacturing companies to produce (tuft) all of his carpets on a contractual basis. Both companies have their own brands, but they also do contract work for other companies. For each manufacturer, Stegall had to agree to use the full output of one manufacturing production line at least one day per month. Each production line was dedicated to producing only one style of carpet, but each manufacturer had production lines capable of running each type of carpet that Wearwell sold.

Stegall signed a contract with a large transport company (CTC), which specializes in carpet-related shipping, to pick up and deliver yarn from the yarn plants to the tufting mills. This company will then deliver the finished product from the tufting mills to Wearwell's ten customers, which are carpet retailers in the ten largest residential building markets in the country. These retailers pay the shipping charges to have the carpets delivered to them. Wearwell maintains a small sales staff (which also doubles as a customer service staff) to deal with the retailers and occasionally with the end customers on quality problems that arise.

Wearwell started selling only one line of carpet, a medium-grade plush, but as new carpet styles were developed, it added two additional lines, a medium-grade berber carpet and a medium-grade textured carpet. Three colors are offered in each carpet style. By selling only medium grades with limited color choices, Stegall felt that he would reach a very large segment of the carpet market without having to deal with a large number of different products. As textured (trackless) carpets have become more popular, sales of plush have diminished substantially.

Required:

a. Describe the value chain for Wearwell Carpet Company, and identify the parties who compose this value chain.

b. Identify and discuss the cost categories that would be included in the cost of the product for financial reporting purposes.

c. Identify and discuss the cost categories that would be included in the cost of the product for pricing and other management purposes.

d. Discuss some of the challenges that Stegall will have trying to apply JIT to regulate the levels of control at Wearwell. Suggest changes that might be necessary to make JIT work.

e. Does Wearwell seem to be an appropriate setting for implementing ABC? If so, what are likely to be the most important activities and related cost drivers?

8–26
Just-in-Time
Performance
Evaluation

The vice president of manufacturing is perplexed. When the new southside plant began operations, it appeared to live up to the expectations of top management. The plant was modern, well lighted, and spacious. Cost variances were favorable, customers were highly satisfied with quality and service, and the plant reported large segment contributions to common costs and profits despite high start-up costs and early period depreciation.

Just three years later, the southside plant seems to be declining into crisis management. Although most cost variances, especially those dealing with cost center efficiency, remain favorable, the plant's segment contribution is declining, and customers are complaining about poor quality and slow delivery. Several customers have suggested that if the firm cannot correct its quality and delivery problems, they will take their business elsewhere. The shop floor is a mess with work-in-process inventory piled everywhere. Production employees complain of difficulty in locating jobs to be worked on, and scheduling personnel have recently requested a larger computer to help track work in process.

The vice president said she does not know where to begin to determine how to solve the plant's problems. She commented, "What is really weird is that we all work so hard. Our facilities are the best in the business, and I know our employees are dedicated, well trained, and hard working. They do exactly what we ask, and we have never had any labor problems. It just seems like the harder we work, the worse our problems become."

Required:

Suggest the nature of the southside plant's problems and recommend how the vice president might begin to determine how to solve the plant's problems.

John Shank Case Recommendation

Booker Jones

With the primary theme of teaching absorption versus direct cost, it has a secondary theme of general business policy with financial reporting as the starting point. It includes the topics of matching, cash flow, borrowing needs, project expansion, and management's role in the entire process of decision making as related to accounting and finance.

Baldwin Bicycle
Company

This case combines financial, marketing, and strategic considerations for a small manufacturing company. It stresses, or at least implies that the students should stress, what is relevant for the decision-making process facing the company. It is a somewhat challenging case, and since it is rather short, it is excellent for in-class group discussion.

Graham, Inc.   This case is also related to absorption versus direct costing. Graham, Inc., illustrates the shock when profits decline while sales are increasing. The basic question is simply "What happened?" It is a short case but with an extensive appendix on GAAP and absorption costing. Because of its short length, it is a very good exercise in the logic of using product costing systems for profit determination.

Solution to Review Problem

a.

	COST PER UNIT	
	Absorption Costing	**Variable Costing**
Direct labor ($200,000 ÷ 50,000)	$ 4.00	$ 4.00
Direct materials ($250,000 ÷ 50,000)	5.00	5.00
Variable manufacturing overhead ($100,000 ÷ 50,000)	2.00	2.00
Fixed manufacturing overhead ($130,000 ÷ 50,000)	2.60	—
Total unit costs	$13.60	$11.00
Ending inventory (units)	10,000	10,000
Unit cost	× $13.60	× $11.00
Ending inventory value	$136,000.00	$110,000.00

b.

Colorado Ski Company
Absorption Costing Income Statement
For the Year Ended December 31, 2004

Sales (40,000 units × $40)		$1,600,000
Cost of goods sold (40,000 units × $13.60)		(544,000)
Gross profit		$1,056,000
Selling and administrative expenses:		
Selling expenses	$ 75,000	
Administrative expenses	112,000	(187,000)
Net income		$ 869,000

Colorado Ski Company
Variable Costing Income Statement
For the Year Ended December 31, 2004

Sales (40,000 units × $40)		$1,600,000
Variable expenses:		
Cost of goods sold (40,000 units × $11.00)	$440,000	
Variable selling expenses	75,000	(515,000)
Contribution margin		$1,085,000
Fixed expenses:		
Manufacturing overhead	$130,000	
Administrative expenses	112,000	(242,000)
Net income		$ 843,000

c. Absorption costing net income .... $ 869,000
   Change in inventories fixed costs:
      Fixed overhead in beginning inventory units .... $ 0
      Less fixed overhead in ending inventory
        (10,000 units × $2.60) .... (26,000)

   Increase (decrease) in inventoried cost .... (26,000)
   Variable costing net income .... $ 843,000

   Variable costing net income .... $ 843,000
   Change in inventoried fixed costs:
   Fixed overhead in ending inventory units
      (10,000 units × $2.60) $26,000
      Less fixed overhead in beginning inventory .... (0)

   Increase (decrease) in inventoried cost 26,000
   Absorption costing net income .... $ 869,000

d. Generally accepted accounting principles require that absorption costing financial statements be used for external reporting. This includes all reports to creditors, stockholders, and governments. Absorption costing financial statements treat all manufacturing costs (fixed and variable) as product costs and assign them to the products produced, the premise being that all products should bear their share of all manufacturing costs. Although many companies use these statements for internal reporting, the analysis of operating results is quite limited because the various cost elements are not separated by fixed and variable behavior.

    For variable costing financial statements, the analysis of cost behavior is required, which in itself provides an additional component in the overall analysis of the operating results. The fixed manufacturing costs are treated as period costs but are not assigned to inventories. Therefore, variable costing provides a decision base for cost-volume-profit analysis, which includes a contribution margin (sales less variable costs) that permits an evaluation of costs that are directly related to the revenues.

STRATEGIC MANAGEMENT OF PRICE, COST, AND QUALITY

After completing this chapter, you should be able to:

LEARNING OBJECTIVE 1 Distinguish between economic and cost-based approaches to pricing.

LEARNING OBJECTIVE 2 Describe target costing and explain why it is gaining widespread acceptance in highly competitive industries.

LEARNING OBJECTIVE 3 Explain the relationship between target costing and continuous improvement costing.

LEARNING OBJECTIVE 4 Distinguish among the four basic types of quality costs and describe how quality cost information can assist in a program of quality management.

LEARNING OBJECTIVE 5 Explain how benchmarking can assist in achieving quality management, continuous improvement, and process reengineering.

TARGET COSTING, CONTINUOUS IMPROVEMENT, AND THE LOW-POLLUTION, FUEL-EFFICIENT CAR

In the late 1990s and early 2000s, strong competition emerged among Japanese, U.S., and European automakers to develop the next generation of cars—the "green cars" that cut pollution and boost fuel economy. The technological, production, and marketing challenges, however, proved significant. Competing technologies included hydrogen fuel cells and hybrid-powered formats. Honda and Toyota favored hybrid car technology that combines gasoline and electric power. Ford, General Motors, and DaimlerChrysler opted to skip the interim hybrid technology and push forward with hydrogen fuel cells that combine hydrogen and oxygen to make electricity and water. Despite competing technological approaches, all of these firms shared an important strategic management issue—convincing customers to buy a green car. To achieve this objective, the firms must price these cars competitively and create reasonable alternatives for potential customers who might be very satisfied with a regular car.

To succeed in this emerging market, these automakers relied on several important management accounting concepts, such as target costing and continuous improvement (Kaizen) costing, to achieve a competitive price that is also profitable. With these tools, managers determine the price that will yield the desired sales level and then set the product cost that will make the product profitable at the target selling price. By constantly improving the design, specifications, or production processes relating to a product, managers expect to lower the cost of an item until it reaches its target cost.

Two hybrid cars made their debut in 1999 and 2000. The Honda Insight and Toyota Prius both had initial price tags of around $20,000 and initial yearly target sales between 4,000 and 12,000 units. During years of development, Toyota relied on continuous improvement to achieve the cost savings necessary to make the Prius profitable. The firm established this price to be competitive with its popular Corolla model.

In hydrogen fuel cell technology, developers observed that during the 1980s, a fuel cell vehicle cost about $20 million and was the size of a bus. In the late 1990s, fuel cell technology could fit in a Ford Taurus for a vehicle cost of $200,000. Like the other manufacturers, the goal was a $20,000 hydrogen fuel cell vehicle sometime between 2004 and 2010. Everyone associated with these projects continuously relies on increased fuel cell performance, reductions in size, and changes in materials to lower the overall cost of this power source. In late 2001, Ford and DaimlerChrysler transferred their hydrogen fuel cell research and development to Ballard Power Systems of Canada—a world leader in hydrogen fuel cell technology. In return, both Ford and DaimlerChrysler received substantial ownership stakes in Ballard. Ballard's mandate from the major automakers is clear: Develop a fuel cell automobile propulsion system that has the right size, weight, range, and cost attributes to become commercially successful.

Within this emerging market for green cars as well as other emerging and existing markets, strategic cost management techniques such as target costing and continuous improvement or Kaizen costing represent important concepts for management professionals involved in the development, manufacture, and marketing of products and services in modern globally competitive markets.

Source: Based on Jeffrey Ball, "Ballard Power Expands Fuel-Cell Drive as Ford, DaimlerChrysler Boost Stakes, *The Wall Street Journal (Interactive Edition),* October 3, 2001; Terril Ye Jones, "Whose Car Is Greener?" *Forbes,* October 18, 1999, p. 60; Keith Naughton, "Can You Have Green Cars Without Red Ink?" *Business Week,* December 29, 1997, p. 50; Keith Naughton, "Detroit's Impossible Dream," *Business Week,* March 2, 1998, pp. 66 & 68; Emily Thornton, Keith Naughton, and David Woodruff, "Toyota's Green Machine," *Business Week,* December 15, 1997, pp. 108-110; David Woodruff and William C. Symonds, "The Hottest Thing in 'Green' Wheels," *Business Week,* April 28, 1997, p. 42.

Strategic cost management techniques, such as *target costing* and *continuous improvement costing,* represent important concepts for management professionals involved in the development, manufacture, and marketing of products and services in modern, globally competitive markets. **The purpose of this chapter is to examine approaches to pricing, the interrelationship between price and cost, and the role of quality costs and benchmarking in meeting customer needs at the lowest possible price.** We begin by investigating the theoretical pricing model presented by economists to explain price equilibrium. After mentioning the limitations of this long-run equilibrium model for actually determining the price of a product or service, we consider the widely used cost-plus approach to identifying initial prices. Then we examine how intense competition (such as that for the forthcoming green car market) has inverted the cost-plus pricing model into one that starts with an acceptable market price and subtracts a desired profit to determine a target cost. We also consider *life cycle costs* and *quality costs* from the perspectives of both the seller, who increasingly plans for all costs before production begins, and the buyer, who regards subsequent operating, maintenance, repair, and disposal costs as important as the purchase price. This leads to efforts to improve quality and minimize quality costs and considerations of quality certification requirements often imposed on vendors. Finally, we consider how *benchmarking* can assist in improving competitiveness and profitability.

THE PRICING DECISION

Pricing products and services is one of the most important and complex decisions facing management. Pricing decisions directly affect the salability of individual products or services, as well as the profitability, and even the survival, of the organization. Many economists have spent their entire careers examining the theoretical foundations of pricing. To respond to the needs of pricing hundreds or thousands of individual items, managers have developed pricing guidelines that are typically based on costs. More recently, global competition has turned cost-based approaches upside down. Managers of world-class organizations increasingly start with a price that customers are willing to pay and then determine allowable costs.

ECONOMIC APPROACHES TO PRICING

In economic models, the firm has a profit-maximizing goal and known cost and revenue functions. Typically, increases in sales quantity require reductions in selling prices, causing **marginal revenue** (the varying increment in total revenue derived from the sale of an additional unit) to decline as sales increase. Increases in production cause an increase in **marginal cost** (the varying increment in total cost required to produce and sell an additional unit of product). In economic models, profits are maximized at the sales volume at which marginal revenues equal marginal costs. Firms continue to produce as long as the marginal revenue derived from the sale of each additional unit exceeds the marginal cost of producing that unit.

Economic models provide a useful framework for considering pricing decisions. The ideal price is the one that will lead customers to purchase all units a firm can provide up to the point at which the last unit has a marginal cost exactly equal to its marginal revenue.

Despite their conceptual merit, economic models are seldom used for day-to-day pricing decisions. Perfect information and an indefinite time period are required to achieve equilibrium prices at which marginal revenues equal marginal costs. In the short run, most for-profit organizations attempt to achieve a target profit rather than a maximum profit. One reason for this is an inability to determine the single set of actions that will lead to profit maximization. Furthermore, managers are more apt to strive to satisfy a number of goals (such as profits for investors, job security for themselves and their employees, and being a "good" corporate citizen) than to strive for the maximization of a single profit goal. In any case, to maximize profits, a company's management would have to know the cost and revenue functions of every product the firm sells. For most firms, this information cannot be developed at a reasonable cost.

COST-BASED APPROACHES TO PRICING

Although cost is not the only consideration in pricing, it has traditionally been the most important for several reasons.

- *Cost data are available.* When hundreds or thousands of different prices must be set in a short time, cost could be the only feasible basis for product pricing.
- *Cost-based prices are defensible.* Managers threatened by legal action or public scrutiny feel secure using cost-based prices. They can argue that prices are set in a manner that provides a "fair" profit.
- *Revenues must exceed costs if the firm is to remain in business.* In the long run, the selling price must exceed the full cost of each unit.

EXHIBIT 9-1

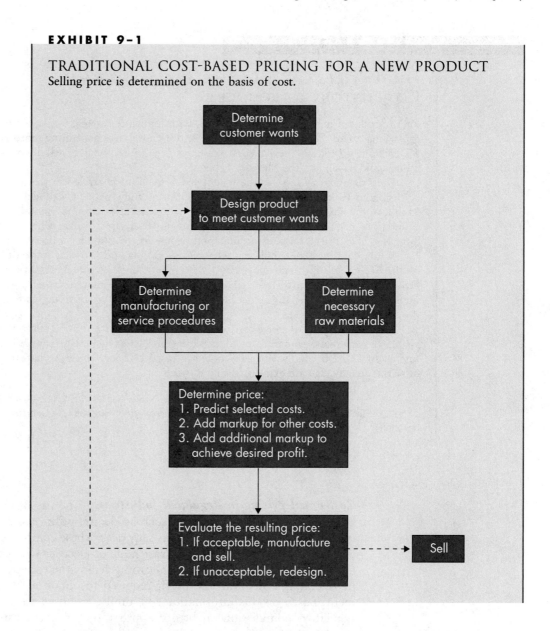

TRADITIONAL COST-BASED PRICING FOR A NEW PRODUCT
Selling price is determined on the basis of cost.

Determine
customer wants

Design product
to meet customer wants

Determine
manufacturing or
service procedures

Determine
necessary
raw materials

Determine price:
1. Predict selected costs.
2. Add markup for other costs.
3. Add additional markup to
   achieve desired profit.

Evaluate the resulting price:
1. If acceptable, manufacture
   and sell.
2. If unacceptable, redesign.

Sell

The general approach to cost-based pricing is illustrated in Exhibit 9–1. The process begins with market research to determine customer wants. If the product requires components to be designed and produced by vendors, the process of obtaining prices may be time consuming. When some costs, such as those at the facility level, are not assigned to specific products, a markup is added to cover these costs. An additional markup is added to achieve a desired profit. The selling price is then set as the sum of the assigned costs, the markup to cover unassigned costs, and the markup to achieve the desired profit.

The proposed selling price should be evaluated with regard to competitive information and what customers are willing to pay. If the price is acceptable, the product or service is produced. If the price is too high, the product might be redesigned, manufacturing procedures might be changed, and different types of materials might be considered until either an acceptable price is achieved or it is determined that the product cannot be produced at an acceptable price. As shown in What's Happening 9–1, managers who ignore customer and competitor reactions to proposed prices do so at their peril.

HIGH PRICES CAUSE CUSTOMERS TO BALK AND COMPETITORS TO POUNCE

First introduced in 1986, the Ford Taurus, with innovative styling and a competitive price, became the top-selling car in the United States. By 1994, the Taurus was generating more than 10 percent of Ford's $73 billion in U.S. auto revenue. Around this time, Ford spent $2.8 billion on the reinvention of the Taurus and its sibling, the Mercury Sable.

Unfortunately, as soon as the redesigned 1996 Taurus arrived in the showroom, sales plummeted as customers balked at the price, up to $24,850 for a fully loaded LX model. "When I think of $20,000, I think of the next level of cars," said a marketing executive who had paid $13,000 for a 1991 Taurus. "I didn't want to pay the higher price," commented a retired teacher who opted for a discounted older Taurus. "They priced this car too high and people are resisting it," observed a former Ford dealer.

While Ford was contemplating what to do, Honda and Chrysler started offering special incentives on the Accord and Plymouth Voyager. "Every manufacturer is attacking our car," said Ross H. Roberts, general manager of Ford Motor's Ford Division. While he placed the cause of soft Taurus sales on a number of factors other than price, Roberts commented, "We're trying to figure out how to keep our dealers competitive."

Ford undertook a major effort to reduce the costs of the 1997 Taurus in ways that would be invisible to customers. Hundreds of ideas were considered, including redesigning the door-hinge pins (a savings of $2). The total savings amounted to just $180 per vehicle, demonstrating that cost reductions after the design stage are extraordinarily difficult.

Source: "Prices Like These Can't Last," *Business Week,* November 20, 1995, pp. 46–47; Bill Nixon and John Innes, "Management Accounting for Design," *Management Accounting: Magazine for Chartered Management Accountants,* September 1997, p. 40.

Cost-Based Pricing in Regulated Industries. The use of cost-based pricing is most apparent in regulated industries such as electric utilities and cable television. In these industries, regulatory commissions set prices. These companies apply to the regulatory commission for a price per kilowatt hour of electricity or per customer for monthly cable service. The company's application details the expected demand for its service, its operating costs, and the profit required to obtain a reasonable return on investment. Based on this information, the utility proposes a rate per unit of service. The regulatory commission might not approve the proposed rate, but the starting point for negotiation is a cost-based price.

Since the 1980s, there has been a movement toward deregulation of the U.S. transportation and communications industries. This movement is now spreading to electric utilities. The deregulation of the airline industry in the United States presented significant opportunities for superefficient airlines, such as Southwest, to profitably compete with low fares. Deregulation also presented problems for less efficient carriers, such as Eastern Airlines, which went out of business.

Cost-Based Pricing for Government Contracts. Defense contractors widely use cost-based pricing. In this case, unique and expensive products are designed and manufactured to government specifications. Because the final cost cannot be known in advance, the government typically enters into a contract that calls for the vendor to be reimbursed for costs incurred in connection with the contract and to receive a profit as specified in the terms of the contract. Obvious problems are how to determine what costs should be assigned to the contract and how to ensure that only allowed costs are assigned. To solve the first problem, the U.S. government established the Cost Accounting Standards Board and gave it the task of specifying what costs are allowable and how those costs should be assigned to government contracts. To solve the second problem, organizations such as the Defense Contract Audit Agency were established to ensure that the costing guidelines are followed on government contracts.

Cost-Based Approaches to Determine Tax Rates. Elected officials set property taxes in most cities, counties, and school districts on the basis of cost. The starting point is typically a proposed budget for the coming year and information on the total assessed valuation on all taxable property in the jurisdiction. The price, a rate per unit of assessed valuation, is determined by dividing the amount of the proposed budget that must be obtained from property taxes by the total taxable assessed valuation. The amount a particular property owner must pay is computed as the assessed valuation of his or her property multiplied by the rate per unit of assessed valuation. Again, although the elected officials (or voters) might decide that the proposed tax rate is so high that the budget needs to be revised, the starting point is based on costs.

Cost-Based Pricing in Single-Product Companies. Implementing cost-based pricing in a single-product company is straightforward if everything is known but the selling price. In this case, all known data are entered into the profit formula, which is then solved for the variable price.

Assume that Bright Rug Cleaners' annual facility-level costs are $200,000 and the unit cost of cleaning a rug is $10. Management desires to achieve an annual profit of $30,000 at an annual volume of 10,000 rugs. To simplify the example, assume that management charges the same price regardless of the type, size, or shape of the rug. Using the profit formula, the cost-based price is determined to be $33:

$$\text{Profit} = \text{Total revenues} - \text{Total costs}$$
$$\$30,000 = (\text{Price} \times 10,000 \text{ rugs}) - (\$200,000 + [\$10 \times 10,000 \text{ rugs}])$$

Solving for the price:

$$(\text{Price} \times 10,000) = \$300,000 + \$30,000$$
$$\text{Price} = \$330,000 \div 10,000$$
$$= \$33$$

A price of $33 to clean a rug will allow Bright to achieve its desired profit. However, before setting the price at $33, management should also evaluate the competitive situation and consider what customers are willing to pay for this service.

Cost-Based Pricing in Multiple-Product Companies. In multiple-product companies, desired profits are determined for the entire company, and standard procedures are established for determining the initial selling price of each product. These procedures typically specify the initial selling price as the costs assigned to products or services plus a markup to cover unassigned costs and provide for the desired profit. Depending on the sophistication of the organization's accounting system, possible cost bases in a manufacturing organization include markups based on (1) a *combination of cost behavior and function* and (2) *activity hierarchy*.

For markups based on behavior and function, the possible cost bases include these:

- Direct materials costs.
- Variable manufacturing costs.
- Total variable costs (manufacturing, selling, and administrative).
- Full manufacturing costs.

For markups based on activity hierarchy, the possible cost bases include the following:

- Unit-level costs.
- Unit- and batch-level costs.
- Unit-, batch-, and product-level costs.

Regardless of the cost base, the general approach to developing a markup is to recognize that the markup must be large enough to provide for costs not included in the base plus the desired profit.

$$\text{Markup on cost base} = \frac{\text{Costs not included in the base + Desired profit}}{\text{Costs included in the base}}$$

First we illustrate a pricing decision with variable costs as the cost base; full manufacturing costs is the cost base in the second illustration.

1. When the markup is based on variable costs, it must be large enough to cover all fixed costs and the desired profit. Assume that the predicted 2005 variable and fixed costs for Magnum Enterprises are as follows:

Variable		**Fixed**	
Manufacturing	$600,000	Manufacturing	$300,000
Selling and		Selling and	
administrative	200,000	administrative	100,000
Total	$800,000	Total	$400,000

Furthermore, assume that Magnum Enterprises has total assets of $1,250,000; management believes that an annual return of 16 percent on total assets is appropriate in Magnum's industry. A 16 percent return translates into a desired annual profit of $200,000 ($1,250,000 × 0.16). Assuming all cost predictions are correct, obtaining a profit of $200,000 requires a 75 percent markup on variable costs:

$$\text{Markup on variable costs} = \frac{\$400,000 + \$200,000}{\$800,000}$$
$$= 0.75$$

If the predicted variable costs for Product A1 are $12 per unit, the initial selling price for Product A1 is $21:

$$\text{Initial selling price} = \$12 + (\$12 \times 0.75)$$
$$= \$21$$

2. When the markup is based on full manufacturing costs, it must be large enough to cover selling and administrative expenses and to provide for the desired profit. Again, it is necessary to determine the desired profit and predict all costs for the pricing period. The initial prices of individual products are then determined as their unit manufacturing costs plus the markup. For Magnum, the markup on manufacturing costs would be 55.6 percent:

$$\text{Markup on manufacturing costs} = \frac{\$300,000 + \$200,000}{\$900,000}$$
$$= 0.556$$

If the predicted manufacturing costs for Product B1 were $10, the initial selling price for Product B1 is $15.56:

$$\text{Initial selling price} = \$10 + (\$10 \times 0.556)$$
$$= \$15.56$$

Cost-Based Pricing for Special Orders. The previous approaches to cost-based pricing focused on organizations providing standard products or services. Many organizations use cost-based pricing to bid on unique projects. If the project requires dedicated assets, the acquisition of new fixed assets, or an investment in employee training, the desired profit on the special order or project should allow for an adequate return on the dedicated assets or additional investment.

A Critique of Cost-Based Pricing.   Cost-based pricing has four major drawbacks:

1. Cost-based pricing requires accurate cost assignments. If costs are not accurately assigned, some products could be priced too high, losing market share to competitors; other products could be priced too low, gaining market share but being less profitable than anticipated.
2. The higher the portion of unassigned costs, the greater is the likelihood of over- or under-pricing individual products.
3. Cost-based pricing assumes that goods or services are relatively scarce and, generally, customers who want a product or service are willing to pay the price.
4. In a competitive environment, cost-based approaches increase the time and cost of bringing new products to market.

Cost-based pricing became the dominant approach to pricing during an era when products were relatively long-lived and there was relatively little competition. Also, these systems, known as **organization-based cost systems**, tend to focus on organizational units such as departments, plants, or divisions and not on activities or cost drivers. While easy to implement, reflecting the need to recover costs and earn a return on investment, and easily justified, cost-based prices might not be competitive. Today's worldwide competition puts intense downward pressure on prices and removes slack from pricing formulas. There is little margin for error in pricing. In a highly competitive market, small variations in pricing make significant differences in success.

ETHICAL AND LEGAL CONSIDERATIONS IN PRICING

In response to intense pressure to achieve an adequate return on investment, managers of competing businesses might be tempted to work together for their mutual benefit. Highway contractors might be tempted to share available business and earn more profits by rigging bids. In an attempt to lessen competition and maintain prices, large automobile manufacturers appeal to the government, protesting that foreign competitors are selling below cost. Large retail organizations pressure manufacturers to give them price concessions not available to other merchants. A major manufacturer that buys more than half of a vendor's product refuses to accept a price increase. A valued customer, experiencing financial problems, requests price reductions and payment terms not available to others. In these circumstances, managers frequently face the problem of trying to determine what is ethical. They must also be aware of laws prohibiting price discrimination and price fixing.

Price discrimination involves illegally charging different purchasers different prices. The **Robinson–Patman Act** prohibits price discrimination when purchasers compete with one another in the sale of their products or services to third parties except in the following instances:

1. The discriminatory lower price is in response to changing conditions in the market for, or marketability of, the commodities involved (such as the sale of discontinued products).
2. The discriminatory lower price is made to meet the equally low price of a competitor.
3. The discriminatory lower price makes due allowance for only specific cost differences such as those resulting from long production runs and bulk shipments.

Efficient, large-volume retailers, such as Wal-Mart, evoke the resentment of smaller merchants because the retailers often sell products for less than the smaller merchants cost of the same products. Although some of the lower prices might be "loss leaders" intended to attract customers, most of the lower prices at large-volume retailers reflect lower operating costs per dollar of sales revenue and lower costs for merchandise. Wholesalers and manufacturers charge Wal-Mart less than they charge smaller independent stores. These lower prices are justified under the Robinson–Patman Act as a result from bulk shipments and reduced order processing costs.

Price fixing, the organized setting of prices by competitors, is prohibited by the **Sherman Antitrust Act.** The goal of price fixing is to reduce competition on the basis of price. The argument in favor of price fixing is that it forces companies to compete on the basis of factors other than price while ensuring that companies remain financially viable. In recent years, the U.S. Justice Department has vigorously enforced regulations against price fixing. The goal of the Justice Department is to enhance competition and lower prices.

For many years, an agency of the U.S. government set airfares. This was done in a belief that a financially viable airline industry was in the nation's best interest and that, without the protection of set prices, financial concerns would reduce airline safety. The airline industry has since been deregulated, and the dramatic reduction in airfares led to a significant increase in air travel. Although the Federal Aviation Administration maintains that increased competition has not affected airline safety, it has led several airlines that were previously protected from competitive pressures into financial difficulty while providing unique growth opportunities for efficient, low-fare operations such as Southwest Airlines. Following the deregulation of the airline industry, the Justice Department charged American, Delta, Continental, Northwest, TWA, and Alaska Airlines with signaling proposed airfares to each other and informally agreeing to set airfares by way of computer systems maintained by the Airline Tariff Publishing Company.

LEARNING OBJECTIVE 2

TARGET COSTING

Peter Drucker has identified cost-based (he calls it "cost-driven") pricing as a "deadly business sin." According to Drucker,

> Most American and practically all European companies arrive at their prices by adding up costs and then putting a profit margin on top. And then, as soon as they have introduced the product, they have to start cutting the price, have to redesign the product at enormous expense, have to take losses—and often have to drop a perfectly good product because it is priced incorrectly."[1]

Drucker believes that cost-based pricing is the reason that, despite its technological success, the United States no longer has a consumer-electronics industry. He believes that the only sound way to price is to start with what the market is willing to pay and then to design a product or service to meet that price. This approach to the pricing and design of new products, referred to as *target costing*, was formalized at Toyota[2] and quickly utilized by other successful Japanese companies such as Nissan, Canon, and Ricoh. On the other hand, the use of target costing is also one of the reasons for the success of U.S.-based personal computer manufacturers such as Compaq, Dell, and Gateway. In the late 1990s, these companies set stretch pricing targets, such as breaking the $1,000 barrier, and worked to design a machine that could be profitable with a retail price of $999 or less.

TARGET COSTING IS A PROACTIVE APPROACH TO COST MANAGEMENT

Target costing starts with determining what customers are willing to pay for a product or service and then subtracts a desired profit on sales to determine the allowable,

---

[1]Peter F. Drucker, "The Five Deadly Business Sins," *The Wall Street Journal*, October 21, 1993, p. A18.
[2]Takao Tanaka, "Target Costing at Toyota," *Journal of Cost Management*, Spring 1993, p. 4.

or target, cost of the product or service. This target cost is then communicated to a cross-functional team of employees representing such diverse areas as marketing, product design, manufacturing, and management accounting. Reflecting value chain concepts and the notion of partnerships up and down the value chain, suppliers of raw materials and components are often included in the teams (recall the supply chain management discussion from Chapter 8). The target costing team is assigned the task of designing a product that meets customer price, function, and quality requirements while providing a desired profit. Its job is not completed until the target cost is met, or a determination is made that the product or service cannot be profitably introduced under the current circumstances. See Exhibit 9–2 for an overview of target costing, and Research Shows 9–1 for some cautions about understanding the market.

Although a formula can be used to determine a markup on cost, it is not possible to develop a formula indicating how to achieve a target cost. Hence, target costing is not a technique. It is more a philosophy or an approach to pricing and cost

EXHIBIT 9-2

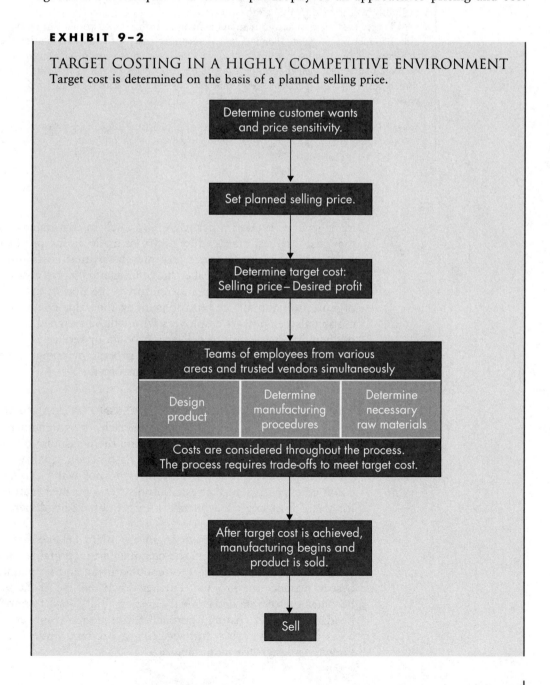

TARGET COSTING IN A HIGHLY COMPETITIVE ENVIRONMENT
Target cost is determined on the basis of a planned selling price.

Determine customer wants and price sensitivity.

Set planned selling price.

Determine target cost: Selling price – Desired profit

Teams of employees from various areas and trusted vendors simultaneously

| Design product | Determine manufacturing procedures | Determine necessary raw materials |

Costs are considered throughout the process. The process requires trade-offs to meet target cost.

After target cost is achieved, manufacturing begins and product is sold.

Sell

UNDERSTANDING TARGET COSTING REQUIRES MARKET KNOWLEDGE

According to Schwendeman and Hartgraves, a certain amount of ambivalence and confusion about target costing remains. Some companies began using target costing only to abandon it because of resistance to change or lack of commitment to carry through to complete implementation. Other attempts failed because the market was ignored.

Managers must understand that target costing is not just about setting cost targets. It is a value chain approach to managing an organization. Target costing requires an understanding of the market: what the customer or prospective customer wants and is willing to pay. It is important to keep customer expectations at the forefront throughout the entire product development cycle. Otherwise, product features could be added in the development stage that don't reflect what customers want. This is one reason many new products do not sell. The decisions made regarding product development must make business sense to the producer. If a product feature does not add value to a customer, in the long run it probably will not add value to the producer.

Target costing first requires management to translate customer value expectations into an acceptable product price. Next, management determines the profit that shareholders expect to make. Netting these two items results in the target cost. Once an organization has determined a product target cost, management must then determine the proper mix of costs that will result in a quality product the customer desires. Customers care only that the cost of the various product features and functions is in line with the value they receive for what they must pay.

Source: David Schwendeman and Al Hartgraves, "Some Myths about Target Costing," *The CPA Letter* (New York: American Institute of CPAs, September 2000), http://www.aicpa.org/pubs.

management. It takes a proactive approach to cost management, reflecting the belief that costs are best managed by decisions made during product development. This contrasts with the more passive cost-plus belief that costs result from design, procurement, and manufacture. Like the value chain, target costing helps orient employees toward the final customer and reinforces the notion that all departments within the organization and all organizations along the value chain must work together. Target costing also empowers employees who will be assigned the responsibility for carrying out activities necessary to deliver a product or service with the authority to determine what activities will be selected. Like process mapping, it helps employees to better understand their role in serving the customer.

TARGET COSTING ENCOURAGES DESIGN FOR MANUFACTURE

In the absence of a target costing approach, design engineers are apt to focus on incorporating leading-edge technology and the maximum number of features in a product. Target costing keeps the customer's function, quality, and price requirements in the forefront at all times. If customers do not want leading-edge technology (which could be expensive and untested) and several product features, they will resist paying for them. Focusing on achieving a target cost keeps design engineers tuned in to the final customer.

Left on their own, design engineers might believe that their job ends when they design a product that meets the customer's functional requirements. The tendency is to simply pass on the design to manufacturing and let manufacturing determine how best to produce the product. Further down the line, if the product needs servicing, it becomes the service department's responsibility to determine how best to service the product. A target costing approach forces design engineers to explicitly consider the costs of manufacturing and servicing a product while it is being designed. This is known as **design for manufacture.**

Minor changes in design that do not affect the product's functioning can often produce dramatic savings in manufacturing and servicing costs. Examples of design for manufacture include the following:

- Using molded plastic parts to avoid assembling several small parts.
- Designing two parts that must be fit together so that joining them in the correct manner is obvious to assembly workers.
- Placing an access panel in the side of an appliance so service personnel can make repairs quickly.
- Using standard-size parts to reduce inventory requirements, to reduce the possibility of assembly personnel inserting the incorrect part, and to simplify the job of service personnel.
- Ensuring that tolerance requirements for parts that must fit together can be met with available equipment.
- Using manufacturing procedures that are common to other products.

The successful implementation of target costing requires employees from all involved disciplines to be familiar with activity-based costing concepts and the notions of value-added and non-value-added activities. When considering the manufacturing process, team members should minimize non-value-added activities such as movement, storage, inspection, and setup. They should also select the lowest-cost value-added activities that will do the job properly.

TARGET COSTING REDUCES TIME TO INTRODUCE NEW PRODUCTS
By designing a product to meet a target cost (rather than evaluating the marketability of a product at a cost-plus price and having to recycle the design through several departments), target costing reduces the time required to introduce new products. Involving vendors in target costing design teams makes the vendors aware of the necessity of meeting a target cost. This facilitates the concurrent engineering of components to be produced outside the organization and reduces the time required to obtain components.

TARGET COSTING CAN APPLY TO COMPONENTS
Although it is most frequently associated with the development of new products, target costing can apply to components. A cost management expert at Isuzu Motors once illustrated target costing for components by taking apart a pen. "This is what we do with our competitors' products. . . . We would analyze the material it is made of, the way it is molded, the process used to assemble it. From this we would determine the product's probable cost." Isuzu would then use the component's probable cost to a competitor as a target cost to meet or beat.[3]

TARGET COSTING REQUIRES DETAILED COST INFORMATION
Implementing target costing requires detailed information on the cost of alternative activities. This information allows decision makers to select design and manufacturing alternatives that best meet function and price requirements. Tables that contain detailed databases of cost information for various manufacturing variables are occasionally used in designing products and selecting processes to meet target costs. The development and use of cost tables were considered in Chapter 5.

TARGET COSTING REQUIRES COORDINATION
The primary limitations of target costing concern employee and supplier attitudes and the many meetings required to coordinate product design and to select manufacturing

---

[3]Ford S. Worthy, "Japan's Smart Secret Weapon," *Fortune,* August 12, 1992, p. 74.

processes. All people involved must have a basic understanding of the overall processes required to bring a product to market and an appreciation of the cost consequences of alternative actions. They must also respect, cooperate, and communicate with other team members and be willing to engage in a negotiation process involving trade-offs. Finally, they must understand that although the total time required to bring a new product to market can be reduced, the countless coordinating meetings could be quite intrusive on the individuals' otherwise orderly schedule. See Exhibit 9–3 for an evaluation of target costing.

This aspect of the process is even more difficult when suppliers must be brought in as part of the coordination process. This concept is frequently referred to as **chained target costing** because the supply chain's support is critical for the product to be both competitively priced and delivered to the final customer in a timely manner. When multiple suppliers are required, the organization must obtain everyone's support or the process will probably not be successful due to gaps in the reliability of delivery, quality, and cost control. Each organization and unit must understand that if the product is not brought to market within the defined constraints, all will lose. They must make firm commitments for the project undertaken and have faith in each other that will carry out whatever part of the supply chain it has promised to fulfill. An example of this process with suppliers of parts and components to Whirlpool Corporation is presented in What's Happening 9–2. Coordination across the supply chain is also vital in the overall process of continuous improvement as discussed later in this chapter.

SHORT PRODUCT LIFE CYCLES INCREASE THE IMPORTANCE OF TARGET COSTING

From a traditional marketing perspective, products with a relatively long life go through four distinct stages during their life cycle:

1. *Startup*. Sales are low when a product is first introduced. Traditionally, initial selling prices are set high, and customers tend to be relatively affluent trendsetters.
2. *Growth*. Sales increase as the product gains acceptance. Traditionally, prices have remained high during this stage because of customer loyalty and the absence of competitive products.
3. *Maturity*. Sales level off as the product matures. Because of increased competition, pressure on selling prices is increasing; some price reductions could be necessary.

EXHIBIT 9–3

PROS AND CONS OF TARGET COSTING

Pros
- Takes proactive approach to cost management.
- Orients organization toward customer.
- Breaks down barriers between departments.
- Enhances employee awareness and empowerment.
- Fosters partnerships with suppliers.
- Minimizes non-value-added activities.
- Encourages selection of lowest-cost value-added activities.
- Reduces time to market.

Cons
- To be effective, requires the development of detailed cost data.
- Requires willingness to cooperate.
- Requires many meetings for coordination.

Quality Parts Make the Product a Success

Industry leaders in electric motor manufacturing are attempting to provide their customers, original equipment manufacturers, with high efficiency and quieter motors at consistently lower costs as part of the supply chain. An example is Emerson Appliance Solutions in St. Louis, which has teamed with Whirlpool Corporation to develop a customized capacitor motor for the new Voyager dishwasher sold under the Sears' Kenmore, Kitchen Aid, and Whirlpool brand names "Energy savings, quiet and increased capacity were the main objectives of the program," says Carl Fischer, Emerson's Whirlpool account manager for dishwashers. "An approximate 20 percent motor energy savings was the result of efforts by engineering teams at both Whirlpool and Emerson that resulted in a smaller, more efficient motor-pump assembly."

Illustrating Emerson's commitment to Whirlpool, the company has three managers who coordinate components for washers, motors, and controls. These managers worked with Whirlpool to achieve its new product objective of emphasizing reduced sound and water consumption while delivering good wash performance. To further enhance the product, Emerson then worked with its supplier, AMP of Harrisburg, Pennsylvania (going up the supply chain), for an improved connection method for the motors' magnet wires and lead wires.

Each member of the supply chain was well aware of Whirlpool's concern about cost of the new product and made every effort to contain costs from development to production. As a result, the new product was within the target set by Whirlpool.

Source: Joe Jancsurak, "Value-Added Power," *Appliance Manufacturer Magazine*, February 26, 2001, http://www.ammagazine.com.

4. *Decline.* Sales decline as the product becomes obsolete. Significant price cuts could be required to sell remaining inventories.

In Exhibit 9–4, the sales revenue over a product's marketing life cycle is represented by the vertical axis, and time is represented by the horizontal axis. Part (a) of Exhibit 9–4 represents a product with a relatively long market life cycle, such as Ford Model T, Coca-Cola's Coke, Levi's blue jeans, or Bounty's paper towels. Some of these products, such as the Model T Ford, have completed their life cycles. Others, such as Coke, seem to remain mature products indefinitely.

Part (b) represents a product with a relatively short market life cycle, such as Microsoft Office 2000 or Intel Pentium IV computer chips. In general, as the rate of technological change increases, product life cycles decrease, especially for products that utilize advanced technology.

Target costing is more important for products with a relatively short market life cycle. Products with a long life cycle, present many opportunities to continuously improve design and manufacturing procedures that are not available when a product has a short life cycle. Hence, extra care must go into the initial planning for short-lived products. This is especially true when short product life cycles are combined with increased worldwide competition. It is important to introduce a product first and at a price that ensures rapid market penetration.

Target Costing Helps Manage Life Cycle Costs

An awareness of the impact of today's actions on tomorrow's costs underlies the notion of **life cycle costs,** which include all costs associated with a product or service ranging from those incurred with the initial conception through design, preproduction, production, and after-production support.

The lower line in Exhibit 9–5 illustrates the cumulative expenditure of funds over the life of a product. For low-technology products with relatively long product lives, decisions committing the organization to spend money are made at approximately the

EXHIBIT 9-4

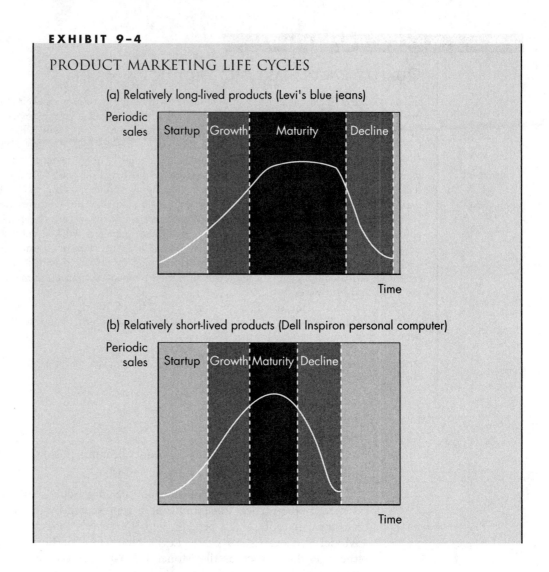

PRODUCT MARKETING LIFE CYCLES

(a) Relatively long-lived products (Levi's blue jeans)

Periodic sales

Startup | Growth | Maturity | Decline

Time

(b) Relatively short-lived products (Dell Inspiron personal computer)

Periodic sales

Startup | Growth | Maturity | Decline

Time

same time the money is spent. However, for high-technology products with relatively short product lives, most of the critical decisions affecting cost, such as product design and the selection of manufacturing procedures, are made before production begins. The top line in Exhibit 9–5 represents decisions committing the organization to expenditures for a product.

Reflecting significant changes in vehicle production since the time of Henry Ford and the Model T, General Motors estimates that 70 percent of the cost of manufacturing truck transmissions is determined during design.[4] Others estimate that up to 95 percent of the total costs associated with high-technology products are committed before the first unit is produced.[5]

Life cycle cost concepts have also been usefully applied to low-technology issues, such as repair versus replace decisions. The New York State Throughway Authority uses life cycle concepts to determine the point at which it is more expensive to repair than to replace bridges. The approach is similar to that employed for cost reduction proposals discussed in Chapter 10.

---

[4]D.E. Whitney, "Manufacturing by Design," *Harvard Business Review,* July–August 1988, pp. 83–91.
[5]Benjamin S. Blanchard, *Design and Manage to Life Cycle Costs* (Portland, OR: M/A Press, 1978), p. 15.

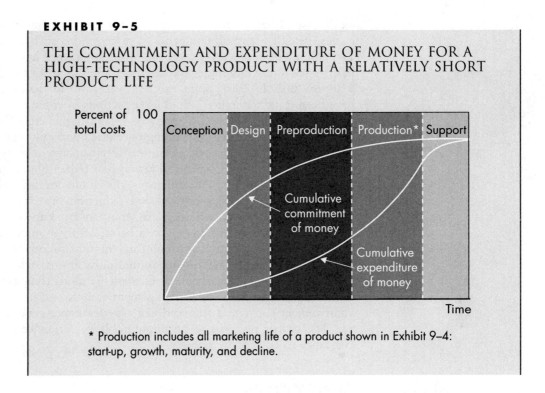

EXHIBIT 9-5

THE COMMITMENT AND EXPENDITURE OF MONEY FOR A HIGH-TECHNOLOGY PRODUCT WITH A RELATIVELY SHORT PRODUCT LIFE

* Production includes all marketing life of a product shown in Exhibit 9–4: start-up, growth, maturity, and decline.

LEARNING OBJECTIVE 3

CONTINUOUS IMPROVEMENT (KAIZEN) COSTING

Continuous improvement (Kaizen) costing calls for establishing cost reduction targets for products or services that an organization is currently providing to customers. Developed in Japan, this approach to cost management is often referred to as *Kaizen costing*. *Kaizen* means "continuous improvement" in Japanese. Continuous improvement costing begins where target costing ends. Target costing takes a proactive approach to cost management during the conception, design, and preproduction stages of a product's life, continuous improvement costing takes a proactive approach to cost management during the production stage of a product's life:

		Time	
Conception	Design	Preproduction	Production
	Target costing		Continuous improvement costing

Continuous improvement costing is accomplished through the use of continuous improvement techniques, such as process mapping (discussed in Chapter 5). Continuous improvement costing adds a specific target to be achieved during a time period to the continuous improvement concept previously discussed. Basically, the mathematics of the concept is quite simple, but its implementation is difficult. Assume that Home Depot wanted to reduce the cost of materials handling in each of its stores, and management set a target reduction of 2 percent a year. If a given store had current annual materials handling costs of $100,000 and expected an increase the next year due to 10 percent growth, the budget for the next year would be $107,800 [($100,000 × 1.10) × 0.98]. The budget for next year based on growth is $110,000 less the continuous improvement factor of 0.02.

Successful world-class companies use continuous improvement costing to avoid complacency. Competitors are constantly striving to win market share through better quality or lower prices. Hewlett-Packard studied Epson to determine its strengths and weaknesses. Isuzu Motors takes competitors' products apart to determine a target cost it must beat. To fend off competition, prices and costs must be continuously reduced. To maintain its competitive position, Hewlett-Packard has reduced the list price of the basic black and white inkjet printer from $365 in 1993 to $250 in 1996 to less than $100 in 2001. In 2001, *color* printers were sold for less than $149. This could not have been done without continuous reductions in costs.

The Daihatsu Motor Company of Osaka, Japan, sets Kaizen cost reduction targets for each cost element, including purchased parts per car, direct materials per car, labor hours per car, and office utilities.[6] Performance reports developed at the end of each month compare targeted and actual cost reductions. If actual cost reductions are more than the targeted cost reductions, the results are favorable; if the actual cost reductions are less than the targeted cost reductions, the results are unfavorable.

Because cost reduction targets are set before it is known how they will be achieved, continuous improvement costing can be stressful to employees. To help reduce this stress at Daihatsu, a period of about three months following the introduction of a new product is allowed before organizational units are expected to meet target costs and Kaizen costing targets. A critical element in motivating employee cooperation and teamwork in aggressive cost management techniques, such as target and continuous improvement costing, is to avoid using performance reports to place blame for failure. The proper response to an unfavorable performance report must be an offer of assistance to correct the failure.

LEARNING OBJECTIVE 4

QUALITY COSTS

Life cycle costs were previously considered from the seller's perspective within the context of developing target costs. From the buyer's perspective, life cycle costs include the total costs associated with a product, such as a refrigerator, furnace, X-ray machine, or tractor, over its entire life. Sophisticated buyers look beyond acquisition cost to life cycle costs in making decisions. Major home appliances come with stickers estimating their annual operating costs, and new automobiles have stickers with information on fuel efficiency. The life cycle costs of a furnace include the purchase price, operating costs such as fuel, maintenance costs such as cleaning the burner, and repair costs such as replacing an exhaust fan. The preferred furnace is the one that provides the desired heat at the lowest life cycle cost.

Applying the life cycle cost concept, the total cost of materials to a manufacturing company includes much more than the purchase price. It also includes costs caused by potential and actual quality problems with materials. A concern that some materials are defective might require purchasing extra materials or inspecting materials. The use of defective materials could cause a manufacturer to incur costs for production downtime and rework. When life cycle costs are considered, purchasing decisions are less likely to be made solely on the basis of price. When the effect of quality on subsequent costs is considered, raw materials quality becomes just as important as price.

Quality, defined as conformance to customer expectations, is an important competitive factor.[7] Successful companies know that they must meet customers' quality and price expectations. In addition to being ethically questionable, reducing quality to achieve a target cost will not lead to long-run profits in today's highly competitive

---

[6] Yasuhiro Monden and John Lee, "How a Japanese Auto Maker Reduces Costs," *Management Accounting,* August 1993, pp. 22–26.

[7] Much of the material in this section is based on Wayne J. Morse, Harold P. Roth, and Kay M. Poston, *Measuring, Planning, and Controlling Quality Costs* (Montvale, NJ: National Association of Accountants, 1987).

worldwide markets. Consistent product quality is a component in the success of companies such as Federal Express, Ford, McDonald's, Toyota, and Intel.

American Airlines found that poor quality (in the form of late arrivals) cost it customer goodwill and millions of dollars a year in "lost" baggage and employee overtime.[8] In manufacturing, Intel found that quality leads to lower manufacturing costs, lower inventory levels, higher productivity, and increased profits. In repetitive activities, such as processing checks at a bank, an emphasis on "doing it right the first time" reduces the need for inspection and for rework.

Quality is an essential element of the JIT approach to inventory management. Purchasing high-quality materials reduces the need to inspect incoming materials, reduces the need for extra inventory, and facilitates the delivery of materials directly to the shop floor. As inventories are reduced, the presence of defective units becomes increasingly disruptive. Indeed, without buffer stocks, manufacturers might have to stop operations as soon as a defective unit is detected. While costly in the short run, these disruptions call attention to quality problems and encourage changes that prevent their recurrence. By eliminating the effort devoted to detecting and reworking or disposing of defective units, organizations are able to increase their productivity and profitability.

Productivity is the relationship between outputs and inputs:

$$\text{Productivity} = \text{Outputs} \div \text{Inputs}$$

Measurement of productivity requires a measure of output and of input. Partial measures of productivity are based on the relationship of units produced to a single input such as the number of employees, direct labor hours, or machine hours. Total measures of productivity convert all inputs into dollars (a common denominator) and restate outputs in terms of sales dollars.

Improvements in quality increase productivity by reducing the inputs required to obtain a given level of output. In turn, these improvements in productivity increase profits by lowering costs for the given level of output. If some of the cost savings are passed on to customers in the form of lower selling prices, an increase in sales volume could generate increased profits. Additionally, if an organization achieves a reputation for quality, it might be able to charge premium prices. The known quality of international brands, such as Coke and Pepsi, allow vendors to sell them at higher prices than they charge for local brands of soft drinks.

QUALITY OF DESIGN AND QUALITY OF CONFORMANCE

A key to improving quality is recognizing that quality is everyone's responsibility. The responsibility for quality starts with determining customer expectations and concludes with the delivery of products and services that conform to these expectations. The process of delivering a quality product or service can be broken into the following five steps:

Step 1 $\longrightarrow$ Step 2 $\longrightarrow$ Step 3 $\longrightarrow$ Step 4 $\longrightarrow$ Step 5
Customer expectations / Functional specifications / Design specifications / Manufacturing specifications / Actual results

1. Quality starts with determining *customer expectations*. An agreement is necessary as to what customers expect and what the vendor will deliver. If customers at a McDonald's restaurant expect table service, lobster, and candlelight, they will be disappointed. If they expect fast, courteous service and low prices, they are likely to be satisfied.
2. The next step in delivering a quality product is to develop *functional specifications* for the product or service. These are explicit statements regarding the service or

---

[8]Wendy Zeller, "Coffee, Tea—And On-Time Arrival," *Business Week*, January 20, 1997, p. 30.

product capabilities, expressed in quantitative terms whenever possible. Functional specifications for a new automobile engine might include specifications for horsepower, fuel consumption, and emissions. Functional specifications at a hotel might refer to the types of services provided for guests, such as prompt room service.

3. The functional specifications then must be turned into *design specifications*. These are detailed statements regarding the physical characteristics of the product and engineering drawings illustrating those physical characteristics. At a Holiday Inn hotel, the number of towels to be left in each room is a design specification.

4. Detailed specifications of how a product will be manufactured to meet design specifications or how a service will be performed must also be developed. At a McDonald's restaurant, *manufacturing specifications* include the specified sequence of activities required to prepare a hamburger.

5. Finally, the *actual results* of a product or service are determined following its delivery in conformance with its design specifications.

For clarity, we have identified five distinct steps in delivering a quality product or service. In reality, these steps are often intermingled. As indicated in the discussion of target costing, teams of employees from various functional areas should work on Steps 1 through 4 concurrently. Many efforts to deliver quality products succeed or fail during the design stage. Quality problems and manufacturing costs increase when a complex design makes manufacture difficult. Warranty costs and buyers' life cycle costs increase when a design does not consider ease of service.

To develop standards for evaluating product quality, it is necessary to distinguish between quality of design and quality of conformance. **Quality of design** refers to the degree of conformance between customer expectations for a product or service and the design specifications of the product or service. **Quality of conformance** refers to the degree of conformance between a product and its design specifications. Conformance to customer expectations requires both the quality of design and the quality of conformance. As shown in Exhibit 9–6, doing the right things wrong (high quality of design but poor quality of conformance) or the wrong things right (poor quality of design but high quality of conformance) results in failure. The only way to win customers is by doing the right things right.

EXHIBIT 9-6

SUCCESS REQUIRES QUALITY OF DESIGN AND CONFORMANCE

	Low	High
High (Quality of design)	Do right things wrong (failure)	**Do right things right** (winner!)
Low (Quality of design)	Do wrong things wrong (failure)	Do wrong things right (failure)

Quality of conformance

TYPES OF QUALITY COSTS

Many managers find financial information related to quality useful for determining the financial significance of quality problems, developing an overall strategy for improving quality, evaluating proposals to invest in quality improvement activities, and appraising the performance of quality improvement activities. The concepts of quality costs serve as the basis for these special-purpose accounting reports for management.

Quality costs are costs incurred because poor quality of conformance does (or could) exist. There are two basic types of quality costs, and each basic type is classified in two subcategories:

1. Quality costs *are incurred because of the possibility of poor conformance* between actual products or services and their design standards:
   a. **Prevention costs** are incurred to prevent nonconforming products from being produced or nonconforming services from being performed.
   b. **Appraisal costs** are incurred to identify nonconforming products or services before they are delivered to customers.
2. Quality costs *are incurred because of poor conformance* between actual products or services and their design standards:
   a. **Internal failure costs** occur when materials, components, products, or services are identified as defective before delivery to customers.
   b. **External failure costs** occur when nonconforming products or services are delivered to customers. For example, State Farm Insurance Company sued Ford Motor Company, claiming it paid millions of dollars for fires caused by faulty ignition switches on Ford vehicles. Ford had previously recalled 8.7 million vehicles due to the faulty switch. State Farm estimated that 26 million more vehicles had the potentially faulty switch.[9]

Quality cost information is periodically summarized in a quality cost report, such as the one in Exhibit 9–7, which also presents examples of costs in each category. Note that quality cost information cuts across organizational boundaries and that quality costs are related to specific activities. By associating costs with activities, activity based costing facilitates the development of quality cost information. To provide a benchmark (see later discussion in this chapter) for comparison between periods with different levels of activity, quality cost information is often restated as a percent of sales or total manufacturing costs.

Notice that in Exhibit 9–7 external failure costs are very high in comparison with other quality costs. This indicates that quality problems are not being identified and corrected before goods are delivered to customers, a situation frequently encountered before the initiation of a quality improvement program. In this case, expenditures on appraisal and prevention might pay off handsomely with reductions in failure costs.

Quality cost information can be prepared for any time period or cost objective such as a machine, department, plant, division, company, product, or product line. Depending on management's information needs, quality cost reports can include fewer than four cost categories. They can even include subjective information such as an estimate of lost sales resulting from quality problems (an external failure cost). Some organizations have devised unique ways of turning the unrecorded opportunity cost of a lost future sale into a current out-of-pocket cost that is booked. To avoid the cost of lost sales due to quality problems, the Ritz-Carlton Hotel Co. authorizes employees to spend up to $2,000 to correct the problem of a guest's grievance. The underlying philosophy is that guests, remembering the level of service and the extra effort taken to resolve problems, will return.

---

[9] "State Farm Sues Ford over Faulty Ignition Switch," *The Huntsville Times*, January 21, 1998.

EXHIBIT 9–7

QUALITY COST REPORT

Best Watch Company
Quality Cost Report
For the Period Ended March 31, 2004

	Amount	Percent of Sales*
Prevention:		
Design for manufacture . . . . $	0	
Quality planning	2,000	
Quality training	3,000	
Supplier verification	0	
Total prevention . . . . $	5,000	0.25%
Appraisal:		
Accuracy review of sales orders . . . . $	0	
Depreciation of testing equipment	1,000	
Field inspection and testing	8,000	
In-process inspection and testing	0	
Total appraisal . . . . $	9,000	0.46%
Internal failure:		
Downtime due to quality problems . . . . . $	0	
Reinspection	400	
Retest	0	
Rework labor and overhead	10,000	
Scrap	1,600	
Total internal failure . . . . $	12,000	0.61%
External failure:		
Complaint adjustment . . . . $	30,000	
Product recalls	60,000	
Returns and allowances	10,000	
Warranty repairs	50,000	
Warranty replacement	80,000	
Insurance for product liability	20,000	
Legal fees for product liability	0	
Total external failure	250,000	12.68%
Total quality costs	$276,000	14.00%

Sales for the period total $1,972,208 (100%).

QUALITY COST TREND ANALYSIS

A *trend analysis* illustrating the effect on quality costs of successfully implementing a quality improvement program is presented in Exhibit 9–8. The most immediate action management can take to prevent the delivery of poor-quality products is to implement a rigorous inspection program and identify defective goods before they are delivered. If the inspection program is successful, there should be a shift in quality costs as a percent of sales, with external failure costs declining and appraisal and internal failure costs increasing. At this stage in a quality improvement program, total known quality costs are likely to increase. The ultimate solution to quality problems is to increase efforts to prevent the occurrence of defects. In addition to reducing external and internal failure costs, a successful quality improvement program will make it possible to reduce appraisal costs when management is confident the job is done right the first time.

EXHIBIT 9-8

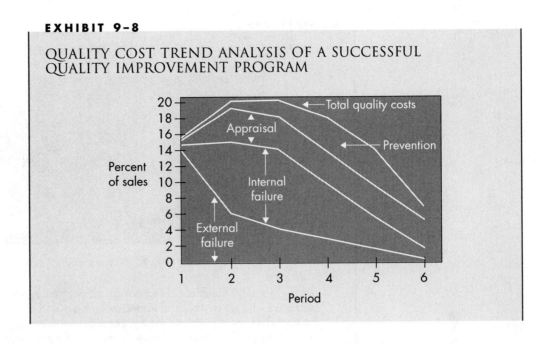

QUALITY COST TREND ANALYSIS OF A SUCCESSFUL
QUALITY IMPROVEMENT PROGRAM

While the implementation of a quality improvement program could have a significant effect on the total amount and distribution of quality costs, it is unlikely that quality costs can be reduced to zero. Management must continue to invest in prevention as new products are introduced and production procedures are changed. Even if the goal of zero defects is reached, some prevention must be required to maintain this ideal state. Appraisal and internal failure costs are better than external failure costs, and prevention costs are preferred to appraisal or failure costs. Quality is not free, but it is less expensive than the alternative.

Exhibit 9–9 shows a hypothesized short-run relationship between the quality of conformance and quality costs. Assuming static conditions with a given technology and level of knowledge, the graph shows that total quality costs are high when quality is low. Total quality costs decline as expenditures for appraisal and prevention produce improvements in quality. As quality nears perfection, the incremental returns to additional efforts to improve quality decline to such an extent that total quality costs begin to rise.

While this hypothesized relationship is a useful way of thinking about quality costs in the short run, remember that these are *static* relationships applicable for a given technology and level of knowledge. Advances in technology or knowledge should have the effect of shifting the prevention and appraisal cost curve down and to the right, increasing the optimal level of quality. The search for quality improvements is never ending. Once a temporary optimal level of quality is achieved, management should strive for advances in technology and knowledge that will permit additional improvements. Competitors who continue to work toward quality improvements could achieve breakthroughs that improve quality, productivity, sales volume, and profitability.

INTERNATIONAL ORGANIZATION FOR STANDARDIZATION (ISO)

The ability to demonstrate a commitment to quality is becoming increasingly important for companies doing business in global markets. As noted in What's Happening 9–3, the opening of former communist countries in Eastern Europe to external competition has had a dramatic impact on how managers and employees in Hungarian companies view customers and the need for quality.

EXHIBIT 9–9

SHORT-RUN ANALYSIS OF THE ECONOMICS OF QUALITY

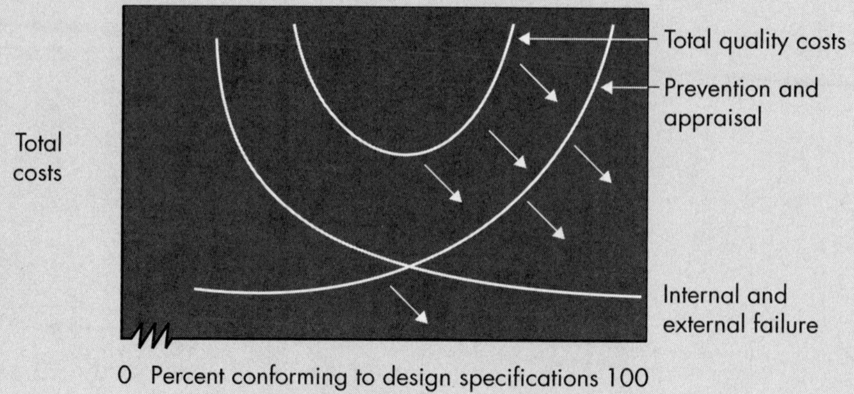

Total costs

Total quality costs

Prevention and appraisal

Internal and external failure

0   Percent conforming to design specifications 100

Arrows represent the effect of technological breakthrough in prevention. They cause the prevention and appraisal cost curve to shift down and to the right. This, in turn, causes the total quality cost curve to shift down and to the right. The net result is an increase in the percentage of conforming that minimizes total quality costs.

ISO 9000 Certification for Quality Management.   The 92-member International Organization for Standardization (ISO) has issued a series of five standards for quality assurance systems. These standards, known as *ISO 9000 standards*, provide organizations with internationally recognized models for the design and operation of a qual-

9-3   WHAT'S HAPPENING?

QUALITY IMPROVEMENTS HELP A HUNGARIAN PAPERBOARD MANUFACTURER IN ITS QUEST TO COMPETE WITH ITS WESTERN COUNTERPARTS

Before the decline of communism in Eastern Europe, the sales staff of Petofi Printing and Packaging of Kecskemet, Hungary, did not make calls on customers. Instead, the sales staff set visiting hours when customers could plead their cases for having their orders accepted. Meanwhile, on the factory floor, employees drank beer, flies got stuck in the paint and pressed into the paperboard, and containers were often delivered in wrong colors and sizes. Having no alternative sources of supply, however, customers did not complain. Instead, they bribed the sales staff with chocolates and liquor to take their orders.

Things changed rapidly after privatization in 1990. Petofi invested $35 million in new equipment, set up a quality assurance lab to inspect materials, and provided incentives for employees to produce quality products. Workers were offered 40 percent pay raises, year-end bonuses, and better working conditions. Customers were brought onto the shop floor, and workers were taken to trade shows to learn firsthand the importance of quality. Opening a beer on the job now results in losing one-third of a month's wages.

With new equipment, employees who are now more motivated and empowered, and relatively low but rising wages, Petofi is competitive in price and is becoming competitive in quality. In a dramatic change from just a few years ago, most of its products are now exported to companies such as Unilever NV of the Netherlands and General Electric of the United States. Petofi's quality "compares very favorably," says Gerry Flanagan, a purchaser for PepsiCo, Inc. "They have filled the gap between competitive quality and best cost."

Source: "New Competitor: East Europe's Industry Is Raising Its Quality and Taking on West," *The Wall Street Journal,* September 21, 1994, pp. A1 and A7.

ity management system. ISO certification means that an organization has documented the procedures used to ensure a quality product and that it follows them consistently. Meeting ISO 9000 standards beyond the first level requires an independent audit by an outside organization. ISO certification does not ensure that specific products or services meet customer expectations. Like developing a process map, the most important benefit of obtaining ISO 9000 certification often comes from forcing everyone involved in a process to carefully consider how their actions relate to each other and the purpose of the process. Once the current practice is documented, areas for improvement are easier to detect.

The European Economic Community requires suppliers of certain products to have ISO 9000 certification. The North Atlantic Treaty Organization, the U.S. Department of Defense, and many U.S. companies, such as IBM and General Electric, also require suppliers to be ISO 9000 certified. Even when it is not a requirement, achieving ISO 9000 certification enables companies to differentiate themselves from competitors. Although initially intended for manufacturing operations, law firms, waste removal companies, and professional associations (such as the American Institute of Certified Public Accountants) have achieved ISO 9000 certification. Even S&H Citadel, an incentive company, is ISO certified. According to S&H marketing vice president Kelly Harper, ISO 9000 certification enhances the organization's position in the marketplace. "No one in our industry has done it before. . . . It also makes it easier on customers who are themselves ISO certified to do business with us."[10]

ISO 14000 Certification for Environmental Management.

Environmental accounting is currently in a situation similar to that of quality costs in the early 1980s. Very few companies measure environmental costs, but awareness of the magnitude and decision usefulness of environmental cost information is increasing.

Environmental costs have traditionally been pooled with other overhead items, causing them to be hidden. When Amoco's Yorktown refinery conducted a special study of environmental costs, management was surprised to learn that environmental costs were 22 percent of operating costs rather than the previously estimated 3 percent. Placing environmental costs into broad overhead cost pools before assigning them to final cost objectives also results in cross-subsidization, with environmental costs misassigned to products that are less environmentally hazardous. The principal environmental issue facing Spectrum Glass was the use and release of cadmium. Although this colorant was used only in a single product, Ruby Red Glass, related overhead costs were assigned to all products by way of an overhead cost pool.[11]

As is the case for quality costs, the development of ABC makes it easier to evaluate environmental costs. One approach to organizing environmental cost information is to use a framework similar to that developed for quality costs:

- *Prevention*—efforts to reduce or prevent environmental hazards from occurring.
- *Appraisal*—inspection to determine whether an environmental problem exists.
- *Failure*—efforts to correct environmental problems.

In the 1990s, the Internal Standards Organization issued a series of more than a dozen environmental management standards. Identified as ISO 14000 standards, they are similar to the ISO 9000 standards in that they focus on systems rather than specific results, they are flexible to meet an organization's specific situation, and they call for external certification. The standards are intended to help management communicate environmental information within and outside the company and to provide management the information to help assess the impact of business decisions on the environment.

---

[10]"Can ISO Certification Boost Sales?" *Sales and Marketing Management*, April 1998, p. 19.

[11]Janet Ranganathan and Daryl Ditz, "Environmental Accounting: A Tool for Better Management," *Management Accounting: Magazine for Chartered Management Accountants*, February 1996, pp. 38–41.

Early results suggest that the ISO 14000 group of standards are helping to make environmental accounting an important management accounting issue rather than simply a financial accounting issue of tracking costs and noting any contingent liability. Quality Chemicals Inc., a maker of herbicides, spent more than $500,000 a year trucking hazardous waste to a disposal site. To prepare for ISO 14000 certification, it reviewed its waste disposal processes and costs and determined it could dispose of its waste locally for less than $50,000 a year by injecting ozone gas to break down the contaminants.[12]

Environmental costs, such as those associated with waste treatment, landfill, hazardous waste disposal, and environmental inspections, are important parts of the life cycle costs of many products. Previously, future costs, such as those associated with removing oil storage tanks and cleaning up any possible pollution, were seldom considered. Including environmental expenditures as part of a product's life cycle costs could reveal that a product with low acquisition costs but high environmental costs is less desirable than a product with a higher initial cost. What's Happening 9–4 reports the overall impact of ISO certification on Jetstream Communications.

LEARNING OBJECTIVE 5

BENCHMARKING

When Isuzu Motors takes a competitor's product apart to determine the competitor's manufacturing costs, or when Hewlett-Packard studies Epson to identify Epson's strengths and weaknesses, each company is engaging in *benchmarking*, a practice that has been around for centuries. In recent years, however, as globalization and increased competitiveness have forced businesses to more aggressively compete on the bases of cost, quality, and service, benchmarking has become more formalized and open. No longer regarded as spying, **benchmarking** is now a systematic approach to identifying the best practices to help an organization take action to improve performance.

9–4   WHAT'S HAPPENING?

QUALITY EMPHASIS LEADS TO ADDITIONAL IMPROVEMENTS

Jetstream Communications, a leader in broadband communications, has received the quality standard certifications ISO 9000 and ISO 14001. "The results of quality control in this market cannot be overestimated, and vendors like Jetstream need to embrace quality as a critical element of their business model," said Bettina Tratz-Ryan, senior analyst of Gartner Dataquest. "Jetstream's successful compliance with quality standards will have a positive impact on their market performance and future product and service development."

With these key quality standards, Jetstream is addressing several major areas of quality management. ISO 14001 is a standard that defines the elements of an environmental management system needed for an organization to effectively manage its impact on the environment. Areas of focus include (1) developing an environmental policy, (2) determining a systematic approach to planning, implementation, and operations management, (3) taking corrective action, and (4) performing regular management review.

With these additional operational emphases, the company has instilled quality standards not only in its products and services but also throughout the organization in its everyday dealings with employees, customers, and suppliers. "This is truly a groundbreaking accomplishment, and we are very pleased to have been involved as the Registrar during this triumphant certification process," said Robert Perry, president, for BSI Americas, Inc., who conducted the certification process. "Jetstream has instituted a comprehensive approach to quality that exemplifies both a leading technology company and a sound business."

Source: "Jetstream Receives ISO 14001 Certification," *ISO 14000, What's New,* January 30, 2001, http://www.iso14000.com.

---

[12]Lisa Sanders, "Going Green with Less Red Tape," *Business Week,* September 1996, pp. 75–76.

The formalization of benchmarking is largely attributed to a book written by Robert Camp of Xerox. Since then, many managers have come to believe that benchmarking is a requirement for success. Although benchmarking can focus on anything of interest, it typically deals with target costs for a product, service, or operation, customer satisfaction, quality, inventory levels, inventory turnover, cycle time, and productivity. Benchmarking initially focused on studying competitors, but benchmarking efforts have changed dramatically in recent years. According to Camp,

> Although you must focus strongly on the competition, if that is the sole objective, playing catch-up is the best you can do. Watching the competition does not tell you how to outdistance them. The mix of our benchmark activities have changed 180 degrees. In the early days, we spent 80 percent of our benchmark time looking at the competition. Today we spend 80 percent of that time outside our industry, because we have found innovative ideas from businesses in other industries.[13]

In considering how to go about benchmarking, an organization must be careful because it must consider nonfinancial limitations. No single numerical measurement can completely describe the performance of a complex device such as a microprocessor or a television camera, but benchmarks can be useful tools for comparing different products, components, and systems. The only totally accurate way to measure the performance of a given product is to test it against other products while performing the exact same activity. What's Happening 9–5 describes how Intel Corporation makes benchmarks available with some information on how to use them.

Benchmarking provides measurements that are useful in setting goals. It can lead to dramatic innovations, and it can help overcome resistance to change. When presented with a major cost reduction target, employees often believe they are being asked

---

9–5   **WHAT'S HAPPENING?**

INTEL MAKES BENCHMARKS AVAILABLE

Via its Web site, Intel Corporation is very open about how it benchmarks its products and how others should benchmark using Intel's products. Benchmark results published by Intel measure specific systems or components using specific hardware and software configurations. Others using its benchmarks are cautioned that any differences between Intel's configurations (including software) and their configuration could very well make those results inapplicable to the component or system being compared.

Intel divides its benchmarks into two types, component and system. *Component benchmarks* measure the performance of specific parts of a computer system, such as a microprocessor or hard disk drive, *system benchmarks* typically measure the performance of the entire computer system. In either case, the performance obtained will almost certainly vary from benchmark performance for a number of reasons. First, individual components must usually be tested in a complete computer system, and it is not always possible to eliminate the considerable effects that differences in system design and configuration have on benchmark results. For instance, vendors sell systems with a wide variety of disk capabilities and speeds, system memory, and video and graphics capabilities, all of which influence how the system components perform in actual use. Differences in software, including operating systems and compilers, also affect component and system performance. Finally, benchmark tests are typically written to be exemplary for only a certain type of computer application, which might or might not be similar to what is being compared.

A benchmark is, at most, only one type of information that an organization might use during the purchasing or manufacturing process. To get a true picture of the performance of a component or system being considered, the organization should consult industry sources, publicly available research reports, and even government publications of related information.

Source: "Benchmark Limitations," April 4, 2001, http://www.intel.com and "SPECmail2001," January 24, 2001, http://www.spec.org/osg.

---

[13]Robert Camp, "A Bible for Benchmarking, by Xerox," *Financial Executive,* July/August 1993, p. 24.

to do the impossible. Benchmarking can be a psychological tool that helps overcome resistance to change by showing how others have already met the target.

Although each organization has its own approach to benchmarking, the following six steps used by Alcoa are typical:

1. Decide what to benchmark.
2. Plan the benchmark project.
3. Understand your own performance.
4. Study others.
5. Learn from the data.
6. Take action.[14]

In recent years, professional organizations, such as the Institute of Management Accountants, have set up clearinghouses for benchmark information or have performed benchmarking studies of interest to members as have certain corporations such as Intel. Research Shows 9–2 summarizes the appliance manufacturing industry's implementation of many topics in this text.

9–2   RESEARCH SHOWS

APPLIANCE MANUFACTURERS PRACTICE WHAT WE PREACH

The 1998 Appliance Manufacturers Market Trends Survey provided the authors of this textbook with a useful benchmark for identifying important management accounting topics. The top ten issues facing appliance manufacturers in 1998 were as follows:

1. Quality
2. Time to market
3. Competing in a global marketplace
4. Product liability
5. International standards
6. Parts reduction
7. Regulatory issues
8. Noise/quiet design
9. Supplier partnerships
10. Energy efficiency

The following selected items are also of interest in relation to this text. The number given is the percentage of affirmative responses.

Expect suppliers to have a JIT delivery program	64%
Expect suppliers to participate in cross-functional teams	47
Expect suppliers to obtain ISO certification	41
Have achieved ISO 9000 certification	47
Have achieved ISO 14000 certification	3
Export to:	
Canada	58
Mexico	47
England	45
South America	42
France	40
Have joint venture in China	13

The number of respondents indicating they had achieved ISO 9000 certification for quality showed a dramatic increase, from 14 percent in 1994 and 29 percent in 1996. In the 1996 edition of this text, we suggested that obtaining ISO 9000 certification provided a competitive advantage; it is increasingly becoming the norm. ISO 14000 certification for environmental programs is very new. It is likely to become increasingly important, first as a competitive edge and then as the norm.

Source: AM Industry News 1998 Market Trends Survey, http://www.ammagazine.com

---

[14]Karen Bemowski, "The Benchmark Bandwagon," *Quality Progress,* January 1991, pp. 22–23.

Summary

Product pricing is one of the most important and complex decisions facing management today. *Cost-based pricing* starts with determining the cost of a product or service and then adding a markup to cover unassigned costs and to provide for a profit. Cost-based pricing assumes that goods or services are relatively scarce and that customers wanting a product or service are willing to pay the price. When these assumptions are incorrect, firms using cost-based pricing could find that their cost structure and the development time for new products or services are not competitive.

Target costing starts with determining what customers will pay for a product and then subtracts a desired profit to determine the target cost of the product or service. Next, a cross-functional team designs a product that meets the customers' price, function, and quality requirements. In addition to achieving a more competitive price by encouraging the concurrent consideration of design, manufacturing, and service issues, target costing focuses more on life cycle costs and can bring products to market in a shorter time.

Meeting customer needs and desires and doing the job right the first time are the essence of quality management. Organizations that continuously strive to improve quality are more apt to attract and retain customers and to meet cost reduction and continuous improvement targets. The concepts of quality costs are often used to understand the cost reduction potential with quality improvements, justify investments in quality-enhancing technology, and serve as cost targets. Increasingly, quality cost concepts are being applied to environmental management.

Organizations have always attempted to obtain information concerning their competitors, often in informal ways. In today's highly competitive environment, benchmarking has become a systematic approach to identifying best practices and taking action to improve performance.

Review Problem

The solution to the review problem is found on page 407. To maximize your learning, you should make a serious attempt to develop a written solution to the review problem before looking at the solution. If there are errors in your solution, you should then attempt to determine their causes.

Cost-Based Pricing and Target Costing

Presented is the 2004 contribution income statement of Knox Company.

Knox Company
Contribution Income Statement
For the Year Ended December 31, 2004

Sales (100,000 units at $12 per unit)		$1,200,000
Less variable costs:		
Manufacturing	$300,000	
Selling and administrative	150,000	(450,000)
Contribution margin		$ 750,000
Less fixed costs:		
Manufacturing	$400,000	
Selling and administrative	200,000	(600,000)
Net income		$ 150,000

Knox has total assets of $2,000,000, and management desires an annual return of 10 percent on total assets.

Required:

a. Determine the dollar amount by which Knox Company exceeded or fell short of the desired annual rate of return in 2004.

b. Given the current sales volume and cost structure, determine the unit selling price required to achieve an annual profit of $250,000.

c. Assume that management wants to state the selling price as a percentage of variable manufacturing costs. Given your answer to requirement (b) and the current sales volume and cost structure, determine the selling price as a percentage of variable manufacturing costs.

d. Restate your answer to requirement (c), dividing into two separate markup percentages:

1. The markup on variable manufacturing costs required to cover unassigned costs.
2. The additional markup on variable manufacturing costs required to achieve an annual profit of $250,000.

e. Market analysis has revealed that the sales volume can be increased to 180,000 units per year if the selling price is set at $9 per unit. At this price and sales volume, determine the target cost that will provide an annual profit of $250,000.

Key Terms

Appraisal costs (p. 383)
Benchmarking (p. 388)
Chained target costing (p. 376)
Continuous improvement (Kaizen) costing (p. 379)
Design for manufacture (p. 374)
External failure costs (p. 383)
Internal failure costs (p. 383)
Life cycle costs (p. 377)
Marginal cost (p. 366)
Marginal revenue (p. 366)
Organization-based cost systems (p. 371)

Prevention costs (p. 383)
Price discrimination (p. 371)
Price fixing (p. 372)
Productivity (p. 381)
Quality (p. 380)
Quality costs (p. 383)
Quality of conformance (p. 382)
Quality of design (p. 382)
Robinson–Patman Act (p. 371)
Sherman Antitrust Act (p. 372)
Target costing (p. 372)

Review Questions

1. Why are economic models seldom used for day-to-day pricing decisions?
2. Identify three reasons that cost-based approaches to pricing have traditionally been important.
3. Identify four drawbacks to cost-based pricing.
4. Distinguish between price discrimination and price fixing.
5. How does target costing differ from cost-based pricing?
6. Why is cost-based pricing more a technique, and target costing is more a philosophy? Which approach takes a more proactive approach to cost management?
7. Distinguish between the marketing life cycles of products incorporating advanced technology (such as household electronic equipment) and those using more traditional technology (such as household paper products). Why would life cycle costing be more important to a manufacturer of household electronic equipment than to a manufacturer of household paper products?
8. What is the relationship between target costing and continuous improvement (Kaizen) costing?

9. Distinguish between the seller's and the buyer's perspective of life cycle costs.
10. Distinguish between quality of design and quality of conformance. Which is used for internal appraisals? What is the ultimate determination of the quality of a product or service?
11. Considering the four types of quality costs, which is most preferred and which is least desirable?
12. What is the purpose of ISO 9000 certification?
13. What advantage is derived from benchmarking against firms other than competitors?

Exercises

9–1
Matching

Match the term or phrase in the left column with the best description in the right column. Use each description only once.

1. Sherman Antitrust Act	a. Prohibits price discrimination when purchasers compete with each other
2. Appraisal cost	
3. Worst type of quality cost	b. Increase the importance of target costing
4. Benchmark	
5. Arguments in favor of cost-based prices	c. Assumes relatively scarce goods or services and customers willing to pay the price
6. Quality of design	d. Provides comparison with customer expectations
7. Argument against cost-based pricing	
8. Target costing	e. Is used to manage costs during product development
9. Robinson–Patman Act	f. Prohibits price fixing
10. Short product life cycles and increased competition	g. Is the best way of performing a task; prices determined by a study of other organizations
	h. Are legally defensible
	i. Results in external failure
	j. Involves inspecting a product before it is delivered to customers

9–2
Product Pricing:
Single Product

Sue Bee Honey is one of the largest processors of the product for the retail market. Assume that it processes honey at one large facility. Its annual fixed costs total $8,000,000, of which $3,000,000 is for administrative and selling efforts. Sales are anticipated to be 800,000 cases a year. Variable costs for processing are $4 per case, and variable selling expenses are 24 percent of selling price. There are no variable administrative expenses.

Required:
If the company desires a profit of $4,000,000, what is the selling price per case?

9–3
Product Pricing:
Single Product

Mary Morgan is planning to open a soft ice cream franchise in a resort community during the summer months. Fixed operating costs for the three-month period are projected to be $5,250. Variable costs per serving include the cost of the ice cream and cone, $0.25, and a franchise fee payable to Snowdrift Cooler, $0.05. A market analysis prepared by Snowdrift Cooler indicates that summer sales in the resort community should total 22,500 units.

Required:

Determine the price Mary should charge for each ice cream cone to achieve a $6,000 profit for the three-month period.

9-4
Product Pricing: Single Product

Presented is the 2003 contribution income statement of Colgate Products.

Colgate Products
Contribution Income Statement
For the Year Ended December 31, 2003

Sales (12,000 units)		$1,440,000
Less variable costs:		
Cost of goods sold	$480,000	
Selling and administrative	132,000	(612,000)
Contribution margin		$ 828,000
Less fixed costs:		
Manufacturing overhead	$520,000	
Selling and administrative	210,000	(730,000)
Net income		$ 98,000

During the coming year, Colgate expects an increase in variable manufacturing costs of $8 per unit and in fixed manufacturing costs of $48,000.

Required:

a. If sales for 2004 remain at 12,000 units, what price should Colgate charge to obtain the same profit as last year?
b. Management believes that sales can be increased to 16,000 units if the selling price is lowered to $107. Is this action desirable?
c. After considering the expected increases in costs, what sales volume is needed to earn a profit of $98,000 with a unit selling price of $107?

9-5
Cost-Based Pricing and Markups with Variable Costs

Johnson Services provides computerized inventory consulting. The office and computer expenses are $600,000 annually. The consulting hours available for the year total 20,000, and the average consulting hour has $20 of variable costs.

Required:

a. If the company desires a profit of $100,000, what should it charge per hour?
b. What is the markup on variable costs if the desired profit is $120,000?
c. If the desired profit is $80,000, what is the markup on variable costs to cover (1) unassigned costs and (2) desired profit?

9-6
Markups

The predicted 2004 costs for Tabor Motors are as follows:

Manufacturing Costs		Selling and Administrative Costs	
Variable	$100,000	Variable	$300,000
Fixed	200,000	Fixed	200,000

Average total assets for 2004 are predicted to be $5,000,000.

Required:

a. If management desires a 12 percent rate of return on total assets, what are the markup percentages for total variable costs and for total manufacturing costs?
b. If the company desires a 10 percent rate of return on total assets, what is the markup percentage on total manufacturing costs for (1) unassigned costs and (2) desired profit?

9-7
Product Pricing:
Two Products

Magic Data manufactures two products, CD-ROMs and zip disks, both on the same assembly lines and packaged 10 disks per pack. The predicted sales are 400,000 packs of CD-ROM and 500,000 packs of zip disks. The predicted costs for the year 2004 are as follows:

	Variable Costs	Fixed Costs
Materials	$200,000	$400,000
Other	300,000	800,000

Each product uses 50 percent of the materials costs. Based on manufacturing time, 40 percent of the other costs are assigned to the CD-ROMs, and 60 percent of the other costs are assigned to the zip disks. The management of Magic Data desires an annual profit of $100,000.

Required:
a. What price should Magic Data charge for each disk pack if management believes the zip disks sell for 20 percent more than the CD-ROMs?
b. What is the total profit per product?
c. Based on your answer to requirement (b), how should the company evaluate the status of the two products?

9-8
Product Pricing:
Two Products

Earthlink, Inc., provides a variety of computer-related services to its clients. Two of the many services offered by each office are Web page design (WPD), and electronic interchange development (EID) services. Assume that each office is expected to earn a 20 percent return on the assets invested. Earthlink has invested $5 million in the Atlanta office since its opening. The annual costs for the coming year are expected to be as follows:

	Variable Costs	Fixed Costs
Consulting support	$600,000	$850,000
Sales and administration	100,000	950,000

The two services expend about equal costs per hour, and the predicted hours for the coming year are 50,000 for WPD and 30,000 for EID.

Required:
a. If markup is based on variable costs, how much revenue must each service generate by the Atlanta office to provide the profit expected by corporate headquarters? What is the anticipated revenue per hour for each service?
b. If the markup is based on total costs, how much revenue must each service generate to provide the expected profit?
c. Explain why answers in requirements (a) and (b) are either the same or different.

9-9
Target Costing

Redback Networks, Inc., provides networking services and related systems hardware to its customers. Assume that it is developing a new networking system that small businesses can use. To attract small business owners, Redback must keep the price low without giving up too many of the features of larger networking systems. A marketing research study conducted on the company's behalf found that the price range must be $25,000 to $30,000. Management has determined a target price to be $26,000. The company's minimum profit percentage of sales is normally 20 percent, but the company is willing to reduce it to 15 percent to get the new product on the market. The fixed costs for the first year are anticipated to be $14,000,000. If sales reach 1,200 installed networks, the company needs to know how much it can spend on variable costs, which are primarily related to installation.

Required:

a. What is the amount of total cost allowed if the 15 percent profit target is allowed and the sales target is met? Show the amount for fixed and for variable costs.

b. What is the amount of total costs allowed if the 20 percent normal profit target is desired at the 1,200 sales target? Show the amount for fixed and for variable costs.

9–10
Target Costing

North Woods Equipment Company wants to develop a new log-splitting machine for rural homeowners. Market research has determined that North Woods could sell 5,000 log-splitting machines per year at a retail price of $500 each. An independent catalog company would handle sales for an annual fee of $2,000 plus $50 per unit sold. The cost of the raw materials required to produce the log-splitting machines amounts to $95 per unit.

Required:

If North Woods' management desires a return equal to 10 percent of the final selling price, what is the target unit cost for conversion and administration?

9–11
Continuous Improvement (Kaizen) Costing

Koto Photo manufactures cameras. At its Pacific plant, cost control has become a concern of management. The actual costs per unit for the years 2003 and 2004 were as follows:

	2003	2004
Direct materials:		
Plastic case	$ 4.00	$ 3.80
Lens set	17.00	17.20
Electrical component set	6.00	5.40
Film track	12.00	10.00
Direct labor	32.00 (1.6 hours)	30.00 (1.5 hours)
Indirect manufacturing costs:		
Variable	8.00	7.10
Fixed	2.00 (100,000 unit base)	1.90 (120,000 unit base)

The company manufactures all of the camera components except the lens sets, which it purchased from several vendors.

The company has used target costing in the past but has not been able to meet the very competitive global pricing. Beginning in 2004, the company implemented a continuous improvement program that requires cost reduction targets.

Required:

If continuous improvement (Kaizen) costing sets a first-year target of a 10 percent reduction of the 2003 base, how successful was the company in meeting 2004 per unit cost reduction targets? Support your answer with appropriate computations.

9–12
Continuous Improvement (Kaizen) Costing

GE Capital, a division of General Electric, has been displeased with the costs of servicing its consumer loans. Assume that it has decided to implement a Kaizen-based cost improvement program. For 2002, GE Capital incurred the following costs:

Loan processing	$14,500,000
Customer relations	3,500,000
Printing, mailing, and postage	800,000

For the next two years, GE Capital expects an increase in consumer loans of 4 percent annually with related increases in costs.

Required:

If the company has a continuous improvement of 1 percent each year, develop a budget for the next two years for the consumer loan department.

9-13
Productivity
Measures:
Manufacturing
Company

Ingram Iron, Inc., has not had strong earnings during the last several quarters of operation. Production management has decided that it needs more information than the current cost accounting system is supplying. The following nonfinancial information is available for the current quarter:

Production in units 20,000
Direct labor hours 14,000
Tons of materials used 5,200
Machine hours 6,000

The standards for the production of each unit are as follows:

41 minutes of direct labor
¼ ton of direct materials
20 minutes of machine time

Required:

Compute several productivity measures that production managers could use. Was the current quarter acceptable in meeting the measures you selected? Explain.

9-14
Productivity
Measures: Service
Company

Assume that Wachovia Bank evaluates each of its branches using both financial and nonfinancial factors. The Piedmont office reported the number or amount of each of the following for March of the current year.

Tellers 10
Customer service employees 2
Customers served 4,000
Teller hours worked 1,600
Customer service hours worked 300
Financial transactions 9,200
Total of all transactions $25,000,000

The bank has the following standards for branch operations, assuming a 20-day month and an 8-hour workday:

Number of teller customers served per hour 20
Number of tellers per 1,000 transactions 1
Number of dollars processed per teller $3,000,000

Required:

a. Determine whether the Piedmont branch met the preceding standards for March.
b. Give four other nonfinancial standards that the bank might use to evaluate its branches.

9-15
Quality Costs:
Service Emphasis

Categorize each of the following quality costs as prevention, appraisal, internal failure, or external failure.

a. Inspecting incoming supplies.
b. Following up of complaints by service department.
c. Training new employees.
d. Reconciling of agency contracts with billing statements.
e. Retraining staff members who are not current in area of expertise.
f. Maintaining toll-free telephone for client questions.
g. Redesigning reception area so clients have privacy during consultations.

(continued)

h. Dismissing staff member found guilty of unethical acts regarding company matters.

i. Senior staff reviewing final report before giving it to client.

9-16
Quality Costs:
Manufacturing
Emphasis

Categorize each of the following quality costs as prevention, appraisal, internal failure, or external failure.

a. Disposal of spoiled work-in-process inventory.
b. Downtime due to quality problems.
c. Expediting of work to meet delivery schedule.
d. Field tests.
e. Internal audits of inventory.
f. Support of complaint department.
g. Opportunity cost of lost sales because of bad reputation for quality.
h. Product liability.
i. Quality circles.
j. Quality training.
k. Reinspection.
l. Revision of computer programs due to software errors.
m. Rework labor and overhead.
n. Scrap.
o. Supplier verification.
p. Technical support provided to vendors.
q. Testing and inspection of equipment.
r. Testing and inspection of purchased raw materials.
s. Utilities used by inspection area.
t. Warranty repairs.

9-17
Quality Costs
Report:
Manufacturing Firm

Expandable Computer had November sales totaling $4,200,000 and incurred the following quality-related costs:

Spoiled work-in-process inventory disposal	$23,000
Downtime due to quality problems	43,000
Field test of new computer	84,000
Support of a customer complaint department	22,000
Product liability insurance	6,000
Quality training	12,000
Reinspection	2,000
Rework labor and overhead	18,000
New vendor verification and facility inspections	28,000
Technical support provided to vendors	3,000
Equipment inspection	33,000
Test and inspection of purchased parts	42,000
Warranty repairs	15,000

Required:
Prepare a quality cost report for November with appropriate classifications.

9-18
Quality Cost Report:
Food Processor

Assume that Hormel Meat Packers incurred the following costs during July:

Livestock inspection at auction yard	$ 4,800
Livestock inspection upon delivery	6,000
Inspector training—finished products	2,000
Redesign of processing procedures and sequence	10,000
Inspection and test of packing procedure	8,200
Product liability insurance	4,000

Product returns	$ 7,400
Scrap disposal	6,600
Downtime due to spoiled products	12,000
Contract negotiations with large vendor	1,500
Rework labor due to processing errors	4,900

Sales for July totaled $4,000,000, and the company's return on investment is expected to be 15 percent for the year.

Required:
Prepare a quality cost report for July with appropriate classifications.

Problems

9–19
Price Setting:
Multiple Products

Sussex Company's predicted 2005 variable and fixed costs are as follows:

	Variable Costs	Fixed Costs
Manufacturing	$400,000	$200,000
Selling and administrative	100,000	50,000
Total	$500,000	$250,000

Sussex produces a wide variety of small tools. Per-unit manufacturing cost information about one of these products, the Type-A Clamp, is as follows:

Direct materials	$ 5
Direct labor	7
Manufacturing overhead:	
Variable	6
Fixed	6
Total manufacturing costs	$24

Variable selling and administrative costs for the Type-A Clamp is $3 per unit. Management has set a 2005 target profit of $150,000 on the sale of Type-A Clamps.

Required:
a. Determine the markup percentage on variable costs required to earn the desired profit.
b. Use variable cost markup to determine a suggested selling price for the Type-A Clamp.
c. For the Type-A Clamp, break the markup on variable costs into separate parts for fixed costs and profit. Explain the significance of each part.
d. Determine the markup percentage on manufacturing costs required to earn the desired profit.
e. Use the manufacturing costs markup to determine a suggested selling price for the Type-A Clamp.
f. Evaluate the variable and the manufacturing cost approaches to determine the markup percentage.

9–20
Price Setting:
Multiple Products

Chesapeake Tackle Company produces a wide variety of commercial fishing equipment. In the past, product managers set prices using their professional judgment. John Marlin, the new controller, believes this practice has led to the significant underpricing of some products (with lost profits) and the significant overpricing of other products (with lost sales volume). You have been asked to assist Marlin in developing a corporate approach to pricing. The output of your work should be a cost-based formula that can be used to develop initial selling prices for each product. Although product managers are allowed to adjust these prices to meet competition and to take advantage of market opportunities, they must explain such deviations in writing.

The following 2003 cost information from the accounting records is available:

	Manufacturing Costs	Selling and Administrative Costs
Variable	$350,000	$ 50,000
Fixed	150,000	200,000

In 2003, Chesapeake reported earnings of $80,000. However, the controller believes that proper pricing should produce earnings of at least $120,000 on the same sales mix and unit volume. Accordingly, you are to use the preceding cost information and a target profit of $120,000 in developing a cost-based pricing formula.

Selling and administrative expenses are not currently associated with individual products. However, you have obtained the following unit production cost information for the Tigershark Reel:

Variable manufacturing costs	$120
Fixed manufacturing costs	60
Total	$180

Required:

a. Determine the standard markup percentage for each of the following cost bases. Round answers to three decimal places.
   1. Full costs, including fixed and variable manufacturing costs, and fixed and variable selling and administrative costs.
   2. Manufacturing costs plus variable selling and administrative costs.
   3. Manufacturing costs.
   4. Variable costs.
   5. Variable manufacturing costs.
b. Explain why the markup percentages become progressively larger from requirement (a) (1) to (a) (5).
c. Determine the initial price of a Tigershark Reel using the manufacturing cost markup and the variable manufacturing cost markup.
d. Do you believe the controller's approach to product pricing is reasonable? Why or why not?

9-21
Predicting External
Failure Costs[15]

In December 1994, Intel offered to replace any Pentium processor that had a "floating-point divide flaw" with an updated version of the Pentium processor. This offer came in response to pressure from computer manufacturers, the communications media, and the general public. Intel's management remained convinced, however, that the floating-point divide flaw was a minor issue that should not cause a problem for most users.

Intel estimated that the replacement of each chip would cost about $200, including service fees. Intel sold a total of 5.3 million flawed Pentium chips before the problem was identified.

The following information is available about the response rate to product recalls:

- The response rate in automobile recalls, where safety is an issue, averages 68 percent.
- Sears reports that the response rate to a recall of a toaster with a safety defect might be as high as 40 percent, but it would be much lower without a safety issue.

---

[15]Based on Jim Carlton, "Humble Pie: Intel to Replace Its Pentium Chips," *The Wall Street Journal*, December 21, 1994, pp. B1, B6

- An independent analyst predicted that 30 to 40 percent of the Pentium processors had been sold to companies and that half of them would not ask for replacements. The analyst also estimated that 90 percent of individual consumers would not ask for a replacement because the flaw does not affect the applications they run.

Required:

Based on the preceding information, develop several alternative predictions of the external failure cost of replacing flawed Pentium processors. If you were to select one estimate, what would it be? Are there any other external failure costs that should be considered?

9–22 Preparing and Analyzing Quality Cost Reports

Assume that Black & Decker Company, concerned about competitive pressures, implemented a program in 2002 to reduce inventory levels, improve productivity, improve on-time delivery of goods to customers, and reduce customer complaints about quality. To help evaluate the success of these efforts, management requested a quality cost report for the year ended December 31, 2002.

After a detailed review of the accounting records and several interviews with key personnel, you have developed the following data for 2002:

Sales	$5,100,000
Inspection of purchased raw materials	50,000
Inspection of finished goods	110,000
Rework	80,000
Disposal cost of spoiled goods	30,000
Reinspection of finished goods	10,000
Development of design-for-manufacture program	5,000
Out-of-warranty adjustments	50,000
Warranty adjustments	60,000
Returns and allowances	8,000
Indirect costs of inspection department	25,000
Development of quality control training programs	8,000
Downtime due to quality problems	210,000

Required:

a. Prepare a quality control cost report with appropriate classifications.
b. Management is concerned about the success of the recently implemented program. The vice president of finance observed, "Although sales were essentially unchanged from 2001, profits declined. Furthermore, the decline in profits appears entirely due to increases in inspection, downtime, rework, and similar costs. Increases in these costs far exceeded the cost savings from lower customer complaints." Prepare a response to the concerns expressed by the vice president of finance.

9–23 Quality Cost Trend Analysis

The following information pertains to quality costs and total sales for Ray Company for the years 1999 through 2003.

	1999	2000	2001	2002	2003
Prevention	$ 20,000	$ 40,000	$ 25,000	$ 10,000	$ 5,000
Appraisal	10,000	10,000	10,000	5,000	5,000
Internal failure	50,000	55,000	40,000	20,000	10,000
External failure	50,000	25,000	15,000	55,000	65,000
Sales	1,000,000	1,500,000	1,600,000	1,200,000	1,000,000

Required:

a. Prepare a quality cost trend analysis based on total dollars of quality costs in each category.
b. Prepare a quality cost trend analysis based on quality costs as a percent of total sales.

(*continued*)

c. Compare the graphs prepared for requirements (a) and (b). Which is more meaningful? Why?

d. Based on the graphs, can any conclusions be made about Ray Company's quality control program?

9–24
Activity-Cost
Analysis: Quality
Costs and Non-
Value-Added Costs

Borroth Manufacturing has developed the following activity cost data for its purchasing and manufacturing activities:

Prepare purchase order and receive order	$ 36.00/order
Unpack and inspect incoming goods	0.50/unit purchased
Move in-process goods	2.50/unit in job
Hold in-process goods (no work being performed)	0.50/unit in job per day
Set up machine	60.00/machine per job
Operate machine A	80.00/hour
Operate machine B	60.00/hour
Perform rework	150.00/hour
Inspect work in process or finished goods	1.50/unit
Pack and ship finished goods	5% of previous costs plus $25.00 per job

Borroth produces only to fill customer orders. Because suppliers deliver on 24-hours' notice, it does not maintain raw materials inventories. Materials are purchased in the required quantities as needed, unpacked and inspected, and sent immediately to the shop floor. Finished goods are inspected, packed, and immediately shipped to customers.

The following information is available for Job 91-Z24, which consisted of 20 units of a special machine part:

Activity

Prepare purchase order 91-B34:		
Material M1	100 units	$1,200 purchase price
Material J2	300 units	300 purchase price
Prepare purchase order 91-B35:		
Material N6	50 units	800 purchase price
Move materials for job to Machine A		
Store at Machine A	1 day	
Set up Machine A		
Run Machine A	4 hours	
Set up Machine B		
Move job to Machine B		
Run Machine B	12 hours	
Move job to inspection		
Inspect goods	20 units	
Move job to rework station		
Store at rework station	2 days	
Perform rework	2.5 hours	
Move job to inspection		
Inspect reworked goods	6 units	
Move to packing and shipping		
Pack and ship finished goods		

Required:

a. Use activity cost data to determine the total cost of Job 91-Z24. Round computations to the nearest cent.

b. Determine the quality costs associated with Job 91-Z24. Assume that 40 percent of the costs of unpacking and inspecting incoming goods are attributable to inspection.

c. Determine the cost of non-value-added activities associated with Job 91-Z24.

Discussion Questions and Cases

9–25
Telephone Pole Rental Rates

Most utility poles carry electric and telephone lines. In areas served by cable television, they also carry television cables. However, cable television companies rarely own any utility poles. Instead, they pay utility companies a rental fee for the use of each pole on a yearly basis. The determination of the rental fee is a source of frequent disagreement between the pole owners and the cable television companies. In one situation, pole owners were arguing for a $7 annual rental fee per pole; this was the standard rate the electric and telephone companies charged each other for the use of poles.

"We object to that," stated the representative of the cable television company. "With two users, the $7 fee represents a rental fee for one-half the pole. This fee is too high because we only use about six inches of each 40-foot pole."

"You are forgetting federal safety regulations," responded a representative of the electric company. "They specify certain distances between different types of lines on a utility pole. Television cables must be a minimum of 40 inches below power lines and 12 inches above telephone lines. If your cable is added to the pole, the total capacity is reduced because this space cannot be used for anything else. Besides, we have an investment in the poles; you don't. We should be entitled to a fair return on this investment. Furthermore, speaking of fair, your company should pay the same rental fee that the telephone company pays us and we pay them. We do not intend to change this fee."

In response, the cable television company representative made two points. First, any fee represents incremental income to the pole owners because the cable company would pay all costs of moving existing lines. Second, because the electric and telephone companies both strive to own the same number of poles in a service area, their pole rental fees cancel themselves. Hence, the fee they charge each other is not relevant.

Required:
Evaluate the arguments presented by the cable television and electric company representatives. What factors should be considered in determining a pole rental fee?

9–26
Target Costing

The president of Household Electronics was pleased with the company's newest product, the HE Versatile CD. The product is portable and can be attached to a computer to play or record computer programs or sound, attached to an amplifier to play or record music, or attached to a television to play or record TV programs. It can even be attached to a camcorder to record videos directly on compact disks rather than on tape. It also can be used with a headset to play or record sound. The proud president announced that this unique and innovative product would be an important factor in reestablishing the North American consumer electronics industry.

Based on development costs and predictions of sales volume, manufacturing costs, and distribution costs, the cost-based price of the HE Versatile CD was determined to be $375. Following a market-skimming strategy, management set the initial selling price at $450. The marketing plan was to reduce the selling price by $50 during each of the first two years of the product's life to obtain the highest contribution possible from each market segment.

The initial sales of the HE Versatile CD were strong, and Household Electronics found itself adding second and third production shifts. Although these shifts were expensive, at a selling price of $450, the product had ample contribution margin to remain highly profitable.

The president was talking with the company's major investors about the desirability of obtaining financing for a major plant expansion when the bad news arrived.

A foreign company had announced that it would shortly introduce a similar product that would incorporate new design features and sell for only $250. The president was shocked. "Why," she remarked, "it costs us $260 to put a complete unit in the hands of customers."

Required:

How could the foreign competitor profitably sell a similar product for less than the manufacturing costs to Household Electronics? What advice do you have for the president concerning the HE Versatile CD? What advice would you have to help Household Electronics avoid similar problems in the future?

9–27
Target Pricing

In April 2001, Marriott International, the large hotel chain, announced that because occupancy rates had declined during the previous quarter, it was raising room rates to cover the cost of its increase in vacant rooms. Although not referring to accounting or economics, several business journalists during the week following the announcement questioned the basis for the rate increases. One stated that "Marriott increases rates of vacant rooms.[16]

Required:

a. Did the *USA Today* journalist mean that vacant rooms would be more expensive? Explain.
b. Do you think Marriott's action to raise room rates was based on economics, accounting, or both?

9–28
Electronic Scanning Errors

Law enforcement officials and the general public are becoming increasingly concerned about errors in electronic checkout scanning systems. Consider the following:

• A survey by Vermont's attorney general found that local outlets of Ames Department Stores, Inc., and Rich's Department Stores had serious errors in their scanning systems.
• Michigan's attorney general announced the detection of errors in scanning systems at Sears and Wal-Mart stores.
• An official of the Morris County New Jersey Office of Weights and Measures found many mistakes at the checkout counter of a Bradlees, Inc., store.[17]

While authorities and retailers say the mistakes are the result of human error rather than fraud, experts believe electronic scanning errors (typically caused by the failure to update price data in computers) represent a serious problem. It most likely occurs when merchandise is placed on sale. Making the problem worse is the fact that electronic scanning allows stores to save money by not placing a price sticker on each item of merchandise. Some communities have responded to concerns about scanning errors by requiring local merchants to continue attaching stickers to each item so that customers can review their bill when they unpack their purchases.

Required:

a. Identify some costs that merchants are likely to incur because of scanning errors.
b. Are these costs related to prevention, appraisal, internal failure, or external failure?
c. Mention several actions a merchant can take to reduce the costs identified in requirement (a). Classify the costs of each action as prevention, appraisal, internal failure, or external failure.

---

[16]"Marriott Increases Rates" *USA Today*, April 16, 2001, p. C1.
[17]Based on Catherine Yank and Willy Stern, "Maybe They Should Call Them Scammers," *Business Week*, January 16, 1995, pp. 32–33.

9–29
Developing Quality
Cost Categories:
Service Company

The management of Good Morning Inn, a national hotel chain, is interested in implementing a total quality control program but is not interested in developing a quality cost reporting system at this time. Nevertheless, the controller believes that the identification of activities and types of costs the hotel might incur in each of the four quality cost categories would be useful as a starting point in initiating the program. However, she is somewhat limited in her knowledge of the four quality cost categories.

Required:
Based on your knowledge of quality costs and the hotel industry, identify relevant activities and costs in each of the four basic quality cost categories.

9–30
Costs of Defective
Work

The production manager and the plant controller of Quartz Limited are disagreeing on the importance and extent of using quality cost reports as part of the normal monthly reporting operations of the Boise plant. The Boise operations are very materials intensive, with most per-unit costs being the actual cost of the materials used. Defective units require substantial replacement of most of the original materials.

The production manager argues that the cost of preparing the report (including major efforts to collect the data) exceeds the benefits to be received. He argues that other than the cost of rework of defective (nonquality) units, the other quality costs are negligible and the quality costs reports would not add anything to the decision model that he does not already know.

The controller disagrees with this assessment of quality cost reports and presents the production manager a list of possible categories that could be used to classify the cost of quality. However, knowing that the production manager is not receptive to more information on quality costs, the controller is planning to provide the manager a list of costs identified as the cost of nonquality work.

Required:
Using the production manager's example of rework as a nonquality cost, assist the controller in developing a list of nonquality costs in addition to rework.

9–31
Ethics and Quality
of Design

In a short period of time, high concentrations of carbon monoxide in the body can cause death. Over a long period, low concentrations can cause a variety of health problems. In 1991, the U.S. Consumer Product Safety Commission, concerned about health problems resulting from carbon monoxide, started a campaign to encourage all homeowners to buy carbon monoxide detectors. The City of Chicago even passed an ordinance mandating the installation of carbon monoxide detectors.

In accordance with Commission guidelines, First Alert, a well-known manufacturer of smoke detectors, designed a carbon monoxide detector to warn when relatively low levels of carbon monoxide were present. By December 1994, First Alert had sold more than 3 million detectors at about $45 each. Most other manufacturers set their detectors so that only life-threatening amounts of carbon monoxide would trigger an alarm.

After nearly 10,000 false carbon monoxide alarms sounded within a 48-hour period in December 1994, Chicago officials were so angry that they threatened to sue First Alert. Although the false alarms were blamed on an unusual temperature inversion that trapped auto exhausts and other pollutants near the ground, officials charged that the First Alert detectors were too sensitive. A fire department representative in another city noted that five of six false carbon monoxide alarms were caused by First Alert detectors.

Despite recommending an increase in the alarm threshold standard set by the Consumer Products Safety Commission, Underwriters Laboratories, Inc., indicated that First Alert detectors warranted its endorsement. First Alert endorsed Underwriters Laboratories' proposed standards although the Carbon Monoxide Safety and Health

Association, a manufacturers' trade group, proposed a standard with an even higher alarm threshold.

Required:
Discuss the issues management of First Alert faced in setting the design standards for its carbon monoxide detector. What arguments can be made in favor of setting relatively low alarm thresholds and in favor of setting relatively high alarm thresholds? Are any ethical issues involved in setting alarm standards? How should First Alert respond to the public relations problem caused by the "false" alarms?

**9–32
Benchmarking**

Your company is developing a new product for the computer printer industry. You have talked to several material vendors about being able to supply quality components for the new product. The product designers are satisfied with the company's ability to make the product in the current facilities. Numerous potential customers also have been surveyed, and most have indicated a willingness to buy the product if the price is competitive.

Required:
What are some means of benchmarking the development and production of your new product?

**9–33
Benchmarking**

"Rampant downsizing has been sweeping across most parts of Corporate America since the early 1990s, producing huge layoffs and shutdowns of operations. Commercial banks, though, have been virtually immune. Despite numerous mergers and consolidations, bank employment has remained remarkably steady. And, even though electronic banking is expanding, bank branches, often regarded as relics of the past, have actually increased."[18]

Presented is benchmark information on the number of bank employees per 1,000 people in various countries:

Germany	3.2
France	3.5
Japan	3.7
Canada	4.9
United States	5.8

Required:
Based on this information, what conclusions can you draw concerning the relative efficiency and operating costs of U.S. commercial banks? Are you aware of any unique circumstances that might lead to these results? What do you predict will happen to employment at U.S. commercial banks during the next several years?

John Shank Case Recommendation

Montclair Paper Mill—The "Deep Color" Grades

The focus of this case is to contrast standard costing with target costing which uses value chain analysis. The case describes a cost management problem in a real but disguised modern company. It centers on how the company's standard cost system was used to address the problem and ask questions about how it could have been solved differently. The students are also challenged to determine what they think the "ideal" cost should be for the situation presented.

---

[18]Kelly Holland, "Blood on the Marble Floors," *Business Week*, February 27, 1995, p. 98.

Dansk Minox This case relates to cost analysis when introducing new products. It emphasizes cost versus market value in the fast-changing consumer food market. Questions arise dealing with product expansions for both product lines and potential customer markets. Related topics of break-even analysis are needed to complete the decision model along with how fixed costs are defined and treated by the accounting system.

Solution To Review Problem

a. Desired annual profit ($2,000,000 × 0.10) $200,000
    Actual profit . . . . (150,000)
       Amount actual profit fell short of achieving the desired return . . . . $ 50,000

b. Predicted costs:
       Variable $450,000
       Fixed 600,000 $1,050,000
    Desired profit 250,000
    Required revenue $1,300,000
    Unit sales . . . . ÷ 100,000
       Required unit selling price . . . . $ 13

c. Variable manufacturing costs per unit = $300,000/100,000 unit = $3
    Selling price as a percent of variable manufacturing costs   = $13/3
                                                                    = 433⅓%

d. Detail of markup on variable manufacturing costs:

    1. Unassigned costs:
       Variable selling and administrative $150,000
       Fixed costs 600,000 $750,000
       Variable manufacturing costs . . . . ÷300,000
       Markup on variable manufacturing costs to cover
          unassigned costs 250%

    2. Desired profit $250,000
       Variable manufacturing costs . . . . ÷300,000
       Additional markup on variable manufacturing costs
          to achieve desired profit ($250,000) 83⅓%

e. Projected revenue (180,000 units × $9) $1,620,000
    Less desired profit . . . . (250,000)
       Target cost $1,370,000

STRATEGIC MANAGEMENT OF CAPITAL EXPENDITURES

After completing this chapter, you should be able to:

LEARNING OBJECTIVE 1   Discuss the role of capital budgeting in long-range planning.

LEARNING OBJECTIVE 2   Apply capital budgeting models, such as the net present value and the internal rate of return, that consider the time value of money.

LEARNING OBJECTIVE 3   Apply capital budgeting models, such as the payback period and the accounting rate of return, that do not consider the time value of money.

LEARNING OBJECTIVE 4   Evaluate the strengths and weaknesses of alternative capital budgeting models.

LEARNING OBJECTIVE 5   Discuss the importance of judgment, attitudes toward risk, and relevant cash flow information in making capital budgeting decisions.

LEARNING OBJECTIVE 6   Determine the net present value of investment proposals with consideration of the effects of taxes.

BUILDING A *MEGALINER*: BIGGER VERSUS FASTER

Analysts in both the airline and aircraft manufacturing markets estimate that air travel will grow by 5 percent per year over the next 20 years. By 2019, airline fleets may include 32,000 airliners, or about double the current number. In this growing environment for commercial aviation, the two world leaders in the production of large airliners—Airbus and Boeing—have recently arrived at different conclusions about the development of the next generation of jumbo jet aircraft.

Airbus estimates the worldwide market for very large commercial passenger jets at about 1,500 planes and has launched an entirely new model to meet this demand. The double-deck A380 will carry 550–650 passengers for 8,150 miles at

565 miles per hour. By mid-2001, Airbus had received a roughly 60–65 orders for this $230-million plane from Air France, Singapore Airlines, Quantas, and FedEx. Engineers estimate that when delivered in 2006, the A380 will be 20 percent cheaper to fly than a Boeing 747-400—the only current plane in this size class.

The A380's performance relies on breakthroughs in design, technology, and manufacturing methods. In order to save 17 tons in weight, Airbus engineers plan to change the center of gravity of the plane, weld parts with lasers instead of fastening them with rivets, and use a greater percentage of carbon fiber and advanced aluminum alloys in the plane's skin and frame. In addition, Airbus managers plan some innovative approaches to cover the estimated $12 billion in development costs. Although Airbus will fund the majority of these costs, managers have developed a risk-sharing plan that relies on funding from vendors and partners.

By contrast, managers at Boeing Company estimate that the market in the next several decades will require only about 500 of these very large commercial planes. At first, Boeing planned to counter the Airbus A380 with a larger version of the successful 747. The new technology and design elements for such a plane would cost only about $4 billion. Potential customers, however, demonstrated a cool attitude to this plan to update a basic design developed 25 or more years ago.

In mid-2001, Boeing shelved the idea of updating the 747 in favor of the development of the Sonic Cruiser—a plane that would carry only 150–300 passengers but would travel 10,000 miles at 625 miles per hour. With a development cost of about $10–$11 billion, the Sonic Cruiser would save one hour of flight time for every 3,000 miles flown when compared with most current aircraft as well as the A380. Also available in 2006, the Sonic Cruiser would address what Boeing managers concluded was a growing fragmentation trend in transcontinental air travel. Rather than flying only from New York to London, many air travelers want the convenience of connections between more cities on each continent. Thus, airline executives would demand smaller, faster planes. Although the Sonic Cruiser had higher estimated operating costs, airlines might charge higher fares on flights that covered the distance in fewer hours. When asked about the differences between the Airbus and Boeing approaches, a senior Boeing executive commented that the two firms just have different views of the world.

As these decisions faced by Airbus and Boeing illustrate, managers face high stakes in capital expenditure decisions. Often, profitability may only be estimated using marketing research information and unproved technology. No analytical tools will eliminate the inherent uncertainty of these decisions, but executives can use management accounting concepts to organize information about a particular decision and evaluate the alternatives.

Sources: "Boeing Plans to Start Taking Orders for Super-Fast Jetliner in Early 2002," *The Wall Street Journal* (Interactive Edition), April 26, 2001; Matthew Brelis, "Faster vs. Bigger," *The Boston Globe*, May 6, 2001, p. C1; Stuart F. Brown, "How to Build a Really, Really, Really Big Plane," *Fortune*, March 5, 2001, pp. 144–154; Stanley Holmes, "Boeing's Sonic Bruiser," *Business Week*, July 2, 2001, pp. 64 & 68; Stanley Holmes, "Rumble Over Tokyo," *Business Week*, April 2, 2001, pp. 80–81; Daniel Michaels and Jeff Cole, "Airbus Employs New Technology to Drop Weight from Jumbo Jet," *The Wall Street Journal* (Interactive Edition), January 19, 2001; Daniel Michaels, "Airbus Sings Up Partners to Help Build Its Jumbo Jet," *The Wall Street Journal* (Interactive Edition), June 21, 2001; and Anne Marie Squeo, "Boeing Scraps Superjumbo Plans to Focus on Building Smaller Jet," *The Wall Street Journal* (Interactive Edition), March 29, 2001.

In the preceding chapters, much of our attention centered on decisions affecting activity and organization cost drivers when we assume that the organization's basic facilities and products or services do not change. In this chapter, we turn our attention to a portion of long-range planning that deals with the identification and evaluation of major investment proposals to expand or change the organization's activities or facilities.

Capital expenditures involve investments of significant financial resources in projects to develop or introduce new products or services, to expand current production or service capacity, or to change current production or service facilities. Capital expenditures are made with the expectation that the new product, process, or service will generate future financial inflows that exceed the initial costs. Capital expenditure decisions affect structural cost drivers. They are made infrequently but once made are difficult to change. They commit the organization to the use of certain facilities and activities to satisfy customer needs. In making large capital expenditure decisions, management might even be risking the future existence of the company.

Although capital expenditure decisions are still fraught with risk, management accounting provides the concepts and tools needed to organize information and evaluate the alternatives. This systematic organization and analysis is the essence of capital budgeting. **The purpose of this chapter is to introduce important capital budgeting concepts and models and to discuss the proper use of accounting data in these models.**

Capital budgeting is a process that involves identifying of potentially desirable projects for capital expenditures, subsequently evaluating capital expenditure proposals, and selecting proposals that meet certain criteria. A number of quantitative models are available to assist managers in evaluating capital expenditure proposals.

The best capital budgeting models are conceptually similar to the short-range planning models used in Chapters 3 and 4. They all emphasize cash flows and focus on future costs (and revenues) that differ among decision alternatives. The major difference is that capital budgeting models involve cash flows over several years, whereas short-range planning models involve cash flows for a year or less. When the cash flows associated with a proposed activity extend over several years, an adjustment is necessary to make the cash flows expected to occur at different points in time comparable.

The *time value of money concept* explains why monies received or paid at different points in time must be adjusted to have comparable values. The time value of money is introduced in Appendix A to this chapter. If you have not previously studied this concept or if you believe you would benefit from reviewing it, read Appendix A of this chapter before continuing.

LONG-RANGE PLANNING AND CAPITAL BUDGETING PROCEDURES

LEARNING OBJECTIVE 1

Most organizations plan not only for operations in the current period but also for the longer term, perhaps 5, 10, or even 20 years in the future. Most planning beyond the next budget year is called *long-range planning*.

Increased uncertainty and an increased number of alternatives increase the difficulty of planning as the horizon increases. Nevertheless, the fact that long-range planning is difficult and involves uncertainties does not relieve management of long-range planning and capital expenditure decisions. Capital expenditure decisions will be made. The question is: How will they be made? Will they be made on the basis of the best information available? Will care be taken to ensure that capital expenditure decisions are in line with the organization's long-range goals? Will the potential consequences, both positive and negative, of capital expenditures be considered? Will important alternative uses of the organization's limited financial resources be considered in a systematic manner? Will managers be held accountable for the results of the major capital expenditure programs they initiate? The alternative to a systematic approach to capital budgeting is the haphazard expenditure of significant resources on the basis of a hunch, immediate need, or persuasion—without accountability by the person(s) making the capital expenditure decisions.

The steps involved in an effective capital budgeting process are outlined in Exhibit 10–1. A basic requirement for a systematic approach to capital budgeting is a clearly defined mission, a set of long-range goals, and a well-defined business strategy. These provide a guideline, thereby reducing the types of capital expenditure decisions management considers. If, for example, KFC's primary goal is to become the largest fast-food restaurant chain in North America, its management should not consider a proposal to purchase and operate a bus line.

A well-defined business strategy will likewise guide capital expenditure decisions. If Hewlett-Packard is following a strategy to obtain technological leadership, it might

EXHIBIT 10–1

CAPITAL BUDGETING PROCEDURES

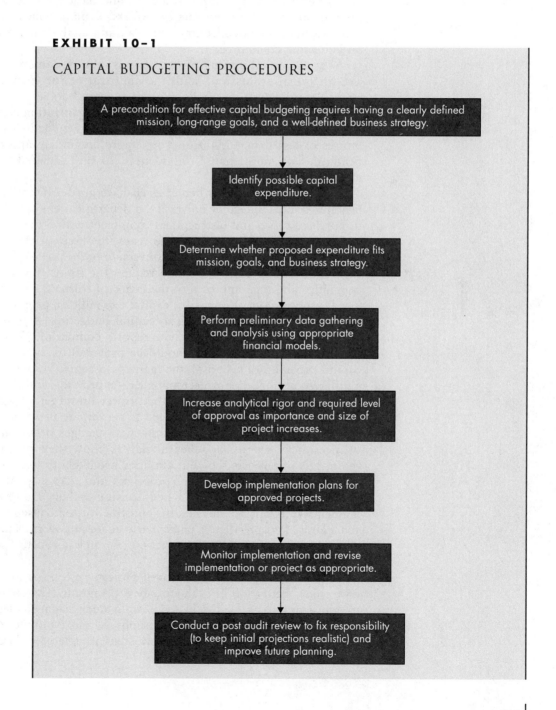

A precondition for effective capital budgeting requires having a clearly defined mission, long-range goals, and a well-defined business strategy.

Identify possible capital expenditure.

Determine whether proposed expenditure fits mission, goals, and business strategy.

Perform preliminary data gathering and analysis using appropriate financial models.

Increase analytical rigor and required level of approval as importance and size of project increases.

Develop implementation plans for approved projects.

Monitor implementation and revise implementation or project as appropriate.

Conduct a post audit review to fix responsibility (to keep initial projections realistic) and improve future planning.

seriously consider a proposal to meet customer needs by investing in innovative production facilities but would not consider a proposal to purchase and refurbish used (but seemingly cost-efficient) equipment.

Management should also developed procedures for the review, evaluation, approval, and post-audit of capital expenditure proposals. In a large organization, a capital budgeting committee that provides guidance to managers in the formulation of capital expenditure proposals is central to these procedures. Additionally, this committee reviews, analyzes, and approves or rejects major capital expenditure proposals. Very significant projects could require the approval of top management and even the board of directors. The capital budgeting committee should include persons knowledgeable in capital budgeting models; financing alternatives and costs; operating procedures; cost estimation and prediction methods; research and development efforts; the organization's goals and basic strategy; and the expectations of the organization's stockholders or owners. A management accountant who is generally expert in data collection, retrieval, and analysis is normally part of the capital budgeting committee.

Not all capital expenditure proposals require committee approval or are subject to formal evaluation. With the approval of top management, the committee might provide guidelines indicating the type and dollar amount of capital expenditures that line managers at each level of the organization can make without formal evaluation or committee approval, or both. The guidelines might state that expenditures of less than $5,000 do not require committee approval and that only expenditures of more than $10,000 need to be evaluated using capital budgeting models.

Typically, managers at higher levels have greater discretion in making capital expenditures. In a college or university, a department chairperson could have authority to purchase office and instructional equipment with a maximum limit of $3,000 per year. A dean may have authority to renovate offices or classrooms with a maximum limit of $20,000 per year, but the conversion of the power plant from fuel oil to wood chips at a cost of $225,000 could require the formal review of a capital budgeting committee and final approval of the board of trustees.

The post-audit of approved capital expenditure proposals is an important part of a well-formulated approach to capital budgeting. A *post-audit* involves the development of project performance reports comparing planned and actual results. Project performance reports should be provided to the manager who initiated the capital expenditure proposal, the manager assigned responsibility for the project (if a different person), the project manager's supervisor, and the capital budgeting committee. These reports help keep the project on target (especially during the initial investment phase), identify the need to reevaluate the project if the initial analysis was in error or significant environmental changes occur, and improve the quality of investment proposals. When managers know they will be held accountable for the results of projects they initiate, they are likely to put more care into the development of capital expenditure proposals and take a greater interest in approved projects. Problems can occur when decision makers are rewarded for undertaking major projects but are not held responsible for the consequences that occur several years later. This problem is particularly acute in government organizations, such as with the city of Denver's construction of a new airport, discussed in What's Happening 10–1.

A post-audit review of approved projects also helps the capital budgeting committee do a better job in evaluating new proposals. The committee might learn how to adjust proposals for the biases of individual managers; learn of new factors that should be considered in evaluating proposals, and avoid the routine approval of projects that appear desirable by themselves but are related to larger projects that are not meeting management's expectations.

EMBLEM OF DENVER'S PROSPERITY BECOMES FINANCIAL BURDEN

In the 1980s, as economic growth and winter storms led to frequent delays at Denver's Stapleton International Airport, city officials committed Denver to build a new airport (DEN). The Federal Aviation Administration predicted that DEN would be the third busiest U.S. airport by the year 2000. At a projected cost of $1.2 billion, the new facility, scheduled to open in 1993, was to be one of the world's largest and most technologically advanced all-weather airports. Plans called for a "showcase" automated baggage system that would move each bag on an underground rail track in its own "telecar."

By October 1993, the projected cost of the new airport had increased to $3.1 billion, and the opening of the airport was delayed due to problems with the automated baggage handling and other systems. In August 1994, Denver's new mayor announced that the baggage handling system just "does not work" and that an additional $50 million was needed to install a manual system. By this time, the projected cost of the airport exceeded $4 billion, and delays in opening were costing the city $2 million a day. The airport finally opened with costs exceeding $5 billion.

United Airlines, with a major hub at Denver, expressed concerns about the increase in landing fees and turnaround time at the new airport. The "new" low-tech baggage handling system would require so much time to move baggage between airplanes that United would have to extend passenger layovers and keep aircraft on the ground longer, thereby increasing operating costs and reducing service.

In an article in a business journal, Paul Dempsey attributed the airport's problems to the egos of designers and politicians who refused to believe that they had not considered every contingency. He pointed as an example to the airport's automated trains, which were the only way to move people between terminals. When asked what would happen if they broke down, designers stated, "They won't." Alas, they did, and the result was chaos.

Today, high airport fees are limiting the growth of air traffic, and passengers who frequently fly through Denver are sticking to carry-on baggage. DEN now has the fewest weather delays among the 20 busiest U.S. airports, but passenger traffic lags behind projections (ranking sixth in U.S. passenger traffic), and airlines are complaining about paying for empty space.

Source: "Still Late for Arrival," *Newsweek,* August 22, 1994, pp. 38–40; "The Rocky Horror Airport Opening," *Business Week,* February 13, 1995, p. 50; Paul Dempsey, "Denver's Own Titanic," *Denver Business Journal,* May 28, 1998, p. 54A; "Mayor, DIA Flunk Critical Test for City," *Denver Business Journal,* October 31, 1997, p. 38A; and "Airports: What $5 Billion Buys" *Air Transport World,* (October 2000, p. 65.)

LEARNING OBJECTIVE 2

CAPITAL BUDGETING MODELS THAT CONSIDER THE TIME VALUE OF MONEY

The capital budgeting models presented in this chapter have gained wide acceptance by for-profit and not-for-profit organizations. You should have at least a rudimentary knowledge of the operation of these models and their strengths and weaknesses. Our primary focus is on the *net present value* and the *internal rate of return models*, which are superior because they consider the time value of money. Later discussions will consider more traditional capital budgeting models, such as the payback period and the accounting rate of return that, while useful under certain circumstances, do not consider the time value of money. Although we briefly consider the cost of financing capital expenditures, we leave a detailed treatment of this topic, as well as a detailed examination of the sources of funds for financing investments, to books on financial management.

ORGANIZING EXPECTED CASH FLOWS

The focus of capital budgeting models that consider the time value of money is on future cash receipts and future cash disbursements that differ under decision alternatives. It is often convenient to distinguish between the following three phases of a project's cash flows:

- Initial investment
- Operation
- Disinvestment

All cash expenditures necessary to begin operations are classified as part of the project's initial investment. Expenditures to acquire property, plant, and equipment are clearly part of the initial investment. Less obvious, but equally important, are expenditures to acquire working capital to purchase inventories and recruit and train employees. Although the initial investment phase often extends over many years, in most textbook examples and problems, we assume that the initial investment takes place at a single point in time.

Cash receipts from sales of goods or services, as well as normal cash expenditures for materials, labor, and other operating expenses, occur during the operation phase. The *operation phase* is typically broken down into one-year periods; for each period, operating cash expenditures are subtracted from operating cash receipts to determine the net operating cash inflow or outflow for the period.

The disinvestment phase occurs at the end of the project's life when assets are disposed of for their salvage value and any initial investment of working capital is recovered. Although this phase might also extend over many years, in textbook examples and problems, we frequently assume disinvestment takes place at a single point in time.

To illustrate the analysis of a project's cash flows, assume the management of Mobile Yogurt Shoppe is considering a capital expenditure proposal to operate a new shop in a resort community in the Ozark Mountains. Each Mobile Yogurt Shoppe is located in a specially constructed motor vehicle that moves on a regular schedule throughout the community it serves. The predicted cash flows associated with the project, which has an expected life of five years, are presented in Exhibit 10–2.

HUMAN BEHAVIOR AND PREDICTING CASH FLOWS

Accurately predicting the cash flows associated with a capital expenditure proposal is critical to properly evaluating the proposal. Managers might be overly optimistic with their predictions, and they are sometimes tempted to modify predictions to justify capital expenditures. Perhaps they are interested in personal rewards. They might also want to avoid a loss of prestige or employment for themselves or to keep a local facility operating for the benefit of current employees and the local economy. Unfortunately, if a major expenditure does not work out, not only the local plant but also the entire company could be forced out of business. For example, under pressure to increase current sales, automobile leasing companies could be tempted to overstate cash receipts during the disinvestment phase of a lease. What's Happening 10–2 considers the financial consequences of overstating residual values for automobile leases.

NET PRESENT VALUE

A project's **net present value,** usually computed as of the time of the initial investment, is the present value of the project's net cash inflows from operations and disinvestment less the amount of the initial investment. In computing a project's net present value, the cash flows occurring at different points in time are adjusted for the time value of money using a **discount rate** that is the minimum rate of return required for the project to be acceptable. Projects with positive net present values (or values at least equal to zero) are acceptable, and projects with negative net present values are unacceptable.

Table Solution Approach. Assuming that management uses a 12 percent discount rate, the net present value of the proposed investment in a Mobile Yogurt Shoppe is

EXHIBIT 10-2

ANALYSIS OF A PROJECT'S PREDICTED CASH FLOWS

Initial investment at time 0:

Vehicle and equipment		$ 90,554
Inventories and other working capital . . .		4,000
Total		$ 94,554

Operation (per year for 5 years):

Sales		$175,000
Cash expenditures:		
Food	$47,000	
Labor	65,000	
Supplies	9,000	
Fuel and utilities	8,000	
Advertising	4,000	
Miscellaneous	12,000	(145,000)
Net annual cash inflow		$ 30,000

Disinvestment (at the end of 5 years):

Sale of vehicle and equipment	$ 8,000
Recovery of investment in inventories and other working capital	4,000
Total	$ 12,000

10-2   WHAT'S HAPPENING?

FALLING RESALE VALUES FOR LEASED SPORT UTILITY VEHICLES MEANS A ROUGH ROAD FOR LEASING COMPANIES

To increase demand for their products by reducing customers' monthly payments, automobile companies encourage customers to lease new vehicles. Important factors in setting vehicles' lease rates include the cost of the vehicle, the cost of capital, the lease period, and the residual values of a vehicle at the end of the lease. The most difficult item to predict is the residual value at the end of the lease. That value, the future selling price of the vehicle, is a function of its condition, economic conditions, actions of competitors, and the popularity of a specific model when the lease expires.

The lease rate (the selling price of the lease) is influenced by predictions of residual value. If residual values are predicted to be high, the monthly lease can be set low enough to attract customers and still earn a profit. Favorable lease terms helped bring down the monthly payments of popular $30,000-plus Ford Explorers and Jeep Grand Cherokees. At the time of the lease, residuals were pegged at $18,000–$19,000.

The profitability of the lease is also partly determined by the residual value. With actual selling prices of $15,000–$16,000 as these leases expired, the leasing companies took a big hit. Commenting on Ford Motor Credit Company's $32.7 billion lease portfolio and General Motors Acceptance Corporation's $24.6 billion lease portfolio, Scott Sprinzen of Standard and Poors observed that a small decrease in the market for used vehicles could cause a substantial loss for manufacturers.

Source: Kathleen Kerwin, "Painful Math for Leasing Companies," *Business Week*, May 19, 1997, p. 38.

shown in Exhibit 10–3 (a) to be $20,400. Since the net present value is more than zero, the investment in the Mobile Yogurt Shoppe is expected to be profitable, even when adjusted for the time value of money.

As an exercise, you should verify the amounts and computations in Exhibit 10–3. Start by tracing the cash flows back to Exhibit 10–2. Next, verify the 12 percent present value factors in Tables 10–1 and 10–2 on pages 439 and 441 in this chapter. The initial investment is assumed to occur at a single point in time (identified as time 0), the start of the project. In net present value computations, all cash flows are restated in terms of their value at time 0. Hence, time 0 cash flows have a present value factor of 1. To simplify computations, all other cash flows are assumed to occur at the end of years 1 through 5, even if they occurred during the year. Although further refinements could be made to adjust for the fact that cash flows occur throughout each year, such adjustments are seldom necessary. Observe that the net operating cash inflows are treated as an *annuity*, whereas the cash flows for the initial investment and the disinvestment are treated as *lump-sum amounts*. If the net operating cash flows varied from year to year, we would have to treat each year's cash flow as a separate amount.

Spreadsheet Solution Approach. Spreadsheet software packages contain functions that compute the present value of a series of cash flows. With this software, simply enter a column or row containing the net cash flows for each period and the appro-

EXHIBIT 10–3

NET PRESENT VALUE ANALYSIS OF A PROJECT'S PREDICTED CASH FLOWS

(a) Table approach:

	Predicted Cash Inflows (outflows) (A)	Year(s) of Cash Flows (B)	12% Present Value Factor (C)	Present Value of Cash Flows (A) × (C)
Initial investment	$(94,554)	0	1.000	$ (94,554)
Operation	30,000	1–5	3.605	108,150
Disinvestment	12,000	5	0.567	6,804
Net present value of all cash flows				$ 20,400

(b) Spreadsheet approach:

Input:

	A	B
1	Year of cash flow	Cash flow
2	1	$30,000
3	2	30,000
4	3	30,000
5	4	30,000
6	5	42,000
7	Present value	=NPV(0.12,B2:B6)
8	Initial investment at time 0	(94,554)
9	Net present value	=B7+B8

Output:

	A	B
1	Year of cash flow	Cash flow
2	1	$30,000
3	2	30,000
4	3	30,000
5	4	30,000
6	5	42,000
7	Present value	$114,952.41
8	Initial investment at time 0	(94,554.00)
9	Net present value	$20,398.41

priate formula. The discount rate of 0.12 is entered as part of the formula. Sample spreadsheet input to determine the net present value of the proposed investment in a Mobile Yogurt Shoppe is shown on the left in Exhibit 10–3 (b). The spreadsheet output is shown on the right, in Exhibit 10–3 (b).

Two cautionary notes follow:

1. The spreadsheet formula for the net present value assumes that the first cash flow occurs at time "1," rather than at time "0." Hence, we cannot include the initial investment in the data set analyzed by the spreadsheet formula when computing the net present value. Instead, the initial investment is subtracted from the present value of future cash flows.
2. Be sure to arrange the cash flows subsequent to the initial investment from *top* to bottom in a column, or *left* to right in a row.

INTERNAL RATE OF RETURN

The **internal rate of return (IRR)**, often called the **time-adjusted rate of return,** is the discount rate that equates the present value of a project's cash inflows with the present value of the project's cash outflows. It is also described in two different ways:

1. The minimum rate that could be paid for the money invested in a project without losing money.
2. The discount rate that results in a project's net present value equaling zero.

Because all practical applications of the IRR model use a calculator or computer, we illustrate determining an IRR only with a spreadsheet in this chapter. The table approach to determining a project's internal rate of return is illustrated in Appendix B of this chapter.

With spreadsheet software, simply enter a column or row containing the net cash flows for each period and the appropriate formula. Spreadsheet input for Mobile Yogurt Shoppe's investment proposal is shown in Exhibit 10–4. Note that the spreadsheet formula for the IRR assumes that the first cash flow occurs at time "0."

The spreadsheet approach requires an initial prediction or guess of the project's internal rate of return. Although the closeness of the prediction to the final solution affects computational speed, for textbook examples almost any number can be used. We use an initial estimate of 0.08 in all illustrations. Because the IRR formula assumes that the first cash flow occurs at time 0, the initial investment is included in

EXHIBIT 10–4

SPREADSHEET APPROACH TO DETERMINING AN INTERNAL RATE OF RETURN

Input:

	A	B
1	Year of cash flow	Cash flow
2	0	$(94,554)
3	1	30,000
4	2	30,000
5	3	30,000
6	4	30,000
7	5	42,000
8	IRR	=IRR(B2:B7,0.08)*

Output:

	A	B
1	Year of cash flow	Cash flow
2	0	$(94,554)
3	1	30,000
4	2	30,000
5	3	30,000
6	4	30,000
7	5	42,000
8	IRR	0.20

The formula is "=IRR(Input data range, guess)." The guess, which can be any likely rate of return, is used as an initial starting point in determining the solution. We use 0.08 in text illustrations.

the data analyzed by the IRR formula. Again, be sure to order the cash flows from top to bottom in a column or left to right in a row. As shown on the right column in Exhibit 10–4, the spreadsheet software computes the IRR as 20 percent.

Although a project's IRR should be compared to the discount rate established by management, such a discount rate is often unknown. In these situations, computing the IRR still provides insights into a project's profitability. Research Shows 10–1 illustrates the use of the IRR model to examine the time-adjusted profitability of Social Security contributions.

The calculated internal rate of return is compared to the discount rate established by management to evaluate investment proposals. If the proposal's IRR is more than or equal to the discount rate, the project is acceptable; if it is less than the discount rate, the project is unacceptable. Because Mobile Yogurt Shoppes has a 12 percent discount rate, the project is acceptable using the IRR model.

Although a computer and appropriate software quickly and accurately perform tedious computations, computational ease increases the opportunity for inappropriate use. The ability to plug numbers into a computer or calculator and obtain an output labeled NPV or IRR could mislead the unwary into believing that capital budgeting models are easy to use. This simply is not true. Training and professional judgment are required to identify relevant costs, to implement procedures to obtain relevant cost information, and to make a good decision once computational results are available. Capital budgeting models are merely decision aids. People, not models, make the decisions. To better illustrate underlying concepts and to assist readers not having a computer available to verify textbook examples, all subsequent textbook illustrations are based on a table approach.

COST OF CAPITAL

When discounting models are used to evaluate capital expenditure proposals, management must determine the discount rate (1) used to compute a proposal's net present value or (2) used as the standard for evaluating a proposal's IRR. An organization's cost of capital is often used as this discount rate.

The **cost of capital** is the average cost an organization pays to obtain the resources necessary to make investments. The cost of capital is the average rate an organization

---

10–1   RESEARCH SHOWS

INTERNAL RATES OF RETURN FROM SOCIAL SECURITY VARY WITH INCOME AND AGE

Under the current Social Security law, 12.4 percent of nearly every U.S. employee's gross annual wage (up to a maximum of $80,400) is contributed to the Old Age and Survivor's Insurance (OASI) program. An important purpose of the program is to provide financial support to employees after retirement.

Caldwell et al. determined the internal rate of return (IRR) for several categories of Social Security participants. The researchers found that the expected IRR for the lowest paid workers is between 4 and 5 percent, for middle income workers is between 1 and 2 percent, and for the highest paid workers is below 1 percent, and for members of this final group born after 1975, could be negative.

These results stem from the design of the Social Security program that provides low-paid workers a higher percentage of their preretirement income. Additional factors include increases in the maximum annual wage subject to Social Security "contributions" and increases in the age required to receive full Social Security benefits.

Source: Kevin Lansing, "Rates of Return from Social Security," *FRBSF Economic Letter*, November 12, 1999, p. 1; and Steven Caldwell et al., "Social Security's Treatment of Postwar Americans," Working Paper 6003, National Bureau of Economic Research. http://www.nber.org

must pay for invested funds. This average rate considers items such as these:

- The effective interest rate on notes or bonds.
- The effective dividend rate on preferred stock.
- The discount rate that equates the present value of all dividends expected on common stock over the life of the organization to the current market value of the organization's common stock.

The cost of capital for a company that has no debt or preferred stock is simply the cost of equity capital, computed as follows:

$$\text{Cost of equity capital} = \frac{\text{Current annual dividend per common share}}{\text{Current market price per common share}} + \frac{\text{Expected dividend}}{\text{Growth rate}}$$

Procedures for determining the cost of capital for more complex capital structures are covered in finance textbooks. Investing in a project that has an internal rate of return equal to the cost of capital should not affect the market value of the firm's securities. Investing in a project that has a return higher than the cost of capital should increase the market value of a firm's securities. If, however, a firm invests in a project that has a return of less than the cost of capital, the market value of the firm's securities should fall.

The cost of capital is the minimum return that is acceptable for investment purposes. Any investment proposal not expected to yield this minimum rate should normally be rejected. Because of difficulties encountered in determining the cost of capital, many organizations adopt a discount rate or a target rate of return without complicated mathematical analysis.

LEARNING OBJECTIVE 3

CAPITAL BUDGETING MODELS THAT DO NOT CONSIDER THE TIME VALUE OF MONEY

For many years, capital budgeting models that do not consider the time value of money were more widely used than were discounting models. Although most large North American organizations use net present value or internal rate of return as their primary evaluation tool, they often use nondiscounting models as an initial screening device. Interestingly, as discussed in Research Shows 10–2, nondiscounting models remain firmly entrenched in small businesses. We consider two nondiscounting models, the *payback period* and the *accounting rate of return*.

PAYBACK PERIOD

The **payback period** is the time required to recover the initial investment in a project from operations. The payback decision rule states that acceptable projects must have less than some maximum payback period designated by management. Payback emphasizes management's concern with liquidity and the need to minimize risk through a rapid recovery of the initial investment. It is frequently used for small expenditures having such obvious benefits that the use of more sophisticated capital budgeting models is not required or justified.

When a project is expected to have equal annual operating cash inflows, its payback period is computed as follows:

$$\text{Payback period} = \frac{\text{Initial investment}}{\text{Annual operating cash inflows}}$$

For Mobile Yogurt Shoppe's investment proposal, outlined in Exhibit 10–2, the payback period is 3.15 years:

NONDISCOUNTING MODELS ARE WIDELY USED IN SMALL BUSINESSES

In spite of the economic importance of small businesses, which employ almost two-thirds of the U.S. workforce, most surveys of the use of capital budgeting models focus on large businesses. Researcher Stanley Block examined firms with less than $5 million sales and fewer than 1,000 employees. He found that most small businesses used the payback period as their primary method of investment analysis. Furthermore, most small businesses required a payback period of less than three years:

Primary Method of Investment Analysis		Minimum Acceptable Payback Period	
Payback period	42.7%	1 year	9.5
Accounting rate of return	22.4	2 years	43.2
Internal rate of return	16.4	3 years	31.1
Net present value	7.3	4 years or more	16.2

Block believes that the predominance of the payback method is attributed to its simplicity, emphasis on liquidity, and response to external financial pressures. He observed, "Bankers are primarily interested in the firm's ability to meet short-term obligations associated with a loan, rather than maximizing the wealth of the owners of the firm. When the small business owner approaches a banker for a loan to finance a capital investment, he better be prepared to demonstrate his capacity to repay the loan within a set period of time. . . ."

Source: Stanley Block, "Capital Budgeting Techniques Used by Small Business Firms in the 1990s," *Engineering Economist,* Summer 1997, pp. 289–302.

$$\text{Payback period} = \frac{\$94,554}{\$30,000}$$
$$= 3.15$$

Determining the payback period for a project having unequal cash flows is slightly more complicated. Assume that Alderman Company is evaluating a capital expenditure proposal that requires an initial investment of $50,000 and has the following expected net cash inflows:

Year	Net Cash Inflow
1	$15,000
2	25,000
3	40,000
4	20,000
5	10,000

To compute the payback period, we must determine the net unrecovered amount at the end of each year. In the year of full recovery, the net cash inflows are assumed to occur evenly and are prorated based on the unrecovered investment at the start of the year. Full recovery of Alderman Company's investment proposal is expected to occur in Year 3:

Year	Net Cash Inflow	Unrecovered Investment
0	$ 0	$50,000
1	15,000	35,000
2	25,000	10,000
3	40,000	

Therefore, $10,000 of $40,000 is needed in Year 3 to complete the recovery of the initial investment. This provides a proportion of 0.25 ($10,000 ÷ $40,000) and a payback period of 2.25 years (2 years plus 0.25 of Year 3). This project is acceptable if management specified a maximum payback period of three years. Because they occur after the payback period, the net cash inflows of Years 4 and 5 are ignored.

ACCOUNTING RATE OF RETURN

The **accounting rate of return** is the average annual increase in net income that results from the acceptance of a capital expenditure proposal divided by either the initial investment or the average investment in the project. This method differs from other capital budgeting models in that it focuses on accounting income rather than on cash flow. In most capital budgeting applications, accounting net income is approximated as net cash inflow from operations minus expenses not requiring the use of cash, such as depreciation.

Consider Mobile Yogurt Shoppe's capital expenditure proposal whose cash flows were outlined in Exhibit 10–2. The vehicle and equipment cost $90,554 and have a disposal value of $8,000 at the end of five years, resulting in an average annual increase in net income of $13,489:

Annual net cash inflow from operations	$30,000
Less average annual depreciation ([$90,554 − $8,000] ÷ 5)	(16,511)
Average annual increase in net income	$13,489

Considering the investment in inventories and other working capital, the initial investment is $94,554 ($90,554 + $4,000), and the *accounting rate of return on initial investment* is 14.27 percent:

$$\text{Accounting rate of return on initial investment} = \frac{\text{Average annual increase in net income}}{\text{Initial investment}} = \frac{\$13,489}{\$94,554} = 0.1427$$

The average investment, computed as the initial investment plus the expected value of any disinvestment, all divided by 2, is $53,277 [($94,554 + $12,000) ÷ 2]. The *accounting rate of return on average investment* is 25.32 percent:

$$\text{Accounting rate of return on initial investment} = \frac{\text{Average annual increase in net income}}{\text{Average investment}} = \frac{\$13,489}{\$53,277} = 0.2532$$

When using the accounting rate of return, management specifies either the initial investment or average investment plus some minimum acceptable rate. Management rejects capital expenditure proposals with a lower accounting rate of return but accepts proposals with an accounting rate of return higher than or equal to the minimum.

LEARNING OBJECTIVE 4

EVALUATION OF CAPITAL BUDGETING MODELS

As a single criterion for evaluating capital expenditure proposals, capital budgeting models that consider the time value of money are superior to models that do not consider it. The payback model concerns merely how long it takes to recover the initial investment from a project, yet investments are not made with the objective of merely getting the money back. Indeed, not investing has a payback period of 0. Investments are made to earn a profit. Hence, what happens after the payback period is more important than is the payback period itself. The payback period model, when used as the sole investment criterion, has a fatal flaw in that it fails to consider cash flows after the payback period. Despite this flaw, payback is a rough-and-ready approach to getting a handle on investment proposals. Sometimes a project is so attractive using payback that, when its life is considered, no further analysis is necessary.

For total life evaluations, the accounting rate of return is superior to the payback period because it does consider a capital expenditure proposal's profitability. Using the accounting rate of return, a project that merely returns the initial investment will have an average annual increase in net income of 0 and an accounting rate of return of 0. The problem with the accounting rate of return is that it fails to consider the timing of cash flows. It treats all cash flows within the life of an investment proposal equally despite the fact that cash flows occurring early in a project's life are more valuable than cash flows occurring late in a project's life. Early period cash flows can earn additional profits by being invested elsewhere. Consider the two investment proposals summarized in Exhibit 10–5. Both have an accounting rate of return of 5 percent, but Proposal A is superior to Proposal B because most of its cash flows occur in the

EXHIBIT 10–5

EVALUATING CAPITAL BUDGETING MODELS WITH DIFFERENCES IN THE TIMING OF CASH FLOWS

Accounting rate of return analysis of Projects A and B:

	Project A	Project B
Predicted net cash inflow from operations:		
Year 1	$ 50,000	$ 10,000
Year 2	50,000	10,000
Year 3	10,000	50,000
Year 4	10,000	50,000
Total	$ 120,000	$ 120,000
Total depreciation	(100,000)	(100,000)
Total net income	$ 20,000	$ 20,000
Project life	÷ 4 years	÷ 4 years
Average annual increase in net income	$ 5,000	$ 5,000
Initial investment	÷ 100,000	÷ 100,000
Accounting rate of return on initial investment	0.05	0.05

Net present value analysis of Project A:

	Predicted Cash Inflows (outflows)	Year(s) of Cash Flows	10% Present Value Factor	Present Value of Cash Flows
Initial investment	$(100,000)	0	1.000	$(100,000)
Operation	50,000	1–2	1.736	86,800
	10,000	3–4	3.170–1.736	14,340
Net present value of all cash flows				$ 1,140

Net present value analysis of Project B:

	Predicted Cash Inflows (outflows)	Year(s) of Cash Flows	10% Present Value Factor	Present Value of Cash Flows
Initial investment	$(100,000)	0	1.000	$(100,000)
Operation	10,000	1–2	1.736	17,360
	50,000	3–4	3.170–1.736	71,700
Net present value of all cash flows				$ (10,940)

first two years. Because of the timing of the cash flows when discounted at an annual rate of 10 percent, Proposal A has a net present value of $1,140 while Proposal B has a negative net present value of $(10,940).

The net present value and the internal rate of return models both consider the time value of money and project profitability. They almost always provide the same evaluation of individual projects whose acceptance or rejection will not affect other projects.[1] The net present value and the internal rate of return models, however, have two basic differences that often lead to differences in the evaluation of competing investment proposals:

1. The net present value model gives explicit consideration to investment size. The internal rate of return model does not.
2. The net present value model assumes that all net cash inflows are reinvested at the discount rate; the internal rate of return model assumes that all net cash inflows are reinvested at the project's internal rate of return.

These differences will be considered later when we discuss mutually exclusive investments.

LEARNING OBJECTIVE 5

ADDITIONAL ASPECTS OF CAPITAL BUDGETING

The capital budgeting models discussed do not make investment decisions. Rather, they help managers separate capital expenditure proposals that meet certain criteria from those that do not. Managers then focus on those proposals that pass the initial screening.

USING MULTIPLE INVESTMENT CRITERIA

In performing this initial screening, management can use a single capital budgeting model or multiple models, including some we have not discussed. Management might specify that proposals must be in line with the organization's long-range goals and business strategy, have a maximum payback period of three years, have a positive net present value when discounted at 14 percent, and have an initial investment of less than $500,000. The maximum payback period might be intended to reduce risk, the present value criterion might be to ensure an adequate return to investors, and the maximum investment size might reflect the resources available for investment. Accounting researchers Arya, Fellingham, and Glover believe the use of multiple criteria is a useful way of evaluating projects from different perspectives. "If many of the criteria suggest the project should be taken, the chance is greater that the project is desirable."[2]

Nonquantitative factors such as market position, operational performance improvement, and strategy implementation often play a decisive role in management's final decision to accept or reject a capital expenditure proposal that has passed the initial screening. Also important at this point are top management's attitudes toward risk and financing alternatives, their confidence in the professional judgment of other managers making investment proposals, their beliefs about the future direction of the economy, and their evaluation of alternative investments. In the following sections, we will focus on evaluating risk to the differential analysis of project cash flows,

---

[1] An exception often occurs when periods of net cash outflows are mixed with periods of net cash inflows. Under these circumstances, an investment proposal could have multiple internal rates of return. For a further discussion of this point, consult a financial management textbook.

[2] Anil Arya, John C. Fellingham, and Jonathan C. Glover, "Capital Budgeting: Some Exceptions to the Net Present Value Rule," *Issues in Accounting Education*, August 1998, pp. 499–508.

predicting differential costs and revenues for high-tech investments, and evaluating mutually exclusive investments.

EVALUATING RISK

All capital expenditure proposals involve many sources of risk, including risk related to

- The cost of the initial investment.
- The time required to complete the initial investment and begin operations.
- Whether the new facilities will operate as planned.
- The life of the facilities.
- The customers' demand for the product or service.
- The final selling price.
- Operating costs.
- Disposal values.

Projected cash flows (such as those summarized for the Mobile Yogurt Shoppe proposal in Exhibit 10–2) are based on management's best prediction as to what will happen. Although these predictions are likely to reflect the professional judgment of economists, marketing personnel, engineers, and accountants, they are far from certain.

Many techniques have been developed to assist in the analysis of the risks inherent in capital budgeting. Suggested approaches include the following:

- To *adjust the discount rate for individual projects based on management's perception of the risks associated with a project*. A project perceived as being almost risk free might be evaluated using a discount rate of 12 percent; a project perceived as having moderate risk may be evaluated using a discount rate of 16 percent; and a project perceived as having high risk might be evaluated using a discount rate of 20 percent.
- To *compute several internal rates of return and/or net present values for a project*. For example, a project's net present value might be computed three times: first assuming the most optimistic projections of cash flows; second assuming the most likely projections of cash flows; and third assuming the most pessimistic projections of cash flows. The final decision is then based on management's attitudes toward risk. A project whose most likely outcome is highly profitable would probably be rejected if its pessimistic outcome might lead to bankruptcy.
- To *subject a capital expenditure proposal to sensitivity analysis*, which was defined in Chapter 3 as a study of the responsiveness of a model's dependent variable(s) to changes in one or more of its independent variables. Management might want to know, for example, the minimum annual net cash inflows that will provide an internal rate of return of 12 percent with other cost and revenue projections being as expected.

Consider the situation presented in Exhibit 10–2 and analyzed using the net present value and the internal rate of return models in Exhibits 10–3 and 10–4. This proposal has a positive net present value when its cash flows are discounted at 12 percent and an expected IRR of 20 percent. Assuming that Mobile Yogurt Shoppes has a 12 percent discount rate, management might wish to know the minimum annual net cash inflow that will meet this criterion.

In Exhibit 10–3, disinvestment cash inflows have a net present value of $6,804. When this amount is subtracted from the initial investment, $87,750 ($94,554 − $6,804) of the initial investment must be recovered from operations. If this amount is to be recovered over a five-year period with equal annual net cash inflows and a 12 percent discount rate, the factor 3.605 (see Table 10–2) must equate the annual net cash inflows with the portion of the initial investment to be recovered from operations. Hence, the minimum annual net cash inflows must be $24,341:

$$\text{Minimum annual net cash inflow} = \frac{\$87,750}{3.605}$$
$$= \$24,341$$

If management could then predict the probability of annual net cash inflows being more than or equal to $24,341, the probability of this project indicates it would meet a 12 percent discount rate. Again, the ultimate decision to accept or reject the proposal rests with management and their attitudes toward risk.

It is interesting to note the similarity of the analysis here, determining the minimum annual net cash inflows, and determining the break-even point in Chapter 3. In effect, $24,341 in annual net cash inflows is a time-adjusted break-even point.

DIFFERENTIAL ANALYSIS OF PROJECT CASH FLOWS

All previous examples assume that capital expenditure proposals will produce additional net cash inflows, but this is not always the case. Units of government and not-for-profit organizations might provide services that do not produce any cash inflows. For-profit organizations might be required to make capital expenditures to maintain product quality or to bring facilities up to environmental or safety standards. In these situations, it is impossible to compute a project's payback period, accounting rate of return, or internal rate of return. It is possible, however, to compute the present value of all life cycle costs associated with alternative ways of providing the service or meeting the environmental or safety standard. Here, the alternative with the smallest negative net present value is preferred.

Capital expenditure proposals to reduce operating costs by upgrading facilities might not provide any incremental cash inflows. Again, we can use a total cost approach and calculate the present value of the costs associated with each alternative, with the low-cost alternative being preferred. Alternatively, we can perform a differential analysis of cash flows and, treating any reduced operating costs as if they were cash inflows, compute the net present value or the internal rate of return of the cost reduction proposal. Recall from Chapter 3 that a differential cost analysis focuses on the costs that differ under alternative actions. Once the differential amounts have been determined, they can be adjusted for the time value of money. To illustrate the differential approach, we consider an example introduced in Chapter 4.

Ace Welding Company uses a Model I welding machine to produce 10,000 Mountain bicycle frames per year. The Model I welding machine is two years old and has a remaining useful life of four years. It cost $90,000 and has an estimated salvage value of zero dollars at the end of its useful life. Its current book value (original cost less accumulated depreciation) is $60,000, but its current disposal value is only $35,000.

Management is evaluating the desirability of replacing the Model I welding machine with a new Model II welding machine. The new machine costs $80,000, has a useful life of four years, and a predicted salvage value of zero dollars at the end of its useful life. Although the new machine has the same productive capacity as the old machine, its predicted operating costs are lower because it requires less electricity. Furthermore, because of a computer control system, the Model II machine will require less frequent and less expensive inspections and adjustments. Finally, the Model II machine requires less maintenance.

A differential analysis of the cash flows associated with this cost reduction proposal, separated into the three phases of the project's life, are presented in Exhibit 10–6. Because the proposal does not have a disposal value, this portion of the analysis could have been omitted. (Readers interested in a detailed explanation of the relevant costs included in this analysis are referred to Exhibit 4–1 and the accompanying

EXHIBIT 10-6

DIFFERENTIAL ANALYSIS OF PREDICTED CASH FLOWS

	DIFFERENTIAL ANALYSIS OF PREDICTED CASH FLOWS		
	Keep Old Model I Machine (A)	Replace with New Model II Machine (B)	Difference (effect of replacement on income) (A) − (B)
Initial investment:			
Cost of new machine		$80,000	$80,000
Disposal value of old machine		(35,000)	(35,000)
Net initial investment			$45,000
Annual operating cash savings:			
Conversion:			
Mountain frames, Model I (10,000 units × $5)	$50,000		
Mountain frames, Model II (10,000 units × $4)		$40,000	$10,000
Inspection and adjustment:			
Mountain frames, Model I (10 × $500)	5,000		
Mountain frames, Model II (5 × $300)		1,500	3,500
Machine maintenance:			
Mountain frames, Model I ($200 × 12 months)	2,400		
Mountain frames, Model II ($200 per year)		200	2,200
Net annual cost savings			$15,700
Disinvestment at end of life:			
Old	$ 0		
New		$ 0	

Chapter 4 discussion of relevant costs.) Assuming that Ace Welding has a discount rate of 12 percent, the proposal's net present value (computed in Exhibit 10–7) is $2,681, and the proposal is acceptable.

PREDICTING DIFFERENTIAL COSTS AND REVENUES FOR HIGH-TECH INVESTMENTS

Special care must be taken when evaluating proposals for investments in the most current technological innovations such as flexible manufacturing systems and computer integrated manufacturing. The three types of errors to consider are: (1) investing in unnecessary or overly complex equipment, (2) overestimating cost saving and (3) underestimating incremental sales.

Investing in Unnecessary or Overly Complex Equipment. A basic error is to simply compare the cost associated with the current inefficient way of doing things with the predicted cost of performing the identical operations with more modern equipment. Although capital budgeting models might suggest that such investments are justifiable, the result could be the costly and rapid completion of non-value-added activities. Consider the following examples.

EXHIBIT 10-7

NET PRESENT VALUE ANALYSIS OF DIFFERENTIAL CASH FLOWS

	Predicted Cash Inflows (outflows) (A)	Year(s) of Cash Flows (B)	12% Present Value Factor (C)	Present Value of Cash Flows (A) × (C)
Initial investment	$(45,000)	0	1.000	$(45,000)
Operation	15,700	1–4	3.037	47,681
Disinvestment	0	4	0.636	0
Net present value of all cash flows				$ 2,681

- A company invests in an automated system to speed the movement of work in process between workstations on the shop floor without first evaluating the plant layout. The firm is still unable to compete with other companies having better organized plants that allow lower cycle times, lower work-in-process inventories, and lower manufacturing costs. Management should have evaluated the plant layout before investing in new equipment. They may have found that rearranging the factory floor would have reduced materials movement and eliminated the need for the investment.

- A company invests in a large automated warehouse to permit the rapid storage and retrieval of goods while competitors work to eliminate excess inventory. The firm is left with large inventories and a large investment in the automated warehouse while competitors, not having to earn a return on similar investments, are able to charge lower prices. Management should have evaluated the need for current inventory levels and perhaps shifted to a just-in-time approach to inventory management before considering the investment in an automated warehouse.

- A company invests in equipment to perform quality inspections while competitors implement total quality management and seek to eliminate the need for quality inspections. While defective products are now detected before shipment to customers, they are still being produced. Furthermore, the company has a higher capital investment than competitors have. The result is, again, a less competitive cost structure. The inspection equipment might not have been needed if management had shifted from inspecting all finished goods for conformance to an emphasis on "doing it right the first time."

- A company invests in automated welding equipment to more efficiently produce printer casings while competitors simplify the product design and shift from welded to molded plastic casings. Although the cost of producing the welded casings might be lower, the company's cost structure is still not competitive.

All of these examples illustrate the limitations of capital budgeting models and the need for professional judgment. *In the final analysis, people, not models, make decisions.* Management must carefully evaluate the situations and determine whether they have considered the proper alternatives and all important cash flows.

Overestimating Cost Savings. When a number of activities drive manufacturing overhead costs, estimates of overhead cost savings based on a single activity cost driver can significantly overestimate cost savings. Assume, for example, that a company containing both machine-intensive and labor-intensive operations develops a cost-estimating equation for manufacturing overhead with direct labor as the only independent variable. Because of this, all overhead costs are associated with direct labor.

The predicted cost savings can be computed as the sum of predicted reductions in direct labor plus predicted reductions in overhead; the predicted reductions in overhead are computed as the overhead per direct labor dollar or labor hour multiplied by the predicted reduction in direct labor dollars or labor hours. Because a major portion of the manufacturing overhead is driven by factors other than direct labor, reducing direct labor will not provide the predicted savings. Capital budgeting models might suggest that the investment is acceptable, but the models are based on inaccurate cost data.

Management should beware of overly simplistic computations of cost savings. This is an area in which management needs the assistance of well-trained management accountants and engineers.

Underestimating Incremental Sales or Cost Savings. In evaluating proposals for investments in new equipment, management often assumes that the baseline for comparison is the current sales level, but this might not be the case. If competitors are investing in equipment to better meet customer needs and to reduce costs, a failure to make similar investments might result in uncompetitive prices and declining, rather than steady, sales. Hence, the baseline for sales without the investment is overstated, and the incremental sales of the investment is understated. Not considering the likely decline in sales understates the incremental sales associated with the investment and biases the results against the proposed investment.

Investments in the most advanced manufacturing technologies, such as flexible manufacturing systems (FMS) and computer integrated manufacturing (CIM), do more than simply allow the efficient production of current products. Such investments also

10-3   WHAT'S HAPPENING?

THE VALUE CHAIN BROADENS THE CAPITAL BUDGETING PERSPECTIVE FOR YAKIMA-OLYMPIA

Yakima-Olympia (Y-O) is a vertically integrated forest product company whose activities range from developing and planting improved seedlings to the retail distribution of wood products. Nevertheless, like most forest product firms, Y-O hires private logging contractors to cut trees (primarily for cost reasons such as nonunion wages). These contractors follow traditional procedures to fell all trees in an area, remove branches with chain saws, and drag trees to loading areas.

Y-O wanted its logging contractors in the Tidewater region of Virginia to switch to harvesting machines that could selectively cut and trim mature trees to meet current production specifications. To do this, a logging contractor would have to make a capital investment of approximately $600,000 in new equipment. Over the harvesting machine's five-year life, it would have annual cash operating costs of approximately $250,000. Following standard rates, the contractor would receive annual revenues of approximately $400,000 from Y-O. With a 12 percent time value of money, the proposed investment's net present value is minus $60,000. Consequently, Y-O met with little success in convincing contractors to switch to harvesting machines.

Analyzing the situation, John Shank and Vijay Govindarajan concluded that the proposal was being rejected because of a failure to analyze costs across Y-O's entire value chain. They noted that across the value chain, the use of harvesting machines would produce significant savings in land management, sorting, reduced waste, and reduced processing costs. Although the investment would produce major financial benefits, the stage in the value chain at which the investment must be made, under traditional pricing policies, would receive none of the benefits. Shank and Govindarajan observed that Y-O should consider a gain-sharing mechanism to convince logging contractors to make the necessary investment. If this is not feasible, Y-O might decide that the economic gains from the investment are large enough to stop outside contracting and internalize logging operations.

Source: John K. Shank and Vijay Govindarajan, "Strategic Cost Analysis of Technological Investments," *Sloan Management Review,* Fall 1992, pp. 39–51.

make possible the rapid, low-cost switching to new products. The result is expanded sales opportunities.

Such investments might also produce cost savings further down the value chain, either within or outside the company. Ace Welding Company's decision to acquire a new Model II welding machine might have the unanticipated consequence of reducing customer warranty claims or increasing sales because customers are attracted to a higher-quality product. What's Happening 10–3 discusses how taking a value chain perspective might affect capital budgeting and other strategic decisions.

Unfortunately, because such opportunities are difficult to quantify, they are often ignored in the evaluation of capital expenditure proposals. The result is a bias against investments in FMS and CIM. The solution to this dilemma involves the application of management's professional judgment, a willingness to take risks based on this professional judgment, and recognition that certain investments transcend capital budgeting models in that they involve strategic as well as long-range planning. At this level of planning, qualitative decisions concerning the nature of the organization are at least as important as quantified factors. What's Happening 10–4 examines the difficulty Aetna Life and Casualty Co. encountered in evaluating strategic investments in information technology.

EVALUATING MUTUALLY EXCLUSIVE INVESTMENTS

Two or more capital expenditure proposals are **mutually exclusive investments** if the acceptance of one automatically causes the rejection of the other(s). Perhaps a builder with a tract of land on the outskirts of Paris is trying to determine the most profitable use of the land. Because of the size of the tract and zoning requirements, the land can be used for only one of three purposes: a shopping center, a housing development, or an office park.

When faced with mutually exclusive investments, management must determine which one to accept. The decision is relatively easy if only one of the proposals meets the organization's investment criteria. If, however, two or more proposals pass the initial screening performed by the investment criteria, management faces the task of selecting the best of the acceptable proposals. To help in this determination, management

---

10–4 WHAT'S HAPPENING?

AETNA LIFE & CASUALTY DOES NOT MEASURE THE RETURN ON INFORMATION TECHNOLOGY

After spending a year trying to determine how to measure the return from investments in information technology, John Loewenberg, senior vice president of information and technology at Aetna Life & Casualty Co., gave up, calling it "an exercise in futility." Loewenberg observed that while there appears to be a correlation between investments in information technology and reductions in cost, it is difficult to say that one caused the other.

Aetna has a complex computer system that links a collection of central databases with computer networks around the country. The system provides up-to-date information so that agents can immediately respond to customer questions. The complexity of the system makes it difficult to evaluate proposals for additional investments in the system. Loewenberg's frustration came from the fact that "once a business unit implemented a new technology solution, the [business and technology] became so integrated that you couldn't tell them apart."

Aetna managers now make the case for additional investments in technology on the basis of business objectives such as customer satisfaction and product improvements. Loewenberg focuses on delivering agreed-upon services as cost-effectively as possible.

Source: "Magic Formula," *The Wall Street Journal,* November 14, 1994, p. R18.

could request that the proposals be ranked on the basis of some criterion such as net present value or internal rate of return. Unfortunately, while these models almost always lead to identical decisions when used to evaluate individual investment proposals, they frequently produce different rankings of acceptable proposals. Assume that management can select only one of three mutually exclusive investment proposals. Relevant information is summarized in Exhibit 10–8.

Assuming that the organization has a 12 percent cost of capital, all projects have a positive net present value and an internal rate of return in excess of 12 percent. Therefore, all are acceptable. The problem is to determine which of these acceptable proposals is most desirable. Ranking the proposals by their net present value indicates that Proposal B is best, while ranking by IRR indicates that Proposal C is best.

A frequent criticism of net present value to rank investment proposals is that it fails to adjust for the size of the proposed investment. To overcome this difficulty, managers can rank projects on the basis of each project's **present value index,** which is computed as the present value of the project's subsequent cash flows divided by the initial investment:

$$\text{Present value index} = \frac{\text{Present value of subsequent cash flows}}{\text{Initial investment}}$$

For Proposal A, the present value of the subsequent cash flows, discounted at 12 percent, is \$30,370,000 (\$10,000,000 × 3.037), and the present value index is 1.129:

$$\text{Present value index} = \frac{\$30,370,000}{\$26,900,000}$$
$$= 1.129$$

Using this criterion, projects that have a present value index of 1.0 or higher are acceptable, and the project with the highest present value index is preferred. Ranking the proposals in Exhibit 10–8 on the basis of their present value index results in Proposal A being ranked number 1.

We now have three acceptable proposals, three criteria, three different rankings, and the task of selecting only one of the three proposals. Many managers would se-

EXHIBIT 10–8

RANKING CAPITAL BUDGETING PROPOSALS

Amounts in Thousands	Proposal A	Proposal B	Proposal C
Predicted cash flows:			
Initial investment (000)	$(26,900)	$(55,960)	$(30,560)
Operation:			
Year 1	10,000	20,000	20,000
Year 2	10,000	20,000	20,000
Year 3	10,000	20,000	0
Year 4	10,000	20,000	0
Disinvestment	0	0	0
Investment criterion:			
Net present value at 12%	$ 3,470	$ 4,780	$ 3,240
Internal rate of return	18%	16%	20%
Present value index	1.129	1.085	1.106
Ranking by investment criterion:			
Net present value	2	1	3
Internal rate of return	2	3	1
Present value index	1	3	2

lect Proposal C because it has the highest IRR or Proposal A because it has the highest present value index. Either selection provides a satisfactory, but not an optimal, solution to the dilemma. If the true cost of capital is 12 percent and other investment opportunities return only 12 percent, the net present value criterion provides the proper choice. This is illustrated in Exhibit 10–9 by evaluating the additional return earned on the differences between Proposals B and A and on the differences between Proposals B and C.

The difference in the net present value and internal rate of return rankings results from differences in their reinvestment assumptions. The net present value model assumes that all net cash inflows from a project are reinvested at the discount rate; the internal rate of return model assumes that all net cash inflows from a project are reinvested at the project's internal rate of return. If unlimited funds are available at the discount rate, marginal investments are made at this rate, and the assumption underlying the net present value model is the correct one. Returning to Exhibit 10–9, if all funds not invested in the chosen project and all funds recovered from the chosen project can earn only the discount rate, the firm is $1,540,000 better off by selecting Proposal B rather than Proposal C.

The present value index eliminates the impact of size from net present value computations. However, size is an important consideration in evaluating investment proposals, especially if funds not invested in a project can earn only the discount rate. In Exhibit 10–9, we see that if funds not invested in the chosen project can be invested only at the discount rate, the firm is $1,310,000 better off by selecting Proposal B rather than Proposal A.

LEARNING OBJECTIVE 6

TAXES IN CAPITAL BUDGETING DECISIONS

To focus on capital budgeting concepts, we deferred consideration of the impact of taxes on capital budgeting until the end of the chapter. Because income taxes affect cash flows and income, their consideration is important in evaluating any business decision.

The cost of investments in plant and equipment is not deducted from taxable revenues in determining taxable income and income taxes at the time of the initial investment. Instead, the amount of the initial investment is deducted as depreciation over the operating life of an asset. To illustrate the impact of taxes on operating cash flows, assume these facts:

- Revenues and operating cash receipts are the same each year.
- Depreciation is the only noncash expense of an organization.

DEPRECIATION TAX SHIELD

Depreciation does not require the use of cash (the funds were spent at the initial investment), but depreciation is said to provide a "tax shield" because it reduces cash payments for income taxes. The **depreciation tax shield** (the reduction in taxes due to the deductibility of depreciation from taxable revenues) is computed as follows:

$$\text{Depreciation tax shield} = \text{Depreciation} \times \text{Tax rate}$$

The value of the depreciation tax shield is illustrated using Mobile Yogurt Shoppe's capital expenditure proposal summarized in Exhibit 10–2. Assuming a tax rate of 34 percent, the annual net income and after-tax cash flows for this investment without depreciation and with straight-line depreciation are shown in Exhibit 10–10. Examine this exhibit, paying particular attention to the lines for depreciation, income taxes, and net annual cash flow.

EXHIBIT 10-9

ANALYSIS OF INCREMENTAL INVESTMENTS

Amounts in Thousands	Proposal B	Proposal A	Difference B − A
Predicted cash flows:			
Initial investment	$(55,960)	$(26,900)	$(29,060)
Operation:			
Year 1	20,000	10,000	10,000
Year 2	20,000	10,000	10,000
Year 3	20,000	10,000	10,000
Year 4	20,000	10,000	10,000
Disinvestment	0	0	0

Net present value of difference (B − A):

	Cash Inflows (outflows)	Year(s) of Cash Flows	12% Present Value Factor	Present Value of Cash Flows
Initial investment	$(29,060)	0	1.000	$(29,060)
Operation	10,000	1–4	3.037	30,370
Disinvestment	0	4	0.636	0
Net present value				$ 1,310

	Proposal B	Proposal C	Difference B − C
Predicted cash flows:			
Initial investment	$(55,960)	$(30,560)	$(25,400)
Operations:			
Year 1	20,000	20,000	0
Year 2	20,000	20,000	0
Year 3	20,000	0	20,000
Year 4	20,000	0	20,000
Disinvestment	0	0	0

Net present value of difference (B − C):

	Cash Inflows (outflows)	Year(s) of Cash Flows	12% Present Value Factor	Present Value of Cash Flows
Initial investment	$(25,400)	0	1.000	$(25,400)
Operation	20,000	2–4	3.037 − 1.690	26,940
Disinvestment	0	4	0.636	0
Net present value				$ 1,540

Mobile Yogurt Shoppe's annual depreciation tax shield, using straight-line depreciation, is $6,158, computed as annual depreciation of $18,111 ($90,554 investment in depreciable assets ÷ 5-year life) multiplied by the tax rate of 34 percent. Without the depreciation tax shield, annual cash payments for income taxes would be $6,158 more, and after-tax cash flows would be $6,158 less.

EXHIBIT 10-10

EFFECT OF DEPRECIATION ON TAXES, INCOME, AND CASH FLOW

Annual Taxes and Income without Depreciation		Annual Taxes and Income with Depreciation	
Sales	$175,000	Sales	$175,000
Operating expenses (except depreciation)	(145,000)	Operating expenses (except depreciation)	(145,000)
Depreciation	0	Depreciation ($90,554 ÷ 5 years)	(18,111)
Income before taxes without depreciation	$ 30,000	Income before taxes with depreciation	$ 11,889
Income taxes (34%)	(10,200)	Income taxes (34%)	(4,042)
Net income	$ 19,800	Net income	$ 7,847

Depreciation reduces income taxes by the amount of depreciation times the tax rate. The difference in taxes, $6,158 ($10,200 − $4,042), is equal to the difference in depreciation multiplied by the tax rate, $6,158 ($18,111 × 0.34).

Annual Taxes and Cash Flow without Depreciation		Annual Taxes and Cash Flow with Depreciation	
Sales	$175,000	Sales	$175,000
Operating expenses (except depreciation)	(145,000)	Operating expenses (except depreciation)	(145,000)
Income taxes	(10,200)	Income taxes	(4,042)
Net annual cash inflow	$ 19,800	Net annual cash inflow	$ 25,958

The deductibility of depreciation for tax purposes reduces cash payments for taxes, thus increasing the net cash flow by the depreciation tax shield. The difference in cash flow, $6,158 ($25,958 − $19,800), is explained by the depreciation multiplied by the tax rate, $6,158 ($18,111 × 0.34). This is the *depreciation tax shield.*

The U.S. Tax Code contains guidelines concerning the depreciation of various types of assets. (A detailed analysis of these guidelines is beyond the scope of this text.) Tax guidelines allow organizations a choice in tax depreciation procedures between straight-line depreciation and an accelerated depreciation method detailed in the Tax Code. Because of the time value of money, profitable businesses should usually select the tax depreciation procedure that provides the earliest depreciation. To illustrate the effect of accelerated depreciation on taxes and capital budgeting, we use double-declining balance depreciation rather than the accelerated method detailed in the Code. When making capital expenditure decisions, managers should, of course, refer to the most current version of the Tax Code to determine the specific depreciation guidelines in effect at that time.

Exhibits 10–11 and 10–12 illustrate the effect of two alternative depreciation procedures, straight-line and double-declining balance, on the net present value of Mobile Yogurt Shoppe's proposed investment.

We assume that the asset is fully depreciated for tax purposes during its five-year life and is sold for a taxable gain equal to its predicted salvage value. The cash flows for this investment were presented in Exhibit 10–2, and the effect of taxes on the

EXHIBIT 10-11

ANALYSIS OF CAPITAL EXPENDITURES INCLUDING TAX EFFECTS: STRAIGHT-LINE DEPRECIATION

	Predicted Cash Inflows (outflows) (A)	Year(s) of Cash Flows (B)	12% Present Value Factor (C)	Present Value of Cash Flows (A) × (C)
Initial investment:				
Vehicle and equipment	$(90,554)	0	1.000	$ (90,554)
Inventory and other				
working capital	(4,000)	0	1.000	(4,000)
Operations:				
Annual taxable income				
without depreciation	30,000	1–5	3.605	108,150
Taxes on income				
($30,000 × 0.34)	(10,200)	1–5	3.605	(36,771)
Depreciation tax shield*	6,158	1–5	3.605	22,200
Disinvestment:				
Sale of vehicle and equipment	8,000	5	0.567	4,536
Taxes on gain on sale				
($8,000 × 0.34)	(2,720)	5	0.567	(1,542)
Inventory and other				
working capital	4,000	5	0.567	2,268
Net present value of all cash flows				$ 4,287

*Computation of depreciation tax shield:
Annual straight-line depreciation ($90,554 ÷ 5) $18,111
Tax rate . . . . × 0.34
    Depreciation tax shield . . . . $ 6,158

investment's annual cash flows were examined in Exhibit 10–10. Ignoring taxes, the investment was shown (in Exhibit 10–3) to have a positive net present value of $20,400 at a discount rate of 12 percent. With taxes, the investment has a positive net present value of $4,287 using straight-line depreciation and $6,084 using double-declining balance depreciation. Although taxes over the entire life of the project are identical, the use of double-declining balance depreciation for taxes results in a higher net present value because it results in lower cash expenditures for taxes in the earlier years of an asset's life.

INVESTMENT TAX CREDIT

From time-to-time, for the purpose of stimulating investment and economic growth, the U.S. federal government has implemented an investment tax credit. An **investment tax credit** reduces taxes in the year a new asset is placed in service by some stated percentage of the cost of the asset. Typically, this is done without reducing the depreciation base of the asset for tax purposes. An investment tax credit reduces cash payments for taxes and, hence, is treated as a cash inflow for capital budgeting purposes. This additional cash inflow increases the probability that a new asset will meet a taxpayer's capital expenditure criteria.

EXHIBIT 10-12

ANALYSIS OF CAPITAL EXPENDITURES INCLUDING TAX EFFECTS:
DOUBLE-DECLINING BALANCE DEPRECIATION

	Predicted Cash Inflows (outflows) (A)	Year(s) of Cash Flows (B)	12% Present Value Factor (C)	Present Value of Cash Flows (A) × (C)
Initial investment:				
Vehicle and equipment	$(90,554)	0	1.000	$ (90,554)
Inventory and other working capital	4,000	0	1.000	(4,000)
Operations:				
Annual taxable income without depreciation	30,000	1–5	3.605	108,150
Taxes on income ($30,000 × 0.34)	(10,200)	1–5	3.605	(36,771)
Depreciation tax shield*				
Year 1	12,315	1	0.893	10,997
Year 2	7,389	2	0.797	5,889
Year 3	4,434	3	0.712	3,157
Year 4	2,660	4	0.636	1,692
Year 5	3,990	5	0.567	2,262
Disinvestment:				
Sale of vehicle and equipment	8,000	5	0.567	4,536
Taxes on gain on sale ($8,000 × 0.34)	(2,720)	5	0.567	(1,542)
Inventory and other working capital	4,000	5	0.567	2,268
Net present value of all cash flows				$ 6,084

*Computation of depreciation tax shield:

Year	Depreciation Base† (A)	Annual Rate (B)	Annual Depreciation (C) (A) × (B)	Tax Rate (D)	Tax Shield (E) (C) × (D)
1	$90,554	2/5	$36,222	0.34	$12,315
2	54,332	2/5	21,733	0.34	7,389
3	32,599	2/5	13,040	0.34	4,434
4	19,559	2/5	7,824	0.34	2,660
5	11,735	balance	11,735	0.34	3,990

†The depreciation base is reduced by the amount of any previous depreciation. The annual rate is twice the straight-line rate. For simplicity, we depreciated the remaining balance in the fifth year and did not switch to straight-line depreciation when the straight-line amount exceeds the double-declining balance amount. This would happen in the fourth year, when $19,559 ÷ 2 = $9,780.

Summary

Capital budgeting involves the identification of potentially desirable projects for capital expenditures, the subsequent evaluation of capital expenditure proposals, and the selection of proposals that meet certain criteria. In this chapter, we studied a number of *capital budgeting models* used to assist managers in evaluating capital expenditure proposals. We concluded that capital budgeting models that consider the *time value of money*, such as *net present value* and *internal rate of return*, are superior to capital budgeting models that do not consider the time value of money, such as the *payback period* and the *accounting rate of return*.

It is important to remember that capital budgeting models do not make investment decisions. Rather, they help managers separate capital expenditure proposals that meet certain criteria from those that do not. In making the final decision to accept or reject a capital expenditure proposal that has passed the initial screening, nonquantitative factors, such as management's attitude toward risk, are apt to play a decisive role.

In the latter portion of this chapter, we outlined some suggested approaches to analyzing risk, illustrated how differential analysis can aid in evaluating capital expenditure proposals that do not produce additional cash inflows, and discussed the problems involved in selecting from among *mutually exclusive investments*. We concluded by considering the impact of *taxes* and the *depreciation tax shield* on capital expenditure proposals.

Appendix A

TIME VALUE OF MONEY

When asked to choose between $500 today or Smith's IOU for $500 to be paid one year later, rational decision makers choose the $500 today. The two reasons for this involve the time *value of money* and the *risk*. A dollar today is worth more than a dollar tomorrow or at some future time. Having a dollar provides flexibility. It can be spent, buried, or invested in a number of projects. If invested in a savings account, it will amount to more than one dollar at some future time because of the effect of interest. The interest paid by a bank (or borrower) for the use of money is analogous to the rent paid for the use of land, buildings, or equipment. Furthermore, we live in an uncertain world, and, for a variety of reasons, the possibility exists that Smith might not pay his debts as they come due.

FUTURE VALUE

Future value is the amount that a current sum of money earning a stated rate of interest will accumulate to at the end of a future period. Suppose you deposit $500 in a savings account at a financial institution that pays interest at the rate of 10 percent per year. At the end of the first year, the original deposit of $500 will total $550 ($500 × 1.10). If you leave the $550 for another year, the amount will increase to $605 ($550 × 1.10). It can be stated that $500 today has a future value in one year of $550, or conversely, that $550 one year from today has a present value of $500. Note that interest of $55 ($605 − $550) was earned in the second year, whereas interest of only $50 was earned in the first year. This happened because interest during the second year was earned on the principal plus interest from the first year ($550). When periodic interest is computed on principal plus prior periods' accumulated interest, the interest is said to be *compounded*. Compound interest is used throughout this text.

To determine future values at the end of one period (usually a year), multiply the beginning amount (present value) by 1 plus the interest rate. When multiple periods are involved, the future value is determined by repeatedly multiplying the beginning amount by 1 plus the interest rate for each period. When $500 is invested for two years at an interest rate of 10 percent per year, its future value is computed as $500 $\times$ 1.10 $\times$ 1.10. The following equation is used to figure future value:

$$fv = pv(1 + i)^n$$

where:

$$fv = \text{future value amount}$$
$$pv = \text{present value amount}$$
$$i = \text{interest rate per period}$$
$$n = \text{number of periods}$$

For our $500 deposit, the equation becomes:

$$fv \text{ of } \$500 = pv(1 + i)^n$$
$$= \$500(1 + 0.10)^2$$
$$= \$605$$

In a similar manner, once the interest rate and number of periods are known, the future value amount of any present value amount is easily determined.

PRESENT VALUE

Present value is the current worth of a specified amount of money to be received at some future date at some interest rate. Solving for pv in the future value equation, the new present value equation is determined as follows:

$$pv = \frac{fv}{(1 + i)^n}$$

Using this equation, the present value of $8,800 to be received in one year, discounted at 10 percent, is computed as follows:

$$pv \text{ of } \$8,800 = \frac{\$8,800}{(1 + 0.10)^1}$$
$$= \frac{\$8,800}{(1.10)}$$
$$= \$8,000$$

Thus, when the discount rate is 10 percent, the present value of $8,800 to be received in one year is $8,000.

The present value equation is often expressed as the future value amount times the present value of $1:

$$pv = fv \times \frac{\$1}{(1 + i)^n}$$

Using the equation for the present value of $1, the present value of $8,800 to be received in one year, discounted at 10 percent, is computed as follows:

$$pv \text{ of } \$8,800 = \$8,800 \times \frac{\$1}{(1 + 0.10)^1}$$
$$= \$8,800 \times 0.909$$
$$= \$8,000$$

The present value of $8,800 two periods from now is $7,273, computed as [$8,800 ÷ $(1.10)^2$] or [$8,800 × $1 ÷ $(1.10)^2$].

If a calculator is not available, present value computations can be done by hand. Tables, such as Table 10–1 for the present value of $1 at various interest rates and time periods, can be used to simplify hand computations. Using the factors in Table 10–1, the present values of any future amount can be determined. For example, with an interest rate of 10 percent, the present value of the following future amounts to be received in one period are as follows:

Future Value Amount		Present Value Factor of $1		Present Value
$ 100	×	0.909	=	$ 90.90
628	×	0.909	=	570.85
4,285	×	0.909	=	3,895.07
9,900	×	0.909	=	8,999.10

To further illustrate the use of Table 10–1, consider the following application. Alert Company wants to invest its surplus cash at 12 percent to have $10,000 to pay off a long-term note due at the end of five years. Table 10–1 shows that the present value factor of $1, discounted at 12 percent per year for five years, is 0.567. Multiplying $10,000 by 0.567, the present value is determined to be $5,670:

$$pv \text{ of } \$10,000 = \$10,000 \times \text{Present value factor for } \$1$$
$$= \$10,000 \times 0.567$$
$$= \$5,670$$

Therefore, if Alert invests $5,670 today, it will have $10,000 available to pay off its note in five years.

Managers also use present value tables to make investment decisions. Assume that Monroe Company can make an investment that will provide a cash flow of $12,000 at the end of eight years. If the company demands a rate of return of 14 percent per year, what is the most it will be willing to pay for this investment? From Table 10–1, we find that the present value factor for $1, discounted at 14 percent per year for eight years, is 0.351:

$$pv \text{ of } \$12,000 = \$12,000 \times \text{Present value factor for } \$1$$
$$= \$12,000 \times 0.351$$
$$= \$4,212$$

If the company demands an annual return of 14 percent, the most it would be willing to invest today is $4,212.

ANNUITIES

Not all investments provide a single sum of money. Many investments provide periodic cash flows called *annuities*. An **annuity** is a series of equal cash flows received or paid over equal intervals of time. Suppose that $100 will be received at the end of each of the next three years. If the discount rate is 10 percent, the present value of this annuity can be determined by summing the present value of each receipt:

$$\text{Year 1 } \$100 \times \$1 \div (1 + 0.10)^1 = \$ 90.90$$
$$\text{Year 2 } \$100 \times \$1 \div (1 + 0.10)^2 = 82.65$$
$$\text{Year 3 } \$100 \times \$1 \div (1 + 0.10)^3 = \underline{75.13}$$
$$\text{Total} \dots \dots \dots \dots \dots \underline{\$248.68}$$

Alternatively, the following equation can be used to compute the present value of an annuity with cash flows at the end of each period:

TABLE 10-1

PRESENT VALUE OF $1

$$\text{Present value of } \$1 = \frac{1}{(1 + r)^n}$$

Periods (n)	Discount rate (r)												
	6%	8%	10%	12%	14%	16%	18%	20%	22%	24%	26%	28%	30%
1	0.943	0.926	0.909	0.893	0.877	0.862	0.847	0.833	0.820	0.806	0.794	0.781	0.769
2	0.890	0.857	0.826	0.797	0.769	0.743	0.718	0.694	0.672	0.650	0.630	0.610	0.592
3	0.840	0.794	0.751	0.712	0.675	0.641	0.609	0.579	0.551	0.524	0.500	0.477	0.455
4	0.792	0.735	0.683	0.636	0.592	0.552	0.516	0.482	0.451	0.423	0.397	0.373	0.350
5	0.747	0.681	0.621	0.567	0.519	0.476	0.437	0.402	0.370	0.341	0.315	0.291	0.269
6	0.705	0.630	0.564	0.507	0.456	0.410	0.370	0.335	0.303	0.275	0.250	0.227	0.207
7	0.665	0.583	0.513	0.452	0.400	0.354	0.314	0.279	0.249	0.222	0.198	0.178	0.159
8	0.627	0.540	0.467	0.404	0.351	0.305	0.266	0.233	0.204	0.179	0.157	0.139	0.123
9	0.592	0.500	0.424	0.361	0.308	0.263	0.225	0.194	0.167	0.144	0.125	0.108	0.094
10	0.558	0.463	0.386	0.322	0.270	0.227	0.191	0.162	0.137	0.116	0.099	0.085	0.073
11	0.527	0.429	0.350	0.287	0.237	0.195	0.162	0.135	0.112	0.094	0.079	0.066	0.056
12	0.497	0.397	0.319	0.257	0.208	0.168	0.137	0.112	0.092	0.076	0.062	0.052	0.043
13	0.469	0.368	0.290	0.229	0.182	0.145	0.116	0.093	0.075	0.061	0.050	0.040	0.033
14	0.442	0.340	0.263	0.205	0.160	0.125	0.099	0.078	0.062	0.049	0.039	0.032	0.025
15	0.417	0.315	0.239	0.183	0.140	0.108	0.084	0.065	0.051	0.040	0.031	0.025	0.020
16	0.394	0.292	0.218	0.163	0.123	0.093	0.071	0.054	0.042	0.032	0.025	0.019	0.015
17	0.371	0.270	0.198	0.146	0.108	0.080	0.060	0.045	0.034	0.026	0.020	0.015	0.012
18	0.350	0.250	0.180	0.130	0.095	0.069	0.051	0.038	0.028	0.021	0.016	0.012	0.009
19	0.331	0.232	0.164	0.116	0.083	0.060	0.043	0.031	0.023	0.017	0.012	0.009	0.007
20	0.312	0.215	0.149	0.104	0.073	0.051	0.037	0.026	0.019	0.014	0.010	0.007	0.005

$$pva = \frac{a}{i} \times \left[1 - \frac{1}{(1 + 0.10)^n}\right]$$

where:

pva = present value of an annuity (also called the *annuity factor*)

i = prevailing rate per period

n = number of periods

a = annuity amount

This equation was used to compute the factors presented in Table 10–2 for an annuity amount of $1. The present value of an annuity of $1 per period for three periods discounted at 10 percent per period is as follows:

$$pva \text{ of } \$1 = \frac{1}{0.10} \times \left[\frac{1 - 1}{(1 + 0.10)^3}\right]$$
$$= 2.4868$$

Using this factor, the present value of a $100 annuity can be computed as $100 × 2.4868, which yields $248.68. To determine the present value of an annuity of any amount, the annuity factor for $1 can be multiplied by the annuity amount.

To further illustrate the use of Table 10–2, assume that Red Kite Company is considering an investment in a piece of equipment that will produce net cash inflows of $2,000 at the end of each year for five years. If the company's desired rate of return is 12 percent, an investment of $7,210 will provide such a return:

$$pva \text{ of } \$2,000 = \$2,000 \times \begin{array}{l}\text{Present value factor for an annuity of}\\ \$1 \text{ for five periods discounted at } 12\%\end{array}$$
$$= \$2,000 \times 3.605$$
$$= \$7,210$$

Here, the $2,000 annuity is multiplied by 3.605, the factor for an annuity of $1 for five periods found in Table 10–2, discounted at 12 percent per period.

Another use of Table 10–2 is to determine the amount that must be received annually to provide a desired rate of return on an investment. Assume that Burnsville Company invests $33,550 and desires a return of the investment plus interest of 8 percent in equal year-end payments for ten years. The minimum amount that must be received each year is determined by solving the equation for the present value of an annuity:

$$pva = a \times (pva \text{ of } \$1)$$
$$a = \frac{pva}{pva \text{ of } \$1}$$

From Table 10–2, we see that the 8 percent factor for ten periods is 6.710. Dividing the $33,550 investment by 6.710, the required annuity is computed to be $5,000:

$$a = \frac{\$33,550}{6.710}$$
$$= \$5,000$$

UNEQUAL CASH FLOWS

Many investment situations do not produce equal periodic cash flows. When this occurs, the present value for each cash flow must be determined independently because the annuity table can be used only for equal periodic cash flows. Table 10–1 is used to determine the present value of each future amount separately. To illustrate, assume that the Atlanta Braves wish to acquire the contract of a popular baseball player who

TABLE 10-2

PRESENT VALUE OF AN ANNUITY OF $1

Present value of an annuity of $1 $= \dfrac{1}{r}\left[1 - \dfrac{1}{(1+r)^n}\right]$

Discount rate (r)

Periods (n)	6%	8%	10%	12%	14%	16%	18%	20%	22%	24%	25%	26%	28%	30%
1	0.943	0.926	0.909	0.893	0.877	0.862	0.847	0.833	0.820	0.806	0.800	0.794	0.781	0.769
2	1.833	1.783	1.736	1.690	1.647	1.605	1.566	1.528	1.492	1.457	1.440	1.424	1.392	1.361
3	2.673	2.577	2.487	2.402	2.322	2.246	2.174	2.106	2.042	1.981	1.952	1.923	1.868	1.816
4	3.465	3.312	3.170	3.037	2.914	2.798	2.690	2.589	2.494	2.404	2.362	2.320	2.241	2.166
5	4.212	3.993	3.791	3.605	3.433	3.274	3.127	2.991	2.864	2.745	2.689	2.635	2.532	2.436
6	4.917	4.623	4.355	4.111	3.889	3.685	3.498	3.326	3.167	3.020	2.951	2.885	2.759	2.643
7	5.582	5.206	4.868	4.564	4.288	4.039	3.812	3.605	3.416	3.242	3.161	3.083	2.937	2.802
8	6.210	5.747	5.335	4.968	4.639	4.344	4.078	3.837	3.619	3.421	3.329	3.241	3.076	2.925
9	6.802	6.247	5.759	5.328	4.946	4.607	4.303	4.031	3.786	3.566	3.463	3.366	3.184	3.019
10	7.360	6.710	6.145	5.650	5.216	4.833	4.494	4.192	3.923	3.682	3.571	3.465	3.269	3.092
11	7.887	7.139	6.495	5.938	5.453	5.029	4.656	4.327	4.035	3.776	3.656	3.544	3.335	3.147
12	8.384	7.536	6.814	6.194	5.660	5.197	4.793	4.439	4.127	3.851	3.725	3.606	3.387	3.190
13	8.853	7.904	7.103	6.424	5.842	5.342	4.910	4.533	4.203	3.912	3.780	3.656	3.427	3.223
14	9.295	8.244	7.367	6.628	6.002	5.468	5.008	4.611	4.265	3.962	3.824	3.695	3.459	3.249
15	9.712	8.559	7.606	6.811	6.142	5.575	5.092	4.675	4.315	4.001	3.859	3.726	3.483	3.268
16	10.106	8.851	7.824	6.974	6.265	5.669	5.162	4.730	4.357	4.033	3.887	3.751	3.503	3.283
17	10.477	9.122	8.022	7.120	6.373	5.749	5.222	4.775	4.391	4.059	3.910	3.771	3.518	3.295
18	10.828	9.372	8.201	7.250	6.467	5.818	5.273	4.812	4.419	4.080	3.928	3.786	3.529	3.304
19	11.158	9.604	8.365	7.366	6.550	5.877	5.361	4.844	4.442	4.097	3.942	3.799	3.539	3.311
20	11.470	9.818	8.514	7.469	6.623	5.929	5.353	4.870	4.460	4.110	3.954	3.808	3.546	3.316

is known to attract large crowds. Management believes this player will return incremental cash flows to the team at the end of each of the next three years in the amounts of $2,500,000, $4,000,000, and $1,500,000. After three years, the player anticipates retiring. If the team's owners require a minimum return of 14 percent on their investment, how much would they be willing to pay for the player's contract?

To solve this problem, it is necessary to determine the present value of the expected future cash flows. Here we use Table 10–1 to find the $1 present value factors at 14 percent for Periods 1, 2, and 3. The cash flows are then multiplied by these factors:

Year	Annual Cash Flow		Present Value of $1 at 14 Percent		Present Value Amount
1	$2,500,000	×	0.877	=	$2,192,500
2	4,000,000	×	0.769	=	3,076,000
3	1,500,000	×	0.675	=	1,012,500
Total					$6,281,000

The total present value of the cash flows for the three years, $6,281,000, represents the maximum amount the team would be willing to pay for the player's contract.

DEFERRED RETURNS

Many times, organizations make investments for which they receive no cash until several periods have passed. The present value of an investment discounted at 12 percent per year, which has a $2,000 return only at the end of Years 4, 5, and 6, can be determined as follows:

Year	Amount		Present Value of $1 at 12 Percent		Present Value Amount
1	$ 0	×	0.893	=	$ 0
2	0	×	0.797	=	0
3	0	×	0.712	=	0
4	2,000	×	0.636	=	1,272
5	2,000	×	0.567	=	1,134
6	2,000	×	0.507	=	1,014
Total					$3,420

Computation of the present value of the deferred annuity can also be performed using the annuity tables if the cash flow amounts are equal for each period. The present value of an annuity for six years minus the present value of an annuity for three years yields the present value of an annuity for Years 4 through 6.

Present value of an annuity for 6 years at 12 percent: $2,000 × 4.111 = $8,222
Present value of an annuity for 3 years at 12 percent: 2,000 × 2.402 = (4,804)
Present value of the deferred annuity $3,418*

The difference between the $3,420 above and the $3,418 here is caused by rounding.

Appendix B

TABLE APPROACH TO DETERMINING THE INTERNAL RATE OF RETURN

We consider the use of present value tables to determine the internal rate of return of a series of cash flows with (1) equal net cash flows after the initial investment and (2) unequal net cash flows after the initial investment.

EQUAL CASH INFLOWS

An investment proposal's internal rate of return is easily determined when a single investment is followed by a series of equal annual net cash flows. The general relationship between the initial investment and the equal annual cash inflows is expressed as follows:

$$\text{Initial investment} = \text{Present value factor for an annuity of \$1} \times \text{Annual net cash inflow}$$

Solve for the appropriate present value factor as follows:

$$\text{Present value factor for an annuity of \$1} = \frac{\text{Initial investment}}{\text{Annual net cash inflows}}$$

Once the present value factor has been calculated, use Table 10–2 and go across the row corresponding to the expected life of the project until a table factor equal to or closest to the project's computed present value factor is found. The corresponding percentage for the present value factor is the proposal's internal rate of return. If a table factor does not exactly equal the proposal's present value factor, a more accurate answer can be obtained by interpolation (which is not discussed in this text).

To illustrate, assume that Mobile Yogurt Shoppe's proposed investment has a zero disinvestment value. Using all information in Exhibit 10–2 (except that for disinvestment), the proposal's present value factor is 3.152:

$$\begin{aligned}\text{Present value factor for an annuity of \$1} &= \frac{\text{Initial investment}}{\text{Annual net cash inflows}}\\ &= \frac{\$94,554}{\$30,000}\\ &= 3.152\end{aligned}$$

Using Table 10–2, go across the row for five periods; the closest table factor is 3.127, which corresponds to an internal rate of return of 18 percent.

UNEQUAL CASH INFLOWS

If periodic cash flows subsequent to the initial investment are unequal, the simple procedure of determining a present value factor and looking up the closest corresponding factor in Table 10–2 cannot be used. Instead, a trial-and-error approach must be used to determine the internal rate of return.

The first step is to select a discount rate estimated to be close to the proposal's IRR and to compute the proposal's net present value. If the resulting net present value is zero, the selected discount rate is the actual rate of return. However, it is unlikely that the first rate selected will be the proposal's IRR. If the computation results in a positive net present value, the actual IRR is higher than the initially selected rate. In this case, the next step is to compute the proposal's net present value using a higher rate. If the second computation produces a negative net present value, the actual IRR is less than the selected rate. Therefore, the actual IRR is between the first and the second rates. This trial-and-error approach continues until a discount rate is found that equates the proposal's cash inflows and outflows. For Mobile Yogurt Shoppe's investment proposal outlined in Exhibit 10–2, the details of the trial-and-error approach are presented in Exhibit 10–13.

Notice in Exhibit 10–13 that the first rate produced a negative net present value, indicating that the proposal's IRR is less than 24 percent. To produce a positive net present value, a smaller rate was selected for the second trial. Since the second rate produced a positive net present value, the proposal's true IRR must be between 16

EXHIBIT 10–13

COMPUTATIONS OF INTERNAL RATE OF RETURN WITH UNEQUAL CASH FLOWS

First trial with a 24 percent discount rate:

	Predicted Cash Inflows (outflows) (A)	Year(s) of Cash Flows (B)	24% Present Value Factor (C)	Present Value of Cash Flows (A) × (C)
Initial investment	$(94,554)	0	1.000	$(94,554)
Operation	30,000	1–5	2.745	82,350
Disinvestment	12,000	5	0.341	4,092
Net present value of all cash flows				$ (8,112)

Second trial with a 16 percent discount rate:

	Predicted Cash Inflows (outflows) (A)	Year(s) of Cash Flows (B)	16% Present Value Factor (C)	Present Value of Cash Flows (A) × (C)
Initial investment	$(94,554)	0	1.000	$(94,554)
Operation	30,000	1–5	3.274	98,220
Disinvestment	12,000	5	0.476	5,712
Net present value of all cash flows				$ 9,378

Third trial with a 20 percent discount rate:

	Predicted Cash Inflows (outflows) (A)	Year(s) of Cash Flows (B)	20% Present Value Factor (C)	Present Value of Cash Flows (A) × (C)
Initial investment	$(94,554)	0	1.000	$(94,554)
Operation	30,000	1–5	2.991	89,730
Disinvestment	12,000	5	0.402	4,824
Net present value of all cash flows				$ 0

and 24 percent. The 20 percent rate selected for the third trial produced a net present value of zero, indicating that this is the proposal's IRR.

Review Problem

The solution to the review problem is found on pages 461–462. To maximize your learning, you should make a serious attempt to develop a written solution to the review problem before looking at the solution. If there are errors in your solution, you should then attempt to determine their causes.

Survey of Capital Budgeting Models

Consider the following investment proposal:

Initial investment:
- Depreciable assets $27,740
- Working capital 3,000

Operations (per year for 4 years):
- Cash receipts $25,000
- Cash expenditures 15,000

Disinvestment:
- Salvage value of plant and equipment $2,000
- Recovery of working capital 3,000

Required:

Determine each of the following:

a. Net present value at a 10 percent discount rate.
b. Internal rate of return. (Refer to Appendix B if you use the table approach.)
c. Payback period.
d. Accounting rate of return on initial investment and on average investment.

Key Terms

Accounting rate of return (p. 421)
Capital budgeting (p. 410)
Capital expenditures (p. 410)
Cost of capital (p. 418)
Depreciation tax shield (p. 431)
Discount rate (p. 414)
Internal rate of return (IRR) (p. 417)
Investment tax credit (p. 434)
Mutually exclusive investments (p. 429)

Net present value (p. 414)
Payback period (p. 419)
Present value index (p. 430)
Time-adjusted rate of return (p. 417)

Appendix Key Terms
Annuity (p. 438)
Future value (p. 436)
Present value (p. 437)

Review Questions

1. What is the relationship between long-range planning and capital budgeting?
2. What tasks are often assigned to the capital budgeting committee?
3. What purposes are served by a post-audit of approved capital expenditure proposals?
4. Into what three phases are a project's cash flows organized?
5. State three alternative definitions or descriptions of the internal rate of return.
6. Why is the cost of capital an important concept when discounting models are used for capital budgeting?
7. What weakness is inherent in the payback period when it is used as the sole investment criterion?
8. What weakness is inherent in the accounting rate of return when it is used as an investment criterion?
9. Why are the net present value and the internal rate of return models superior to the payback period and the accounting rate of return models?
10. State two basic differences between the net present value and the internal rate of return models that often lead to differences in the evaluation of competing investment proposals.

11. Identify several nonquantitative factors that are apt to play a decisive role in the final selection of projects for capital expenditures.
12. In what way does depreciation affect the analysis of cash flows for a proposed capital expenditure?

Exercises

10–1
Time Value of Money: Basics (Appendix A)

Using the equations and tables in Appendix A of this chapter, determine the answers to each of the following independent situations:

a. The future value in two years of $1,000 deposited today in a savings account with interest compounded annually at 8 percent.
b. The present value of $9,000 to be received in five years, discounted at 12 percent.
c. The present value of an annuity of $2,000 per year for five years discounted at 16 percent.
d. An initial investment of $32,010 is to be returned in eight equal annual payments. Determine the amount of each payment if the interest rate is 10 percent.
e. A proposed investment will provide cash flows of $20,000, $8,000, and $6,000 at the end of Years 1, 2, and 3, respectively. Using a discount rate of 20 percent, determine the present value of these cash flows.
f. Find the present value of an investment that will pay $5,000 at the end of Years 10, 11, and 12. Use a discount rate of 14 percent.

10–2
Time Value of Money: Basics (Appendix A)

Using the equations and tables in Appendix A of this chapter, determine the answers to each of the following independent situations:

a. The future value in two years of $3,000 invested today in a certificate of deposit with interest compounded annually at 10 percent.
b. The present value of $8,000 to be received in five years, discounted at 8 percent.
c. The present value of an annuity of $10,000 per year for four years discounted at 12 percent.
d. An initial investment of $14,740 is to be returned in six equal annual payments. Determine the amount of each payment if the interest rate is 16 percent.
e. A proposed investment will provide cash flows of $6,000, $8,000, and $20,000 at the end of Years 1, 2, and 3, respectively. Using a discount rate of 18 percent, determine the present value of these cash flows.
f. Find the present value of an investment that will pay $6,000 at the end of Years 8, 9, and 10. Use a discount rate of 14 percent.

10–3
NPV, IRR: Equal Annual Net Cash Inflows

Blue Company is evaluating a capital expenditure proposal that requires an initial investment of $9,350, has predicted cash inflows of $2,000 per year for 15 years, and has no salvage value.

Required:
a. Using a discount rate of 14 percent, determine the net present value of the investment proposal.
b. Determine the proposal's internal rate of return. (Refer to Appendix B if you use the table approach.)
c. What discount rate would produce a net present value of zero?

10–4
NPV, IRR: Equal Annual Net Cash Inflows

Sky Company is evaluating a capital expenditure proposal that requires an initial investment of $32,160, has predicted cash inflows of $7,500 per year for seven years, and has no salvage value.

Required:

a. Using a discount rate of 16 percent, determine the net present value of the investment proposal.
b. Determine the proposal's internal rate of return. (Refer to Appendix B if you use the table approach.)
c. What discount rate would produce a net present value of zero?

10–5
NPV, IRR: Unequal Annual Net Cash Inflows

Lake Ski Company is evaluating a capital expenditure proposal that has the following predicted cash flows:

Initial investment	$(42,580)
Operation:	
Year 1	18,000
Year 2	25,000
Year 3	20,000
Salvage	0

Required:

a. Using a discount rate of 12 percent, determine the net present value of the investment proposal.
b. Determine the proposal's internal rate of return. (Refer to Appendix B if you use the table approach.)

10–6
NPV, IRR: Unequal Annual Net Cash Inflows

Alpine Ski Company is evaluating a capital expenditure proposal that has the following predicted cash flows:

Initial investment	$(40,860)
Operation:	
Year 1	20,000
Year 2	30,000
Year 3	10,000
Salvage	0

Required:

a. Using a discount rate of 14 percent, determine the net present value of the investment proposal.
b. Determine the proposal's internal rate of return. (Refer to Appendix B if you use the table approach.)

10–7
Payback Period, Accounting Rate of Return

Presented is information pertaining to three capital expenditure proposals:

	Proposal X	Proposal Y	Proposal Z
Initial investment:			
Depreciable assets	$60,000	$120,000	$90,000
Working capital	0	0	10,000
Net cash inflow from operations (per year for 4 years)	20,000	40,000	25,000
Disinvestment:			
Depreciable assets	0	20,000	10,000
Working capital	0	0	10,000

Required:

a. Determine each proposal's payback period.
b. Determine each proposal's accounting rate of return on:
   1. Initial investment.
   2. Average investment.
c. Why is the accounting rate of return higher on an average investment than on an initial investment?

10–8
Payback Period,
IRR, Minimum Cash
Flows

The management of Kingston, Limited is currently evaluating the following investment proposal:

	Time 0	Year 1	Year 2	Year 3	Year 4
Initial investment	$240,000				
Net operating cash inflows		$100,000	$100,000	$100,000	$100,000

Required:
a. Determine the proposal's payback period.
b. Determine the proposal's internal rate of return. (Refer to Appendix B if you use the table approach.)
c. Given the amount of the initial investment, determine the minimum annual net cash inflows required to obtain an internal rate of return of 18 percent. Round the answer to the nearest dollar.

10–9
Time-Adjusted Cost-
Volume-Profit
Analysis

Seventh Avenue Treat Shop is considering the desirability of producing a new chocolate candy called Pleasure Bombs. Before purchasing the new equipment required to manufacture Pleasure Bombs, Tracy Sealer, the shop's proprietor performed the following analysis:

Unit selling price	$1.25
Variable manufacturing and selling costs	(1.15)
Unit contribution margin	$0.10

Annual fixed costs:
Depreciation (straight line for 3 years)	$ 4,000
Other (all cash)	8,000
Total	$12,000

Annual break-even sales volume = $12,000 ÷ $0.10 = 120,000 units

Because the expected annual sales volume is 130,000 units, Tracy Smith decided to undertake the production of Pleasure Bombs. This required an immediate investment of $12,000 in equipment that has a life of three years and no salvage value. After three years, the production of Pleasure Bombs will be discontinued.

Required:
a. Evaluate the analysis performed by Tracy Smith.
b. If Seventh Avenue Treat Shop has a time value of money of 14 percent, should it make the investment with projected annual sales of 130,000 units?
c. Considering the time value of money, what annual unit sales volume is required to break even?

10–10
Time-Adjusted Cost-
Volume-Profit
Analysis with
Income Taxes

Assume the same facts as given in Exercise 10–9.

Required:
With a 40 percent tax rate and a 14 percent time value of money, determine the annual unit sales required to break even on a time-adjusted basis.

Problems

10–11
Ranking Investment Proposals: Payback Period, Accounting Rate of Return, and Net Present Value

Presented is information pertaining to the cash flows of three mutually exclusive investment proposals:

	Proposal X	Proposal Y	Proposal Z
Initial investment	$45,000	$45,000	$45,000
Cash flow from operations:			
Year 1	40,000	22,500	45,000
Year 2	5,000	22,500	
Year 3	22,500	22,500	
Disinvestment	0	0	0
Life	3 years	3 years	1 year

Required:

a. Rank these investment proposals using the payback period, the accounting rate of return on initial investment, and the net present value criteria. Assume that the organization's cost of capital is 14 percent. Round calculations to four decimal places.

b. Explain the difference in rankings. Which investment would you recommend?

10–12
Ranking Investment Proposals: NPV and Present Value Index

Assume that Alpo is considering the replacement of its traditional canned dog food with dog food packaged in either resealable plastic containers or in disposable foil-lined pouches. Although either alternative will produce significant cost savings and marketing benefits, limitations on available shelf space in stores require management to select only one alternative. Cash flow information on each alternative follows.

	Plastic Containers	Lined Pouches
Initial investment in necessary equipment	$50,000	$150,000
Increase in annual net cash flows	$20,000	$56,000
Life of equipment (years)	5	5
Salvage value of equipment	$10,000	$12,000

Alpo has a 10 percent cost of capital.

Required:

a. Evaluate the investment alternatives using the net present value and the present value index criteria.

b. Explain the difference in rankings. Which investment would you recommend?

10–13
Ranking Investment Proposals: NPV and Present Value Index

Sea Breeze Cat Sand Company is considering the replacement of its traditional bag packaging of cat sand with either reusable plastic or aluminum pails. Customers would make a refundable deposit on the container each time they purchased cat sand. Because the pails would be reusable, the net cost of cat sand to customers who returned the pail for a refund would be lower than the cost of cat sand sold in bags. Sea Breeze has a 16 percent cost of capital. Cash flow information on each alternative follows.

	Plastic	Aluminum
Initial investment	$80,000	$68,000
Increase in annual net cash flows	$35,000	$30,000
Life of equipment (years)	4	4
Disposal value of equipment	$8,000	$9,000

Required:

a. Evaluate the investment alternatives using the net present value and the present value index criteria.

b. Explain the difference in rankings. Which investment would you recommend if unlimited funds were available at Sea Breeze's cost of capital?

10–14
Cost Reduction Proposal: IRR, NPV, and Payback Period

BJ Company currently discharges liquid waste into Calgary's municipal sewer system. However, the Calgary municipal government has informed BJ that a surcharge of $4 per thousand cubic liters will soon be imposed for the discharge of this waste. This has prompted management to evaluate the desirability of treating its own liquid waste.

A proposed system consists of three elements. The first is a retention basin, which would permit unusual discharges to be held and treated before entering the downstream system. The second is a continuous self-cleaning rotary filter required where solids are removed. The third is an automated neutralization process required where materials are added to control the alkalinity-acidity range.

The system is designed to process 500,000 liters a day. However, management anticipates that only about 200,000 liters of liquid waste would be processed in a normal workday. The company operates 300 days per year.

The initial investment in the system would be $400,000, and annual operating costs are predicted to be $150,000. The system has a predicted useful life of ten years and a salvage value of $50,000.

Required:

a. Determine the project's net present value at a discount rate of 18 percent.

b. Determine the project's approximate internal rate of return. (Refer to Appendix B if you use the table approach.)

c. Determine the project's payback period.

10–15
NPV with Income Taxes: Straight-Line versus Accelerated Depreciation

John Paul Jones Inc. is a conservatively managed boat company whose motto is, "The old ways are the good ways." Management has always used straight-line depreciation for tax and external reporting purposes. Although they are reluctant to change, they are aware of the impact of taxes on a project's profitability.

Required:

For a typical $100,000 investment in equipment with a five-year life and no salvage value, determine the present value of the advantage resulting from the use of double-declining balance depreciation as opposed to straight-line depreciation. Assume an income tax rate of 40 percent and a discount rate of 16 percent. Also assume that there will be a switch from double-declining balance to straight-line depreciation in the fourth year.

10–16
Payback Period, NPV, and PVI: Taxes and Straight-Line Depreciation

Spara is considering the various benefits that might result from shortening its production cycle time by changing from the company's present manual system to a computer-aided design/computer-aided manufacturing (CAD/CAM) system. The proposed system can provide productive time equivalency close to the 20,000 hours currently available with the manual system. The out-of-pocket costs of maintaining the manual system are $20 per hour.

The annual out-of-pocket costs of maintaining the CAD/CAM system are estimated to be $200,000, with an initial investment of $480,000. The estimated life of this system is six years with no salvage value. The tax rate is 30 percent, and Spara will use straight-line depreciation for tax purposes. Spara requires a minimum after-tax return of 20 percent on projects of this type. Full capacity will be utilized.

Required:

a. Compute the relevant annual after-tax cash flows related to the CAD/CAM project.

b. Based on the computation in (a), compute each of the following:
   1. Payback period.
   2. Net present value.
   3. Present value index.

(CPA Adapted)

10-17
NPV: Taxes and Accelerated Depreciation

Assume the same facts as given in Exercise 10–16, except that Spara intends to use double-declining balance depreciation with a switch to straight-line depreciation (applied to any undepreciated balance) starting in Year 5.

Required:

Determine the project's net present value.

10-18
NPV Total and Differential Analysis of Replacement Decision

Gusher Petro is evaluating a proposal to purchase a new processor that would cost $120,000 and have a salvage value of $12,000 in five years. Gusher's cast of capital is 16. It would provide annual operating cash savings of $15,000, as follows:

	Old Processor	New Processor
Salaries	$34,000	$44,000
Supplies	6,000	5,000
Utilities	13,000	6,000
Cleaning and maintenance	22,000	5,000
Total cash expenditures	$75,000	$60,000

If the new processor is purchased, Gusher will sell the old processor for its current salvage value of $30,000. If the new processor is not purchased, the old processor will be disposed of in five years at a predicted scrap value of $2,000. The old processor's present book value is $50,000. If kept, the old processor will require repairs predicted to cost $40,000 in one year.

Required:

a. Use the total cost approach to evaluate the alternatives of keeping the old processor and purchasing the new processor. Indicate which alternative is preferred.

b. Use the differential cost approach to evaluate the desirability of purchasing the new processor.

10-19
NPV Total and Differential Analysis of Replacement Decision

White Snow Automatic Laundry must either have a complete overhaul of its current dry-cleaning system or purchase a new one. Its cost of capital is 20 percent. White Snow's accountant has developed the following cost projections:

	Present System	New System
Purchase cost (new)	$40,000	$50,000
Remaining book value	15,000	
Overhaul needed	20,000	
Annual cash operating costs	35,000	20,000
Current salvage value	10,000	
Salvage value in 5 years	2,500	10,000

If White Snow keeps the old system, it will have to be overhauled immediately. With the overhaul, the old system will have a useful life of five more years.

Required:

a. Use the total cost approach to evaluate the alternatives of keeping the old system and purchasing the new system. Indicate which alternative is preferred.

b. Use the differential cost approach to evaluate the desirability of purchasing the new system.

10–20
NPV Differential
Analysis of
Replacement
Decision

The management of Essen Manufacturing Company is currently evaluating a proposal to purchase a new, innovative drill press as a replacement for a less efficient piece of similar equipment, which would then be sold. The cost of the equipment, including delivery and installation, is $175,000. If the equipment is purchased, Essen will incur a $5,000 cost in removing the present equipment and revamping service facilities. The present equipment has a book value of $100,000 and a remaining useful life of ten years. Because of new technical improvements that have made the present equipment obsolete, it now has a disposal value of only $40,000.

Management has provided the following comparison of manufacturing costs:

	Present Equipment	New Equipment
Annual production (units)	400,000	400,000
Annual costs:		
Direct labor (per unit)	$0.075	$0.05
Overhead:		
Depreciation (10% of asset's book value)	$10,000	$17,500
Other	$48,000	$20,000

Additional information follows:

- Management believes that if the current equipment is not replaced now, it will have to wait ten years before replacement is justifiable.
- Both pieces of equipment are expected to have a negligible salvage value at the end of ten years.
- Management expects to sell the entire annual production of 400,000 units.
- Essen's cost of capital is 14 percent.

Required:
Evaluate the desirability of purchasing the new equipment

Discussion Questions and Cases

10–21
Post-Audit Review
of Capital
Expenditures

What's Happening 10–1, Emblem of Denver's Prosperity Becomes a Financial Burden, examines a capital budgeting decision to construct and operate a major international airport.

Required:

a. Identify the errors made in developing the capital expenditure proposal for the airport.

b. What factors are preventing the airport from achieving the planned passenger volume?

10–22
Payback Period

In response to a significant increase in energy costs, American Energy Systems of Hutchinson, Minnesota, introduced a stove that uses dry-shelled field corn as fuel. Depending on the size of the house and weather conditions, tests indicated that heating an average house requires 15 to 30 bushels of corn per month. In 2001 the stove sold for $2,170 and, with corn at a historical low cost of $2 a bushel, heating with corn was ten times cheaper than gas or heating oil and seven times cheaper than electricity.[3]

Required:

a. Determine the range of possible payback periods in months.

b. What other factors should be considered before purchasing a stove that uses corn?

c. Assuming the corn stove has a life of ten years, do you feel comfortable making this decision using only the payback capital budgeting model? Why or why not?

10–23
Determining Terms
of Automobile
Leases (Requires
Spreadsheet)

Avant-Garde Motor Company has asked you to develop lease terms for the firm's popular Avant-Garde Challenger, which has an average selling price (new) of $25,000.

You know that leasing is attractive because it assists consumers in obtaining new vehicles with a small down payment and "reasonable" monthly payments. Market analysts have told you that to attract the widest number of young professionals, the Challenger must have an initial down payment of no more than $1,000, monthly payments of no more than $450, and lease terms of no more than three years.

When the lease expires, Avant-Garde will sell the used Challengers at the automobile's resale market price at that time. It is difficult to predict the future price of the increasingly popular Challenger, but you have obtained the following information on the average resale prices of used Challengers:

Age	Resale Price
1 year	$20,000
2 years	18,500
3 years	16,000
4 years	13,500
5 years	12,500

Avant-Garde's cost of capital is 18 percent per year, or 1.5 percent per month.

Required:

a. With the aid of spreadsheet software, develop a competitive and profitable lease payment program. Assume the down payment and the first lease payment are made immediately and that all subsequent lease payments are made at the start of the month. [*Hint:* Most software packages include a function such as the following: PMT(rate,nper,pv,fv,type), where rate = the time value of money; nper = the number of periods; pv = the present value; fv = the future value; and type = 0 (when the payment is at the end of the period) or 1 (when the payment is at the beginning of the period). For monthly payments, *rate* should be set at the annual rate divided by 12, and *npr* should be set at the number of months in the lease. Here, *fv* is the residual value. Be sure to consider the residual value as a future value and enter it as a negative number, indicating the lessor has not paid for full cost of the car.]

b. Reevaluate the lease program assuming a down payment of $2,000.

c. Reevaluate the lease program assuming a down payment of $1,000 and a $2,000 increase in residual values.

d. Reevaluate the lease program assuming a down payment of $2,000 and a $2,000 increase in residual values.

e. What is your final recommendation? What risks are associated with your recommendation? Are there any other actions to consider?

---

[3]Based on Laurie Freeman, "Oil Shock: Throw Another Cob on the Fire," *Business Week*, March 12, 2001.

**10–24
Evaluating Data
and Using Payback
Period for an
Investment Proposal**

To determine the desirability of investing in a 17-inch SVGA monitor with a SVGA card (as opposed to the typical 14-inch monitor that comes with a new personal computer), the editors of *PC Computing* developed an experiment testing the time required to perform a set of tasks. The tasks included the following:

- Setting up a meeting using electronic mail.
- Reviewing meeting requests.
- Checking an on-line schedule.
- Embedding a video file into a document.
- Searching a customer database to find a specific set of contracts.
- Copying a database into a spreadsheet.
- Modifying a slide presentation.

The editors assumed this was a typical set of tasks performed by a manager. They determined that there was a 9 percent productivity gain using the 17-inch monitor. One test manager commented that the largest productivity gain came from being able to have multiple applications open at the same time and from being able to view several slides at once.

Required:

- Accepting the 9 percent productivity gain as accurate, what additional information is needed to determine the payback period of an investment in one 17-inch SVGA monitor and a SVGA card that is to be used by a manager?

- Make any necessary assumptions and obtain whatever data you can (perhaps from computer component advertisements) to determine the payback period for the proposed investment.

**10–25
IRR, NPV with
Performance
Evaluation Conflict**

Pepperoni Pizza Company owns and operates fast-service pizza parlors throughout North America. The firm operates on a regional basis and provides almost complete autonomy to the manager of each region. Regional managers are responsible for long-range planning, capital expenditures, personnel policies, pricing, and so forth. Each year the performance of regional managers is evaluated by determining the accounting return on fixed assets in their regions; a return of 14 percent is expected. To determine this return, regional net income is divided by the book value of fixed assets at the start of the year. Managers of regions earning a return of more than 16 percent are identified for possible promotion, and managers of regions with a return of less than 12 percent are subject to replacement.

Mr. Light, with a degree in hotel and restaurant management, is the manager of the Northeast region. He is regarded as a "rising star" and will be considered for promotion during the next two years. Light has been with Pepperoni for a total of three years. During that period, the return on fixed assets in his region (the oldest in the firm) has increased dramatically. He is currently considering a proposal to open five new parlors in the Boston area. The total project involves an investment of $640,000 and will double the number of Pepperoni pizzas sold in the Northeast region to a total of 600,000 per year. At an average price of $6 each, total sales revenue will be $3,600,000.

The expenses of operating each of the new parlors include variable costs of $4 per pizza and fixed costs (excluding depreciation) of $80,904 per year. Because each of the new parlors has only a five-year life and no salvage value, yearly straight-line depreciation will be $25,600 [($640,000 ÷ 5 parlors) ÷ 5 years].

Required:

a. Evaluate the desirability of the $640,000 investment in new pizza parlors by computing the internal rate of return and the net present value. Assume a time value of money of 14 percent. (Refer to Appendix B if you use the table approach.)

b. If Light is shrewd, will he approve the expansion? Why or why not? (Additional computations are suggested.)

10-26
**NPV, Project
Reevaluation with
Taxes, Straight-Line
Depreciation**

In 2004, the Bayside Chemical Company prepared the following analysis of an investment proposal for a new manufacturing facility:

	Predicted Cash Inflows (outflows) (A)	Year(s) of Cash Flows (B)	12% Present Value Factor (C)	Present Value of Cash Flows (A) × (C)
Initial investment:				
Fixed assets	$(800,000)	0	1.000	$ (800,000)
Working capital	(100,000)	0	1.000	(100,000)
Operations:				
Annual taxable income				
without depreciation	300,000	1–5	3.605	1,081,500
Taxes on income				
($300,000 × 0.34)	(102,000)	1–5	3.605	(367,710)
Depreciation tax shield	54,400*	1–5	3.605	196,112
Disinvestment:				
Site restoration	80,000	5	0.567	(45,360)
Tax shield of restoration				
($80,000 × 0.34)	27,200	5	0.567	15,422
Working capital	100,000	5	0.567	56,700
Net present value of all cash flows				$ 36,664

*Computation of depreciation tax shield:
Annual straight-line depreciation ($800,000 ÷ 5) $160,000
Tax rate .... × 0.34
Depreciation tax shield .... $ 54,400

Because the proposal had a positive net present value when discounted at Bayside's cost of capital of 12 percent, the project was approved; all investments were made at the end of 2004.

Shortly after production began in January 2005, a government agency notified Bayside of required additional expenditures totaling $200,000 to bring the plant into compliance with new federal emission regulations. Bayside has the option either to comply with the regulations by December 31, 2005, or to sell the entire operation (fixed assets and working capital) for $250,000 on December 31, 2005. The improvements will be depreciated over the remaining four-year life of the plant using straight-line depreciation. The cost of site restoration will not be affected by the improvements.

If Bayside elects to sell the plant, any book loss can be treated as an offset against taxable income on other operations. This tax reduction is an additional cash benefit of selling.

Required:
a. Should Bayside sell the plant or comply with the new federal regulations? To simplify calculations, assume that any additional improvements are paid for on December 31, 2005.
b. Would Bayside have accepted the proposal in 2004 if it were aware of the forthcoming federal regulations?
c. Do you have any suggestions that might increase the project's net present value? (No calculations are required.)

10-27
**NPV Analysis of
Labor Saving
Investment: Cross-
Subsidization**

Heavy Loading Company's plant has three production departments. Presented are the actual cost functions for each department (DLH = direct labor hour; MH = machine hour):

D1—Total annual overhead = $150,000 + $5DLH + $12MH

D2—Total annual overhead = $185,000 + $2DLH + $10MH

D3—Total annual overhead = $50,000 + $10DLH

The direct labor rate is $12 per hour in all departments. Departments 1 and 2 are machine intensive; Department 3 is labor intensive. The fixed overhead in Departments 1 and 2 is related to building occupancy, machine depreciation, and machine maintenance. The fixed overhead in Department 3 is related to building occupancy.

Required:

(The requirements are interrelated and concern a decision to introduce labor-saving equipment into Department 3.)

a. Management is not aware of the actual overhead cost functions. A plantwide overhead rate (based on the historic relationship between the plant's total annual overhead and total direct labor hours) is used to assign overhead to departments and products.

Presented are the actual number of direct labor hours and machine hours for a typical year:

	Department 1	Department 2	Department 3
Direct labor hours	2,000	5,000	10,000
Machine hours	5,000	20,000	

Determine the plantwide overhead rate per direct labor hour and the annual overhead assigned to Department 3.

b. Management is concerned about the high cost of products subject to Department 3 manufacturing operations. It is evaluating a proposal to invest in a machine that would substantially reduce the labor content of Department 3 operations. The machine would require an initial investment of $500,000. In addition to fixed maintenance costs of $35,000 per year, the machine would have operating costs of $15 per machine hour. It is predicted to operate 4,000 hours during a typical year. Direct labor savings would amount to 7,000 hours per year. The machine is estimated to have a life of five years with no salvage value.

Heavy Loading's cost of capital is 16 percent. In evaluating the investment proposal, management included overhead cost savings at the plantwide rate per direct labor hour as determined in requirement (a). Following management's procedures, determine the investment proposal's net present value. Based on this analysis, indicate whether management should accept the proposal.

c. Assuming no change in costs (except in Department 3), determine the plantwide overhead rate per direct labor hour if the proposal is accepted. Why does the rate change from that computed in requirement (a)? Also determine the annual overhead now assigned to Department 3.

d. Evaluate the decision to invest in the new machine. Was this the correct decision? Why or why not? (Provide additional analysis as appropriate.)

e. Assume that Heavy Loading did invest in the machine. Because the machine is a special purpose one, it does not have any resale value, and its scrap value is exactly equal to removal costs. Based on your analysis in requirement (d), what should management do now?

10–28
NPV Analysis of Replacement and Expansion: Relevant Costs

Illinois Products Company manufactures several different products. One of its principal products sells for $20 per unit. The sales manager of Illinois Products has stated repeatedly that he could sell more units of this product if they were available. In an attempt to substantiate his claim, the sales manager conducted a market research study last year at a cost of $44,000 to determine potential demand for this product. The study indicated that Illinois Products could sell 18,000 units of this product annually for the next five years.

The equipment currently in use has the capacity to produce 11,000 units annually. The variable production costs are $9 per unit. The equipment has a book value of $60,000 and a remaining useful life of five years. The salvage value is negligible now and will be zero in five years.

A maximum of 20,000 units could be produced annually on a new machine, which could be purchased for $300,000. The new machine has an estimated life of five years and no salvage value. Illinois Products' production manager has estimated that the new equipment would enhance production efficiency, thereby reducing the variable production costs to $7 per unit.

The sales manager believed so strongly that additional capacity was needed that he attempted to prepare an economic justification for the equipment even though this was not part of his responsibilities. His analysis (as follows) disappointed him because it did not justify acquiring the equipment.

Required investment:	
Purchase price of new equipment	$300,000
Loss on disposal of old equipment	60,000
Cost of market research study	44,000
Total investment	$404,000
Annual returns:	
Contribution from product:	
Using new equipment (20,000 × [$20 − $7])	$260,000
Using existing equipment (11,000 × [$20 − $9])	(121,000)
Increase in contribution	$139,000
Less depreciation ($300,000 ÷ 5 years)	(60,000)
Increase in income	$ 79,000
Less cost of capital on additional required investment (0.20 × $404,000)	(80,800)
Net annual return of proposed investment in new equipment	$ (1,800)

Illinois Products Company has a 20 percent cost of capital.

Required:

a. The controller of Illinois Products Company plans to prepare a discounted cash flow analysis of this investment proposal and has asked you to prepare correct calculations of
   1. The required investment in the new equipment.
   2. The recurring annual cash flows.
   Explain the treatment of each item you consider differently from the original analysis prepared by the sales manager.
b. Calculate the net present value of the proposed investment in the new equipment and indicate whether the investment proposal is acceptable.

(CMA Adapted)

10-29
Project Screening and Evaluation with Risk: Multiple Criteria

Transhemisphere uses a capital budgeting committee to evaluate and approve capital expenditure proposals. Because the committee is composed of busy executives, a staff has been assigned to assist the committee in the mechanical aspects of proposal evaluation. As a member of this staff, you have been requested to evaluate five mutually exclusive capital expenditure proposals.

Transhemisphere uses multiple criteria in evaluating capital expenditure proposals. The criteria are designed to consider the time period for which monies invested in a project are unavailable for other purposes, the maximum possible time-adjusted loss on a project, and the time-adjusted relative profitability of a project. To assist in monitoring accepted proposals, the committee also requests information regarding the minimum annual cash flows required for a time-adjusted break-even point. The criteria are applied on a sequential basis, with only proposals that meet the earlier criteria receiving further evaluation.

The following specific procedures are to be followed in the evaluation:

1. Only proposals having an expected bailout and/or payback period of three years or less are subject to further evaluation. The bailout period is the time it takes to recover the investment in a project from any source, including disposal.
2. Evaluate the net present value of the pessimistic cash flows associated with each project using Transhemisphere's cost of capital of 16 percent. Projects whose pessimistic cash flows have a negative net present value of $50,000 or more are eliminated from further consideration.
3. Rank the remaining projects on the basis of the internal rate of return of their expected cash flows. (Refer to Appendix B if you use the table approach.)
4. For the highest ranked project, determine the minimum annual net cash inflows needed to provide an internal rate of return equal to the company's cost of capital.

Information pertaining to the five capital expenditure proposals you have been asked to evaluate follows in thousands of dollars (000):

		DISPOSAL VALUE AT END OF YEAR			PESSIMISTIC		EXPECTED	
Proposal	Initial Investment	1	2	3	Annual Net Cash Inflow	Life	Annual Net Cash Inflow	Life
A	$196	$150	$100	$ 0	$ 40	7 years	$ 50	10 years
B	500	400	350	0	75	10 years	110	12 years
C	400	300	100	0	40	8 years	50	10 years
D	420	250	200	150	100	7 years	100	10 years
E	250	150	75	0	15	9 years	75	12 years

The nature of the investments is such that none of them has a disposal value after the end of its third year.

Required:
a. Following Transhemisphere's capital budgeting procedures, evaluate the five proposals. (Round calculations to the nearest dollar; do not interpolate.)
b. Regardless of Transhemisphere's procedures, which proposal do you recommend and why?

10–30
Post-Audit and Reevaluation of Investment Proposal: NPV

Anthony Company's capital budgeting committee is evaluating a capital expenditure proposal for the production of a stereo tuner to be sold as an add-on feature for television sets not equipped for stereophonic sound. The proposal calls for an independent contractor to construct the necessary facilities by December 31, 2005, at a total cost of $250,000. Payment for all construction costs will be made on that date. An additional $50,000 in cash will also be made available on December 31, 2005, for working capital to support sales and production activities.

Management anticipates that the stereo tuner has a limited market life; there is a high probability that by 2012 all quality television sets will have built-in stereo tuners. Accordingly, the proposal specifies that production will cease on December 31, 2011. The investment in working capital will be recovered on that date, and the production facilities will be sold for $30,000. Predicted net cash inflows from operations for 2006 through 2011 are as follows:

2006 . . . . . $100,000
2007 100,000
2008 100,000
2009 40,000
2010 40,000
2011 40,000

Anthony Company has a time value of money of 16 percent. For capital budgeting purposes, all cash flows are assumed to occur at the end of each year.

Required:

a. Evaluate the capital expenditure proposal using the net present value method. Should Anthony accept the proposal?

b. Assume that the capital expenditure proposal is accepted, but construction delays caused by labor problems and difficulties in obtaining the necessary construction permits delay the completion of the project. Payments totaling $200,000 were made to the construction company on December 31, 2005, for that year's construction. However, completion is now scheduled for December 31, 2006, and an additional $100,000 will be required to complete construction. If the project is continued, the additional $100,000 will be paid at the end of 2006, and the plant will begin operations on January 1, 2007.

   Because of the cost overruns, the capital budgeting committee requests a reevaluation of the project in early 2006, before agreeing to any additional expenditures. After much effort, the following revised predictions of net operating cash inflows are developed:

2007 . . . . . $120,000
2008 100,000
2009 40,000
2010 40,000
2011 40,000

   The working capital investment and disinvestment and the plant salvage values have not changed, except that the cash for working capital would now be made available on December 31, 2006.

   Use the net present value method to reevaluate the *initial* decision to accept the proposal. Given the information currently available about the project, should it have been accepted in 2005? (*Hint:* Determine the net present value as of December 31, 2005, assuming management has not committed Anthony to the proposal.)

c. Given the situation that exists in early 2006, should management continue or cancel the project? Assume that the facilities have a current salvage value of $50,000. (*Hint:* Assume that the decision is being made on January 1, 2006.)

10-31
Post-Audit and Reevaluation of Investment Proposal: IRR

Throughout his four years in college, Ronald King worked at the local Beef Burger Restaurant in College City. Although the working conditions were good and the pay was not bad, Ron believed he could do a much better job of managing the restaurant than the current owner-manager. In particular, Ron believed that the proper use of marketing campaigns and sales incentives, such as selling a second burger for a 25 percent discount, could increase annual sales by 50 percent.

Just before graduation in 2006, Ron inherited $500,000 from his great uncle. He seriously considered buying the restaurant. It seemed like a good idea because he liked the town and its college atmosphere, knew the business, and always wanted to work for himself. He also knew that the current owner wanted to sell the restaurant and retire to Florida.

As part of a small business management course, Ron developed the following income statement for the restaurant's 2005 operations:

Beef Burger Restaurant: College City
Income Statement
For the Year Ended December 31, 2005

Sales		$450,000
Expenses:		
Cost of food	$150,000	
Supplies	20,000	
Employee expenses	140,000	
Utilities	28,000	
Property taxes	20,000	
Insurance	10,000	
Advertising	8,000	
Depreciation	60,000	436,000
Net income		$ 14,000

Ron believed that the cost of food and supplies were all variable, the employee expenses and utilities were one-half variable and one-half fixed in 2005, and all other expenses were fixed.

If Ron purchased the restaurant and followed through on his plans, he believed there would be a 50 percent increase in unit sales volume and all variable costs. Of the fixed costs, only advertising would increase by $12,000. The use of discounts and special promotions would, however, limit the increase in sales revenue to only 40 percent even though sales volume increased 50 percent.

Required:

a. Determine
   1. The current annual net cash inflow.
   2. The predicted annual net cash inflow if Ron executes his plans and his assumptions are correct.

b. Ron believes his plan would produce equal net cash inflows during each of the next 15 years, the period remaining on a long-term lease for the land on which the restaurant is built. At the end of that time, the restaurant would have to be demolished at a predicted net cost of $80,000. Assuming Ron would otherwise invest the money in stock expected to yield 12 percent, determine the maximum amount he should pay for the restaurant.

c. Assume that Ron accepts an offer from the current owner to buy the restaurant for $400,000. Unfortunately, although the expected increase in sales volume does occur, customers make much more extensive use of the promotions than Ron had anticipated. As a result, total sales revenues are 8 percent below projections. Furthermore, to improve employee attitudes, Ron gave a 10 percent raise immediately after purchasing the restaurant.

   Reevaluate the initial decision using the actual sales revenue and the increase in labor costs, assuming conditions will remain unchanged over the remaining life of the project. Was the investment decision a wise one? (Round calculations to the nearest dollar.)

d. Ron can sell the restaurant to a large franchise operator for $300,000. Alternatively, he believes that additional annual marketing expenditures and changes in promotions costing $20,000 per year could bring the sales revenues up to their original projections, with no other changes in costs. Should Ron sell the restaurant or keep it and make the additional expenditures? (Round calculations to the nearest dollar.) (*Hint*: Ron has just bought the restaurant.)

John Shank Case Recommendation

"Marvis Machine Shop" This deceptively short case discusses an equipment replacement decision with strategic considerations. It is set in a metal working shop in West Virginia that produces drill bits for oil exploration. While the normal capital budgeting models are considered, the meat of the case concerns predicting cash flows and strategic issues. Students should think long and hard before responding to the final case requirement: "What decision would you recommend?"

Solution to Review Problem

Basic computations:

Initial investment:
Depreciable assets	$27,740
Working capital	3,000
Total	$30,740

Operation:
Cash receipts	$25,000
Cash expenditures	(15,000)
Net cash inflow	$10,000

Disinvestment:
Sale of depreciable assets	$ 2,000
Recovery of working capital	3,000
Total	$ 5,000

a. Net present value at a 10 percent discount rate:

	Predicted Cash Inflows (outflows) (A)	Year(s) of Cash Flows (B)	10% Present Value Factor (C)	Present Value of Cash Flows (A) × (C)
Initial investment	$(30,740)	0	1.000	$(30,740)
Operation	10,000	1–4	3.170	31,700
Disinvestment	5,000	4	0.683	3,415
Net present value of all cash flows				$ 4,375

b. Internal rate of return:
Using a spreadsheet, the proposal's internal rate of return is readily determined to be 16 percent:

	A	B
1	Year of cash flow	Cash flow
2	0	$(30,740)
3	1	10,000
4	2	10,000
5	3	10,000
6	4	15,000
7	IRR	0.16

The table approach requires additional analysis. Because the proposal has a positive net present value when discounted at 10 percent, its internal rate of return must be higher than 10 percent. Through a trial-and-error approach, the internal rate of return is determined to be 16 percent.

	Predicted Cash Inflows (outflows) (A)	Year(s) of Cash Flows (B)	16% Present Value Factor (C)	Present Value of Cash Flows (A) × (C)
Initial investment	$(30,740)	0	1.000	$(30,740)
Operation	10,000	1–4	2.798	27,980
Disinvestment	5,000	4	0.552	2,760
Net present value of all cash flows				$ 0

c. Payback period = $30,740 ÷ $10,000
= 3.074 years

d. Accounting rate of return on initial and average investments:

Annual net cash inflow from operations $10,000
Less average annual depreciation
([$27,740 − $2,000] ÷ 4) .... (6,435)
Average annual increase in net income ..... $ 3,565

Average investment = ($30,740 + $5,000) ÷ 2
= $17,870

$$\text{Accounting rate of return on initial investment} = \frac{\$3,565}{\$30,740}$$
= 0.1160, or 11.6%

$$\text{Accounting rate of return on average investment} = \frac{\$3,565}{\$17,870}$$
= 0.1995, or 19.95%

OPERATIONAL BUDGETING

After completing this chapter, you should be able to:

LEARNING OBJECTIVE 1   Discuss the importance of budgets.

LEARNING OBJECTIVE 2   Describe the basic approaches to budgeting.

LEARNING OBJECTIVE 3   Develop an activity-based budget.

LEARNING OBJECTIVE 4   Explain the interrelationships among the elements of a master budget and develop a basic budget.

LEARNING OBJECTIVE 5   Discuss the interrelationship between budget development and human behavior.

THE PRIMACY OF THE SALES FORECAST

Managers rely on the budgeting process to integrate the various components of the firm and provide insights into the appropriate scale of operations for upcoming months or quarters. By linking marketing, operations, and financial information, an effective budget can assist all three functional areas as managers respond to the inevitable changes that lie ahead for every organization. The sales forecast represents a starting point in the budget process. In this step, managers estimate the volume of goods and/or services that customers will purchase in the short term. These volumes, in turn, drive the level of activities and resulting costs the firm will incur. To effectively forecast sales, managers must evaluate leading economic indicators, potential changes in consumer preferences, and possible changes in competition.

In general, macroeconomic variables such as income levels and interest rates provide basic information for sales forecasters. Many firms and industry segments rely on specialized economic indicators that signal upcoming activity levels. The volume of corrugated boxes represents one of these leading economic indicators. During the economic expansion of the 1990s, corrugated box production increased 27 percent. Known commonly as cardboard boxes, these corrugated boxes lead expansionary times because manufacturers usually increase their box orders before expanding production. Although 1,500 firms make these boxes, four firms dominate the industry: Smurfit-Stone (with a 20 percent market share), Weyerhaeuser (12 percent), International Paper (10 percent), and Georgia Pacific (9 percent). Industry associations track the volumes of corrugated boxes shipped by these firms, and managers throughout the economy study this leading indicator information.

Over time, consumers' preferences change, and as a result, some product volumes soar while others slide. In the late 1990s and early 2000s, one interesting shift in consumer tastes concerned the relative demand for carbonated versus noncarbonated soft drinks. As consumers have shifted their interest from carbonated soda to noncarbonated juice drinks and water, this latter market has grown 15 times faster than the traditional soda market. Industry estimates suggest that water and juice drinks will make up 50 percent of soft-drink growth between 2000 and 2005. At 7-11's 5,200 stores, two-thirds of the cooler space reserved for nonalcoholic drinks is devoted to noncarbonated juice and bottled water. This trend in beverage consumption has a significant impact on the budgets of bottlers of all types within the industry.

While consumer preference may not change for some products, the competitive environment may change significantly. For example, nonprofit charities and civic organizations often relied on Christmas tree sales as a major fundraising activity. In recent years, however, large retailers such as Wal-Mart, Home Depot, and Target, and many local supermarkets have added Christmas trees to their garden centers during the holiday season. These stores offer Christmas tree customers expanded shopping hours and prices that often beat the nonprofit organizations' lots by $10–$15 per tree. Although managers at smaller lots complain, the major stores contend that the nonprofits have a natural advantage because of the public's appreciation for their various causes. To maintain their volume levels, the nonprofits have increased marketing efforts and added services for their customers.

Budgets benefit managers by providing insight into the impact of the inevitable adjustments required as circumstances change. The budget, however, is no better than the quality of the sales forecast upon which the budget is built. Managerial accounting not only helps managers with the general relationships within a budget but also provides some guidelines by which to assess the quality of the sales forecast.

Source: Based on Kelly Greene, "Boy Scout Troops Face Stiff Competition from Big Retailers Selling Cheap Trees," *The Wall Street Journal* (Interactive Edition), December 19, 2000; Carol Hymowitz, "Managers Must Adjust Quickly in Changing Economic Environment," *The Wall Street Journal* (Interactive Edition) January 9, 2001; Betsy McKay, "Consumers' Appetite for Soda Is Going Flat," *The Wall Street Journal* (Interactive Edition), September 19, 2000; and Dan Morse, "Sales of Corrugated Boxes Offer One Measure of Economy's Health," *The Wall Street Journal* (Interactive Edition), February 12, 2001.

The process of projecting the operations of an organization and their financial impact into the future is called **budgeting.** A **budget** is a formal plan of action expressed in monetary terms. **The purpose of this chapter is to examine the concepts, relationships, and procedures used in budgeting.** Our emphasis is on **operating budgets,** which concern the development of detailed plans to guide operations throughout the budget period. We will consider the reasons that organizations budget and alternative approaches to budget development. We will also examine budget assembly and consider issues related to human behavior and managing the budgeting process. The chapter appendix considers budgeting for manufacturing activities.

LEARNING OBJECTIVE 1 ## REASONS FOR BUDGETING

Operating managers frequently regard budgeting as a time-consuming task that diverts attention from current problems. Indeed, the development of an effective budget is a difficult job. It is also a necessary one. Organizations that do not plan are likely to wander aimlessly and ultimately succumb to the swirl of current events. The formal development of a budget helps to ensure both success and survival; it compels planning; it improves communications and coordination among organizational elements; it provides a guide to action; and it provides a basis of performance evaluation.

BUDGETS COMPEL PLANNING

Formal budgeting procedures require people to think about the future. Without formal planning procedures, busy operating managers would not find time to plan. Immediate needs would consume all available time. Formal budgeting procedures, with specified deadlines, force managers to plan for the future by making the completion of the budget another immediate need. Budgeting moves an organization from an informal "reactive" style to a formal "proactive" style of management. As a result, management and other employees spend less time solving unanticipated problems and more time on positive measures and preventative actions.

BUDGETS IMPROVE COMMUNICATION AND COORDINATION

When operating responsibilities are divided, it is difficult to synchronize activities. Production must know what marketing intends to sell. Purchasing and personnel must know the factory's material and labor requirements. The treasurer must plan to ensure the availability of the cash to support receivables, inventories, and capital expenditures. Budgeting forces the managers of these diverse functions to communicate their plans and coordinate their activities. It helps ensure that plans are feasible (Can purchasing obtain adequate inventories to support projected sales?) and that they are synchronized (Will inventory be available in advance of an advertising campaign?). The final version of the budget emerges after an extensive (often lengthy) process of communication and coordination. As examined in Research Shows 11–1, recent advances in computer software allow organizations to better coordinate budget development.

BUDGETS PROVIDE A GUIDE TO ACTION

Once the budget has been finalized, the various operating managers know what is expected of them, and they can set about doing it. If employees do not have a guide to action, their efforts could be wasted on unproductive or even counterproductive activities.

BUDGETS PROVIDE A BASIS OF PERFORMANCE EVALUATION

After employees accept the budget as a guide to action, they can be held responsible for their portion of the budget. When results do not agree with plans, managers attempt to determine the cause of the divergence. This information is then used to adjust operations or to modify plans.

Budgeting is an important part of **management by exception,** whereby management directs attention only to those activities not proceeding according to plan. Without the budget, management might spend an inordinate amount of time seeking explanation of past activities and not enough time planning future activities. The process of developing a budgeting system could produce unexpected benefits.

LEARNING OBJECTIVE 2   **GENERAL APPROACHES TO BUDGETING**

Approaches to developing a budget can be placed into two broad categories:

1. Budgeting with unit-level cost drivers.
2. Budgeting with unit- and nonunit-level cost drivers.

11-1 ▸ **RESEARCH SHOWS**

BUDGET MANAGEMENT SOFTWARE AND DATA WAREHOUSING GIVE MANAGERS CONTROL

A multi-user budgeting system provides shared access to a single database (data warehouse) through which everyone involved in the budgeting process can access common revenue and expense definitions, use similar layouts, use the same encoding and decoding structures, and, therefore, quickly share budget projections. This type of budgeting system allows the budget manager more control over the entire process while providing the top executives with better overviews. Some of the characteristics of a good multi-user budgeting system include the following:

1. Support for changes to hierarchy so that different levels of budgets can be examined.
2. Shared access to common data warehouses.
3. Automatic mapping of imported data for use in multiple applications.
4. Numerous "what-if" functions.

This type of system is effective only if the data warehouse is well designed and managed. The design team for and management of a data warehouse should include technical personnel who are available to monitor and maintain the system, including the following:

1. Technical data warehouse designer (created the database structure and assists in its maintenance).
2. Systems analyst/programmer (continually evaluates and creates new programs as needed).
3. End-user analyst (evaluates and monitors users' needs).
4. Database administrator (creator of physical database structure who continues to monitor performance).
5. Technical support (maintain system's integrity and reliability).

The result of a successful implementation is that the data warehouse consists of a group of technologies that integrates the operational information of all budget centers into a single database. This allows authorized individuals access to the data and gives them the ability to generate budgets to their own specifications.

Sources: Guy Haddleton, "10 Rules for Selecting Budget Management Software," *Management Accounting*, January 1998, pp. 24, 26–27; and Marc Levine and Joel Siegel, "What the Accountant Must Know about Data Warehousing," *The CPA Journal*, January 2001, pp. 37, 39–42.

BUDGETING WITH UNIT-LEVEL COST DRIVERS

The traditional approach to developing a budget assumed that resource requirements and costs responded to changes in unit-level cost drivers, such as units sold or sales dollars. Costs that responded to changes in unit-level cost drivers were budgeted using an output/input approach. Costs that did not respond to unit-level cost drivers were budgeted using an incremental approach.

Output/Input Approach. The **output/input approach** budgets physical inputs and costs as a function of planned unit-level activities. This approach is often used for service, merchandising, manufacturing, and distribution activities that have clearly defined relationships between effort and accomplishment. If each unit produced requires 2 pounds of direct materials that cost $5 each, and the planned production volume is 25 units, the budgeted inputs and costs for direct materials are 50 pounds (25 units × 2 pounds per unit) and $250 (50 pounds × $5 per pound).

Note that the budgeted inputs are a function of the planned outputs. The output/input approach starts with the planned outputs and works backward to budget the inputs. It is difficult to use this approach for costs that do not respond to changes in unit-level cost drivers.

Incremental Approach. The **incremental approach** budgets costs for a coming period as a dollar or percentage change from the amount budgeted for (or spent during) some previous period. This approach is often used when the relationships between inputs and outputs are weak or nonexistent. For example, it is difficult to establish a clear relationship between sales volume and advertising expenditures. Consequently, the budgeted amount of advertising for a future period is often based on the budgeted or actual advertising expenditures in a previous period. If budgeted advertising expenditures for 2003 were $200,000, the budgeted expenditures for 2004 would be some increment, say 5 percent, above $200,000. In evaluating the proposed 2004 budget, management would accept the $200,000 base and focus attention only on justifying the increment.

The incremental approach is widely used in government and not-for-profit organizations. In seeking a budget appropriation, a manager using the incremental approach need only justify proposed expenditures in excess of the previous budget. The primary advantage of the incremental approach is that it simplifies the budget process by considering only the increments in the various budget items. A major disadvantage is that existing waste and inefficiencies could escalate year after year.

Minimum Level Approach. As the portion of costs not responding to unit-level drivers increased throughout the twentieth century, an increasing portion of costs was budgeted using the less precise incremental approach. This lack of good budgetary control led to further increases in costs. Before the development of hierarchical approaches to cost analysis, management attempted to better control costs by employing a number of variations on the incremental approach. The minimum level approach is representative of these attempts to control the growth of costs not responding to unit-level drivers.

Using the **minimum level approach**, an organization establishes a base amount for budget items and requires explanation or justification for any budgeted amount above the minimum (base). This base is usually significantly less than the base used in the incremental approach. It likely is the minimum amount necessary to keep a program or organizational unit viable. For example, the corporate director of product development would need some basic amount to avoid canceling ongoing projects. Additional increments might also be included, first to support the current level of product development and second to undertake desirable new projects.

Some organizations, especially units of government, employ a variation of the minimum level approach, identified as *zero-based budgeting*. Under **zero-based budgeting** every dollar of expenditure must be justified. The essence of zero-based budgeting is breaking an organizational unit's total budget into program packages with related costs. Management then ranks all program packages on the basis of the perceived benefits in relationship to their costs. Program packages are then funded for the budget period using this ranking. High-ranking packages are most likely to be funded and low-ranking packages are least likely to be funded.

The minimum level approach improves on the incremental approach by questioning the necessity for costs included in the base of the incremental approach, but it is very time consuming. In addition, it is still based on the traditional distinction between variable costs that respond to unit-level cost drivers and fixed costs that do not respond to unit-level cost drivers. As noted in previous chapters, more complete tools are now available to examine cost behavior.

All three approaches are often used within the same organization. A manufacturing firm might use the output/input approach to budget distribution expenditures, the incremental approach to budget administrative salaries, and the minimum level approach to budget research and development.

BUDGETING WITH UNIT- AND NONUNIT-LEVEL COST DRIVERS
In recent years, managers have made an increasing use of cost hierarchies that consider unit-level and nonunit-level cost drivers. We used this hierarchy for cost analysis in Chapter 2, profitability analysis in Chapter 3, decision making in Chapter 4,

and numerous other purposes in subsequent chapters. This hierarchy can also be used for budgeting.

Activity-Based Approach.   The **activity-based approach** to budgeting uses an activity cost hierarchy to budget physical inputs and costs as a function of planned activity. While mechanically similar to the output/input approach, the addition of nonunit-level cost drivers allows managers using the activity-based approach to take control of costs previously budgeted with the less precise incremental or minimum level approaches. In evaluating the proposed budget, managers focus more on identifying the optimal set of activities and spend less time considering vaguely defined and packaged cost increments.

The activity-based approach budgets costs on the basis of the anticipated consumption of cost drivers. Activity-based budgeting incorporates costs at different levels (such as batch, order, or customer) that are not easily handled by the output/input approach and then budgeted using the incremental approach.

Although it is possible to develop an activity-based budget for an entire organization, as in Research Shows 11–2, most applications of this approach focus on processes, services, products, or departments. Even when an activity approach is used, management might still use the incremental or minimum level approaches to budget product-level, market segment, or facility-level costs.

Continuous Improvement (Kaizen) Approach.   The **continuous improvement (Kaizen) approach** to budgeting incorporates a targeted improvement (reduction) in costs. The continuous improvement approach can be used in conjunction with any previously discussed approach to budgeting and can be applied to every budget category throughout the entire organization or to specific areas selected by management. When used with the activity-based approach, the focus is typically on redesigning products or improving processes rather than simply cutting costs.

In a typical application, the continuous improvement approach might target the costs of some program, product, or process to be reduced by a specified improvement

---

11–2   RESEARCH SHOWS

STRATEGY-BASED COSTING INTEGRATES ALL BUDGET ELEMENTS

Operating budgets cannot be prepared in isolation of the organization's capital budgets discussed in the last chapter. The organization's overall strategy must be considered when preparing annual operating budgets and, according to Latimer, one way to incorporate all elements is to develop strategy-based costing.

This method determines where organizational spending is concentrated and then analyzes according to the categories of strategic, obligatory, and elective. *Strategic costs* include those areas typically considered as capital budgeting and those necessary to preserve and grow the organization. *Obligatory costs* stem from efforts related to current and potential customers, vendors, creditors, regulators, and other stakeholders (operational budgeting). *Elective costs* are self-imposed and are primarily procedural in nature. They include such things as employee training, systems obsolescence, exception analysis, and management intervention (known as *oversupervision*) and generally are part of operational budgeting rather than being developed as a separate budget.

Once the categories have been defined, it is important for management to make efforts to shift costs from the elective category to the other two. Some elective costs will always exist, but the organization should direct its resources to concentrate on strategic and obligatory activities. Before the resource allocation is changed, management should consider whether the existing cost structure can support its objectives as defined by being strategic, obligatory, or elective.

Source: Michael F. Latimer, "Linking Strategy-Based Costing and Innovation-Based Budgeting," *Strategic Finance,* March 2001, pp. 38–42.

factor each quarter or month. With January's budget set at $24,000 and an improvement factor of 0.997, the budget for February is $23,928 ($24,000 × 0.997), for March is $23,856 ($23,928 × 0.997); and so forth for each month of the current budget.

When the continuous improvement or Kaizen approach is related to products, the stage of a product's life cycle should be considered. During the early stages, the Kaizen approach might expect significant improvements as learning takes place and technological improvements are implemented. As a product nears the maturity stage in its life cycle, the amount of continuous improvements will likely decline.

LEARNING OBJECTIVE 3 ## ACTIVITY-BASED BUDGETS

Although the master budget illustrated in the next section provides an overview of developing a budget for an entire organization, management is often interested in budgets for specific types of activities, products, or processes. If management were interested in improving quality or environmental awareness, they might develop an organizationwide budget for quality costs or environmental costs. In a similar manner, specific budgets might be developed for telephone expenditures, travel costs, or any other item of interest. These specialized budgets typically cut across organization boundaries. Their usefulness is enhanced if they focus on activities and activity costs.

Assume that Atlantic Magnetic Inc. produces a variety of products including compact disks (CDs), components of hard disk drives, and 3½-inch floppy disks. Because management is interested in examining the detailed cost of CDs, perhaps as a starting point for a continuous improvement program, they develop an activity-based budget for this product. The 2004 activity-based budget for CDs is shown in Exhibit 11–1.

To simplify the illustration, we omitted computational details, combined many activities, and clearly labeled the activities as unit, batch, or product level. This activity-based budget cuts across functional areas to bring together all budgeted costs for CDs. Observe that it is based on activities (such as developing and designing the product, procuring, setting up, operating, inspecting, and packaging), rather than on expense categories such as direct labor and overhead. Also note that the budget reflects an activity cost hierarchy with total cost at the unit level, batch level, and product level.

EXHIBIT 11–1

ACTIVITY-BASED BUDGETING FOR A PRODUCT

Atlantic Magnetic Inc.
Activity-Based Budget for Compact Disks
For the Year Ending December 31, 2004

Unit-level costs:		
Direct materials	$180,000	
Assembling	245,000	
Packaging	380,000	
Distributing	60,000	$ 865,000
Batch-level costs:		
Procuring	$ 30,000	
Setting up	80,000	
Inspecting	70,000	180,000
Product-level costs:		
Developing and design	$ 50,000	
Advertising product	120,000	170,000
Total product costs		$1,215,000

Facility-level costs are not included in such a budget unless the organization manufactures only one product.

To illustrate another possible type of activity-based budget, the 2004 activity-based budget for the Purchasing Department of Atlantic Magnetic is presented in Exhibit 11–2. Once again, to simplify the illustration, we omitted computational details and combined many activities.

In examining Exhibit 11–2, note the following:

- The activity-based budget emphasizes the activities performed by the Purchasing Department, including screening vendors and performing quality certification, and placing, verifying, and receiving orders. A more traditional budget would emphasize expense categories such as salaries, office supplies, and maintenance.
- Because the Purchasing Department conducts activities for several products, the procurement expenses in Exhibit 11–2 exceed those in Exhibit 11–1. Some Purchasing Department costs, such as those for vendor screening and quality certification and those classified as facility level, might not be assigned to any products.
- In comparing Exhibits 11–1 and 11–2, procuring is classified differently: as a batch cost from the viewpoint of the product CDs and as a unit cost from the viewpoint of the Purchasing Department. From the perspective of the product, an order is placed for a batch of direct materials. From the perspective of the Purchasing Department, whose job is to acquire direct materials, each purchase order is a unit.

LEARNING OBJECTIVE 4

THE MASTER BUDGET

The final step in budgeting is to prepare a master budget for an entire organization that considers all interrelationships among organization units. The **master budget** groups together all budgets and supporting schedules and coordinates all financial and operational activities, placing them into an organizationwide set of budgets for a given time period.

EXHIBIT 11–2

ACTIVITY-BASED BUDGETING FOR A DEPARTMENT

Atlantic Magnetic Inc.
Activity-Based Budget for Purchasing Department
For the Year Ending December 31, 2004

Budgeted activities:			
Screening new vendors		130	
Placing orders		1,200	
Receiving and inspecting shipments		1,400	
Budgeted costs:			
Screening vendors and performing quality certification (unit level per vendor)			$ 30,000
Procuring (unit level per purchase order):			
Placing orders	$50,000		
Verifying orders	25,000		
Receiving orders	16,000		
Inspecting orders	8,000		99,000
General administration and maintenance (facility level)			25,000
Total purchasing department costs			$154,000

Because it explicitly considers organizational interrelationships, the master budget is more complex than budgets developed for products, services, organization units, or specific processes. The elements of the master budget depend on the nature of the business, its products or services, processes and organization, and management needs.

A major goal of developing a master budget is to ensure the smooth functioning of a business throughout the budget period and the organization's operating cycle. As shown in Exhibit 11–3, the operating cycle involves the conversion of cash into other assets, which are intended to produce revenues in excess of their costs. The cycle generally follows a path from cash, to inventories, to receivables (via sales or services), and back to cash. There are, of course, intermediate processes such as the purchase or manufacture of inventories, payments of accounts payable, and the collection of receivables. The master budget is merely a detailed model of the firm's operating cycle that includes all internal processes.

Most for-profit organizations begin the budgeting process with the development of the sales budget and conclude with the development of budgeted financial statements. Exhibit 11–4 depicts the annual budget assembly process in a retail merchandising organization. Note that most of the budget data flow from sales toward cash and then toward the budgeted financial statements.

To illustrate the procedures involved in budget assembly, a quarterly budget for the year 2005 is developed for Backpacks Galore Inc. (BGI), a retail organization that sells backpacks. Although BGI sells many types of backpacks, for our purposes they are classified as either school or hiking. The assembly sequence follows the overview illustrated in Exhibit 11–4. Each element of the budget process in Exhibit 11–4 is illustrated in a separate exhibit. Because of the numerous elements in the budget process illustrated for BGI, you will find it useful to refer to Exhibit 11–4 often.

The activities of a business can be summarized under three broad categories: operating activities, financing activities, and investing activities. To simplify the illustration, assume that Backpacks Galore engaged in no investing activities during the budget period and that the only financing activity was short-term borrowing. Normal profit-related activities performed in conducting the daily affairs of an

EXHIBIT 11–3

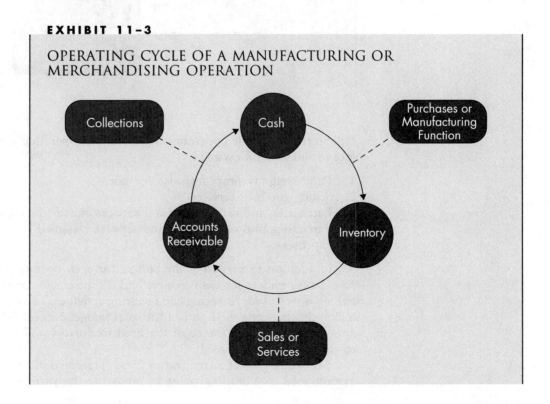

OPERATING CYCLE OF A MANUFACTURING OR MERCHANDISING OPERATION

EXHIBIT 11–4

OVERVIEW OF BUDGET ASSEMBLY PROCESS IN A
MERCHANDISING FIRM

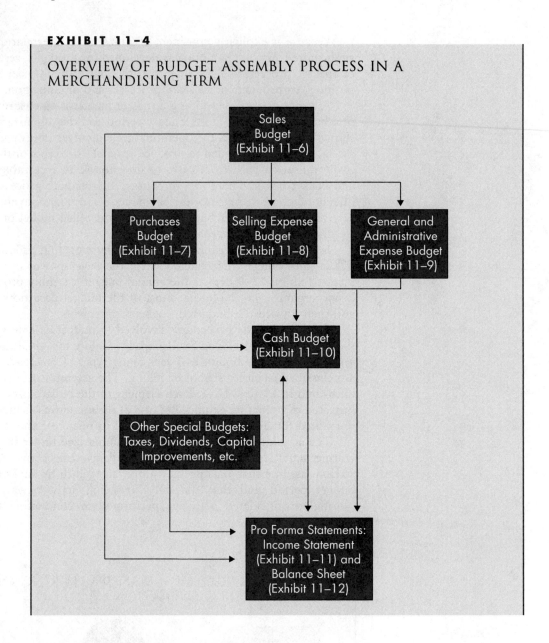

organization are called **operating activities.** The operating activities of Backpacks Galore include the following:

1. Purchasing inventory intended for sale.
2. Selling goods or services.
3. Purchasing and using goods and services classified as selling expenses.
4. Purchasing and using goods and services classified as general and administrative expenses.

In addition to preparing the budget for each operating activity, companies prepare a cash budget for cash receipts and disbursements related to their operating activities as well as for financing and investing activities. The importance of cash planning makes this budget a vital part of the total budget process. Management must, for example, be aware in advance of the need to borrow and have some idea when borrowed funds can be repaid.

The balance sheet at the end of 2004, presented in Exhibit 11–5, contains information used as a starting point in preparing the various budgets. To reduce com-

EXHIBIT 11-5

INITIAL BALANCE SHEET

Backpacks Galore Inc.
Balance Sheet
December 31, 2004

Assets

Current assets:			
Cash			$ 15,000
Accounts receivable (net)			21,600
Inventory:			
School backpacks (5,000 × $10)	$ 50,000		
Hiking backpacks (1,600 × $60)	96,000	146,000	$182,600
Property and equipment:			
Land		$ 60,000	
Buildings and equipment	$260,000		
Less accumulated depreciation	(124,800)	135,200	195,200
Total assets			$377,800

Liabilities and Stockholders' Equity

Current liabilities:			
Accounts payable			$ 40,000
Stockholders' equity:			
Capital stock		$150,000	
Retained earnings		187,800	337,800
Total liabilities and stockholders' equity			$377,800

plexity, we use the output/input approach to budget variable costs and assume that the budgets for other costs were previously developed using the incremental approach. Budgets to be prepared include those for sales, purchases, selling expense, general and administrative expense, and cash.

SALES BUDGET

The **sales budget** includes a forecast of unit sales volume and sales revenue, and it can also contain a forecast of sales collections. Because sales drive almost all other activities in a for-profit organization, developing a sales budget is the starting point in the budgeting process. Managers use the best available information to accurately forecast future market conditions. These forecasts, when considered along with merchandise available, promotion and advertising plans, and expected pricing policies, should lead to the most dependable sales budget. The sales budget of BGI for 2005 is presented in Exhibit 11-6.

The information in the sales budget and the predictions of the expected portion of cash sales and the timing of collections from credit sales are used to detail cash receipts. In the event of a projected cash shortfall, management could consider ways to increase cash sales or to accelerate the collection of receipts from credit sales.

PURCHASES BUDGET

The **purchases budget** indicates the merchandise that must be acquired to meet sales needs and ending inventory requirements. It can be referred to as a *merchandise budget* if it contains only purchases of merchandise for sale. However, it often contains office and selling supplies. For simplicity, BGI's purchases budget, shown in Exhibit 11-7, includes only purchases of merchandise.

EXHIBIT 11–6

SALES BUDGET

Backpacks Galore Inc.
Sales Budget
For the Year Ending December 31, 2005

	First Quarter	Second Quarter	Third Quarter	Fourth Quarter	Year Total
Sales (units):					
School backpacks	4,000	3,400	3,650	3,950	15,000
Hiking backpacks	1,100	1,600	2,500	1,300	6,500
Sales (dollars):					
School backpacks					
(unit sales × $20)	$ 80,000	$ 68,000	$ 73,000	$ 79,000	$300,000
Hiking backpacks					
(unit sales × $100)	110,000	160,000	250,000	130,000	650,000
Total	$190,000	$228,000	$323,000	$209,000	$950,000

EXHIBIT 11–7

PURCHASES BUDGET

Backpacks Galore Inc.
Purchases Budget
For the Year Ending December 31, 2005

	First Quarter	Second Quarter	Third Quarter	Fourth Quarter	Year Total
Purchase units:					
School backpacks:					
Current sales	4,000	3,400	3,650	3,950	
Desired ending inventory*	4,400	4,650	4,950	5,100†	
Total needs	8,400	8,050	8,600	9,050	
Less beginning inventory	(5,000)	(4,400)	(4,650)	(4,950)	
Purchases	3,400	3,650	3,950	4,100	15,100
Hiking backpacks:					
Current sales	1,100	1,600	2,500	1,300	
Desired ending inventory*	2,100	3,000	1,800	1,700†	
Total needs	3,200	4,600	4,300	3,000	
Less beginning inventory	(1,600)	(2,100)	(3,000)	(1,800)	
Purchases	1,600	2,500	1,300	1,200	6,600
Purchase dollars:					
School backpacks	$ 34,000	$ 36,500	$ 39,500	$ 41,000	$151,000
Hiking backpacks	96,000	150,000	78,000	72,000	396,000
Total	$130,000	$186,500	$117,500	$113,000	$547,000

*Next quarter's sales plus base inventory of 1,000 school backpacks and 500 hiking backpacks.
†Projected sales for the first quarter of 2002 are 4,100 school backpacks and 1,200 hiking backpacks.

In reviewing BGI's purchases budget, note the following:

- Management desires to have all inventory needed to fill the following quarter's sales in stock at the end of the previous quarter.
- To provide for a possible delay in the receipt of inventory, BGI also carries a safety stock of 1,000 school backpacks and 500 hiking backpacks.
- The total inventory needs equal current sales plus desired ending inventory, including safety stock.
- Budgeted purchases are computed as total inventory needs less the beginning inventory.

If BGI's suppliers were willing to make more frequent deliveries, BGI could adopt an inventory system that would no longer require BGI to begin each quarter with enough inventory to satisfy the quarter's entire sales. This would reduce inventory investment and the space needed to store the inventory.

The information in the purchases budget and the information on expected timing of payments for purchases are used to budget cash disbursements for purchases. In the event of a projected cash shortfall, management can consider ways to delay the purchase of inventory or the payment for inventory purchases.

SELLING EXPENSE BUDGET

The **selling expense budget** presents the expenses the organization plans to incur in connection with sales and distribution. Budgeted selling expenses, including variable selling expenses and fixed selling expenses, are $4,500 per quarter. Note in the selling expense budget, Exhibit 11–8, that the budgeted variable selling expenses are determined as a percentage of budgeted sales dollars. The budgeted fixed selling expenses are based on amounts obtained from the manager of the sales department. To simplify the presentation of the cash budget, assume that BGI pays its selling expenses in the quarter they are incurred.

EXHIBIT 11-8

SELLING EXPENSE BUDGET

Backpacks Galore Inc.
Selling Expense Budget
For the Year Ending December 31, 2005

	First Quarter	Second Quarter	Third Quarter	Fourth Quarter	Year Total
Budgeted sales (from Exhibit 11–6)	$190,000	$228,000	$323,000	$209,000	$950,000
Selling costs and disbursements:					
Variable costs:					
Setup/Display (1% sales)	$ 1,900	$ 2,280	$ 3,230	$ 2,090	$ 9,500
Commissions (2% sales)	3,800	4,560	6,460	4,180	19,000
Miscellaneous (1% sales)	1,900	2,280	3,230	2,090	9,500
Total	$ 7,600	$ 9,120	$12,920	$ 8,360	$38,000
Fixed costs:					
Advertising	$ 2,250	$ 2,250	$ 2,250	$ 2,250	$ 9,000
Office expenses	1,250	1,250	1,250	1,250	5,000
Miscellaneous	1,000	1,000	1,000	1,000	4,000
Total	$ 4,500	$ 4,500	$ 4,500	$ 4,500	$18,000
Total selling expenses	$12,100	$13,620	$17,420	$12,860	$56,000

GENERAL AND ADMINISTRATIVE EXPENSE BUDGET

The **general and administrative expense budget** presents the expenses the organization plans to incur in connection with the general administration of the organization. Included are expenses for the accounting department, the computer center, and the president's office, for example. BGI's general and administrative expense budget is presented in Exhibit 11–9.

Note that the depreciation of $2,000 per quarter is a noncash item and is not carried forward to the cash budget. Also observe that no variable general and administrative costs are included because most expenditures categorized as general and administrative are related to top-management operations that do not vary with unit-level cost drivers. To simplify the presentation of the cash budget, assume that BGI's general and administrative expenses, except depreciation, are paid in the quarter they are incurred.

CASH BUDGET

The **cash budget** summarizes all cash receipts and disbursements expected to occur during the budget period. Cash is critical to survival. Income is like food and cash is like water. Food is necessary to survive and prosper over time, but you can get along without food for a short period of time. You cannot survive very long without water. Hence, cash budgeting is very important, especially in a small business, such as the one considered in What's Happening 11–1.

After it makes sales predictions, an organization uses information on credit terms, collections policy, and prior collection experience to develop a cash collections budget. Collections on sales normally include receipts from the current period's sales and collections from sales of prior periods. An allowance for bad debts, which reduces each period's collections, is also predicted. Other items often included are cash sales, sales discounts, allowances for volume discounts, and seasonal changes of sales prices and collections.

BGI's cash budget is presented in Exhibit 11–10. As you review this exhibit, note the following:

EXHIBIT 11-9

GENERAL AND ADMINISTRATIVE EXPENSE BUDGET

Backpacks Galore Inc.
General and Administrative Expense Budget
For the Year Ending December 31, 2005

	First Quarter	Second Quarter	Third Quarter	Fourth Quarter	Year Total
Costs and disbursements:					
Compensation	$20,000	$20,000	$20,000	$20,000	$ 80,000
Research and development	5,000	5,000	5,000	5,000	20,000
Insurance	2,000	2,000	2,000	2,000	8,000
Depreciation	2,000	2,000	2,000	2,000	8,000
Property taxes	3,000	3,000	3,000	3,000	12,000
Miscellaneous	1,000	1,000	1,000	1,000	4,000
Total general and administrative expenses	$33,000	$33,000	$33,000	$33,000	$132,000

GOING BROKE GETTING RICH

Frank used his own cash plus some borrowed from his bank to start a business. In the first two years, Frank's company showed a small operating loss that he considered acceptable. In the third year, it showed a profit of more than $100,000. Frank thought this was great until the accountant told him that the company did not have enough cash to pay income taxes. Frank did not believe his accountant until the differences between income and cash flow were explained and the accountant showed him a cash flow statement for his business.

Because income is not the same as cash inflow, cash budgets are critical to all businesses, especially small ones. Managers who do not understand cash flow can really have problems, even when profits are evident. Cash can be tied up in inventory purchased in anticipation of sales growth. When sales are on account, additional cash is tied up in receivables rather than being available to pay bills. Worse, the money Frank borrowed to start the business might come due just as the business starts to turn a profit, even though it still has critical cash needs to support future growth.

Managers must understand the operating cycle and relationship between income and cash flows. For Frank, a cash budget would show the cash generated by operations, the cash outflow needed for paying back his loan, and the amount of cash tied up in inventory and receivables.

Source: Gary Gibbs, "Managing Cash Flow: A Constant Business Challenge," *Wichita Business Journal*, December 1997, pp. 8b–14b.

- Management estimates that one-half of all sales are for cash and the other half are on the company's credit card.[1] Seventy-five percent of the credit sales are collected in the quarter of sale, and 24 percent are collected in the following quarter. Bad debts are budgeted at 1 percent of credit sales. This resource flow is graphically illustrated as follows:

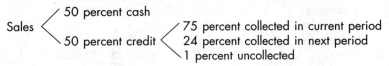

- Payments for purchases are made 50 percent in the quarter purchased and 50 percent in the next quarter.
- Information on cash expenditures for selling expenses and for general and administrative expenses is based on budgets for these items. Note that the quarterly cash expenditures for general and administrative expenses are $31,000 rather than $33,000. The $2,000 difference relates to depreciation, which does not require the use of cash.
- BGI's accountant provided tax information. Income taxes are determined on the basis of predicted taxable income following rules established by the Internal Revenue Service.
- The dividend information is provided by BGI's board of directors.
- The cash budget shows the cash operating deficiencies and surpluses expected to occur at the end of each quarter. This information is used to plan for borrowing and loan payment.
- The cash maintenance policy for Backpacks Galore specifies maintaining a minimum balance of $15,000.
- BGI has a line of credit with a bank, with any interest on borrowed funds computed at the simple interest rate of 12.0 percent per year, or 1.0 percent per month.

---

[1]When sales are on bank credit cards, the collection is immediate, less any bank user fee.

EXHIBIT 11–10

CASH BUDGET

Backpacks Galore Inc.
Cash Budget
For the Year Ending December 31, 2005

	First Quarter	Second Quarter	Third Quarter	Fourth Quarter	Year Total
Cash balance, beginning	$ 15,000	$ 15,750	$ 15,180	$ 56,155	$ 15,000
Collections on sales:					
Cash sales	$ 95,000	$ 114,000	$ 161,500	$ 104,500	$ 475,000
Credit sales:					
Current quarter	71,250	85,500	121,125	78,375	356,250
Prior quarter	21,600*	22,800	27,360	38,760	110,520
Total	$ 187,850	$ 222,300	$ 309,985	$ 221,635	$ 941,770
Total available from operations	$ 202,850	$ 238,050	$ 325,165	$ 277,790	$ 956,770
Less budgeted disbursements:					
Purchasing (Exhibit 11–7):					
Current quarter (50%)	$ 65,000	$ 93,250	$ 58,750	$ 56,500	$ 273,500
Previous quarter (50%)	40,000†	65,000	93,250	58,750	257,000
Total	$ 105,000	$ 158,250	$ 152,000	$ 115,250	$ 530,500
Selling (Exhibit 11–8)	12,100	13,620	17,420	12,860	56,000
General and administrative (Exhibit 11–9)	31,000‡	31,000	31,000	31,000	124,000
Other:					
Income taxes	22,000	22,000	22,000	11,200	77,200
Dividends	20,000	20,000	20,000	30,000	90,000
Total disbursements	$(190,100)	$(244,870)	$(242,420)	$(200,310)	$(877,700)
Excess (deficiency) cash available over disbursements	$ 12,750	$ (6,820)	$ 82,745	$ 77,480	$ 79,070
Short-term financing§:					
New loans	$ 3,000	$ 22,000			$ 25,000
Repayments			$ (25,000)		(25,000)
Interest#			(1,590)		(1,590)
Net cash flow from financing	$ 3,000	$ 22,000	$ (26,590)		$ (1,590)
Cash balance, ending	$ 15,750	$ 15,180	$ 56,155	$ 77,480	$ 77,480

*This is based on the fourth quarter 2004 credit sales.
†Unpaid balance at December 31, 2004, reflects prior year payment terms.
‡Amounts for cash flow exclude depreciation.
§Loans are obtained in $1,000 increments to maintain cash at a minimum balance of $15,000 at all times. New loans required are budgeted for the beginning of the quarter, and repayments are budgeted for the end of the quarter. Loan repayments are made on a first-borrowed, first-repaid basis, and interest is paid only at the time of repayment.
#Interest for $25,000 is $1,590 ($3,000 × 9 months × 0.01 = $270) + ($22,000 × 6 months × 0.01 = $1,320).
Note: The accounts receivable balance on December 31, 2005, is $25,080 ($104,500 − $78,375 − $1,045).

All necessary borrowing is assumed to occur at the start of each quarter in increments of $1,000. Repayments are assumed to occur at the end of the quarter. Interest is paid when loans are repaid.

- The cash budget indicates that BGI will need to borrow $3,000 at the beginning of the first quarter and $22,000 at the beginning of the second quarter. At the end of the third quarter, BGI will be able to repay both loans.

BUDGETED FINANCIAL STATEMENTS

The preparation of the master budget culminates in the preparation of budgeted financial statements. **Budgeted financial statements** are hypothetical statements that reflect the "as-if" effects of the budgeted activities on the actual financial position of the organization. That is, the statements reflect the results of operations assuming all budget predictions are correct. Spreadsheets that permit the user to immediately determine the impact of any assumed changes facilitate developing budgeted financial statements. The budgeted income statement can follow the functional format traditionally used for financial accounting or the contribution format introduced in Chapter 3. In either case, the balance sheet amounts reflect the corresponding budgeted entries.

Exhibit 11–11 presents the budgeted income statement for the year ending December 31, 2005. If all predictions made in the operating budget are correct, Backpacks Galore will produce a net income of $138,460 for the year. Note that almost every item on the budgeted income statement comes from one of the budget schedules.

EXHIBIT 11-11

BUDGETED INCOME STATEMENT

Backpacks Galore Inc.
Budgeted Income Statement (Functional Format)
For the Year Ending December 31, 2005

Sales (Exhibit 11–6)			$950,000
Expenses:			
Cost of goods sold:			
Beginning inventory (Exhibit 11–5)	$146,000		
Purchases (Exhibit 11–7)	547,000		
Cost of merchandise available	$693,000		
Ending inventory, 12/31/05*	(153,000)	$540,000	
Selling operations (Exhibit 11–8)		56,000	
General and administrative (Exhibit 11–9)		132,000	
Bad debt expense[†]		4,750	(732,750)
Income from operations			$217,250
Other expenses:			
Interest expense (Exhibit 11–10)			(1,590)
Net income before taxes			$215,660
Allowance for income taxes			(77,200)
Net income			$138,460

*(School backpacks, 5,100 × $10 = $51,000) + (Hiking backpacks, 1,700 × $60 = $102,000) = $153,000 (Exhibit 11–7).
[†]Bad debt is 1 percent of credit sales ($475,000 × 0.01).

The budgeted balance sheet, presented in Exhibit 11–12, shows the anticipated financial position of BGI at the end of 2005, assuming that all budget predictions are correct. Sources of the budgeted balance sheet data are included as part of the exhibit.

FINALIZING THE BUDGET

After studying the BGI example, you might conclude that developing the master budget is a mechanical process. That is not the case. Understanding the basics of budget assembly is not the end; it is a tool to assist in efficient and effective budgeting. Before finalizing the budget, the following two questions must be addressed:

- Is the proposed budget feasible?
- Is the proposed budget acceptable?

To be feasible, the organization must be able to actually implement the proposed budget. Without the line of credit, BGI's budget is not feasible because the company would run out of cash by the end of the second quarter. Knowing this, management

EXHIBIT 11–12

BUDGETED BALANCE SHEET

Backpacks Galore Inc.
Budgeted Balance Sheet
December 31, 2005

Assets

Current assets:			
Cash (Exhibit 11–10)		$ 77,480	
Accounts receivable (net) (Exhibit 11–10)		25,080	
Merchandise inventory (Exhibit 11–11)		153,000	$255,560
Property and equipment:			
Land		$ 60,000	
Buildings and equipment	$260,000		
Less accumulated depreciation	(132,800)	127,200	187,200
Total assets			$442,760

Liabilities and Stockholders' Equity

Current liabilities:			
Accounts payable (Exhibit 11–10)			$ 56,500
Stockholders' equity:			
Capital stock		$150,000	
Retained earnings		236,260	386,260
Total liabilities and stockholders' equity			$442,760

Sources of data:
1. *The balance in accounts receivable is 24 percent of the fourth quarter credit sales ($104,500 × 0.24).*
2. *Land and buildings and equipment are the same as their respective balances at the end of 2004.*
3. *Accumulated depreciation is equal to the balance at the end of 2004 increased by the 2005 depreciation ($124,800 + $8,000) (Exhibit 11–9).*
4. *The balance in accounts payable is 50 percent of the fourth quarter purchases ($113,000 × 0.50).*
5. *Capital stock is the same as its balance at the end of 2004.*
6. *Retained earnings is equal to the 2004 year-end balance plus budgeted net income less dividends ($90,000) reported in the cash budget.*

can take timely corrective action. Possible actions include obtaining equity financing, issuing long-term debt, reducing the amount of inventory on hand at the end of each quarter, or obtaining a line of credit. Other constraints that would make the budget infeasible include the availability of merchandise and, in the case of a manufacturing organization, production capacity.

Once management determines that the budget is feasible, they still need to determine if it is acceptable. To evaluate acceptability, management might consider various financial ratios, such as return on assets. They might compare the return provided by the proposed budget with past returns, industry averages, or some organizational goal.

<table>
<tr><td>LEARNING OBJECTIVE 5</td><td></td></tr>
</table>

BUDGET DEVELOPMENT AND HUMAN BEHAVIOR

Organizations are composed of individuals who perform a wide variety of activities in pursuit of the organization's goals. To accomplish these goals, management must recognize the effects that budgeting and performance evaluation methods have on the behavior of the organization's employees.

EMPLOYEE PARTICIPATION

Budgeting should be used to promote productive employee behavior directed toward meeting the organization's goals. While no two organizations use exactly the same budgeting procedures, two approaches to employee involvement in budgeting represent possible end points on a continuum. These approaches are sometimes referred to as *top-down* and *bottom-up* methods.

With a **top-down** or **imposed budget,** top management identifies the primary goals and objectives for the organization and communicates them to lower management levels. Because relatively few people are involved in top-down budgeting, an imposed budget saves time. It also minimizes the slack that managers at lower organizational levels are sometimes prone to build into their budgets. However, this nonparticipative approach to budgeting can have undesirable motivational consequences. Personnel who do not participate in budget preparation might lack a commitment to achieve their part of the budget.

With a **bottom-up** or **participative budget,** managers at all levels—and in some cases, even nonmanagers—are involved in budget preparation. Budget proposals originate at the lowest level of management possible and are then integrated into the proposals for the next level, and so on, until the proposals reach the top level of management, which completes the budget.

Participation helps ensure that important issues are considered and that employees understand the importance of their roles in meeting the organization's goals. It also provides opportunities for problem solving and fosters employee commitment to agreed-upon goals. Hence, budget predictions are likely to be more accurate, and the people responsible for the budget are more likely to strive to accomplish its objectives. These *self-imposed budgets* reinforce the concept of participative management and should strengthen the overall budgeting process.

Participative approaches to budgeting have a few disadvantages. Because they require the involvement of many people, the preparation period is longer than that for an imposed budget. Another disadvantage is the tendency of some managers to intentionally understate revenues or overstate expenses to provide **budgetary slack.** A manager might do this to reduce his or her concern regarding unfavorable performance reviews or to make it easier to obtain favorable performance reviews. If a department consistently produces favorable variances (actual results versus budget) with little apparent effort, this might be a symptom of budgetary slack.

ROLE OF THE BUDGET COMMITTEE

Because of the complexity of budget development, many organizations have a **budget committee,** composed of top-level managers, responsible for supervising budget preparation. The committee also evaluates requests for discretionary cost items and new projects.

Larger companies sometimes have a **budget office,** responsible to the controller, that assists the budget committee and others involved in budgeting. The budget office is responsible for preparing, distributing, and processing forms used in gathering budget data; it handles most of the work of actually formulating the budget schedules and reports. The budget office staff may also assist by preparing various analyses and special reports. Some large organizations even have a full-time budgeting staff working year-round on the budget. This does not mean that it takes 12 months to prepare the budget or that once the annual budget is completed, the budgeting staff has nothing else to do until the next year. The final budget is really never final—changing circumstances could require its revision during the course of the budget period. Furthermore, the multi-year plans of many companies are continuously updated to reflect changing conditions. Revisions and updating are part of the responsibility of the budget office.

BUDGETING PERIODS

Although most organizations use a one-year budget period, some organizations budget for shorter or longer periods. In addition to fixed-length budget periods, two other types of budget periods commonly used are life cycle budgeting and continuous budgeting.

When a fixed time period is not particularly relevant to planning, an organization can use **life cycle budgeting,** which involves developing a budget for a project's entire life. An ice cream vendor at the beach might develop a budget for the season. A general contractor might budget costs for the entire (multiple-year) time required to construct a building.

Under **continuous budgeting,** the budget (sometimes called a **rolling budget**) is based on a moving time frame. For example, an organization on a continuous four-quarter budget system adds a quarter to the budget at the end of each quarter of operations, thereby always maintaining a budget for four quarters into the future. Under this system, plans for a full year into the future are always available, whereas under a fixed annual budget, operating plans for a full year ahead are available only at the beginning of the budget year. Because managers are constantly involved in this type of budgeting, the budget process becomes an active and integral part of the management process. Managers are forced to be future oriented throughout the year rather than just once each year.

FORECASTS

Budget preparation requires the development of a variety of forecasts. The sales forecast is based on a variety of interrelated factors such as historical trends, product innovation, general economic conditions, industry conditions, and the organization's strategic position for competing on the basis of price, product differentiation, or market niche. Many organizations first determine the industry forecast for a given product or service and then extract from it their sales estimations.

Although the sales forecast is primary to most organizations, other types of forecasts of varying importance include the following:

1. Collection period for sales on account.
2. Percent of uncollectable sales on account.
3. Cost of materials, supplies, utilities, and so forth.
4. Employee turnover.

5. Time required to perform activities.
6. Interest rates.
7. Development time for new products or services.

What's Happening 11–2 examines the forecasts used by Qwest and the way it deals with uncertainty in forecasting.

ETHICS

Because most wrongful activities related to budgeting are unethical, rather than illegal, organizations often have difficulty dealing with them. However, when managers' actions cross the gray area between ethical and fraudulent behavior, organizations are not reluctant to dismiss employees or even pursue legal actions against them.[2]

Although most managers have a natural inclination to be conservative in developing their budgets, at some level the blatant padding or building slack into the budget becomes unethical. In an extreme case, it might even be considered theft if an inordinate level of budgetary slack creates favorable performance variances that lead to significant bonuses or other financial gain for the manager. Another form of falsifying budgets occurs when managers include expense categories in their budgets that are not needed in their operations and subsequently use the funds to pad other budget categories. The deliberate falsification of budgets is unethical behavior and is grounds for dismissal in most organizations.

Ethical issues might also arise in the reporting of performance results, which usually compares actual data with budgeted data. Examples of unethical reporting of

---

11-2   WHAT'S HAPPENING?

BUDGET FORECASTING AT QWEST INCLUDES A RANGE OF ESTIMATES

The operation budgets of an organization should consider its current and future economic environment. Items to consider include the required resources, potential of new markets and products, changing technology, and direction of the economy in the countries where it operates and sells. These areas are then evaluated to help forecast revenue targets, changing costs, technological implementations, and targeted profits.

In addition to the basics just mentioned, planners at Qwest require budget estimates to include high, middle, and low ranges for each major category. The middle estimate is considered the most likely, but management desires to know the parameters for the best- and worst-case scenarios. Some of the key questions that management requires to be answered for each budget planning cycle include these:

1. How fast could revenue grow?
2. What costs will likely increase?
3. How large will the market be?
4. What consumer trends are likely to affect our products?
5. What business trends are likely to affect our products?

In recent years, Qwest's revenue growth has exceeded that of the industry, and management contributes this industry leadership to its annual economic reality checks of the items just mentioned. To help keep the company's perspective in line with its environment, management divides data sources into five areas: (1) demographic, (2) government, (3) consumer spending, (4) production and employment, and (5) business environment. Primary sources of information for each area are maintained and furnished to budget planners as needed throughout the budget planning cycle.

Source: Dianne W. Green, "Using Economic Data in Your Strategic Plan," *Management Accounting*, January 1997, pp. 28–32.

---

[2]*Fraud Survey Results 1993*, (New York: KPMG Peat Marwick, 1993).

actual performance data include misclassification of expenses, overstating revenues or understating expenses, postponing or accelerating the recording of activities at the end of the accounting period, or creating fictitious activities. The insightful views of the former CEO of Phillips Petroleum on this type of behavior and the competitive environment from which it is often motivated are summarized in What's Happening 11–3.

DEVELOPING BUDGETS THAT WORK

It is important for management to understand that budgets are not perfect. Mistakes in prediction and judgment are made, and unforeseen circumstances often develop, necessitating modification of the budget. Unless top management is willing to recognize that changes in the budget are needed, support for the budget at lower levels will quickly erode. If an organization is to receive maximum benefit from the budget process, support for the budget at the top management level, as well as at lower levels, must be maintained. Achieving this support could be the most difficult challenge facing an organization undertaking budgeting for the first time. Lower-level managers are not likely to respect the budget and the related performance reports if they perceive a lack of commitment by top management. Disregard for the budget by top management can quickly destroy the effectiveness of the budget throughout the organization.

Managers who follow the suggestions listed here are more likely to be successful in using budgets as a positive motivational tool for accomplishing organizational goals through people.

1. Emphasize the importance of budgeting as a planning device.
2. Encourage wide participation in budget preparation at all levels of the organization.
3. Demonstrate that the budget has the complete support of top management.
4. Recognize that the budget is not unalterable; that is, it could require modification if conditions change.
5. Use budget performance reports not just to identify poor performers but also to recognize good performance.

11–3   WHAT'S HAPPENING?

"ETHICS: THE HEART OF EVERY DECISION"

Regarding the issue of ethics, C. J. Silas, retired CEO of Phillips Petroleum, stated, "What we are all called upon to do, whatever professional field we have chosen, is to make ethics the heart of every decision we make, from boardroom to the mailroom."

In his discussion of moral dilemmas, Silas cites several examples of managers making the wrong decisions, one including a budget-related situation. This particular person, a plant manager at a glass container plant, inflated the results of operations not slightly but by 33 percent over actual levels. When the plant manager confessed to his wrongdoings, he stated that the actual results were so unfavorable that he "was afraid the company would close the aging plant, throwing [him] and 300 employees out of work."

As Silas noted, "It's a lot harder to resist temptation when honesty and integrity could mean the end of your job, your company, even your town." Organizations should establish policies of operations that do not cause direct conflicts with managers' decisions, a concept Silas labeled "the moral dimension of competitiveness." An example is an executive order to a manager to cut costs but not to cut customer satisfaction. Organizations should provide guidelines and expectations of actions, not blatant orders for which the means and goals seem to conflict.

Source: C. J. Silas, "The Moral Dimension of Competitiveness," *Management Accounting,* December 1994, p. 72. Reprinted with permission of the Ethics Resource Center, Inc.

BUDGETING INTERFACES WITH RESPONSIBILITY

To facilitate the budgeting process, SIGNAL Inc. developed strategic service centers with budget responsibility, and General Dynamics uses a management control system called Cost Account Directive (CAD) as a means of securing both employee adherence to budgets and schedules and cooperation across functional lines. Both systems provide a means of bringing budgeting and management responsibility together to improve planning and control.

SIGNAL's strategic service center approach works well because more people at lower levels have input to the budget. People in the service centers are accountable for their performance against the budget and, as a result, have more realistic expectations for the budget. This approach has helped increase profitability, streamlined decision making, and increased employees' levels of preapproved responsibility over their budgets.

For General Dynamics, CAD describes the work to be completed (in a detailed task description) and helps build a project spreadsheet (the personnel, materials, expenses, computer time, and schedule necessary for the project). The four goals of each cost account directive are (1) coordinating the goals of a project's manager with the goals of project team members from different functional groups; (2) motivating employees through specific goal setting; (3) monitoring the project's progress through budgeting; and (4) providing more accurate time and cost estimates. Although such a budget control process appears time consuming and complicated, it is a useful management tool when implemented correctly.

As these two corporations have discovered, employee cooperation is critical to developing a successful budget. For both companies, budgeting had been traditionally limited to corporate personnel only with little input from operations. Now the budget is everyone's responsibility. Also, by including more people in budget planning, additional levels of detail are contributed to the process. "Details are critical in the budget because this is the way to identify savings," says Michael Murphy of Delta Air Lines. "If you can identify it, you can save it." Responsibility leads to detailed analysis, and detailed analysis leads to control.

Source: Joanne Sammer, "Seven Ways to Build Better Budgets," *Controller Magazine*, September 1997, pp. 29–33; and Terence J. Plaza and Mary M. K. Fleming, "Cost Account Directive—An Effective Management Tool," *Management Accounting*, May 1987, pp. 49–54.

6. Conduct programs in budget education to provide new managers information about the purposes of budgets and to dispel erroneous misconceptions that they might have.

Properly used, an operating budget is an effective mechanism for motivating employees to higher levels of performance and productivity. Improperly developed and administered, budgets can foster feelings of animosity toward management and the budget process. Behavioral research has generally concluded that when employees participate in the preparation of budgets and believe that the budgets represent fair standards for evaluating their performance, they receive personal satisfaction from accomplishing the goals set in the budgets. See What's Happening 11–4 for ways that General Dynamics and SIGNAL, Inc., implemented a management control system involving many operating levels within the organization.

Summary

Operating budgets represent an integral part of the overall planning and control system as well as management's expectations about the events and activities scheduled to occur during a specified future period. Budgets provide the basis for evaluating actual performance and modifying subsequent plans. Budgeting offers many potential benefits for organizations, including forcing managers to look at the future of the company; improving communication; improving coordination between various departments and functions in the organization; and motivating managers to achieve organizational objectives.

The *output/input approach* to budget planning is based on unit-level cost drivers. The *activity-based approach* is based on unit- and nonunit-level cost drivers. It focuses on determining the cost of planned activities for a process, department, service, or product. The *incremental approach* requires budget review of proposals in excess of the budgeted or actual expenditures for the previous period. The *minimum level approach* requires review of any budgeted amounts in excess of some minimum amount. The budgeting process is usually implemented on an annual schedule, although companies in certain industries find the cyclical approach more appropriate. *Continuous budgeting* consists of adding a new time unit to the end of the budget period upon completing the current unit of time.

Feedback is an essential part of budgeting. Without interpretation of actual performance, much of the benefit, including that of motivating people, can be lost. To receive maximum benefits from budgeting, the process requires participation by all levels of management, commitments by top management, and both positive and negative feedback.

Pitfalls of operations budgeting include placing excessive time demands on managers and expecting accurate and reliable predictions of all general economic and industry conditions. Additionally, the failure of top management to support the budget, poorly established organization lines of authority and responsibility, and possible budget slack further impede the process.

Appendix

Manufacturing Budgets

To illustrate budget development in a manufacturing organization, we use the Backpacks Galore example rather than developing an entirely new illustration. The basic modification to the existing example is the assumption that the company must now manufacture the school backpacks and the hiking backpacks because the supplier's quality declined to an unacceptable level. Manufacturing budgets are also illustrated in the chapter's second review problem.

After the sales budget has been completed, the manufacturing manager determines how much to produce instead of how many units of merchandise to order. The production budget in Exhibit 11–13 is based on the sales budget in Exhibit 11–4. However, because of an assured source of supply and increased coordination between production and sales, starting in the year 2005, the desired finished goods inventory at the end of each quarter is set at 10 percent of the following quarter's sales. The finished goods inventory at the start of the first quarter of 2005 consisted of 1,000 school backpacks and 500 hiking backpacks. Assume that the projected sales for the first quarter of 2006 are the same as those for the first quarter of 2005.

In Exhibit 11–13, the arrows indicate the mechanics of determining ending finished goods inventories. They also indicate the relationship between ending and beginning inventories.

BGI must now purchase the raw materials required to manufacture these products. This requires developing a purchases budget for raw materials. The previous purchases budget for merchandise inventory was based directly on budgeted sales, but the new purchases budget is based on budgeted production. The goal is for inventories to meet the needs detailed in the production budget.

Before developing budgets for purchases and manufacturing costs, management uses the information contained in the bill of materials and operations list to develop

EXHIBIT 11–13

PRODUCTION BUDGET

Backpacks Galore Inc.
Production Budget
For the Year Ending December 31, 2005

	First Quarter	Second Quarter	Third Quarter	Fourth Quarter	Year Total
School backpacks, units:					
Budgeted sales (Exhibit 11–6) ...	4,000	3,400	3,650	3,950	15,000
Plus desired ending inventory* ...	340	365	395	400	400
Total inventory requirements	4,340	3,765	4,045	4,350	15,400
Less beginning inventory†	(1,000)	(340)	(365)	(395)	(1,000)
Budgeted production	3,340	3,425	3,680	3,955	14,400
Hiking backpacks, units:					
Budgeted sales (Exhibit 11–6) ...	1,100	1,600	2,500	1,300	6,500
Plus desired ending inventory* ...	160	250	130	110	110
Total inventory requirements	1,260	1,850	2,630	1,410	6,610
Less beginning inventory†	(500)	(160)	(250)	(130)	(500)
Budgeted production	760	1,690	2,380	1,280	6,110
Total units	4,100	5,115	6,060	5,235	20,510

*Desired ending inventory of finished goods is 10 percent of the following quarter's sales. Projected sales for the first quarter of 2006 are the same as for the first quarter of 2005.
†Beginning inventory of each quarter is equal to the ending inventory of the previous quarter. For the first quarter the beginning inventory is 1,000 school backpacks and 500 hiking backpacks.

a budgeted cost for each unit of final product. Such a unit-level budget is often referred to as a **standard cost.** Variable standard cost information for school backpacks and hiking backpacks is as follows:

	School Backpacks			Hiking Backpacks	
Direct materials:					
Fabric	1 square yard × $7	.. $ 7	1½ square yards × $10	..$15	
Kits (zipper, etc.) ..	1 kit × $5	....	5	1 kit × $5	5
Direct labor	¼ hour × $20	5	⅓ hour × $24		8
Variable overhead ...	$2 per unit	2	$2 per unit		2
Total		$19			$30

The information on materials requirements and costs is used to develop the purchases budget for raw materials in units and dollars. Also assume the following:

- Management desires to have ending raw materials inventories equal to 10 percent of the production needs of the following quarter.
- January 1, 2005, raw materials inventories are in line with this policy.
- Production in the first quarter of 2006 is projected to be the same as the first quarter of 2005.

The purchases budget for the manufacturing operation of Backpacks Galore is shown in Exhibit 11–14.

In a manufacturing operation, management should develop a **manufacturing cost budget.** This budget details the direct materials, direct labor, and manufacturing overhead costs that should be incurred in the manufacturing operations in producing the

EXHIBIT 11-14

MANUFACTURING PURCHASES BUDGET

Backpacks Galore Inc.
Purchases Budget
For the Year Ending December 31, 2005

	First Quarter	Second Quarter	Third Quarter	Fourth Quarter	Year Total
Production budget (units):					
School backpacks	3,340	3,425	3,680	3,955	14,400
Hiking backpacks	760	1,690	2,380	1,280	6,110
Total units	4,100	5,115	6,060	5,235	20,510
Purchases (units):					
School backpack fabric:					
Current needs for production					
(1 square yard per unit) . .	3,340.0	3,425.0	3,680.0	3,955.0	14,400
Plus desired ending inventory*	342.5	368.0	395.5	334.0	334
Total requirements	3,682.5	3,793.0	4,075.5	4,289.0	14,734
Less beginning inventory	(334.0)	(342.5)	(368.0)	(395.5)	(334)
Purchases in units	3,348.5	3,450.5	3,707.5	3,893.5	14,400
Hiking backpack fabric:					
Current needs for production					
(1.5 square yards per unit) .	1,140.0	2,535.0	3,570.0	1,920.0	9,165
Plus desired ending inventory* .	253.5	357.0	192.0	114.0	114
Total requirements	1,393.5	2,892.0	3,762.0	2,034.0	9,279
Less beginning inventory	(114.0)	(253.5)	(357.0)	(192.0)	(114)
Purchases in units	1,279.5	2,638.5	3,405.0	1,842.0	9,165
Kits:					
Current needs for production					
(1 kit per backpack)	4,100	5,115	6,060	5,235	20,510
Plus desired ending inventory*	512[†]	606	524[†]	410	410
Total requirements	4,612	5,721	6,584	5,645	20,920
Less beginning inventory	(410)	(512)	(606)	(524)	(410)
Purchases in units	4,202	5,209	5,978	5,121	20,510
Purchases (dollars):					
School backpack materials					
($7 per yard)	$23,439.50	$24,153.50	$25,952.50	$27,254.50	$100,800.00
Hiking backpack materials					
($10 per yard)	12,795.00	26,385.00	34,050.00	18,420.00	91,650.00
Kits (1 each; $5 per kit) . . .	21,010.00	26,045.00	29,890.00	25,605.00	102,550.00
Totals	$57,244.50	$76,583.50	$89,892.50	$71,279.50	$295,000.00

*Desired ending inventories of raw materials are 10 percent of the following quarter's production requirements.
[†]Purchase of kits must be in whole units.

number of units called for in the production budget. This budget is based on budgeted production and standard cost information. Because fixed manufacturing overhead does not vary with production volume, assume that fixed manufacturing costs are budgeted at $10,000 per quarter. BGI's 2005 manufacturing cost budget is presented in Exhibit 11–15.

EXHIBIT 11-15

MANUFACTURING COST BUDGET

Backpacks Galore Inc.
Manufacturing Cost Budget
For the Year Ending December 31, 2005

	First Quarter	Second Quarter	Third Quarter	Fourth Quarter	Year Total
Production budget (units) (Exhibit 11-13):					
Budgeted production:					
School backpacks	3,340	3,425	3,680	3,955	14,400
Hiking backpacks	760	1,690	2,380	1,280	6,110
Total units	4,100	5,115	6,060	5,235	20,510
Direct materials:					
Fabric for school backpacks (1 square yard × $7)	$23,380	$ 23,975	$ 25,760	$ 27,685	$100,800
Fabric for hiking backpacks (1.5 square yard × $10)	11,400	25,350	35,700	19,200	91,650
Kits (1 per unit × $5)	20,500	25,575	30,300	26,175	102,550
Total direct materials	$55,280	$ 74,900	$ 91,760	$ 73,060	$295,000
Direct labor:					
School backpacks (¼ hour × $20)	$16,700	$ 17,125	$ 18,400	$ 19,775	$ 72,000
Hiking backpacks (⅓ hour × $24)	6,080	13,520	19,040	10,240	48,880
Total direct labor	22,780	30,645	37,440	30,015	120,880
Manufacturing overhead:					
Variable (total units × $2)	$ 8,200	$ 10,230	$ 12,120	$ 10,470	$ 41,020
Fixed	10,000	10,000	10,000	10,000	40,000
Total manufacturing overhead	18,200	20,230	22,120	20,470	81,020
Total manufacturing costs	$96,260	$125,775	$151,320	$123,545	$496,900

To focus attention on the differences between merchandising and manufacturing, the cash budget is not developed, but one is illustrated in Review Problem 2. Also, it is possible to continue the manufacturing example to include a budgeted income statement and a budgeted balance sheet. However, because no new concepts are involved, this is omitted from this text. Complete manufacturing examples can be found in most cost accounting texts.

Review Problems

The solutions to the review problems are found on pages 509–513. To maximize your learning, you should make a serious attempt to develop written solutions to the review problems before looking at the solutions. If there are errors in your solutions, you should then attempt to determine their causes.

1.
Operating Budget for a Merchandising Organization

Stumphouse Cheese Company is a wholesale distributor of blue cheese and ice cream. The following information is available for April 2005.

Estimated sales:
Blue cheese . . . . . . 160,000 hoops at $10 each
Ice cream . . . . 240,000 gallons at $5 each

Estimated costs:
Blue cheese . . . . . . $8 per hoop
Ice cream . . . . $2 per gallon

Desired inventories:

	Beginning	**Ending**
Blue cheese	10,000	12,000
Ice cream	4,000	5,000

Financial information follows:

- Beginning cash balance is $400,000.
- Purchases of merchandise are paid 60 percent in the current month and 40 percent in the following month. Purchases totaled $1,800,000 in March and are estimated to be $2,000,000 in May.
- Employee wages, salaries, and commissions are paid for in the current month. Employee expenses for April totaled $156,000.
- Overhead expenses are paid in the next month. The accounts payable amount for these expenses from March is $80,000 and for May will be $90,000.
- Sales are on credit and are collected 70 percent in the current period and the remainder in the next period. March's sales were $3,000,000, and May's sales are estimated to be $3,200,000. Bad debts average 1 percent of sales.
- Selling and administrative expenses are paid monthly and total $450,000, including $40,000 of depreciation.
- All unit costs for April are the same as they were in March.

Required:
Prepare the following for April:

a. Sales budget in dollars.
b. Purchases budget.
c. Cash budget.
d. Budgeted income statement.

2.
Operating Budget for a Manufacturing Organization (Appendix)

Handy Company manufactures and sells two industrial products in a single plant. The new manager wants to have quarterly budgets and has prepared the following information for the first quarter of 2004. The following information is available:

Budgeted sales:
Drills . . . . . . 60,000 at $100 each
Saws . . . . . . 40,000 at $125 each

Budgeted inventories:

	Beginning	**Ending**
Drills, finished	20,000	25,000
Saws, finished	8,000	10,000
Metal, direct materials	32,000 pounds	36,000 pounds
Plastic, direct materials	29,000 pounds	32,000 pounds
Handles, direct materials	6,000 each	7,000 each

Standard variable costs:

	Drills		Saws	
Direct materials:				
Metal	5 pounds × $8.00	$40.00	4 pounds × $8.00	$32.00
Plastic	3 pounds × $5.00	15.00	3 pounds × $5.00	15.00
Handles	1 handle × $3.00	3.00		
Total		$58.00		$47.00
Direct labor	2 hours × $12.00	24.00	3 hours × $16.00	48.00
Variable manufacturing overhead	2 hours × $1.50	3.00	3 hours × $1.50	4.50
Total		$85.00		$99.50

Fixed factory overhead is $214,000 per quarter (including noncash expenditures of $156,000) and is allocated on total units produced.

Financial information follows:

- Beginning cash balance is $1,800,000.
- Sales are on credit and are collected 50 percent in the current period and the remainder in the next period. Last quarter's sales were $8,400,000. There are no bad debts.
- Purchases of direct materials and labor costs are paid for in the quarter acquired.
- Manufacturing overhead expenses are paid in the quarter incurred.
- Selling and administrative expenses are all fixed and are paid in the quarter incurred. They are budgeted at $340,000 per quarter, including $90,000 of depreciation.

Required:

For the first quarter of 2004, prepare the following:

a. Sales budget in dollars.
b. Production budget in units.
c. Purchases budget.
d. Manufacturing cost budget.
e. Cash budget. (*Hint:* See Review Problem 1.)
f. Budgeted contribution income statement.

3.
Activity-Based Budget

Holtzendorff Industries has the following budget information available for February:

General administration	$22,000
Advertising Product X	$10,000
Assembly	½ hour per unit of Product X × $16
Direct materials	2 gallons per unit of Product X × $3
Inspection	$200 per batch of 1,000 units
Finishing	$2 per unit of Product X
Product development	$15,000 for Product X
Sales units	20,000 units × $20
Setup cost	$100 per batch of 1,000 units

Required:

Prepare a February activity-based budget for Product X.

Key Terms

Review Questions

1. What are the primary phases in the planning and control cycle?
2. Does budgeting require formal or informal planning? What are some advantages of this style of management?
3. Identify the advantages and disadvantages of the incremental approach to budgeting.
4. Explain the minimum level approach to budgeting.
5. How does activity-based budgeting predict a cost objective's budget?
6. Explain the continuous improvement concept of budgeting.
7. Which budget brings together all other budgets? How is this accomplished?
8. What budgets are normally used to support the cash budget? What is the net result of cash budget preparations?
9. Define *budgeted financial statements*.
10. Contrast the top-down and bottom-up approaches to budget preparation.
11. Is budgetary slack a desirable feature? Can it be prevented? Why or why not?
12. Why are annual budgets not always desirable? What are some alternative budget periods?
13. Explain how continuous budgeting works.
14. In addition to the sales forecast, what forecasts are used in budgeting?
15. Why should motivational considerations be a part of budget planning and utilization? List several ways to motivate employees with budgets.

Exercises

11-1
Department Budget Using Output/Input Approach

The following data are from the general records of Department 16 for October.

• Each unit of product requires 6 direct labor hours, 20 liters of direct materials, and 1 container.
• Each liter of material processed requires $12 of manufacturing overhead.

- Average wages for direct laborers are $15 per hour.
- Direct materials currently cost $2 per liter.
- Containers cost $8 each.
- Direct material waste amounts to 10 percent of materials started in process.

Required:

Prepare an October department budget for Department 16 if planned production is 2,000 units of output.

11–2
Department Budget Using Incremental Approach

Assume that the Assembly Department of Applied Materials' Texas plant prepares its budget using the incremental approach for both fixed and variable costs. For 2004 assume that the following costs were incurred for the production of 100,000 units.

Direct materials	$200,000
Direct labor	600,000
Supervision	80,000
Depreciation, equipment (straight line)	32,000
Variable overhead ($1.20 per unit)	120,000

Assume that each unit takes one-half hour to assemble.

Required:

Prepare a budget for the Assembly Department that allows for a 4 percent inflation rate if the Texas plant sets a production level of 140,000 for 2005.

11–3
Activity-Based Budget

Fike Industries Inc. has the following budget information available for February:

Administration	$30,000
Advertising	$10,000
Assembly	½ hour per unit × $8
Direct materials	2 pounds per unit × $3
Inspection	$200 per batch of 1,000 units
Manufacturing overhead	$2 per unit
Manufactured units	$20,000
Product development	$15,000
Sales units	20,000 units × $20
Setup cost	$10 per batch of 1,000 units

Required:

Prepare a February activity-based budgeted income statement.

11–4
Product and Department Budgets Using Activity-Based Approach

The following data are from the general records of the Loading Department of Bowman Freight Company for November.

- Cleaning incoming trucks, 20 minutes.
- Obtaining and reviewing shipping documents for loading truck and instructing loaders, 30 minutes.
- Loading truck, 1 hour and 30 minutes.
- Cleaning shipping dock and storage area after each loading, 10 minutes.
- Employees perform both cleaning and loading tasks and are currently averaging $16 per hour in wages and benefits.
- The supervisor spends 10 percent of her time overseeing the cleaning activities; 60 percent overseeing various loading activities; and the remainder of her time making general plans and managing the department. Her current salary is $4,000 per month.
- Other overhead of the department amounts to $10,000 per month, 20 percent for cleaning and 80 percent for loading.

Required:

Prepare an activities budget for cleaning and loading in the Loading Department for November, assuming 20 working days and the loading of an average of 14 trucks per day.

11-5
Activity-Based
Budgeting

Piedmont Hospital is preparing its budget for the coming year. It uses an activity-based approach for all costs except physician care. Its emergency room has three activity areas with cost drivers as follows:

1. *Reception*—paperwork of incoming patients. Cost driver is the number of forms completed.
2. *Treatment*—initial diagnosis and treatment of patients. Cost driver is the number of ailments treated.
3. *Cleaning*—general cleaning plus preparing treatment facilities for next patient. Cost driver is the number of people visiting emergency room (patients plus person(s) accompanying them).

Activity Area	Cost Driver Rates	BUDGETED AMOUNT OF COST DRIVER	
		Outpatients	Admitted Patients
Reception	$30	7,400 forms	5,000 forms
Treatment	90	7,000 ailments	4,200 ailments
Cleaning	10	6,400 people	2,400 people

Required:

a. Prepare the total budgeted cost for each activity.
b. How might you adjust the budget approach if you found that outpatients were kept in the emergency room for one hour on average while admitted patients remained for two hours?
c. What advantage does an activity-based approach have over the hospital's former budgeting method of basing the next year's budget on the last year's actual amount plus a percentage increase?

11-6
Continuous
Improvement
Approach to
Budgeting

Assume that the Macon branch of BankAmerica is being used as a test facility for the bank's implementation of Kaizen costing. Since the bank uses quarterly reporting, it has established improvement factors for the following cost categories. This and other information follows.

Category	Improvement Factor	First Quarter Budget	Third Quarter Actual
Teller operations	0.99	$400,000	$380,000
Loan operations	0.98	300,000	290,000
Branch management	0.97	100,000	91,000
Computer support	0.99	80,000	78,450

Required:

a. Prepare quarterly budgets for the second and third quarters using the first quarter as the base.
b. Compute the variances for the third quarter.

11-7
Continuous
Improvement
Approach to
Budgeting

Assume that Blockbuster Video will implement its budget for the coming year using a Kaizen approach. The initial monthly operating budget for January for a Louisville store's receiving department is $5,000. The store manager has concurred with the budget manager that labor-related efficiencies can be targeted for implementation during the next year. These efficiencies will reduce overall costs by a factor of 0.99 each month for the next 12 months.

Required:

a. Compute the operating budget amounts for January, February, and March.

b. Compute the variances for each month if actual costs per month were $4,950.

11–8
Sales Budget

Jennifer's T-Shirt Shop has very seasonal sales. For 2005, Jennifer is trying to decide whether to establish a sales budget based on average sales or on sales estimated by quarter. The unit sales for 2005 are expected to be 10 percent higher than 2004 sales. Unit shirt sales by quarter for 2004 were as follows:

	Children's	Women's	Men's	Total
Winter quarter	200	200	100	500
Spring quarter	200	250	200	650
Summer quarter	400	300	200	900
Fall quarter	200	250	100	550
Total	1,000	1,000	600	2,600

Children's T-shirts sell for $4 each, women's sell for $8, and men's sell for $7.

Required:

Assuming a 10 percent increase in sales, prepare a sales budget for each quarter of 2005 using the following:

a. Average quarterly sales. (*Hint:* Winter quarter children's shirts are 275 [1,000 × 1.10 ÷ 4].)

b. Actual quarterly sales. (*Hint:* Winter quarter children's shirts are 220 [200 × 1.10].)

c. Suggest advantages of each method.

11–9
Sales Budget

Assume that Datek, a leader in on-line stock trading, is preparing for a surge in growth with a new set of stock trading fees. The following information is available:

Category	Number of Shares	Current Fee	New Fee as of July	Revenue
A	0–10,000	$ 11	$ 10	$1,210,000
B	10,001–50,000	50	40	50,000
C	50,001 and above	200	150	20,000

With the new fees, Datek expects to take many big volume traders from its competitors. Anticipated monthly growth is expected to be 10 percent, 20 percent, and 30 percent, respectively, for each category for the first four months after the new rates go into effect.

Required:

a. What are the anticipated revenues per month for July and August?

b. Is the new fee structure satisfactory? Explain.

11–10
Purchases Budget in Units and Dollars

Budgeted sales of The Record Shop for the first six months of 2005 are as follows:

Month	Unit Sales	Month	Unit Sales
January	120,000	April	210,000
February	160,000	May	180,000
March	200,000	June	240,000

Beginning inventory for 2005 is 40,000 units. The budgeted inventory at the end of a month is 40 percent of units to be sold the following month. Purchase price per unit is $3.

Required:

Prepare a purchases budget in units and dollars for each month, January through May.

11-11
Purchases Budget in Units and Dollars (Appendix)

Unit sales estimates for Snow King Plow Company for next year are as follows:

Month	Unit Sales	Month	Unit Sales
January	45,000	March	90,000
February	60,000	April	93,000

At the beginning of January, 10,000 units of finished goods were in inventory. Plans are to have an inventory of finished product equal to one-third of the sales for the next month.

Each unit produced requires 400 pounds of materials. Each pound of material costs $10. Inventory levels for materials are to equal one-fourth of the needs for the next month. Materials inventory on January 1 was 5.5 million pounds.

Required:
a. Prepare a production budget for January, February, and March.
b. Prepare a purchases budget in pounds and dollars for January and February.

11-12
Cash Budget

Wilson's Retail Company is planning a cash budget for the next three months. Estimated sales revenue is as follows:

Month	Sales Revenue	Month	Sales Revenue
January	$300,000	March	$200,000
February	225,000	April	175,000

All sales are on credit; 40 percent is collected during the month of sale, and 60 percent is collected during the next month.

Cost of goods sold is 70 percent of sales. Payments for merchandise sold are made in the month following the month of sale. Operating expenses total $41,000 per month and are paid during the month incurred.

The cash balance on February 1 is estimated to be $20,000.

Required:
Prepare monthly cash budgets for February, March, and April.

11-13
Cash Budget

Boston Tea Company began July with a cash balance of $142,000. A cash receipts and payments budget for each six-month period is prepared in advance. Sales have been estimated as follows:

Month	Sales Revenue	Month	Sales Revenue
May	$120,000	September	$ 80,000
June	140,000	October	100,000
July	80,000	November	100,000
August	60,000	December	120,000

All sales are on credit with 75 percent collected during the month of sale, 20 percent collected during the next month, and 5 percent collected during the second month following the month of sale.

Cost of goods sold averages 70 percent of sales revenue. Ending inventory is one-half of the next month's predicted cost of sales. The other half of the merchandise is acquired during the month of sale. All purchases are paid for in the month after purchase.

Operating costs are estimated at $18,000 each month and are paid for during the month incurred.

Required:
Prepare monthly cash budgets for the six months from July to December. (*Hint:* Prepare monthly purchases budgets for June through November.)

11–14
Cash Receipts

The sales budget for Cards Inc. is forecasted as follows:

Month	Sales Revenue
May	$60,000
June	80,000
July	90,000
August	60,000

To prepare a cash budget, the company must determine the budgeted cash collections from sales. Historically, the following trend has been established regarding cash collection of sales:

- 60 percent in the month of sale.
- 20 percent in the month following sale.
- 15 percent in the second month following sale.
- 5 percent uncollectible.

The company gives a 2 percent cash discount for payments made by customers during the month of sale. The accounts receivable balance on April 30 is $24,000, of which $7,000 represents uncollected March sales and $17,000 represents uncollected April sales.

Required:
Prepare a schedule of budgeted cash collections from sales for May, June, and July. Include a three-month summary of estimated cash collections.

11–15
Cash Receipts

Chicago Metal Company is currently estimating cash receipts for the next six months. The accounts receivable balance is also to be estimated at the end of each month. Cash sales are estimated at 10 percent of sales for the month. The balance of sales should be collected as follows:

- 50 percent during the month of sale.
- 40 percent during the following month.
- 10 percent during the second month following month of sale.

The accounts receivable balance at April 1 was $93,600. Budgeted and actual sales are as follows:

Month	Sales Revenue
January	$200,000
February	190,000
March	170,000
April	150,000
May	180,000
June	200,000

Required:
Prepare a schedule of budgeted cash collections for each month of the second quarter. Determine the estimated balance of Accounts Receivable at the end of each month.

11–16
Cash Disbursements

Oregon Timber Company is in the process of preparing its budget for next year. Cost of goods sold has been estimated at 70 percent of sales. Lumber purchases and payments are to be made during the month preceding the month of sale. Wages are estimated at 15 percent of sales and are paid during the month of sale. Other operating costs amounting to 10 percent of sales are to be paid in the month following the month of sale. Additionally, a monthly lease payment of $10,000 is paid to BMI for computer services. Sales revenue is forecast as follows:

Month	Sales Revenue
February	$100,000
March	160,000
April	180,000
May	210,000
June	180,000
July	230,000

Required:

Prepare a schedule of cash disbursements for April, May, and June.

11-17
Cash Disbursements

Assume that Russell Manufacturing manages its cash flow from its home office. Russell controls cash disbursements by category and month. In setting its budget for the next six months, beginning in July, it used the following managerial guidelines:

Category	Guidelines
Accounts payable	Pay half in current and half in following month.
Payroll	Pay 80 percent in current month and 20 percent in following month.
Loan payments	Pay total amount due each month.

Predicted balances and due amounts for selected months follow:

Category	May	June	July	August	September	October
Accounts payable	$ 40,000	$ 44,000	$ 48,000	$ 50,000	$ 44,000	$ 46,000
Payroll	100,000	110,000	120,000	100,000	108,000	112,000
Notes payable	10,000	10,000	10,000	15,000	15,000	15,000

Required:

Prepare a schedule showing cash disbursements by account for July and August.

11-18
Budgeted Income
Statement

Pendleton Company, a merchandising company, is developing its master budget for 2005. The income statement for 2004 is as follows:

Pendleton Company
Income Statement
For the Year Ending December 31, 2004

Gross sales	$750,000
Less estimated uncollectible accounts	(7,500)
Net sales	$742,500
Cost of goods sold	(430,000)
Gross profit	$312,500
Operating expenses (including $25,000 depreciation)	(200,500)
Net income	$112,000

The following are management's goals and forecasts for 2005:

1. Selling prices will increase by 8 percent, and sales volume will increase by 5 percent.
2. The cost of merchandise will increase by 4 percent.
3. All operating expenses are fixed and are paid in the month incurred. Price increases for operating expenses will be 10 percent.
4. The estimated uncollectibles are 1 percent of budgeted sales.

Required:

Prepare a budgeted traditional income statement for 2005.

11–19
Budgeted Income Statement

Big Burger Drive-In is planning a budget for the next fiscal year. The estimate of sales revenue is $1,000,000 and of cost of goods sold is 70 percent of sales revenue. Depreciation on the office building and fixtures is budgeted at $50,000. Salaries and wages should amount to 15 percent of sales revenue. Advertising has been budgeted at $75,000, and utilities should amount to $20,000. Income tax is estimated at 40 percent of operating income.

Required:
Prepare a budgeted income statement for the next fiscal year.

11–20
Budgeted Income Statement with Activity-Based Emphasis

Greenwood Company, a merchandising store, is developing its master budget for 2005. The income statement for 2004 is as follows:

Greenwood Company
Income Statement
For the Year Ending December 31, 2004

Sales	$700,000
Less estimated uncollectible accounts	(7,000)
Net sales	$693,000
Cost of goods sold	(400,000)
Gross profit	$293,000
Operating expenses (including $25,000 depreciation)	(175,000)
Net income	$118,000

The following are management's goals and forecasts for 2005:

1. Selling prices will increase by 5 percent, and sales volume will increase by 4 percent.
2. The cost of merchandise will increase by 4 percent.
3. All operating expenses are fixed and are paid in the month incurred. Price increases for operating expenses will be 9 percent.
4. The estimated uncollectibles are 1 percent of budgeted sales.
5. The company's activity cost drivers are product development, manufacturing, marketing, and distribution.
6. Product development averages 10 percent of estimated cost of goods sold. The remaining estimate of cost of goods sold is for merchandise.
7. Operating expenses are primarily composed of marketing and distribution efforts, with marketing historically consuming 70 percent.

Required:

a. Prepare a budgeted traditional income statement for 2005.
b. Prepare a budgeted income statement for 2005 using the activity categories. (You might need to refer to Chapter 3.)

Problem

11–21
Cash Budget

Cash budgeting for Carolina Apple, a merchandising firm, is performed on a quarterly basis. The company is planning its cash needs for the third quarter of 2004, and the following information is available to assist in preparing a cash budget.

Budgeted income statements for July through October 2004 are as follows:

	July	August	September	October
Sales	$18,000	$24,000	$28,000	$36,000
Cost of goods sold	(10,000)	(14,000)	(16,000)	(20,000)
Gross profit	$ 8,000	$10,000	$12,000	$16,000
Less other expenses:				
Selling	$ 2,300	$ 3,000	$ 3,400	$ 4,200
Administrative	2,600	3,000	3,200	3,600
Total	(4,900)	(6,000)	(6,600)	(7,800)
Net income	$ 3,100	$ 4,000	$ 5,400	$ 8,200

Additional information follows:

1. Other expenses, which are paid monthly, include $1,000 of depreciation.
2. Sales are 30 percent for cash and 70 percent on credit.
3. Credit sales are collected 20 percent in the month of sale, 70 percent one month after sale, and 10 percent two months after sale.
4. May sales were $15,000, and June sales were $16,000. Merchandise is paid for 50 percent in the month of purchase; the remaining 50 percent is paid in the following month. Accounts payable for merchandise at June 30 totaled $6,000.
5. The company maintains its ending inventory levels at 25 percent of the cost of goods to be sold in the following month. The inventory at June 30 is $2,500.
6. An equipment note of $5,000 per month is being paid through August.
7. The company must maintain a cash balance of at least $5,000 at the end of each month. The cash balance on June 30 is $5,100.
8. The company can borrow from its bank as needed. Borrowings and repayments must be in multiples of $100. All borrowings take place at the beginning of a month, and all repayments are made at the end of a month. When the principal is repaid, interest on the repayment is also paid. The interest rate is 12 percent per year.

Required:

a. Prepare a monthly schedule of budgeted operating cash receipts for July, August, and September.
b. Prepare a monthly purchases budget and a schedule of budgeted cash payments for purchases for July, August, and September.
c. Prepare a monthly cash budget for July, August, and September. Show borrowings from the company's bank and repayments to the bank as needed to maintain the minimum cash balance.

11-22
Cash Budget

The Mobile Supply Company sells for $30 one product that it purchases for $20. Budgeted sales in total dollars for next year are $720,000. The sales information needed for preparing the July budget is as follows:

Month	Sales Revenue
May	$30,000
June	42,000
July	48,000
August	60,000

Account balances at July 1 include these:

Cash	$15,000
Merchandise inventory	16,000
Accounts receivable (sales)	23,000
Accounts payable (purchases)	15,000

The company pays for one-half of its purchases in the month of purchase and the remainder in the following month. End-of-month inventory must be 50 percent of the budgeted sales in units for the next month.

A 2 percent cash discount on sales is allowed if payment is made during the month of sale. Experience indicates that 50 percent of the billings will be collected during the month of sale, 40 percent in the following month, 8 percent in the second following month, and 2 percent will be uncollectible.

Total budgeted selling and administrative expenses (excluding bad debts) for the fiscal year are estimated at $186,000, of which one-half is fixed expense (inclusive of a $20,000 annual depreciation charge). Fixed expenses are incurred evenly during the year. The other selling and administrative expenses vary with sales. Expenses are paid during the month incurred.

Required:

a. Prepare a schedule of estimated cash collections for July.
b. Prepare a schedule of estimated July cash payments for purchases. (Round calculations to the nearest dollar.)
c. Prepare schedules of all July selling and administrative expenses and of those requiring cash payments.
d. Prepare a cash budget in summary form for July.

11-23
Budgeted Income Statement with Continuous Improvement

Townville Orthodontist's accountant is planning a budget for the next fiscal year. Patient revenue is estimated by Dr. I. C. Klearly to be $2,000,000. Approximately 4 percent of revenue is uncollectible. Based on the prior year's results, the cost of dental supplies is estimated to be 10 percent of gross revenue. Depreciation of equipment and fixtures is budgeted at $30,000 annually. Salaries of nurses and office staff should increase 5 percent over the current level of $250,000. Professional dues, fees, and meetings have been budgeted at $35,000. Utilities and other overhead items should amount to $20,000. Income tax is estimated at 30 percent of operating income.

Required:

Prepare a budgeted income statement for the next fiscal year if all costs (except depreciation) are to show a Kaizen improvement factor of 0.98 per quarter. Use the first quarter as base.

11-24
Budgeted Statements

Madison Butter Sales Company is preparing a budget for January and February of next year. The balance sheet as of December 31, 2004 follows:

Madison Butter Sales Company
Balance Sheet
December 31, 2004

Assets		Liabilities and Stockholders' Equities	
Cash	$100,000	Accounts payable	$125,000
Accounts receivable	60,000	Operating expenses payable	10,000
Inventory	30,000	Miscellaneous payable	20,000
Equipment leasehold	60,000	Capital stock	25,000
		Retained earnings	70,000
Total assets	$250,000	Total liabilities and stockholders' equities	$250,000

Monthly sales data for the current year and the budgeted data for the next year are as follows:

November 2001	$180,000	February 2002	$250,000
December 2001	100,000	March 2002	260,000
January 2002	240,000	April 2002	280,000

For 2005, the following are expected:

- Forty percent of the sales revenue is collected during the month of sale, with the balance collected during the following month.
- Cost of goods sold is 60 percent of sales. Merchandise inventory sufficient for 20 percent of the next month's sales is to be maintained at the end of each month. All butter purchased for resale is paid for in the month following the month of purchase.
- Operating expenses for each month are estimated at 10 percent of sales revenue. All operating expenses are paid for during the following month.
- Income taxes are estimated at 40 percent of income before taxes. Income taxes are paid 15 days after the end of the quarter. There were no taxes payable on December 31. The miscellaneous payables at December 31, 2004, are to be paid during January 2005.

Required:
a. Prepare a contribution budgeted income statement for the quarter ending March 31, 2005. Do not prepare monthly statements.
b. Prepare a budgeted balance sheet as of March 31, 2005. (*Hint:* Prepare purchases and cash budgets.)

11-25
Developing a
Master Budget

Peyton Department Store prepares budgets quarterly. The following information is available for use in planning the second quarter budgets for 2004.

Peyton Department Store
Balance Sheet
March 31, 2004

Assets		Liabilities and Stockholders' Equity	
Cash	$ 3,000	Accounts payable	$26,000
Accounts receivable	25,000	Dividends payable	17,000
Inventory	30,000	Rent payable	2,000
Prepaid insurance	2,000	Stockholders' equity	40,000
Fixtures	25,000		
Total assets	$85,000	Total liabilities and stockholders' equity	$85,000

Actual and forecasted sales for selected months in 2004 are as follows:

Month	Sales Revenue
January	$60,000
February	50,000
March	40,000
April	50,000
May	60,000
June	70,000
July	90,000
August	80,000

Monthly operating expenses are as follows:

Wages and salaries	$25,000
Depreciation	100
Utilities	1,000
Rent	2,000

Cash dividends of $17,000 are declared during the third month of each quarter and are paid during the first month of the following quarter. Operating expenses, except insurance, rent, and depreciation are paid as incurred. Rent is paid during the following month. The prepaid insurance is for five more months. Cost of goods sold is equal to 50 percent of sales.

Beginning inventories are sufficient for 120 percent of the next month's sales. Purchases during any given month are paid in full during the following month. All sales are on account, with 50 percent collected during the month of sale, 40 percent during the next month, and 10 percent during the month thereafter.

Money can be borrowed and repaid in multiples of $1,000 at an interest rate of 12 percent per year. The company desires a minimum cash balance of $3,000 on the first of each month. At the time the principal is repaid, interest is paid on the portion of principal that is repaid. All borrowing is at the beginning of the month, and all repayment is at the end of the month. Money is never repaid at the end of the month it is borrowed.

Required:

a. Prepare a purchases budget for each month of the second quarter ending June 30, 2004.

b. Prepare a cash receipts schedule for each month of the second quarter ending June 30, 2004. Do not include borrowings.

c. Prepare a cash disbursements schedule for each month of the second quarter ending June 30, 2004. Do not include repayments of borrowings.

d. Prepare a cash budget for each month of the second quarter ending June 30, 2004. Include budgeted borrowings and repayments.

e. Prepare an income statement for each month of the second quarter ending June 30, 2004.

f. Prepare a budgeted balance sheet as of June 30, 2004.

11–26
Inventory and
Purchases Budgets
(Appendix)

Midwest Belt Company manufactures men's and boys' belts that are cut to order. Each foot or fraction thereof sells for $2.00. Small belts average 2 feet, and large belts average 3 feet in length. The leather is purchased from a local tannery for $0.90 cents per foot. The buckles are purchased at $2.00 for the small size and $2.50 for the large size. No changes are expected in any of the purchasing and selling prices.

Sales should increase 20 percent this year over last year. Last year the company sold 300 small belts and 140 large belts during January and February. The inventories are as follows:

December 31 (actual)		February 28 (target)	
Leather (feet)	900	Leather (feet)	800
Small buckles	200	Small buckles	200
Large buckles	300	Large buckles	250

Purchases are made to provide sufficient stock for each two-month period.

Required:

a. Prepare a purchases budget in units for total January and February purchases of buckles and leather.

b. Compute the budgeted cost of the direct materials to be used in manufacturing small and large belts during January and February.

11–27
Purchases Budget
(Appendix)

Crown Candy Company manufactures various products to sell to retail stores. A sales budget for pecan turtles for the next several months is as follows:

Month	Budgeted Units (in boxes)
June	20,000
July	24,000
August	30,000
September	36,000
October	40,000

Chapter 11

No inventory of turtles is on hand at June 1. During the summer, the company desires an ending finished goods inventory of 10 percent of the following month's sales. The direct materials must be purchased one month before they are needed in production. The June 1 direct materials inventory meets this requirement.

Pecan turtles require direct materials as follows:

Direct Material	Pounds of Materials (per box)
Caramel	3
Pecans	2
Chocolate	5

Required:

Prepare a purchases budget of each ingredient in pounds for June and July. (*Hint:* A production budget will be helpful.)

11-28
Production and Purchases Budgets (Appendix)

Topper Toys makes plastic riding tractors that require 3 pounds of material. The company wants raw materials on hand at the beginning of each month equal to 50 percent of the month's production needs. This requirement was met on April 1, the start of the second quarter. There are no work-in-process inventories. A sales budget in units for the next four months follows:

Month	Unit Sales
April	15,000
May	18,000
June	24,000
July	26,000

Finished goods inventory at the end of each month must be equal to 40 percent of the next month's sales. On March 31, the finished goods inventory totaled 7,500 units.

Required:
a. Prepare a production budget for April, May, and June.
b. Prepare a purchases budget for April and May.

11-29
Developing a Master Budget for a Manufacturer (Appendix)

Overton Products assembles computer terminals in a single plant. The controller has decided to begin a new evaluation system, which includes quarterly budgets. She has prepared the following information for the first quarter of next year:

Estimated sales: 20,000 units × $100 each

Predicted inventories:

	Beginning	Ending
Finished units	5,000	6,000
Frames, raw materials	2,000	3,000
Tubes, raw materials	1,000	1,200

Manufacturing requirements per unit:

Direct Materials	Direct Labor
1 frame × $16	2 hours × $15 per hour
1 tube × $20	

Variable manufacturing overhead is applied at the rate of $5 per direct labor hour. Fixed manufacturing overhead is $147,000 per quarter (including noncash expenditures of $30,000) and is allocated to total units completed.

Financial information follows:

- Beginning cash balance is $300,000.
- Purchases of direct materials are paid for in the quarter acquired; direct labor costs are paid in the month incurred.
- Overhead expenses are paid in the next quarter. The accounts payable for these expenses from the last quarter was $320,000.
- Sales are on credit and are collected 40 percent in the current period and the remainder the next period. Last quarter's sales were $1,800,000. There are no bad debts.
- Selling and administrative expenses are paid quarterly and total $240,000, including $70,000 of depreciation.
- All unit costs for the next quarter were the same as they were for the last quarter.

Required:

For the next quarter, prepare the following items:

a. Sales budget in dollars.
b. Production budget in units.
c. Purchases budget.
d. Manufacturing disbursements budget.
e. Manufacturing cost budget.
f. Budgeted income statement. (*Hint:* First determine the total costs per unit.)

**11-30
Developing a
Master Budget for a
Manufacturer
(Appendix)**

Tuscaloosa Tire Company manufactures plastic tires for automated cleaning machines. It is completing its financial plans for 2005 and needs assistance in the budgeting phase. You are provided the following information that could be useful in preparing the necessary budgets and schedules for 2005:

**Tuscaloosa Tire Company
Balance Sheet
December 31, 2005**

Assets

Current assets:			
Cash		$200,000	
Accounts receivable (net)		294,000	$494,000
Plant, property, and equipment:			
Land		$100,500	
Buildings and equipment	$350,000		
Less accumulated depreciation	(118,000)	232,000	332,500
Total assets			$826,500

Liabilities and Stockholders' Equity

Current liabilities:		
Accounts payable		$132,000
Stockholders' equity:		
Capital stock	$400,000	
Retained earnings	294,500	694,500
Total liabilities and stockholders' equity		$826,500

Estimated sales:

	First Quarter	Second Quarter	Third Quarter
Sales (units)	15,000	16,000	18,000
Sales ($30 each)	$450,000	$480,000	$540,000

All sales are on credit and are collected 30 percent in the quarter of sale and 70 percent in the quarter following sale. The company has a history of no bad debts. The sales from the last quarter of 2000 were $420,000.

The company will have no inventories at the beginning of the year. Management desires 5,000 pounds of unmolded plastic at the end of the first quarter and 6,000 pounds at the end of the second quarter. Each wheel takes 2 pounds of plastic, including waste trimmings. Tuscaloosa should have 2,000 wheel rims at the end of the first quarter and 2,500 at the end of the second quarter. Finished inventory should total 1,000 wheels at the end of the first quarter and 1,500 at the end of the second quarter.

Manufacturing requirements per wheel follow:

	Direct Materials	**Direct Labor**
Plastic	2 pounds × $3	0.5 hour
Rims	1 each × $2	

Variable factory overhead is applied at the rate of $3 per direct labor hour for each finished unit. Fixed factory overhead is $170,000 per quarter, including noncash expenditures of $54,000, and is allocated on the total number of units completed. Direct labor averages $20 per hour.

Additional information follows:

- Purchases of direct materials are paid for in the quarter acquired; direct labor costs are paid in the quarter incurred.
- Overhead expenses are paid in the next quarter.
- The accounts payable on the balance sheet is for overhead expenses from the last quarter of 2005.
- Selling and administrative expenses are paid quarterly and total $40,000, including $10,000 of depreciation.

Required:

For the first and second quarters of 2006, prepare the following items:

a. Sales budget in dollars.
b. Production budget in units.
c. Purchases budget.
d. Manufacturing cost budget.
e. Cash budget.

Discussion Questions and Cases

**11–31
Behavioral
Implications of
Budgeting**

Andrea Rawls, controller of Data Scientific, believes that effective budgeting greatly assists in meeting the organization's goals and objectives. She argues that the budget serves as a blueprint for the operating activities during each reporting period, making it an important control device. She believes that sound management evaluations can be based on the comparisons of performance and budgetary schedules and that employees respond more favorably when they participate in the budgetary process.

Jeff Cooke, treasurer of Data Scientific, agrees that budgeting is essential for overall organization success, but he argues that human resources are too valuable to spend much time planning and preparing the budgetary process. He thinks that the roles people play in budgetary preparation are not important in the final analysis of a budget's effectiveness.

Required:

Contrast the participative versus imposed budgeting concepts and indicate how the ideas of Rawls and Cooke fit the two categories.

11-32
Behavioral
Considerations
and Budgeting

Scott Weidner, the controller in the Division of Social Services for the state, recognizes the importance of the budgetary process for planning, control, and motivation purposes. He believes that a properly implemented participative budgeting process for planning purposes and a management by exception reporting procedure based on that budget will motivate his subordinates to improve productivity within their particular departments. Based on this philosophy, Weidner has implemented the following budget procedures.

- An appropriation target figure is given to each department manager. This amount is the maximum funding that each department can expect to receive in the next fiscal year.
- Department managers develop their individual budgets within the following spending constraints as directed by the controller's staff.
  1. Expenditure requests cannot exceed the appropriation target.
  2. All fixed expenditures should be included in the budget; these should include items such as contracts and salaries at current levels.
  3. All government projects directed by higher authority should be included in the budget in their entirety.
- The controller consolidates the departmental budget requests from the various departments into one budget that is to be submitted for the entire division.
- Upon final budget approval by the legislature, the controller's staff allocates the appropriation to the various departments on instructions from the division manager. However, a specified percentage of each department's appropriation is held back in anticipation of potential budget cuts and special funding needs. The amount and use of this contingency fund are left to the discretion of the division manager.
- Each department is allowed to adjust its budget when necessary to operate within the reduced appropriation level. However, as stated in the original directive, specific projects authorized by higher authority must remain intact.
- The final budget is used as the basis of control for a management by exception form of reporting. Excessive expenditures by account for each department are highlighted on a monthly basis. Department managers are expected to account for all expenditures over budget. Fiscal responsibility is an important factor in the overall performance evaluation of department managers.

Weidner believes that his policy of allowing the department managers to participate in the budget process and then holding them accountable for their performance is essential, especially during these times of limited resources. He also believes that department managers will be positively motivated to increase the efficiency and effectiveness of their departments because they have provided input into the initial budgetary process and are required to justify any unfavorable performances.

Required:
a. Explain the operational and behavioral benefits that generally are attributed to a participative budgeting process.
b. Identify deficiencies in Weidner's participative budgetary policy for planning and performance evaluation purposes. For each deficiency identified, recommend how the deficiency can be corrected.

(CMA Adapted)

11-33
Budgetary Slack
with Ethical
Considerations

Alene Adams was promoted to department manager of a production unit in Dallas Industries three years ago. She enjoys her job except for the evaluation measures that are based on the department's budget. After three years of consistently poor annual evaluations based on a set annual budget, she has decided to improve the evaluation situation. At a recent budget meeting of junior-level managers, the topic of budgetary slack was discussed as a means to maintain some consistency in budgeting matters.

As a result of this meeting, Adams decided to take the following steps in preparing the upcoming year's budget:

1. Use the top quartile for all wage and salary categories.
2. Select the optimistic values for the estimated production ranges for the coming year. These are provided by the marketing department.
3. Use the average of the three months in the current year with poorest production efficiency as benchmarks of success for the coming year.
4. Base equipment charges (primarily depreciation) on replacement values furnished by the purchasing department.
5. Base other fixed costs on current cost plus an inflation rate estimated for the coming year.
6. Use the average of the ten newly hired employees' performance as a basis of labor efficiency for the coming year.

Required:

a. For each item on Adams' list, explain whether it will create budgetary slack. Use numerical examples as necessary to illustrate.
b. Given the company's use of static budgets as one of the performance evaluation measures of its managers, can the managers justify the use of built-in budgetary slack?
c. What would you recommend as a means for Adams to improve the budgeting situation in the company? Provide some specific examples of how the budgeting process might be improved.

**11-34
Budgetary Slack
with Ethical
Considerations**

Norton Company, a manufacturer of infant furniture and carriages, is in the initial stages of preparing the annual budget for next year. Scott Ford recently joined Norton's accounting staff and is interested to learn as much as possible about the company's budgeting process. During a recent lunch with Marge Atkins, sales manager, and Pete Granger, production manager, Ford initiated the following conversation:

Ford: Since I'm new around here and am going to be involved with the preparation of the annual budget, I'd be interested to learn how the two of you estimate sales and production numbers.

Atkins: We start out very methodically by looking at recent history, discussing what we know about current accounts, potential customers, and the general state of consumer spending. Then we add that usual dose of intuition to come up with the best forecast we can.

Granger: I usually take the sales projections as the basis for my projections. Of course, we have to make an estimate of what this year's closing inventories will be, which is sometimes difficult.

Ford: Why does that present a problem? There must have been an estimate of closing inventories in the budget for the current year.

Granger: Those numbers aren't always reliable since Marge makes some adjustments to the sales numbers before passing them on to me.

Ford: What kind of adjustments?

Atkins: Well, we don't want to fall short of the sales projections, so we generally give ourselves a little breathing room by lowering the initial sales projection anywhere from 5 to 10 percent.

Granger: So, you can see why this year's budget is not a very reliable starting point. We always have to adjust the projected production rates as the year progresses; of course, this changes the ending inventory estimates. By the way, we make similar adjustments to expenses by adding at least 10 percent to the estimates; I think everyone around here does the same thing.

Required:

a. Marge Atkins and Pete Granger have described the use of budgetary slack.
   1. Explain why Atkins and Granger behave in this manner, and describe the benefits they expect to realize from the use of budgetary slack.
   2. Explain how the use of budgetary slack can adversely affect Atkins and Granger.

b. As a management accountant, Scott Ford believes that the behavior described by Marge Atkins and Pete Granger could be unethical and that he might have an obligation not to support this behavior. By citing specific standards of competence, confidentiality, integrity, and/or objectivity from "Statements on Management Accounting Number 1C," *Standards of Ethical Conduct for Management Accountants*, Chapter 1 Appendix, explain why the use of budgetary slack could be unethical.

(CMA Adapted)

Solutions to Review Problems

1.
Operating Budget for a Merchandising Organization

a.

Stumphouse Cheese Company
Sales Budget
For the Month of April 2005

	Units	Price	Sales
Blue cheese	160,000	$10	$1,600,000
Ice cream	240,000	5	1,200,000
Total			$2,800,000

b.

Stumphouse Cheese Company
Purchases Budget
For the Month of April 2005

	Blue Cheese	Ice Cream	Total
Units:			
Sales needs	160,000	240,000	
Desired ending inventory	12,000	5,000	
Total	172,000	245,000	
Less beginning inventory	(10,000)	(4,000)	
Purchases	162,000	241,000	
Dollars:			
Sales needs	$1,280,000	$480,000	
Desired ending inventory	96,000	10,000	
Total	$1,376,000	$490,000	
Less beginning inventory	(80,000)	(8,000)	
Purchases needed	$1,296,000	$482,000	$1,778,000

c.

Stumphouse Cheese Company
Cash Budget
For the Month of April 2005

Cash balance, beginning		$ 400,000
Collections on sales:		
Current month's sales ($2,800,000 × 0.70)	$1,960,000	
Previous month's sales ($3,000,000 × 0.29)	870,000	2,830,000
Cash available from operations		$3,230,000
Less budgeted disbursements:		
March purchases ($1,800,000 × 0.40)	$ 720,000	
April purchases ($1,778,000 × 0.60)	1,066,800	
Labor	156,000	
Overhead (March)	80,000	
Selling and administrative		
($450,000 − $40,000 depreciation)	410,000	(2,432,800)
Cash balance, ending		$ 797,200

d.

Stumphouse Cheese Company
Budgeted Income Statement
For the Month of April 2005

Sales (sales budget)		$2,800,000
Allowance for bad debts		(28,000)
Net sales		$2,772,000
Costs of merchandise sold:		
Blue cheese (160,000 × $8)	$1,280,000	
Ice cream (240,000 × $2)	480,000	$1,760,000
Wages and salaries	$ 156,000	
Overhead	80,000	
Selling and administrative	450,000	686,000	(2,446,000)
Net income		$ 326,000

2.
Operating Budget for a Manufacturing Organization (Appendix)

a.

Handy Company
Sales Budget
For the First Quarter of 2004

	Units	Price	Sales
Drills	60,000	$100	$ 6,000,000
Saws	40,000	125	5,000,000
Total			$11,000,000

b.

Handy Company
Production Budget
For the First Quarter of 2004

	Drills	Saws
Budget sales	60,000	40,000
Plus desired ending inventory	25,000	10,000
Total inventory requirements	85,000	50,000
Less beginning inventory	(20,000)	(8,000)
Budgeted production	65,000	42,000

c.

Handy Company
Purchases Budget
For the First Quarter of 2004

	Drills	Saws	Total
Metal purchases:			
Production units (production budget):	65,000	42,000	
Metal (pounds)	× 5	× 4	
Production needs (pounds)	325,000	168,000	493,000
Desired ending inventory (pounds)			36,000
Total metal needs (pounds)			529,000
Less beginning inventory (pounds)			(32,000)
Purchases needed (pounds)			497,000
Cost per pound			× $8
Total metal purchases			$3,976,000
Plastic purchases:			
Production units (production budget):	65,000	42,000	107,000
Plastic (pounds)			× 3
Production needs (pounds)			321,000
Desired ending inventory (pounds)			32,000
Total plastic needs (pounds)			353,000
Less beginning inventory (pounds)			(29,000)
Purchases needed (pounds)			324,000
Cost per pound			× $5
Total plastic purchases			$1,620,000
Handle purchases:			
Production units (production budget)	65,000		65,000
Handles			× 1
Production needs			65,000
Desired ending inventory			7,000
Total handle needs			72,000
Less beginning inventory			(6,000)
Purchases needed			66,000
Cost per handle			× $3
Total handle purchases			$198,000
Total purchases:			
Metal			$3,976,000
Plastic			1,620,000
Handles			198,000
Total purchases			$5,794,000

d.

Handy Company
Manufacturing Cost Budget
For the First Quarter of 2004

	Drills	Saws	Total
Direct materials:			
Metal:			
Production units (production budget)	65,000	42,000	
Metal per unit of product (pounds) . . .	× 5	× 4	
Production needs for metal (pounds) . . .	325,000	168,000	
Unit cost	× $8	× $8	
Cost of metal issued to production	$2,600,000	$1,344,000	$3,944,000
Plastic:			
Production units (production budget)	65,000	42,000	
Plastic (pounds)	× 3	× 3	
Production needs for plastic (pounds) . . .	195,000	126,000	
Unit cost	× $5	× $5	
Cost of plastic issued to production	$ 975,000	$ 630,000	1,605,000
Handles:			
Production units (production budget)	65,000		
Handles	× 1		
Production needs for handles	65,000		
Unit cost	× $3		
Cost of handles issued to production	$ 195,000		195,000
Total			$5,744,000
Direct labor:			
Budgeted production	65,000	42,000	
Direct labor hours per unit	× 2	× 3	
Total direct labor hours	130,000	126,000	
Labor rate	× $12	× $16	
Labor expenditures	$1,560,000	$2,016,000	3,576,000
Variable factory overhead:			
Direct labor hours	130,000	126,000	
Variable factory overhead rate	× $1.50	× $1.50	
Total variable overhead	$ 195,000	$ 189,000	384,000
Fixed factory overhead:			214,000
Total			$9,918,000

e.

Handy Company
Cash Budget
For the First Quarter of 2004

Cash balance, beginning		$ 1,800,000
Collections on sales:		
Current quarter's sales (0.50)	$5,500,000	
Previous quarter's sales (0.50)	4,200,000	9,700,000
Cash available from operations		$11,500,000
Less budgeted disbursements:		
Materials (purchases budget)	$5,794,000	
Labor (manufacturing cost budget)	3,576,000	
Manufacturing overhead (manufacturing cost budget) ($598,000 − 156,000)	442,000	
Selling and administrative ($340,000 − $90,000 depreciation)	250,000	(10,062,000)
Cash balance, ending		$ 1,438,000

f.

Handy Company
Contribution Income Statement
For the First Quarter of 2004

Sales (sales budget)		$11,000,000
Less variable costs of goods sold:		
Drills (60,000 × $85.00)	$5,100,000	
Saws (40,000 × $99.50)	3,980,000	(9,080,000)
Gross profit		$ 1,920,000
Less fixed costs:		
Manufacturing overhead	$ 214,000	
Selling and administrative expenses	340,000	(554,000)
Net income		$ 1,366,000

3.
Activity-Based
Budget

Holtzendorff Industries
Activity-Based Budget for Product X
For the Month of February

Unit-level costs:		
Direct materials (2 gallons × 20,000 × $3)	$120,000	
Assembly (½ × 20,000 × $16)	160,000	
Finishing (20,000 × $2)	40,000	$320,000
Batch-level production costs:		
Setup (20 batches × $100)	$ 2,000	
Inspection (20 batches × $200)	4,000	6,000
Product-level costs:		
Advertising	$ 10,000	
Product development	15,000	25,000
Total product costs		$351,000

Note: Administration is not a product cost.

PERFORMANCE ASSESSMENT

After completing this chapter, you should be able to:

LEARNING OBJECTIVE 1   Explain responsibility accounting and differentiate between financial and nonfinancial performance measures.

LEARNING OBJECTIVE 2   Differentiate between static and flexible budgets used in performance reporting.

LEARNING OBJECTIVE 3   Determine and interpret direct materials and direct labor cost variances.

LEARNING OBJECTIVE 4   Prepare a performance report for a revenue center.

THE FALLACY OF THE *13-MINUTE SERVICE CALL*

Managers use standards, benchmarks, and metrics to assess organizational performance in a variety of settings. In addition to assisting managers in their efforts to gauge organizational performance, standards and metrics also carry significant motivational content. These issues are evident in the recent history of the Gateway Corporation.

Over 15 years in the late 1980s and 1990s, Gateway grew into the fourth largest seller of personal computers with a low-cost–high-volume strategy. At one point, the firm had 20,000 employees, 300 stores, 15 call centers, and 5 domestic and international plants. As the century closed, however, the slumping economy and falling personal computer sales proved to be quite a challenge. During 2000, the firm's income fell 26 percent to $316 million. In 2001, results were even worse as Gateway lost $524 million on first-quarter sales of $3.5 billion.

A closer look at Gateway operations reveal much more than a response to a changing economy. In 1998, founder Ted Waitt concluded that the company needed a more professional management approach. Over the next several years, he retired from active involvement with the firm and ceded executive authority to a handpicked successor and a new management team. The firm went from a rather freewheeling management style to one of rules and procedures.

Of particular interest was a new policy that impacted the service representatives who answered technical questions for customers. The new policy stated that service reps would not receive their monthly bonus if they spent more than 13 minutes with a caller. The management goal was to control overall service costs better. The motivational impact on employees and ultimate results, how-

ever, were quite predictable. Service reps emphasized solving these service problems quickly in order to preserve their bonus. Their strategies included sending out new parts for customers to install themselves, replacing entire computers if problems could not be diagnosed quickly, or simply hanging up in the middle of a call claiming that the phone was not working properly. As a result of this and other management decisions, selling, general, and administrative costs rose from 14 percent of revenues in the fourth quarter of 1999 to 20 percent of revenues in the fourth quarter of 2000. The 13-minute standard had just the opposite effect from the intention.

In addition, senior management began to emphasize the sale of expensive add-on products and services rather than the computers themselves. By raising commissions on the add-on items, management encouraged sales reps to be very casual about selling the basic computers that had been the firm's mainstay. As a result of these changes, customer satisfaction slumped, and referrals fell from 50 percent of sales to 30 percent.

In early 2001, Ted Waitt resumed his active management of the company. Emphasizing a back-to-basics approach, he eliminated numerous rules—including the 13-minute standard—and raised the commission on the basic computers. Other elements of the recovery strategy included cutting prices to match industry leaders, eliminating noncore business operations, and rewarding employees for cost saving ideas.

While not all of Gateway's management challenges resulted from the 13-minute service call standard, this policy and others like it profoundly impacted operations of the firm and the resulting customer satisfaction ratings. Managerial accounting provides a multidimensional lens that emphasizes the technical, motivational, and strategic implications of standards, benchmarks, and metrics.

Sources: Katrina Brooker, "I Built This Company, I Can Save It," *Fortune*, April 30, 2001, pp. 94–102; and Arlene Weintraub and Andrew Park, "Can Gateway Survive in a Smaller Pasture?" *Business Week*, September 10, 2001.

Managers in many organizations face these same performance challenges; Management accounting tools aid in the assessment of the performance of the firm as a whole or any of its various components. Indeed, feedback in the form of performance reports is essential if the benefits of budgeting and other types of planning are to be fully realized. Managers need to know how actual results compare with current budgets and standards to control current operations and to improve future operations. These performance reports should be prepared in accordance with the concept of **responsibility accounting,** which is the structuring of performance reports addressed to individual (or group) members of an organization in a manner that emphasizes the factors they are able to control.

The purpose of this chapter is to introduce responsibility accounting and performance assessment. We begin by examining responsibility accounting and identifying various types of responsibility centers. We then take a close look at performance assessment for service representatives used by Gateway Corporation. We conclude the chapter by considering performance reports for revenue centers. (Responsibility accounting for major business segments, is considered in Chapter 13.) Appendices to this chapter take a close look at overhead variances and illustrate the reconciliation of budgeted and actual income.

LEARNING OBJECTIVE 1

RESPONSIBILITY ACCOUNTING

Performance reports that include comparisons of actual results with plans or budgets serve as assessment tools and attention-directors to help managers determine and control activities. According to the concept of *management by exception*, the absence of significant differences indicates that activities are proceeding as planned whereas the presence of significant differences indicates a need to either take corrective action or revise plans. These evaluations and actions are made within the framework of an organization's overall mission, goals, and strategies as discussed in Chapter 1. Specifically, the responsibility accounting system should address the organization's strategic positions that relate to cost leadership, product/service differentiation, and market niche. Relevant implementations of Kaizen costing and quality cost issues (refer to Chapter 9) should be incorporated into the planning phase of the reporting system.

Responsibility accounting may focus on specific units within the organization or various aspects of the value chain that are accountable for the accomplishment of specific activities or objectives. Performance reports are customized to emphasize the activities of each specific organizational unit or value chain element. For example, a financial performance report addressed to the head of a production department contains manufacturing costs controllable by the department head; it does not contain costs (such as advertising, sales commissions, or the president's salary) that the head of the production department cannot control. Including noncontrollable costs in the report distracts the manager's attention from the controllable cost, thereby diluting a manager's efforts to deal with controllable items. Lower-level managers could also become frustrated with the entire performance reporting system if they believe upper-level managers expect them to control costs they cannot influence. However, some companies insist on reporting all related revenues and expenses in the same report. When this is the case, the noncontrollable items should be clearly labeled.

A poorly designed responsibility accounting system can lead to unethical practices by managers in key positions. If too much pressure is placed on managers to meet performance targets, they sometimes take actions that are not in the best interest of the organization. What's Happening 12–1 presents examples of such actions involving a vice president of Bausch & Lomb and the CEO of Sunbeam who forced sales in one year to the detriment of the company's sales the following year. The designers of an organization's responsibility accounting system need to be aware of the potential pressures that such a system can place on managers. The decision-making model of the organization should be such that managers are not influenced to make undesirable decisions just to receive bonuses or promotions.

PERFORMANCE REPORTING AND ORGANIZATION STRUCTURES

Before implementing a responsibility accounting system, all areas of authority and responsibility within an organization must be clearly defined. Organization charts and other documents should be examined to determine an organization's authority and responsibility structure. **Organization structure** is the arrangement of lines of responsibility within the organization. These structures vary widely. Some companies have functional-based structures along the lines of marketing, production, research, and so forth; other companies use products, services, customers, or geography as the basis of organization. When an attempt is made to implement a responsibility accounting system, management could find instances of overlapping duties, authority not commensurate with responsibility, and expenditures for which no one appears responsible. These circumstances can make the development of a responsibility accounting system difficult. General Electric overcame many of these problems with the use of teams and a new measurement tool as explained in What's Happening 12–2. (For discussions and examples of organization structures, consult a basic principles of management text.)

SALES STRATEGY REFLECTS CONFLICT BETWEEN ETHICS AND RESPONSIBILITY ACCOUNTING

In late 1993, the contact lens division of Bausch & Lomb, Inc., was experiencing lower-than-anticipated sales levels. In December, the head of the division called a meeting of its independent distributors and told them that the company had changed its sales strategy. Effective immediately, each distributor would have to boost its inventory of contact lenses if it wanted to remain a distributor of Bausch & Lomb products.

The strategy was for distributors to buy only in very large quantities (some as much as a two-year supply) with prices increased by amounts up to 50 percent. Also, the distributors had to place these large orders by December 24, 1993. As one distributor stated, "When your No. 1 vendor says you'd better take it or else, what're you going to do?" All but two of Bausch & Lomb's distributors complied with the new sales strategy demands; those two were dropped as customers in January 1994.

Initially the strategy paid off; the sales in the last few days of December totaled about $25 million and amounted to one-half of the division's profit for the entire year. The division manager was delighted, of course; sales and profits soared, and his operations were in great shape. However, the long-term results were not favorable. By June 1994, the company announced that the high inventories of its distributors would severely reduce sales and profits for the year. The profit decline was approximately 37 percent.

The ending? The manager got what he wanted: increased sales and a nice profit for the year. But the company and its stockholders paid the price of one manager's poor decision. In the summer of 1994, after the company made the announcement about the sales decline, the company's stock fell from $50 to $32. After this disclosure, the manager was forced to step down from his position, and stockholders filed a class-action lawsuit accusing the company of falsely inflating sales and earnings.

History repeated itself in 1997 when Al Dunlap, CEO of Sunbeam, followed the Bausch & Lomb manager's plan to force sales to show how well his management style (firing employees and closing plants) was working; history did repeat, and quickly. Dunlap instituted a "bill and hold" plan that called for products to be produced in large quantities and sold to customers for delivery at a later date. While this made the financial report for 1997 very favorable, it had a detrimental effect on the 1998 report. In late March 1998, the company acknowledged that first quarter income would be below expectations, and in fact, a loss. The 1997 results were so exaggerated that stockholders quickly filed lawsuits charging deception. Mr. Dunlap was fired on June 13, 1998.

Source: "Numbers Game at Bausch & Lomb?" *Business Week,* December 19, 1994, pp. 108–10; and "How Al Dunlap Self-Destructed," *Business Week,* July 6, 1998, pp. 58–61, 64.

Although performance reports can be developed for areas of responsibility as narrow as a single worker, the basic responsibility unit in most organizations begins with the department and progresses to division and corporate levels. In manufacturing plants, separate performance reports can be used for responsibility centers comprising production or service departments or for processes of manufacturing cells. In large universities, separate responsibility centers are set up for individual academic departments (e.g., accounting, psychology, and mathematics) and staff and service departments (e.g., human resources, cafeteria, and maintenance). When a large department performs a number of diverse and significant activities, responsibility accounting can be further refined so that a single department contains several responsibility centers with performance reports prepared for each.

FINANCIAL PERFORMANCE MEASURES

Commensurate with their authority, individual department heads have quite narrow responsibility. Commensurate with greater authority, responsibility is broader at higher levels in the organization. Consider the structure of Mall Realty, a company that owns

RESPONSIBILITY ACCOUNTING CAN BE INVOLVED

During the 1990s General Electric found that to continue its world dominance, it had to improve quality without ignoring costs and that its managers had to be responsible for controlling the combination of quality and costs. Five years after implementing its new responsibility accounting program, called Six Sigma, GE had increased its annual productivity 266 percent and increased its operating margin from 14.4 to 18.4 percent.

Six Sigma, a statistically derived name, is a means of measuring problems (errors or defects) within a system. It relates to quality by measuring the defect level (rate) of any activity. For each area, activity, service, and so on, a target for improvement is set and a manager is assigned the responsibility to achieve the target. The reporting system centers on the rate of improvement as measured by reduced defects or errors. The program has five basic steps:

1. *Define problem:* Teams generally work to define problems related to some process or customer satisfaction.
2. *Measure:* Determine what is wrong with the existing process or service.
3. *Analyze:* Determine reasons for what is wrong.
4. *Improve:* Define and develop a plan of action.
5. *Control:* To ensure that changes are installed and used effectively, implement measures to keep problems from recurring.

Because of the involvement of teams and the support of top management, the acceptance of the system has been very high. GE has been very pleased with it because the system not only improved quality but also saved the company millions of dollars in operating expenses.

Source: Sridhar Seshadri and Gregory T. Lucier, "GE Takes Six Sigma beyond the Bottom Line," *Strategic Finance,* May 2001, pp. 40–46.

and leases space in shopping malls. The firm's short-run objective is to earn a profit by renting space in company-owned malls. While the president is responsible for overall operations and profitability, the authority to incur costs in connection with the actual rental spaces (stores) is delegated to the vice president of operations, who in turn delegates a portion of this authority to each mall manager. Finally, each mall manager delegates the authority to incur costs in connection with specific rental activities to department heads.

A series of performance reports, illustrating expanding authority for operating costs is presented in Exhibit 12–1. A mall manager is responsible for more costs than is a department head; the vice president of operations is responsible for more costs than is a single mall manager. Note the way the financial performance reports tie together. The totals for the head of the Security Department are included as one line in the mall manager's report, and the totals for the manager of Mall 2 are included as one line in the report for the vice president of operations. This aggregation takes place because the managers closest to actual activities need detailed information to control day-to-day activities, whereas upper-level managers spend less time controlling activities and more time planning them. This same logic also applies to the nonfinancial measures discussed in the next section.

All product and service activities result in financial measures. The common financial performance measures are income statements, variance reports of actual to budget, variance reports of actual to standard, and return on investment. The variance measures, in particular, are usually available at all levels in the organization. A department head needs to know whether department labor costs are within acceptable ranges; a plant manager needs to know whether plant labor costs are within acceptable ranges; and a division manager needs to know whether division labor costs are within acceptable ranges.

EXHIBIT 12-1

RESPONSIBILITY ACCOUNTING REPORTS WITH FINANCIAL MEASURES

	Actual Cost	Allowed Cost	Variance*
Vice President: Operations			
Mall 1	$ 55,000	$ 54,800	$ 200 U
➤ Mall 2	69,600	68,400	1,200 U
Vice pres.'s office (itemized)	10,900	12,000	1,100 F
Total	$135,500	$135,200	$ 300 U
Manager: Mall 2			
Maintenance department	$ 25,400	$ 24,700	$ 700 U
Advertising department	17,500	18,000	500 F
➤ Security department	20,500	19,900	600 U
Mall mgr.'s office (itemized)	6,200	5,800	400 U
Total	$ 69,600	$ 68,400	$1,200 U
Head: Security Department			
Supplies	$ 3,000	$ 2,000	$1,000 U
Staff wages	9,500	10,000	500 F
General overhead (itemized)	8,000	7,900	100 U
Total	$ 20,500	$ 19,900	$ 600 U

*F = Favorable if actual costs are lower than allowed costs; U = unfavorable if actual costs are higher than allowed costs.

Basic performance reports are almost always stated in terms of dollars, a common additive unit of measure for all activities. Once the dollar impact of each activity is determined, the dollar measures can be summarized and reported up the corporate ladder. Furthermore, both the immediate supervisor of an activity and managers far removed from the activity can understand the impact of dollars on cash flow and income.

NONFINANCIAL PERFORMANCE MEASURES

Limited nonfinancial information is routinely collected and reported along with financial information in most performance assessment systems. Examples of traditionally reported nonfinancial information include sales volume in units, production output in units, reporting bases (such as labor and machine hours), absenteeism rates, various quantity measures of materials used (i.e., pounds, liters, etc.), and cycle times of processes. Several external measures also are nonfinancial in nature: measures of customer satisfaction, returned units per product per period, on-time deliveries, and various rankings within the industry (such as employees per unit of output). A major advantage of many nonfinancial measures is that they encourage managers to consider concerns beyond that which is financially quantifiable. They can be reported almost instantly, whereas many financial measures take several days or weeks to report. For example, a manufacturer can have daily reports of units reworked, and a restaurant can determine the number of meals served hourly. However, as discussed in Research Shows 12–1, the use of nonfinancial information is often limited and does not always match what executives think is important.

In extending the performance report of Mall Realty, several nonfinancial measures could be relevant in the overall management of operations. Exhibit 12–2 shows examples of both additive and relative measures. While financial measures are usually

SURVEY INVESTIGATES THE USE OF NONFINANCIAL MEASURES

To gauge the use of nonfinancial performance measures, a survey of 800 large corporations in Canada and the United States was conducted; 253 usable responses were received. The top executives of these companies were asked about the measurement and the use of five critical nonfinancial areas: customer service, market performance, goal achievement, innovation, and employee involvement. Each area was divided into segments for which nonfinancial measures could be taken. Our example area, marketing performance, was divided into the following segments (see the graph below): marketing effectiveness, market growth, and market share.

For each area segment, the executive was asked to evaluate its importance, whether it was measured by the company, and whether its measurement was used. The surprising result was that while most executives considered each area important, their companies' measurement and subsequent use of the measurement was considerably less.

While executives placed much emphasis on market share and market growth, their companies did not do much with market effectiveness. Even though they rated it almost as high as the other categories, only about 27 percent measured it and only 17 percent used it.

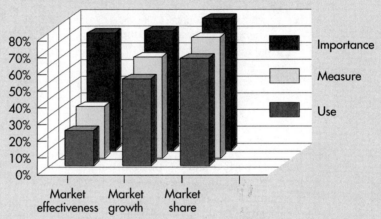

Nonfinancial Measures as Percentages

Source: Bonnie P. Stivers, Teresa J. Covin, Nancy G. Hall, and Steven W. Smalt, "How Nonfinancial Performance Measures Are Used," *Management Accounting*, February 1998, pp. 44–49.

additive (can be combined without distorting the facts) from one level to the next, nonfinancial measures are usually a mix of additive and relative (cannot be combined mathematically for meaningful purposes) measures. The additive measure of complaints per week can be evaluated for each sublevel and summed as it progresses up the management levels. However, the percentage occupancy goal of the company could not be summed because the various units have different benchmarks of expectations due to size, age, demographics, and so forth. The same is true for the absenteeism rate. Different units have a different mix of employees as to education, experience, age, and so on, and the mix influences the amount of absenteeism. Also notice that the nonfinancial measures do not use the same measurement base or the same time frame. Occupancy and absenteeism are percentages while the complaints are expressed as the number per week.

Nonfinancial performance measures should be used along with traditional financial measures in most situations. A favorable financial variance that resulted from an unethical or illegal action should not be rewarded. Short-sighted managers can also take actions that appear favorable in the short run but are detrimental to the organi-

EXHIBIT 12-2

RESPONSIBILITY ACCOUNTING REPORTS WITH NONFINANCIAL MEASURES

	Actual Activity	Expected Activity	Variance*
Vice President: Operations			
Percentage occupancy	92%	98%	6% U
Absenteeism rate	8%	4%	4% U
Complaints per week	45	50	5 F
Manager: Mall 2			
Percentage occupancy	87%	94%	7% U
Absenteeism rate	10%	5%	5% U
Complaints per week:			
General	4	4	0 F
Maintenance	7	6	1 U
Security	4	6	2 F
Total complaints	15	16	1 F
Head: Security Department			
Absenteeism rate	12%	6%	6% U
Security complaints per store per week	4	6	2 F

*F = favorable; U = unfavorable.

zation in the long run. Excessive pressure for employee productivity could result in strikes and employee turnover, and bargain purchases of raw materials could result in excess waste. These examples illustrate the need for upper-level management to inquire about the causes of favorable as well as unfavorable financial variances. Variances of any substantial amount should be indicators (red flags) that something in the process is not operating as it should; nonfinancial measures can often identify causes of variances outside the norm. Keep these types of explanations in mind when studying the variance methods discussed later in the chapter.

From the perspective of an organization's goals and objectives, sometimes nonfinancial aspects can be as important as the financial objectives. Rather than concentrating only on the profit motive, sometimes it is more important to consider items such as customer satisfaction, vendor relations, and environmental factors. As noted in What's Happening 12–3, the results of focusing on a critical nonfinancial issue can reap unexpected financial rewards.

TYPES OF RESPONSIBILITY CENTERS

Under responsibility accounting, performance reports are prepared for departments, segments of departments, or groupings of departments that operate under the control and authority of a responsible manager. Each organization unit for which performance reports are prepared is identified as a responsibility center. For the purpose of evaluating their financial performance, responsibility centers can be classified as cost centers, revenue centers, profit centers, or investment centers. Within each of the centers there could be responsibility for interrelationships with the value chain of the organization so that no aspect of operations is overlooked, or even worse, ignored.

Cost Center. A cost center is a responsibility center whose manager is responsible for managing only costs; there is no revenue responsibility. A cost center can be as small as a segment of a department or large enough to include a major aspect of the

CLINIC REALIZES FINANCIAL RESULTS FROM NONFINANCIAL DECISIONS

What started out as an effort to make an outpatient clinic more user friendly in a competitive local market resulted in a significant improvement in financial results. The changes implemented by the outpatient clinic in Salt Lake City, Utah, were intended to provide users with faster, friendlier, and more efficient visits. The changes were in response to a new organization objective implemented by the nurses (*not* top management) of the clinic.

The first goal was to reduce patient waiting time. Physicians were found to be the main culprits of delays. Many did not get to the clinic at their appointed starting times, thus delaying many activities during their particular shift. Chronically late physicians were provided data as to the number of patients the clinic was not serving because of their delays.

Patients were also targeted for improved relations by such changes as letting them wear their personal underwear (versus the hospital gowns) and walking to operating rooms (versus riding in a wheel chair). Services for those accompanying the patients were also addressed. A kitchen stocked with free refreshments for family members of patients was made available. The results of the changes include happier patients (and happier relatives), shorter recovery times, and an increased turnover rate of the outpatient rooms.

Unexpectedly, the management of the clinic, as well as the executives of the associated hospital, were overjoyed. By reducing the time a patient occupies a treatment room, the capacity of the clinic increased by 50 percent with no increase in personnel. In the following months, the revenue of the clinic increased greatly with the only new cost being that of the waiting room kitchen. By striving for a set of nonfinancial goals, this organization realized very real financial rewards.

Source: "Nurses Discover the Healing Power of Customer Service," *The Wall Street Journal*, February 17, 1998, p. B1.

organization, such as all manufacturing activities. The financial performance reports in Exhibit 12–1 illustrate an increasing responsibility for cost management. Each department head is responsible only for costs incurred for his or her department, but each mall manager is also responsible for all mall operating costs. Cost centers are established for value chain activities, operating activities, and nonoperating activities and are found in manufacturing, merchandising, service, and not-for-profit organizations. Typical examples of these cost centers include the following:

Organization	Cost Center
Manufacturing plant	Tooling department
	Assembly activities
Retail store	Inventory control function
	Maintenance department
TV station	Audio/video engineering
	Buildings and grounds
College	History department
	Student registration unit
City government	Public safety (police and fire)
	Road maintenance

Revenue Center. A **revenue center** is a responsibility center whose manager is responsible for the generation of sales revenues. Even though the basic performance report of a revenue center emphasizes sales, revenue centers are likely to be assigned responsibility for the controllable costs they incur in generating revenues. If revenues and costs are evaluated separately, the center has dual responsibility as a revenue center and as a cost center. If controllable costs are deducted from revenues to obtain some bottom-line contribution, the center is, in fact, being treated more like a profit center than a cost center.

Profit Center. A **profit center** is a responsibility center whose manager is responsible for revenues, costs, and resulting profits. It could be an entire organization, but it is more frequently a segment of an organization such as a product line, marketing territory, or store. In the context of performance evaluation, the word "profit" does not necessarily refer to the bottom line of an income statement; instead, it likely refers to the profit center's contribution to common corporate costs and profit. Profit is computed as the center's revenues less all costs associated with operating the center. In addition to a center's profits, other measures of performance can include quality assessments, service ratings, and operating efficiencies.

A large retail organization might evaluate each of its stores as a profit center with the store manager being the administrative officer. The store manager, who has responsibility for the store's overall operation, accepts the store's physical structure and the organization's investment in the store as "givens." Having limited authority regarding the size of the store's total assets, the store manager is not held responsible for the relationship between profits and assets.

Investment Center. An **investment center** is a responsibility center whose manager is responsible for the relationship between its profits and the total assets invested in the center. Investment center managers have a high degree of organization autonomy. In general, the management of an investment center is expected to earn a target profit per dollar invested. Investment center managers are evaluated on the basis of how well they use the total resources entrusted to their care to earn a profit. An investment center is the broadest and most inclusive type of responsibility center. Managers of these centers have more authority and responsibility than other managers and are primarily responsible for planning, organizing, and controlling firm activities. Because of their authority regarding the size of corporate assets, they are held responsible for the relationship between profits and assets. (Investment centers are discussed further in Chapter 13.)

<table>
<tr><td>LEARNING OBJECTIVE 2</td><td>

PERFORMANCE REPORTING FOR COST CENTERS

</td></tr>
</table>

Financial performance reports for cost centers should always include a comparison of actual and budgeted (or allowed) costs and should always identify the difference as a **variance.** *Allowed costs* are used in performance reports as the flexible budget amounts for the actual level of activity. The variance is favorable if actual costs are less than budgeted (or allowed) costs and unfavorable if actual costs are more than budgeted (or allowed) costs. These comparisons are made in total and individually for each type of controllable cost assigned to the cost center.

DEVELOPMENT OF FLEXIBLE BUDGETS

A budget that is based on a prediction of sales and production is called a *static budget.* The operating budget explained in Chapter 11 is a **static budget.** Budgets can also be set for a series of possible production and sales volumes, or budgets can be adjusted to a particular level of production after the fact. These budgets, based on cost-volume or cost-activity relationships, are called **flexible budgets;** they are used to determine what costs should have been for an attained level of activity. For example, if the college cafeteria budgets $10,000 for food during April for 5,000 meals but provides 6,000 meals, the budget needs to be adjusted to the original food budget rate of $2 ($10,000 ÷ 5,000 meals). Otherwise, the amount spent on food will not be a fair evaluation of the cost per the original budget. If $11,500 was spent on food during the month, the analysis might appear as follows:

Budget Item	Actual	Budget	Difference
Static analysis:			
Food	$11,500	$10,000 (5,000 meals × $2)	$1,500 over budget
Flexible analysis:			
Food	$11,500	$12,000 (6,000 meals × $2)	$500 under budget

The cafeteria manager is better evaluated based on what actually happened with the flexible budget than with the static budget, especially if the manager had no control over how many student meals were requested.

Before developing a flexible budget, management must understand how costs respond to changes in activity. Some costs respond to unit or volume activity; others respond to batch activity. There are always fixed costs that generally do not respond to either units or volume and are usually classified as product or facility level items. Research Shows 12-2 demonstrates how the advantages of multiple drivers can often be realized when only one or two drivers do not properly explain what is taking place.

For an in-depth example, assume that McMillan Company, which produces leather compact disk carrying cases, has three departments: Production, Sales, and Administration. The focus in this section is on the development of financial performance reports for the Production Department, a department with highly automated processes performing most of the work. Since direct labor composes only a small portion of the processing cost, the work effort for processing will be labeled "assembly." The flexible budget cost-estimating equations for total monthly production costs of cases are based on production standards with unit- and batch-level costs being variable and product- and facility-level costs being fixed. The standards follow:

Unit level:
   Direct materials—2 pounds per unit at $5 per pound, or $10 per unit
   Assembly—0.25 hour per unit at $24 per hour, or $6 per unit
   Waterproofing and inspection—$8 per unit
Batch level:
   Setup costs—$400 per batch of 1,000 units, or $0.40 per unit
   Test run—$100 per batch of 1,000 units, or $0.10 unit
Product level items—fixed costs per month of $20,000
Facility level items—fixed costs per month of $32,000

If management plans to produce 10,000 cases (10 batches of 1,000 cases) in July, requiring 4,000 machine hours and 20,000 pounds of materials, the budgeted manufacturing costs for the month will amount to $297,000:

McMillan Company
Manufacturing Budget
For the Month of July

Manufacturing costs:
Unit level:

Direct materials (10,000 × 2 pounds × $5)	$100,000
Assembly (10,000 × 0.25 hours × $24)	60,000
Waterproofing and inspection (10,000 × $8)	80,000
Batch level:	
Setup (10 batches × $400)	4,000
Test run (10 batches × $100)	1,000
Product level	20,000
Facility level	32,000
Total	$297,000

FLEXIBLE BUDGETS EMPHASIZE PERFORMANCE

If actual production happened to equal 10,000 units produced in 10 batches, the performance of the Production Department in controlling costs could be based on a comparison of actual and budgeted manufacturing costs. If production was at some volume other than that planned in the original manufacturing budget, however, it would be inappropriate to compare actual manufacturing costs with the costs predicted in the original static budget. Doing so would intermix two separate Production Department responsibilities, namely, the manufacturing responsibility for production volume and the financial responsibility for cost control.

The original budget for production volume was set on the basis of predicted needs for sales and inventory requirements, taking into consideration materials, labor, and facilities constraints. In the absence of any changes in these needs, the Production Department's manufacturing responsibility for production volume is evaluated by comparing the actual and budgeted production volumes. If, however, production needs change, perhaps due to an unexpected increase or decrease in sales volume, the Production Department should attempt to make appropriate changes in its production volume. When the actual production volume is anything other than the originally budgeted amount, the Production Department's financial responsibility for cost control should be based on the actual level of production or an adjustment to the level of planned production.

For the purpose of evaluating the financial performance of cost centers, a flexible budget is tailored, after the fact, to the actual level of activity. A **flexible budget variance** is computed for each cost as the difference between the actual cost and the flexible budget cost of producing a given quantity of product or service. Assume that actual production for July totaled 11,000 units in 11 batches rather than the 10,000 units that were budgeted. Examples of a performance report for July manufacturing costs based on static and flexible budgets are presented in Exhibit 12–3. When the Production Department's financial performance is evaluated using the static budget, the actual cost of producing 11,000 units is compared to the budgeted cost of producing 10,000 units. The result is a series of unfavorable static budget variances totaling $20,600.

When the Production Department's financial performance is evaluated by comparing actual costs with costs allowed in a flexible budget drawn up for the actual production volume, however, the results are mixed. Direct materials have a $2,000 favorable flexible budget variance. Assembly has a $4,000 unfavorable flexible budget variance. The unit-level variable overhead variance is $7,000 favorable. The batch-level costs have a $100 unfavorable variance, and the fixed overhead variances (product level and facility level) have not changed since the static and flexible fixed budgets stay the same. The net flexible budget variance is $3,900 favorable, a substantial change from the static variance of $20,600 unfavorable. Notice that there are no

EXHIBIT 12-3

FLEXIBLE BUDGETS AND PERFORMANCE EVALUATION

McMillan Company
Production Department Performance Report
For the Month of July

	Based on Static Budget			Based on Flexible Budget		
	Actual	Original Budget	Static Budget Variance	Actual	Flexible Budget*	Flexible Budget Variance
Volume	11,000	10,000		11,000	11,000	
Unit level:						
Direct materials ..	$108,000	$100,000	$ 8,000 U	$108,000	$110,000	$2,000 F
Assembly	70,000	60,000	10,000 U	70,000	66,000	4,000 U
Waterproofing and						
inspection	81,000	80,000	1,000 U	81,000	88,000	7,000 F
Batch costs:						
Setup		4,000			4,400	
Test runs		1,000			1,100	
Total	5,600	5,000	600 U	5,600	5,500	100 U
Fixed overhead:						
Product	22,000	20,000	2,000 U	22,000	20,000	2,000 U
Facility	31,000	32,000	1,000 F	31,000	32,000	1,000 F
Totals	$317,600	$297,000	$20,600 U	$317,600	$321,500	$3,900 F

Flexible budget manufacturing costs: (Actual level × Budgeted unit cost)
Direct materials (11,000 units × 2 pounds × $5)
Assembly (11,000 units × 0.25 labor hour × $24)
Waterproofing and inspection (11,000 units × $8)
Setup (11 batches × $400)
Test runs (11 batches × $100)

budget variances for batch-level items because McMillan decided not to track them individually, a frequent option for smaller dollar items.

It should be obvious that the flexible budget variances provide a much better indicator of performance than do the static budget variances, which do not consider the increased level of production (11,000 units rather than 10,000 units). Almost anyone could have guessed that when production increases by 10 percent, the static budget variances would be unfavorable. Likewise, when actual production is substantially below the planned level of activity, the static variances are usually favorable. While it is important to isolate variances and explain their causes, the financial-based performance report is not the appropriate place to mix volume-created variances with those related to the actual production levels.

STANDARD COSTS

A **standard cost** indicates what it should cost to provide an activity or produce one batch or unit of product under planned and efficient operating conditions. In a standard costing environment, the flexible budget is based on standard unit costs. Traditionally, standard costs have been developed from an engineering analysis or from an analysis of historical data adjusted for expected changes in the product, production technology, or costs. When standards are developed using historical data, management must be careful to ensure that past inefficiencies are excluded from current standards. Target costing and continuous improvement costing (see Chapters 5, 9, and 11) can also be used to set standard costs. In target costing, an allowance for profit is subtracted from a desired selling price to determine the maximum allowable cost. In continuous improvement costing, the maximum allowable cost is set as the current cost less a target reduction in cost. What's Happening 12–4 examines performance reports based on continuous improvement costing.

To obtain the full benefit of standard costs, the standards must be based on realistic expectations. The standard variable product cost for assembly is $6.00 per unit. Some organizations intentionally set "tight" standards to motivate employees toward higher levels of production. The management of McMillan Company might set their standards for assembly at 0.22 hours per unit rather than at the expected 0.25 hours per unit, hoping that employees will strive toward the lower time and, consequently, the lower cost of $5.28 ($24 × 0.22). The use of tight standards often causes planning and behavioral problems. Management expects them to result in unfavorable variances. Accordingly, tight standards should not be used to budget input requirements and cash flows because management expects to incur more labor costs than the standards allow. The use of tight standards can have undesirable behavioral effects if lower-level managers and employees find that a second set of standards is used in the "real" budget or if they are constantly subject to unfavorable performance reports. These employees could come to distrust the entire budgeting and performance evaluation system, or they may quit trying to achieve any of the organization's standards.

Tight standards are more likely to occur in an imposed budget and less likely to occur in a participation budget for which employees are actively involved in preparing. In a participation budget, the problems may be to avoid loose standards that are easily attained and to avoid overstating the costs required to produce a product. Loose standards may fail to properly motivate employees and may make the company uncompetitive due to costs and prices that are higher than those of competitors.

| 12–4 | WHAT'S HAPPENING? |

KAIZEN COSTING CAN BE AN AGGRESSIVE TOOL IN VARIANCE ANALYSIS

Recall from Chapters 5 and 11 that continuous improvement costing, also known as *Kaizen costing*, takes target costing one step further in that it provides a means of ensuring continuous improvement activities after the target costs have been developed. It seems to reduce current costs below previous standard costs. Kaizen costing activities are defined as those activities that sustain the current level of existing production and are very specific with respect to each department and each accounting period.

The actual production costs of the prior period serve as the cost base of the current period. The target of the Kaizen method seeks to reduce the cost base during the current period. The ratio of the target reduction amount to the base amount is the target reduction rate. After the target reduction amount for each activity is determined, the actual cost of the activity is then compared to the target amounts for the computation of variances. For each activity being controlled, the process flows as follows (with example):

Item	Cost Base →	Continuous Improvement Target Ratio →	Continuous Improvement Target Costs →	Actual Costs →	Variance
Indirect labor (per day) . .	$14,000 ×	0.92	= $12,880	− $13,100	= $220 U

The key is the selection of the target ratio by members of management and the area or department involved with the activity. Once Kaizen costing is established for a period, it becomes a very aggressive tool for cost reduction.

Source: Yasuhiro Monden and John Lee, "How a Japanese Auto Maker Reduces Costs," *Management Accounting*, August 1993, pp. 22–26.

RELATIONAL AND DISCRETIONARY COST CENTERS

A distinction is often made between relational and discretionary cost centers. A **relational (cause-and-effect) cost center** has clearly defined relationships between effort and accomplishment. A **discretionary cost center** does not have clearly defined relationships between effort and accomplishment.

The financial performance of relational cost centers is evaluated with the aid of flexible budgets drawn up for the actual level of activity. A production department is the most obvious example of a relational cost center. The growth of services and service industries and the resultant need to control service costs, however, has led to an expanding use of relational cost centers in these types of organizations. Relational cost centers can be established for any segment of a business for which it is possible to develop output/input relationships and standard costs per unit or batch of activity. Possible applications include the costs of packaging, transportation, commissions, utilities, room cleaning, residential fire inspection, laundry, automobile repair, and processing loan applications.

Discretionary costs are set at a fixed amount at the judgment of management. Changing these costs does not affect production or service capacity in the short term. Because a relationship between effort and accomplishment is weak, the financial performance of a discretionary cost center cannot be evaluated with the aid of a flexible budget. Indeed, it is difficult to evaluate the performance of a discretionary cost center by any financial assessment means. The best monetary evaluation is based on a comparison of the actual and budgeted costs for a given period, with the results identified as being over or under the budget. This is an area for which nonfinancial measures are generally the best indicators of success. In a research and development department, the best assessments could be the number of successful new products developed, the quality improvements in existing products, and the number of new ideas generated (even though some could have failed).

If a research and development budget for 2002 contained authorized expenditures of $1.5 million but the actual 2002 expenditures amounted to $1.2 million, the $300,000 difference is not necessarily favorable. Research and development was $300,000 under budget. Whether this is good or bad depends on what was accomplished during the year. If the money was saved by canceling a program critical to the organization's future, the net result is hardly favorable. Again, all the variance does is inform management that actual results were not in line with plans. Management must investigate further to determine the significance of the variance. This is an area in which the use of nonfinancial performance measures can be beneficial.

Although it is difficult to evaluate the underbudget performance of a discretionary cost center, an overbudget performance has an undesirable implication, regardless of the results achieved. If, after the budget is approved, the manager of a discretionary cost center realizes the center's budget is inadequate, the manager should request additional funds or notify his or her supervisor of the need to reduce activity. Going over the budget implies that the manager is unable to operate within the budgeted resources. Obviously, a manager should not be allowed unlimited use of the organization's resources. Also, a cost center that was initially established as a discretionary cost center could be changed to a relational cost center once management determines the relationships between the center's operating costs and measures of its activity. A management that desires to better plan and control costs will encourage the evolution from discretionary to relational cost centers wherever practical.

LEARNING OBJECTIVE 3

VARIANCE ANALYSIS FOR PRIMARY VARIABLE COSTS

To use and interpret standard cost variances properly, managers must understand both the standard-setting process and the framework for computing and analyzing standard cost variances. While these are preliminary tools for decision analysis regarding activities and operations, they nevertheless give managers a starting point as to the general movement toward efficiency (or lack thereof) of the defined activities being evaluated. The variances alone do not explain, however, why the activity is different from expectations. Underlying causes of variances must always be investigated before final judgment is passed on the effectiveness and efficiency of an operation or activity. Later chapter sections consider possible explanations as to why variances occur in each area.

Standard cost variance analysis provides a system for examining the flexible budget variance, which is the difference between the actual cost and flexible budget cost of producing a given quantity of product or service. Actual cost is determined from the organization's economic transactions. Flexible budget cost is determined by multiplying standard quantities allowed for the output times the standard price per unit. In other words, the flexible budget can also be computed as actual output times standard unit cost. Recall that standard unit cost represents what it *should* cost to produce a completed unit of product or service under efficient operating conditions. To determine standard unit cost, management establishes separate quantity and price (or rate) standards for each input production component. Following activity-based costing (ABC) concepts, each manufacturing activity could have its own standard costs that focus on underlying concepts and cost drivers, and companies even develop their own set of variances as discussed in What's Happening 12–5. However, to provide a

---

12–5   WHAT'S HAPPENING?

BEING FLEXIBLE IN UTILIZING STANDARD COSTING CAN MEET MANAGEMENT NEEDS

The traditional variances presented in this text are not the only ones used by many companies. In fact, many companies develop their own variances to meet the needs of their managers when confronted with unusual activities. Such is the case with Parker Brass.

Two of the primary concerns of the production managers at Parker Brass concerned the timing of product cost information and providing an effective cost control system. As the managers were struggling with new and different decisions, they decided that additional information was needed to keep their decision making on the cutting edge. The company developed three new variances, standard run quantity variance, materials substitution variance, and method variance.

The standard run quantity variance measures the amount of setup cost that was not recovered because the batch size was smaller than the predetermined optimal batch size. Because the company had been including setup cost with labor, the managers were having difficulty explaining all of the labor variances. By pulling out the amounts related to batch sizes, the remainder of the analysis became easier to explain.

The materials substitute variance is relevant when the standard materials have to be substituted because of lack of inventory or because a customer wants something different than normal. This often helps explain both materials price variances and usage variances so these two variances do not have to be used to justify all differences between standard and actual cost.

The method variance is used when different machines or processes can be used to produce the same output. For example, if a process requires three labor hours and two machine hours but due to machine demand by other products, the process can be completed with seven labor hours and one machine hour, the resulting standard versus actual cost variances will be different even when all costs are perfectly controlled.

When managers know that the accounting system is flexible in helping them meet their decision demands, there is more coordination between those who develop the system and those who use it. Parker Brass has modified its standard costing system to better meet the needs of its managers without disrupting the traditional cost accounting system.

Source: David Johnsen and Parvez Sopariwala, "Standard Costing Is Alive and Well at Parker Brass, *Management Accounting Quarterly,* Winter 2000, pp. 12–20.

more defined focus, our illustrations use only one direct cost for assembly and three variable cost drivers for overhead.

Standard cost variance analysis identifies the general causes of the total flexible budget variance by breaking it into separate price and quantity variances for each production component. Two possible reasons that actual cost could differ from flexible budget cost for a given amount of output produced are (1) a difference between actual and standard prices paid for the production components—the price variance—and (2) a difference between the actual quantity and the standard quantity allowed for the production components—the quantity variance. It should be noted that the variances have different names for different cost categories, as follows:

Cost Component	Price Variance Name	Quantity Variance Name
Direct materials	Materials price variance	Materials quantity variance
Direct labor	Labor rate variance	Labor efficiency variance
Variable overhead	Variable overhead spending variance	Variable overhead effectiveness variance

Fixed overhead is excluded from the unit standard costs because, within the relevant range of normal activity, it does not vary with the volume of production. To facilitate product costing, however, many organizations develop a standard fixed overhead cost per unit.

In the following sections, we analyze the flexible budget cost variances for materials and labor (assembly); variable overhead analysis is covered in Appendix A of this chapter. Our illustration of variance analysis is based on the July activity and costs of McMillan Company's Production Department. There were 11 batches and 4,100 machine hours during the month.

McMillan Company—Production Department
Actual Manufacturing Costs
For the Month of July

Actual units completed	11,000

Manufacturing costs:
Unit level:

Direct materials (24,000 pounds × $4.50)	$108,000
Assembly (2,800 hours × $25.00)	70,000
Waterproofing and inspection	81,000
Batch level	5,600
Product level (fixed overhead)	22,000
Facility level (fixed overhead)	31,000
Total	$317,600

MATERIALS STANDARDS AND VARIANCES

The two basic elements contained in the standards for direct materials are the *standard price* and the *standard quantity*. Materials standards indicate how much an organization should pay for each input unit of direct materials and the quantity of direct materials it allows to produce one unit of output. The standard price per unit of direct materials should include all reasonable costs necessary to acquire the materials. These costs include the invoice price of materials, less planned discounts plus freight, insurance, special handling, and any other costs related to the acquisition of the materials. The standard quantity represents the number of units of raw materials allowed for the production of one unit of finished product. This amount should include the amount dictated by the physical characteristics of the process and the product, plus a reasonable allowance for normal spoilage, waste, and other inefficiencies. The quantity standard can be determined by engineering analysis, professional judgment, or by averaging the actual amount used for several periods. An average of actual past materials usage may not be a good standard because it could include excessive wastes and inefficiencies in the standard quantity.

McMillan Company has a direct materials quantity standard of 2.0 pounds per finished unit produced. In fact, each unit can physically contain only 1.8 pounds of raw materials, with the additional 0.2 pound representing the amount allowed by the standards for normal spoilage, waste, and other inefficiencies. This is an area for which the company could consider implementing quality cost analysis to see whether the situation can be improved.

The **materials price variance** is the difference between the actual materials cost and the standard cost of actual materials inputs. The **materials quantity variance** is the difference between the standard cost of actual materials inputs and the flexible budget cost for materials. The direct materials variances for McMillan Company follow.

Standard Cost Variance Analysis

Input component: Direct materials   **Output: 11,000 cases**

Actual Cost	Standard Cost of Actual Inputs	Flexible Budget Cost
Actual quantity (AQ) .. 24,000	Actual quantity (AQ) .. 24,000	Standard quantity allowed (SQ) .. 22,000*
Actual price (AP) .... × $4.50	Standard price (SP) ... × $5.00	Standard price (SP) .... × $5.00
$108,000	$120,000	$110,000

Materials price variance $12,000 F

Materials quantity variance $10,000 U

Total flexible budget materials variance $2,000 F

*11,000 units × 2 pounds per unit

McMillan Company had a favorable materials price variance of $12,000 because the actual cost of materials used ($108,000) was less than the standard cost of actual materials used ($120,000). Stated another way, for the materials actually used, the total price paid was $12,000 less than the price allowed by the standards. The price variance can also be viewed as the actual quantity (AQ) used times the difference between the actual price (AP) and the standard price (SP). McMillan Company paid $0.50 per pound below the standard price for 24,000 pounds for a total savings of $12,000. This is readily shown using the formula approach:

$$\text{Materials price variance} = AQ(AP - SP)$$
$$= 24{,}000(\$4.50 - \$5.00)$$
$$= 24{,}000 \times \$0.50$$
$$= \$12{,}000 \text{ F}$$

The unfavorable quantity variance of $10,000 occurred because the standard cost of actual materials used, $120,000 (24,000 × $5), was higher than the cost of materials allowed by the flexible budget, $110,000 (22,000 × $5). A total of 22,000 pounds of materials is allowed to produce 11,000 units of finished outputs. This is computed as 11,000 finished units times 2.0 pounds of direct materials per unit. The materials quantity variance can also be computed as the standard price (SP) per pound times the difference between the number of pounds actually used (AQ) and the number of pounds allowed (SQ). This is also readily shown using the formula approach:

$$\begin{aligned}
\text{Materials quantity variance} &= SP(AQ - SQ) \\
&= \$5(24{,}000 - 22{,}000) \\
&= \$5 \times 2{,}000 \\
&= \$10{,}000 \text{ U}
\end{aligned}$$

Interpreting Materials Variances.   After computing variances, managers must understand how to use them in making decisions relevant to the items being evaluated. A *favorable materials price variance* indicates that the employee responsible for materials purchases paid less per unit than the price allowed by the standards. This could result from receiving discounts for purchasing more than the normal quantities, effective bargaining by the employee, purchasing substandard-quality materials, purchasing from a distress seller, or other factors. Ordinarily, when a favorable price variance is reported, the employee's performance is interpreted as favorable. However, if the favorable price variance results from the purchase of materials of lower than standard quality (importance of value chain) or from a purchase in more than desirable quantities, the employee's performance would be questionable. Consistent and highly favorable variances could indicate situations that are undermining the responsibility accounting system by building slack into the standards or using incorrect data. These situations should be thoroughly investigated for causes and corrections.

An *unfavorable materials price variance* means that the purchasing employee paid more per unit for materials than the price allowed by the standards. This could be caused by failure to buy in sufficient quantities to receive normal discounts; purchase of higher-quality materials than called for in the product specifications; failure to place materials orders on a timely basis, thereby requiring a more expensive shipping alternative; uncontrollable price changes in the market for the materials; failure to bargain for the best available prices; or other factors. It should be emphasized that an unfavorable variance does not always mean that the employee performed unfavorably. Many noncontrollable factors surround the purchasing function due to timing problems, changing vendors, and changes in materials required by production.

A *favorable materials quantity variance* means that the actual quantity of raw materials used was less than the quantity allowed for the units produced. This could result from factors such as less materials waste than allowed by the standards, better than expected machine efficiency, direct materials of higher quality than required by the standards, and more efficient use of direct materials by employees. An *unfavorable materials quantity variance* occurs when the quantity of raw materials used exceeds the quantity allowed for the units produced. This could result from incurring more waste than provided for in the standards, poorly maintained machinery, requiring larger amounts of raw materials, raw materials of lower quality than required by the standards, or poorly trained employees who were unable to use the materials at the level of efficiency required by the standards.

The preceding examples of materials variances assumes an inventory system for which the amount of materials awaiting use in the production facilities is minimal. For situations in which substantial purchases occur in accounting periods other than the one in which the materials are used, a split materials variance is used. This method computes the materials price variance at the time of purchase rather than at the time of usage. The timing difference provides the manager an immediate evaluation of the purchasing function. The split method has no effect on the materials quantity variance; it is still computed at the time of usage. The split method is preferred when supply is scarce, prices fluctuate, or special purchase opportunities occur. Timely reporting of price variance information is often as necessary for making pricing decisions as it is for making other decisions based on current replacement costs. This is particularly true when you consider the relationships up and down the value chain and the impact prices (costs) have on other aspects of overall operations.

LABOR (ASSEMBLY) STANDARDS AND VARIANCES

To evaluate management performance in controlling labor costs by using a standard cost system, it is necessary to determine the *standard labor rate* for each hour allowed and the *standard time allowed* to produce a unit. Setting labor rate standards can be quite simple or extremely complex. If only one class of employee is used to make each product and if all employees have the same wage rate, determining the standard cost is relatively easy: Simply adopt the normal wage rate as the standard labor rate. If several different classes of employees are used to make each unit of product, separate efficiency and rate standards could be established for each class. If assembly is a combination of labor and automation, rates can vary as to skill of employee and complication of automation, and determining an overall rate could be more difficult. For McMillan Company, a weighted-average labor-automation rate is assumed.

The standard labor (assembly) time per unit can be determined by an engineering approach or an empirical observation approach. When using an engineering approach, industrial engineers ascertain the amount of time required to produce a unit of finished product by applying time and motion methods or other available techniques. Normal operating conditions are assumed in arriving at the labor standard. Therefore, allowances must be made for normal machine downtime, employee personal breaks, and so forth. Under the empirical approach, the long-run average time required in the past to produce a unit under normal operating conditions is used as a basis for the standard. Use of normal operating conditions automatically factors inefficiencies such as machine downtime and employee breaks into the standard.

Using the general variance model for materials, we can compute the labor rate and efficiency variances. The **labor rate (spending) variance** is the difference between the actual cost and the standard cost of actual labor inputs. The **labor efficiency variance** is the difference between the standard cost of actual inputs and the flexible budget cost for labor. These are known as the **assembly rate variance** and the **assembly efficiency variance** for which direct labor is a minor expense of assembly, as with the McMillian Company.

McMillan Company's assembly standards provide for 0.25 hour of assembly per unit produced. During July, 2,800 hours were assigned to assembly at a cost of $25 per hour. Using these data, the assembly rate (price) variance and assembly efficiency (quantity) variance can be computed as shown in the following illustration.

Standard Cost Variance Analysis

Input component: Assembly (direct labor)   **Output: 11,000 cases**

Actual Cost		Standard Cost of Actual Inputs		Flexible Budget Cost	
Actual hours (AH)	2,800	Actual hours (AH)	2,800	Standard hours allowed (SH)	2,750*
Actual rate (AR)	× $25	Standard rate (SR)	× $24	Standard rate (SR)	× $24
	$70,000		$67,200		$66,000

Assembly rate variance $2,800 U   Assembly efficiency variance $1,200 U

Total flexible budget assembly variance $4,000 U

11,000 units × 0.25 hour per unit

The assembly rate variance can also be computed in formula form as the actual number of hours used times the difference between the actual rate and the standard rate. The symbols are the same as in the diagram.

$$\text{Assembly rate variance} = AH(AR - SR)$$
$$= 2,800(\$25 - \$24)$$
$$= 2,800 \times \$1$$
$$= \$2,800\ U$$

This computation of the assembly rate variance shows that the company paid $1 more than the standard rate for each of the 2,800 hours worked. Stated another way, the assembly actually used was $2,800 more than allowed by the standards.

Since 11,000 units of product were finished during the period and 0.25 hour of assembly was allowed for each unit, the total number of standard hours allowed was 2,750. The assembly efficiency variance can also be computed as the standard rate times the difference between the actual assembly hours and the standard hours allowed for the output achieved:

$$\text{Assembly efficiency variance} = SR(AH - SH)$$
$$= \$24(2,800 - 2,750)$$
$$= \$24 \times 50$$
$$= \$1,200\ U$$

This computation of the assembly efficiency variance indicates that the company used 50 more assembly hours than the budget permitted and that each of these hours costs $24, or a total of $1,200 more than the standards allowed. Since our illustration avoids the use of more complicated evaluations with multiple drivers, a multiple driver example is provided in What's Happening 12–6. The approach in this illustration can be used for labor (assembly), direct labor, or variable overhead.

Interpreting Labor (Assembly) Variances. The possible explanations for labor (assembly) rate variances are rather limited. An *unfavorable labor rate variance* can be caused by the use of higher paid laborers or more expensive equipment than the standards provided. Also, a new labor union contract increasing wages could have been implemented after the standards were set. In this case, the standards should have been revised to account for the wage rate change. In a nonunion situation when a negotiated contract does not control wages, a manager could arbitrarily increase employee wages above the standard rate. This also can cause an unfavorable labor rate variance. A *favorable labor rate variance* occurs if lower paid workers or less expensive equipment (part of value chain) was used or if actual wage rates declined.

Unfavorable labor efficiency variances occur when workers or machines require more than the number of hours allowed by the standards to produce a given amount of output. This could be caused by a management decision to use poorly trained workers or poorly maintained machinery or by downtime resulting from the use of low-quality materials. Low employee morale and generally poor working conditions could also adversely affect the efficiency of workers, resulting in an unfavorable labor efficiency variance.

A *favorable labor efficiency variance* occurs when fewer hours are used than are allowed by the standards. This above-normal efficiency can be caused by the company's use of higher skilled (and higher paid) workers, better machinery, or raw materials of higher quality than the standards provided. High employee morale, improved job satisfaction, or generally improved working conditions could also account for the above-normal efficiency of the workers.

It is important to understand the potential interactive effect of the use of labor, direct materials, and machinery on the overall efficiency of the production process.

MULTIPLE COST DRIVERS ARE USED IN HIGHLY AUTOMATED SETTING

Supporting a highly structured activity-based reporting system usually requires the performance reports to indicate, to the extent possible, all relevant cost drivers associated with the activities being evaluated. This is a very popular approach in highly automated settings such as those of Hewlett-Packard, Advanced Micro Devices, AT&T, and IBM. In these manufacturing environments, labor, as a cost driver, does not dominate. The manufacture and assembly of products are completed in distinct stages, each somewhat independent of all others. To illustrate this type of setting, assume that an operating department has three automated processes performing three different tasks. The variances for each activity could be presented as follows:

Standard Cost Variance Analysis

Input component: Materials fabrication   **Output: 100 units**

Activity	Actual Cost	Standard Cost of Actual Inputs			Flexible Budget Cost		
Cutting	$ 3,400	160 cuts	× $20.00 =	$ 3,200	150 cuts	× $20.00 =	$ 3,000
Shaping . . .	7,100	8,000 turns	× $ 0.90 =	7,200	8,100 turns	× $ 0.90 =	7,290
Fitting	18,000	80,000 fittings	× $ 0.20 =	16,000	63,700 fittings	× $ 0.20 =	12,740
	$28,500			$26,400			$23,030

Activity spendings:		Activity efficiencies:	
Cutting	$ 200 U	Cutting	$ 200 U
Shaping . . .	100 F	Shaping . . .	90 F
Fitting	2,000 U	Fitting	3,260 U
Total spending variance	$2,100 U	Total efficiency variance	$3,370 U

Total flexible budget variance $5,470 U

Source: James M. Reeve, "Projects, Models, and Systems—Where Is ABM Headed?" *Journal of Cost Management,* Summer 1996, pp. 5–16.

These three factors must be combined efficiently to produce a unit of finished product of optimal quality. The quality of one factor usually affects the efficiency in using the other two components. Because of these interactive relationships, the interpretation of one variance is often interrelated with the interpretation of other variances. As a result of these relationships, some companies have begun to use procedure variances as discussed in Research Shows 12–3. Seldom are there clear-cut and isolated explanations for each variance reported. Because of complexities of this sort, using variances is far more challenging than computing them.

OVERHEAD STANDARDS AND VARIANCES

The traditional unit-level approach usually separates overhead costs into fixed and variable elements for control purposes. This separation is necessary because the variance between actual costs and expected costs is caused by different factors for fixed and variable costs. Unlike direct materials costs, which represent specific cost components, manufacturing overhead represents *groups* of different costs. Consequently, setting standards is often more difficult for overhead costs than it is for materials costs. For mixed manufacturing overhead costs (those that have variable and fixed components),

| 12-3 | **RESEARCH SHOWS** |

INCREASED USE OF MIX VARIANCES SUPPORT BETTER DECISION MAKING

According to the author of a recent article, it is not easy for some companies to divide their costs into direct materials, direct labor, and overhead. In these cases, the use of the mixed cost concept is helpful. Sales mix has been used for years to explain why actual revenues differed from the budget (i.e. the proportion of products sold was different from the proportion of products that was planned to be sold). Mix is also used in direct materials variances when the actual mix of materials in a product, per customers' requests, differs from what was planned per engineering specifications.

If customer satisfaction is upmost on a company's list of objectives, the mix of materials, labor, and overhead is likely to vary from the plans for the period. To avoid using only material, labor, and overhead variances, cost activities (procedures) are defined and their own variances determined. The standards set for a given procedure might include 5 units of materials, 8 hours of labor, 3 hours of machine time, 45 minutes of computer time, and 10 minutes of testing time. At the end of the period, the actual activity mix is determined along with the total costs for all procedures. This is then compared to the standards with at least part of the variance explained by any differences in the activity mix.

The author concludes that oversimplification of costs into material, labor, and overhead, along with the two behavior categories of variable and fixed, is not enough for today's decision makers. There must be more use of mix variances and evaluations because "significant costs must be modeled more accurately in order for management accounting systems to better support executive deliberation and decision making."

Source: Kennard T. Wing, "Using Enhanced Cost Models in Variance Analysis for Better Control and Decision Making," *Management Accounting Quarterly,* Winter 2000, pp. 27–35.

an estimation technique, such as the high-low method, regression analysis (least-squares), or scatter diagram, is often used to separate the fixed and variable overhead components. (These techniques were discussed in Chapter 2.) If management concludes that the observations used in estimating variable costs reflect normal operating conditions, managers will probably adopt the estimate as the standard variable cost.

Because it includes many heterogeneous costs, manufacturing overhead poses a unique problem in measuring standard quantity and standard price. Direct materials have a natural physical measure of quantity such as tons, barrels, pounds, and liters. Similarly, labor or assembly is measurable in hours. However, no single quantity measure is common to all overhead items. Overhead is a cost group that can simultaneously include costs measurable in hours, pounds, liters and kilowatts.

To deal with the problem of multiple quantity measures in variable manufacturing overhead, most companies use an artificial (substitute) measure of quantity for all items in a given group. Typical substitute measures are machine hours, units of finished product, direct labor hours, and direct labor dollars. The variable overhead standard is then stated in terms of this single-factor base, and the amount of variable overhead budgeted is based on this artificial activity measure. A detailed discussion of both variable and fixed overhead standards and variances is included in the appendices to this chapter.

In recent years, some organizations have used hierarchical approaches to overhead variance analysis. This approach, although somewhat complex, allows the manager to analyze: unit level, batch level, and product level costs and activities.[1]

---

[1]For a detailed discussion of this topic, refer to an article by Jack M. Ruhl, "Activity-Based Variance Analysis," *Journal of Cost Management,* Winter 1995, pp. 38–47.

LEARNING OBJECTIVE 4   **PERFORMANCE REPORTS FOR REVENUE CENTERS**

The financial performance reports for revenue centers (defined earlier) include a comparison of actual and budgeted revenues, with the difference identified as a variance similar to those of the cost centers. Controllable costs can be deducted from revenues to obtain some bottom-line contribution margin. If the center is then evaluated on the basis of this contribution, it is being treated as a profit center.

If the organization is to meet its budgeted profit goal for a period, with its budgeted fixed and variable costs, the organization's revenue centers must meet their original revenue budgets. Consequently, the original budget (a static budget) rather than a flexible budget is used to evaluate the financial performance of revenue centers.

Assume that McMillan Company's July sales budget for cases called for the sale of 10,000 units at $40 each. If McMillan Company actually sold 11,000 units at $39 each, the total revenue variance is $29,000:

$$
\begin{array}{lr}
\text{Actual revenues (11,000} \times \text{\$39)} & \text{\$429,000} \\
\text{Budgeted revenues (10,000} \times \text{\$40)} & \underline{(400,000)} \\
\text{Revenue variance} & \underline{\text{\$ 29,000}} \text{ F}
\end{array}
$$

The **revenue variance** is the difference between the budgeted sales volume at the budgeted selling price and the actual sales volume at the actual selling price. Because actual revenues exceeded budgeted revenues, the revenue variance is favorable. It can be presented as follows:

Revenue variance = (Actual volume × Actual price) − (Budgeted volume × Budgeted price)

After the revenue variance is computed, the impact of changing prices and volume on revenue is then analyzed with the sales price and sales volume variances. The **sales price variance** is computed as the change in selling price times the actual sales volume:

Sales price variance = (Actual selling price − Budgeted selling price) × Actual sales volume

For McMillan, the sales price variance for July is as follows:

$$
\begin{aligned}
\text{Sales price variance} &= (\$39 - \$40) \times 11{,}000 \text{ units} \\
&= \$11{,}000 \text{ U}
\end{aligned}
$$

The **sales volume variance** indicates the impact of the change in sales volume on revenues, assuming there was no change in selling price. The sales volume variance is computed as the difference between the actual and the budgeted sales volumes times the budgeted selling price:

Sales volume variance = (Actual sales volume − Budgeted sales volume) ×
Budgeted selling price

For McMillan, the sales volume variance for July would be as follows:

$$
\begin{aligned}
\text{Sales volume variance} &= (11{,}000 \text{ units} - 10{,}000 \text{ units}) \times \$40 \\
&= \$40{,}000 \text{ F}
\end{aligned}
$$

Notice that the net of the sales price and the sales volume variances is equal to the revenue variance:

Sales price variance	$11,000 U
Sales volume variance	40,000 F
Revenue variance	$29,000 F

The interpretation of these variances is subjective. In this case, we could say that if the increase in sales volume had not been accompanied by a decline in selling price, revenues would have increased $40,000 (1,000 units × $40) instead of $29,000. The $1 per unit decline in selling price cost the company $11,000 in revenues. Alternatively, we might note that a $1 reduction in the unit selling price was more than offset by an increase in sales volume. An economic analysis could explain the relationship as volume being sensitive to price (price elasticity).

In any case, variances are merely signals that actual results are not proceeding according to plan. They help managers identify potential problems and opportunities. An investigation into their cause(s) could even indicate that a manager who received a favorable variance was doing a poor job, whereas a manager who received an unfavorable variance was doing an outstanding job. Consider McMillan Company's favorable revenue variance. This occurred because actual sales exceeded budgeted sales by 1,000 units (10 percent), which on the surface indicates good performance. But what if the total market for the company's products exceeded the company's forecast by 15 percent? In this case, McMillan Company's sales volume falls below its expected percentage share of the market; the favorable variance could occur (despite a poor marketing effort) because of strong customer demand that competitors could not fill.

INCLUSION OF CONTROLLABLE COSTS

Controllable costs should also be considered when evaluating the overall performance of revenue centers. A failure to consider costs could encourage uneconomic selling practices, such as excessive advertising and entertaining, and spending too much time on small accounts. The controllable costs of revenue centers include variable and fixed selling costs. These costs are sometimes further classified into order-getting and order-filling costs. **Order-getting costs** are incurred to obtain customers' orders (for example, advertising, salespersons' salaries and commissions, travel, telephone, and entertainment). **Order-filling costs** are incurred to place finished goods in the hands of purchasers (for example, storing, packaging, and transportation).

The performance of a revenue center in controlling costs can be evaluated with the aid of a flexible budget drawn up for the actual level of activity. Assume that the McMillan Company's July budget for the Sales Department calls for fixed costs of $10,000 and variable costs of $5 per unit sold. If the actual fixed and variable selling expenses for July are $9,500 and $65,000, respectively, the total cost variances assigned to the Sales Department are $9,500 unfavorable. In evaluating the Sales Department's performance as both a cost center and a revenue center, management would consider these cost variances as well as the revenue variances shown in Exhibit 12–4. Note that although the revenue variances are based on the original budget, the cost variances are based on the flexible budget.

REVENUE CENTERS AS PROFIT CENTERS

Even though we have computed revenue and cost variances for McMillan's Sales Department, we are still left with an incomplete picture of this revenue center's performance. Is the Sales Department's performance best represented by the $29,000 favorable revenue variance, by the $9,500 unfavorable cost variance, or by the net favorable variance of $19,500 ($29,000 F − $9,500 U)? Actually, it is inappropriate to attempt to obtain an overall measure of the Sales Department's performance by combining these separate revenue and cost variances. The combination of revenue and cost variances is appropriate only for a profit center; so far, we have left out one important cost that must be assigned to the Sales Department before it can be treated as a profit center. That cost is the *standard variable cost of goods sold.*

As a profit center, the Sales Department acquires units from the Production Department and sells them outside the firm. Its total responsibilities include revenues, the standard variable cost of goods sold, and actual selling expenses. Note that the Sales Department is assigned the *standard,* rather than the *actual, variable cost of goods sold.* Because the Sales Department does not control production activities, it

EXHIBIT 12-4

SALES DEPARTMENT PERFORMANCE REPORT

McMillan Company
Sales Department Performance Report
For the Month of July

	Based on Static Budget			Based on Flexible Budget		
	Actual	**Original Budget**	**Static Budget Variance**	**Actual**	**Flexible Budget***	**Flexible Budget Variance**
Revenue:						
Units	11,000	10,000	1,000 F			
Dollars	$429,000	$400,000	$29,000 F			
Selling expenses:						
Variable				$65,000	$55,000	$10,000 U
Fixed				9,500	10,000	500 F
Total				$74,500	$65,000	$ 9,500 U

Flexible budget formulas:
  Sales ($40 per unit)
  Variable selling expenses ($5 per unit)
  Fixed selling expenses ($10,000 per month)

should not be assigned actual production costs. Doing so results in passing the Production Department's variances on to the Sales Department. Fixed manufacturing costs are not assigned to the Sales Department because short-run variations in sales volume do not normally affect the total amount of these costs.

To evaluate the Sales Department as a profit center, the net sales volume variance must be computed. The **net sales volume variance** indicates the impact of a change in sales volume on the contribution margin given the budgeted selling price *and* the standard variable costs. It is computed as the difference between the actual and the budgeted sales volumes times the budgeted unit contribution margin.

$$\text{Sales volume variance} = (\text{Actual volume} - \text{Budgeted volume}) \times \text{Budgeted contribution margin}$$

Using the $40 budgeted selling price, the standard costs presented for the product (see example introduction on page 524), and the standard variable selling expenses from Exhibit 12–4, the budgeted contribution margin is $10.50, computed as follows:

Sales			$40.00
Direct materials		$10.00	
Assembly		6.00	
Variable manufacturing overhead:			
Unit level	$8.00		
Batch level	0.50*	8.50	
Selling	. . . .	5.00	29.50
Contribution margin			$10.50

For simplicity because production is in complete batches of 1,000 units, we are combining unit- and batch-level costs ($0.40 + $0.10).

Using the formula presented, the net sales volume variance is computed as follows:

$$\text{Net sales volume variance} = (11,000 - 10,000) \times \$10.50$$
$$= \$10,500 \text{ F}$$

As a profit center, the Sales Department has responsibility for the sales price variance, the sales volume variance, and any cost variances associated with its operations. For July, these cost variances net to $11,340 unfavorable:

Sales price variance	$11,000 U
Net sales volume variance	10,500 F
Selling expense variance	9,500 U
Sales Department variances, net	$10,000 U

In an attempt to improve their overall performance, managers often commit themselves to unfavorable variances in some areas, believing that these variances will be more than offset by favorable variances in other areas. In the case preceding, the favorable sales volume variance appears not to have been sufficient to offset the price reductions and the higher selling expenses. Also note that the more complete evaluation of the Sales Department as a profit center (with a $10,000 unfavorable variance) gives a very different impression than the evaluation of the Sales Department as a pure revenue center (with a $29,000 favorable variance) or as a revenue center responsible only for its own direct costs (with a $9,500 unfavorable cost variance).

Summary

Responsibility accounting is the structuring of performance reports addressed to individual members of an organization in a manner that emphasizes the factors that each member controls. Each organization unit for which performance reports are prepared is identified as a *responsibility center*. Each of these units has a manager responsible for the activities in, and the performance of, the unit. For the purpose of evaluating their financial performance, responsibility centers are classified as *investment centers, profit centers, revenue centers*, or *cost centers*. An *investment center* manager is responsible for the relationship between its profits and the total assets invested in the center. A *profit center* manager is responsible for the difference between revenues and costs. Although a *revenue center* manager is responsible for generating sales revenue, the manager is often assigned responsibility for the controllable costs incurred in generating revenues. The manager of a *cost center*, which is often further classified as either a standard or discretionary cost center, is financially responsible only for the occurrence of costs.

Cost centers that have a predictable relationship between production inputs and outputs often use standard costs for controlling costs and evaluating manager performance. Standard cost systems require that cost standards be developed for each type of product (or service) and that they include standard unit costs for materials, labor, and overhead. Periodically, actual costs are compared with standard costs, and cost variances are reported to managers for possible corrective action. The performance of a standard cost center is evaluated by comparing actual costs with the costs allowed in a flexible budget drawn up for the actual level of activity.

A *discretionary cost center* does not have clearly defined relationships between activity and accomplishment. It is evaluated, for accounting purposes, by comparing the actual and budgeted costs for a given period. The difference is identified as over- or underbudget.

Variance analysis involves breaking down flexible budget variances into specific variances caused by price and quantity departures from standards. Both price and quantity variances are reported for labor (assembly), materials, and variable overhead.

Appendix A

VARIABLE OVERHEAD VARIANCES

To illustrate the computation of variable factory overhead variances, assume that McMillan Company's standard unit-level variable overhead costs for waterproofing and inspection (see page 524) consist of the following:

Variable Overhead Cost Item	Quantity Consumed per Pound of Direct Materials	Standard Cost per Pound of Direct Materials*
Indirect materials:		
Sealant coating	2 fluid ounces	$1.10
Hinge lubricants	3 milliliters	0.40
Indirect labor:		
Inspection workers	6 minutes	2.50
Total variable cost per pound of direct materials used		$4.00

Standard unit-level variable overhead requires 2 pounds of direct materials at $4 per pound for a standard overhead cost per unit of $8. Management assigns 2 pounds of materials as the best base for measuring this part of related costs.

The general model for computing standard cost variances for materials and labor can also be used in computing variable overhead variances. The actual costs of inputs, such as indirect materials, indirect labor, and utilities, are ordinarily obtained, however, directly from the accounting records rather than being computed as quantity times cost.

The **variable overhead spending variance** is the difference between the actual variable overhead cost and the standard variable overhead cost for the actual inputs of the measurement base. The **variable overhead effectiveness variance** is the difference between the standard variable overhead cost for the actual inputs of the measurement base and the flexible budget cost allowed for variable overhead based on outputs.

For McMillan Company, the actual unit variable overhead for waterproofing and inspection is $81,000. This represents the actual cost of overhead items such as indirect materials. Since actual variable overhead is expected to vary with pounds of direct materials used, the standard cost of actual inputs is calculated as actual pounds of materials (AP) times the standard variable overhead rate per pound (SRP):

$$\text{Standard cost of actual inputs} = (AP \times SRP)$$
$$= 24,000 \times \$4$$
$$= \$96,000$$

The flexible budget cost for variable overhead allowed for the actual outputs is based on the 22,000 pounds of materials allowed (SP) for the units produced during the period (11,000 units × 2 pounds). The allowed quantities are multiplied by the standard prices (SRP). The resulting variable overhead flexible budget cost is $88,000:

$$\text{Flexible budget cost} = (SP \times SRP)$$
$$= 22,000 \times \$4$$
$$= \$88,000$$

Using these data, the variable overhead spending (price) variance and the variable overhead effectiveness (quantity) variance are shown as follows.

Standard Cost Variance Analysis

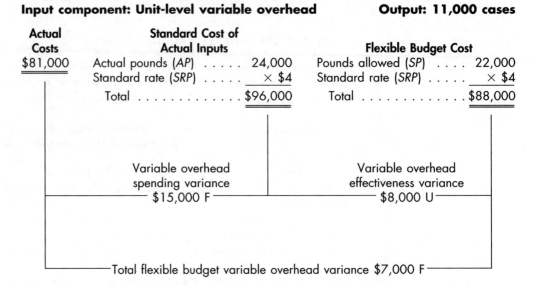

Input component: Unit-level variable overhead **Output: 11,000 cases**

Actual Costs	Standard Cost of Actual Inputs		Flexible Budget Cost	
$81,000	Actual pounds (AP)	24,000	Pounds allowed (SP)	22,000
	Standard rate (SRP)	× $4	Standard rate (SRP)	× $4
	Total	$96,000	Total	$88,000

Variable overhead spending variance $15,000 F

Variable overhead effectiveness variance $8,000 U

Total flexible budget variable overhead variance $7,000 F

An alternative to the computation of the variable overhead effectiveness variance is as follows:

$$\text{Variable overhead effectiveness variance} = SRP(AP - SP)$$
$$= \$4(24,000 - 22,000)$$
$$= \$8,000 \text{ U}$$

This approach emphasizes that the 2,000 extra pounds saved should have increased variable overhead savings by $8,000 at the standard rate of $4 per pound.

INTERPRETING VARIABLE OVERHEAD VARIANCES

A *favorable spending variance* encompasses all factors that cause actual expenditures to be less than the amount expected for the actual inputs of the measurement base, including consumption and payment. Conversely, an *unfavorable spending variance* results when the actual expenditures are more than expected for the inputs of the measurement base. This is caused by consuming more overhead items than expected, or by paying more than the expected amount for overhead items consumed, or by both. Thus, the term *spending variance* is used instead of *price variance*.

The key to understanding the variable overhead spending variance is recognizing that the amount of variable overhead cost allowed is determined by the level of the measurement bases used. Any deviation from this spending budget—due to uncontrolled or mismanaged variable overhead price or quantity variables—causes a spending variance to occur.

The variable overhead effectiveness variance measures the difference between the standard variable overhead cost for the actual use of the measurement base and the standard variable overhead cost for the allowed use of the measurement base. This variance measures the amount of variable overhead that should have been saved (or incurred) because of the efficient (or inefficient) use of the measurement base. It provides no information about the degree of efficiency in using variable overhead items such as indirect materials and indirect labor. This information is reflected in the spending variance. Because of the connection of the efficiency variance to material quantity or machine or labor (assembly) efficiency, the effectiveness variance label will always be the same as the material quantity or machine or labor (assembly) efficiency variance; favorable material quantity results in favorable overhead effectiveness, and vice versa.

Appendix B

FIXED OVERHEAD VARIANCES

By definition, the quantity of goods and services purchased by fixed expenditures is not expected to change in proportion to short-run changes in the level of production. For example, in the short run, the production level does not affect the amount of depreciation on buildings, the number of fixed salaried employees, or the amount of real property subject to property taxes. Whether the organization produces 10,000 or 15,000 cases, the same quantity of fixed overhead is expected to be incurred, as long as the production level is within the relevant range of activity provided by the current fixed overhead items. Therefore, an effectiveness variance is ordinarily not computed for fixed overhead costs.

Even though the components of fixed overhead are not expected to be affected by the production activity level in the short run, the actual amount spent for fixed overhead items can differ from the amount budgeted by management. For example, higher than budgeted supervisors' salaries could be paid, longer than normal working shifts could cause heating or cooling costs to exceed budget, and price increases could cause the amounts paid for equipment to be higher than expected. Fixed overhead costs in excess of the amount budgeted are reflected in the fixed overhead budget variance. The **fixed overhead budget variance** is the difference between budgeted and actual fixed overhead. Using the facility-level fixed costs of McMillan Company as an example:

$$\text{Fixed overhead budget variance} = \text{Actual fixed overhead} - \text{Budgeted fixed overhead}$$
$$= \$31,000 - \$32,000$$
$$= \$1,000 \text{ F}$$

The fixed overhead budget variance is always the same as the total fixed overhead flexible budget variance. Because budgeted fixed overhead is the same for all outputs within the relevant range, the budget variance explains the total flexible budget variance between actual and allowed fixed overhead. Similar to variable overhead, fixed overhead variances can be caused by a combination of price and quantity factors.

Recall that predetermined overhead rates are computed by dividing the predicted overhead costs for the period by the predicted activity of the period. The motivation for using a standard fixed overhead rate is the same as the motivation for using a predetermined overhead rate; namely, quicker product costing and smoothing the workload of the cost accountants. Furthermore, the use of a standard fixed overhead rate results in assigning identical fixed costs to identical products, regardless of when they are produced during the year.

When a standard fixed overhead rate is used, total fixed overhead costs assigned to production behave as variable costs. As production increases, the total fixed overhead assigned to production increases. Because total budgeted fixed overhead does not vary, differences arise between budgeted and assigned fixed overhead, and managers often inquire about the cause of the differences.

The standard fixed overhead rate is computed as the budgeted fixed costs divided by some budgeted standard level of activity. Since budgeted fixed overhead is the same for all levels of output (within the relevant production range), the standard fixed overhead rate varies, depending on the budgeted level of activity. To simplify the illustration, assume that McMillan develops its standard fixed overhead rate monthly, instead of annually, and that it bases the rate on a budgeted activity level of 4,000 machine hours per month for facility-level costs. The standard fixed overhead rate per machine hour is $8.

Standard fixed overhead rate = Budgeted total fixed overhead ÷ Budgeted activity level

$$= \$32,000 \div 4,000 \text{ hours}$$

$$= \$8 \text{ per machine hour}$$

The total fixed overhead assigned to production is computed as the standard rate of $8 multiplied by the standard hours allowed for the units produced. Therefore, the assigned fixed overhead cost equals the budgeted monthly fixed overhead cost only if the allowed activity equals the budgeted activity of 4,000 hours. If the company operates less than 4,000 hours, the fixed overhead assigned to production is less than the $32,000 budgeted; if it operates more than 4,000 hours, the fixed overhead assigned to production is more than the amount budgeted.

Even though total fixed overhead is not affected by production below or above the standard activity level, the fixed overhead assigned to production increases at the rate of $8 per allowed machine hour. The difference between total budgeted fixed overhead and total standard fixed overhead assigned to production is called the **fixed overhead volume variance.** This variance is sometimes referred to as the **capacity variance,** a term that emphasizes the maximum output of an operation. The fixed overhead volume variance indicates neither good nor poor performance by the production personnel. Instead, it indicates the difference between the activity allowed for the actual output and the budget level used as the denominator in computing the standard fixed overhead rate.

To explain the difference between actual fixed overhead and standard fixed overhead assigned to production, two fixed overhead variances are computed and illustrated for McMillan: the fixed overhead budget variance and the fixed overhead volume variance. The fixed overhead budget variance represents the difference between actual fixed overhead and budgeted fixed overhead. The budget variance is caused by a combination of price and quantity factors related to the use of fixed overhead goods and services (e.g., depreciation, insurance, supervisors' salaries). The $1,000 favorable budget variance for McMillan was caused either by using fewer quantities of fixed overhead goods and services, or by paying lower prices than expected for those items, or both.

The volume variance represents the difference between budgeted and assigned fixed overhead and is caused by a difference between the activity level allowed for the actual output and the budgeted activity used in computing the fixed overhead rate. The $3,200 favorable volume variance for McMillan indicates that the activity level allowed for the actual output was more than the budgeted activity level. As previously stated, this variance ordinarily cannot be used to control costs. If the budgeted activity is based on production capacity, an unfavorable variance alerts management that facilities are underutilized, and a favorable variance alerts management that facilities are utilized above their expectations.

Standard Cost Variance Analysis

Input component: Fixed manufacturing overhead   **Output: 11,000 cases**

Actual Cost	**Budgeted Cost**	**Budgeted Cost Assigned**

Actual hours (AH) . . . .   NA*   Budgeted hours (BH) . . .   4,000*   Standard hours allowed (SH) . . . . .   4,400†
Actual rate (AR) . . . . . .   × NA   Standard price (SP) . . .   × 8   Standard price (SP) . . . .   × $8
                             $31,000 $32,000 $35,200

Fixed overhead
budget variance
——— $1,000 F‡ ———

Fixed overhead
volume variance
——— $3,200 F ———

———Total fixed manufacturing overhead variance $4,200 F———

*Not applicable
†11,000 units × 0.40
‡Also the flexible budget fixed overhead variance

Appendix C

RECONCILING BUDGETED AND ACTUAL INCOME

It is possible to reconcile the difference between budgeted and actual net income for an entire organization. This can be done either by (1) assigning all costs and revenues to responsibility centers and summarizing the financial performance of each responsibility center or (2) developing a detailed reconciliation of actual and budgeted costs and revenues for the organization as a whole (see cost accounting texts for this approach). McMillan Company's budgeted and actual income statements, in a contribution format, for July are presented in Exhibit 12–5.

Following the first reconciliation approach, assume that McMillan Company contains three responsibility centers: a Production Department, a Sales Department, and an Administration Department. Also assume that the Production and the Administration Departments are cost centers, and the Sales Department is a profit center. The Production Department's variances, as itemized in Exhibit 12–3, net to $3,900 F. The Sales Department's variances itemized in Exhibit 12–6 net to $10,000 U. The only variance for the Administration Department is the $200 difference between actual and budgeted fixed administrative costs ($3,800 actual − $4,000 budget). Because the Administration Department is a discretionary cost center, this variance is best identified as being underbudget. For consistency in the performance reports, however, it is labeled favorable. By assigning all variances to these three responsibility centers, the reconciliation of budgeted and actual income is as shown in Exhibit 12–6.

EXHIBIT 12-5

BUDGETED AND ACTUAL INCOME STATEMENTS: CONTRIBUTION FORMAT

McMillan Company
Budgeted Income Statement
For the Month of July

Sales (10,000 units × $40)			$400,000
Less variable costs:			
Variable cost of goods sold:			
Direct materials (10,000 units × $10)	$100,000		
Assembly (10,000 units × $6)	60,000		
Manufacturing overhead*	85,000	$245,000	
Selling (10,000 units × $5)		50,000	(295,000)
Contribution margin			$105,000
Less fixed costs:			
Manufacturing overhead†		$ 52,000	
Selling		10,000	
Administrative		4,000	(66,000)
Net income			$ 39,000

*Unit (20,000 pounds × $4) + Batch [(10 batches × $400) + 10 batches × $100] = $85,000.
†Product ($20,000) + Facility ($32,000) = $52,000

McMillan Company
Actual Income Statement
For the Month of July

Sales (11,000 units × $39)			$429,000
Less variable costs:			
Variable cost of goods sold:			
Direct materials	$108,000		
Assembly	70,000		
Manufacturing overhead*	86,600	$264,600	
Selling		65,000	(329,600)
Contribution margin			$ 99,400
Less fixed costs:			
Manufacturing overhead†		$ 53,000	
Selling		9,500	
Administrative		3,800	(66,300)
Net income			$ 33,100

*Unit ($81,000) + Batch ($5,600) = $86,600
†Product ($22,000) + Facility ($31,000) = $53,000

EXHIBIT 12-6

RECONCILIATION OF BUDGETED AND ACTUAL INCOME

McMillan Company
Actual Income Statement
For the Month of July

Budgeted net income $39,000
Sales department variances:
   Sales price variance . . . . ($39 − $40) × 11,000 = $11,000 U
   Net sales volume variance . . . . (11,000 − 10,000) × $10.50* = 10,500 F
   Variable expense variance . . . . (11,000 × $5) − $65,000 = 10,000 U
   Fixed expense variance . . . . $9,500 − $10,000 =   500 F   10,000 U
Production department variances . . . . See Exhibit 12–4   3,900 F
Administration department variances . . . . $3,800 − $4,000 =   200 F

Actual net income $33,100

The budgeted variable cost per unit includes production costs of $24.50 and selling expenses of $5.00. The variable production costs are computed as the total budgeted variable costs in the original budget divided by budgeted production ($245,000 ÷ 10,000 = $24.50). See Exhibit 12–3.

Review Problem

The solution to this problem is found on pages 566–567. To maximize your learning, you should make a serious attempt to develop a written solution to the review problem before looking at the solution. If there are errors in your solution, you should then attempt to determine their causes.

Standard Cost Variance Analysis

The flexible budget performance report for Sunset Enterprises Inc. for March follows. The company manufactures only one product, folding chairs.

	Actual Costs	Flexible Budget Cost	Flexible Budget Variances
Output units	5,000	5,000	
Direct materials	$104,125	$100,000	$ 4,125 U
Direct labor	82,400	75,000	7,400 U
Variable manufacturing overhead:			
Category 1	31,000	30,000	1,000 U
Category 2	18,000	20,000	2,000 F
Fixed manufacturing overhead	42,000	40,000	2,000 U
Total	$277,525	$265,000	$12,525 U

The standard unit cost for folding chairs is as follows:

Direct materials (4 pounds × $5.00 per pound) $20
Direct labor (1.25 hours × $12.00 per hour) 15
Variable overhead, Category 1 (1.25 hours × $4.80) 6
Variable overhead, Category 2 ($4 per finished unit) 4
Total standard variable cost per unit $45

Actual cost of materials is based on 21,250 pounds of direct materials purchased and used at $4.90 per pound; actual cost of assembly is based on 7,000 labor hours. Variable overhead is applied on labor hours for Category 1 and finished units for Category 2.

Required:
a. Calculate all standard cost variances for direct materials and direct labor.
b. Calculate all standard cost variances for variable manufacturing overhead (Appendix A).

Key Terms

Assembly efficiency variance (p. 533)
Assembly rate variance (p. 533)
Cost center (p. 521)
Discretionary cost center (p. 528)
Flexible budget variance (p. 525)
Flexible budgets (p. 523)
Investment center (p. 523)
Labor efficiency variance (p. 533)
Labor rate (spending) variance (p. 533)
Materials price variance (p. 531)
Materials quantity variance (p. 531)
Net sales volume variance (p. 539)
Order-filling costs (p. 538)
Order-getting costs (p. 538)
Organization structure (p. 516)
Profit center (p. 523)
Relational (cause-and-effect) cost center (p. 528)
Responsibility accounting (p. 515)

Revenue center (p. 522)
Revenue variance (p. 537)
Sales price variance (p. 537)
Sales volume variance (p. 537)
Standard cost (p. 526)
Standard cost variance analysis (p. 529)
Static budget (p. 523)
Variance (p. 523)

Appendix Key Terms
Capacity variance (p. 544)
Fixed overhead budget variance (p. 543)
Fixed overhead volume variance (p. 544)
Variable overhead effectiveness variance (p. 541)
Variable overhead spending variance (p. 541)

Review Questions

1. What is responsibility accounting? Why should noncontrollable costs be excluded from performance reports prepared in accordance with responsibility accounting?
2. How can responsibility accounting lead to unethical practices?
3. Responsibility accounting reports must be expanded to include what nonfinancial areas? Give some examples of nonfinancial measures.
4. What is a cost center? Give some examples.
5. How is a cost center different from either an investment or a profit center?
6. What problems can result from the use of tight standards?
7. Distinguish between a relational cost center and a discretionary cost center.
8. What is a standard cost variance, and what is the objective of variance analysis?
9. Standard cost variances can usually be broken down into two basic types of variances. Identify and describe these two types of variances.
10. Identify possible causes for (1) a favorable materials price variance; (2) an unfavorable materials price variance; (3) a favorable materials quantity variance; and (4) an unfavorable materials quantity variance.
11. How is standard assembly (labor) time determined? Explain the two ways.

12. In the standard cost system, what is the appropriate treatment of a change in wage rates (per new labor union contract) that dominate the cost of assembly?
13. Explain the difference between the revenue variance and the sales price variance.
14. Explain the net sales volume variance and list its components.
15. Explain the difference between how the *actual costs* and the *standard cost of actual inputs* are computed in variable overhead analysis. (Appendix A)
16. Explain what the fixed overhead volume variance measures. (Appendix B)
17. In this chapter, what method is used to reconcile budgeted and actual income? What elements are used in the reconciliation? (Appendix C)

Exercises

**12-1
Responsibility
Accounting Reports**

Teapot Café, a developer and manager of a chain of tea houses in Europe and Australia, has not had good financial results for the last few years. The organization was changed from a president/vice president model, to one with a CEO and two division presidents who are in charge of the company's two main geographic regions, Europe and Australia. The actual and allowed costs (in thousands) of each division and their key costing centers for last year were as follows:

	Actual Cost	Allowed Cost
Europe headquarters	$155,000	$150,000
Australia headquarters	296,000	300,000
Operations (vice president):		
Europe	735,400	730,000
Australia	944,000	940,000
Advertising (manager):		
Europe	13,500	15,900
Australia	14,000	13,400
Supplies/other (manager):		
Europe	13,000	20,000
Australia	34,000	35,000

Each division was to provide a measure of success based on the number of customers, customer satisfaction, and the share of local market. The company's goal was to have average occupancy per café during the peak tea times of 70 percent during the morning hours and 85 percent during the afternoon hours. Customer satisfaction goals were 90 percent and 94 percent, respectively, for Europe and Australia. For the year under review, the market share for European cafés was expected to reach 10 percent of the market, while the Australian cafés were expected to reach 15 percent.

	Actual Activity
Café occupancy:	
Europe: AM	55%
PM	83
Australia: AM	71
PM	88
Customer satisfaction:	
Europe	78
Australia	95
Market share:	
Europe	8
Australia	15

Required:
a. Develop for the CEO of Teapot Café a responsibility accounting report that includes both financial and nonfinancial measures.
b. What problem areas might you point out to the CEO?

12-2
Flexible Budgets and Performance Evaluation

Presented is the January performance report for the Production Department of Thompson Company.

Thompson Company
Production Department Performance Report
For the Month of January

	Actual	Budget	Variance
Volume	30,000	28,000	
Manufacturing costs:			
Direct materials	$ 89,600	$ 84,000	$ 5,600 U
Assembly	165,000	140,000	25,000 U
Variable overhead	64,000	56,000	8,000 U
Fixed overhead	27,500	28,000	500 F
Total	$346,100	$308,000	$38,100 U

Required:
a. Evaluate the performance report.
b. Prepare a more appropriate performance report.

12-3
Materials Variances

Assume that Lenscrafters uses standard costs to control the materials in its made-to-order sunglasses. The standards call for 2 ounces of material for each pair of lens. The standard cost per ounce of material is $15. During July, the Palm Beach location produced 4,800 pairs of sunglasses and used 8,800 ounces of materials. The cost of the materials during July was $15.20, and there were no beginning or ending inventories.

Required:
a. Determine the flexible budget materials cost for the completion of the 4,800 pairs of glasses.
b. Determine the actual materials cost incurred for the completion of the 4,800 pairs of glasses and compute the total materials variance.
c. How much of the difference between the answers to requirements (a) and (b) was related to the price paid to purchase the materials?
d. How much of the difference between the answers to requirements (a) and (b) was related to the quantity of materials used?

12-4
Materials Price Variance Based on Purchases and Usage

Charleston Company manufactures decorative weather vanes that have a standard cost of $1.50 per pound for direct materials used in the manufacturing process. During September, 11,000 pounds of materials were purchased at $1.55 per pound, and 10,000 pounds were actually used in making 4,800 weather vanes. There were no beginning inventories.

Required:
a. Determine the materials price variance, assuming that it is determined when materials are purchased.
b. Determine the materials price variance, assuming that it is determined when materials are used.
c. Determine the materials quantity variance if the standard materials for each weather vane is 2 pounds. Does the price variance method influence the computation of the quantity variance? Explain.
d. Discuss the issues involved in determining the price variance at the point of purchase versus the point of consumption.

12–5
Direct Labor
Variances

Assume that Nortal manufactures specialty electronic circuitry through a unique photo-electronic process. One of the primary products, Model ZX40, has a standard labor time of 0.5 hour and a standard labor rate of $13.50 per hour. During February, the following activities pertaining to direct labor for ZX40 were recorded:

Direct labor hours used 2,150
Direct labor cost $34,000
Units of ZX40 manufactured 4,600

Required:
a. Determine the labor rate variance.
b. Determine the labor efficiency variance.
c. Determine the total flexible budget labor cost variance.

12–6
Direct Labor
Variances

Assume that Springs Mills, Inc., operates its Charlotte plant using a combination of hourly and incentive wage programs for production employees. The guaranteed minimum wage is $14 per hour but with incentive outputs, the wage can increase to $22 per hour. For dye processing, the standard output per hour is 1,000 pounds of yarn processed and dyed. During June, the dye process had an average wage rate of $16 with 920,000 pounds of dyed yarn completing production. Production hours totaled 950.

Required:
a. Compute rate and efficiency variances using the minimum wage.
b. Compute rate and efficiency variance using the maximum wage with incentives.
c. Why does changing the standard used for the hourly rate change the efficiency variance?
d. Explain which set of variances is most useful for management.

12–7
Assembly Variances

Assume that 3M Company figures standard assembly cost with direct labor hours as the cost driver. Standard assembly cost has been set at $10 per unit of output based on 2 hours allowed to produce each finished unit. Last month, 3,000 direct labor hours were used, and 1,400 units of output were manufactured at an assembly cost of $16,000.

Required:
a. Determine the assembly spending variance.
b. Determine the assembly efficiency variance.
c. If the company used fewer direct labor hours than those reflected in the standards, in which variance would the resulting cost savings be reflected? Explain.

12–8
Causes for
Variances (including
appendices)

During January, Mayday Company reported the following variances in the production of flagpoles, its only product.

1. Materials price variance
2. Materials quantity variance
3. Labor rate variance
4. Labor efficiency variance
5. Variable overhead spending variance
6. Variable overhead efficiency variance
7. Fixed overhead budget variance

Required:
a. Identify the variances that are caused primarily by price factors.
b. Identify the variances that are caused primarily by quantity usage factors.
c. Identify the variances that are caused by both price and quantity factors.

12–9
Setting Standards

Oconee Inc. has just completed one month's testing of a new machine. The manufacturer listed the operating capacity of the machine at 100 feet of material per hour if operated by a skilled employee using top-quality materials. During the month, Oconee used some of its highly skilled employees and medium grade materials (the best price at the time). Test results produced 88 feet per hour on average. Oconee's average work force is 25 percent highly skilled, 65 percent skilled, and 10 percent trainees. Historically, skilled employees work 20 percent faster than trainees and 10 percent slower than the highly skilled employees. All workers will be trained to operate the new equipment.

Required:
What should Oconee set as the standard output per hour? Justify with assumptions as necessary.

12–10
Sales Variances

Presented is information pertaining to an item sold by Winding Creek General Store:

	Actual	Budget
Unit sales	150	125
Unit selling price	$26	$25
Unit standard variable costs	(20)	(20)
Unit contribution margin	$ 6	$ 5
Revenues	$3,900	$3,125
Standard variable costs	(3,000)	(2,500)
Contribution margin at standard costs	$ 900	$ 625

Required:
Compute the revenue, sales price, and the sales volume variances net sales variance.

12–11
Sales Variances

Assume that Casio sells handheld communication devices for $100 during August as a back-to-school special. The normal selling price is $150. The standard variable cost for each device is $70. Sales for August had been budgeted for 400,000 units nationwide; however, due to the slowdown in the economy, sales were only 340,000.

Required:
Compute the revenue, sales price, and the sales volume variance.

12–12
Variable Overhead Variances (Appendix A)

Assume that the best cost driver that Intel has for variable factory overhead in the assembly department is machine hours. During April, the company budgeted 480,000 machine hours and $5,000,000 for its Texas plant's assembly department. The actual variable overhead incurred was $5,200,000, which was related to 490,000 machine hours.

Required:
a. Determine the variable overhead spending variance.
b. Determine the variable overhead effectiveness variance.

12–13
Variable Overhead Variances (Appendix A)

Tea Leaf Company bases standard variable overhead cost on direct labor hours as the cost driver. Standard variable overhead cost has been set at $15 per unit of output based on $5 of variable overhead per direct labor hour for 3 hours allowed to produce 1 finished unit. Last month, 4,300 direct labor hours were used, and 1,400 units of output were manufactured. The following actual variable overhead costs were incurred:

Indirect materials	$ 4,500
Indirect labor	8,200
Utilities	5,800
Miscellaneous	3,500
Total variable overhead	$22,000

Required:

a. Determine the variable overhead spending variance.
b. Determine the variable overhead effectiveness variance.
c. How is the variable overhead effectiveness variance related to labor efficiency?
d. If the company used smaller quantities of indirect materials than those reflected in the standards, in which variance would the resulting cost savings be reflected? Explain.

12–14
Fixed Overhead
Variances
(Appendix B)

Gainesville Company uses standard costs for cost control and internal reporting. Fixed costs are budgeted at $7,500 per month at a normal operating level of 10,000 units of production output. During October, actual fixed costs were $7,900, and actual production output was 9,500 units.

Required:

a. Determine the fixed overhead budget variance.
b. Assume that the company applied fixed overhead to production on a per-unit basis. Determine the fixed overhead volume variance.
c. Was the fixed overhead budget variance from requirement (a) affected because the company operated below the normal activity level of 10,000 units? Explain.
d. Explain the possible causes for the volume variance computed in requirement (b). How is reporting of the volume variance useful to management?

12–15
Fixed Overhead
Variances
(Appendix B)

Assume that Phillips Petroleum uses a standard cost system for each of its refineries. For the Tulsa refinery, the monthly fixed overhead budget is $21,000,000 for a planned output of 10,000,000 barrels. For September, the actual fixed cost was $22,000,000 for 11,000,000 barrels. The Tulsa refinery's capacity is 12,000,000 barrels.

Required:

a. Determine the fixed overhead budget variance.
b. If fixed overhead is applied on a per-barrel basis, determine the volume variance.
c. What is the refinery's capacity variance?

12–16
Reconciling
Budgeted and
Actual Income
(Appendix C)

Fromer Company is a merchandising firm that buys and sells a single product. Presented is information from Fromer's 2004 and 2003 income statements.

	2004	2003
Unit sales	220,000	250,000
Sales revenue	$770,000	$750,000
Cost of goods sold	(506,000)	(500,000)
Gross profit	$264,000	$250,000

Required:

a. Reconcile the variation in sales revenue using appropriate sales variances. Use 2003 as the base or standard.
b. Reconcile the variation in gross profit using appropriate sales and cost variances. Use 2003 as the base or standard.

**12-17
Causes of Standard
Cost Variances
(Comprehensive)**

Following are ten unrelated situations that would ordinarily be expected to affect one or more standard cost variances:

1. A salaried production supervisor is given a raise, but no adjustment is made in the labor cost standards.
2. The materials purchasing manager gets a special reduced price on raw materials by purchasing a train carload. A warehouse had to be rented to accommodate the unusually large amount of raw materials. The rental fee was charged to Rent Expense, a fixed overhead item.
3. An unusually hot August caused the company to use 25,000 kilowatts more electricity than provided for in the variable overhead standards.
4. The local electric utility company raised the charge per kilowatt-hour. No adjustment was made in the variable overhead standards.
5. The plant manager traded in his leased company car for a new one in July, increasing the monthly lease payment by $150.
6. A machine malfunction on the assembly line (caused by using cheap and inferior raw materials) resulted in decreased output by the machine operator and higher than normal machine repair costs. Repairs are treated as variable overhead costs.
7. The production maintenance supervisor decreased routine maintenance checks, resulting in lower maintenance costs and lower machine production output per hour. Maintenance costs are treated as fixed costs.
8. An announcement that vacation benefits had been increased resulted in improved employee morale. Consequently, raw materials pilferage and waste declined, and production efficiency increased.
9. The plant manager reclassified her secretary to administrative assistant and gave him an increase in salary.
10. A union contract agreement calling for an immediate 5 percent increase in production worker wages was signed. No changes were made in the standards.

Required:
For each of these situations, indicate by letter which of the following standard cost variances would be affected. More than one variance will be affected in some cases.

a. Materials price variance.
b. Materials quantity variance.
c. Labor rate variance.
d. Labor efficiency variance.
e. Variable overhead spending variance.
f. Variable overhead efficiency variance.
g. Fixed overhead budget variance.

Problems

**12-18
Multiple Product
Performance Report**

Creative Products manufactures two models of cassette tape storage cases: regular and deluxe. Presented is standard cost information for each model:

	Regular		Deluxe	
Direct materials:				
Lumber	2 board feet × $3 =	$ 6.00	3 board feet × $3 =	$ 9.00
Assembly kit	=	2.00	=	2.00
Assembly	1 hour × $4 =	4.00	1.25 hours × $4 =	5.00
Variable overhead	1 labor hr. × $2 =	2.00	1.25 labor hrs. × $2 =	2.50
Total		$14.00		$18.50

Budgeted fixed manufacturing overhead is $15,000 per month. During July, Creative Products produced 5,000 regular and 3,000 deluxe storage cases while incurring the following manufacturing costs:

Direct materials	$ 80,000
Assembly	34,000
Variable overhead	16,000
Fixed overhead	17,500
Total	$147,500

Required:

Prepare a flexible budget performance report for the July manufacturing activities.

12–19
Computation of Variable Cost Variances

The following information pertains to the standard costs and actual activity for Tyler Company for September:

Standard cost per unit:
Direct materials . . . . 4 units of material A × $2.00 per unit
1 unit of material B × $3.00 per unit
Direct labor . . . . 3 hours × $8.00 per hour
Activity for September:
Materials purchased:
  Material A . . . . 4,500 units × $2.05 per unit
  Material B . . . . 1,100 units × $3.10 per unit
Materials used:
  Material A . . . . 4,150 units
  Material B . . . . 1,005 units
Direct labor used . . . . 2,950 hours × $8.20 per hour
Production output . . . . 1,000 units

There were no beginning direct materials inventories.

Required:

a. Determine the materials price and quantity variances.
b. Determine the labor rate and efficiency variances.

12–20
Variance Computations and Explanations

Outdoor Company manufactures camping tents from a lightweight synthetic fabric. Each tent has a standard materials cost of $20, consisting of 4 yards of fabric at $5 per yard. The standards call for 2 hours of assembly at $12 per hour.

The following data were recorded for October, the first month of operations:

Fabric purchased . . . . 9,000 yards × $4.90 per yard
Fabric used in production of 1,700 tents . . . . . 7,000 yards
Direct labor used . . . . 3,600 hours × $12.50 per hour

Required:

a. Compute all standard cost variances for materials and assembly.
b. Give one possible reason for each of the preceding variances.
c. Determine the standard variable cost of the 1,700 tents produced, separated into direct materials and assembly.

12–21
Determining Unit Costs, Variance Analysis, and Interpretation (including Appendix A)

Harmon Company, a manufacturer of dog food, produces its product in 1,000-bag batches. The standard cost of each batch consists of 8,000 pounds of direct materials at $0.30 per pound, 48 direct labor hours at $8.50 per hour, and variable overhead cost (based on machine hours) at the rate of $10 per hour with 16 machine hours per batch.

The following variable costs were incurred for the last 1,000-bag batch produced:

Direct materials . . . . 8,200 pounds costing $2,378 were purchased and used
Direct labor . . . . 45 hours costing $450
Variable overhead $200
Machine hours used 18

Required:
a. Determine the actual and standard variable costs per bag of dog food produced, separated into direct materials, direct labor, and variable overhead.
b. For the last 1,000-bag batch, determine the standard cost variances for direct materials, direct labor, and variable overhead.
c. Explain the possible causes for each of the variances determined in requirement (b).

12–22
Computation of Variances and Other Missing Data (including Appendix A)

The following data for O'Keefe Company pertain to the production of 300 units of Product X during December. Selected data items are omitted.

Direct materials (all materials purchased were used during period):
  Standard cost per unit: (a) pounds at $3.20 per pound
  Total actual cost: (b) pounds costing $5,673
  Standard cost allowed for units produced: $5,760
  Materials price variance: (c)
  Materials quantity variance: $96 U
Direct labor:
  Standard cost: 2 hours at $7.00
  Actual cost per hour: $7.25
  Total actual cost: (d)
  Labor rate variance: (e)
  Labor efficiency variance: $140 U
Variable overhead:
  Standard costs: (f) hours at $4.00 per direct labor hour
  Actual cost: $2,250
  Variable overhead spending variance: (g)
  Variable overhead efficiency variance: (h)

Required:
Complete the missing amounts lettered (a) through (h).

12–23
Measuring the Effects of Decisions on Standard Cost Variances (Comprehensive)

The following five unrelated situations affect one or more standard cost variances for materials, labor (assembly), and overhead:

1. Lois Jones, a production worker, announced her intent to resign to accept another job paying $1.20 more per hour. To keep Lois, the production manager agreed to raise her salary from $7.00 to $8.50 per hour. Lois works an average of 175 regular hours per month.
2. At the beginning of the month, a supplier of a component used in our product notified us that, because of a minor design improvement, the price will be increased by 15 percent above the current standard price of $100 per unit. As a result of the improved design, we expect the number of defective components to decrease by 80 units per month. On average, 1,200 units of the component are purchased each month. Defective units are identified prior to use and are not returnable.
3. In an effort to meet a deadline on a rush order in Department A, the plant manager reassigned several higher-skilled workers from Department B, for a total of 300 labor hours. The average salary of the Department B workers was $1.85 more than the standard $7.00 per hour rate of the Department A workers. Since they

were not accustomed to the work, the average Department B worker was able to produce only 36 units per hour instead of the standard 48 units per hour. (Consider only the effect on Department A labor variances.)

4. Rob Celiba is an inspector who earns a base salary of $700 per month plus a piece rate of 20 cents per bundle inspected. His company accounts for inspection costs as manufacturing overhead. Because of a payroll department error in June, Rob was paid $500 plus a piece rate of 30 cents per bundle. He received gross wages totaling $1,100.

5. The materials purchasing manager purchased 5,000 units of component K2X from a new source at a price $12 below the standard unit price of $200. These components turned out to be of extremely poor quality with defects occurring at three times the standard rate of 5 percent. The higher rate of defects reduced the output of workers (who earn $8 per hour) from 20 units per hour to 15 units per hour on the units containing the discount components. Each finished unit contains one K2X component. To appease the workers (who were irate at having to work with inferior components), the production manager agreed to pay the workers an additional $0.25 for each of the components (good and bad) in the discount batch. Variable manufacturing overhead is applied at the rate of $4 per direct labor hour. The defective units also caused a 20-hour increase in total machine hours. The actual cost of electricity to run the machines is $2 per hour.

Required:

For each of the preceding situations, determine which standard cost variance(s) will be affected, and compute the amount of the effect for one month on each variance. Indicate whether the effect is favorable or unfavorable. Assume that the standards are not changed in response to these situations. (Round calculations to two decimal places.)

12–24
Fixed Overhead
Budget and
Volume Variance
(Appendix B)

Starling Company assigns fixed overhead costs to inventory for external reporting purposes by using a predetermined standard overhead rate based on direct labor hours. The standard rate is based on a normal (or denominator) activity level of 10,000 standard allowed direct labor hours per year. There are five standard allowed hours for each unit of output. Budgeted fixed overhead costs are $200,000 per year. During 2004, Starling Company produced 2,100 units of output, and actual fixed costs were $205,000.

Required:

a. Determine the standard fixed overhead rate used to assign fixed costs to inventory.
b. Determine the amount of fixed overhead assigned to inventory in 2004.
c. Determine the fixed overhead budget variance.
d. Determine the fixed overhead volume variance.
e. Even though the cost of security guards is controlled as a fixed cost, the number of hours worked by the guards could fluctuate somewhat. If the number of hours worked by the guards in 2004 had been smaller, which fixed overhead variance would have been affected? Explain. If the wage rate for security guards had increased during the year (with no revision of the standard), which variance would have been affected? Explain.
f. What information does the fixed overhead volume variance computed convey to management?

12–25
Profit Center
Performance Report
(Appendix C)

Record Rack is a store that specializes in the sale of recordings of classical music. Due to a recent upsurge in the popularity of J. S. Bach's works, Record Rack has established a separate room, Bach's Concert Room, dealing only in recordings of Bach's music. The cd's are purchased from a wholesaler for $4.25 each. Although the standard retail price is $7.75 per cd, the manager of Bach's Concert Room can undertake price reductions and other sales promotions in an attempt to increase sales volume. With the exception of the cost of cd's, the operating costs of Bach's Concert Room are fixed.

Presented are the budgeted and the actual August contribution statements of Bach's Concert Room.

Record Rack—Bach's Concert Room
Budgeted and Actual Contribution Statements
For the Month of August

	Actual	Budget
Unit sales	4,200	4,000
Unit selling price	$7.25	$7.75
Sales revenue	$30,450	$31,000
Cost of goods sold	(17,850)	(17,000)
Gross profit	$12,600	$14,000
Operating costs	(5,000)	(6,000)
Contribution to corporate costs and profits	$ 7,600	$ 8,000

Required:

Compute variances to assist in evaluating the performance of Bach's Concert Room as a profit center. Use these variances to reconcile the budgeted and actual contribution to corporate costs and profits. Was the performance satisfactory? Explain.

12-26
Comprehensive
Performance Report

Presented are the budgeted and actual contribution income statements of World Encyclopedia, Limited, for October.

World Encyclopedia contains three responsibility centers: a Production Department, a Sales Department, and an Administration Department. Both the Production and Administration Departments are cost centers, and the Sales Department is a profit center.

World Encyclopedia, Limited
Budgeted Contribution Income Statement
For the Month of October

Sales (900 × $300)			$270,000
Less variable costs:			
Variable cost of goods sold:			
Direct materials (900 × $50)	$45,000		
Direct labor (900 × $20)	18,000		
Manufacturing overhead (900 × $30)	27,000	$ 90,000	
Selling (900 × $70)		63,000	(153,000)
Contribution margin			$117,000
Less fixed costs:			
Manufacturing overhead		$ 40,000	
Selling		50,000	
Administrative		10,500	(100,500)
Net income			$ 16,500

World Encyclopedia, Limited
Actual Contribution Income Statement
For the Month of October

Sales (1,000 × $320)			$320,000
Less variable costs:			
Cost of goods sold:			
Direct materials	$50,000		
Direct labor	22,000		
Manufacturing overhead	35,000	$107,000	
Selling		100,000	(207,000)
Contribution margin			$113,000
Less fixed costs:			
Manufacturing overhead		$ 38,000	
Selling		65,000	
Administrative		12,000	(115,000)
Net income (loss)			$ (2,000)

Required:

a. Prepare a performance report for the Production Department that compares actual and allowed costs.
b. Prepare a performance report for selling expenses that compares actual and allowed costs.
c. Determine the sales price and the net sales volume variances.
d. Prepare a report that summarizes the performance of the Sales Department.
e. Determine the amount by which the Administration Department was over- or under budget.
f. Prepare a report reconciling budgeted and actual net income. Your report should focus on the performance of each responsibility center.

Discussion Questions and Cases

12–27
Discretionary Cost Center Performance Reports

Buggywhip Products had been extremely profitable at the turn of the twentieth century, but the company has been "whipped" in recent years by competition and a failure to introduce new consumer products. In 1998, Tom Bright became head of Consumer Products Research (CPR) and began a number of product development projects. Although the group had good ideas that led to the introduction of several promising products at the start of 2003, Bright was criticized for poor cost control. The financial performance reports for CPR under Bright's leadership were consistently unfavorable. Management was quite concerned about cost control because profits were low, and the company's cash budget indicated that additional borrowing would be required throughout 2003 to cover out-of-pocket costs.

Because of his inability to exert proper cost control, Bright was relieved of his responsibilities in 2003, and John Tight became head of Consumer Products Research. Tight vowed to improve the performance of CPR and scaled back CPR's development activities to obtain favorable financial performance reports.

By the end of 2004, Buggywhip Products had improved its market position, profitability, and cash position. At this time, the board of directors promoted Tight to president, congratulating him for the contribution CPR made to the revitalization of the company, as well as his success in improving the financial performance of CPR. Tight assured the board that the company's financial performance would improve even more in the future as he applied the same cost-reducing measures that had worked so well in CPR to the company as a whole.

Required:

a. For the purpose of evaluating financial performance, what responsibility center classification should be given to the Consumer Products Research Department? What unique problems are associated with evaluating the financial performance of this type of responsibility center?

b. Compare the performances of Bright and Tight in the role as head of Consumer Products Research. Did Tight do a much better job, thereby making him deserving of the promotion? Why or why not?

**12–28
Discretionary Cost
Center Performance
Reports**

The budget for the Literature Department of Classic University is set by the dean of the School of Liberal Arts in consultation with the chairperson of the Literature Department. It is a line item budget with separate appropriations for such things as faculty salaries, secretarial support, travel, research, equipment, and instructional supplies. The budget for each year is a function of the budget for the previous year, with an adjustment for certain items that were funded at an excess or inadequate level during the previous year.

The chairperson has done a good job in controlling most departmental costs, but the dean is concerned about the chairperson's inability to keep instructional supplies in line with the budget. Prior to meeting with the dean to discuss the 2004 departmental budget, the chairperson developed the following summary of the financial performance of the Literature Department in controlling the cost of instructional supplies:

Classic University—Literature Department
Summary of Financial Performance for Instructional Supplies
For the Years 2000–2004

	Student Enrollment	Actual	Budget	Budget Variance
2000	4,500	$15,500	$12,000	$3,500 U
2001	6,000	20,000	13,750	6,250 U
2002	5,250	17,750	16,875	875 U
2003	6,300	20,900	16,438	4,462 U
2004	5,500	18,500	18,669	169 F

Required:
Comment on the financial performance of the Literature Department. What budgetary planning and control problem is illustrated by the given data?

**12–29
Evaluating
Alternative Sales
Compensation Plans**

Pre-Fab Corporation, a relatively large company in the manufactured housing industry, is known for its aggressive sales promotion campaigns. Pre-Fab's innovative advertising and sales strategies have resulted in generally satisfactory performance in the last few years.

One of Pre-Fab's objectives is to increase sales revenue by at least 10 percent annually. This objective has been obtained. Return on investment is considered good and had increased annually until last year when net income decreased for the first time in nine years. The latest economic recession could be the cause of the change, but other factors, such as sales growth, discount this reason.

A significant portion of Pre-Fab's administrative expenses are fixed, but the majority of the manufacturing expenses are variable in nature. The increases in selling prices have been consistent with the 12 percent increase in manufacturing expenses. Pre-Fab has consistently been able to maintain a companywide contribution margin of approximately 30 percent. However, the contribution margin on individual product lines varies from 15 to 45 percent.

Sales commission expenses increased 30 percent over the past year. The prefabricated housing industry has always been sales-oriented, and Pre-Fab's management has believed in generously rewarding the efforts of its sales personnel. The sales force compensation plan consists of three segments:

- A guaranteed annual salary, which is increased by about 6 percent per year. The salary is below industry average.
- A sales commission of 9 percent of total sales dollars. This is higher than the industry average.
- A year-end bonus of 5 percent of total sales dollars to each salesperson when his or her total sales dollars exceed the prior year by at least 12 percent.

The current compensation plan has resulted in an average annual income of $62,500 per sales employee, compared with an industry annual average of $50,000. The compensation plan has been effective in generating increased sales. Further, the Sales Department employees are satisfied with the plan. Management, however, is concerned about the financial implications of the current plan. They believe the plan has caused higher selling expenses and a lower net income relative to the sales revenue increase.

At the last staff meeting, the controller suggested that the sales compensation plan be modified so that sales employees could earn an annual average income of $57,500. The controller believed that such a plan would still be attractive to its sales personnel and, at the same time, allow the company to earn a more satisfactory profit.

The vice president for sales voiced strong objection to altering the current compensation plan because employee morale and incentive would drop significantly if there were any change. Nevertheless, most of the staff believed that the area of sales compensation merited a review. The president stated that all phases of a company operation can benefit from a periodic review, no matter how successful they have been in the past.

Several compensation plans known to be used by other companies in the manufactured housing industry are:

- Straight commission as a percentage of sales
- Straight salary
- Salary plus compensation based on sales to new customers
- Salary plus compensation based on contribution margin
- Salary plus compensation based on unit sales volume

Required:
a. Discuss the advantages and disadvantages of Pre-Fab Corporation's current sales compensation plan with respect to (1) the financial aspects of the company and (2) the behavioral aspects of the sales personnel.
b. For each of the alternative compensation plans known to be used by other companies in the manufactured housing industry, discuss whether the plan would be an improvement over the current plan in terms of (1) the financial performance of the company and (2) the behavioral implications for the sales personnel.

(CMA Adapted)

12–30
Developing Cost
Standards for
Materials and Labor

After several years of operating without a formal system of cost control, Carlsen Company, a tools manufacturer, has decided to implement a standard cost system. The system will first be established for the department that makes lug wrenches for automobile mechanics. The standard production batch size is 100 wrenches. The actual materials and labor required for eight randomly selected batches from last year's production are as follows:

Batch	Materials Used (in pounds)	Labor Used (in hours)
1	504.0	10.00
2	508.0	9.00
3	506.0	9.00
4	521.0	5.00
5	516.0	8.00
6	518.0	7.00
7	520.0	6.00
8	515.0	8.00
Average	513.5	7.75

Management has obtained the following recommendations concerning what the materials and labor quantity standards should be:

- The manufacturer of the equipment used in making the wrenches advertises in the toolmakers' trade journal that the machine Carlsen uses can produce 100 wrenches with 500 pounds of direct materials and 5 labor hours. Carlsen's engineers believe the standards should be based on these facts.
- The Accounting Department believes more realistic standards would be 504 pounds and 5 hours.
- The production supervisor believes the standards should be 513.5 pounds and 7.75 hours.
- The production workers argue for standards of 525 pounds and 8 hours.

Required:
a. State the arguments for and against each of the recommendations, as well as the probable effects of each recommendation on the quantity variance for materials and labor.
b. Which recommendation provides the best combination of cost control and motivation to the production workers? Explain.

12-31
Behavioral Effect of Standard Costs

Delaware Corp. has used a standard cost system for evaluating the performance of its responsibility center managers for three years. Top management believes that standard costing has not produced the cost savings or increases in productivity and profits promised by the accounting department. Large unfavorable variances are consistently reported for most cost categories, and employee morale has fallen since the system was installed. To help pinpoint the problem with the system, top management asked for separate evaluations of the system by the plant department manager, the accounting department manager, and the personnel department manager. Their responses are summarized here.

Plant Manager—The standards are unrealistic. They assume an ideal work environment that does not allow materials defects or errors by the workers or machines. Consequently, morale has gone down and productivity has declined. Standards should be based on expected actual prices and recent past averages for efficiency. Thus, if we improve over the past, we receive a favorable variance.

Accounting Manager—The goal of accounting reports is to measure performance against an absolute standard and the best approximation of that standard is ideal conditions. Cost standards should be comparable to "par" on a golf course. Just as the game of golf uses a handicap system to allow for differences in individual players' skills and scores, it could be necessary for management to interpret variances based on the circumstances that produced the variances. Accordingly, in one case, a given unfavorable variance could represent poor performance; in another case, it could represent good performance. The managers are just going to have to recognize these subtleties in standard cost systems and depend on upper management to be fair.

Personnel Manager—The key to employee productivity is employee satisfaction and a sense of accomplishment. A set of standards that can never be met denies managers of this vital motivator. The current standards would be appropriate in a laboratory with a controlled environment but not in the factory with its many variables. If we are to recapture our old "team spirit," we must give the managers a goal that they can achieve through hard work.

Required:

Discuss the behavioral issues involved in Delaware Corp.'s standard cost dilemma. Evaluate each of the three responses (pros and cons) and recommend a course of action.

12–32
Evaluating a
Companywide
Performance Report

Mr. Micawber, the production supervisor, bursts into your office, carrying the company's 2004 performance report and thundering, "There is villainy here, sir! And I shall get to the bottom of it. I will not stop searching until I have found the answer! Why is Mr. Heep so down on my department? I thought we did a good job last year. But Heep claims my production people and I cost the company $31,500! I plead with you, sir, explain this performance report to me."

Trying to calm Micawber, you take the report from him and ask to be left alone for 15 minutes. The report is as follows:

Crupp Company, Limited
Performance Report
For the Year 2004

	Actual	Budget	Variance
Unit sales	7,500	5,000	
Sales	$262,500	$225,000	$37,500 F
Less manufacturing costs:			
Direct materials	$ 55,500	$ 47,500	$ 8,000 U
Direct labor	48,000	32,500	15,500 U
Manufacturing overhead	40,000	32,000*	8,000 U
Total	(143,500)	(112,000)	(31,500) U
Gross profit	$119,000	$113,000	$ 6,000 F
Less selling and administrative expenses:			
Selling (all fixed)	$ 60,000	$ 40,000	$20,000 U
Administrative (all fixed)	55,000	50,000	5,000 U
Total	(115,000)	(90,000)	(25,000) U
Net income	$ 4,000	$ 23,000	$19,000 U

Performance summary:

Budgeted net income			$23,000
Sales department variances:			
Sales revenue	$ 37,500 F		
Selling expenses	20,000 U	$17,500 F	
Administration department variances		5,000 U	
Production department variances		31,500 U	19,000 U
Actual net income			$ 4,000

Includes fixed manufacturing overhead of $22,000.

Required:

a. Evaluate the performance report. Is Mr. Heep correct, or is there "villainy here"?
b. Assume that the Sales Department is a profit center and that the Production and Administration Departments are cost centers. Determine the responsibility of each for cost, revenue, and income variances, and prepare a report reconciling budgeted and actual net income. Your report should focus on the performance of each responsibility center.

12–33
Evaluating
Companywide
Performance: The
Case of Multiple
Profit Centers

Computeraid produces a variety of computer accessories. To improve financial incentives, the Production Department and the Sales Department are both treated as profit centers, with all goods produced in the Production Department being "sold" to the Sales Department at 150 percent of variable cost. The costs of the Administration Department are allocated equally to the Production and Sales Departments. The following performance reports are for the Production and Sales Departments for the year 2004:

Computeraid
Production Department Performance Report
For the Year 2004

	Actual	Budget	Variance
Unit sales	10,000	7,000	
Sales revenue	$241,500	$147,000	
Less variable manufacturing costs:			
Direct materials	$ 69,000	$ 35,000	
Direct labor	32,000	21,000	
Manufacturing overhead	60,000	42,000	
Total	(161,000)	(98,000)	
Contribution margin	$ 80,500	$ 49,000	
Less fixed costs:			
Manufacturing overhead	$ 24,000	$ 25,000	
Administrative	15,000	10,000	
Total	(39,000)	(35,000)	
Manufacturing profit	$ 41,500	$ 14,000	$27,500 F

Computeraid
Sales Department Performance Report
For the Year 2004

	Actual	Budget	Variance
Unit sales	10,000	7,000	
Sales revenue	$310,000	$217,000	
Less variable costs:			
Cost of goods sold	$241,500	$147,000	
Selling and distribution	50,000	35,000	
Total	(291,500)	(182,000)	
Contribution margin	$ 18,500	$ 35,000	
Less fixed costs:			
Selling and distribution	$ 8,000	$ 8,000	
Administrative	15,000	10,000	
Total	(23,000)	(18,000)	
Selling profit (loss)	$ (4,500)	$ 17,000	$21,500 U

Management congratulated the Production Department supervisor for another outstanding performance and offered him a raise. The manager of the Sales Department, on the other hand, was called to a special meeting of the board of directors and told that unless she provided an adequate explanation of her department's performance, she would be terminated.

Required:
Extremely concerned about her future with the organization, the manager of the Sales Department has asked you (1) to evaluate the 2004 performance reports for each department and (2) to assist in preparing revised 2004 performance reports for each department and Computeraid as a whole.

12–34
Evaluating Cost Center Performance Reports with Behavioral Implications

Denny Daniels is production manager of the Alumalloy Division of WRT Inc. Alumalloy has limited contact with outside customers and no sales staff. Most of its customers are other divisions of WRT. All sales and purchases with outside customers are handled by other corporate divisions. Therefore, Alumalloy is treated as a cost center for reporting and evaluation purposes rather than as a revenue or profit center.

Daniels perceives accounting as a historical number-generating process that provides little useful information for conducting his job. Consequently, the entire accounting process is regarded as a negative motivational device that does not reflect how hard or how effectively he works as a production manager. Daniels tried to discuss these perceptions and concerns with John Scott, the controller for the Alumalloy Division. Daniels told Scott, "I think the cost report is misleading. I know I've had better production over a number of operating periods, but the cost report still says I have excessive costs. Look, I'm not an accountant; I'm a production manager. I know how to get a good quality product out. Over a number of years, I've even cut the raw materials used to do it. But the cost report doesn't show any of this. Basically, it's always negative, no matter what I do. There's no way you can win with accounting or the people at corporate headquarters who use those reports."

Scott gave Daniels little consolation. "The accounting system and the cost reports generated by headquarters," Scott stated, "are just part of the corporate game and almost impossible for an individual to change. Although these accounting reports are pretty much the basis for evaluating the efficiency of your division and the means corporate management uses to determine whether you have done the job they want, you shouldn't worry too much. You haven't been fired yet! Besides, these cost reports have been used by WRT for the last 25 years."

Daniels perceived (from talking to the production manager of the Zinc Division) that most of what Scott said was probably true. However, some minor cost reporting changes for Zinc had been agreed to by corporate headquarters. Daniels also knew from the trade grapevine that the turnover of production managers was considered high at WRT, even though relatively few were fired. Most seemed to end up quitting, usually in disgust, because of beliefs that they were not being evaluated fairly. Typical comments of production managers who have left WRT follow:

- "Corporate headquarters doesn't really listen to us. All they consider are those misleading cost reports. They don't want them changed, and they don't want any supplemental information."
- "The accountants may be quick with numbers, but they don't know anything about production. As it was, I had to either ignore the cost reports entirely or pretend they are important even though they didn't tell how good a job I had done. No matter what they say about not firing people, negative reports mean negative evaluations. I'm better off working for another company."

A recent copy of the cost report prepared by corporate headquarters for the Alumalloy Division follows. Daniels does not like this report because he believes it fails to properly reflect the division's operations, thereby resulting in an unfair evaluation of performance.

Alumalloy Division
Cost Report
For the Month of April 2004

	Original Budget	Actual Cost	Excess Cost
Aluminum	$ 400,000	$ 437,000	$37,000
Labor	560,000	540,000	
Overhead	100,000	134,000	34,000
Total	$1,060,000	$1,111,000	$71,000

Required:

a. Comment on Daniels' perceptions of Scott (the controller), corporate headquarters, the cost report, and himself as a production manager. Discuss how his perceptions affect his behavior and probable performance as a production manager and employee of WRT.

b. Identify and explain three changes that could be made in the cost information presented to the production managers that would make the information more meaningful and less threatening to them.

(CMA Adapted)

John Shank Case Recommendation

Arctic Insulation

This case covers basic concepts in cost analysis for cost control and managerial decisions. The case is very good for class discussion. Perhaps because of the unusual industry, the case is intriguing to students who enjoy thinking about business issues in different environments. Also, the topics have a high common-sense appeal for certain students. If students have not been exposed to this topic, it is seen as very relevant; if they have been exposed to these issues previously, it is seen as a review in a "fun" business setting.

Kinkead Equipment

This case focuses on profit variance with particular attention to the strategic context of the business. It is for a manufacturing company with multiple lines of business. It is a very short case. It requires the student to analyze the situation and write a report detailing whether the year just completed was as good as it first appeared.

RC Blake Co.

Cost reduction with technology is the theme of this case. How does changing operations relate to meaningful financial analysis? This question must be addressed by the student before a correct analysis can be made. How the assessment will be made is critical to getting on the right track in solving the case. Does the new technology save anything or just cause management more headaches?

Solution to Review Problem

a. **Standard Cost Variance Analysis**

Input component: Direct labor   **Output: 5,000 units**

Actual Costs	Standard Cost of Actual Inputs		Flexible Budget Cost	
$82,400	Actual hours (AH) . . .	7,000	Standard hours allowed (SH) . .	6,250*
	Standard rate (SR) . . .	× $12	Standard rate (SR)	× $12
	Total	$84,000	Total	$75,000

Labor rate variance $1,600 F   Labor efficiency variance $9,000 U

Total flexible budget labor variance $7,400 U

*5,000 units × 1.25 hours per unit

Input component: Direct materials   **Output: 5,000 units**

Actual Cost		Standard Cost of Actual Inputs		Flexible Budget Cost	
Actual quantity (AQ) . . .	21,250	Actual quantity (AQ) . . .	21,250	Standard quantity allowed (SA) . . .	20,000*
Actual price (AP)	× $4.90	Standard price (SP) . . .	× $5.00	Standard price (SP)	× $5.00
	$104,125		$106,250		$100,000

Materials price variance $2,125 F

Materials quantity variance $6,250 U

Total flexible budget materials variance $4,125 U

5,000 units × 4 pounds per unit produced

b.   **Standard Cost Variance Analysis**

Input component: Variable overhead   **Output: 5,000 units**

Actual Costs		Standard Cost of Actual Inputs		Flexible Budget Cost	
Category 1	$31,000	Actual labor hours	7,000	Standard hours allowed	6,250
Category 2	18,000	Standard rate	× $4.80	Standard rate	× $4.80
Total	$49,000	Driver total	$33,600	Driver total	$30,000
		Finished units	5,000	Finished units	5,000
		Standard rate	× $4.00	Standard rate	× $4.00
		Driver total	$20,000	Driver total	$20,000
		Total	$53,600	Total	$50,000

Variable overhead spending variance $4,600 F

Variable overhead efficiency variance $3,600 U

Total flexible budget variable overhead variance $1,000 F

PROFITABILITY ANALYSIS OF STRATEGIC BUSINESS SEGMENTS

After completing this chapter, you should be able to:

LEARNING OBJECTIVE 1   Recognize a strategic business segment.

LEARNING OBJECTIVE 2   Discuss centralized and decentralized organization structures.

LEARNING OBJECTIVE 3   Understand the development and use of segment reports.

LEARNING OBJECTIVE 4   Evaluate transfer-pricing alternatives, including international transfers.

LEARNING OBJECTIVE 5   Discuss the issues that cause difficulty in evaluating decentralized operations.

LEARNING OBJECTIVE 6   Calculate, explain, and compare return on investment, residual income, and economic value-added residual income measures for divisional performance.

LEARNING OBJECTIVE 7   Understand the concept of comprehensive performance measurement when financial and nonfinancial concepts are integrated.

MANAGING BUSINESS SEGMENTS

Many businesses provide a variety of products or services for a wide spectrum of consumers. These products or services often relate to a common area such as technology, financial services, or consumer products. Many firms organize these products and services into units called divisions *or* strategic business segments. *While managers of the strategic business segments make most of the operating decisions for their respective units, senior organization managers focus on strategic issues such as the investment of assets and the evaluation of performance. Three firms in very different business sectors, Procter & Gamble, Verizon, and C. H. Robinson Worldwide, illustrate the challenges of managing these strategic business segments.*

In managing a major consumer products company, senior executives of Procter & Gamble focus on the success of the firm's many familiar brands. P&G's major products include brands such as Tide (38 percent market share in laundry detergent), Bounty (39 percent market share in paper towels), Downy (46 percent market share in fabric softener), and Folgers (33 percent share in packaged coffee). Although these brands have been traditionally successful, seven of P&G's

nine most successful brands recently lost market share. In addition, P&G's performance in 16 of 27 major product categories has dropped. Observers comment that P&G's diverse product line has fallen victim to a group of smaller, more nimble niche firms that can focus on their specific products and markets. At the senior management level, P&G executives must make the appropriate resource allocation decisions to rejuvenate their brands.

In the telecommunications services industry, Verizon has emerged as a major provider. Created through a merger of GTE and Bell Atlantic, the firm had sales of about $60 to 65 billion in 2000. With $8 billion of income and $3.5 billion available for capital expenditures, Verizon managers expect the firm's sales to top $100 billion by 2005. Boasting the best collection of assets in the industry, the firm offers services including data transmission; wireless communications; local, long distance, and international calling; transmission lines; pay phones; and phone books. Although a telecommunications firm offers many services that share common assets, senior managers must still decide where to invest in the next capital projects that will expand the firm's capability in one of several business directions.

Managers at C. H. Robinson Worldwide, a much smaller firm than either Verizon or Procter & Gamble, take a very decentralized approach to managing the firm's 138 branches. This logistics company with yearly sales of about $450 million and income around $78 million owns no vehicles and ships none of its own freight. Robinson serves as an intermediary between the companies with trucks, ships, and planes and the companies with cargo to move. The firm acts as broker for about 2.5 million shipments per year using an operating philosophy that the CEO summarizes as "hire good people and let them attack the marketplace." This very decentralized approach allows each of the branch managers to control the branches' own budget, hiring, marketing, and compensation. Essentially, each branch represents a profit center for the firm.

Senior managers need to evaluate the performance of their strategic business segments (the different brands, different services, or different geographical locations). Managerial accounting provides a variety of tools with which to analyze the performance of these units and/or their managers.

Source: Robert Berner. "Can Procter & Gamble Clean Up Its Act?" *Business Week*, March 12, 2001, pp. 80–83; Joanne Gordon, "Green Machine," *Forbes*, October 29, 2001, p. 150; and Scott Woolley, "The New Ma Bell," *Forbes*, April, 16, 2001, pp. 68–71.

Large and diverse organizations that maintain multiple product lines or that operate in several industries or in multiple markets around the globe often adopt a decentralized organization structure in which managers of major business units or strategic segments enjoy a high degree of autonomy. Examples of strategic business segments include the Chrysler Group of DaimlerChrysler and the Asia Pacific Group of The Coca-Cola Company. Sometimes companies establish segments within segments such as at Coca-Cola, whose Asia Pacific Group has separate business units for individual countries (Japan, Korea, etc.). In organizations such as DaimlerChrysler and Coca-Cola, upper management typically sets specific performance and profitability objectives for each segment and allows the manager of the segment the decision-making freedom to achieve those objectives.

The purpose of this chapter is to examine the ways that an organization evaluates strategic business segments. It also considers transfer pricing and some of the problems that occur when one segment provides goods or services to another segment in the same organization. Finally, it examines nonfinancial performance measures for evaluating strategic segments, including the balanced scorecard.

STRATEGIC BUSINESS SEGMENTS

A **strategic business segment** has its own mission and set of goals. Its mission influences the decisions that its top managers make in both short-run and long-run situations. The organization structure dictates to a large extent the type of financial segment reporting and other measures used to evaluate the segment and its managers. In decentralized organizations, for example, the reporting units (typically called *divisions*) normally are quasi-independent companies, often having their own computer system, cost accounting system, and administrative and marketing staffs. With this type structure, top management monitors the segments to ensure that these independent units are functioning for the benefit of the entire organization.

Although segment reports are normally produced to coincide with managerial lines of responsibility, some companies also produce segment reports for smaller slices of the business that do not represent separate responsibility centers. These parts of the business are not significant enough to be identified as "strategic" business units as defined, but management could want information about them on a continuing basis. For example, BellSouth Corporation has several strategic business units, including Bell-South Telecommunications Company (BST), which provides traditional regulated telephone services to customers using telephone lines. Within BST are several strategic business units, including units for residential customers, large businesss customers, and small business customers. Financial reports are prepared for each of these units. Within the residential division, BST can also prepare segment reports on a more detailed basis to determine the profitability of its smaller segments, such as single-line and multi-line customers. The point is that segment reporting is not constrained by lines of responsibility. A segment report can be prepared for any part of the business for which management believes more detailed information is useful in managing that portion of the business.

MANAGEMENT PHILOSOPHIES OF DECENTRALIZED OPERATIONS

Decentralization is the delegation of decision-making authority to successively lower management levels in an organization. The lower in the organization that authority is delegated, the greater is the decentralization. The most compelling argument for decentralization is the need for decisions to be made by managers who are close to and knowledgeable about operations. In decentralized organizations, managers closely associated with problems and situations make most of the key operating decisions. This experience in decision making at lower management levels helps provide a supply of managers trained for higher level positions when they become available. Most decisions also are made locally without having to feed information up the chain of command and then wait for a response. Under a decentralization philosophy, corporate management can concentrate on strategic planning and policy, and divisional management can concentrate on operating decisions. By actively participating in decision making, managers in decentralized organizations are more likely to be committed to the success of programs and more willing to accept responsibility for the consequences of their actions. Managers in a decentralized organization typically have fewer performance objectives, have more flexibility in responding to changing conditions, and are better able to keep their focus on the tasks at hand.

Despite the benefits of decentralization, a high level of decentralization can introduce problems. In organizations with many decentralized units, it could be difficult to keep all operating units on the same measurement system with regard to reporting periods, methods of reporting, and consistency of data collection. It is also difficult to keep each unit focused on operating for the benefit of the entire organization rather than for its own selfish benefit. Top management must keep in mind that it is only natural for decision makers to look out for themselves regarding expectations for promotions, raises, and bonuses. Decentralization can also lead to increased cost and decreased efficiency due to duplication of efforts in areas such as payroll processing, employee hiring and training, and legal work.

Centralization exists when top management has a wide span of control, including direct control over all major functions of an organization (such as manufacturing, sales, accounting, computer operations, marketing, research and development, and management control). Highly centralized organizations have fewer management levels; therefore, they are often referred to as *flat organization structures*. A centralized organization structure overcomes some of the problems of decentralization, although it introduces others. One of the most significant benefits of centralization is the economies of scale realized from combining similar resources and activities into more efficient operations. Another benefit is that the direct lines of authority provide better control of resources, and improved control permits the organization to shift resources rapidly to achieve changing corporate goals. Centralization can give top managers a clearer perspective of the operation of the business because they are in closer contact with more activities than they are in a decentralized company. The downside of centralization is its loss of most of the benefits of decentralization, including management's ability to provide focused direction to each area of the company and speedy decisions.

As organizations expand in size and complexity, centralized control becomes more difficult. Planning, organizing, and controlling can eventually overwhelm top management in a large centralized organization. The solution to this problem is the decentralization of the organization into smaller operating units. With proper planning and staffing of each unit or division, the organization can overcome the disadvantages of decentralization and improve overall organizational performance. See What's Happening 13–1 for an example of a diversified international company that credits decentralization for much of its success.

13–1   WHAT'S HAPPENING?

TECHNOLOGICAL REVOLUTION AIDS DECENTRALIZED STRUCTURE AT ACE LTD.

ACE Ltd. is an 8,000-employee, diversified, global insurance company headquartered in Bermuda that has undergone massive growth and diversification through acquisitions over the past few years. ACE has a highly diversified organization structure that allows local managers who are thoroughly familiar with local market conditions to run the company's business units. ACE's CEO, Brian Duperrault, stated that "it is important to allow managers to have some room to maneuver. You have to give them some feeling of ownership in the organization."

To ensure that ACE has an effective system of companywide standards, it has an internal board of directors (in addition to its external board) made up of the CEOs of its five subsidiaries. This internal board coordinates corporate policy to ensure that things are being done for the common good of the company. Duperrault emphasized that the company's diversification and decentralized structure are being aided by the technological revolution. He stated that "there is no way that we could run a global organization out of Bermuda without having the ability to communicate, and communicate rapidly, on a global scale. The whole communication revolution has allowed us to weave together an organization that is 50 countries wide in a way that has actually added to the organization."

Source: Lisa A. Howard, "Ace's CEO Likes Decentralization," *Information Access Company*, July 7, 2000.

In most decentralized organizations, a division is a largely autonomous organizational unit, whose manager is responsible for its sales, production, and administration. Division managers frequently have control over all activities, although capital budgeting and long-range planning activities could be limited. These two activities are often centralized within corporate headquarters, with the various division managers given control over the investments once they have been made. As generally organized, the division is the most common example of an investment center.

Exhibit 13–1 illustrates a decentralized organizational structure. The theory behind this structure is to delegate enough responsibility to each division manager for the division to operate as a quasi-independent business. The division management group usually includes managers of information technology, personnel, marketing, accounting (controller), and production. Often in decentralized organizations, functional managers within divisions report to both the division manager and the corporate functional manager, which could lead to problems. The dashed lines in Exhibit 13–1 represent each staff member's responsibility to corporate headquarters; the solid lines connect each staff to the division vice president who has day-to-day authority. For example, the division controller (the division's chief accountant) has a dual responsibility to the vice president of Division B who exercises line authority, the corporate controller (the company's chief accountant) who exercises functional authority, and to other corporate staff. The division controller must follow certain firmwide accounting procedures specified by the corporate controller. Sometimes the division controller is regarded as an extension of the corporate controller or as a "front-office" employee. In that case, the division controller would have a direct-line relationship with the corporate controller and a staff-line relationship with the division vice president.

LEARNING OBJECTIVE 3   **SEGMENT REPORTING**

Segment reports are income statements for portions or segments of a business. Segment reporting is used primarily for internal purposes, although generally accepted ac-

EXHIBIT 13-1

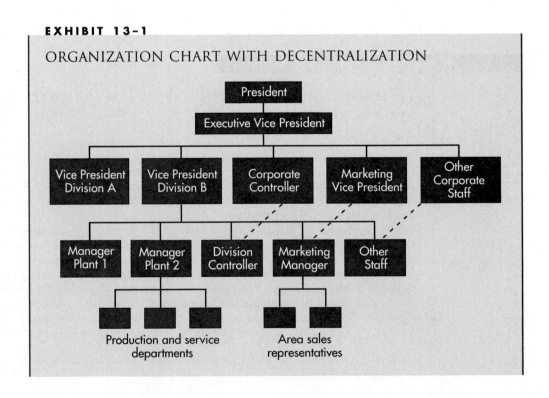

ORGANIZATION CHART WITH DECENTRALIZATION

counting principles also require some disclosure of segment information for some public corporations. Even though there are many different types of segment reports, at least three steps are basic to the preparation of all segment reports:

1. Identify the segments.
2. Assign direct costs to the segments.
3. Allocate indirect costs to the segments.

The format of segment income statements varies depending on the approach adopted by a company for reporting income statements internally. The various income statement formats illustrated earlier in this text including the functional format, contribution format, and cost hierarchy format, can be used for segment reporting. Data availability can, however, dictate the format used. Regardless of the format adopted, it is essential that costs be separable into those directly traceable to the segments and those not directly traceable to segments.

Determining the segment reporting structure is often a more difficult decision than choosing the format for the segment income statements. As indicated earlier in this chapter, companies could or could not structure segment reporting along the lines of responsibility reporting. Also, it is necessary to decide whether segment reports will be prepared only on one level or on several levels. For example, consider the case of Digital Communications Company (DCC) that has two market divisions, three products, and two geographic territories. DCC's two divisions include the National Division (serving large national accounts) and the Regional Division (serving smaller regional and local accounts). DCC's three product lines are fiber optic cable, twisted pair cable, and coaxial cable. The company is organized into two geographic territories, Atlantic and Pacific. If DCC were using only a single-level segment reporting approach for all three groupings, one report would show the total company income statement broken down into the two divisions, a second report would show the total company income statement broken down into the three products, and a third report would show the total company income statement broken down into the two geographic territories.

MULTI-LEVEL SEGMENT INCOME STATEMENTS

If top management of DCC wants to know how much a particular product is contributing to the income of one of the two divisions or how much income a particular product in one of its two geographic territories contributes, it is necessary to prepare multilevel segment income statements. Since DCC sells three products and operates through two divisions in two territories, many combinations of divisions, products, and territories could be used in structuring the company's multilevel segment reporting. Obviously, the goal is not to slice and dice the revenue and cost data in as many ways as possible but it is to provide useful and meaningful information to management. Therefore, deciding what type of reporting structure is most useful in managing the company is important. This decision will be constrained to a great extent by the data availability and cost. If there were no data constraints, DCC could look at the company's net income for every possible combination of division, product, and territory. The more data required to support a reporting system, however, the more costly it is to maintain the system, so management must determine the value and the cost of the additional information and make an appropriate cost-benefit judgment.

Panel A of Exhibit 13–2 illustrates multi-level segment reporting for DCC in which the first level shows the total company income statement segmented into the two market divisions, National Accounts and Regional Accounts. Panel B of Exhibit 13–2 shows a second-level report for DCC in which the National Division's segment income statement is broken down into its three product lines, fiber optic cable, twisted pair cable, and coaxial cable. Panel C then provides a third-level income statement for the National Division's fiber optic sales in each of the company's two geographic

EXHIBIT 13–2

MULTI-LEVEL SEGMENT REPORTS

Panel A: First-Level Segment Report of Digital Communications Company—For Divisions (in thousands)

	SEGMENTS (DIVISIONS)		
	National Accounts	Regional Accounts	Company Total
Sales	$100,000	$200,000	$300,000
Less variable costs	(55,000)	(95,000)	(150,000)
Contribution margin	$ 45,000	$105,000	$150,000
Less direct fixed costs	(20,000)	(60,000)	(80,000)
Division margin	$ 25,000	$ 45,000	$ 70,000
Less allocated common costs	(10,000)	(25,000)	(35,000)
Division income	$ 15,000	$ 20,000	$ 35,000
Less unallocated common costs			(12,000)
Net income			$ 23,000

Panel B: Second-Level Segment Report of the National Division—For Products (in thousands)

	SEGMENTS (PRODUCTS)			National Division Total
	Fiber Optic	Twisted Pair	Coaxial	
Sales	$30,000	$40,000	$30,000	$100,000
Less variable costs	(15,000)	(19,000)	(21,000)	(55,000)
Contribution margin	$15,000	$21,000	$ 9,000	$ 45,000
Less direct fixed costs	(9,000)	(4,000)	(2,000)	(15,000)
Product margin	$ 6,000	$17,000	$ 7,000	$ 30,000
Less allocated division costs	(5,000)	(4,000)	(1,000)	(10,000)
Product income	$ 1,000	$13,000	$ 6,000	$ 20,000
Less unallocated costs				(5,000)
National Division income				$ 15,000

Panel C: Third-Level Segment Report of the Fiber Optic Product Line in the National Division—For Geographic Territories (in thousands)

	SEGMENTS (TERRITORIES)		Fiber Optic Total
	Atlantic	Pacific	
Sales	$20,000	$10,000	$30,000
Less variable costs	(11,000)	(4,000)	(15,000)
Contribution margin	$ 9,000	$ 6,000	$15,000
Less direct fixed costs	(3,000)	(4,000)	(7,000)
Territory margin	$ 6,000	$ 2,000	$ 8,000
Less allocated division costs	(2,000)	(3,000)	(5,000)
Territory income	$ 4,000	$ (1,000)	$ 3,000
Less unallocated common costs			(2,000)
Fiber optic income			$ 1,000

territories, the Atlantic and Pacific territories. The example in Exhibit 13–2 shows only part of the segment reports for DCC. The complete three-level set of segment reports would also break down the Regional Accounts Division into its product lines and all product lines for both divisions into geographic territories.

In the DCC example in Exhibit 13–2, the first reporting level is the company's divisions, its second reporting level is product lines, and the third is geographic territories. Another approach could be to structure the segment reports with product lines as the first level, geographic territories as the second level, and divisions as the third level. Another approach would be to make product lines the first level, divisions the second level, and geographic territories the third level. Regardless of how many different ways the company segments the income statements, at least one set of segment reports follows the company's responsibility reporting system; therefore, one of the segment reports has the operating divisions as the first level. If each division has a product manager for each product, the division segment reports are broken down by products. Finally, if each product within each division has a territory manager, the product segment reports are broken down by territories.

INTERPRETING SEGMENT REPORTS AND DECISION MAKING

Notice that in Exhibit 13–2 costs are reported in four categories: variable costs, direct fixed costs, allocated common costs, and unallocated common costs. Variable costs vary in proportion to the level of sales and are subtracted from sales in calculating contribution margin. **Direct segment fixed costs** are nonvariable costs directly traceable to the segments incurred for the specific benefit of the respective segments. **Segment margin** equals the contribution margin minus the direct segment fixed costs. For DCC, segment margins are referred to as *division margins, product margins,* and *territory margins.* Segment margins represent the amount that a segment contributes directly to the company's profitability in the short run.

Common segment costs are incurred for the common benefit of all related segments shown on a segment income statement. In some cases, allocating some common costs may be reasonable even though they cannot be directly traced to the various segments based on benefits received. For example, if segments share common space, allocating all space-related costs to the segments based on building space occupied could be appropriate. If there is no reasonable basis for allocating common costs, they should not be allocated to the segments. In Panel C of Exhibit 13–2, if advertising costs to promote the company's fiber optic products on national television could not be reasonably allocated to the two geographic territories, they would be charged to the fiber optic product line as an unallocated common cost, not to the individual territories.

If some portion of common costs can be reasonably allocated to the segments, those allocated costs are subtracted from the segment margins to determine segment income. Hence, **segment income** represents all revenues of the segment minus all costs directly or indirectly charged to it. To properly interpret segment income, we should ask whether segment income represents the amount by which net income of the company will change if that segment is discontinued. For example, if DCC discontinues the coaxial product line in the National Division, does this mean that DCC's net income will decrease by $6 million? Also, does it mean that if the National Division stops selling fiber optic cable in the Pacific territory, DCC's net income will increase by $1 million?

The answer to these questions depends on whether the costs allocated to the segments are avoidable. **Avoidable common costs** are allocated common costs that eventually can be avoided (that is, can be eliminated) if a segment is discontinued. If all allocated common costs are avoidable, the effect of discontinuing the segment on corporate profitability equals the amount of segment income. In most cases, the short-term impact of discontinuing a segment equals the segment margin because allocated costs are capacity costs that cannot be adjusted in the short run. Over time, the company should be able to adjust capacity and eliminate some, or possibly all, of the allocated common costs or find productive uses for that capacity in other segments of the business. The unallocated common costs cannot be changed readily in the short term or the long term without causing major disruptions to the company and its strategy. Therefore, over the long term, the impact of discontinuing a segment should approximate its segment income.

If DCC discontinues selling fiber optic cable in the Pacific territory (see Exhibit 13–2, Panel C) the short-term effect on the company's profits will probably be a $2 million reduction of profits, which equals the Pacific territory's margin. The revenues and costs that make up the Pacific territory margin would all be lost if fiber optic sales were discontinued in the Pacific territory, but the $3 million of common costs allocated to the Pacific territory would continue, at least in the short term. Over the long term, however, after adjusting the capacity for selling this product in the Pacific territory and eliminating the $3 million of allocated common costs, the effect of discontinuing fiber optics in the Pacific territory on profits should be an increase of about $1 million, which is the amount of the segment income for fiber optics in the Pacific territory. To summarize, segment margin is relevant for measuring the short-term effects of decisions to continue or discontinue a segment; however, segment income is relevant for measuring the long-term effects of decisions to continue or discontinue.

SEGMENT REPORTING AND ACTIVITY-BASED COSTING

Meaningful segment reports can be produced only if accurate revenue and cost data are attributed to the various segments. The approach illustrated for DCC in the previous section entailed separating costs into variable and fixed costs and then separating fixed costs into direct and indirect common costs. As we have discussed throughout this text, separating costs into variable and fixed categories is often difficult because costs tend not to vary with a single cost driver. Companies that use activity-based costing often categorize costs into cost pools that reflect a hierarchy of cost drivers, such as unit, batch, product, and facilities. An activity-based costing approach to segment reporting is likely to give a more accurate assignment of costs to segments for companies that have a more complicated operating environment.

LEARNING OBJECTIVE 4

TRANSFER PRICING

To determine whether each division is achieving its organizational objectives, managers must be accountable for the goods and services they acquire, both externally and internally. When goods or services are exchanged internally between segments of a decentralized organization, the way that the transferor and the transferee will report the transfer must be determined. A **transfer price** is the internal value assigned a product or service that one division provides to another. The transfer price is recognized as revenue by the division providing goods or services and as expense (or cost) by the division receiving them. Transfer-pricing transactions normally occur between profit or investment centers rather than between cost centers of an organization; however, managers often consider cost allocations between cost centers as a type of transfer price. The focus in this chapter is on transfers between responsibility centers that are evaluated based on profits.

MANAGEMENT CONSIDERATIONS

The desire of the selling and buying divisions of the same company to maximize their individual performance measures often creates transfer-pricing problems. Acting as independent units, divisions could take actions that are not in the best interest(s) of the organization as a whole. The three examples that follow illustrate the need for organizations to maintain a *corporate* profit-maximizing viewpoint while attempting to allow *divisional* autonomy and responsibility.

OmniTech, Inc., has five divisions, some of which transfer products and product components to other OmniTech divisons. The BioTech Division manufactures two products, Alpha and Beta. It sells Alpha externally for $50 per unit and transfers Beta to the GenTech Division for $60 per unit. The costs associated with the two products follow:

	PRODUCT	
	Alpha	**Beta**
Variable costs:		
Direct materials	$15	$14
Direct labor	5	10
Variable manufacturing overhead	5	16
Selling	4	0
Fixed Costs:		
Fixed manufacturing overhead	6	15
Total	$35	$55

An external company has just proposed to supply a Beta substitute product to the GenTech Division at a price of $52. From the company's viewpoint, this is merely a make or buy decision. The relevant costs are the differential outlay costs of the alternative actions. Assuming that the fixed manufacturing costs of the BioTech Division are unavoidable, the relevant costs of this proposal from the company's perspective are as follows:

Buy		$52
Make:		
Direct materials	$14	
Direct labor	10	
Variable manufacturing overhead	16	(40)
Difference		$12

From the corporate viewpoint, the best decision is for the product to be transferred since the relevant cost is $40 rather than to buy it from an external source for $52. The decision for the GenTech Division management is basically one of cost minimization: Buy from the source that charges the lowest price. If BioTech is not willing to transfer Beta at a price of $52 or less, the GenTech management could go to the external supplier to maximize the division's profits. (Although GenTech's managers are concerned about the cost of Beta, they are also concerned about the quality of the goods. If the $52 product does not meet its quality standards, GenTech could decide to buy from BioTech at the higher price. For this discussion, assume that the internal and external products are identical; therefore, acting in its best interest, GenTech purchases Beta for $52 from the external source unless BioTech can match the price.)

Prior to GenTech's receipt of the external offer, BioTech had been transferring Beta to GenTech for $60. BioTech must decide whether to reduce the contribution margin on its transfers of Beta to GenTech and, therefore, lower divisional profits or to try to find an alternative use for its resources. Of course, corporate management could intervene and require the internal transfer even though it would hurt BioTech's profits.

As the second example, assume that the BioTech Division has the option to sell an equivalent amount of Beta externally for $60 per unit if the GenTech Division discontinues its transfers from BioTech. Now the decision for BioTech's management is simple: Sell to the buyer willing to pay the most. From the corporate viewpoint, it is best for BioTech to sell to the external buyer for $60 and for GenTech to purchase from the external provider for $52.

To examine a slightly different transfer-pricing conflict, assume that the BioTech Division can sell all the Alpha that it can produce (it is operating at capacity). Also assume that there is no external market for Beta, but there is a one-to-one trade-off between the production of Alpha and Beta, which use equal amounts of the BioTech Division's limited capacity.

The corporation still regards this as a make or buy decision, but the costs of producing Beta have changed. The cost of Beta now includes an outlay cost and an opportunity cost. The outlay cost of Beta is its variable cost of $40 ($14 + $10 + $16), as previously computed. Beta's opportunity cost is the net benefit forgone if the BioTech Division's limited capacity is used to produce Beta rather than Alpha:

Selling price of Alpha			$50
Outlay costs of Alpha:			
Direct materials		$15	
Direct labor		5	
Variable manufacturing overhead		5	
Variable selling		4	(29)
Opportunity cost of making Beta			$21

Accordingly, the relevant costs in the make or buy decision follow.

Make:		
Outlay cost of Beta	$40	
Opportunity cost of Beta	21	$61
Buy		$52

From the corporate viewpoint, GenTech should purchase Beta from the outside supplier for $52 because in this case it costs $61 to make the product. If there were no outside suppliers, the corporation's relevant cost of manufacturing Beta is $61. This is another way of saying that the GenTech Division should not produce and process Beta further unless its revenues cover all outlay costs (including the $40 in the BioTech Division) and provide a contribution of at least $21 ($61 − $40). From the corporate viewpoint, the relevant costs in make or buy decisions are the external price, the outlay costs to manufacture, and the opportunity cost to manufacture. The opportunity cost is zero if there is excess capacity.

DETERMINING TRANSFER PRICES

As illustrated, the transfer price of goods or services can be subject to much controversy. The most widely used and discussed transfer prices are covered in this section. See What's Happening 13–2 for a discussion of transfer-pricing. Although a price must be agreed upon for each item or service transferred between divisions, the selection of the pricing method depends on many factors. The conditions surrounding the transfer determine which of the alternative methods discussed subsequently is selected.

Although no method is likely to be ideal, one must be selected if the profit or investment center concept is used. In considering each method, observe that each transfer results in a revenue entry on the supplier's books and a cost entry on the receiver's books. Transfers can be considered as sales by the supplier and as purchases by the receiver.

Market Price. When there is an existing market with established prices for an intermediate product and the transfer actions of the company will not affect prices, market prices are ideal transfer prices. If divisions are free to buy and sell outside the firm, the use of market prices preserves divisional autonomy and leads divisions to act in a manner that maximizes corporate goal congruence. Unfortunately, not all product transfers have equivalent external markets. Furthermore, the divisions should carefully evaluate whether the market price is competitive or controlled by one or two large

13-2   WHAT'S HAPPENING?

CITIGROUP EXPERIENCES DECENTRALIZATION AND TRANSFER-PRICING PROBLEMS

Fortune magazine interviewed Sandy Weill, the high-profile CEO of Citigroup, in connection with it's annual "Fortune 500" article, which ranked Citigroup the sixth largest company in the United States. Citigroup is a diversified financial company that includes such major financial brands as Primerica, Salomon Smith Barney, Citibank, and Travelers. The following is an excerpt from that article discussing some of the problems of decentralization and transfer pricing at Citigroup.

Weill, who'd never scheduled more than a monthly management meeting at Citi, says he was initially dubious about weekly sessions because he wasn't sure there'd be that much to talk about—which, when you think about it, says a lot about Weill's view of management. But the meetings have turned out to be so valuable that people even tune in by phone when they're out of town.

The get-togethers are useful because in a company of Citi's size and complexity, there are dozens of issues—business overlaps, competitive threats, regulations—that cut across divisions. In an institution that promotes cross-selling, for example, there is always the question of how the financial spoils are divided up between the two divisions—a matter that goes under the name "transfer pricing." For example, suppose that a Salomon Smith Barney financial consultant sells a mutual fund "manufactured" by Citi's investment management division. What's the price that the IM division receives? The answer, since it determines profit, is extremely important to executives getting paid (and paying their people) according to what their own bottom line looks like. One former Citi executive says that difficult questions like these have sometimes aggravated business heads to the point of their "barely speaking to each other."

Asked about transfer pricing pains at Citi, Weill says testily that he wishes people "would think about doing the business first, and worry about who gets the credit second." But, trying to mediate, he also has his financial people studying plans for internally double counting revenues, so as to make profits (or losses) accrue to both parties involved in a cross-selling event. He adds that the weekly meeting of the business heads has the potential—he obviously hopes—to soothe disagreements like those about cross-selling, because it encourages these people to "relate."

Source: Carol J. Loomis, "The Fortune 500, No. 6 Sandy Weill's Monster," *Fortune,* April 16, 2001.

companies. When substantial selling expenses are associated with outside sales, many firms specify the transfer price as market price less selling expenses. The internal sale may not require the incurrence of costs to get and fill the order.

To illustrate using the OmniTech example, assume that product Alpha of the BioTech Division can be sold competitively at $50 per unit or transferred to a third division, the Quantum Division, for additional processing. Under most situations, The Biotech Division will never sell Alpha for less than $50, and The Quantum Division will likewise never pay more than $50 for it. However, if any variable expenses related to marketing and shipping can be eliminated by divisional transfers, these costs are generally subtracted from the competitive market price. In our illustration in which variable selling expenses are $4 for Alpha, the transfer price could be reduced to $46 ($50 − $4). A price between $46 and $50 would probably be better than either extreme price. To the extent that these transfer prices represent a nearly competitive situation, the profitability of each division can then be fairly evaluated.

Variable Costs.   If excess capacity exists in the supplying division, establishing a transfer price equal to variable costs leads the purchasing division to act in a manner that is optimal from the corporation's viewpoint. The buying division has the corporation's variable cost as its own variable cost as it enters the external market. Unfortunately, establishing the transfer price at variable cost causes the supplying division to report zero profits or a loss equal to any fixed costs. If excess capacity does not exist, establishing a transfer price at variable cost would not lead to optimal action because the supplying division would have to forgo external sales that include a markup for fixed costs and profits. If Beta could be sold externally for $60, the BioTech Division would not want to transfer Beta to the GenTech Division for a $40 transfer price based on the following variable costs:

Direct materials	$14
Direct labor	10
Variable manufacturing overhead	16
Total variable costs	$40

The BioTech Division would much rather sell outside the company for $60, which covers variable costs and provides a profit contribution margin of $20:

Selling price of Beta	$60
Variable costs	(40)
Contribution margin	$20

Variable Costs Plus Opportunity Costs. From the organization's viewpoint, this is the optimal transfer price. Because all relevant costs are included in the transfer price, the purchasing division is led to act in a manner optimal for the overall company, whether or not excess capacity exists.

With excess capacity in the supplying division, the transfer price is the variable cost per unit. Without excess capacity, the transfer price is the sum of the variable and opportunity costs. Following this rule in the previous example, if the BioTech Division had excess capacity, the transfer price of Beta would be set at Beta's variable costs of $40 per unit. At this transfer price, the GenTech Division would buy Beta internally, rather than externally at $52 per unit. If the BioTech Division cannot sell Beta externally but can sell all the Alpha it can produce and is operating at capacity, the transfer price per unit would be set at $61, the sum of Beta's variable and opportunity costs ($40 + $21). (Refer back to page 578.) At this transfer price, the GenTech Division would buy Beta externally for $52. In both situations, the management of the GenTech Division has acted in accordance with the organization's profit-maximizing goal.

There are two problems, however, with this method. First, when the supplying division has excess capacity, establishing the transfer price at variable cost causes the supplying division to report zero profits or a loss equal to any fixed costs. Second, determining opportunity costs when the supplying division produces several products is difficult. If the problems with the previously mentioned transfer-pricing methods are too great, three other methods can be used: absorption cost plus markup, negotiated prices, and dual prices.

Absorption Cost Plus Markup. According to absorption costing, all variable and fixed manufacturing costs are product costs. Pricing internal transfers at absorption cost eliminates the supplying division's reported loss on each product that can occur using a variable cost transfer price. Absorption cost plus markup provides the supplying division a contribution toward unallocated costs. In "cost-plus" transfer pricing, "cost" should be defined as standard cost rather than as actual cost. This prevents the supplying division from passing on the cost of inefficient operations to other divisions, and it allows the buying division to know its cost in advance of purchase. Even though cost-plus transfer prices could not maximize company profits, they are widely used. Their popularity stems from several factors, including ease of implementation, justifiability, and perceived fairness. Once everyone agrees on absorption cost plus markup pricing rules, internal disputes are minimized.

Negotiated Prices. *Negotiated transfer prices* are used when the supplying and buying divisions independently agree on a price. As with market-based transfer prices, negotiated transfer prices are believed to preserve divisional autonomy. Negotiated transfer prices can lead to some suboptimal decisions, but this is regarded as a small price to pay for other benefits of decentralization. When they use negotiated transfer prices, some corporations establish arbitration procedures to help settle disputes between divisions. However, the existence of an arbitrator with any real or perceived authority reduces divisional autonomy.

Negotiated prices should have market prices as their ceiling and variable costs as their floor. Although frequently used when an external market for the product or component exists, the most common use of negotiated prices occurs when no identical-product external market exists. Negotiations could start with a floor price plus add-ons such as overhead and profit markups or with a ceiling price less adjustments for selling and administrative expenses and allowances for quantity discounts. When no identical-product external market exists, the market price for a similar completed product can be used, less the estimated cost of completing the product from the transfer stage to the completed stage.

Dual Prices. Dual prices exist when a company allows a difference in the supplier's and receiver's transfer prices for the same product. This method allegedly minimizes internal squabbles of division managers and problems of conflicting divisional and corporate goals. The supplier's transfer price normally approximates market price, which allows the selling division to show a "normal" profit on items that it transfers internally. The receiver's price is usually the internal cost of the product or service, calculated as variable cost plus opportunity cost. This ensures that the buying division will make an internal transfer when it is in the best interest of the company to do so.

LEARNING OBJECTIVE 5

SUBOPTIMIZATION

Suboptimization exists when divisions, acting in their own best interests, set transfer prices or make decisions based on transfer prices that are not in the best interest of the organization as a whole. The most desirable situation occurs when divisions operate in industries for which the markets for their products are well established and the divisions are free to transfer products within the firm or to buy and sell outside the firm. In most cases, a market-based transfer price achieves the optimal outcome for both the divisions and the company as a whole. As discussed earlier, an exception occurs when a division is operating below full capacity and has no alternative use for its excess capacity. In this case, it is best for the company to have an internal transfer; therefore, to ensure that the receiving division makes an internal transfer, the company must require the internal transfer as long as its price does not exceed the established market rate. The only time an external price is more attractive when excess capacity exists is when the external price is below the variable cost of the providing internal division, and that scenario is highly unlikely.

A potential transfer pricing problem exists when divisions exchange goods or services for which no established market exists. For example, suppose that a company is operating its information technology (IT) service department as a profit center that transfers services to other profit center departments using a cost-plus transfer price. If the departments using IT services can choose to use those services or to replicate them inside their departments, users might not make a decision that is best for the company. It could be best for the company to have all IT services come from the IT department, but other profit centers could believe that they can provide those services for themselves at lower cost. In this case, the company must decide how important it is to maintain the independence of its profit center. In the interest of maintaining a strong profit center philosophy, top management can decide that it is acceptable to suboptimize by allowing profit centers to provide IT services for themselves.

The ideal transfer pricing arrangement is seldom the same for both the providing and receiving divisions for every situation. In these cases, what is good for one division is likely not to be good for the other division resulting in no transfer, even though a transfer could achieve corporate goals. These conflicts are sometimes overcome by having a higher ranking manager impose a transfer price and insist that a transfer be made. Managers in organizations that have a policy of decentralization, however, often regard these orders as undermining their autonomy. Therefore, the imposition of a price could solve the corporate profit optimization problem but create other problems regarding the company's organization strategy. Transfer pricing thus becomes a problem with no ideal solutions.

INTERNATIONAL TRANSFER PRICING

To this point we have emphasized the behavioral and motivational issues surrounding transfer pricing in decentralized organizations. If the divisions exchanging goods are located in different countries with different tax rate structures, the key determinant of transfer prices could be based largely on a tax strategy of minimizing overall corporate taxes. For example, assume that a unit of the Chrysler Division of DaimlerChrysler in the United States manufactures a particular emission control component used by the Mercedes Division of DaimlerChrysler in Germany. Since Germany's corporate income tax rates are higher than U.S. rates, DaimlerChrysler could minimize its overall corporate income taxes by shifting profit from Germany to the United States. Setting the highest possible transfer price on the component sold by the Chrysler Division to the Mercedes Division would increase the revenues and profits of the Chrysler Division as well as the costs of the Mercedes Division, thereby decreasing its profits.

Assume that for a recent year, both the Chrysler Division and the Mercedes Division had taxable income of $200 million before considering the revenue and expense effects of the emission component transfer. During the year, Chrysler transferred 300,000 units of the emission control component to the Mercedes Division. The component had a variable cost per unit of $20 and a fixed cost per unit of $5; similar units sold in the automotive parts market had a market price of $40. Furthermore, assume that the marginal tax rates were 50 percent for Mercedes and 35 percent for Chrysler. The table at the top of the following page calculates the total taxes that DaimlerChrysler would pay for the year, assuming that the emission control unit is transferred at variable cost, full cost, and estimated market price. To simplify the calculations, we express all monetary amounts in U.S. dollars.

From the perspective of minimizing total income taxes, DaimlerChrysler wanted to use the highest possible transfer price, namely, the market price. Using the market price shifts $20 per unit (or $6,000,000) more income to the Chrysler Division than using variable cost as the transfer price. The tax savings for the overall company from using the higher transfer price equaled $900,000, calculated as $169,100,000 less $168,200,000 or as $6,000,000 times the tax rate difference of 15 percent between Germany and the United States.

Companies do not have complete latitude in setting transfer prices. In the United States, the Internal Revenue Code has guidelines for setting a transfer price at a value that approximates fair market value. Tax treaties between countries also include guidelines for setting transfer prices in an attempt to counteract attempts to manipulate transfer prices to avoid reporting income in the higher tax rate countries. Despite these restrictions, managers can still exercise some latitude in setting transfer prices that could have only a small effect on the price of a given unit transferred between two divisions. If a company gains a few dollars or perhaps just a few cents in total tax savings for each transfer of a product or component between international divisions, the total tax savings on thousands of transfers can accumulate to a substantial amount.

	USING TRANSFER PRICE BASED ON		
	Variable Cost	**Full Cost**	**Market Price**
Taxable income of the Mercedes Division, excluding the transfer	$200,000,000	$200,000,000	$200,000,000
Cost of emission components to Mercedes Division:			
Variable cost ($20 × 300,000)	(6,000,000)		
Full cost ($25 × 300,000)		(7,500,000)	
Market price ($40 × 300,000)			(12,000,000)
Taxable income	$194,000,000	$192,500,000	$188,000,000
Mercedes Division income taxes (50%)	$ 97,000,000	$ 96,250,000	$ 94,000,000
Taxable income to the Chrysler Division, excluding the transfer	$200,000,000	$200,000,000	$200,000,000
Revenue from emission components Mercedes Division:			
Variable cost ($20 × 300,000)	6,000,000		
Full cost ($25 × 300,000)		7,500,000	
Market price ($40 × 300,000)			12,000,000
Taxable income	$206,000,000	$207,500,000	$212,000,000
Chrysler Division income taxes (35%)	$ 72,100,000	$ 72,625,000	$ 74,200,000
Total DaimlerChrysler income taxes			
($97,000,000 + $72,100,000)	$169,100,000		
($96,250,000 + $72,625,000)		$168,875,000	
($94,000,000 + $74,200,000)			$168,200,000

LEARNING OBJECTIVE 6

EVALUATION MEASURES

Three of the most common measures of investment center performance, return on investment, residual income, and economic value added, are discussed in the following sections. Several supporting components of these measures that help clarify the applications are also presented.

RETURN ON INVESTMENT

Return on investment (ROI) is a measure of the earnings per dollar of investment.[1] The return on investment of an investment center is computed by dividing the income of the center by its asset base (usually total assets):

$$ROI = \frac{\text{Investment center income}}{\text{Investment center asset base}}$$

ROI is also computed as investment turnover times the return-on-sales ratio (also called *margin*, *income percentage of revenue*, and *income-sales ratio*). This approach, commonly known as the *DuPont method of profitability analysis*, is computed as follows:

$$ROI = \text{Investment turnover} \times \text{Return-on-sales ratio}$$

---

[1]This assumes that financing decisions are made at the corporate level rather than the division level. Hence, the corporation's investment in the division equals the division's asset base. The computation of ROI, as presented here, is similar to that for return on assets.

where

$$\text{Investment turnover} = \frac{\text{Sales}}{\text{Investment center asset base}}$$

and

$$\text{Return-on-sales ratio} = \frac{\text{Investment center income}}{\text{Sales}}$$

When investment turnover is multiplied by the return-on-sales ratio, the product is the same as investment center income divided by investment center asset base:

$$\text{ROI} = \frac{\text{Sales}}{\text{Investment center asset base}} \times \frac{\text{Investment center income}}{\text{Sales}}$$

$$= \frac{\text{Investment center income}}{\text{Investment center asset base}}$$

Once ROI has been computed, it is compared to some previously identified performance criteria. These include the investment center's previous ROI, overall company ROI, the ROI of similar divisions, or the ROI of nonaffiliated companies that operate in similar markets. The breakdown of ROI into investment turnover and return-on-sales ratio is useful in determining the source of variance in overall performance.

To illustrate the computation and use of ROI, the following information is available concerning the 2004 operations of North American Steel:

Division	Net Assets	Sales	Divisional Income
Maine	$8,000,000	$12,000,000	$1,440,000
Alberta	4,000,000	8,000,000	960,000
Missouri	7,500,000	5,000,000	1,650,000
Tijuana	3,800,000	5,700,000	1,026,000

Using this information and the preceding equations, a set of Dupont performance measures can be presented as shown in Exhibit 13–3. To illustrate, Maine Division earned a return on its investment base of 18 percent ($1,440,000 ÷ $8,000,000), consisting of an investment turnover of 1.50 ($12,000,000 ÷ $8,000,000) and a return-on-sales ratio of 0.12 ($1,440,000 ÷ $12,000,000). Using such an analysis, the company has three measurement criteria with which to evaluate the performance of Maine Division: (1) ROI, (2) investment turnover, and (3) return-on-sales ratio.

For 2004, North American chose to evaluate its divisions based on company ROI and its interrelated components of investment turnover and return-on-sales ratio. Because each division is different in size, the company evaluation standard is not a simple average of the divisions but is based on desired relationships between assets, sales, and income.

Based on ROI, the Tijuana Division had the best performance, the Alberta Division excelled in investment turnover, and the Missouri Division had the highest return-on-sales ratio. From Exhibit 13–3, the Tijuana Division clearly had the best year because it was the only division that exceeded each of the company's performance criteria. For 2004, each division equaled or exceeded the minimum ROI established by the company even though the component criteria of ROI were not always achieved.

To properly evaluate each division, the company should study the underlying components of ROI. For the Maine Division, management would want to know why the minimum investment turnover was exceeded while the return-on-sales ratio minimum was not. The Maine Division could have incurred unfavorable cost variances by producing inefficiently. As a result of inefficient production, the return-on-sales ratio declined to a point below the minimum desired level. Evaluating a large operating division based on one financial indicator is difficult. Management should select

EXHIBIT 13-3

PERFORMANCE EVALUATION DATA

North American Steel
Performance Measures
For the Year Ending June 30, 2004

	PERFORMANCE MEASURES		
	Investment Turnover	× Return-on-Sales Ratio	= ROI
Operating unit:			
Maine	1.50	0.12	0.18
Alberta	2.00	0.12	0.24
Missouri	0.67	0.33	0.22
Tijuana	1.50	0.18	0.27
Company performance criteria:			
Projected minimums	1.20	0.15	0.18

several key indicators of performance when conducting periodic reviews of its operating segments.

A similar analysis of ROI and its components is useful for planning. In developing plans for 2005, management wants to know the possible effect of changes in the major elements of ROI for the Maine Division. Sensitivity analysis can be used to predict the impact of changes in sales, the investment center asset base, or the investment center income.

Assuming the investment base is unchanged, a projected ROI can be determined for the Maine Division for a sales goal of $16,000,000 and an income goal of $1,600,000:

$$\text{ROI} = \frac{\text{Sales}}{\text{Investment center asset base}} \times \frac{\text{Investment center income}}{\text{Sales}}$$

$$= \frac{\$16,000,000}{\$8,000,000} \times \frac{\$1,600,000}{\$16,000,000}$$

$$= 2.0 \times 0.10$$

$$= 0.20, \text{ or } 20 \text{ percent.}$$

Note that ROI increased from 18 to 20 percent, even though the return-on-sales ratio decreased from 12 to 10 percent. The change in turnover from 1.5 to 2.0 more than offset the reduced return-on-sales ratio.

Sensitivity analysis can involve changing only one factor or a combination of factors in the ROI model. When more than one factor is changed, it is important to analyze exactly how much change is caused by each factor.

Statistics such as ROI, investment turnover, and return-on-sales ratio mean little by themselves. They take on meaning only when compared with an objective, a trend, another division, a competitor, or an industry average. Many businesses establish minimum ROIs for each of their divisions, expecting them to attain or exceed this minimum return. The salaries, bonuses, and promotions of division managers can be tied directly to their division's ROI. Without other evaluation techniques, managers often strive for ROI maximization, sometimes to the long-run detriment of the entire organization.

INVESTMENT CENTER INCOME

Despite the relevance and conceptual simplicity of ROI, a division's ROI cannot be determined until management decides how to measure divisional income and investment. Divisional income equals divisional revenues less divisional operating expenses. Determining divisional revenues is usually a relatively easy task since revenues are typically generated and recorded at the division level, but determining total operating expenses for divisions is more complicated. Because many expenses are incurred at the corporate level for the common benefit of the various operating divisions and to support corporate headquarters operations, the cost assignment issues discussed early in this chapter affect investment center income.

Direct division expenses are always included in division operating expenses, but there are conflicting viewpoints about how to deal with common corporate expenses. In corporate annual reports, many companies are required to provide segment revenues and expenses segmented by product lines, geographic territories, customer markets, and so on. Companies also show operating income for their various segments in their annual reports, but they include a category called *corporate* or *unallocated* for company expenses that cannot be reasonably allocated to the various segments. For example, the Ericsson, Inc. annual report for the year 2000 includes the following breakdown of its operating income by segments (stated in millions of Swedish kronas):

Network operators and service providers	33,072 SEK
Consumer products	(16,195)
Enterprises solutions	22
Other operations	1,708
Unallocated	(1,858)
Total operating income	16,749 SEK

A footnote in the Ericsson report indicates that "unallocated consists mainly of costs for corporate staffs, certain goodwill amortization and non-operational gains and losses."

For internal segment reporting, some companies do not allocate corporate costs that cannot be associated closely with individual segments. Other companies insist on allocating all common corporate costs to the operating divisions to emphasize that the company does not earn a profit until revenues have covered all costs. Some top managers believe that since only operating divisions produce revenues, they should also bear all costs, including corporate costs. These managers want to ensure that the sum of the division income for the various segments equals the total operating income for the company.

Division managers do not control corporate costs; therefore, these costs are seldom relevant in evaluating a division manager's performance. To deal with this conflict, some companies allocate some, or possibly all, common corporate costs in reporting segment operating income, but for ROI calculation purposes exclude allocated corporate costs that are not closely associated with the divisions. These companies include in the ROI calculation costs that represent an identifiable benefit to the divisions but not general corporate costs that provide no identifiable benefits to the divisions. In practice, the treatment of corporate costs for division performance evaluation varies widely.

INVESTMENT CENTER ASSET BASE

Because the primary purpose for computing ROI is to evaluate the effectiveness of a division's operating management in using the assets entrusted to them, most organizations define *investment* as the average total assets of a division during the evaluation period. For most companies, the *investment base* is defined as each division's operating assets. These normally include those assets held for productive use, such as accounts receivable, inventory, and plant and equipment. Nonproductive assets, such as land for a future plant site, are not included in the investment base of a division but in the investment base for the company.

General corporate assets allocated to divisions should not be included in their bases. Although the divisions might need additional administrative facilities if they were truly independent, they have no control over the headquarters' facilities. The joint nature and use of facility-level expenses make any allocation arbitrary.

OTHER VALUATION ISSUES

Once divisional investment and income have been operationally defined and ROI computations have been made, the significance of the resulting ratios can still be questioned. Return on investment can be overstated in terms of constant dollars because inflation as well as arbitrary inventory and depreciation procedures cause an undervaluation of the inventory and fixed assets included in the investment center asset base. Asset measurement is particularly troublesome if inventories are valued at last-in, first-out (LIFO) cost and fixed assets were acquired many years ago. A division manager could hesitate to replace an old, inefficient asset with a new, efficient one because the replacement could lower income and ROI through an increased investment base and increased depreciation.

To improve the comparability between divisions with old and new assets, some firms value assets at original cost rather than at net book value (cost less accumulated depreciation), in ROI computations. This procedure does not reflect inflation, however. An old asset that cost $120,000 ten years ago is still being compared with an asset that costs $200,000 today. A better solution could be to value old assets at their replacement cost, although obtaining replacement cost data can be a problem.

RESIDUAL INCOME

Residual income is an often-mentioned alternative to ROI for measuring investment center performance. **Residual income** is the excess of investment center income over the minimum rate of return set by top management. The minimum rate of return represents the rate that can be earned on alternative investments of similar risks, which is the opportunity cost of the investment.

The minimum dollar return is computed as a percentage of the investment center's asset base. When residual income is the primary basis of evaluation, the management of each investment center is encouraged to maximize residual income rather than ROI. To illustrate the computation, assume that a company requires a minimum return of 12 percent on each division's investment base. The residual income of a division with an annual net operating income of $2,000,000 and an investment base of $15,000,000 is $200,000:

Division income	$2,000,000
Minimum return ($15,000,000 × 0.12)	(1,800,000)
Residual income	$ 200,000

ECONOMIC VALUE ADDED

In recent years, a variation of residual income, referred to as **economic value added** or **EVA**®[2], has gained in popularity with many large corporations. EVA is equal to income after taxes less the cost of capital employed. The three significant changes from the residual income computation are the use of an organization's weighted average cost of capital as the minimum return, net assets as the evaluation base, and after-tax income (although some residual income proponents also use after-tax income). **Weighted**

---

[2]The term *EVA* is a registered trademark of the financial consulting firm of Stern Stewart and Company.

average cost of capital is an average of the after-tax cost of all long-term borrowing and the cost of equity; **net assets** are total assets less current liabilities. Economic value is added only after a division's taxable income exceeds its net cost of investing.

Using the preceding situation, assume that the company has a cost of capital of 10 percent, $1,800,000 in current liabilities, and a 30 percent tax rate. The economic value-added residual income becomes $80,000, computed as follows:

Division income after taxes ($2,000,000 × 0.70) $1,400,000
Cost of capital employed ([$15,000,000 − $1,800,000] × 0.10) . . . . . (1,320,000)

Economic value added . . . . $ 80,000

Another differentiating characteristic of the EVA model is that it usually corrects for potential distortions in economic net income caused by generally accepted accounting principles (GAAP). In calculating EVA, the user can abandon any accounting principles that are viewed as distorting the measurement of wealth creation. In practice, EVA consultants have identified up to 150 different adjustments to GAAP income and equity that must be made to restore equity and income to their true economic values. Most companies use no more than about five adjustments (such as the capitalization of research and development cost and the elimination of goodwill write-offs).

Proponents of EVA argue that it is the best measure of managerial performance from the standpoint of maximizing the market value added to a firm through managerial decisions. They maintain that **market value added (MVA)**, which is the increase in market value of the firm for the period, is the definitive measure of wealth creation and that MVA is maximized by maximizing EVA. By maximizing the excess of economic net income over the cost of all outside capital invested in the firm, the firm should maximize its MVA in the long run. One might ask why we should use EVA to estimate managerial contribution to the maximization of MVA, when we could simply measure how much market value has been added to the firm by considering changes in stock prices. In theory, measuring market success on stock price changes would work, but in practice this does not work well because of short-run changes in market prices caused by overall market factors, not just firm-specific factors. Also, many firms are not publicly traded, which makes determining market value changes difficult. Finally, companies want to measure managerial performance over specific segments of a firm, as well as the firm as a whole, but market values for individual segments are seldom available.

EVA provides a good operational metric for assessing how effective managers are performing in terms of maximizing MVA over time. An advantage of EVA is that it is a model than can also be used to guide managerial action. Companies that use EVA for evaluating performance use it in making a broad range of decisions such as evaluating capital expenditure proposals, adding or dropping a product line, or acquiring another company. Research Shows 13–1 discusses the impact of adopting an EVA financial management system on performances.

WHICH MEASURE IS BEST?

Many executives view either residual income method as a better measure of managers' performance than ROI. They believe that residual income encourages managers to make profitable investments that managers would reject if being measured exclusively by ROI. To illustrate, assume that three divisions of Color Company have an opportunity to make an investment of $100,000 that requires $10,000 of additional current liabilities and that will generate a return of 20 percent. The manager of the Rainbow Division is evaluated using ROI, the manager of the Ink Division is evaluated using residual income, and the manager of the Dye Division is evaluated using economic value added. The current ROI of each division is 24 percent. Each division has a current income of $120,000, a minimum return of 18 percent on invested capital, and a

EMPIRICAL EVIDENCE SUPPORTS EVA

A variety of research projects has focused on the effectiveness of EVA in leading companies to superior performance. Stern Stewart and Company tested the relationship between EVA and MVA for the largest companies in the United States and found that EVA statistically explains about 50 percent of the total movement in company MVA, whereas accounting earnings and cash flow explained about 18 percent and 22 percent respectively. Another study found that low MVA and EVA numbers more than double the chance that a company's CEO will be fired. For firms with MVAs above the median, 8.6 percent had fired their CEO, but for firms with MVAs below the median, the firing rate was 20.0 percent. The CEO turnover rate was 9.0 percent when EVA was above the median and 19.3 percent when it was below the median.

Source: Al Ehrbar, "Using EVA to Measure Performance and Assess Strategy," *Strategy & Leadership*, May/June 1999.

cost of capital of 14 percent. If each division has a current investment base of $500,000, current liabilities of $40,000, and a tax rate of 30 percent, the effect of the proposed investment on each division's performance is as follows:

	Current	+ Proposed	= Total
Rainbow Division:			
Investment center income	$120,000	$20,000	$140,000
Asset base	$500,000	$100,000	$600,000
ROI	24%	20%	23.3%
Ink Division:			
Asset base	$500,000	$100,000	$600,000
Investment center income	$120,000	$ 20,000	$140,000
Minimum return (0.18 × base)	(90,000)	(18,000)	(108,000)
Residual income	$ 30,000	$ 2,000	$ 32,000
Dye Division:			
Assets	$500,000	$100,000	$600,000
Current liabilities	(40,000)	(10,000)	(50,000)
Evaluation base	$460,000	$ 90,000	$550,000
Investment center income	$120,000	$ 20,000	$140,000
Income taxes (30%)	(36,000)	(6,000)	(42,000)
Income after taxes	$ 84,000	$ 14,000	$ 98,000
Cost of capital (0.14 × base)	(64,400)	(12,600)	(77,000)
Economic value added	$ 19,600	$ 1,400	$ 21,000

The Rainbow Division manager will not want to make the new investment because it reduces the current ROI from 24 percent to 23.3 percent. This is true, even though the company's minimum return is only 18 percent. Not wanting to explain a decline in the division's ROI, the manager will probably reject the opportunity even though it could have benefited the company as a whole.

The Ink Division manager will probably be happy to accept the new project because it increases residual income by $2,000. Any investment that provides a return more than the required minimum of 18 percent will be acceptable to the Ink Division manager. Given a profit maximization goal for the organization, the residual income method is preferred over ROI evaluations because it encourages division managers to accept all projects with returns above the 18 percent cutoff. The same is true for the Dye Division manager, although the EVA increase is not as high as that of the residual income because it has a different base. However, the EVA is often considered a better evaluation tool than residual income because it is believed to be a better measure of economic profit.

The primary disadvantage of the residual income and EVA methods as comparative evaluation tools is that they measure performance in absolute terms. Although they can be used to compare period-to-period results of the same division or with similar-size divisions, they cannot be used to compare the performance of divisions of substantially different sizes. For example, the residual income of a multimillion dollar sales division is expected to be higher than that of a half-million dollar sales division. Because most performance evaluations and comparisons are made between units or alternative investments of different sizes, ROI continues to be extensively used.

COMPREHENSIVE PERFORMANCE MEASUREMENT SYSTEMS

LEARNING OBJECTIVE 7

Now that you have been introduced to some of the more important aspects of performance measurement in management accounting, how do you use them in making decisions in the corporate environment? Although financial measures have been emphasized throughout this text—after all, this is an accounting text—several sections stress that other measures, specifically qualitative measures, are important in evaluating managerial performance. This section examines one popular method of performance evaluation using both financial and nonfinancial information.

Why not use just financial measures? First, no single financial measure captures all performance aspects of an organization. To begin with, then, more than one measure needs to be used. Second, financial measures have reporting time lags that could hinder timely decision making. Finally, financial measures might not accurately capture the information needed for current decision making because of the time lag that occurs between making financial investments and receiving their results. For example, building a new operating plant can take several years with total assets increasing the entire time without generating revenues.

Comprehensive performance measurement systems have been discussed since the turn of the century. The basic premise is to establish a set of diverse key performance indicators to monitor performance. As this concept evolved, it became known as the **balanced scorecard**, a performance measurement system that includes financial and operational measures related to a firm's goals and strategies. The balanced scorecard comprises several categories, the most common of which include the following:

- Financial
- Customer satisfaction
- Internal processes
- Innovation and learning

The balanced scorecard is not a one-model-fits-all measurement and evaluation system. It must be adapted to the needs of the organization as explained in Research Shows 13–2. A balanced scorecard is usually a set of reports required of all common operating units in an organization. To facilitate the periodic evaluation of performance, a cover sheet (or sheets for a large operation) can be used to summarize the performance of each area using the established criteria for each category. For example, a chain of bagel shops might have a balanced scorecard that looks something like the one in Exhibit 13–4. The balanced scorecard uses four categories for evaluation and includes financial and nonfinancial information. Each category being monitored has information from the previous period and the standard related to the category. The report should always include the current period, at least one previous period, and some standard. Each store manager should attach documentation and an appropriate explanation as to the movement of the measurements during the reporting period.

BALANCED SCORECARDS SHOULD FIT THE ORGANIZATION

Balanced scorecards can be found in manufacturing, retail, service, and governmental organizations. However, an organization should not try to force someone else's model to meet its own needs. Developing a balanced scorecard involves a process of custom designing a strategic management measurement system. The process begins by making a preliminary assessment of the overall business strategy with a focus on the integration of the entire economic process. Once the overall process, goals, and objectives have been identified, the measures believed best to capture the essence of the organization's progress toward these goals and objectives should be selected.

Examples of successful balanced scorecard applications are quite varied in the categories that are used to measure performance as follows.

Commercial bank:
   Shareholder return
   Customer service
   Employee satisfaction
   Community involvement

Biotechnology company:
   Customer perceptions
   Internal business perspective (efficiency)
   Innovation and technological leadership
   Building shareholder value

Food processing company:
   Financial growth
   Customer satisfaction
   Internal efficiency
   Learning and growth

Electronics company:
   Customer perspective
   Internal capabilities
   Innovation
   Financial perspective
   Employee and community perspective

Each of the four examples has some common elements of financial and customer perspectives, but it varies in the other areas of evaluation emphasis. Differences in perspective can be related to size, position in industry, type of business, phase in life cycle, and structure of organization.

Source: Chee W. Chow, Kamal M. Haddad, and James E. Williamson, "Applying the Balanced Scorecard to Small Companies," *Management Accounting*, August 1997, pp. 21–27.

EXHIBIT 13-4

BALANCED SCORECARD FOR BEN'S BAGELS FOR FEBRUARY

	Standard	January	February
Key financial indicators:			
Cash flow	$25,000	$(4,000)	$21,000
ROI	0.18	0.22	0.19
Economic value added	$130,000	$133,000	$123,000
Sales	$4,400,000	$4,494,000	$4,342,000
Key customer indicators:			
Average customers per hour	75	80	71
Number of customer complaints per month	22	21	17
Number of sales returns per month	10	8	5
Key operating indicators:			
Bagels sold/produced ratio per day	0.96	0.93	0.91
Daily units lost (burned, dropped, etc.)	25	32	34
Employee turnover per month	0.10	0.07	0.00
Key growth and innovation indicators:			
New products introduced during month	1	1	0
Products discontinued during month	1	1	1
Number of sales promotions	3	3	2
Special offers, discounts, etc.	4	5	3

In making assessments with the evaluation categories, it is important to consider both trailing and leading performance measures. *Trailing measures* look backward at historical data while *leading measures* provide some idea of what to expect currently or in the near future. For example, in the financial category, ROI is a trailing indicator while a budget of production units and costs for the next month is a leading indicator. In the customer category, a chart of sales units per store might tell us whether each store is maintaining its customer base (a trailing indicator) while a weekly chart of product complaints per 100 units sold might be a leading indicator of customer satisfaction, quality control problems, and future sales.

The use of balanced scorecard systems to monitor and assess managerial and organizational performance is increasing worldwide. What's Happening 13–3 provides insights into the key performance indicators used by a group of Australian firms.

A balanced scorecard gives management a perspective of the organization's performance on a recurring set of criteria. Since each reporting unit knows what reports are expected, no one is surprised by changing monthly requests for data. Because the multiple perspectives provide management a broad analysis of the organization's performance, it allows them to determine how and where the goals and objectives are either being achieved or not achieved. For most management teams, the balanced scorecard highlights trade-offs between measures. For example, a substantial increase in customer satisfaction can result in a short-run decrease in ROI because the extra effort to please customers is expensive, thereby reducing ROI. Finally, a balanced scorecard can be filtered down the organization with successively lower operating units having their own scorecards that mimic those of the larger units, thereby providing all levels of management an opportunity to evaluate operations from more than just a financial perspective.

13-3 WHAT'S HAPPENING?

BALANCED SCORECARD IS LINKED TO SIZE AND MARKET FACTORS

A survey of 66 Australian firms found that a balanced scorecard performance assessment model is more widely used by larger firms and that firms having a higher proportion of new products are more likely to include in their scorecard measures related to new products. On the other hand, no relationship was found between size of market share of companies and whether or not they used the balanced scorecard. Results also indicated that the usage of the balanced scorecard is associated with improved performance of companies regardless of company size, stage of product life cycle, or market position. The following were the most commonly used key performance indicators of the surveyed firms:

Financial perspective:
  Operating income
  Sales growth
  Return on investment
Customer perspective:
  Customer satisfaction
  Number of customer complaints
  Market share
  Percentage of shipments returned
    due to poor quality
  On-time delivery
  Warranty repair cost
  Customer response time
  Cycle time from order to delivery

Internal perspective:
  Labor efficiency variance
  Rate of material scrap loss
  Material efficiency variance
  Manufacturing lead time
  Ratio of good output to total output
  Percentage of defective products shipped
Innovation and learning perspective:
  Number of new product launches
  Number of new patents
  Time to market new products

Source: Zahirul Hoque and Wendy James, "Linking Balanced Scorecard Measures to Size and Market Factors: Impact on Organizational Performance," *Journal of Management Accounting Research,* Vol. 12, 2000.

As with all management tools and techniques, the use of the balanced scorecard must be incorporated with the other information sources within the organization. Just as the accounting information system cannot stand alone in managing a business, neither can the balanced scorecard. Some areas could need extensive accounting information in great detail to make the best possible decision while other areas need great detail in production or service integration to be at the right place at the right time. By using a multi-faceted approach to managing, however, the organization should be able to better establish an operating strategy that coincides with its overall goals and objectives.

BALANCED SCORECARD AND STRATEGY IMPLEMENTATION

When a balanced scorecard system is fully utilized to monitor and evaluate an organization's progress, it becomes a system for operationalizing the organization's strategy. Having a goal to maximize shareholder value or generate a certain income or EVA does not constitute a strategy. Maximizing shareholder value can be an overarching corporate goal, but it will not likely be realized without a well-developed strategy that identifies and establishes a balanced set of goals on various dimensions of performance. A balanced scorecard can be the primary vehicle for translating strategy into action and establishing accountability for performance. The balanced scorecard identifies the areas of managerial action that are believed to be the drivers of corporate achievement. If the corporate goal is to increase ROI or EVA, the balanced scorecard should include key performance indicators that drive ROI or EVA.

An interesting parallel to the successful management of a company can be drawn by considering the key performance indicators the manager of a professional baseball team uses in setting goals and evaluating progress. Joe Torre, the manager of the New York Yankees, does not just tell his players and managers at the beginning of the baseball season that the team's goal is to win the World Series or even a certain number of ball games. The win-loss record is only one metric used to set goals and evaluate performance for a baseball team. The manager looks at many different strategic drivers of success related to hitting, pitching, and fielding, including the earned run averages of the pitchers, the batting and on-base averages of hitters, the number of errors per game by fielders, and the number of bases stolen by base runners. At the end of the season, Joe Torre measures success not just by whether the Yankees won the World Series, but also by the batting average, number of home runs, and number of bases stolen by individual players, and whether or not a team member won a Golden Glove award or the Cy Young award. These are all measures by which to evaluate achievement and strategic accomplishment. By achieving the goals for each of these areas of the game, the win-loss ratio will take care of itself. If the win-loss results are not acceptable, then Joe Torre adjusts his strategic goals with respect to the key performance indicators.

Like a baseball team, a company can use a balanced scorecard to develop performance metrics for managers from the top of the company to the lowest-level manager. The scorecard becomes a vehicle for communicating the factors that are key to the success of managers, factors that upper management will monitor in evaluating the success of lower managers in carrying out the corporate strategy.

Summary

When an organization expands in size, management must decide whether to adopt a centralized or decentralized structure. As individual units within an organization become large enough to be separately evaluated as quasi-independent businesses, management generally decides to decentralize its operations into investment centers. Such a change requires the development of sound practices of responsibility accounting.

The selection of the evaluation method to be used for each responsibility center should be determined by what the center can realistically be responsible for in its operations. Centers that receive no revenues can hardly be considered profit centers, but centers that sell goods or services externally can be considered profit or investment centers.

Segment reports are income statements that show operating results for portions or segments of a business. The format and frequency of segment reports are limited only by management's needs and willingness to incur the cost of these reports.

Distinguishing between direct segment costs and indirect, or common, segment costs is important in segment reporting. Direct segment costs are specifically identifiable with a particular segment of a business. By subtracting a segment's direct costs from its revenues, segment margin is obtained. Indirect, or common, segment costs are not directly traceable to a particular segment but are necessary to support the activities of two or more segments. Indirect segment costs can be allocated to segments for a variety of reporting purposes, but unavoidable indirect segment costs should not be allocated in internal reports used for management decisions such as whether to continue or discontinue a segment.

Organizations having internal transfers between profit or investment centers must establish transfer prices for recorded transfers between internal units. Seldom does a single transfer price meet all the criteria for inducing division managers to make decisions that are congruent with corporate goals. The best transfer price depends on the circumstances. Furthermore, the optimal price for internal purposes can differ from that employed for external needs, including tax requirements.

To properly evaluate each responsibility center, management must select some type of measurement system with (preferably) quantitative and qualitative requirements. The three most popular financial methods of evaluating investment center performance are *return on investment (ROI), residual income,* and *economic value added (EVA).* For the qualitative areas, something in the areas of customer satisfaction and internal processes should be included as a minimum. Both the quantitative and qualitative areas can be combined into a *balanced scorecard* of key performance indicators that measure how well managers are achieving strategic objectives.

Review Problem

The solution to the review problem is found on pages 617–618. To maximize your learning, you should make a serious attempt to develop a written solution to the review problem before looking at the solution. If there are errors in your solution, you should then attempt to determine their causes.

Measures for Divisional Performance

Pareto International, a decentralized organization that manufactures specialty construction products, has three divisions, Commercial, Industrial, and Residential. Corporate management desires a minimum return of 15 percent on its investments and has a 20 percent tax rate with an average cost of capital of 12 percent.

The divisions' 2004 results were as follows (in thousands):

Division	Income	Investment	Current Liabilities
Commercial	$30,000	$200,000	$10,000
Industrial	50,000	250,000	30,000
Residential	22,000	100,000	5,000

The company is planning an expansion project in 2005 that will cost $50,000,000 and return $9,000,000 per year. It will result in a $10,000 increase in current liabilities.

Required:

a. Compute the ROI for each division for 2004.

b. Compute the residual income for each division for 2004.

c. Compute the economic value-added residual income for each division for 2004.

d. Rank the divisions according to their ROI, residual income, and EVA.

e. Assume that other income and investments will remain unchanged. Determine the effect of the project by itself. What is the effect on ROI, residual income, and economic value-added residual income if the new project is added to each division?

Key Terms

Avoidable common costs (p. 575)

Balanced scorecard (p. 590)

Centralization (p. 571)

Common segment costs (p. 575)

Decentralization (p. 570)

Direct segment fixed costs (p. 575)

Economic value added (EVA) (p. 587)

Market value added (MVA) (p. 588)

Net assets (p. 588)

Residual income (p. 587)

Return on investment (ROI) (p. 583)

Segment income (p. 575)

Segment margin (p. 575)

Segment reports (p. 572)

Strategic business segment (p. 570)

Suboptimization (p. 581)

Transfer price (p. 576)

Weighted average cost of capital (p. 587)

Review Questions

1. What are the primary advantages of having a decentralized organization structure?
2. How can the problems of decentralization be minimized?
3. What is the relationship between segment reports and product reports?
4. What is a reporting objective? How is it determined?
5. Can a company have more than one type of first-level statement in segment reporting?
6. Explain the relationships between any two levels of statements in segment reporting.
7. How do you distinguish between direct and indirect segment costs?
8. What types of information are needed before management should decide to drop a segment?
9. In what types of organizations and for what purpose are transfer prices used?
10. What problems arise when transfer pricing is used?
11. When do transfer prices lead to suboptimization? How can suboptimization be minimized? Can it be eliminated? Why or why not?
12. How do income tax issues affect transfer prices on transfers between divisions in different countries?
13. For what purpose do organizations use return on investment? Why is this measure preferred to net income?
14. What advantages do residual income and EVA have over ROI for segment evaluations?
15. Contrast the difference between residual income and EVA.
16. Explain how a balanced scorecard helps with the evaluation process of internal operations.
17. How can a balanced scorecard be used as a strategy implementation tool?

Exercises

13–1
Centralization versus Decentralization

Tell whether for each of the following activities, characteristics, and applications it is generally found in a centralized organization, in a decentralized organization, or in both types of organizations.

a. Cost centers
b. Profit centers
c. Maximization of benefits over costs
d. Minimization of duplication of functions
e. Few interdependencies among divisions
f. Very little suboptimization
g. Faster responsiveness to user needs
h. Greater freedom for managers at lower organizational levels to make decisions

13–2
Multiple Levels of Segment Reporting

Abraham Appliances manufactures four different lines of household appliances: cooking, cleaning, convenience, and safety. Each of the product lines is produced in all of the company's three plants: Abbeyville, Bakersville, and Charlottesville. Marketing efforts of the company are divided into five regions: East, West, South, North, and Central.

Required:
a. Develop a reporting schematic that illustrates how the company might prepare single-level reports segmented on three different bases.
b. Develop a segment reporting schematic that has three different levels. Be sure to identify each segment's level. Briefly explain why you chose the primary-level segment.

13–3
Income Statements Segmented by Territory

Writing Products, Inc., has two product lines. The September income statements of each product line and the company are as follows:

Writing Products, Inc.
Product Line and Company Income Statements
For the Month of September

	PRODUCT LINES		Company Totals
	Pens	Pencils	
Sales	$20,000	$30,000	$50,000
Less variable expenses	(8,000)	(12,000)	(20,000)
Contribution margin	$12,000	$18,000	$30,000
Less direct fixed expenses	(8,000)	(7,000)	(15,000)
Product margin	$ 4,000	$11,000	$15,000
Less common fixed expenses			(6,000)
Net income			$ 9,000

Pens and pencils are sold in two territories, Alaska and Alabama, as follows:

	Alaska	Alabama
Pen sales	$12,000	$ 8,000
Pencil sales	9,000	21,000
Total sales	$21,000	$29,000

The preceding common fixed expenses are traceable to each territory as follows:

> Alaska fixed expenses $2,000
> Alabama fixed expenses 3,000
> Home office administration fixed expenses 1,000
> Total common fixed expenses $6,000

The direct fixed expenses of pens, $8,000, and of pencils, $7,000, cannot be identified with either territory. The company's accountants were unable to allocate any of the common fixed expenses to the various segments.

Required:

a. Prepare income statements segmented by territory for September, including a column for the entire firm.

b. Why are the direct expenses of one type of segment report not necessarily the direct expenses of another type of segment report?

**13–4
Income Statements
Segmented by
Products**

Clayton Consulting Firm provides three types of client services in three health care-related industries. The income statement for July is as follows:

Clayton Consulting Firm
Income Statement
For the Month of July

Sales		$800,000
Less variable costs		(535,000)
Contribution margin		$265,000
Less fixed expenses:		
Service	$70,000	
Selling and administrative	65,000	(135,000)
Net income		$130,000

The sales, contribution margin ratios, and direct fixed expenses for the three types of services are as follows:

	Hospitals	Physicians	Nursing Care
Sales	$250,000	$250,000	$300,000
Contribution margin ratio	30%	40%	30%
Direct fixed expenses of services	$20,000	$18,000	$16,000
Allocated common fixed services expense	$1,000	$1,000	$1,500

Required:

Prepare income statements segmented by client categories. Include a column for the entire firm in the statement.

**13–5
Transfer Pricing and
Divisional Profit**

Leitch Consulting Company has two divisions: Tax Consultants and Financial Consultants. In addition to its external sales, each division performs work for the other division. The external fees earned by each division in April were $400,000 for Tax and $700,000 for Financial. Tax worked 3,000 hours for Financial, and Financial worked 1,200 hours for Tax. The costs of services performed were $220,000 for Tax and $480,000 for Financial.

Required:

a. Determine the gross profit in April for each division and for the company as a whole if the transfer price from Tax to Financial is $30 per hour and the transfer price from Financial to Tax is $25 per hour.

b. Determine the gross profit in April for each division and for the company as a whole if the transfer price for each division is $30 per hour.

c. What are the gross profit results in April for the divisions and the company as a whole if the two divisions net their hours and charge a transfer fee of $25 per excess hour? Which division manager would favor this arrangement?

13-6
Internal or External Acquisitions: No Opportunity Costs

The Van Division of CP Corporation has offered to purchase 180,000 wheels from the Wheel Division for $52 per wheel. At a normal volume of 500,000 wheels per year, production costs per wheel for the Wheel Division are as follows:

Direct materials	$20
Direct labor	10
Variable overhead	6
Fixed overhead	20
Total	$56

The Wheel Division has been selling 500,000 wheels per year to outside buyers at $68 each. Capacity is 700,000 wheels per year. The Van Division has been buying wheels from outside suppliers at $65 per wheel.

Required:
a. Should the Wheel Division manager accept the offer? Show computations.
b. From the standpoint of the company, will the internal sale be beneficial?

13-7
Appropriate Transfer Prices: Opportunity Costs

Plains Peanut Butter Company recently acquired a peanut-processing company that has a normal annual capacity of 4,000,000 pounds and that sold 2,800,000 pounds last year at a price of $2.00 per pound. The purpose of the acquisition is to furnish peanuts for the peanut butter plant, which needs 1,600,000 pounds of peanuts per year. It has been purchasing peanuts from suppliers at the market price.
Production costs per pound of the peanut-processing company are as follows:

Direct materials	$0.50
Direct labor	0.25
Variable overhead	0.12
Fixed overhead at normal capacity	0.20
Total	$1.07

Management is trying to decide what transfer price to use for sales from the newly acquired Peanut Division to the Peanut Butter Division. The manager of the Peanut Division argues that $2.00, the market price, is appropriate. The manager of the Peanut Butter Division argues that the cost price of $1.07 (or perhaps even less) should be used since fixed overhead costs should be recomputed.
Any output of the Peanut Division up to 2,800,000 pounds that is not sold to the Peanut Butter Division could be sold to regular customers at $2.00 per pound.

Required:
a. Compute the annual gross profit for the Peanut Division using a transfer price of $2.00.
b. Compute the annual gross profit for the Peanut Division using a transfer price of $1.07.
c. What transfer price(s) will lead the manager of the Peanut Butter Division to act in a manner that will maximize company profits?

13-8
Negotiating a Transfer Price with Excess Capacity

The Weaving Division of Carolina Textiles Inc. produces cloth that is sold to the company's Dyeing Division and to outside customers. Operating data for the Weaving Division for 2004 are as follows:

	To the Dyeing Division	To Outside Customers
Sales:		
300,000 yards × $5.00	$1,500,000	
200,000 yards × $6.00		$1,200,000
Variable expenses at $2.00	(600,000)	(400,000)
Contribution margin	$ 900,000	$ 800,000
Fixed expenses*	(750,000)	(500,000)
Net income	$ 150,000	$ 300,000

*Allocated on the basis of unit sales.

The Dyeing Division has just received an offer from an outside supplier to supply cloth at $4.30 per yard. The Weaving Division manager is not willing to meet the $4.30 price. She argues that it costs her $4.50 per yard to produce and sell to the Dyeing Division, so she would show no profit on the Dyeing Division sales. Sales to outside customers are at a maximum, 200,000 yards.

Required:
a. Verify the Weaving Division's $4.50 unit cost figure.
b. Should the Weaving Division meet the outside price of $4.30 for Dyeing Division sales? Explain.
c. Could the Weaving Division meet the $4.30 price and still show a profit for sales to the Dyeing Division? Show computations.

13–9
Dual Transfer Pricing

The Greek Company has two divisions, Beta and Gamma. Gamma Division produces a product at a variable cost of $6 per unit, and sells 150,000 units to outside customers at $10 per unit and 40,000 units to Beta Division at variable cost plus 40 percent. Under the dual transfer price system, Beta Division pays only the variable cost per unit. Gamma Division's fixed costs are $250,000 per year.

Beta Division sells its finished product to outside customers at $23 per unit. Beta has variable costs of $5 per unit, in addition to the costs from Gamma Division. Beta Division's annual fixed costs are $170,000. There are no beginning or ending inventories.

Required:
a. Prepare the income statements for the two divisions and the company as a whole.
b. Why is the income for the company less than the sum of the profit figures shown on the income statements for the two divisions? Explain.

13–10
Transfer Prices at Full Cost with Excess Capacity: Divisional Viewpoint

Dairy Company's Cheese Division produces cheese that sells for $12 per unit in the open market. The cost of the product is $8 (variable manufacturing of $5, plus fixed manufacturing of $3). Total fixed manufacturing costs are $210,000 at the normal annual production volume of 70,000 units.

The Overseas Division has offered to buy 15,000 units at the full cost of $8. The Producing Division has excess capacity, and the 15,000 units can be produced without interfering with the current outside sales of 70,000 units. The total fixed cost of the Cheese Division will not change.

Required:
Explain whether the Cheese Division should accept or reject the offer. Show calculations.

13-11
Transfer Pricing with Excess Capacity: Divisional and Corporate Viewpoints

Boyett Art Company has a Print Division that is currently producing 100,000 prints per year but has a capacity of 150,000 prints. The variable costs of each print are $30, and the annual fixed costs are $900,000. The prints sell for $40 in the open market.

The company's Retail Division wants to buy 50,000 prints at $28 each. The Print Division manager refuses the order because the price is below variable cost. The Retail Division manager argues that the order should be accepted because it will lower the fixed cost per print from $9 to $6.

Required:
a. Should the Retail Division order be accepted? Why or why not?
b. From the viewpoints of the Print Division and the company, should the order be accepted if the manager of the Retail Division intends to sell each print in the outside market for $42 after incurring additional costs of $10 per print?
c. What action should the company take, assuming it believes in divisional autonomy?

13-12
ROI, Residual Income, and EVA: Basic Computations

Watkins Associated Industries is a highly diversified company with three divisions: Trucking, Seafood, and Construction. Assume that the company uses return on investment, residual income, and economic value-added residual income as three of the evaluation tools for division managers. The company has a minimum desired rate of return on investment of 12 percent and a weighted average cost of capital of 10 percent with a 30 percent tax rate.

Selected operating data for three divisions of the company follow.

	Trucking Division	Seafood Division	Construction Division
Sales	$600,000	$750,000	$900,000
Operating assets	300,000	250,000	350,000
Net operating income	51,000	56,000	59,000
Current liabilities	20,000	10,000	30,000

Required:
a. Compute the return on investment for each division. (Round answers to three decimal places.)
b. Compute the residual income for each division.
c. Compute the economic value-added residual income for each division.
d. Which divisional manager is doing the best job based on ROI? Based on residual income? Based on economic value-added residual income? Why?

13-13
ROI and Residual Income: Impact of a New Investment

The Firebird Division of Central Motors had an operating income of $90,000 and net assets of $400,000. Central Motors has a target rate of return of 16 percent.

Required:
a. Compute the return on investment.
b. Compute the residual income.
c. Firebird has an opportunity to increase operating income by $20,000 with an $85,000 investment in assets.
   1. Compute the Firebird Division's return on investment if the project is undertaken. (Round your answer to three decimal places.)
   2. Compute the Firebird Division's residual income if the project is undertaken.

**13-14
ROI: Fill in the
Unknowns**

Provide the missing data in the following situations:

	North American Division	Asian Division	European Division
Sales	?	$5,000,000	?
Net operating income	$100,000	$200,000	$144,000
Operating assets	?	?	$800,000
Return on investment	16%	10%	?
Return-on-sales ratio	0.04	?	0.12
Investment turnover	?	?	1.5

**13-15
ROI, Residual
Income, and EVA
with Different Bases**

Macrosoft Company requires a return on capital of 12 percent. The following financial information is available for October:

	SOFTWARE DIVISION VALUE BASE		CONSULTING DIVISION VALUE BASE		VENTURE CAPITAL DIVISION VALUE BASE	
	Book	Current	Book	Current	Book	Current
Sales	$100,000	$100,000	$200,000	$200,000	$800,000	$800,000
Income	12,000	10,000	16,000	17,000	50,000	52,000
Assets	60,000	80,000	90,000	100,000	600,000	580,000
Current liabilities	10,000	10,000	14,000	14,000	40,000	40,000

Required:

a. Compute the return on investment using both book and current values for each division. (Round answers to three decimal places.)
b. Compute the residual income for both book and current values for each division.
c. Compute the economic value-added residual income for both book and current values for each division if the tax rate is 30 percent and the weighted average cost of capital is 10 percent.
d. Does book value or current value provide better basis for performance evaluation? Which division do you consider the most successful?

**13-16
Selection of
Balanced Scorecard
Items**

The International Accountants' Association is a professional association for accountants. Its current membership totals 110,000 worldwide. The association operates from a central headquarters in New Zealand but has local membership chapters throughout the world. The local chapters hold monthly meetings to discuss recent developments in accounting and to hear professional speakers on topics of interests. The association's journal, *International Accountant,* is published monthly with feature articles and topical interest areas. The association publishes books and reports and sponsors continuing education courses. A recent statement of revenues and expenses follows:

**International Accountants' Association
Statement of Revenues and Expenses
For the Year Ending November 30, 2004**

Revenues		$30,275,000
Expenses:		
Salaries	$14,000,000	
Other personnel costs	3,400,000	
Occupancy costs	2,000,000	
Reimbursement to local chapters	800,000	
Other membership services	500,000	
Printing and paper	320,000	
Postage and shipping	114,000	
General and administrative	538,000	(21,672,000)
Excess of revenues over expenses		$ 8,603,000

Additional information follows:

- Membership dues are $200 per year, of which $50 is considered to cover a one-year subscription to the association's journal. Other benefits include membership in the association and chapter affiliation.
- One-year subscriptions to *International Accountant* are sold to nonmembers for $80 each. A total of 2,500 of these subscriptions were sold. In addition to subscriptions, the journal generated $200,000 in advertising revenue. The cost per magazine was $20.
- A total of 30,000 technical reports were sold by the Books and Reports Department at an average unit selling price of $45. Average costs per publication were $12.
- The association offers a variety of continuing education courses to both members and nonmembers. During 2004, the one-day course, which cost participants an average of $75 each, was attended by 34,400 people. A total of 2,630 people took two-day courses at a cost of $125 per person.
- General and administrative expenses include all other costs incurred by the corporate staff to operate the association.
- The organization has net capital assets of $44,000,000 and prefers to maintain a cost of capital of 10 percent.

Required:
a. Give some examples of financial measures (no computations needed) that could be part of a balanced scorecard for the organization.
b. Using the categories of customer information and operating criteria, give several evaluation measures (no computations needed) for a balanced scorecard.

13-17
Balanced Scorecard
Preparation

The following information is in addition to that presented in Exercise 13–16 for the International Accountants' Association. For the year ended November 30, 2004, the organization had set a membership goal of 100,000 members with the following anticipated results:

International Accountants' Association
Planned Revenues and Expenses
For the Year Ending November 30, 2004

Revenues		$28,000,000
Expenses:		
Salaries	$13,950,000	
Other personnel costs	3,450,000	
Occupancy costs	1,900,000	
Reimbursement to local chapters	780,000	
Other membership services	525,000	
Printing and paper	300,000	
Postage and shipping	103,000	
General and administrative	550,000	(21,558,000)
Excess of revenues over expenses		$ 6,442,000

Additional information follows:

- Membership dues were increased from $180 to $200 during the year.
- One-year subscriptions to *International Accountant* are anticipated to be 2,400 units.
- Advertising revenue was budgeted at $225,000. Each magazine was budgeted at $18.
- A total of 28,000 technical reports were anticipated at an average price of $40 with average costs of $11.

- The budgeted one-day courses had an anticipated attendance of 32,000 with an average fee of $80. The two-day courses had an anticipated attendance of 3,000 with an average fee of $125 per person.
- The organization began the year with net capital assets of $40,000,000 with a planned cost of capital of 10 percent.

Required:

a. Prepare a balanced scorecard with examples in the categories of financial information, customer information, and operating criteria.
b. Which of the evaluation areas you selected indicated success and which indicated failure?
c. Give some explanations of the successes and failures.

Problems

13-18
Segment Reporting

Seattle Promotions Company has provided you the following information about its operations:

1. It has two products, umbrellas and hats.
2. It has two sales territories, Southeast and Northwest.
3. Monthly traceable direct fixed costs are $15,000 in the Southeast territory and $14,000 in the Northwest territory.
4. During January, Southeast sold $40,000 of umbrellas and $20,000 of hats; Northwest sold $10,000 of umbrellas and $30,000 of hats.
5. Variable cost of sales and selling expenses total 40 percent for umbrellas and 70 percent for hats.
6. Of Northwest's direct fixed costs, $5,000 is traceable to umbrellas and $5,000 to hats.
7. Of Southeast's direct fixed costs, $4,000 is traceable to umbrellas and $2,000 to hats.
8. Seattle Company's total fixed costs were $40,000 during January.
9. Seattle Company's total variable costs were $55,000 during January.
10. Common fixed expenses of $3,000 and $2,000, respectively, could be allocated to the Southeast and the Northwest.

Required:

a. Prepare January segment income statements for both territories. Include a column for the entire firm.
b. Prepare income statements segmented by product within each territory. Include a column for the entire firm.
c. What conclusions can management draw from evaluating the segment statements prepared in requirements (a) and (b)?

13-19
Multiple Segment Reports

Earth Products Incorporated sells throughout the world in three sales territories: Europe, Asia, and the Americas. For July, all $50,000 of administrative expense is traceable to the territories, except $10,000, which is common to all units and cannot be traced or allocated to the sales territories. The percentage of product line sales made in each of the sales territories and the assignment of traceable fixed expenses follow:

	SALES TERRITORY			
	Europe	Asia	The Americas	Total
Cookware sales	40%	50%	10%	100%
China sales	40	40	20	100
Vases sales	20	20	60	100
Fixed administrative expense . . .	$15,000	$15,000	$10,000	$ 40,000
Fixed selling expense	$30,000	$60,000	$60,000	$150,000

The manufacturing takes place in one large facility with three distinct manufacturing operations. Selected product-line cost data follow.

	Cookware	China	Vases	Total
Variable costs	$ 9	$ 9	$ 5	
Depreciation and supervision	15,000	15,000	12,000	$ 45,000*
Other mfg. overhead (common)				10,000
Fixed administrative expense (common)				50,000
Fixed selling expense (common)				150,000

Includes common costs of $3,000

The unit sales and selling prices for each product follow.

	Unit Sales	Selling Price
Cookware	10,000	$10
China	20,000	15
Vases	15,000	20

Required:

a. Prepare an income statement for July segmented by product line. Include a column for the entire firm.
b. Prepare an income statement for July segmented by sales territory. Include a column for the entire firm.
c. Prepare an income statement for July by product line for The Americas sales territory. Include a column for the territory as a whole.

13–20
Segment Reporting and Analysis

Midwest Bakery Incorporated bakes three products: donuts, pies, and cakes. It sells them in the cities of Chicago and Milwaukee. For March, the following income statement was prepared:

Midwest Bakery, Incorporated
Territory and Company Income Statements
For the Month of March

	CITY		Company Total
	Chicago	Milwaukee	
Sales	$2,100	$500	$2,600
Cost of goods sold	(1,500)	(300)	(1,800)
Gross profit	$ 600	$200	$ 800
Selling and administrative expenses	(400)	(100)	(500)
Net income	$ 200	$100	$ 300

Sales and selected variable expense data are as follows:

	PRODUCTS		
	Donuts	Pies	Cakes
Fixed baking expenses	$200	$140	$100
Variable baking expenses as a percentage of sales	50%	50%	60%
Variable selling expenses as a percentage of sales	4%	4%	5%
City of Chicago, sales	$800	$900	$400
City of Milwaukee, sales	$200	$100	$200

The fixed selling expenses were $260 for March, of which $210 was a direct expense of the Chicago market and $50 was a direct expense of the Milwaukee market. Fixed administrative expenses were $130, which management has decided not to allocate when using the contribution approach.

Required:

a. Prepare a segment income statement for each sales territory for March. Include a column for the entire firm.

b. Prepare segment income statements for each product. Include a column for the entire firm.

c. If the cake line is dropped and fixed baking expenses do not change, what is the product margin for donuts and pies?

13–21
Segment Reporting and Analysis

Accounting Publishers, Inc. has prepared income statements segmented by divisions, but management is still uncertain about actual performance. Financial information for May is given as follows:

SEGMENTS

	Textbook Division	Professional Division	Company Total
Sales	$180,000	$410,000	$590,000
Less variable expenses:			
Manufacturing	$ 32,000	$205,000	$237,000
Selling and administrative	4,000	20,500	24,500
Total	(36,000)	(225,500)	(261,500)
Contribution margin	$144,000	$184,500	$328,500
Less direct fixed expenses	(15,000)	(220,000)	(235,000)
Net income	$129,000	$ (35,500)	$ 93,500

Management is concerned about the Professional Division and requests additional analysis. Additional information regarding May operations of the Professional Division is as follows:

	Accounting	Executive	Management
Sales	$140,000	$140,000	$130,000
Variable manufacturing expenses as a percentage of sales	60%	40%	50%
Other variable expenses as a percentage of sales	5%	5%	5%
Direct fixed expenses	$50,000	$75,000	$50,000
Allocated common fixed expenses	$5,000	$2,000	$7,000

The professional accounting books are sold to auditors and controllers. The current information on these markets is as follows:

SALES MARKET

	Auditors	Controllers
Sales	$30,000	$110,000
Variable manufacturing expenses as a percentage of sales	60%	60%
Other variable expenses as a percentage of sales	16%	2%
Direct fixed expenses	$5,000	$25,000
Allocated common fixed expenses	$7,000	$8,000

Required:

a. Prepare an income statement segmented by product for the Professional Division. Include a column for the division as a whole.

b. Prepare an income statement segmented by market for the accounting books of the Professional Division.

c. Evaluate which accounting books the Professional Division should keep or discontinue in the short run.

d. What is the correct long-run decision?

13-22
Segment Reports

The Entertainment Corporation produces and sells three products. The three products, CDs, DVDs, and videotapes, are sold in a local market and in a regional market. At the end of the first quarter of 2004, the following income statement was prepared:

Entertainment Corporation
Territory and Company Income Statements
First Quarter of 2004

	Local	Regional	Company
Sales	$1,000,000	$300,000	$1,300,000
Cost of goods sold	(775,000)	(235,000)	(1,010,000)
Gross profit	$ 225,000	$ 65,000	$ 290,000
Selling expenses	$ 60,000	$ 45,000	$ 105,000
Administrative expenses	40,000	12,000	52,000
Total	(100,000)	(57,000)	(157,000)
Net income	$ 125,000	$ 8,000	$ 133,000

Management has expressed special concern with the Regional Market because of the extremely poor return on sales. This market was entered a year ago because of excess capacity. Management originally believed that the return on sales would improve with time, but after a year, no noticeable improvement could be seen from the results as reported in the preceding quarterly statement.

In attempting to decide whether to eliminate the Regional Market, the following information has been gathered:

	PRODUCTS		
	CD	DVD	Videotape
Sales	$500,000	$400,000	$400,000
Variable manufacturing expenses as a percentage of sales	60%	70%	60%
Variable selling expenses as a percentage of sales	3%	2%	2%

SALES BY MARKETS

Product	Local	Regional
CD	$400,000	$100,000
DVD	300,000	100,000
Videotape	300,000	100,000

All administrative expenses and fixed manufacturing expenses are common to the three products and the two markets; these expenses are fixed for the period. The remaining selling expenses are fixed for the period and separable by market. All fixed expenses are based on a prorated yearly amount.

Required:

a. Prepare the quarterly income statement showing contribution margins by market (territories). Include a column for the company as a whole.

b. Assuming there are no alternative uses for Entertainment Corporation's present capacity, would you recommend dropping the regional market? Why or why not?

c. Prepare the quarterly income statement showing contribution margins by product. Include a column for the company as a whole.

d. It is believed that a new product can be ready for sale next year if Entertainment Corporation decides to go ahead with continued research. The new product can be produced by simply converting equipment now used to produce videotapes. This conversion will increase fixed costs by $10,000 per quarter. What must be the minimum contribution margin per quarter for the new product to make the changeover financially feasible?

(CMA Adapted)

13–23
Segment Reports and Cost Allocations

Pacific Products, Inc. has three sales divisions. One of the key evaluation inputs for each division manager is the performance of his or her division based on division income. The division statements for August are as follows:

	DIVISION			Company Total
	Kiwi	Queensland	Hawaii	
Sales	$400,000	$500,000	$450,000	$1,350,000
Cost of sales	$200,000	$240,000	$230,000	$ 670,000
Division overhead	100,000	110,000	110,000	320,000
Divisional expenses	(300,000)	(350,000)	(340,000)	(990,000)
Division contribution	$100,000	$150,000	$110,000	$ 360,000
Corporate overhead	(70,000)	(90,000)	(80,000)	(240,000)
Division income	$ 30,000	$ 60,000	$ 30,000	$ 120,000

The Hawaii manager is unhappy that his profitability is the same as that of the Kiwi Division and one-half that of the Queensland Division when his sales are halfway between these two divisions. The manager knows that his division must carry more product lines because of customer demands, and many of these additional product lines are not very profitable. He has not dropped these marginal product lines because of idle capacity; all of the products cover their own variable costs.

After analyzing the product lines with the lowest profit margins, the divisional controller for Hawaii provided the following to the manager:

Sales of marginal products		$90,000
Cost of sales	$50,000	
Avoidable fixed costs	20,000	(70,000)
Product margin		$20,000
Proportion of corporate overhead		(16,000)
Product income		$ 4,000

Although these products were 20 percent of Hawaii's total sales, they contributed only about 13 percent of the division's profits. The controller also noted that the corporate overhead allocation was based on a formula of sales and divisional contribution margin.

Required:

a. Prepare a set of segment statements for August assuming that all facts remain the same except that Hawaii's weak product lines are dropped and corporate overhead is allocated as follows: Kiwi, $80,000; Queensland, $95,000; and Hawaii, $65,000. Does the Hawaii Division appear better after this action? What will be the responses of the other two division managers?

b. Suggest improvements for Pacific Products' reporting process that will better reflect the actual operations of the divisions. Keep in mind the utilization of the reporting process to assist in the evaluation of the managers. What other changes could be made to improve the manager evaluation process?

13–24
Transfer Pricing

Southern Brick Company owns its own clay mine that supplies clay for the Brick Division. The clay is charged to the Brick Division at market price. Income statements for March were as follows:

Southern Brick Company
Divisional Income Statements
For the Month of March

	Clay Mine	Brick Division
Sales	$800,000	$2,000,000
Production costs:		
Materials	$ —	$ 800,000
Labor	380,000	500,000
Overhead	160,000	300,000
Total	(540,000)	(1,600,000)
Gross profit	$260,000	$ 400,000
Selling and administrative costs	(120,000)	(300,000)
Income of division	$140,000	$ 100,000

In March and April, the clay mine sold 20,000 tons of clay. In April, the market price of clay increased 50 percent and conversion costs increased 10 percent, whereas the Brick Division increased its price by 10 percent. Income statements for April were as follows:

Southern Brick Company
Divisional Income Statements
For the Month of April

	Clay Mine	Brick Division
Sales	$1,200,000	$2,200,000
Production costs:		
Materials	$ —	$1,200,000
Labor	418,000	550,000
Overhead	176,000	330,000
Total	(594,000)	(2,080,000)
Gross profit	$ 606,000	$ 120,000
Selling and administrative costs	(120,000)	(330,000)
Income (loss) of division	$ 486,000	$ (210,000)

Corporate management is concerned about the Brick Division's April loss.

Required:
a. Prepare income statements for the company for March and April.
b. Evaluate the company's performance in April.
c. What should be the transfer price for clay? Discuss.

13-25
Various
Performance
Evaluation
Calculations

Following are data for BellSouth Corporation's four major business segments taken from its 2000 corporate annual report, along with other assumed data and selected ratio calculations (dollars in millions): (A) wireline communcations, (B) domestic wireless, (C) international operations, and (D) advertising and publishing.

	SEGMENTS			
	A	B	C	D
Segment sales	$18,063	$4,205	$2,771	$2,178
Segment net income (pretax)	3,503	(f)	(h)	637
Segment investment asset base	29,892	8,133	7,742	(j)
Segment current liabilities	9,266	2,521	2,400	(k)
Return-on-sales ratio	(a)	(g)	(i)	29.2%
Investment turnover	(b)	0.517	0.358	(l)
ROI	(c)	4.4%	(3.2%)	33.6%

	A	B	C	D
Minimum capital charge	10%	10%	10%	10%
Residual income	(d)	(456)	(944)	448
Weighted average cost of capital	16%	16%	16%	16%
Effective income tax rate	36%	36%	36%	36%
EVA	(e)	(669)	(964)	200

Required:

Calculate the amount for the lettered items (a) through (l) in the preceding table.

**13-26
ROI, Residual
Income, and EVA:
Impact of a New
Investment**

Office Equipment Inc. is a decentralized organization with four autonomous divisions. The divisions are evaluated on the basis of the change in their return on invested assets. Operating results in the Retail Division for 2004 follow:

**Office Equipment Inc.—Retail Division
Income Statement
For the Year Ending December 31, 2004**

Sales	$2,500,000
Less variable expenses	(1,250,000)
Contribution margin	$1,250,000
Less fixed expenses	(900,000)
Net operating income	$ 350,000

Operating assets for the Retail Division currently average $1,800,000. The Retail Division can add a new product line for an investment of $300,000. Relevant data for the new product line are as follows:

Sales	$800,000
Variable expenses (% of sales)	0.60
Fixed expenses	$300,000
Increase in current liabilities	$20,000

Required:

a. Determine the effect on ROI of accepting the new product line. (Round calculations to three decimal places.)

b. If a return of 6 percent is the minimum that any division should earn and residual income is used to evaluate managers, would this encourage the division to accept the new product line? Explain and show computations.

c. If EVA is used to evaluate managers, should the new product line be accepted if the weighted average cost of capital is 8 percent and the investment tax rate is 40 percent?

**13-27
Valuing Investment
Center Assets**

Six Flags Theme Parks, Inc., operates theme parks in the United States, Mexico, and Europe. One of its first theme parks, Six Flags over Georgia, was built in the 1960s in Atlanta on a large tract of land that has appreciated enormously over the past 35 years. Although most of the rides and other attractions have a fairly short life, some of the major buildings that are still in use on the property have been fully depreciated since they were built. Assume that Six Flags over Georgia operates as an investment center with total assets that have a book value of $150 million and current liabilities of $20 million. Assume also that in 2004, this particular theme park had sales of $60 million and pretax division income of $20 million. The replacement cost of all the assets in this park is estimated to be $250 million. The company's cost of capital is 16 percent, and it has a 35 percent tax rate.

Required:

a. Calculate the ROI, residual income, and EVA for Six Flags over Georgia using book value as the valuation basis for the investment center asset base.

b. Repeat requirement (a) using replacement cost as the investment center asset value.

c. Which valuation, accounting book value or replacement cost do you think the company uses to evaluate the managers of its various theme parks? Discuss.

Discussion Questions and Cases

13-28 Transfer Price Decisions

The Consulting Division of IBM Corporation is often involved in assignments for which IBM computer equipment is sold as part of a systems installation. The Computer Equipment Division is frequently a vendor of the Consulting Division in cases for which the Computer Division purchases the equipment from the Computer Equipment Division. The Consulting Division does not view itself as a sales arm of the Computer Equipment Division but as a strong competitor to the major consulting firms of information systems. The Consulting Division's goal is to maximize its profit contribution to the company, not necessarily to see how much IBM equipment it can sell. If the Consulting Division is truly an autonomous investment center, it has the freedom to purchase equipment from competing vendors if the consultants believe that a competitor's products serve the needs of a client better than the comparable IBM product in a particular situation.

Required:

a. In this situation, should corporate managment be concerned about whether the Consulting Division sells IBM products or those of other computer companies? Should the Consulting Division be required to sell only IBM products?

b. Discuss the transfer pricing issues that both the Equipment Division manager and the Consulting Division manager should consider. If top management does not have a policy on pricing transfers between these two divisions, what alternative transfer prices should the division managers consider?

c. What is your recommendation regarding how the managers of the Consulting and Equipment Divisions can work together in a way that will benefit each of them individually and the company as a whole?

13-29 Decentralization and Autonomy

Edwin Hall, chairman of the board and president of Arrow Works Products Company, founded the company in the mid-1990s. He is a talented and creative engineer. He started Arrow Works with one of his inventions, an intricate die-cast item that required a minimum of finish work. Arrow Works manufactured the item in a Gary, Indiana, foundry. The product sold well in a wide market.

The company issued common stock in 1998 to finance the purchase of the Gary foundry. Additional shares were issued in 1999 when Arrow purchased a fabricating plant in Cleveland to meet the capacity requirement of a defense contract.

The company now consists of five divisions, each of which is headed by a manager who reports to Hall. The Chicago Division contains the product development and engineering department and the finishing (assembly) operation for the basic products. The Gary Division and Cleveland Division are the other two segments engaged in manufacturing operations. All products manufactured are sold through two selling divisions. The Eastern Sales Division is located in Pittsburgh and covers the country from Chicago to the East Coast. The Western Sales Division, which covers the rest of the country, is located in Denver. The Western Sales Division is the newer operation and was established just eight months ago.

Hall, who still owns 53 percent of the outstanding stock, actively participates in the management of the company. He regularly travels to all the company's plants and offices. He says, "Having a business with locations in five different cities spread over half the country requires all my time." Despite his regular and frequent visits, he believes that the company is decentralized, with the managers having complete autonomy. "They make all the decisions and run their own shops. Of course, they don't understand the total business as I do, so I have to straighten them out once in a while. My managers are all good people, but they can't be expected to handle everything alone. I try to help all I can."

The last two months have been a period of considerable stress for Hall. During this period, John Staple, manager of the fabricating plant, was advised by his physician to request a six-month sick leave to relieve the work pressures that had made him nervous and tense. This request had followed (by three days) a phone call in which Hall had directly and bluntly blamed Staple for the lagging production output and increased rework and scrap of the fabricating plant. Hall made no allowances for the pressures created by the operation of the plant at volumes in excess of normal and close to its maximum rated capacity for the previous nine months.

Hall thought he and Staple had had a long and good relationship before this event. Hall attributed his loss of temper in this case to his frustration with several other management problems that had arisen in the past two months. The sales manager of the Denver office had resigned shortly after a visit from Hall. The letter of resignation stated he was seeking a position with greater responsibility. The sales manager in Pittsburgh asked to be reassigned to a sales position in the field; he did not believe he could cope with the pressure of management.

Required:

a. Explain the difference between centralized and decentralized management.
b. Is Arrow Works Products Company decentralized as Edwin Hall believes? Explain your answer.
c. Could the events that have occurred over the past two months in Arrow Works Products Company have been expected? Explain your answer.

(CMA Adapted)

13-30
Transfer Pricing at Absorption Cost

The Fabrication Division of Metro Sign Company produces large metal numbers that are sold to the Sign Division. This division uses the numbers in constructing signs that are sold to highway departments of local governments.

The Fabrication Division contains two operations, stamping and finishing. The unit variable cost of materials and labor used in the stamping operation is $100. The fixed stamping overhead is $800,000 per year. Current production (20,000 units) is at full capacity.

The variable cost of labor used in the finishing operation is $12 per number. The fixed overhead in this operation is $340,000 per year.

The company uses an absorption-cost transfer price. The price data for each operation presented to the Sign Division by the Fabrication Division follow.

Stamping:
Variable cost per unit $100
Fixed overhead cost per unit ($800,000 ÷ 20,000 units) 40 $140

Finishing:
Labor cost per unit . . . . $ 12
Fixed overhead cost per unit ($340,000 ÷ 20,000 units) 17   29

Total cost per unit $169

An outside company has offered to lease machinery to the Sign Division that would perform the finishing part of the number manufacturing for $200,000 per year. With the new machinery, the labor cost per frame would remain at $12. If the Fabrication Division transfers the units for $140, the following analysis can be made:

Current process:
Finishing process costs (20,000 × $29) $580,000
New process:
Machine rental cost per year $200,000
Labor cost ($12 × 20,000 units) 240,000 (440,000)
Savings $140,000

The manager of the Sign Division wants approval to acquire the new machinery.

Required:
a. How would you advise the company concerning the proposed lease?
b. How could the transfer-pricing system be modified or the transfer-pricing problem eliminated?

**13–31
Transfer Pricing
with and without
Capacity Constraints**

National Carpet Company has just acquired a new backing division that produces a rubber backing, which it sells for $2.00 per square yard. Sales are about 1,200,000 square yards per year. Since the Backing Division has a capacity of 2,000,000 square yards per year, top management is thinking that it might be wise for the company's Tufting Division to start purchasing from the newly acquired Backing Division.

The Tufting Division now purchases 600,000 square yards per year from an outside supplier at a price of $1.80 per square yard. The current price is lower than the competitive $2.00 price as a result of the large quantity discounts.

The Backing Division's cost per square yard follows.

Direct materials $1.00
Direct labor 0.20
Variable overhead 0.25
Fixed overhead (1,200,000 level) 0.10
Total cost $1.55

Required:
a. If both divisions are to be treated as investment centers and their performance evaluated by the ROI formula, what transfer price would you recommend? Why?
b. Determine the effect of making the backing on corporate profits.
c. Based on your transfer price, would you expect the ROI in the Backing Division to increase, decrease, or remain unchanged? Explain.
d. What would be the effect on the ROI of the Tufting Division using your transfer price? Explain.
e. Assume that the Backing Division is now selling 2,000,000 square yards per year to retail outlets. What transfer price would you recommend? What will be the effect on corporate profits?
f. If the Backing Division is at capacity and decides to sell to the Tufting Division for $1.80 per square yard, what will be the effect on the company's profits?

**13–32
Transfer Pricing and
Special Orders**

Continental Communications Company has several manufacturing divisions. The Pacific Division produces a component part that is used in the manufacture of electronic equipment. The cost per part for July is as follows:

Variable cost . . . . $ 90
Fixed cost (at 2,000 units per month capacity) 60
Total cost per part $150

Some of Pacific Division's output is sold to outside manufacturers, and some is sold internally to the Atlantic Division. The price per part is $175.

The Atlantic Division's cost and revenue structure follow.

Selling price per unit		$1,000
Less variable costs per unit:		
Cost of parts from the Pacific Division	$175	
Other variable costs	400	(575)
Contribution margin per unit		$ 425
Less fixed costs per unit (at 200 units per month)		(100)
Net income per unit		$ 325

The Atlantic Division received an order for 10 units. The buyer wants to pay only $500 per unit.

Required:

a. From the perspective of the Atlantic Division, should the $500 price be accepted? Explain.
b. If both divisions have excess capacity, would the Atlantic Division's action benefit the company as a whole? Explain.
c. If the Atlantic Division has excess capacity but the Pacific Division does not and can sell all of its parts to outside manufacturers, what would be the advantage or disadvantage of accepting the ten-unit order at the $500 price to the Atlantic Division?
d. To make a decision that is in the best interest of the company, what transfer-pricing information does the Atlantic Division need?

13–33
An Evaluation of
Market-Based
Transfer Prices

Worldwide Products, a large diversified corporation, operates its divisions on a decentralized basis. Division Alpha makes Product X, which can be sold either to Division Beta or to outside customers.

At current levels of production, the variable cost of making Product X is $3.50 per unit, the fixed cost is $0.50, and the market price is $7.00 per unit. There are no separate selling costs.

Division Beta processes Product X into Product Y. The additional variable cost of producing Product Y is $4.00 per unit.

Top management is developing a corporate transfer-pricing policy. The bases for setting transfer prices being reviewed are full absorption cost, total variable costs, and market price.

Required:

a. In order to maximize company profits, which of the transfer-pricing bases being reviewed should be used and why?
b. In the short run, which of the transfer-pricing bases would tend to encourage the best use of the corporation's productive capacity? Why would this not be true in the long run?
c. Identify two possible advantages that Division Beta might expect if it purchased Product X from Division Alpha at the current market price.
d. What possible disadvantage might accrue to Division Alpha if it were committed to sell all its production of Product X to Division Beta at the current market price?

(CIA Adapted)

13–34
Evaluating ROI

International Consulting Group has several decentralized divisions whose managers are responsible for service revenue, cost of operations, acquisition and financing of divisional assets, and working capital management.

The vice president of general operations is considering changing from annual to multi-year evaluations of division managers. Currently, a review of the performance, attitudes, and skills of management is undertaken annually. As a trial run, two managers will be selected for the new evaluation procedure. The selection has been narrowed to the managers of Divisions 1 (the Canadian practice) and 4 (the Scandinavian practice).

Both managers became division managers in 2004. Their divisions had the following operating results (in thousands) for the last three years:

	DIVISION 1			DIVISION 4		
	2004	2005	2006	2004	2005	2006
Estimated industry sales	$1,000,000	$1,200,000	$1,300,000	$500,000	$600,000	$650,000
Division sales	100,000	110,000	121,000	45,000	60,000	75,000
Variable costs	30,000	32,000	34,500	13,500	17,500	21,000
Fixed operating costs	40,000	40,500	42,000	17,000	20,000	23,000
Fixed administrative costs	27,500	32,500	32,500	14,000	20,000	25,000
Total costs	97,500	105,000	109,000	44,500	57,500	69,000
Net income	2,500	5,000	12,000	500	2,500	6,000
Net assets	22,700	23,500	24,500	12,300	14,000	17,000
Return on investment	?	?	?	?	?	?

Required:

a. Determine each manager's ROI for each year.
b. Is ROI an appropriate measurement for manager evaluation? Why or why not?
c. What additional measures could be used?
d. Per year, which manager performed better?
e. Over three years, which manager performed better?

(CMA Adapted)

13-35
Transfer Pricing
Dispute

MBR Inc. consists of three divisions that were formerly three independent manufacturing companies. Bader Corporation and Roper Company merged in 1995, and the merged corporation acquired Mitchell Company in 1996. The name of the corporation was subsequently changed to MBR Inc., and each company became a separate division retaining the name of its former company.

The three divisions have operated as if they were still independent companies. Each division has its own sales force and production facilities. Each division management is responsible for sales, cost of operations, acquisition and financing of divisional assets, and working capital management. The corporate management of MBR evaluates the performance of the divisions and division management on the basis of return on investment.

Mitchell Division has just been awarded a contract for a product that uses a component manufactured by the Roper Division and also by outside suppliers. Mitchell used a cost figure of $3.80 for the component manufactured by Roper in preparing its bid for the new product. Roper supplied this cost figure in response to Mitchell's request for the average variable cost of the component; it represents the standard variable manufacturing cost and variable selling and distribution expenses.

Roper has an active sales force that is continually soliciting new prospects. Roper's regular selling price for the component Mitchell needs for the new product is $6.50. Sales of this component are expected to increase. The Roper management has indicated, however, that it could supply Mitchell the required quantities of the component at the regular selling price less variable selling and distribution expenses. Mitchell's management has responded by offering to pay standard variable manufacturing cost plus 20 percent.

The two divisions have been unable to agree on a transfer price. Corporate management has never established a transfer-pricing policy because interdivisional transactions have never occurred. As a compromise, the corporate vice president of finance suggested a price equal to the standard full manufacturing cost (i.e., no selling and distribution expenses) plus a 15 percent markup. The two division managers have also rejected this price because each considered it grossly unfair.

The unit cost structure for the Roper component and the three suggested prices follow.

Standard variable manufacturing cost	$3.20
Standard fixed manufacturing cost	1.20
Variable selling and distribution expenses	0.60
	$5.00

Regular selling price less variable selling and distribution expenses ($6.50 − $0.60)	$5.90
Standard full manufacturing cost plus 15% ($4.40 × 1.15)	$5.06
Variable manufacturing plus 20% ($3.20 × 1.20)	$3.84

Required:

a. What should be the attitude of the Roper Division's management toward the three proposed prices?

b. Is the negotiation of a price between the Mitchell and Roper Divisions a satisfactory method of solving the transfer-pricing problem? Explain your answer.

c. Should the corporate management of MBR Inc. become involved in this transfer-price controversy? Explain your answer.

(CMA Adapted)

13–36
Segmented Reports by Revenue Center

Music Teachers Inc. is an educational association for music teachers that had 20,000 members during 2004. The association operates from a central headquarters but has local membership chapters throughout the United States and Canada. The local chapters hold monthly meetings to discuss recent developments on topics of interest to music teachers. The association's journal, *Teachers' Forum*, is issued monthly with features about recent developments in the field. The association publishes books and reports and sponsors professional courses that qualify for professional continuing education credit. The statement of revenues and expenses follows:

Music Teachers Inc.
Statement of Revenues and Expenses
For the Year Ending November 30, 2004

Revenues		$3,275,000
Expenses:		
Salaries	$920,000	
Personnel costs	230,000	
Occupancy costs	280,000	
Reimbursement to local chapters	600,000	
Other membership services	500,000	
Printing and paper	320,000	
Postage and shipping	176,000	
Instructors' fees	80,000	
General and administrative	38,000	(3,144,000)
Excess of revenues over expenses		$ 131,000

The board of directors has requested that a segmented statement of operations be prepared showing the contribution of each revenue center (i.e., Membership, Magazine Subscriptions, Books and Reports, and Continuing Education). Mickie Doyle, who has been assigned this responsibility, has gathered the following data prior to statement preparation:

- Membership dues are $100 per year, of which $20 is considered to cover a one-year subscription to the association's journal. Other benefits include membership in the association and chapter affiliation. The portion of the dues covering the magazine subscription ($20) should be assigned to the Magazine Subscriptions revenue center.

- A total of 2,500 one-year subscriptions to *Teachers' Forum* were sold to non-members and libraries at $30 each. In addition to subscriptions, the magazine generated $100,000 in advertising revenue. The costs per magazine subscription were $7 for printing and paper and $4 for postage and shipping.
- The Books and Reports Department sold a total of 28,000 technical reports and professional texts at an average unit selling price of $25. Average costs per publication were as follows:

Printing and paper	$4
Postage and shipping	2

- The association offers a variety of continuing education courses to both members and nonmembers. During 2004, the one-day course, which cost participants $75 each, was attended by 2,400 people. A total of 1,760 people took two-day courses at a cost of $125 per person. Outside instructors were paid to teach some courses.
- Salary and occupancy data were as follows:

	Salaries	Square Footage
Membership	$210,000	2,000
Magazine subscriptions	150,000	2,000
Books and reports	300,000	3,000
Continuing education	180,000	2,000
Corporate staff	80,000	1,000
Totals	$920,000	10,000

- The Books and Reports Department also rents warehouse space at an annual cost of $50,000. Personnel costs are 25 percent of salaries.
- Printing and paper costs other than those for magazine subscriptions, books, and reports relate to the Continuing Education Department.
- General and administrative expenses include all other costs incurred by the corporate staff to operate the association.

Doyle has decided to assign all revenues and expenses to the revenue centers that can be (1) traced directly to a revenue center or (2) allocated on a reasonable and logical basis to a revenue center. The expenses that can be traced or assigned to corporate staff, as well as any other expenses that cannot be assigned to revenue centers, will be grouped with the general and administrative expenses and not allocated to the revenue centers. She believes that allocations often tend to be arbitrary and are not useful for management reporting and analysis. She believes that any further allocation of the general and administrative expenses associated with the operation and administration of the association would be arbitrary.

Required:
a. Prepare a segmented statement of revenues and expenses that presents the contribution of each revenue center and includes the common costs of the organization that are not allocated to the revenue centers.
b. If the association adopts segmented reporting for continued use, discuss the ways the association can utilize the information provided by the report.
c. Mickie Doyle decided not to allocate some indirect or nontraceable expenses to revenue centers because she believes that allocations tend to be arbitrary.
   1. Besides the arbitrary argument, what reasons are often presented for not allocating indirect or nontraceable expenses to revenue centers?
   2. Under what circumstances might the allocation of indirect or nontraceable expenses to revenue centers be acceptable?

(CMA Adapted)

John Shank Case Recommendation

Bridgewater Castings, Inc.

This heavily disguised case is set in the "mature" woodstoves business in 1986. The issue is product line strategy based on product line profitability analysis. The case requires students to evaluate cost allocations for manufacturing, selling, and shipping expenses and to evaluate profitability using the return on assets ratio. It also poses the question of whether to keep or drop an established product line.

Montclair Paper Mill—The APL Line

This case explores all of the links in a supply chain, looking for a way to revise the chain to improve profitability to the manufacturing. It presents profitability data for two profitability segments and requires the students to evaluate them utilizing the DuPont model framework. It combines profitability analysis with value chain analysis by requiring the student to evaluate profitability at various stages in the value chain.

Solution to Review Problem

a.
$$\text{Return on investment} = \frac{\text{Investment center income}}{\text{Investment center asset base}}$$

$$\text{Commercial Division} = \$30,000 \div \$200,000$$
$$= 0.15, \text{ or } 15 \text{ percent}$$
$$\text{Industrial Division} = \$50,000 \div \$250,000$$
$$= 0.20, \text{ or } 20 \text{ percent}$$
$$\text{Residential Division} = \$22,000 \div \$100,000$$
$$= 0.22, \text{ or } 22 \text{ percent}$$

b. Residual income = Investment center income − (Investment center asset base × Minimum return)

$$\text{Commercial Division} = \$30,000 - (0.15 \times \$200,000)$$
$$= \$0.00$$
$$\text{Industrial Division} = \$50,000 - (0.15 \times \$250,000)$$
$$= \$12,500$$
$$\text{Residential Division} = \$22,000 - (0.15 \times \$100,000)$$
$$= \$7,000$$

c. EVA = After tax income − (Net assets × Weighted average cost of capital)

$$\text{Commercial Division} = (\$30,000 \times 0.80) - [(\$200,000 - \$10,000) \times 0.12]$$
$$= \$1,200$$
$$\text{Industrial Division} = (\$50,000 \times 0.80) - [(\$250,000 - \$30,000) \times 0.12]$$
$$= \$13,600$$
$$\text{Residential Division} = (\$22,000 \times 0.80) - [(\$100,000 - \$5,000) \times 0.12]$$
$$= \$6,200$$

d. ROI ranks the Residential Division first, the Industrial Division second, and the Commercial Division third. Residual income ranks the Industrial Division first, the Residential Division second, and the Commercial Division third.

   Because the investments for each division are different, it is somewhat misleading to rank the divisions according to residual income. The Industrial Division had the highest residual income, but it also had the largest investment. The Residential Division's residual income was 56 percent of the Industrial Division's income but only 40 percent of the investment of the Industrial Division. This fact, along with the best ROI ranking, probably justifies the Residential Division being evaluated as the best division of Pareto Company.

e. Return on investment:

$$\text{Investment} = \$9,000 \div \$50,000$$
$$= 0.18, \text{ or } 18 \text{ percent}$$
$$\text{Commercial Division} = (\$30,000 + \$9,000) \div (\$200,000 + \$50,000)$$
$$= 0.156, \text{ or } 15.6 \text{ percent}$$
$$\text{Industrial Division} = (\$50,000 + \$9,000) \div (\$250,000 + \$50,000)$$
$$= 0.1967, \text{ or } 19.67 \text{ percent}$$
$$\text{Residential Division} = (\$22,000 + \$9,000) \div (\$100,000 + \$50,000)$$
$$= 0.2067, \text{ or } 20.67 \text{ percent}$$

ROI will increase for the Commercial Division but decrease for the Industrial and Residential Divisions, even though the project's ROI of 18 percent exceeds the company's minimum return of 15 percent.

Residual income:

$$\text{Commercial Division} = (\$30,000 + \$9,000) - [0.15 \times (\$200,000 + \$50,000)]$$
$$= \$1,500$$
$$\text{Industrial Division} = (\$50,000 + \$9,000) - [0.15 \times (\$250,000 + \$50,000)]$$
$$= \$14,000$$
$$\text{Residential Division} = (\$22,000 + \$9,000) - [0.15 \times (\$100,000 + \$50,000)]$$
$$= \$8,500$$

Because the project's ROI exceeds the company's minimum return, the residual income of all divisions will increase.

Economic value-added:

$$\text{Commerical Division} = [(\$30,000 + \$9,000) \times 0.80] - [(\$200,000 + \$50,000 - \$20,000) \times 0.12]$$
$$= \$3,600$$
$$\text{Industrial Division} = [(\$50,000 + \$9,000) \times 0.80] - [(\$250,000 + \$50,000 - \$40,000) \times 0.12]$$
$$= \$16,000$$
$$\text{Residential Division} = [(\$22,000 + \$9,000) \times 0.80] - [(\$100,000 + \$50,000 - \$15,000) \times 0.12]$$
$$= \$8,600$$

The EVA does not shift the same way the residual income does because of the additional relationships between the level of current liabilities and the tax rate. However, in this situation, all divisions have an increase when the new investment is made.

GLOSSARY

A

Absorption costing an approach to product costing that treats both variable and fixed manufacturing costs as product costs.

Accounting rate of return the average annual increase in net income that results from acceptance of a capital expenditure proposal divided by either the initial investment or the average investment in the project.

Activities list *see* **operations list.**

Activity a unit of work.

Activity cost drivers specific units of work (activities) performed to serve customer needs that consume costly resources.

Activity costing the determination of the cost of specific activities performed to fill customer needs.

Activity dictionary a standardized list of processes and related activities.

Activity-based budgeting an approach to budgeting that uses an activity cost hierarchy to budget physical inputs and costs as a function of planned activity. It is mechanically similar to the output/input approach to budgeting where physical inputs and costs are budgeted as a function of planned activity.

Activity-based costing (ABC) used to develop cost information by determining the cost of activities and tracing their costs to cost objectives on the basis of the cost objective's utilization of units of activity.

Activity-based management (ABM) the identification and selection of activities to maximize the value of the activities while minimizing their cost from the perspective of the final consumer.

Annuity a series of equal cash flows received or paid over equal intervals of time.

Appraisal costs quality costs incurred to identify nonconforming products or services before they are delivered to customers.

Assembly efficiency variance the difference between the standard cost of actual assembly inputs and the flexible budget cost for assembly.

Assembly rate variance the difference between the actual cost and the standard cost of actual assembly inputs.

Automatic identification systems (AIS) the use of bar coding of products and production processes that allows inventory and production information to be entered into a computer without writing or keying.

B

Backflush costing an inventory accounting system used in conjunction with JIT in which costs are assigned initially to cost of goods sold. At the end of the period, costs are backed out of cost of goods sold and assigned to appropriate inventory accounts for any inventories that may exist.

Balance sheet a picture of the economic health of an organization at a specific time, showing the organization's assets and the claims on those assets.

Balanced scorecard a performance measurement system that includes financial and operational measures which are related to the organizational goals. The basic premise is to establish a set of indicators that can be used to monitor performance progress and then compare the goals that are established with the results.

Batch level activity an activity performed for each batch of product produced.

Benchmarking a systematic approach to identifying the best practices to help an organization take action to improve performance.

Bill of materials a document that specifies the kinds and quantities of raw materials required to produce one unit of product.

Bottom-up budget a budget where managers at all levels—and in some cases even nonmanagers—become involved in the budget preparation.

Break-even point the unit or dollar sales volume where total revenues equal total costs.

Budget a formal plan of action expressed in monetary terms.

Budget committee a committee responsible for supervising budget preparation. It serves as a review board for evaluating requests for discretionary cost items and new projects.

Budget office an organizational unit responsible for the preparation, distribution, and processing of forms used in gathering budget data. It handles most of the work of actually formulating the budget schedules and reports.

Budgetary slack occurs when managers intentionally understate revenues or overstate expenses in order to produce favorable variances for the department.

Budgeted financial statements hypothetical statements that reflect the "as if" effects of the budgeted activities on the actual financial position of the organization. They reflect what the results of operations will be if all the predictions in the budget are correct.

Budgeting projecting the operations of an organization and their financial impact on the future.

C

Capacity costs *see* **committed fixed costs.**

Capital budgeting a process that involves the identification of potentially desirable projects for capital expenditures, the subsequent evaluation of capital expenditure proposals, and the selection of proposals that meet certain criteria.

Capital expenditures investments of significant financial resources in projects to develop or introduce new products or services, to expand current production or service capacity, or to change current production or service facilities.

Cash budget summarizes all cash receipts and disbursements expected to occur during the budget period.

Centralization when top management controls the major functions of an organization (such as manufacturing, sales, accounting, computer operations, marketing, research and development, and management control).

Chained target costing bringing in suppliers as part of the coordination process to attain a competitively priced product that is delivered to the customer in a timely manner.

Coefficient of determination (R^2) a measure of the percent of variation in the dependent variable that is explained by variations in the independent variable when the least-squares estimation equation is used.

Committed fixed costs (capacity costs) costs required to maintain the current service or production capacity or to fill a previous legal commitment.

Common cost a cost incurred for the benefit of two or more cost objectives—an indirect cost.

Common segment costs costs related to more than one segment and not directly traceable to a particular segment. These costs are referred to as common costs because they are incurred at one level for the benefit of two or more segments at a lower level.

Computer-aided design (CAD) a method of design that involves the use of computers to design products.

Computer-aided manufacturing (CAM) a manufacturing method that involves the use of computers to control the operation of machines.

Computer-integrated manufacturing (CIM) the ultimate extension of the CAD, CAM, and FMS concepts to a completely automated and computer-controlled factory where production is self-operating once a product is designed and the decision to produce is made.

Continuous budgeting budgeting based on a moving time frame that extends over a fixed period. The budget system adds an identical time period to the budget at the end of each period of operations, thereby always maintaining a budget of exactly the same time length.

Continuous improvement an approach to activity-based management where the employees constantly evaluate products, services, and processes, seeking ways to do better.

Continuous improvement (Kaizen) budgeting an approach to budgeting that incorporates a targeted improvement

(reduction) in costs; management requests that a given process will be improved during the budgeting process. This may be applied to every budget category or to specific areas selected by management. Kaizen budgeting is based upon prior performance and anticipated operating conditions during the upcoming period.

Continuous improvement (Kaizen) costing establishing cost reduction targets for products or services that an organization is currently providing to customers.

Contribution income statement an income statement format in which variable costs are subtracted from revenues to figure contribution margin, and fixed costs are then subtracted from contribution margin to calculate net income.

Contribution margin the difference between total revenues and total variable costs; this amount goes toward covering fixed costs and providing a profit.

Contribution margin ratio the portion of each dollar of sales revenue contributed toward covering fixed costs and earning a profit.

Controlling the process of ensuring that results agree with plans.

Conversion cost the combined costs of direct labor and manufacturing overhead incurred to convert raw materials into finished goods.

Cost allocation base a measure of volume of activity, such as direct labor hours or machine hours, that determines how much of a cost pool is assigned to each cost objective.

Cost behavior how costs respond to changes in an activity cost driver.

Cost center a responsibility center whose manager is responsible only for managing costs.

Cost driver a factor that causes or influences costs.

Cost driver analysis the study of factors that influence costs.

Cost estimation the determination of the relationship between activity and cost.

Cost objective an object to which costs are assigned. Examples include departments, products, and services.

Cost of capital the average cost of obtaining the resources necessary to make investments.

Cost of production report used in a process costing system; summarizes unit and cost data for each department or process for each period.

Cost pool a collection of related costs, such as departmental manufacturing overhead, that is assigned to one or more cost objectives, such as products.

Cost prediction error the difference between a predicted future cost and the actual amount of the cost when, or if, it is incurred.

Cost prediction the forecasting of future costs.

Cost reduction proposal a proposed action or investment intended to reduce the cost of an activity that the organization is committed to keeping.

Cost-volume-profit (CVP) analysis a technique used to examine the relationships among total volume of some independent variable, total costs, total revenues, and profits during a time period (typically a month or a year).

Cost-volume-profit graph an illustration of the relationships among activity volume, total revenues, total costs, and profits.

Customer level activity an activity performed to obtain or maintain each customer.

Cycle efficiency the ratio of value-added to nonvalue-added manufacturing activities.

Cycle time the total time required to complete a process. It is composed of the times needed for setup, processing, movement, waiting, and inspection.

D

Decentralization the delegation of decision-making authority to successively lower management levels in an organization. The lower in the organization the authority is delegated, the greater the decentralization.

Degree of operating leverage a measure of operating leverage, computed as the contribution margin divided by income before taxes.

Denominator variance *see* **fixed overhead volume variance.**

Depreciation tax shield the reduction in taxes due to the deductibility of depreciation from taxable revenues.

Descriptive model a model that merely specifies the relationships between a series of independent and dependent variables.

Design for manufacture explicitly considering the costs of manufacturing and servicing a product while it is being designed.

Differential cost analysis an approach to the analysis of relevant costs that focuses on the costs that differ under alternative actions.

Direct costing *see* **variable costing.**

Direct department cost a cost directly traceable to a department upon its incurrence.

Direct labor wages earned by production employees for the time they spend working on the conversion of raw materials into finished goods.

Direct materials the costs of primary raw materials that are converted into finished goods.

Direct method a method of allocating service department costs to producing departments based only on the amount of services provided to the producing departments. It does not recognize any interdepartmental services.

Direct segment fixed costs costs that would not be incurred if the segment being evaluated were discontinued. They are specifically identifiable with a particular segment.

Discount rate the minimum rate of return required for the project to be acceptable.

Discretionary cost center a cost center that does not have clearly defined relationships between effort and accomplishment.

Discretionary fixed costs costs set at a fixed amount each period at the discretion of management.

Division margin the amount each division contributes toward covering common corporate expenses and generating corporate profits. It is computed by subtracting all direct fixed expenses identifiable with each division from the contribution margin.

E

Economic value-added (EVA) a variation of residual income calculated as income after taxes less the cost of capital employed.

Electronic data interchange (EDI) the electronic communication of data between organizations.

Enterprise Resource Planning (ERP) enterprise management information systems that provide organizations an integrated set of operating, financial, and management systems.

Equivalent completed units the number of completed units that is equal, in terms of production effort, to a given number of partially completed units.

Ethics the moral quality, fitness, or propriety of a course of action that may injure or benefit people.

External failure costs quality costs incurred when nonconforming products or services are delivered to customers.

F

Facility level activity an activity performed to maintain general manufacturing or marketing capabilities.

File a collection of related records.

Financial accounting an information processing system that generates general-purpose reports of financial operations (income statement and cash flows statement) and financial position (balance sheet) for an organization.

Financial reporting the process of preparing financial statements (income statement, balance sheet, and statement of cash flows) for a firm in accordance with generally accepted accounting principles.

Finished goods inventories the completely manufactured products held for sale to customers.

First-in, First-out (FIFO) method in process costing, a costing method that accounts for unit costs of beginning inventory units separately from those started during the current period. The first costs incurred each period are assumed to have been used to complete the unfinished units left over from the previous period.

Fixed costs costs unrelated to unit level activity. With a unit level cost driver as the independent variable, fixed costs are a constant amount per period of time.

Fixed manufacturing overhead all fixed costs associated with converting raw materials into finished goods.

Fixed overhead budget variance the difference between budgeted and actual fixed overhead.

Fixed overhead volume variance the difference between total budgeted fixed overhead and total standard fixed overhead assigned to production.

Fixed selling and administrative costs all fixed costs other than those directly associated with converting raw materials into finished goods.

Flexible budget variance computed for each cost as the difference between the actual cost and the flexible budget cost of producing a given quantity of product or service.

Flexible budgets budgets that are drawn up for a series of possible production and sales volumes or adjusted to a particular level of production after the fact. These budgets, based on cost-volume or cost-activity relationships, are used to determine what costs should have been for an attained level of activity.

Flexible manufacturing systems (FMS) an extension of computer-aided manufacturing techniques through a series of manufacturing operations. These operations include the automatic movement of units between operations and the automatic and rapid setup of machines to produce each product.

For-profit organization an organization that has profit as a primary mission.

Full absorption cost *see* **absorption costing.**

Full costing *see* **absorption costing.**

Full costs include all costs, regardless of their behavior patterns (variable or fixed) or activity level.

Functional income statement a type of income statement where costs are classified according to function, rather than behavior. It is typically included in external financial reports.

Future value the amount a current sum of money earning a stated rate of interest will accumulate to at the end of a future period.

G

General and administrative expense budget presents the expenses the organization plans to incur in connection with the general administration of the organization. Included are expenses for such things as the accounting department, the computer center, and the president's office.

Goal a definable, measurable objective.

H

High-low method of cost estimation utilizes data from two time periods, a *representative* high activity period and a *representative* low activity period, to estimate fixed and variable costs.

I

Imposed budget *see* **top-down budget.**

Income statement a summary of economic events during a period of time, showing the revenues generated by operating activities, the expenses incurred in generating those revenues, and any gains or losses attributed to the period.

Incremental budgeting an approach to budgeting where costs for a coming period are budgeted as a dollar or percentage change from the amount budgeted for (or spent during) some previous period.

Indirect department cost a cost reassigned, or allocated, to a department from another cost objective.

Indirect segment costs *see* **common segment costs.**

Inspection time the amount of time it takes units to be inspected.

Integer programming a variation of linear programming that determines the solution in whole numbers.

Interdepartmental services services provided by one service department to other service departments.

Internal failure costs quality costs incurred when materials, components, products, or services are identified as defective before delivery to customers.

Internal rate of return (IRR) (often called the **time-adjusted rate of return**) the discount rate that equates the present value of a project's cash inflows with the present value of the project's cash outflows.

Inventory turnover the annual demand in units divided by the average inventory in units. It is also computed (in dollars) as cost of goods sold divided by the cost of average inventory.

Investment center a responsibility center whose manager is responsible for the relationship between its profits and the total assets invested in the center. In general, the management of an investment center is expected to earn a target profit per dollar invested.

Investment tax credit a reduction in income taxes of a percent of the cost of a new asset in the year the new asset is placed in service.

Irrelevant costs costs that do not differ among competing decision alternatives.

J

Job cost sheet a document used to track the status of and accumulate the costs for a specific job in a job cost system.

Job order production the manufacturing of products in single units or in batches of identical units.

Job production *see* **job order production.**

Joint costs all materials and conversion costs of joint products incurred prior to the split-off point.

Joint products two or more products simultaneously produced by a single process from a common set of inputs.

Just-in-time (JIT) inventory management a comprehensive inventory management philosophy that stresses policies, procedures, and attitudes by managers and other workers that result in the efficient production of high-quality goods while maintaining the minimum level of inventories.

K

Kanban system *see* **materials pull system.**

Kaizen costing *see* **continuous improvement costing.**

L

Labor efficiency variance the difference between the standard cost of actual labor inputs and the flexible budget cost for labor.

Labor rate (spending) variance the difference between the actual cost and the standard cost of actual labor inputs.

Least-squares regression analysis uses a mathematical technique to fit a cost estimating equation to the observed data in a manner that minimizes the sum of the vertical squared estimating errors between the estimated and actual costs at each observation.

Life-cycle budgeting an approach to budgeting when the entire life of the project represents a more useful planning horizon than an artificial period of one year.

Life-cycle costs from the seller's perspective, all costs associated with a product or service ranging from those incurred with initial conception through design, preproduction, production, and after-production support. From the buyer's perspective, all costs associated with a purchased product or service, including initial acquisition costs and subsequent costs of operation, maintenance, repair, and disposal.

Linear algebra method (reciprocal) method a method of allocating service department costs using a series of linear algebraic equations, which are solved simultaneously, to allocate service department costs both interdepartmentally among service departments and to the producing departments.

Linear programming an optimizing model used to assist managers in making decisions under constrained conditions when linear relationships exist between all variables.

M

Managed fixed costs *see* **discretionary fixed costs.**

Management accounting a discipline concerned with financial and related information used by managers and other persons inside specific organizations to make strategic, organizational, and operational decisions.

Management by exception an approach to performance assessment whereby management directs attention only to those activities not proceeding according to plan.

Manufacturing cost budget a budget detailing the direct materials, direct labor, and manufacturing overhead costs that should be incurred by manufacturing operations to produce the number of units called for in the production budget.

Manufacturing margin the result when direct manufacturing costs (variable costs) are deducted from product sales.

Manufacturing organizations organizations that process raw materials into finished products for sale to others.

Manufacturing overhead all manufacturing costs other than direct materials and direct labor.

Margin of safety the amount by which actual or planned sales exceed the break-even point.

Marginal cost the varying increment in total cost required to produce and sell an additional unit of product.

Marginal revenue the varying increment in total revenue derived from the sale of an additional unit.

Market segment level activity performed to obtain or maintain operations in a market segment.

Master budget the grouping together of all budgets and supporting schedules. This budget coordinates all the financial and operational activities and places them into an organizationwide set of budgets for a given time period.

Materials price variance the difference between the actual materials cost and the standard cost of actual materials inputs.

Materials pull system an inventory production flow system in which employees at each station work to replenish the inventory used by employees at subsequent stations. The building of excess inventories is strictly prohibited. When the number of units in inventory reaches a specified

limit, work at the station stops until workers at a subsequent station pull a unit from the in-process storage area.

Materials push system an inventory production flow system in which employees work to reduce the pile of inventory building up at their work stations. Workers at each station remove materials from an in-process storage area, complete their operation, and place the output in another in-process storage area. Hence, they push the work to the next work station.

Materials quantity variance the difference between the standard cost of actual materials inputs and the flexible budget cost for materials.

Materials requisition form a document used to record the type and quantity of each raw material issued to the factory.

Merchandising organizations organizations that buy and sell goods without performing manufacturing operations.

Minimum level budgeting an approach to budgeting that establishes a base amount for all budget items and requires explanation or justification for any budgeted amount above the minimum (base).

Mission the basic purpose toward which an organization's activities are directed.

Mixed costs costs that contain a fixed and a variable cost element.

Model a simplified representation of some real-world phenomenon.

Movement time the time units spend moving between work or inspection stations.

Mutually exclusive investments two or more capital expenditure proposals where the acceptance of one investment automatically causes the rejection of the other(s).

N

Net assets total assets less current liabilities.

Net present value the present value of a project's net cash inflows from operations and disinvestment less the amount of the initial investment.

Net sales volume variance indicates the impact of a change in sales volume on the contribution margin, given the budgeted selling price and the standard variable costs. It is computed as the difference between the actual and the budgeted sales volumes times the budgeted unit contribution margin.

Non-value-added activity an activity that does not add value to a product or service from the viewpoint of the customer.

Not-for-profit organization an organization that does not have profit as a primary goal.

O

Objective function in linear programming models, the goal to be minimized or maximized.

Operating activities normal profit-related activities performed in conducting the daily affairs of an organization. These are the major concerns of management in preparing operating budgets.

Operating budget detailed plans to guide operations throughout the budget period.

Operating leverage a measure of the extent that an organization's costs are fixed.

Operations list a document that specifies the manufacturing operations and related times required to produce one unit or batch of product.

Opportunity cost the net cash inflow that could be obtained if the resources committed to one action were used in the most desirable other alternative.

Optimal solution in linear programming models, the feasible solution than maximizes or minimizes the value of the objective function, depending on the decision maker's goal.

Optimizing model a model that suggests a specific choice between decision alternatives.

Order-filling costs costs incurred to place finished goods in the hands of purchasers (for example, storing, packaging, and transportation).

Order-getting costs costs incurred to obtain customers' orders (for example, advertising, salespersons' salaries and commissions, travel, telephone, and entertainment).

Order level activity an activity performed for each sales order.

Organization chart an illustration of the formal relationships existing between the elements of an organization.

Organization structure the arrangement of lines of responsibility within the organization.

Organizational cost drivers choices concerning the organization of activities and the involvement of persons inside and outside the organization in decision making.

Organizational-based cost systems used for financial reporting, these systems focus on organizational units such as a company, plant, or department rather than on processes and activities.

Organizing the process of making the organization into a well-ordered whole.

Outcomes assessment *see* **performance measurement.**

Outlay costs costs that require future expenditures of cash or other resources.

Output/input budgeting an approach to budgeting where physical inputs and costs are budgeted as a function of planned unit level activities. The budgeted inputs are a function of the planned outputs.

Outsourcing the external acquisition of services or components.

P

Participation budget *see* **bottom-up budget.**

Payback period the time required to recover the initial investment in a project from operations.

Performance measurement the determination of the extent to which actual outcomes correspond to planned outcomes.

Period costs expired costs not related to manufacturing inventory; they are recognized as expenses when incurred.

Physical model a scaled-down version or replica of physical reality.

Planning the process of selecting goals and strategies to achieve those goals.

Practical capacity the maximum possible activity, allowing for normal repairs and maintenance.

Predetermined manufacturing overhead rate an overhead rate established at the start of each year by dividing the predicted overhead costs for the year by the predicted volume of activity in the overhead base for the year.

Present value the current worth of a specified amount of money to be received at some future date at some interest rate.

Present value index the present value of the project's subsequent cash flows divided by the initial investment.

Prevention costs quality costs incurred to prevent nonconforming products from being produced or nonconforming services from being performed.

Price discrimination illegally charging different purchasers different prices.

Price fixing the organized setting of prices by competitors.

Process a collection of related activities intended to achieve a common purpose.

Process manufacturing a manufacturing environment where production is on a continuous basis.

Process map (or process flowchart) a schematic overview of all the activities required to complete a process. Each major activity is represented by a rectangle on the map.

Process reengineering the fundamental redesign of a process to serve internal or external customers.

Processing time the time spent working on units.

Product costs all costs incurred in the manufacturing of products; they are carried in the accounts as an asset (inventory) until the product is sold, at which time they are recognized as an expense (cost of goods sold).

Product level activity an activity performed to support the production of each different type of product.

Product margin computed as product sales less direct product costs.

Production order a document that contains a job's unique identification number and specifies details for the job such as the quantity to be produced, the total raw materials requirements, the manufacturing operations and other activities to be performed, and perhaps even the time when each manufacturing operation should be performed.

Productivity the relationship between outputs and inputs.

Profit center a responsibility center whose manager is responsible for revenues, costs, and resulting profits. It may be an entire organization, but it is more frequently a segment of an organization such as a product line, marketing territory, or store.

Profitability analysis an examination of the relationships between revenues, costs, and profits.

Profit-volume graph illustrates the relationship between volume and profits; it does not show revenues and costs.

Project-level activity an activity performed to support the completion of each project.

Purchases budget indicates the merchandise or materials that must be acquired to meet current needs and ending inventory requirements.

Q

Quality conformance to customer expectations.

Quality circles groups of employees involved in the production of products who have the authority, within certain parameters, to address and resolve quality problems as they occur, without seeking management approval.

Quality costs costs incurred because poor quality of conformance does (or may) exist.

Quality of conformance the degree of conformance between a product and its design specifications.

Quality of design the degree of conformance between customer expectations for a product or service and the design specifications of the product or service.

Quantitative model a set of mathematical relationships.

R

Raw materials inventories the physical ingredients and components that will be converted by machines and/or human labor into a finished product.

Record a related set of alphabetic and/or numeric data items.

Relational (cause-and-effect) cost center a cost center that has clearly defined relationships between effort and accomplishment (cause and effect).

Relevant costs future costs that differ between competing decision alternatives.

Relevant range the range of activity within which a linear cost function is valid.

Residual income the excess of investment center income over the minimum rate of return set by top management. The minimum dollar return is computed as a percentage of the investment center's asset base.

Responsibility accounting the structuring of performance reports addressed to individual (or group) members of an organization in a manner that emphasizes the factors they are able to control. The focus is on specific units within the organization that are responsible for the accomplishment of specific activities or objectives.

Return on investment (ROI) a measure of the earnings per dollar of investment. The return on investment of an investment center is computed by dividing the income of the center by its asset base (usually total assets). It can also be computed as investment turnover times the return-on-sales ratio.

Revenue center a responsibility center whose manager is responsible for the generation of sales revenues.

Revenue variance the difference between the budgeted sales volume at the budgeted selling price and the actual sales volume at the actual selling price.

Revenues inflows of resources from the sale of goods and services.

Robinson-Patman Act prohibits price discrimination when purchasers compete with one another in the sale of their products or services to third parties.

Rolling budget *see* **continuous budgeting.**

S

Sales budget a plan of unit sales volume and sales revenue for a future period. It may also contain a forecast of sales collections.

Sales mix the relative portion of unit or dollar sales derived from each product or service.

Sales price variance the impact on revenues of a change in selling price, given the actual sales volume. It is computed as the change in selling price times the actual sales volume.

Sales volume variance indicates the impact on revenues of change in sales volume, assuming there was no change in selling price. It is computed as the difference between the actual and the budgeted sales volumes times the budgeted selling price.

Scatter diagram a graph of past activity and cost data, with individual observations represented by dots.

Segment income all revenues of a segment minus all costs directly or indirectly charged to it.

Segment margin the amount that a segment contributes toward the common (indirect) costs of the organization and toward profits. It is computed as segment sales less direct segment costs.

Segment reports income statements that show operating results for portions or segments of a business. Segment reporting is used primarily for internal purposes, although generally accepted accounting principles also require disclosure of segment information for some public corporations.

Selling expense budget presents the expenses the organization plans to incur in connection with sales and distribution.

Semivariable costs *see* **mixed costs.**

Sensitivity analysis the study of the responsiveness of a model to changes in one or more of its independent variables.

Service costing the process of assigning costs to services performed.

Service department a department that provides support services to production and/or other support departments.

Service organizations nonmanufacturing organizations that perform work for others, including banks, hospitals, and real estate agencies.

Setup time the time required to prepare equipment to produce a specific product.

Sherman Antitrust Act prohibits price fixing.

Simplex method a mathematical approach to solving linear programming models containing three or more variables.

Split-off point the point in the process where joint products become separately identifiable.

Standard cost variance analysis a system for examining the flexible budget variance, which is the difference between the actual cost and flexible budget cost of producing a given quantity of product or service.

Standard cost a budget that indicates what it should cost to provide an activity or produce one batch or unit of product under efficient operating conditions.

Statement of cash flows a summary of resource inflows and outflows stated in terms of cash.

Statement of cost of goods manufactured a report that summarizes the cost of goods completed and transferred into finished goods inventory during the period.

Static budget a budget based on a prior prediction of expected sales and production.

Step costs costs that are constant within a narrow range of activity but shift to a higher level with an increased range of activity. Total step costs increase in a step-like fashion as activity increases.

Step method A method of allocating service department costs that gives partial recognition to interdepartmental services by using a methodology that allocates service department costs sequentially to both the remaining service departments and the producing departments.

Storyboard a process map developed by employees who perform the component activities within a process.

Strategic business segment a segment that has its own mission and set of goals to be achieved. The mission of the segment influences the decisions that its top managers make in both short-run and long-run situations.

Strategic cost management making decisions concerning specific cost drivers within the context of an organization's business strategy, its internal value chain, and its place in a larger value chain stretching from the development and use of resources to the final consumers.

Strategic plan a guideline or framework for making specific medium-range or short-run decisions.

Strategic position analysis an organization's basic way of competing to sell products or services.

Strategic position how an organization wants to place itself in comparison to the competition.

Strategy a course of action that will assist in achieving one or more goals.

Structural cost drivers fundamental choices about the size and scope of operations and technologies employed in delivering products or services to customers. These choices affect the types of activities and the costs of activities performed to satisfy customer needs.

Suboptimization when managers or operating units, acting in their own best interests, make decisions that are not in the best interest of the organization as a whole.

Sunk costs costs resulting from past decisions that cannot be changed.

T

Target costing establishes the allowable cost of a product or service by starting with determining what customers are willing to pay for the product or service and then subtracting a desired profit on sales.

Theory of constraints every process has a bottleneck (constraining resource), and production cannot take place faster than it is processed through the bottleneck. The theory's goal is to maximize throughput in a constrained environment.

Throughput sales revenue minus direct materials costs. *See also* **theory of constraints**.

Time-adjusted rate of return *see* **internal rate of return**.

Top-down budget a budget where top management decides on the primary goals and objectives for the organization and communicates them to lower management levels.

Transfer price the internal value assigned a product or service that one division provides to another.

U

Unit contribution margin the difference between the unit selling price and the unit variable costs.

Unit level activity an activity performed for each unit of product produced or sold.

Unit level approach an approach to analyzing cost behavior that assumes changes in costs are best explained by changes in the number of units or sales dollars of products or services provided for customers.

V

Value the worth in usefulness or importance of a product or service to the customer.

Value chain the set of value-producing activities stretching from basic raw materials to the final consumer.

Value chain analysis the study of value-producing activities, stretching from basic raw materials to the final consumer of a product or service.

Value-added activity an activity that adds value to a product or service from the viewpoint of the customer.

Variable cost ratio variable costs as a portion of sales revenue.

Variable costing an approach to product costing that treats variable manufacturing costs as product costs and fixed manufacturing costs as period costs.

Variable costs costs that are an identical amount for each incremental unit of activity. Their total amount increases as activity increases, equaling zero dollars when activity is zero and increasing at a constant amount per unit of activity.

Variable manufacturing overhead all variable costs, except direct labor and direct materials, associated with converting raw materials into finished goods.

Variable overhead effectiveness variance the difference between the standard variable overhead cost for the actual inputs and the flexible budget cost for variable overhead based on outputs.

Variable overhead spending variance the difference between the actual variable overhead cost and the standard variable overhead cost for the actual inputs.

Variable selling and administrative costs all variable costs other than those directly associated with converting raw materials into finished goods.

Variance a comparison of actual and budgeted (or allowed) costs or revenues which are usually identified in financial performance reports.

Virtual integration the use of information technology and partnership concepts to allow two or more entities along a value chain to act as if they were a single economic entity.

W

Waiting time the time units spend in temporary storage waiting to be processed, moved, or inspected.

Weighted average cost of capital an average of the after-tax cost of all long-term borrowing and the cost of equity.

Weighted average method in process costing, a costing method that spreads the combined beginning inventory cost and current manufacturing costs (for materials, labor, and overhead) over the units completed and those in ending inventory on an average basis.

Work ticket a document used to record the time a job spends in a specific manufacturing operation.

Work-in-process inventories partially completed goods consisting of raw materials that are in the process of being converted into a finished product.

Z

Zero-based budgeting a variation of the minimum level approach to budgeting where every dollar of expenditure must be justified.

INDEX

CHAPTER 2

2-6	(a)	Average cost for 100 servings $126
2-7	(a)	2. Total costs of automatic process at 50,000 units, $93,000
2-8	(a)	2. Total costs of collating machine at 1,500,000 units, $1,525
2-9		Fixed costs, $38,000
2-10	(a)	Fixed costs, $5,000
2-11	(a)	Fixed costs, $2,900
2-12	(b)	Fixed costs, $7,300
2-13	(b)	$6.875
2-15	(b)	Fixed costs, $930
2-16	(c)	Total costs, $26,900
2-18	(b)	Total overhead $30,000
2-19	(e)	Total cost, $182
2-20	(a)	Total cost, $117,125
2-21	(c)	Average unit cost of Product A, $17
2-22	(c)	Average unit cost of Product A, $29
2-28	(a)	Cost of X1, $56.78
2-29	(c)	Fixed costs, $4,034

CHAPTER 3

3-1	(a)	Contribution margin, $90,000
3-2	(b)	$40,000
3-3	(d)	Revised break-even point, $500,000
3-7	(a)	500,000 hot dogs
3-8	(b)	$475,000
3-10	(a)	2. Labor intensive break-even point, 175,000 units
	(c)	2. Capital intensive operative leverage, 6.25
3-11	(c)	32 percent decrease
3-13	(e)	$5,937.50
3-14		36,000 units
3-15	(b)	Margin of safety, $137,500
3-18	(c)	23,200 units
3-19	(b)	7,500 units
3-20	(c)	$5,454,545 (rounded)
3-21	(b)	Net decrease, $(606,660)
3-22	(d)	Loss, $(17,600)
	(f)	Decrease $2.97 per pair
3-23	(c)	$3,928.289 million
3-24	(e)	1. $180,000
3-25	(b)	Break-even point, 1,500 units
3-26	(c)	$4,900
3-27	(a)	2. Break-even point, $57,635
3-30	(c)	After-tax profit, $448,200
	(f)	After-tax profit, $404,250

CHAPTER 4

4-5		Advantage of replacement $60,000
4-7	(a)	$1,750
4-8	(a)	$5.00
4-9	(a)	$255,000
4-10	(a)	Advantage of buying, $35,000
4-11	(a)	Advantage of making, $2,500
4-13		Disadvantage of further processing, $700
4-15	(a)	1. Contribution, $1,000
4-16	(b)	$4,900
4-17	(b)	Value of objective function, $680
4-18	(b)	Value of objective function, $24,000
4-21	(b)	Advantage of replacement, $30,000
4-22	(c)	1. Opportunity cost $22,500
4-23	(b)	Coupon redemptions for break-even, 3,600
	(d)	Profit $240
4-24	(b)	Decrease in monthly profit, $8,200
	(f)	Advantage of selling unassembled, $5,000
4-25	(b)	Decrease in monthly profit, $2,100
	(f)	Advantage of full service, $7,800
4-26	(b)	Value of objective function, $5,950
4-27		Coefficient of B1, $1.61
4-28	(b)	Value of objective function, $46,000
4-32	(b)	Value of objective function, $9,000
	(d)	Value of objective function, $22,200

CHAPTER 5

5-11		Cost per introductory student, $54.375
5-12		Batch level salary, $20,000
5-13		$24,798
5-14		$24,770
5-15		Cost per unit of J26 cams, $62.10
5-16		Cost per gallon of Mirlite, $7.61
5-17	(b)	Cost per casement, $69.80
5-18	(a)	Activity cost variance, $200U
5-19	(a)	Consumer unit cost, $5.28
5-20	(a)	Unit cost of standard product A, $13.042
5-21	(c)	Activity overhead cost per unit of product Standard A, $10.20
5-22	(b)	Manufacturing cost per unit of Gas, $680
5-23	(b)	ABC cost per resident day for class A, $220.21
5-24	(a)	Activity cost per unit of Plutocrat, $5.24
5-25	(b)	Cost for Loan #5429, $610.56
5-26	(a)	Non-value added activity cost for Executive Chair, $1,090
5-27	(b)	Unit level costs, $108,750

5-28	(a)	Total average cost per unit, $57.156
5-36	(b)	Total activity cost per Routine Trip, $10.21
5-37	(a)	Purchasing department costs for Standard, $2,507

CHAPTER 6

6-6	(c)	Underapplied overhead, end of February, $30,000
6-7	(d)	Overapplied overhead, $30,000
6-8		Ending Work-in-Process, $9,500
6-9	(3)	Debit Manufacturing Overhead, $4,800
6-10		Ending Finished Goods Inventory, $10,500
6-11	(5)	Debit Manufacturing Overhead, $12,000
6-12		Ending overapplied Studio Overhead, $40
6-13	(3)	Debit Videos-in-Process, $65,000
6-14	(c)	$8,000
6-15	(d)	$6,000
6-18	(b)	Ending Work-in-Process, $12,640
6-19		Total cost per equivalent unit in process, $10.48
6-20		Total cost per equivalent unit in process, $27.60
6-21		Cost of goods manufactured, $278,700
6-22		Net Income, $72,000
6-23		Case 4 Net Income, $7,000
6-24	(a)	Cost of goods manufactured $144,200
6-25	(a)	Ending Work-in-Process, $1,185
6-26		Ending Work-in-Process, $27,600
6-27		Ending Work-in-Process, $16,100
6-28	(a)	Conversion cost for equivalent unit in process, $7.00
6-29	(b)	Cost of goods manufactured, $1,434,800
6-30	(a)	Variable cost per unit, $33.00
6-32		Profit per unit for Other Products, $1.00
6-33		Actual gross profit (loss) for Lion Tamer, ($27,820)

CHAPTER 7

7-1	(a)(1)	P1 cost after allocations, $145,000
7-2	(b)	Total Melting Department overhead, $164,130
7-3	(c)	Overhead cost per unit of Q45, $114.60
7-4	(c)	Furniture Department costs after allocation, $17,446
7-5		Total P1 cost after allocations, $77,103
7-6		Total P1 cost after allocation, $72,324
7-7		Total P1 cost after allocation, $73,575.32
7-8	(b)	Assembling cost after allocation, $515,750
7-9	(b)	P2 cost after allocation, $294,822
7-10	(d)	Milling Department overhead rate, $320 per DLR
7-11	(b)	Total Job 845 cost, $15,980
7-12	(b)	Unit cost of Gas Cooker, $111.52
7-13	(b)	Unit cost of Z205, $40.60
7-14	(a)	Job 201 cost, $42,570
7-15	(b)	Stamping overhead cost, $46.00 per machine hour
7-16	(b)	P1 cost after allocation, $3,760
7-17	(a)(2)	Total Cafeteria costs allocated to Mixing, $99,000

7-18	(b)	Medical cost per patient, $34.00
7-19	(b)	Budgeted cost per pound, $3.07
7-20	(c)	West Division income, $400
7-21	(b)	A2 job cost, $11,759
	(c)	A1 job cost using step allocation method, $15,960
7-22	(b)	A2 total job cost, $11,767
7-23	(c)	$3,840
7-24	(c)	Cost per unit of forceps, $43.50
7-25	(a)	Total product BB costs, $9,900
7-26	(c)	ABC overhead cost per unit of shafts, $6.725
7-27		Total On-Line cost per minute, $0.76
7-29	(b)	Branch net income, $26,000

CHAPTER 8

8-1		June absorption costing ending inventory, $180,000
		July variable costing ending inventory, $96,000
8-2		Absorption costing inventory, $24,000
8-3		Variable costing cost of goods sold, $186,000
8-4	(a)	Absorption cost per unit, $21
	(b)	Variable costing net income, $50,000
8-5	(b)	Variable costing net income, $30,000
8-6	(a)	Absorption costing unit cost, $8.20
	(b)	Variable costing net income, $26,000
8-7		Absorption costing net income for 2004, $1,600
8-8	(a)	Absorption costing net income for 2004, 350,000
	(b)	Variable costing net income for 2004, $150,000
8-9		Contribution margin, $285,000
8-10		Net income, $54,000
8-11	(a)	$1.00
	(b)	$2.00
8-12	(a)	$45
	(b)	$130
8-13	(a)	$483,000
	(b)	Finished goods inventory, $10,000
8-14	(a)	System A, 77
	(b)	System A, 0.52
8-15	(a)	First quarter income, $426,000
	(b)	First quarter income, $446,000
8-16	(a)	Net income, 2004, $3,900,000
	(b)	Net income, 2004, $3,900,000
8-17	(a)	Net income, 2004, $101,000
	(b)	Net income, 2004, $76,000
8-18	(a)	Absorption costing net income, 2004, $5,625
	(b)	Variable costing net income, 2005, $110,000
8-19	(a)	Absorption cost per unit for February, $14
	(c)	Variable costing net income for February, $26,000
8-20	(a)	Absorption costing net income (loss), ($124,800)
8-21	(a)	Theory of constraints unit cost, $10.00
		Traditional absorption unit cost, $15.425
	(b)	Variable costing inventory, $7,187.50
		Traditional and ABC incomes, $152,587.50
8-22		Total savings, $117,500
8-23		2004 inventory turnover, 5

CHAPTER 9

9-4	(a)	$132
9-5	(a)	$55
9-6	(a)	Variable markup, 250%, fixed markup, 367%
9-7	(a)	$2.16
9-8	(a)	WPD revenue per hour $43.75
9-9	(a)	$12,520,000
9-10		$304.60
9-11		Plastic case variance, $0.20U
9-12		2003, $19,356,480
9-13		Labor standard, 1.46 units per hour
9-17		Internal failure, 2.048% of sales
9-18		Preventive, 0.2875% of sales
9-19	(d)	Manufacturing cost markup, 0.50
9-20	(a)	1. Full cost markup, 0.16
9-21		Internal failure, 6.471% of sales
9-24	(a)	Total cost, $4,751.05
	(c)	Total nonvalue-added cost, $1,219.05

CHAPTER 10

10-1	(e)	$25,686
10-2	(e)	$23,006
10-3	(a)	$2,934
10-4	(a)	$(1,867)
10-5	(a)	$7,659
10-6	(a)	$6,500
10-7	(a)	Proposal X, 3 years
10-8	(c)	$88,219
10-9	(b)	Net present value, $(390)
10-11	(a)	Proposal X accounting rate of return, 0.1667
10-12	(a)	Plastic containers present value index, 1.6406
10-13	(a)	Plastic present value index, 1.2793
10-14	(a)	Net present value of investment, $14,010
10-15		Advantage of double-declining balance, $2,866
10-16	(b)	3. Present value index, 1.14
10-17		Net present value, $91,880
10-18	(a)	Time adjusted advantage of old processor, $1,650
10-19	(a)	Time adjusted advantage of new system, $27,880
10-20		Net present value, $58,208
10-26	(a)	Net present value of additional investment, $648,187
10-27	(a)	Overhead assigned to Department 3, $450,000
	(c)	Overhead assigned to Department 3, $267,000
10-28	(b)	Net present value, $37,983
10-30	(a)	Net present value, $14,960
10-31	(a)	2. Net cash inflow, $115,000

CHAPTER 11

11-1		Direct labor, $180,000
11-2		Variable overhead, $174,720
11-3		Unit level contribution margin, $160,000
11-4		Cleaning costs, $4,640
11-5		Reception costs, $372,000
11-6	(a)	Second quarter, $866,200
11-7		February variance, $0F
11-8	(a)	Winter total, $4,455
	(b)	Winter total, $3,410
11-9		July, $1,277,500
11-10		January purchases, 144,000 units
11-11	(a)	January production, 55,000 units
11-12		February cash available, $290,000
11-13		July cash ending balance, $141,000
11-14		May receipts, $49,030
11-15		April ending accounts receivable, $82,800
11-16		April disbursements, $200,000
11-17		July, $174,000
11-18		Net sales, $841,995
11-19		Gross margin, $300,000
11-20	(a)	Gross profit, $324,116
11-21	(a)	July cash receipts, $16,810
	(b)	July budgeted purchases, $11,000
	(c)	July ending cash balance, $5,010
11-22	(a)	Cash collections, $42,720
	(b)	Cash payments, $33,000
11-23		Net revenue with improvements, $1,922,368
11-24	(b)	Total assets, $504,400
11-25	(a)	April budgeted purchases, $31,000
	(e)	April net income, $(3,750)
11-26	(b)	Small belts budgeted cost of materials, $1,368
11-27		June pecan purchases, 49,200 pounds
11-28	(b)	April budgeted purchases, 52,650 pounds
11-29	(b)	Total inventory needs, 26,000 units
	(b)	Frame purchases, $352,000
	(e)	Total manufacturing costs, $1,743,000
11-30	(a)	First quarter cash collections, $429,000
	(d)	First quarter total manufacturing costs, $482,000

CHAPTER 12

12-1	(a)	European headquarters variance, $5,000U
12-2		Flexible budget variance, direct materials, $400F
12-3	(a)	$144,000
12-4	(a)	Material price variance, $550U
12-5		Labor rate variance, $4,975U
12-6	(a)	Labor efficiency variance, $420U
12-7	(a)	Spending variance, $1,000U
12-10		Sales price variance, $150F
12-11		Revenue variance, $26,000,000U
12-12		Variance spending variance, $94,200U
12-13	(a)	Standard variable costs for actual inputs, $21,500
12-14	(a)	Budgeted fixed overhead costs, $7,500
12-15	(a)	Fixed overhead budget variance, $1,000,000U
12-16	(a)	Sales price variance, $110,000F
12-18		Total variance, $7,000U
12-19	(a)	Material A price variance, $207.50U
12-20	(a)	Assembly rate variance, $1,800U
12-21	(b)	Material quantity variance, $60U

12-22	(b)	Actual quantity in units, 1,830 pounds
12-23	(l)	Effect on labor rate variance, $262.50U
12-24	(a)	Fixed overhead rate, $20 per direct labor hour
12-25		Net sales volume variance, $700F
12-26	(a)	Direct materials variance, $0F
12-33		Total production department variance, $20,000U

CHAPTER 13

13-3	(a)	Alabama territory margin, $14,400
13-4		Hospitals product income, $54,000
13-5	(b)	Financial Consultants gross profit, $166,000
13-6	(a)	Contribution margin, $16
13-7	(b)	Peanut Division gross profit, $2,232,000
13-8	(c)	Net loss, $(60,000)
13-9	(a)	Gamma net income, $446,000
13-10		Proposed net income, $325,000

13-11	(a)	Proposed net income, $0.00
13-12	(c)	EVA for Construction, $9,300
13-13	(b)	Residual income, $26,000
13-14		European Division ROI, 18%
13-15	(c)	EVA using current value for Consulting, $3,300
13-17	(a)	Residual income actual, $4,203,000
13-18	(a)	Southeast territory income, $12,000
13-19	(b)	Asia territory margin, $23,000
13-20	(b)	Donuts product margin, $260
13-21	(b)	Controllers market income, $8,800
13-22	(a)	Local territory margin, $310,000
13-23	(a)	Kiwi division income, $20,000
13-24	(a)	March net income, $240,000
13-25	(e)	$(1,058)
13-26	(c)	EVA, $(10,400)
13-27	(b)	Residual income, $(20) million
13-31	(b)	Net income increase, $210,000
13-36	(a)	Membership segment margin, $191,500